The endurance horse

Frontispiece. The late Wendell Robie, father of modern endurance riding. (Western States Trail Foundation)

The endurance horse

A world survey from ancient civilizations to modern competition

Ann Hyland

J. A. Allen
London

British Library Cataloguing in Publication Data

Hyland, Ann
The endurance horse.
1. Livestock : Horses. Endurance riding – Manuals
I. Title
798.2'3
ISBN 0-85131-4376

Published in Great Britain in 1988 by
J. A. Allen & Company Limited,
1, Lower Grosvenor Place, Buckingham Palace Road,
London, SW1W 0EL

Printed in Great Britain

To my
Magnet Regent
1960–1987
a great-hearted mare who introduced me to endurance
riding and who died during the production of this book

Foreword

For those of you who have suffered long and dry (with your horse) on either Competitive Trail or Endurance Rides, there is special message in this work of Ann Hyland's. We are shown that message in a panoramic sweep of hard-riding history: *others have done it before*!

Done what? Stayed in the saddle (and/or led or tailed on the ground) for extended distances and periods of time with ourselves and our mounts, enduring the wear and tear of terrain and weather conditions.

This book will provide the riding reader with some classical, comparative stress formats that we all can relate to if we have smelled the sweat of hard and fit trail horses. Ann Hyland's research is not just noteworthy and interesting to endurance riding buffs – it is also challenging! The details of past episodes in effective (but sometimes not so humane) horse use in battles and wars; in land acquisition; in communication and transport and so many other equine exploits and exploitation will give all of us pause to consider our own small victories as we 'put miles on our horse'.

The interesting vignettes projecting today's riders – horsemen and horsewomen – add a special charm to this work as we 'meet' the people who have made some modern history in the endurance sport competition. With Ann's thorough pursuit of factual data, we are led through a variety of geographic rides: European, British, South African, Australian and North American, to name but a few.

And finally, a most effective outline of helpful training and management techniques is given which will prove of tremendous value (if followed) to all those riders out there who ride to finish and with condition enough in their horses to GO ON. We see in Ann Hyland's work a realistic view of man's relationship to stressful endurance competition – a horse should be *used* ... but not *used up*!

Richard B. Barsaleau, DVM
California 1987

Contents

CONTENTS

Part Two: The practical side

CONTENTS

List of illustrations

Acknowledgements

In writing this book I have relied to a very great extent on the generosity of many people who have supplied me with information, particularly for the reference section. To the Secretaries of all the associations and national societies mentioned I would like to extend my heartfelt thanks. Appreciation is also tendered to the many riders worldwide who have taken the trouble to write to me about their own special horses whom readers will meet in this book, and to supply photographs and the permission to reproduce them here.

My especial thanks must also go to several people who helped in vital areas where information was difficult to come by, and in all the other areas where their assistance has been of value in making this book what I hope will be an enjoyable and informative survey of the sport of long distance riding. My thanks to: Dr Richard Barsaleau, DVM, who took time out from his very busy schedule not only to send his own and his horses' endurance feats, but also to write the foreword which necessitated reading the whole manuscript through beforehand. To Dr David Snow, MRCVS, BSc., for advising me on the veterinary section, writing his own piece on muscle fatigue, and then reading the whole veterinary chapter for error before it was submitted. To Penelope Dauster, who not only sent me all the ELDRIC and German information, but also prompted answers from Germany's leading riders and translated all their answers before sending them to me! To Hazel McCort for doing half my work in gathering all the information from the New Zealand representatives. To Terry Woods for sending me data he had received from Bob Sample, and in turn to Bob Sample for permission to use it here. To my friend Sharon Saare who chased up elusive information, and to Julie Suhr who kept me up to date with recent information, as did Louise Hermelin from Sweden. To the Patee Museum for their extremely helpful information on the Pony Express. To Jim Kerr, MRCVS, Veterinary Adviser to the Endurance Horse and Pony Society of Great Britain, for his contribution, to my friend Lieutenant Colonel Stephen Jenkins for reading the whole typescript before it was submitted, even though he is not a horse afficionado, and to my editor Elizabeth O'Beirne-Ranelagh who has made sure that the work is as error free as it is humanly possible so to do. And finally my gratitude to the two equines who have given me my initial love of the sport and who each in their own way have had a tremendous impact on it in Britain. To my Magnet Regent, who was my first endurance mount in the United States and the mother of my current long distance horse Granicus, and to Nizzolan who was my top horse in Britain for many years. Without Magnet Regent's effortless performances in the USA I would never have been started and kept on the long distance trail that led to the founding of the EHPS of GB.

Ann Hyland
Leverington
December 1987

Introduction

The endurance horse! Twentieth-century understanding of the title is of the competition horse par excellence: an equine athlete that can happily cover great distances over any and every type of terrain, under clement skies and, all too frequently, under the reverse – lowering clouds that throw bitter elements into the already tough challenge of covering courses that stretch 100 miles in a gruelling day's toll-taking trial.

To me, and to a rapidly growing core of endurance horse enthusists, the long-distance horse overshadows all other equine athletes in the scale of his achievements, whether this be the moderate mileage expected of novice horses, or the acme of the 100-mile champions. The endurance horse follows no prepared trail; has no covered hall to compete in; tackles no carefully paced course set on 'suitable going'; encircles no close-cropped show ring; meets no judge with likes and dislikes who chooses winner and runners-up. An endurance ride winner is judged against his own fitness criteria assessed by a skilled team of veterinary surgeons.

Today we ask a lot of our endurance horses. We hope for great achievements at the end of months and often years of careful training. In turn, our tough horses receive the best of care and everything veterinary science can offer to protect their health – good food, warm stabling, regular health checks, frequent shoeing by skilled farriers, careful fitting of quality equipment, and continuous research into their physiological makeup. Our horses are there for our pleasure, no matter that such pleasure is frequently achieved in a rather masochistic way by riders who choose to ride across 100 miles of demanding territory. Rewards in most cases, and in most countries, are the rewards of great achievement. The lack of major commercial involvement keeps endurance riding a sport for any who desire to compete, from early novice rides to the top echelons.

Achievement is a key word throughout this book. In history, the achievements of countless horses have gone unrecorded and largely unmarked. Conquering armies owe their conquests to the horse and his endurance. This may be a sweeping statement but it is one backed by proof.

Mention of equines is found as far back as Sumerian times, fully 2500 years before Christ, in the semi-legendary Epic of Gilgamesh where we are given a picture of war chariots drawn by mules and warriors mounted on the 'stallion magnificent in battle'. War is nothing if not a feat of endurance. Then, slender though the references are, occasional sightings of the horse filter through the dust and heat haze and the tramp of armies over the centuries across Western Asia, until in the thirteenth century BC we get the first actual treatise on horse training. Written by Kikkuli, a Mitanni groom in the Mari king's stables, it gives the outlines of training horses, whether harnessed to a chariot or unharnessed, the latter involving great distances to be travelled to ensure fitness. Kikkuli lays down the duration of training as 169 days, almost the exact time it takes today to bring a horse intended for 100 miling up to peak performance. He stipulates weight to be carried; the type of ground the horse should traverse; which gait he should use and at what speed he should travel – not so very different from today's rules for a Competitive Trail Ride.

Once man realized how to profit from the horse there was hardly a nation that does not owe its successful emergence and subsequent domination over new lands to either chariotry or cavalry. In ancient times the distances travelled were of epic proportions and the conditions suffered by both horse and rider were such as to ensure that man and beast endured in the fullest sense of the word.

Literature is punctuated by references to the horse, some casual as if the horse were considered merely an adjunct to the man. Indeed we are rarely given a valid description of the ancient horse, and as time closes over him we must speculate to a large degree about what he looked like. But we are left in no doubt as to what he did, where he went, and what he encountered, and today's endurance riders can only have admiration for what was to history's horse an everyday feat.

Valued though he was for what he could achieve and help his masters conquer, he was subjected to what we would now consider calculated cruelty. Today's horse is in the favoured position of being used for man's pleasure and relaxation and his sporting achievements – a far happier partnership, though not necessarily a less close one than that of history's warhorses. But through the centuries the horse has been man's partner and at many times his friend. In this book I shall attempt to chart the changes which took place, as well as how and where today's endurance horse covers the miles to achieve prestigious acclaim and solicitous care.

Along the way there will be many equine characters, and many other fields of endeavour that merit the term endurance, though not always in the number of miles travelled. All these horses, some wiling, some unwitting partners, deserve recognition. In the fields of war, exploration, communications, business, travel and sport there are many uncrowned champions.

PART ONE

ENDURANCE FEATS OF HISTORY

1 The expansion of the early empires

Homer

While Assyrian ferocity swathed its way to greater empires on its western limits, the tiny hilltop town of Troy, Homer's famed city of Ilium, was waging its ten-year battle with the ship-borne Achaeans encamped in the plains below. Long thought to be a poet's fantasy, the finding of Priam's Troy, or Truva in modern Turkey, gave new evidence that the town had in truth existed. As with many writings in the ancient world much of what was thought total fantasy has been found through archaeological evidence to be a mixture of fact and fiction. Homer (ninth century BC), writing at least 400 years after the ten-year conflict between Trojans and Achaeans, was no different; but throughout his saga there is such detailed description, of the sort that makes total sense, that we know we are witnessing what could and did happen in those far-off bloodthirsty times. Only in the scale, and occasionally where he forgets that Troy fell in the age of bronze and not in his own age of iron, does he step aside from what we are convinced is fact.

As a raconteur using author's licence he portrays the clangour of battle: bronze smiting bronze; the whistling spear; the cleaving sword; the rattle of chariots and thunder of hooves; and as the story unfolds we get a glimpse of those far-off warhorses that have endured through nearly three millennia and are still fresh off the page as they gather in formation for a massed chariot charge. Horses from Tros, famed for speed; Pylian steeds, courageous but slow, from the royal herds of King Neleus; the huge white horses from far-off Thrace; the chestnut horses of Achaean Pthia; a swirl of colour, a maelstrom of movement with high stepping, high necked horses full of fire and courage, hitched variously – four, three and two abreast – to chariots bedecked with gold, silver or royal purple, fit for heroes but soundly built withal.

Lightweight poplar provided the felloes, clad in bronze tyres with the eight spokes fitting into the silvered hub of the iron axle, while the double-railed chariot car supported the charioteer and his spearman on a tightly woven springy platform.

After the battle we learn how the horses were cared for: the washing down with cool water and salving oil, the ration of white barley and rye, and how the stallions stalled in Troy ate from marble mangers whereas those of the Achaeans were hobbled on the plain.

Horses from Tros fought on both sides. They were clearly the spoils of Agamemnon's Achaean victories, as throughout the ten years of siege skirmish followed skirmish. (Surely, from the size of the ruined city and the distance it lies on its heights above the plain and bordering shore, fighting must have been in the nature of skirmishes, for all Homer portrays the armies as vast concourses.) The hinterland of Truva, called in the *Iliad* a breeding ground, must have been a haven of thick pastures for the Trojan breeding stock, just as today Turkey boasts at least a double crop per year from the very fertile grounds bordering her rivers and streams, rocky and barren though great stretches of country remain. The legendary Scamander could have been no different.

The horses of Tros were valued highly, Troy having suffered attack long before Helen stirred up emotions, when Argives came looting for Laomedon's mares, the dams of the Trojan breed. Their value is shown more clearly in the funeral games for Patroclus. Second prize in the chariot race is a mare in foal to a jackass or 'with a little mule in her womb', while the fourth prize is two talents of gold! Horses were indeed prized and expensive, hard to rear on thin soil except in favoured regions such as Macedonia, Thessaly and the hinterlands of Troy, and yet they were endowed with toughness and the ability to withstand constant use in wars. Some of these must have seemed interminable, or as in other periods of Greek history they were petty city feuds that saw chariots constantly on the move. Homer's horses were bred to withstand strain and stress; they were strong, fast, tough of hoof – shoes were not then invented – and often ended in a bloody heap of mangled horse and shattered chariot, hamstrung, as Homer would have it, by a god. Yet in one line we see a shade of today's feeling when Pandarus, a Lycian, will not bring his beloved horses to Troy for fear they will go short of fodder.

Horses of Achaea, horses of Ilium; although their feats of endurance lie in legend, it is a legend gilded with more than a hint of fact.

Assyria

The Assyrian came down like the wolf on the fold,
And his cohorts were gleaming in purple and gold;
And the sheen of their spears was like stars on the
sea,
When the blue wave rolls nightly on deep Galilee.

And there lay the steed with his nostril all wide,
But through it there roll'd not the breath of his
pride:
And the foam of his gasping lay white on the turf,
And cold as the spray of the rock-beating surf.

Destruction of Sennacherib, Lord Byron (1788–
1824)

Ferocity was the Assyrian legacy. Their annals resound with deeds of 'frightfulness': tales of retribution, deportation, atrocities so brutal that Assyria's name has been anathema in the unwinding of the world's history. Yet there was a vision and a purpose obscured by three millennia of opprobrium where only their vicious deeds were told.

In the cradle of civilization on the Mesopotamian Plain, Assyria rose on the banks of the middle Tigris in the second half of the second millennium BC as a people thrusting towards nationhood from an even older nomadic heritage thousands of years in the dimmest past. A vassal state owing allegiance to Mitannian overlords who ruled east of the Euphrates, Assyria grasped freedom when Mitanni and the Hittites, the two greatest nations of the era, went to war against each other.

From nuclear Assyria, the size of England's East Anglia or America's state of Connecticut, this fledgling nation grew into the greatest empire the ancient world had ever known. From their heartland centred on the capital, Ashur, they ranged even further, and they ranged on horseback.

Earlier nomadic tribes had ridden out of an Asian dawn with the horse a part of their culture, but it was the Assyrians who pioneered the world's first far-ranging cavalry. Their expansionist policies depended in large measure on the horse, especially at the empire's zenith. Far from being a disorganized horde of bloodthirsty butchers, the Assyrian army was a highly disciplined force. The scale of their conquests needed meticulous planning, with cohorts of cavalry and infantry fighting fit.

A fourteenth-century BC king, Ashur-Uballit (1365–1330), noted the tribute paid to him from a small client kingdom: 40 chariots complete with drivers and gear and 460 horses 'broke to the yoke' highest in value on the list. But it was not until the reign of eleventh-century Tiglath Pileser I (1115–1077) that the chariot arm developed into a major strike force. Building up the horse herds was a prime royal consideration. It was another two centuries before specialized cavalry forces were developed under Tukulti Ninurta II (890–884). By that time Assyria had begun on her massive expansion. Before, though she had gradually conquered her closest neighbours, the fighting had been sporadic, of the nature of razzias (raids). Having no natural boundaries she had early developed the tactic of strike to defend.

With increasing success and aggressive confidence, aided by the mobility that chariots and cavalry afforded, her boundaries were pushed rapidly outwards until her kingdom finally stretched from Egypt, the border regions of Iraq, Syria, Turkey, Armenia and Iran, and southwards to the Persian Gulf – an area measuring roughly 1000 miles on each border. Into this area poured massive tribute, and successive kings constantly record the thousands of horses received from conquered nations. Iran, Armenia and Cilicia provided the bulk of the cavalry's mounts. Herds were also raised on the heartland plains, as well as purchases being made by merchants acting as middlemen. Sargon II (721–705) recorded a single shipment of 760 horses, although purchase was the least used method of acquiring mounts.

With present-day long-distance rides offering every aid to competing horses, the feats of history's first cavalry bear noting. In the ninth century BC, Ashurnasirpal II (883–859) heard of a revolt in an Aramean city on the Lower Khabur 200 miles away, and forced his cavalry through the Mesopotamian summer heat rising to 120 °F. Yet another campaign route of 350 miles, covered at a steady 20 miles per day, had the file of deportee prisoners dying of thirst in the Euphrates desert. The distress of the cavalry's mounts can well be imagined.

But it was Tiglath Pileser III (745–727), credited with being the founder of the surging empire, who brought new vigour to Assyria. He established a standing army; operated a system whereby client kingdoms provided conscripts, along with a never-ending supply of mounts; made the occasional deportation of people a general policy, transporting whole populations away from their homelands in an effort to break the back of resistance; and greatly extended long-distance campaigns, ranging 550 miles from his capital Nimrud (Calah) into neighbouring Iran, close to modern Tehran. Three years later, after minor razzias, he was again on a long-haul campaign across the breadth of the empire, to the Mediterranean trouble spots of Tyre and Sidon.

Tiglath Pileser III left several inscriptions regarding horses and it is from his reign that we get an insight into the Assyrians' preferences in horseflesh. By his time Iran was providing a constant stream of the best horses as annual tribute, as was Urartu (Armenia), when it was not at war with Assyria. In wartime, tribute changed its title and became spoils of war! In their campaign against Syria and her ally King Sardur IV of Urartu, the Assyrians laughed derisively at the beaten Sardur, who made his getaway from the battle mounted on a mare – a cowardly action to a nation of fierce cavalrymen who prided themselves on riding only stallions.

However, cowardly though Sardur might have been, his country, Urartu, bred some of the finest horses and her warriors were renowned for their horsemanship. We find Tiglath Pileser III's successor, Sargon II, praising them unstintingly, and at the same time throwing light on their training methods: 'their like does not exist for skill with cavalry horses. The foals ... which are reared for the royal contingents and caught yearly, until they are taken to the land of Subi (for training) and it is seen what they are capable of, will never have had anyone straddling their backs, will not have been taught advancing, wheeling, retreating, or battle drill.' Clearly once Urartu was crushed her spoils and tribute were highly desirable, and the three most noted of Assyria's breeds, the Kusian, the Mesian, and the Turanian from the north and east of Assyria, must have originally come from Armenia and Iran where the bulk of remounts were obtained.

Sargon had need of fine horses. His campaigns had him ranging across the breadth of his empire – to the north against Urartu who had risen defiantly again, and far down south in Babylon where Merodach Baladan was revolting. In his campaign against Urartu he covered 300 miles across the Zagros range of mountains, coming up with the Urartian army in a pass walled by sheer precipices south of Tabriz. The campaign had taken such a heavy toll of his army that the infantry were exhausted and near to mutiny, so leading the way in his battle chariot, he took his chariots and household cavalry on alone and we find it recorded in his annals in a letter to the god Ashur how he set his sappers to work: 'the crags of high mountains they caused to fly in splinters; they improved the passage. I took the head of my troops. The chariots, the cavalry, the fighters who went beside me I made to fly over this mountain like valiant eagles.'

Later we find Sargon's son, Sennacherib (704–681), concerned for his horses' welfare, shipping grain and hay to the Persian Gulf prior to his assault on Elam (southwest Iran), a neighbouring

7

country which in concert with Babylon was threatening Assyria's border. As well as coming down 'like the wolf on the fold' of Jerusalem, Sennacherib visited siege on Babylon, destroying the city, his troops ravaging and rampaging through the streets. Among the spoils he numbered 7200 horses.

His successor Esarhaddon (680–669) was altogether a milder ruler, at pains to repair the damage to Babylon. He also had to contend with new waves of nomads pouring into the borderlands. The Cimmerians, followed by the Scythians, were pushing out of Russia on their tough little steppe ponies. Esarhaddon's 1200-mile long northern and eastern border was threatened, and throughout his reign he made repeated cavalry raids into Iranian territory where the Medes were also massing. Holding them at bay he levied tribute of horses, his ranks being largely mounted on horses of Median breed.

By the end of Esarhaddon's brief reign the Assyrian Empire was almost at its zenith. His son Ashurbanipal (668–627) pushed the frontiers to their limit. He has gone down in history for two totally opposite facets of his character – as a man of learning, gathering a massive library to which we owe much of our knowledge of Assyrian history, and as a man reviled for the ferocity of his campaigns, his scorched earth policy, the flaying alive, the impalements, and the bloody butchery. In one campaign he totally depopulated Elam, leaving it a desert, and in doing so sowed the seeds of Assyria's destruction as the Persians took root, their erstwhile overlords having taught them the way to victory.

Egypt too felt the heel of Assyria grind her down. This campaign was made possible by aid from Arabia, with whom Assyria had a centuries old tradition of trade. Arabia accepted Assyria's suzerainty in return for help in disputes over tribal succession, paying tribute in the currency of Assyrian times – yet more horses. And in this we can surely trace the source of much of the blood of Assyrian mounts. [This is if we accept the premise that the Arabian horse (not then so entitled, of course) did stem as a separate breed from that region, as one school of thought avers. Other reasoning suggests that instead the breed stemmed from the Oriental

types bred in centres in Asia Minor.] Desert Arabs, however loth they might have been to part with prized bloodstock, would scarcely risk Assyrian atrocity being visited on them.

Ashurbanipal is frequently displayed on the bas-reliefs from Nineveh hunting on horseback, or in his ceremonial chariot, and his horses show quality and size in relation to the rider. The horses' heads are concave, nostrils flared, necks arched and carried proudly showing stallion crest; their bodies are short coupled and muscular, well rounded, with a high-set tail carriage, while the legs show tendons clearly delineated, and in the case of the chariot horses the gait is the pace (or possibly, without the instant recall offered by photography, the artist's representation of a walk). Elsewhere, reliefs show horses being groomed and watered, and though not so finely carved or in such detail the horses are of fair size in relation to their attendants and show a certain refinement in their breeding.

Clearly Assyrian horses were valued in quality and sheer numbers, as well as being the first of their kind to engage in planned epic marches across the breadth of Asia Minor from Egypt to the Caspian Sea, from the headwaters of the Tigris and Euphrates to the Persian Gulf, along 800 miles of torrid desert and sun-baked plain. Surely these were horses with endurance in their genes.

Persia

As the Assyrian Empire outgrew its strength and waned, the Medes were ready to step on to the scene. In the passage of history they were only a link between the two Middle Eastern colossi, with the Persians coming strongly forward on to the stage of world history in the mid sixth century BC when Cyrus the Great (560/59–530), first of the Achaemenid kings, enforced Persian domination over his Median maternal grandfather Astyages. Thenceforwards Persia was paramount, though the Medes had considerable influence in the formation of the Persian Empire. Cyrus acquired a ready-made strong cavalry arm, as Herodotus informs us that the Median King Cyaxares, Cyrus' maternal great-grandfather, had already united all Asia to the River Halys, in modern Turkey, using his cavalry units of archer spearmen.

Herodotus' spotlight on the cavalry of this ancient civilization opens up a body of information about the Persian attitude to horses, their use, their provenance, their importance in Persian culture; even the incorporation of the word for horse, *aspa*, in many of the Persian names. In the 200 years following Cyrus the Persian Empire rolled ever outwards from the focal point of Susa until it covered an incredible 3000 by 1500 miles. As with the Assyrians the shock force, the hard-hitting troops, were the cavalry, constantly buttressed by levies from subject peoples.

At the beginning of Cyrus' reign his army was mainly infantry, but with his sights set on mobility and expansion he rapidly built up a crack cavalry arm of 10,000 Persians to match the famous Premier Persian Corps. This glittering contingent was known as the Immortals and was kept close to the king and always at full strength. Complementing the Persian divisions Cyrus raised similar cohorts from his Median subjects.

The biggest coup from a cavalryman's aspect was the acquisition of Astyages' Nisean Plains, breeding grounds of the famed Median Nisean horses which stood a full hand taller than regular tribute horses levied from western Asia Minor. In Achaemenid times the Great Kings ran herds of up to 150,000 head of these heavy, high crested, muscular horses (as shown in the Apandana frieze at Persepolis). The Zagros region provided ideal pasturage with a highly nutritious clover known as Median Grass.

Casting covetous eyes further westward to the rich lands of Croesus, King of Lydia, Cyrus employed his newly acquired cavalry in a whirlwind campaign of aggression. Lydia at that time possessed formidable chariotry and a cavalry whose main weapon was the long spear. Against them Cyrus sent a swooping horde of fast-moving mounted archers and a corps of camels, no doubt recruited from Arabia via the Babylonians with whom he initially had good diplomatic relations. Terrified by the unusual stink, Croesus' cavalry and chariotry panicked, leaving the open Lydian plains to the Persians.

The main drawback in conquering Lydia was the shortage of infantry and siege engines to reduce the many fortified cities, but its capital, Sardis, finally fell to a weakness in its outer walls when a besieged Lydian was seen climbing down to retrieve his fallen helmet – no doubt he was careless on watch, and even more careless in retrieving it. Consequently Sardis was taken, and with it Lydia and its king.

Educating a noble Persian started in infancy. To ride, shoot the bow, and tell the truth equipped the young *kardake* (young adult in training) to fight honourably in the Great King's army. In Cyrus' thirty-year rule there was plenty to attract an aspiring young cavalryman.

The victorious Cyrus then turned his acquisitive eyes to his erstwhile friend, Nabonidus of Babylon. The distance between Sardis and Babylon is roughly 1500 miles, just a shade shorter than the famous Royal Road from Sardis to Susa. The pressure on troops and cavalry must have been great. The conditions of travel, let alone the sheer mileage, must have been a severe test of endurance. Both horses and men suffered intense and immense discomfort, as the terrain alternated from the flat, torrid windless wastes of Elamite Media, through marshy swamps in low-lying riverine belts, to the flat but wind-scored plains of Babylon.

With Babylon conquered the Persian Empire mushroomed. Subject peoples paid tribute, and were assimilated at the lower levels, thankfully without the ferocity of the Assyrians. Noble Persians and high-ranking allied soldiers were well rewarded with fiefs from which they were obliged to provide either bowmen, cavalrymen, or chariots according to their status, in a similar way to the later medieval fiefdoms of Europe. Commanders of armies and the king's relatives were awarded satrapies (governorships) where the financial rewards were enormous. One Satrap of Assyria, Tritantaechmen, had as his personal property, no doubt levied from disgruntled subjects, 800 stallions and 16,000 mares, twenty per stallion. And he owned warhorses in addition. Even allowing for ancient historians' exaggeration it marked Assyria as one of the wealthiest satrapies, capable of providing remounts by the drove.

Throughout the duration of the empire tribute

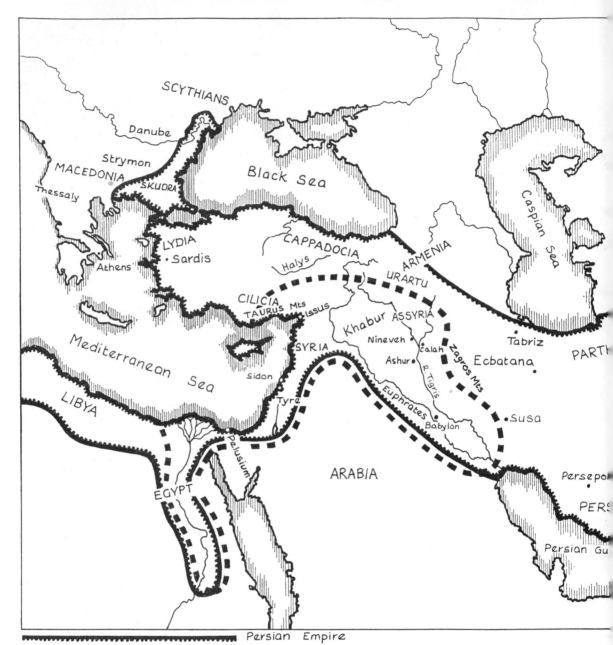

Map 1 The Assyrian and Persian Empires, seventh and fifth centuries BC.

came in by the herd, the main suppliers being Cilicia, Cappadocia (Turkey), Urartu (Armenia), and of course for the highest-ranking Persian Corps and officers the famed Nisean chargers.

Cyrus, who ruled 'like a father', was succeeded by his unbalanced, tyrannical son Cambyses (530–522), who launched his cavalry of archers against the new Egyptian Pharaoh Psammetichus III in 526 BC. Stationed in Abarnahara (Syria), the cavalry had to cross the desiccated sands east of Gaza where temperatures rise to furnace heat. Again, as in Assyrian times, the Arabs obliged with camel

SOGDIANA

SCYTHIANS

BACTRIA

SIND

ARACHOSIA

Indus

rian Empire ■ ■ ■ ■ ■ ■ ■ ■ ■ ■ ■ ■ ■

wine amphorae. Much of Herodotus is fact, a great deal hearsay to which he admits, and some fable, but unlikely as it seems it is possible to cache water in the desert (witness the African Bushmen in the Kalahari with their ostrich egg mini-reservoirs). Later Darius was to cross the Arabian Desert when Egypt revolted, and the cavalry and infantry depended on adequate water supplies. Ancient amphorae were resin-coated inside so that water would not have evaporated. Also the Arabs were credited with building cisterns in the desert.

Cambyses' successor Darius I (522–486) is reputed to have 'grabbed' power (a word he himself constantly used in his inscriptions) through the clever agency of his groom Oebares and a randy stallion who obligingly neighed loudly at a pre-arranged spot. The cunning groom had previously taken the stallion to a mare at the designated spot and the stallion thought his luck was in once again. Partly fable, the legend has endured for 2500 years and it throws light on the hippomancy in Persian religion. Horses were sacred to Ahuramazda and the eager stallion's neigh was taken as a good omen.

Whereas Cyrus built and Cambyses tyrannized, Darius consolidated the gains, adding others and keeping the Persian might in force, quelling early revolts. He was quick to offer due recognition to Ahuramazda in his many rockface inscriptions recounting his deeds, praising the god for 'good land possessed of good horses and good men', with the accent on horses before men. Throughout his reign horses loomed large. The ever-expanding army needed a never-ending supply of remounts as Darius pushed the borders to far greater lengths than Cyrus had. The Persepolis inscriptions tally twenty-eight nations subject to Darius at one time, and later others also succumbed. The Behistun inscriptions number twenty-nine – from Put (Libya) to Sind (India). In addition to the Nisean horses huge royal studs were established in Armenia and Cappadocia. In the Daskyleion satrapy (in Turkey), crack Iranian cavalry was garrisoned. It is from the upper satrapies of Bactria and Sogdiana (now within the USSR, around the region of Samarkand) that the best cavalry came. The men were warlike, physically large, and breeders of

trains carrying water supplies. Once through the desert the Persian cavalry routed the Egyptian archers at Pelusium to begin the long Persian occupation of Egypt.

The Persians are credited by Herodotus with laying in stocks of water in the Sinai desert in used good horses, particularly in Ferghana, a region leaving a legacy of first-rate horseflesh through the ages.

Almost as soon as he took power Darius had need of a good strike force. Within weeks of his accession he was marching southwards to Babylon where two successful engagements made him master of the ancient city. Before the second engagement he was reputedly jeered at from the walls of the citadel by Babylonians who said he would take the city 'when mules have foals'. Five days after Darius crossed the Tigris, on 18 December 522, Babylon fell. According to Herodotus, the omens were favourable when one of Darius' generals, Zopyrus, reported that one of the baggage mules had foaled. [This is not impossible; see Robert Miller DVM, 'Pilgrim the Mule', *Western Horseman* (March 1984), recording mules foaling and fourteen documented cases in the USA.]

In his first year of rule Darius captured nine kings and conducted nineteen battles, at many of which he himself was present. Within three years he had fought his way from the southern reaches of his kingdom to the furthest northern stretches 2000 miles away, crossing the Danube in an effort to subdue the Scythians. Here his toughened cavalry endured two months of forced marches, never engaging the nomad Scythians. Superior horsemen, they led the Persians on a frustrating march in a scorched earth wasteland, always out of reach and refusing to give battle, until the exhausted army finally recrossed the Danube and, as in a later Mongol invasion, Europe was saved from Oriental domination. What few successes Darius did achieve were accorded to his pack donkeys whose braying terrified the Scythians' horses who had never seen them before.

Darius reigned for thirty-four years. Xerxes I (486–465), succeeding his father, had even greater ambitions, fielding a huge army at the end of five years' preparation aimed at solving the eternal Greek problem. With the constant internecine warfare occupying the myriad Greek city-states it is difficult to sort out the pro- and the anti-Persian cities, especially as current expedience often dictated which side they fought on. The Battle of Marathon in 490 had been an infantry engagement and a disaster for Darius, and Xerxes was determined to settle the Greek question once and for all. Subject nations provided the means – infantry, supplies, cavalry, horses, horse transports and other ships – and in 481 the Persian juggernaut rolled up the Royal Road from Susa to winter 1600 miles away at Sardis before launching an attack on mainland Greece.

The numbers involved were enormous, though Herodotus' fanciful computations running to over five million with infantry, cavalry and camp attendants, quartermasters, mule drivers, and the inevitable camp followers are outrageous. A more likely figure for the fighting force has been computed at around 360,000, and with all ancillaries boosted to around three-quarters of a million. Even that marching must have shaken the earth and instilled fear along the Royal Road. Of this number approximately 60,000 were cavalry. What we can reliably gather is the type of troops who marched with Xerxes, and the horses they rode. Xerxes himself rode in a chariot drawn by Nisean horses. Other white mares drew the god's chariot, and at the River Strymon white horses were sacrificed by the Magi to the river.

As Persia's greatness grew so too did the size of her army, but unfortunately as with many other armies throughout history success eventually softened the striking force, and Xerxes' cavalry was no exception. Though numbering tens of thousands it in no way matched the infantry for sheer numbers, although it was more disciplined. The cavalry force that thundered down the Royal Road consisted of eight different corps from as many national backgrounds: the elite Persian Corps mounted on 10,000 Nisean chargers, complemented by the Medes and Cashites, all archer spearmen carrying shields. Additionally there were three corps of horsed archers – Bactrian, Caspian and Paricanian. To his cost Xerxes neglected to recruit a special Scythian corps, the world's best horsed archers, incorporating what he had into the Bactrian archers instead. The Indian archers, unlike the others, were armed with the stave bow. The 8000-strong contingent of Sagartians were armed with lariats. As this was their national armament it must have been effective, though without stirrups or means of attaching to the saddle, if indeed saddles were used, they must have relied on superb training of horses to stop in mid-gallop and thus jerk their victims down. As the army rolled onwards disaffected Greek cavalry from Thessaly and Boetia swelled the numbers.

From Herodotus we learn something of the training of a cavalry mount and the fate awaiting an unreliable animal, as well as how morale depended on good cavalry commanders. Three of the cavalry commanders specifically mentioned are Artybius, whose horse was trained to rear and strike with both front feet and savage with his teeth; Pharnuces, who sustained a bad fall due to his mount shying at a dog – retribution was swift, the horse being immediately destroyed by severing its front legs; and Masistius, the cavalry commander left behind with Mardonius. It was Masistius' death at Plataea that started the rout that finished the Persians as a great force in Greece.

The sheer size of the armies and the great distances travelled meant endurance on all counts for such an unwieldy mass. Months in the field on route march, scant water, heat, sand, short commons – no army of that size can carry enough fodder, or stockpile or forage sufficient quantities however much they extorted, and much of the terrain traversed was arid infertile ground. The Persian colossus was rolling towards Greece and its eventual ruin. Thermopylae gave Xerxes an early victory in 480, an infantry engagement, followed by the fall of Athens which had been denuded of people except for a small garrison which succumbed to the Great King, who then turned his attention seawards. False information lured his fleet into the Sound of Salamis where the mass of Persian ships, over 1000 triremes and countless smaller craft, fell foul of the Greek navy. The losses were so heavy that, without his fleet and provisions to back his enormous land army, what had started as a campaign of conquest turned into a retreat to Sardis before winter set in.

Leaving a third of his land forces under Mardonius and the cavalry commander Masistius, Xerxes headed home. In all the vast panoply of war so far his cavalry horses and his weary infantry had mar-

ched 3000 miles, only to return empty-handed.

Mardonius and Masistius wintered in Thessaly and descended in the following year (479) to re-open hostilities, their force replenished and ready to retrieve Persian losses and honour. Facing the Greek hoplites at Plataea were 35,000 infantry, 12,000 cavalry and 15,000 disaffected Greeks, among them crack Thessalian cavalry, and almost immediately cavalry weight began to tell. Even after Masistius' horse was killed, followed by the commander himself, the cavalry inflicted heavy damage on the Greek infantry, harrying it for two days, cutting it off from water and supplies and the possibility of orderly retreat. Meanwhile the undisciplined Persian infantry held apart, giving the Greeks the chance of a night withdrawal. With the Greeks retreating Mardonius ordered a concerted attack of cavalry and infantry. Once the Persians were committed with the heavy infantry to the fore, the Greeks turned and forming their dreaded hoplite phalanx fought one of the bloodiest battles in history. Persian cavalry without its commander was ineffective, and on the field of Plataea over 30,000 Persians died, leaving the pitiful few to make their escape back to Sardis. Seeing the tide turn against the Persians the mercenaries fled the field, with the exception of the Boetian cavalry which formed a protective shield which the harrying Greeks could not penetrate. Thus ended Xerxes' grand design, and the Greeks were freed from Persian dominance.

As the Persian Empire grew so too had grown the army – too great to deploy successfully, far too large to provision adequately as it ranged thousands of miles from the heart of the empire. It had been bulked up with huge numbers of infantry and cavalry. Though enormous, it had not kept pace with the added needs of controlling an ever-lengthening border. To the Greeks at Plataea must have fallen the choicest chargers, and in the next few decades a Macedonian, Philip II, was to rise to prominence to give the Greeks a cavalry par excellence, which in his son's reign would carry out an epic journey lasting eleven years and covering over 20,000 miles.

2　The conquests and legacy of Alexander

Alexander the Great

During the late fifth century before Christ the myriad petty Greek city-states were still enmeshed in internecine quarrels, each wanting autonomy, each jealous of its neighbours. Their inward-looking quarrels blinded them to the looming Persian danger. In an attempt to bolster their strength some Greek states sought Persian help; other Greeks hired themselves out as mercenaries to the highest bidder.

When Hippias, the Athenian tyrant, was deposed he appealed to Darius I of Persia for help. Athens refused Darius' demand to accept Hippias back, and this launched the series of offensives known as the Persian Wars. Faced at last with the huge Persian war machine the Greek states temporarily united, sufficiently to deploy their justly famed hoplite infantry in a concerted effort to repel the Persians who had grown over-confident and massively unwieldy, and had failed to use their main weapon, cavalry, efficiently; indeed at Marathon, in ideal cavalry terrain, they did not use it at all, inexplicably re-embarking it prior to the engagement. The subsequent battles – Marathon, Salamis (a sea battle), and Plataea, in which the Persian cavalry was used but not effectively once their commander Masistius was killed – gave Greece resounding victories and a pool of prized Persian horseflesh as one of the spoils of war. Instead of consolidating their victory, within ten years they were entrenched in internecine warfare again, leaving the way clear in the fourth century BC for Macedon under the Temenid kings to wax strong.

The Temenids had their own inter-family struggles stemming from multiple legal claimants to the throne of Macedon, until the rise of the warrior and statesman, Philip II, father of Alexander the Great. Elected regent to an infant king,

Philip brilliantly reorganized the Macedonian army and created ancient history's finest bred and trained cavalry. In one sweep he routed the strong force of invading Illyrians who had overrun Macedon. Subsequently elected king he unified Macedon, reorganized the economy and agriculture, and with revenues from this and the country's mines maintained a virtually invincible army which suppressed opposing northern Greek states. With Thessaly he concluded an alliance, and sought to end the discord among the Greek city-states. When they refused to unite he gave battle at Chaeronea in 338 BC. Victorious, Philip formed the unifying League of Corinth with himself at its head.

It was at Chaeronea that Philip's son, Alexander, fought his first cavalry engagement, exploding on to the world battle scene in the first of a string of victories in his whirlwind career across Europe, Asia and India.

Within two years of Chaeronea Philip was dead, assassinated, and Alexander the ruler of Macedon and inheritor of his father's superb army. Philip had invented the twenty-foot long sarissa (pike) of cornel wood, and the dreaded Macedonian phalanx formation, perfected and used to devastating effect by his son. More important from Alexander's point of view was the Macedonian cavalry, which Philip had brought to a state of pre-eminence, at one time, so Pliny the Elder tells us, importing 20,000 Scythian mares to improve the indigenous breeds of the Macedonian plains.

Owing to the poor soil of much of Greece horses were not raised in great numbers, but three regions did produce quality horseflesh and became known for their cavalry: Boeotia, Thessaly, and on the borders Thrace, which had a very strong horse culture. These more fertile regions gave rise to several breeds of horse that became prized cavalry mounts. By 334 Alexander's Thessalian allies had the strongest cavalry unit in the contemporary world.

Alexander was imbued with a love of all things Greek, his father having introduced much of the culture to his court at Pella. As tutor to his son he had engaged the Greek philosopher Aristotle who was to have such an influence over the young king. Alexander always sent fruits of victory to Athens, but never in return received the desired acceptance from that restless city, the orator Demosthenes, who despised all Macedonians as barbarians, constantly inveighing against him. Despite this Alexander determined to make reparation to Athens for the desecration wrought in an earlier era by Xerxes, the great Persian king. However, before invading Asia he first had to secure his northern boundaries against Triballians and Getae, and then his western border against incursive Illyrians. In these engagements at the very outset of his reign he set the pattern for future victories, using his lightning strike force, the elite Companion Cavalry composed of eight squadrons, seven of just over 200 horses each and spearheaded by the Royal Squadron of 300 from whose nobles were drawn governors and generals.

The mounts of these highborn Macedonians were no less noble, being horses from Thessaly which were rated the best possible chargers for warfare. They were larger and heavier than the usual Greek horses, and had in antiquity acquired the description 'bull-headed' from the shape of the head, which had small ears set well apart on a wide brow with a large poll. It was from this breed that the famed charger Bucephalus came. The name by which he is known to posterity means 'bull head', being in effect his actual description. From the description of his head other characteristics may be inferred. Many horses of the common, carty, heavier type have coarse, long heads with narrow brows, often accompanied by long, close-set coarse ears. The description of the 'bull-head' puts one in mind of that other horse of antiquity, the Arabian, in two respects: both have small ears and both have wide brows; and in the latter it is accepted that the broad brow gives the necessary added room for the Arabian's measuredly larger

brain. Alexander's charger Bucephalus was credited throughout his long life with acts that today we would describe as intelligent and courageous.

The story told by many ancient writers – Plutarch and Pliny especially – recounts that a dealer, Philoneicus, had brought the Thessalian stallion to Pella where he was being tried by grooms in front of Philip. He refused to submit to a rider, repeatedly plunging and rearing. Twelve-year-old Alexander, seeing that the horse was scared of its wildly moving shadow, challenged the grooms, offering the price of the horse, a massive sixteen talents of silver (also variously noted as thirteen and eighteen talents), should he fail to master it. Calming the horse and turning it into the sun he mounted and successfully rode it. So was born the dual legend of man and horse, and Philip's prideful prediction that Alexander must look for a kingdom to match him as Macedon was not large enough. The partnership between Alexander and Bucephalus was to endure for sixteen years, and before Bucephalus died at the age of thirty he had covered well over half of Alexander's massive 22,000 mile total and had been his battle charger in all of his major victories across Europe, Asia and India.

During the border wars Thebes revolted, inciting other city-states to rebellion and also killing the garrison's Macedonian officers. In a swift reprisal Alexander swooped southwards over mountainous territory so quickly that the Thebans, thinking he had died in the northern campaign, presumed it was Antipater who had been left commanding Greece. Refusing all mediation they received no mercy from Alexander when the city fell. It was the only city Alexander destroyed and the incident served to bring the rest of Greece to heel under Antipater's governorship. As usual Alexander was in the thick of the battle, and Bucephalus was wounded. Pliny tells of the horse's courage when he would not permit Alexander to change to another mount. No doubt maddened with pain he proved fearsome, as ancient warhorses, unlike docile modern mounts, were usually stallions and trained and encouraged to offensive use of tooth and heel.

A year had passed since Alexander's accession, and with his back secured he turned his army of 30,000 foot and 5000 cavalry towards the Dardanelles and crossed into Asia at the start of the most extraordinary endurance feat of all time, where the loyalty and courage of both men and horses was tested to the full. Once on Asian soil he was in Persian-dominated territory. He brought with him a reputation for invincibility so that Darius III was advised to send a force into Macedonia to harry Alexander's back and prevent reinforcements of men, horses and provisions reaching the Macedonian. He was also advised to retreat before Alexander's army in a scorched earth policy. But Darius, no military strategist, refused, feeling it showed fear of a general too young to claim superiority over the massive Persian juggernaut. Instead the Persian forces stood ready on the far bank of the River Granicus with four times the number of men Alexander could deploy, and with their heavy cavalry mounted on Nisean chargers massed in the centre.

Over the years Alexander was repeatedly criticized for rashness, his strategy being to take the initiative with his Companion Cavalry striking at lightning speed in their sharpened wedge formation. This, coupled with the impact of the feared Macedonian phalanx of pikemen, proved invincible. At the Granicus, against the advice of senior generals, he took the offensive, gambling on speed to unnerve the enemy. Thirteen squadrons of cavalry surged across the dangerous depths of the racing river, scrambling up the steep and slippery banks, which fortunately crumbled and eased the passage for the following foot. They were met by the waiting Persian cavalry and hand-to-hand fighting ensued, a swirling mass of horseflesh and biting iron, arrows raining down, swords slicing. Gradually the Macedonian horse thrust forwards, the infantry scrambling up the crumbled bank behind and forming into their dreaded phalanx. Stupidly the Persians had deployed their mercenary Greek infantry behind their cavalry, rendering them powerless. With his strategist's eye Alexander reacted by directing his Companions' charge at the Persians' weakest point, as Arrian described it 'at the double'. At the centre of the mêlée Alexander drew Persian fire and, his lance shattered, dealt fatal blows with his sword until he was half stunned by a blow to the head, being saved by his foster

brother Black Cleitus. Irresistably the Macedonians carved into the Persian centre which broke and fled, leaving 20,000 dead on the field. Macedonian losses were slight – a reported twenty-five Companions and even fewer infantry falling, though most sources favourable to Alexander tended to exaggerate Persian losses and underestimate Macedonian dead.

Thus in one brief battle in May of 334 BC, Alexander destroyed the Persian army stationed in Asia Minor. The next year he spent clearing all Persian opposition at the sea ports along the southern coast of Asia Minor, especially Miletus which had been stiffened by Memnon, a Greek mercenary and the most able general and adviser in Darius' employ. In Memnon Alexander had his most worthy opponent, and he was forced to fight his way around the coast in a winter campaign until Memnon died fighting at Lesbos. With the threat from the Persian fleet over Alexander secured the rest of the coastline, subduing marauding hill tribes, and thus earning the coastal towns' gratitude and securing his rear by friendship. His army wintered at Phaeselis, resting and enjoying games until spring when campaigning was renewed, with various contingents meeting at Gordium in modern Turkey, before the downwards march through the Taurus mountains of Phrygia to the narrow pass of the Cicilian Gates. As usual Alexander's march was so rapid that the Persian governor neglected to man the pass efficiently, so allowing the Macedonians through with ease. Here Alexander took a fever, delaying his meeting with Darius who foolishly presumed that the young king was scared to meet him. In spite of his three years of invincible campaigning neither Greece nor Persia had taken the measure of the man, or his determination and uncanny knack of outwitting all opponents, usually by forced cavalry marches considered to be impossible. In the eighteen months since Granicus Alexander had ridden over 1000 miles, fighting engagement after engagement, often in mountainous country and winter weather and in lands offering scant provender for horses pushed to their limits, yet his cavalry, still comprised of Thessalian stock, was fit and ready to assail the Persian might.

On the Issus Plain Darius waited with his army.

Without realizing it he had cut Alexander's line of communications, but he failed to take advantage of this. Bereft of Memnon, his ablest adviser, he had foolishly drawn up his forces with their right flank to the sea, and was bounded on the other two sides by a range of mountains to the left and the River Pinarius in front, although this had been fortified with stakes against the expected Macedonian attack. The only well-deployed Persians were the massed cavalry under Nabarsanes. Initial skirmishes cleared the foothills of Persians. Unhurriedly, with no semblance of massing for the charge, Alexander and the Companions rode steadily on until within bowshot range he gave the order to charge. No army ever withstood a charge of Macedonian heavy cavalry in all its history, and as it drove right into the Persians both sides suffered heavy losses. The infantry locking with the Greek mercenaries also suffered heavy losses until aided by Alexander, and in concert with the phalanx, the Macedonians drove straight for the Great King's chariot. Darius, fearing capture was imminent, fled, whereat the Persian forces collapsed, joined by Nabarsanes and his cavalry. Darkness prevented a protracted chase, and the Macedonians returned to the battlefield and the incredible richness of the Persian spoils. In all his campaigns Alexander kept the loyalty of his troops and was careful to reward them with deserved riches, keeping little to himself.

Though precipitate when occasion demanded Alexander never once left his rear and flanks unprotected. After Issus, instead of moving directly to the Mesopotamian heartland of Darius' empire, he secured his flank and rear down the coast of the Mediterranean, city after city falling quickly with the exception of Tyre, to which he laid siege for seven months. When it finally fell he enslaved 30,000 civilians and crucified 2000 of the opposing military. Everywhere he left Macedonian garrisons. After Tyre he marched on Egypt which, denuded of its Persian garrisons which had fallen at Issus, received him joyfully. Wintering in Egypt for four months he founded Alexandria, which at a later date under his general Ptolemy was to receive his embalmed body. When the campaigning season of 332 unrolled the Macedonian army had been strengthened. Antipater sent cavalry and infantry reinforcements from home, and many of the mercenaries formerly in Darius' pay elected to go over to Alexander. Before him stretched the vast core of the Persian empire and his greatest test yet.

Darius had at last realized that Alexander was bent on total subjugation of Persia and he had massed an army of 35,000 cavalry, 200 scythed chariots, and 65,000 infantry on the Plain of Gaugemela. To counter this host Alexander had 40,000 infantry and 7000 cavalry, and he was marching further and further from his line of supply. Darius' vast array could not be taken by his usual storming methods so Alexander deployed his cavalry in an ever-extending line, drawing the desired response from the Persians who sent increasing numbers of their cavalry to intercept. Thinking Alexander's line had been weakened, Darius sent his chariots in. The Macedonian infantry lines opened to let them roll through. Only then, with the bulk of the Persian cavalry drawn off and the chariots spent, did Alexander revert to his usual tactics. The Companion Cavalry, held in readiness, charged, driving straight for the Great King who again panicked as he had at Issus, and mounting a horse fled.

While Darius was fleeing on horseback, Mazeus, the Satrap of Babylon, had led his contingent of Persian and Indian cavalry in a sortie against Alexander's senior general Parmenion, who countered with a phalanx formation which opened up to envelop Mazeus' contingent. However, instead of turning to fight the phalanx the Persians and Indians raged on in an undisciplined charge, intent on looting the Macedonian baggage lines. The phalanx closed, turning the enemy towards the charge of the Companion Cavalry from which those Persians who could fled in a final rout. The cost in lives had been huge, estimates of Persian dead being recorded as between 40,000 and 90,000, while the Macedonians lost only 500. Again these estimates must be treated with caution as they are taken from pro-Macedonian histories, but the stark fact of Macedonian discipline over Persian chaos is clear.

In horseflesh the cost was high. In the 35-mile chase after Darius over 1000 horses perished, but

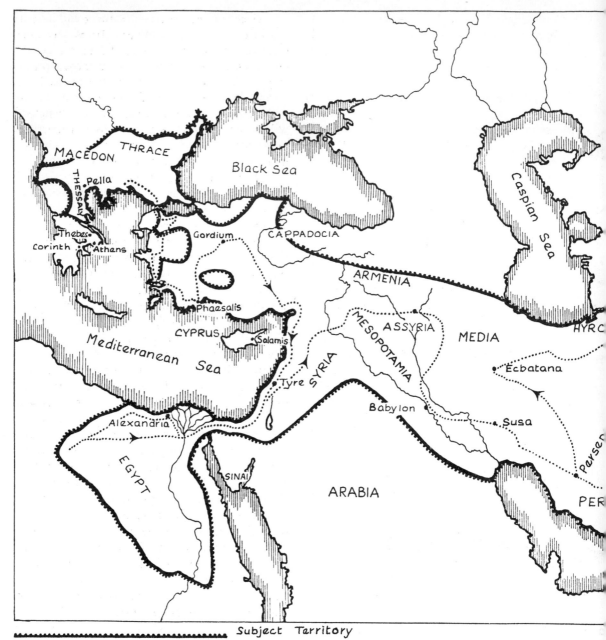

Map 2 Alexander's conquests, fourth century BC.

to balance their losses the Macedonians were the richer, not only by the usual Persian spoils, but by the wealth of the enemy's now riderless horses. At this battle Bucephalus was twenty-four years of age and had been in the thick of the fighting as usual.

After Gaugemela Alexander was undisputed conqueror of Asia, and he followed it up with a lightning march of 300 miles to invest Babylon which, instead of resisting, opened her gates in festive welcome, so hated had been the Persian

FERGHANA

BACTRIA Zariaspa (Bactra) HINDU KUSH RANGE Nicaea

HIA

Hydaspes

GEDROSIA

Indus

ander's Route ....

his Macedonians' dislike. In his turn he was alarmed at some of the young officers becoming softened with luxury and warned them they would fare ill on active service if, in times of relaxation, they left the care of their horses to menials. This throws light on the attitude prevalent in care of horses, it being the duty of the individual, whether officer or enlisted, to care for his own mount, with its resultant benefits to both. Possibly in modern times in our own endurance sport, where such individual care is essential to achieve rapport and understanding, we are only learning from the ancients whose safety depended on thorough understanding of their mount's wellbeing.

In the next six months, the winter and spring of 331–330, Alexander marched on Susa, 200 miles from Babylon, then further south to Persepolis where he unleashed his anger against Persia's desecration of Athens in burning much of the fabled city. Wintering in Persepolis recharged the army's energies for the 330 spring campaign, its first objective being Ecbatana 550 miles away, where Alexander had heard that Darius had wintered and was raising troops. However, Darius had again fled, this time being held captive by one of his own Satraps, Bessus of Bactria. There ensued one of the most dramatic endurance rides of history. Racing over 400 miles through the waterless Parthian desert in the furnace heat of midsummer with a picked troop of light cavalrymen, Alexander took eleven days to close with the fleeing Darius and his captors. Of the initial corps of 500 only sixty remained at the end of the chase, attrition being savage, with men and horses succumbing to heat and the worst enemy – thirst. They caught up with Darius and with the usual Macedonian tactics charged the unprepared sleeping Persian camp at dawn. Bessus, panicking, murdered his king and fled onwards, leaving Alexander to find and bury Darius with full Persian pomp at his erstwhile capital of Persepolis.

Bessus, still loose, assumed the Persian kingship, and the Macedonians pursued him from the torrid desert, climbing into the mountains dividing Parthia from Hyrcania. It was in Hyrcania that Alexander showed how he valued his charger Bucephalus. A group of forest-dwelling Mardians,

domination. There the Macedonians spent a month in relaxation, games and festivals, before the inexorable take over of the fallen Persian Empire continued. In Persia on state occasions Alexander adopted Persian dress and protocol, to in the manner of many outlaw tribes, swooped down and stole the stallion while he was being led by grooms. Enraged, Alexander threatened to wipe out the province's population unless the horse was returned, but anger turned to relief and he relented, even rewarding the captors, when Bucephalus was returned to the camp. His horse had now endured six whole years of campaigning, and when it is considered he did not even start on the 12,000 plus miles of his partnership in conquest with his master until he was twenty-two years of age, he must have been one of the toughest of even the renowned Thessalian breed, many others of which were the companions in battle and route march for the elite cavalry contingents. Throughout the first six years of conquests Alexander continued to receive fresh cavalry horses from his homeland as well as acquiring the wealth of horseflesh Persia bred, plus tribute from conquered tribes in the time-honoured fashion.

Bessus wintered confidently in Bactria, having laid waste the land through which he expected Alexander to lead his army. Again the conqueror did the impossible and least expected, taking the harsher route over the freezing snow-clad heights of the Hindu Kush in the depths of winter at well over 11,000 feet. To hunger and cold was added the risk of mountain sickness in the rarified air. Alarmed, Bessus fled to Sogdiana. Relentlessly Alexander pursued, and in turn Bessus' supporters turned traitor, delivering him up to Alexander for execution. In all Bessus and his usurpation had cost Alexander a year and nearly 4000 miles of hard-ridden pursuit with heavy losses of men and horses, but at last Persia was indisputably his, as many former foes came over to the conqueror's side.

After replenishing his army with recruits and horses his next objective was to subdue the harrying mountain tribes, amongst them the famed horsed archers of Scythia. It was in this later campaign of 329 that Alexander suffered a serious wound and subsequently fell sick with dysentery. The Scythians with their swift shooting and riding tactics also inflicted heavy losses on the Macedonians. To turn the tide Alexander led his Companions in close formation and drove the Scythians off,

killing 1000 and taking many prisoners. But he still had to deal with the only Persian holding out against him. Disappointed that after Bessus was surrendered Alexander did not return to Europe, Spitamenes, the Sogdian satrap who had fled to the land of the Massagetai north of Sogdiana, continued to cause him trouble, heading a revolt. He induced his followers to raid into Sogdiana, and across the chain of defensive forts built by Alexander, into Bactria. Finally, fearing Macedonian reprisals they turned on Spitamenes, delivering his head to Alexander as token of submission. After two years of continuous forced marches and fighting Alexander's army wintered in Bactra-Zariaspa.

Alexander's army was steadily incorporating large numbers of Persians and neighbouring peoples, but the number of Macedonians was steadily shrinking, as garrisons of his loyal countrymen were left wherever he had planted Macedonian sovereignty. He held the loyalty of his personal guard and leading generals – Ptolemy, Nearchus and Craterus amongst them – plus a handful of nobleman who had been with him right from the start. They were to stay loyal to him up to his death at Babylon and beyond, during the infancy of his posthumous son until the child was murdered by Cassander, Antipater's son, and the wars of the Diadochi rent Alexander's empire into multiple kingdoms. Unlike Persian royalty, the Macedonian kings were used to their noblemen speaking frankly, and Alexander had also created a rapport with the rank and file, so that when the Thessalian cavalry was offered the chance to retrace their steps homewards they chose to stay with the Commander in Chief. It was two years before things changed.

After Bactria came the push to the Punjab and the furthest limits of this extraordinary genius' empire. With his troops' loyalty, fired by tales of Indian riches and spoils, he entered the last phase of conquest beset by marauding tribes, especially in the area of Gandara (Afghanistan). Alexander was aided by King Taxiles whose lands stretched from the Cophen (today's Kabul) River to the Indus. Taxiles' warring neighbour was Porus, whose lands were south of the Hydaspes (modern Jhelum). In the winter and spring campaign of 326 which covered over 1000 miles in the region of the Indus and its tributaries, Alexander was to fight the last of his great battles.

The Indian King Porus had ranged a vast army across the River Hydaspes which was raging in spate after an overnight storm. The Macedonians and their horses breasted the waters with great difficulty. The water was level with the infantry-men's chests and the horses forded the river with water at wither height, their heads barely above the torrent. [From this can be deduced the size of the Greek horses in Alexander's cavalry. Macedonians were relatively tall for the times, and giving an approximate height of five foot nine for the average cavalryman (Roman cavalrymen were originally required to be six foot – five foot ten in our measurement – but this was reduced to five foot seven – five foot five our size – in the late empire; in ancient times cavalrymen tended to come from the richer, better fed and therefore better grown classes), it can be worked out that a five foot nine man walking chest to wither height with his horse would mean that the horse was around 14.2 to 15 hands. Pictures of the Parthenon frieze bear this out as the dangling bareback leg position of the men on the horses gives a position in relation to the horses' knees the same as today when a similar sized 14.2 to 15 hand horse is ridden by a rider of approximately five foot nine. (The author at five foot nine can verify this, and also from swimming in a fast river current that a rider without benefit of saddle would be best alongside the horse.) Remember that the frieze was meant to be looked up to, not at eye level, which would alter the perspective in favour of a larger animal than we are led to believe is the case by some historians. Also references to many coins from Macedon and Thessaly shows such a relation in man/horse size.]

King Porus' army was double the strength of Alexander's. However, in this one battle Alexander had greater cavalry numbers than his opponent, but he did not have the terror-inspiring elephants that were Porus' strength. Knowing the Macedonian horses would refuse to engage such fearsome beasts, Alexander used guile and strategy plus good land reconnaissance to inveigle Porus into making just the tactical blunder he needed in order to use his cavalry efficiently. Coming in at an oblique angle, instead of his usual frontal attack, he induced the Indian cavalry to turn and meet him or be enveloped by Macedonians. The tactic worked, with the infantry courageously attacking the elephants and rendering them useless so that they in fact wreaked more havoc amongst their own lines by turning and rampaging in pain, totally out of control.

Macedonian invincibility and discipline told after eight hours of concerted effort by cavalry and infantry, and Alexander emerged the inevitable winner. Once more it was a battle where training and loyalty outweighed massed troops whose main strength lay entirely in numbers. But victory had been bought at the price of his thirty-year-old charger who had carried him into the thick of the fighting and taken thrust after javelin thrust until, weakened from loss of blood, he collapsed. The partnership had endured for sixteen years and well over half of the 22,000 miles of conquest. In those miles he had suffered wounds and theft, and crossed burning deserts and freezing mountain ranges where man and beast fell prey to mountain sickness. Many times the fleeing enemy had scorched the earth bare of sustenance, making hunger part of the war hazard. Persia, Media, Armenia, Cappadocia – all part of Alexander's conquests – bred cavalry mounts in the tens of thousands and Alexander culled much tribute in horses, yet he repeatedly sent back to Macedon for horse replenishments. No better accolade could be found to the Thessalian breed's toughness and qualities of endurance than that 12,000 miles from home and with the wealth of horsebreeding countries, including the superhorses of the Nisean plains, to call on Alexander still chose horses of Thessalian breeding on which to mount his cavalry. Bucephalus himself must have made a great impact and had a strong and endearing as well as enduring character, because about this one factual horse alone ancient historians have left specific stories culled from written memoirs of those present with Alexander. In all earlier instances except for legend a warrior's mount has come down merely as warhorse or charger. Where his horse fell Alexander raised the city of Bucephala in tribute to his memory.

Alexander was to survive his mount by a mere two years, and the Hydaspes was the last of his great victories. His troops finally refused to go further, having been absent from home for eight years, but the incredible exploits were to continue. Not least on the return journey was the crossing of the Gedrosian desert – one of the most inhospitable areas then known where intense heat prevented travel by day only to change to icy biting cold by night. Wells were few; guides lost track of direction; sudden storms swept baggage, tents and animals away, leaving many dead. In the stagnant pools which were left lurked infection to add to hunger. Yet after sixty days in this torrid wilderness both cavalry and infantry came through in good order, though horses and men were skeletal. The heaviest toll was taken from camp followers and non-combatants. But with the final victory at the Hydaspes the highpoint of the most remarkable career in the whole of history had been passed – remarkable for the length of his communications line; for the loyalty of Macedonians to their king, particularly when viewed against the repeated treachery of Persian against Persian; for the vision of a king who treated all men by their worth, not their race, incorporating all races and creeds into his empire on equal terms, but reserving his strongest affections for his own Macedonians. Though many fell short of the trust placed in them others stayed loyal until after his death in 323.

Down the centuries even until today his impact is felt, as is the imprint of the Thessalian and Nisean horses he used on campaigns. Today some Afghans purport to trace their descent from Alexander's Macedonians, and some claim that their horses are lineal descendants of Alexander's cavalry mounts. China improved her cavalry mounts by importing descendants of the 'Blood Sweating' horses of Ferghana, reputed to have been left there by Alexander the Great. From Golden Samarkand and Ferghana the Russians too claim that the golden-coated Akhal Teke breed stems from horses imbued with blood of Nisean and Thessalian chargers carried down the generations.

The horses of Ferghana

Alexander had stretched his conquests farther than any military leader up to his own time and well beyond, and he left a legend behind him that has endured for well over 2000 years. The descendants of the horses which he left behind – horses from his homeland, horses captured from the Persians, the spoils of many wars – became a living legend grazing the fertile pastures of Ferghana near Samarkand and prized and coveted even as far away as China.

It was the Emperor Wu Ti of the early Han Dynasty who cast covetous eyes towards Ferghana. In the late second century BC the Chinese were at war with the Huns who were superior in cavalry. The Chinese, mounted on horses indigenous to East Asia, needed an improvement in their stock, especially in the speed and endurance attributes. The Huns, similarly mounted, were superior in horsemanship, and Emperor Wu, knowing the conflict was likely to be long drawn out, believed that eventual success would depend largely on his cavalry arm. A returning envoy had excited his imagination with a report of the fabled warhorses known as the Blood Sweating Horses of Ferghana. [The syndrome known as 'blood sweating' is caused by a minute parasite that gorges on the horse's blood to such an extent that it appears as if the horse is sweating blood, when in fact he is simply host to a multitude of parasites.] Legend had it that they were descended from those left behind by Alexander, who at the furthest reach of his conquests invested Samarkand, which lies in the province bordering Ferghana. The Ferghana thoroughbreds had just the mix of attributes Wu Ti needed to infuse into his native stock, possessing both speed and endurance. In 106 BC the emperor sent his initial expedition, under the brother of one of his concubines, along the hazardous route to prize future Chinese foundation stock from Ferghana. Of the several thousand strong task force only a few reached Ferghana and this remnant were soundly defeated by the Persians and driven back empty-handed. The emperor had lost face – a soul-destroying state for an Oriental monarch.

In 102 BC Wu Ti, determined on success, once

more sent an armed expedition to Ferghana, only this time it was 100,000 strong. The 4000-mile journey across icy mountain ranges and scorching deserts cost the lives of half the force as they fought their way past hostile terrain and tribes. The remainder of the Chinese army attacked, this time in sufficient strength for success and the prized horseflesh was theirs.

The journey back for these highly bred horses must have been a living hell, used as they were to fertile valleys, lush grazing and the care due to and received by prized possessions of a wealthy nobility. They now had to tackle the 4000 mile journey through some of the most inhospitable terrain imaginable. From Golden Samarkand the journey skirted the icy Pamirs and the Karakorams, heading into China through Yarkand en route to Shahidula and Khotan before tackling the searing heat of the Takla Makan desert in Sinkiang Province. Then skirting Tibet before dropping down to Lanchow in Kansu Province, they finally reached their goal in Shansi Province. Debilitated by hunger –

for mountain and desert offer little sustenance – thirst, dehydration with loss of body salts, exacerbated by mountain cold and desert furnace, the emaciated remnants of the band arrived at the emperor's court. Wu Ti had what he desired – a select band of a few dozen of the toughest endurance horses imaginable.

Recovered from their astounding journey this select band did indeed help China to score a resounding victory over the nomadic Huns, driving them from the territory and putting an end to their repeated incursions into Chinese lands. This victory also resulted in the opening of trade routes across the whole of Central Asia. As cavalry mounts the descendants of the Ferghana thoroughbreds were one more instance where without the horse conquest, peace, and subsequent trade would not have progressed. They have come down to us in the wealth of Chinese art where these fabled equines are recorded in some of the finest art of the Han period.

3 Cavalry and chariots in ancient Rome

Cavalry

When we think of ancient Rome it is not primarily as a horse-owning or riding nation, but definitely as a war-machine enmeshing much of the then known world. People after people fell to the legions – a conquest that escalated for many centuries. At the height of her power Rome controlled the whole of the Mediterranean and bordering countries in an area extending 3000 by 1300 miles, excluding Britain and client states who found it advisable and profitable to owe allegiance to such a powerful empire while staying outside its actual boundaries. However, it was only in the mid third century BC that Rome started her foreign conquests during the first Punic War.

Carthage was to prove a constant thorn in Rome's side for over a century, and gave her her first major lesson in cavalry tactics under the hooves of Hannibal Barca's Numidian light cavalry. Again and again, up and down the length of Italy these horsemen were to play a crucial part in the Barcid triumphs – at Ticinus, Trebia, Trasimene, Cannae. These desert horsemen were renowned for deadly accuracy as mounted archers. They had already endured the long haul from Carthage on the African coast to Cartagena in Spain, then a Carthaginian province. From Cartagena they marched north the length of Spain, crossed the Pyrenees into Narbonnensis (France), and thence to the Alps, crossing into Italy in bitter mountain conditions where all the famous elephants perished and many of the horses. [Polybius tells us that Hannibal did have one surviving elephant which he continued to use as his personal mount.] Those that survived, a force of approximately 6000, already had a journey of 1500 miles behind them, not including the sea passage. Hannibal himself, long resident in Spain, knew the value of blood horses with inherited toughness, and used

Numidian horses. Numidian cavalry, especially their deadly accurate javelin men, repeatedly proved invincible, winning Hannibal his major victories under the Carthaginian cavalry commander Maharbal. Using the now seemingly simple tactic of extending the battle line with cavalry wings, leaving the centre relatively soft, Maharbal enticed the enemy to strike, upon which the wings folded inward enveloping the enemy from sides and rear.

It took Rome sixteen years to get it right by cutting Hannibal's supply line from Spain. Finally recalled to Carthage, Hannibal met his match at Zama in 202 BC. Publius Cornelius Scipio, the greatest general of the Roman Republic, turned Hannibal's best-known tactic against him. Having concluded a treaty with King Masinissa of Numidia, Scipio had strengthened his army with formidable Numidian cavalry and it was this that was Hannibal's undoing.

Though Scipio, named Africanus for his Zama victory, had shown the way to use cavalry Rome continued to put more faith in her infantry legions. In 53 BC the lesson that superb disciplined cavalry would defeat infantry was rammed home a second time. Crassus, in an endeavour to match Julius Caesar's Gallic victories, had launched an offensive against the Parthians and, blindly trusting to his seven legions, failed to study Persian tactics. From the time of Alexander the Great and even earlier, Persia had been renowned for the quality and size of its horses from the Nesean Plains in Media. Confronted at Carrhae by massed Parthian cataphracts (heavy-armoured cavalry), Crassus' auxiliary cavalry was obliterated in the first clash, leaving the infantry wide open to light cavalry armed with powerful recurve bows. Well-prepared, the Parthian general, Surenas, had arranged a back-up in a camel train loaded with spare arrows.

Carrhae, fought on the plains of Mesopotamia, meant Rome's legions were a good 1500 miles and more from home. As the reason for her defeat sank in so did the realization that a crack cavalry arm was vital. Now to the tramp of legions would be added the hoofbeats of the cavalry alae (wings), at first small in number – about 120 per legion; but as the empire grew so did the cavalry units to Ala Quingenaria of 500 and Ala Milliaria of 1000 strength.

Though greedy for power Rome lacked the ferocity and rapacity of earlier conquerors of Asiatic nations, putting her new territories under a relatively light yoke, and gradually assimilating them rather than grinding them out of the empire. From these nations she successively drew her mounted warriors so that the cavalry alae showed great diversification in mount and man and weapons. Each new auxiliary brought with him a mount which had endurance as a vital factor in his makeup, and which was therefore well suited to the Roman style of far-flung warfare.

While drafting these new auxiliary forces into the legions Rome also paid due attention to enlarging the pool from which replacements in horseflesh could be drawn. Spain, one of her earlier acquisitions, became a breeding ground for the alae's mounts. Pliny the Elder in his *Natural History* says that the Gallic and Asturian tribes bred a horse called the Theldones, and that there was a civilian type of riding pony called the 'Cob' with a smooth trot, and which also paced and ambled – a little confusing, but as with twentieth-century horses which are capable of many types of gait other than walk, trot, canter, and gallop, quite possible. Numidian horses with their greater size were used to cross on to the native Spanish stock. Dio Cassius, a historian well acquainted with the history of the Carrhae débâcle, made a strong plea for good horseflesh: 'above all we need to have an abundant supply of the best horses for the army'.

Tribute was frequently in the form of horses. Gaul thus became, along with Spain and Numidia, one of the suppliers of cavalry mounts, but of a lighter type not suitable for the heavy mailed cavalryman. These were introduced as a regular component of the cavalry alae in the time of Hadrian. Eventually Rome was drawing cavalry from all corners of her empire, particularly Dacia (Rumania), Belgica and Osrhoene (Mesopotamia), with their sagitarii (bowmen) being largely of eastern origin.

From the early days of the empire Rome had been harrassed by one nomad nation, almost a precursor in Europe of the later Mongols. The Sarmatians, inheritors and successors to the Scythians, migrated thousands of miles from their central Asian base around the Altai Mountains. They crossed into southern Russia and thence to Eastern Europe where they moved westwards into Central Europe and Roman-held lands, challenging Rome in Pannonia (Hungary), southern Russia and the Crimea, coming right down to the empire's borders on the Danube. Two tribes in particular were to cause havoc for centuries. Both were superlative horsemen – the light cavalry of the Iazyges clad in leather caps and jerkins and shooting with deadly accuracy from bows reinforced with inlaid bone, and the heavy armoured cavalry of the Roxolani whose horses and riders were clad in chain armour, each link stitched to a fabric lining, and the rider armed with bows and heavy lance.

According to Pliny the Elder Sarmatians rode mares because they can urinate on the move. The same writer gives us a glimpse of the enduring attributes of the Sarmatian mounts. Before long forays they were denied fodder the day before and allowed only a little water. Then they were fit for a 150-mile non-stop trek. As with much of Pliny there are seeds of truth mixed with the chaff of legend, but it is certainly obvious from his notes that the Sarmatians knew enough not to overburden their warhorses' digestive tracts, even if the continuous march can be doubted, especially if they were denied water. The distances these nomad tribes covered were to them not unusual. The mounts, far from being only scruffy steppe ponies, had the tough blood of Ferghana thoroughbreds running in their veins. No record has come down of the exact type of horse used, but considering that the tribes originally stemmed from central Asia it would be fairly safe to assume that they rode descendants of the same type of horse used by their original forebears. Specimens of these horses were unearthed in the Pazryk burials in the Altai Mountains of Mongolia and showed both Ferghana and Mongol pony types with the very wide differentiation in size. In the course of their migration ever westwards the blood of other breeds must have been blended, and using as a guide Trajan's column, which depicts Sarmatians with their horses, they are definitely not of the Mongolian pony type, but show both more size and more refinement.

In their seesaw relations with Rome the Sarmatians fought against the Romans, made peace pacts, paid tribute, fought beside them, and then reverted and fought against them once again. Such was the constant trouble that in AD 63 Plautius Silvanus Aelianus defeated and transported 100,000 Sarmatians to Roman territory, but it took until AD 175 in Marcus Aurelius' reign finally to defeat the Iazyges. They came to terms, returned 100,000 Roman captives, and agreed to an alliance which was sealed with tribute of 8000 Sarmatian cavalry, 5500 of which were immediately sent to Britain to help quell unrest that had been simmering there since AD 162. Rome frequently used the policy of displacing whole tribes or large masses of troublesome peoples, and in those days isolated, sea-locked Britain fulfilled much the same role as today Siberia does for Russian dissidents.

There are several interesting points, which if they can be proved conclusively would account for a great percentage of the Sarmatians' ability as horsemen. They are credited with having hard saddles (remains have been unearthed), while at that period other nations either rode bareback, on a saddle cloth, or on a soft, girthed-up pad. More importantly some historians credit them with use of and indeed invention of the metal stirrup and spur. If this is true it is difficult to understand, given the fact that they were considered such superlative horsemen, why other nations failed to copy them, particularly the Romans who usually turned their enemies' attributes to their own advantage. Maybe in the future evidence will come to light to prove conclusively what to the horseman interested in the history of the horse is such a milestone in progress.

Once in Britain the Sarmatian auxiliaries became part of the Roman task force. In Britain we get a glimpse of cavalry training, including the long distances they had to ride on their training trips.

As early as the time of the Boudiccan uprising in AD 60 a gyrus, or horse-training ring, had been built at the Lunt, a Roman Army fort in Warwickshire, England. In area it is very similar to that occupied by a modern dressage arena, except that it is round and has high sides; it could more reliably be likened to a Western ranch's round-pen breaking corral, except on a much larger scale. It was used to break in both horses and newly recruited cavalrymen. It is situated at the top of a flattened hill, so that once the recruits had the rudiments of staying aboard the hill was suitable for training horse and rider to cope with a steep slope at speed. Other cavalry training grounds in Britain with basilica exercitatoria (indoor riding schools) have been located at Brecon Gaer, Newstead and Haltonchesters. Disused hill forts supplied gradient and speed work. Swimming across rivers in full gear weighing 100 lb or more was part of the training. The Batavians, a Germanic tribe from the Rhine, were especially noted for this, according to Tacitus.

In the third century AD the cavalry of Cohors Equitatae I Verdullorum Milliaria used a training ground at Gloster Hill 25 miles from their Risingham base. To reach the training ground much the same terrain as is offered by a modern Competitive Trail Ride was crossed, including rough going and rivers, but without the benefit of saddles or stirrups – indeed, one of the ailments cavalrymen were prone to in Roman times was swelling of the lower legs. The return trip, after manoeuvres, would have qualified even the raw recruits for a modern completion award, though I should think that, although the horses would have passed the veterinary inspection, many of the riders would have failed in the lameness department. Once trained, like the Sarmatians sent to Britain, the British-born troops were sent overseas away from their own home territories.

During the third century AD cavalry had become a predominant part of the army, and the Equites Dalmatae, an elite unarmoured corps, was pioneered by the Emperor Gallienus who also put a new thrust into horsebreeding by crossing Numidian stock on to indigenous Spanish types.

Also during the third century Sassanid Persia was again causing trouble and threatening the Roman Limes (frontiers) in Syria. Mounted on the heavier Persian-bred horses the Sassanians put a formidable force into the field against the Romans, and they have come down to us known as clibanarii, or oven men. Each rider was covered in scale or chain armour made of bronze or iron with a one-piece helmet encasing the head, while the horse had his head covered by a metal plate (a chamfron), his body by a mail blanket, and his legs by metal greaves. Ever ready to adopt, Aurelian introduced this cataphract into the Roman army, using cobby animals with muscular bodies and short thick legs, but unlike poorly bred horses these mounts had small heads. It was quickly found that though the Sassanians might be able to operate clibanarii on their own Persian plains they were unsuited to the Roman habits of long marches over uneven going and roads choked with dust. Good in a head-on charge they lacked the agility and mobility of Sarmatian and Parthian sagitarii.

By now Rome had started her slow decline. Partition meant rule from both east and west, and though she had striven to improve her cavalry, which had finally become a major part of her army, it still lacked the mobility of the far-ranging nomad horsemen who had plagued her boundaries. People with no fixed homes are always harder to control, and the nomads not only roamed, but they roamed on horseback, and it was another such group that sounded the empire's death knell.

The Eastern Emperor Valens probing into Thrace (Bulgaria) pitted himself against the Goths at Adrianople. Fighting in blistering 100 °F heat on the 9 August 378, at first he was successful against the Gothic commanders Alatheus and Saphrax. Then he saw his victory turn to a crushing defeat as the Gothic cavalry, which had been foraging, unexpectedly returned, annihilating the Roman forces and killing Valens.

The year AD 378 is considered the turning point in the fall of Rome. Throughout her history, while victory followed victory, her most bitter defeats were always at the hands of cavalry. Superior cavalry; cavalry that had been able to march for hundreds of miles in scorching desert or icy steppe with horses whose breeds must have been a byword for toughness. Softness creeping into the empire as she became all-powerful and rich has been given as one of the reasons for her downfall. Rarely has the horse been accorded his true merit. Without him aiding her enemies Rome's legions would have remained invincible.

Rome and racing

Good cavalry, or the lack of it, may have been Rome's Achilles' Heel, but she certainly fared better in the racing field – racing not as we know it, but in the Circus with all the glamour and clamour of wealthy Rome on holiday.

Almost all racehorses were hitched to chariots – either the two-horse biga, or the four-horse quadriga, with occasional variations of three, six, eight, or even ten. The most common was the quadriga, so that a full complement with all twelve starting stalls filled meant forty-eight horses stretched across the track. The largest racetrack was Rome's Circus Maximus measuring 650 by 220 yards, with a Spina (central barrier) 233 yards long, and from visiting the Circus it appears that jockeying for room must have occurred early on in the races as the track, though on an enormous scale taken as a whole, must have meant axle to axle driving at the start of each race. Underfoot conditions were hard, with raked sand on top, and each race lasted for approximately fifteen minutes and covered seven laps, a total distance of approximately 5 miles (8.4 km). Considering that the sharp turns at each end of the central Spina dictated a modicum of braking, or loss of ground on a wide-arced turn, the races must have been run in a blur of speed at 20 mph.

Roman racehorses must have been specially tough to withstand the stresses and strains of Circus racing – no soft going, and no easy distances, nor early retirement to stud for the successful racer such as modern racing equines enjoy. The Roman racer must have matched some of our best endurance equines with heavy demands made on bone and sinew, joints and wind – it is no mean feat to gallop flat out for 5 miles incorporating the constant turns around that Spina. Attrition was high, with carnage part of the exciting spectacle. It took a skilful driver to negotiate the fourteen turns and avoid the all too common pile-ups. Only quick-thinking charioteers could cut themselves loose from the reins wrapped around their waists and walk unaided from a tangle of wrecked harness and splintered chariot. Historians' writings and inscriptions in stone make it clear that a charioteer's life was all too often short, and the wastage in horseflesh must have been enormous, both from accidents on the track and injury to limbs and backs with the pounding, turning and twisting.

Racing was under the auspices of special magistrates and organized into Factions, similar to today's training stables, who each employed the necessary vets, trainers, chariot-makers and drivers. Rome scoured her empire for likely prospects, but repeatedly turned to the same sources that she used for cavalry improvements – Africa and Spain. She also imported from Greece, Cyrene, and from the Moors – all of which indicates strains of Arabian blood running in the horses' veins. Italy also produced notable horses, mostly from Lucania and Apulia. One of the most noted breeders, but sadly not for his success on the racetrack, was the infamous Ofonius Tigellinus, a man responsible for some of the worst excesses of the Neronian period, and also responsible for sparking the Emperor Nero's compulsive delight in chariot racing, when he was prefect of the Praetorian Guard.

From the Factions grew the famous four – the Reds, Blues, Greens and Whites – and in Domitian's time a further two, the Purple and Gold, though these two were short lived. Pliny the Elder tells us that horses were broken at two but not subjected to the rigours of racing until they were five, though we may assume that the races offered for young maiden horses were less harsh and of shorter duration. At five and fully inducted it took a special type of horse to endure the ensuing years.

In Roman chariot racing we have one of the few areas where the individual horses have come down to us by name. Among them are the Africans Ferox, Icarus and Cupido; the big winners Coryphaeus and Hirpinus; and the team of four belonging to Porphyrius, a charioteer of the Eastern Empire. Their names – Aristides, Palaestiniarches, Purros and Euthunikos – now grace the Turkish Archaeological Museum in Istanbul. Then there was the Imperial favourite Volucer, who raced for the Greens at the time of Marcus Aurelius. Not an avid racegoer, Marcus Aurelius was ascetic for a Roman Emperor, but his co-Emperor Lucius was an inveterate racing 'buff', using the highly organized Roman Post Road system to have the latest despatches about his favourite galloped to him by courier, even when he was in the furthest eastern parts of the empire. As a constant reminder of Volucer, Lucius had a golden statue of the horse erected wherever he set up camp. The man in the street, while not knowing much of his own pedigree, would be fully aware of the bloodlines of the top racing horses, and the drivers themselves were accorded the status and mass adulation that is reserved for modern pop stars, and with better reason: to survive in the tough world of chariot racing was a great achievement and an endurance feat which needed real talent.

Few charioteers reached old age, and only the best horses would have come through fifteen years of racing sound. Pliny tells us that they retired to stud at twenty and that one mare lived to be seventy-five years of age – again, as with his cavalry statistics I suspect the grain among the chaff, but it does at least indicate longevity amongst the breeds preferred, and therefore a testament to inherent soundness.

The annals of Rome are some of the few ancient writings that specifically give individual statistics of horses, rather than merely lumping them together collectively. From them we know of many successful drivers: C. Appuleius Diocles who notched up a total with quadrigae of 1462 first prizes and bigae 2900 places, racing for all four Factions and with prize money close to four million sesterces (some sources even go several million higher). He retired in AD 150 in one piece, a multi-millionaire by modern reckoning, and rather luckier than Crescens the Moor who had a brilliant ten-year career, dying at the age of twenty-two with one and a half million sesterces already credited. Most likely he was vic-

1 Roman chariot horses immortalized in mosaics from African studs. (Sousse Museum, Tunisia)

2 These chariot horses stand underneath the palm tree which signifies victory. (Sousse Museum, Tunisia)

tim of one of the lethal pile-ups too common in the frenzy of flying hooves. P. Aelius Calpurnianus erected a monument to himself charting his 1127 wins. Primarily won racing an African team for the Blues, his best horse clocked up 105 wins, giving a total of over 500 miles flat out on rock-hard going – a creditable distance for an endurance horse at a more leisured pace on better going, let alone a horse pounding through the hurly-burly of Roman racing.

The Roman Circus anticipated the famous Levi Ride and Tie by two thousand years. The Pedibus et Quadrigam was a four-horse chariot race with two men up, and as the charioteer flashed his team across the finish line his companion leapt down and pounded up the track; the first team to have both horses and runner in was declared the winner.

Witness to the grip which chariot racing exerted on the Equites and Plebs alike was Cassius Dio's cryptic memorandum of an Imperial edict: 'No horseracing is to be encouraged outside Rome as it distracts the people who get hooked.' Presumably inside Rome it was felt that a contented mob was a safe mob, but racing flourished throughout the empire nevertheless with the resulting steady improvement in bloodstock breeding.

Romans en masse at the various games and circus spectacles were not noted for their finer sentiments, being as quick to condemn as to cheer, but at least some of the horses must have endeared themselves to the masses, for in Africa there is a mosaic recording the legend to a famous horse: 'Whether you win or lose we love you Polidoxus.'

The Mongol invasion of Europe

That some of the seeds of retribution sown in 1215 at the signing of Magna Carta would take a quarter of a century to burst into the hideous flower of the Mongol invasion of Europe might seem as remote as the great Khagan's tented capital at Karakorum, 6000 miles from the meadow at Runnymede where King John was forced into signing his famous Charter by his disaffected barons. These banded together to protect their estates and ancient rights and privileges which were being constantly abused by King John by demands for his interminable and costly efforts to regain Normandy for the British Crown. The king signed and then took what, to a medieval knight, was one of the worst types of vengeance – reconciled with the Pope after years of wrangling John secured the excommunication of many of the Charter barons. Amongst these was Robert Fitzwalter, and in his household was a chaplain who suffered excommunication along with his patron. Never named, his existence is referred to in several medieval manuscripts, including those of Mathew Paris, the thirteenth-century St Albans chronicler. In these writings this unknown Englishman is also indicted as largely responsible for behind-the-scenes planning of Batu Khan's invasion of Europe.

Excommunicated and exiled, the English cleric went first to Europe but there was no safe haven for him. By an unknown impulse he headed out on what at the time seemed a one-way journey to the furthest reaches of Christendom, crossed the lands of Islam and rode into the Shamanistic regions of the Mongol Empire. Unwittingly, and definitely uncomfortably, he made what was probably the first major endurance ride undertaken by an Englishman – a 6000-mile journey starting on an ambling palfrey or plodding mule, and once into the Mongols' sphere of influence transferring to a bone-jarring, jolting Mongolian pony. In those days monks and clerics did undertake circuitous routes proselytizing for the faith. The Mongols, toughened and acquisitive warriors, were also very tolerant and inquisitive about strange religions, welcoming holy men of many faiths to their vast empire. At the borders the English cleric would have been advised, as had so many other journeyers, to leave their western horses behind and transfer to a Mongolian mount who knew how to dig for the grass beneath the snows. Once into Mongolian territory, provided he had the required cachet, the frequent posthouses would ensure fresh mounts.

Once at Karakorum he was safe from European retribution, but Europe was anything but safe from him as he soon became a valued adviser to the great Chingis Khagan more commonly known as Genghis Khan; but 'khagan' denotes the head or chief, and 'khan' the lesser rulers (like 'king' and 'prince'), able to tell the great Mongol ruler much of value about the lands of Europe. At the time of England's Magna Carta, Chingis had subdued China and was expanding his empire westwards. The Khwarizmian Empire had fallen in 1220 to the incomparable Mongol general Subutei, who, when Muhammad Shar of Khwarizm died on 10 January 1221, personally carried the news to Chingis at his military headquarters at Samarkand. It took him just seven days to ride the 1200 miles! Azerbaijan also felt the Conqueror's heel, and the Atabeg of Tabriz, rather than risk his city, surrendered monumental tribute in silver together with many thousands of horses. These the Mongols herded back to their camp on the Caspian delta lands of the rivers Kura and Arax, where they were broken and trained to warfare. Neighbouring Armenia, long a land of horsebreeding, also fell to the Mongols. Over Persia, Rum, and even as far as

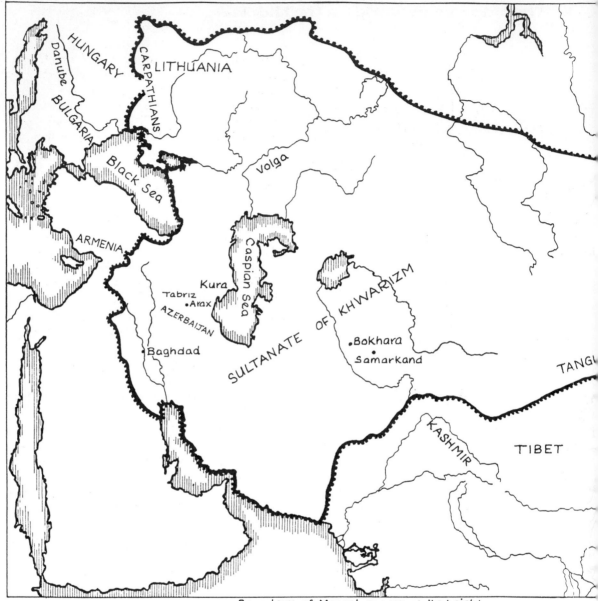

Map 3 The Mongol power at its height in the thirteenth century.

Syria the hordes of Mongol ponies converged in their tens of thousands. And all along the way tribute, often in prized horseflesh, was levied for a city left unrazed, or herds were taken from depopulated lands.

By 1227 when Chingis died the name Mongol was feared wherever tidings of conquest had travelled. The Khagan's legacy to his grandson Batu Khan was 'all the lands northwest of Karakorum for as far as a Mongol pony can take you'. Inherent in his legacy was the acknowledgement made to their indispensable counterpart in war, the

Karakorum

Yellow River

descendants of Alexander's Ferghana horses and the great studs of Persia.

In the ensuing decade a triumvirate worked in harmony: Batu Khan, the unnamed English adviser, and the great strategist Subutei. Under his nine-horsetail banner Batu Khan determined on a literal obedience to his grandfather, for his Mongol pony was to carry him the full 6000 miles from the heart of the Mongol Empire at Karakorum to the very gates of Vienna. But as yet that was in the future. More lands waited to be conquered and the logistics of such an expedition would take years of planning. With typical Mongolian thoroughness the army would not be going into uncharted territory. Subutei, in concert with three other commanders – Jebe Khan, Noyan Khan and Jochi Khan – set forth on a reconnoitering campaign that in two years involved 5500 miles of continuous travel, interspersed with a dozen battles, at the end of which time in 1237 Batu Khan was ready to march on Europe. With him went his interpreter and envoy, the English friar.

Europe was about to have 'the golden bit' put in its mouth, as the Mongols euphemistically described conquest, but they were still five years away from the gates of Vienna. During these years Europe became increasingly more frightened. The fables about the Great Khan and his Il Khans were shattered to be replaced by a terrible reality. The 'civilized' nations of Europe were to learn in a devastating way the lessons the Tartar Khan's Englishman had swiftly learnt at the Mongol court.

Far from being the undisciplined bandits and barbarians of European imagination the Mongols had a highly developed military force. Boys were trained from an early age to ride, to shoot and to hunt, and by the time they were grown to manhood they were ready to serve in a Mongol tuman of cavalry. Consisting of 10,000 mounted warriors, each tuman was under the command of a lesser khan (an Il Khan), usually either a member of the Great Khan's family, or a highly rated cavalry commander such as Subutei. The Mongol troops were not paid. They rode for their honour and the honour of their Khan, and, as well, offered their officers tribute in good horses, cattle and prized felt. A Mongol warrior's whole life centred on his pony.

pony of the plains, small, tough, ugly, but even then merging for the better with the uncountable thousands of head that had been captured or levied from all the countries along their march of conquest. Amongst these ranged the fiery hot bloods of Arabia, Oriental breeds, and also the legendary

He was all but welded to the saddle, eating, drinking and even sleeping there, and at times when short of food slitting a vein in the weakest pony's leg and drinking its blood to sustain himself, plugging the slit when he had drawn off sufficient blood. It was an iron discipline that turned the Mongol youth into the feared Mongol warrior.

Even peacetime exercises mimicked war, for the hunt was used to induct lads and horses into the rigours expected of them on later marches. A Mongol hunt, like the hordes themselves, was on a vast scale using the whole army stretched on as much as an 80-mile front. For days the quarry would be driven, with orders to hold the *coup de grace*. Whole herds of game were pushed into an ever-shrinking area and before the warriors were let loose for the kill the khans had first thrust at creatures turned at bay. A better proving ground for the rigours of war could not have been devised, for not all the hunted were fearful grazing animals. Amongst the prey would be angry tusked boars and big cats with razor-sharp teeth and claws.

The horses too were raised with one thing in mind. They were needed in their hundreds of thousands to mount the tumans. Indeed Batu Khan's horde alone numbered 150,000, meaning fifteen tumans of 10,000 warriors. Each warrior would normally have a string of ponies, one to ride and at least three to follow. These horses were raised on a vast scale and each animal was highly valued. In his first two years, once grown to sufficient size, he would be broken and ridden hard to bend his will to his master, for the Mongol warrior demanded discipline amongst his horses, as much as his commander demanded it from him. Then at two the horses were turned away to graze for three years, being brought up again as five year olds when they would be trained in battle tactics. Their herd instincts were fostered so that each warrior's string would follow willingly. Their stamina was brought to a peak and then tested in races of endurance proportions, but to make sure that no horse won by his rider's guile the jockeys would be inexperienced children, so that each horse's true merits would emerge. Nothing was left to chance. Mares were preferred as warhorses – they were gentler, having neither the fractiousness and un-

ruliness nor the noisy trumpeting of stallions. As they were also used as broodmares and allowed to lactate for three months they carried with them food for foal and man, and when burnt up or weakened they also provided meat. Their milk would be dried and carried as 'iron rations' by warriors who on route march carried ten days' food supply. They were hardy, toughened little beasts, covering the immense distances demanded of them unshod, and subsisting on a diet of grass and roots which in winter they pawed from the ground. The luxury of a corn feed was rare, except when passing through a conquered province when they would sweep the fields as clean as would locusts.

Between such disciplined warriors and hardy mounts grew a bond of interdependence. Held in affection, a favourite warhorse would never be killed for food, but when he died he would pass to the beyond buried with his master.

Each tuman rode horses of a different colour, white horses being both sacred and reserved for khans and princes. One of the most favoured colours, still extant today in many of the modern Mongolian ponies, was piebald (pinto). Together these disciplined men and highly trained horses marching en masse must have presented an awesome sight, strung out on a line of march hundreds of miles wide. Heavy cavalrymen wore armour, a coat of mail and iron or oxhide cuirass, or leather covered in iron scales. Sometimes they depended on a quilted kalat (like a gambeson) without armour. Underneath their armour or kalat they wore a silk shirt, not for sybaritic purposes or the undenied warmth offered by silk, but because when pierced by an arrow the arrowhead would take the silk with it in a spiralling motion, which made it much easier and less damaging to the injured man when withdrawing the arrow with the twist of the silk.

These then were the hordes being unleashed on a quailing Europe in 1237. Riddled with superstition and ignorant of tactical warfare, the European commanders continued in the false notion that the Mongols were undisciplined, attributing their feats to the Devil, for they believed that no mortal man could accomplish what the Asiatic *ordus* repeatedly achieved. Used to the slow, defensive, internecine warfare of one petty baron against another, the Europeans could not understand how the Mongols worked as a cohesive whole over many thousands of miles. This was not warfare, European style! In the Age of Chivalry the baron and prince headed his own Menie (household knights), the richer mounted on lumbering destriers, the mounted man at arms on a lesser, lighter rouncey. It was an age of individual challenge, and the mass charge of undisciplined knights on almost as unmanageable stallions, both eager to be the first in the fray. No European knight would demean himself by riding a mare. Their levies would for the most part be peasant masses armed the best way they could find, often with nothing better than sharpened farm implements. They were also used to the slow, defensive type of campaign withstanding a siege, inside the walls, or waiting outside for the fortress to fall or surrender. They could not comprehend the complete reversal of everything they considered normal. The aggressive onward drive of the Mongol horde sweeping everything before it; the tales of mindless atrocities committed; the utter devastation and havoc; everything confirmed their belief that the vast forces converging on Europe were unstoppable, and they were all but paralysed. Yet on almost all counts the bigoted Chivalry of Europe was mistaken. Winter ice and floods were no barrier to the aggressors, for in a reversal of normal warfare the Mongols paid as little heed to the bitter weather, to storms, ice and snows, as they did to the furnace heat of desert summers. But most of all it was the sheer speed at which they travelled that defied Europe's understanding.

Bulgaria was the first European country to fall to Batu Khan and Subutei in 1237, followed quickly by all of Russia where Mangku Khan and Budjek Khan were the first to reach the Volga River. Even today Russia bears the mark of the 200 years of Mongol occupation in her modern populace. Then it was the turn of Lithuania, Poland and Hungary. The hordes spread over a 600-mile line of disciplined advance. To the Poles and Hungarians the numbers launched against them seemed endless, as for every warrior there would be three replacement mounts.

In battles training of horse and rider paid off,

each tuman working as a unit, signals being sped to commanders and officers by means of flags by day and flares by night. Smoke bombs were used to mask manoeuvres. Though they did have limited firepower they lacked heavy artillery. On the rare occasions when smaller divisions met with successful resistance the Mongols never fought recklessly but used their iron discipline, always withdrawing if outfaced and retreating at speed. And this speed was phenomenal! Whole armies could ride 80 miles a day, keeping up the pace on the tough little ponies for as many days as were necessary to place them at advantage. Iced-over river crossings proved no barrier. The unshod hooves of their ponies gripped on the ice and the lighter weight meant safe passage. Where necessary the hooves would be wrapped in felt to prevent slipping, repeating an old trick that their mentor Chingis had used when he routed the Tangut cavalry at the Yellow River back in 1226.

Their communications too were superlative, news travelling at the rate of 500 miles a day using a combination of fast-riding messengers and strategically placed signals. Never had a host depended so utterly on the endurance qualities of their horses and riders. No wonder that in the superstitious climate of medieval Europe they earned the appellation of 'Devil's Horsemen'. Though commanding their separate *ordus* all the khans worked in a concerted effort, so that when Baidar and Kadan were terrorizing Poland and Leignitz fell to the Mongols, Kuyuk, 600 miles away at Hermanstadt in Rumania, was informed by signal and courier and a day later was able to march against the army of Transylvania and destroy it.

In Poland today the razing of Krakow is remembered still, and I have heard the clarion call of the daily ceremony echoing from the crown-shaped tower of the Cathedral where a trumpeter, on that fateful day in 1241, was cut off in mid-warning by a Mongol arrow. Today the trumpeted call echoes down the centuries still cut off in midnote.

Krakow razed and Poland overrun, the hordes were crowding closer. With Hungary the gateway to Europe their king, Bela IV, made a gallant effort to stem the Mongol tide, but within his borders he had allowed the Cuman peoples to settle after they

35

had been driven from their homes beyond the Aral by the Mongols. The Hungarians detested them, and the Cumans on their part behaved like barbarians in their country of refuge, but Bela would not eject them. He had given his word. So while he and his nobles argued, the Mongols under Batu Khan were swarming down from the Carpathians at the rate of 60 miles a day through the last of the icy blasts of winter. It was March 1242 and Batu Khan was close to success. Subutei was racing up the River Tisza and Kuyuk was already entrenched, feeding disinformation to the ill-organized Hungarian soldiery by mounting dummies on spare horses and visibly swelling his numbers.

Wherever the Mongols had gone they had depopulated whole regions, massacring entire towns and villages, not so much in wanton killing as to make sure that no enemy was left at their backs, and for dread effect to force people to submit to them. Turncoat soldiers were welcomed, and then when least expecting it they would be murdered, for the Mongols had no use for traitors who could turn yet again. But a brave opponent they sometimes honoured, acknowledging his courage with the gift of life.

Bela held out against the Mongols, trying to stiffen his people's resistance, but in the end he too acknowledged defeat and fled. It is from Bela's captured golden tent that Batu Khan's tumans became known as the Golden Horde.

After Hungary, Austria waited like a lamb for the slaughter as the invincible Golden Horde marched to the gates of Vienna in the summer of 1242. Batu Khan's English envoy had gone to demand surrender while the horde waited. Then a miracle happened, or so it seemed to the terrified citizens. They woke to find Batu Khan, Subutei, and all the vast hordes and their herds of horses gone. The lands beyond the walls were empty – the Mongols had simply disappeared. Yet it was no miracle. With the ultimate prize within his grasp the discipline that had stiffened his whole life called Batu Khan back to Karakorum. Ogodei, the Khagan, Chingis' successor, had died and Mongol law required all Princes of the Blood to convene as soon as possible at the Mongol capital to elect a new Khagan. So Batu Khan had turned about and be-

gun the 6000-mile journey back into the wastes of the Gobi desert. Europe and its much depleted population was saved by the very characteristic that the arrogant barons claimed the Mongols lacked – discipline.

As for our English cleric: one month later in the little Austrian town of Wiener Neustadt he was executed. Without him the invasion would still have taken place, for there was no end to the length a Mongol pony could travel. He had but helped to guide its passage, and he paid with his life.

The opening of the Americas

Just as in very ancient days the horse ensured the expansion of many civilizations, carrying conquerors from victory to victory, and also in the more recent past when Europe quailed before the mounted Mongol hordes, so too the horse made it possible for the successful incursions of many Europeans into the New World of the Americas. Although the French, English and Dutch were ably aided by the horses they introduced into the eastern part of America, it was the Spaniards who left the most enduring mark. Centuries later their successors are today's horsemen who bear the appellation 'Western rider'.

Initially it was gold hunger that brought the Spaniards to the Americas, allied with proselytizing fervour, but it was the horse that made Spanish exploration possible. It was the Spaniards who introduced the horse, once indigenous but now extinct, back into America. In the late 1490s they established studs in the Antilles, using prize Cordoban horses as foundation stock. In the favourable climate and on lush pasturage the initial few multiplied rapidly. From these studs, augmented with fresh imports from the mother country, the Conquistadores drew the horses that carried them on their plundering raids into the Central and South American mainland.

In 1519 Hernando Cortés set out with his initial small band of comrades. It is to Captain Bernal Diaz de Castillo, a Spanish historian accompanying Cortés, that we owe the description of the sixteen horses and riders who accompanied Cortés. [Translators have differed in the coloration of some of these horses, bay often being interchanged for chestnut, piebald for dun and cream. In this translation from the original, both options are given.]

Captain Cortés, a black bay [dark chestnut] horse that died in San Juan de Ulua.

Pedro de Alvarado and Hernando Lopez de Avila, a very good bay [chestnut] mare for tilting and racing; and when we reached Mexico Pedro de Alvarado bought his share of the mare, or took it by force.

Alonzo Hernandez Puertocarrero, a grey mare with good speed, that was bought by Cortés for a gold ornament.

Juan Velasquez de Leon, another grey mare, very strong, which we called La Rabona (Bobtail), with a good mouth and fast.

Christobal de Oli, a dark chestnut [dark brown] horse, very good.

Francisco de Montejo and Alonso de Avila, a dark chestnut horse: it was unfit for war.

Francisco de Morla, a dark bay [chestnut] horse, very fast and well bitted.

Juan de Escalante, a light bay [chestnut] horse with three white feet, no good.

Diego de Ordas, a grey mare, barren, a pacer but not fast.

Gonzalo Dominguez, an extremely fine horseman, a dark brown [chestnut] horse, very good and with excellent speed.

Pedro Gonzalez de Trujillo, a good bay [chestnut] horse, of perfect colour, which ran very well.

Vaeno from Trinidad, an overo piebald [dun] horse: he was worth nothing.

Moron of Vaimo [Bayamo], an overo [creamcoloured] horse, with a very good mouth.

Lares, a very fine horseman, a very good horse, light bay [light chestnut] in colour and a good galloper.

Ortiz the Musician, and one Bartolome Garcia, a goldmine owner, a very good black horse called El Arriero (Drover): this was one of the best horses we had on the fleet.

Juan Sedeno from Havana, a brown mare, this mare foaled on the ship.

Along with the sixteen horses came 700 years of experience of fighting war on horseback. A later historian, Inca Garcilaso de la Vega, son of a Conquistador and an Inca princess, wrote: 'my country was won *a la gineta*', which meant riding after the Moorish short stirrup fashion which was then prevalent in Spain. This gave the rider a great advantage in delivering a downwards sword thrust, or enabled him to increase the force behind a bow when he rose in the stirrups.

Among the sixteen were eleven stallions and five mares, some of which had initially made the journey from Spain two months' distance away and were already endurance survivors, many horses being cast overboard in the Horse Latitudes where water was short and decisions to save some were made at the expense of others. Then came the fortnight's journey from the Antilles to the landing at the mouth of the Tabasco River. Once on mainland soil they had a scant day's rest before embarking on a reconnaissance that was the precursor of the main conquest. In the first skirmish with Indians eight horses were injured, and in the second Cortés' stallion was killed under him. He first changed to the grey mare, but later on took to riding the black horse that has come down in Indian legend as a god – Morzillo.

The Conquistadores' initial probes into the hinterland took them through jungle territory, where in debilitating and starving conditions they fought rearguard actions against Indians who both feared and resented the incursions of the predatory Spaniards. The fear was mainly engendered by the strange beasts which they initially took to be some sort of large dog, and by the spitting firesticks wielded by the riders who at first they considered part of the horses they rode.

After early attempts to probe the interior Cortés conducted a temporary retreat from Mexico with heavy losses of 300 men and twenty horses, with all twelve surviving horses injured. After a year's rest he returned with far greater numbers and headed south to Honduras, making a daily average of six leagues (18 miles) in territory that tested the endurance of men and horses to the utmost. Used to the drier climate of their European home the men suffered abominably, as did the horses, some of which were Spanish bred and also used to Spain's more favourable climate. Even the Antilles stock found the going tough, exchanging the burgeoning studs where they had been raised for the hazards of inhospitable country that challenged them at every step as they crossed fever-ridden marshes; climbed icy mountain ranges; dropped back to fetid jungles thick with insufferable heat; crossed rivers spanned by swaying liana rope bridges that terrified the horses with their instability. Worse still were the bridgeless rivers swarming with alligators. On land it was not much better, the dense vegetation concealing boa constrictors and venomous snakes which could strike silently and fatally. Overhead the trees were alive with chattering monkeys shrilling danger. The morion- and cuirass-clad men on their strange beasts frightened the Indians into offering their treasures which, instead of buying off the invaders, only aggravated their avarice into full-scale oppression and plunder.

The horses fed off the land; maize was grown by the Indians, but other fodder in jungle areas was scarce, and with hunger allied to overwork, heat and exhaustion they began to drop. The Indian tribes, holding deer sacred, had tamed them and they fed docilely close by the villages, offering the chance of fresh meat and the excitements of the chase, which the Spaniards – excellent riders but bad horsemasters – failed to resist, thus exacerbating their horses' already debilitated state. In addition they were still maintaining their southwards Mexico to Honduras push, and the expeditionary army of Spaniards, although now augmented by allied Mexican Indians, gradually diminished as the route lengthened. Attrition amongst the horses was heavy, sixty-eight animals dying in one mountain pass alone from overwork. Yet others perished falling down precipices too steep to negotiate in their weakened condition. Thirst had also become a killer, for in spite of incessant torrential rains the precipitous route lacked water catchments.

The final force that marched from mountain and jungle to the Honduran coast numbered pitifully few – various historians estimate losses at 250 to 300 for the Spanish leaders, 3000 for the Mexican dead, while the cavalry numbered only 120 still mounted. After a trek which military historians rank as one of the greatest of all time, their journey's end was marked by founding the city of Puerto Cortés.

In the next half century more and more Spaniards set foot on Central and South American soil, bringing with them their prized Cordoban stock, descended from the best of Barb and Arabian blood. The Antilles supplied bulk contingents of horses from now well-established studs, while Spain continued to send infusions of fresh blood, plus fresh adventurers avid for loot. They brought their diseases, and their religion, neither of which the Indians wanted. They took treasure immeasurable, but they did leave a heritage of horseflesh. Many horses survived – escapees, or those left behind too weak to be of use – and it was not long before the Indians lost their fear and began capturing them from the rapidly increasing herds that bred prolifically and unfortunately indiscriminately in their new-found ranges.

But it was not only in the West and in Southern America that Spain's heavy mailed fist was felt. While France and England were making inroads further north, King Charles V of Spain commissioned Hernando de Soto to conquer Florida for the Spanish Empire. Inca Garcilaso de la Vega wrote of the exploits of de Soto's Florida Intrepids.

De Soto was born in the province of Badajoz in Estremadura and made repeated forays to the Americas, always accompanied by cavalry reinforcements, including his own favourite mount Aceituno. On the Florida expedition he was accompanied by a Captain Balthasarde de Gallegos and by Goncalo de Silvestre, who left his native Herrera de Alcantara in Cáceres at the age of twenty. Under Captain de Gallegos, de Silvestre was one of the advance party sent by de Soto to explore Florida and report back. De Silvestre had a reputation for fine horsemanship, and scouting tested it to the full. With his three companions he scouted far into the interior, covering over twenty-five leagues in the first two days. The horses were fresh from several months at sea but they were carrying about 16 stone (224 lb) including man, saddle, armour, and other equipment including iron rations, and they rode by the sun, returning to de Soto with full descriptions to fire the expedition on.

Thereafter Goncalo de Silvestre was de Soto's number one scout, always in the thick of any excitement, trusting to his horsemanship and tough Cordoban mount to extricate him from danger. The Florida Indians were also terrified of horses, but, unlike the Mexican Indians earlier encountered by Cortés, the Florida tribes were fiercer – even today Seminole ferocity is legendary.

De Silvestre's next test came when, travelling with de Soto and a band of 100 cavalry, they found themselves brought up short by a vast swamp. At the end of eight days they managed to discover a way through the swamp only to find themselves cut off from the main army. De Silvestre and Juan Lopez Cacho were despatched to report to the main camp and order up supplies. They travelled light, de Silvestre's chestnut and Cacho's bay making good time over the 15 miles of plains until they came up against the swamp, where they took the wrong route. The horses took over, resisting their rider's directions and retracing their steps to the right spot to cross the swamp. There they were assailed by Indians who pursued them in canoes as they skirted the swamp, until in desperation as the Indians closed with them they plunged into the morass, endeavouring to ford it before they were trapped. Arrows hailed across the water, bouncing off armour as the horses swam onwards. Both men and horses emerged unscathed at the far side to be met by the main army. After arranging for the supplies to come through and indicating safe ground, de Silvestre alone returned to de Soto, an exhausted Cacho remaining to recuperate.

His next venture was with the army, marching the 450 miles to Apalache, until he was needed as scout once more. This time he had thirty of the best horses and riders in the army. His mission: to fetch de Soto's lieutenant Pedro Calderon and his men so the two armies could amalgamate in strength for the winter.

De Silvestre rode directly into danger – swamp, infested rivers, desert and open plains – constantly assailed by Indians, this time armed with more powerful bows so that only Milanese armour proved effective against their arrows. On the first day he covered 39 miles in little-known territory, passing the Apalache swamp, and then rode 36 miles nearly to Osachile, an Indian town. They holed up until night fell and then risked a hair-raising gallop directly through the settlement, not drawing rein for 3 miles, after which they spent the night in watch. The next day the journey totalled 39 miles, the first 15 at a gallop to put distance between them and the Indians. The horses endured the constant pressure despite lack of food and being kept constantly alert. On reaching the Osachile River they swam over at midday, pressing on a further 12 miles to Vitachico where they had successfully engaged Indians a month before. The following days were a hazy blur covering successively 57 miles on the third and 51 miles on the fourth day, which was interrupted by attacking a small band of Indians before riding a further 15 miles to set camp.

The next day they were pressed from both rear and front. Indians were closing on them as they tried to ford the Ochali River and hostiles menaced the landing side, the horses courageously charging the Indians until the whole party was safely landed. In awe of the horses, the Indians had pulled back, giving the Spaniards some respite that night as they waited in Ochale Town. One of the scouts, Juan Lopez Cacho, had succumbed to exposure in freezing conditions and was in a very bad way. While it was still dark they set out, covering 18 miles before dawn, killing any Indians en route. By this time more caballeros were succumbing to the conditions. It was the sixth day and they covered 60 miles, followed on the seventh by another 60 and the loss of Pedro de Atienca, who died in the saddle. The next night Juan de Soto also died at the Great Swamp. Winter conditions had made the crossing so bad with ice and winds that the horses finally refused to go further until the midday sun warmed the water.

They camped at night around huge fires, but failed to warm themselves in the howling wind. Men and horses were exhausted and near starving, but at dawn they picked up the trail and rode 39 miles, followed by a further 18 miles the next day, during the course of which they came on some Indians roasting fish over a fire. They charged the

Indians and, famished, fell on the food. Only Cacho's horse had given out so he took that of a fallen comrade for the last 18 miles to Hirihigua. Sensing journey's end the horses broke into a gallop. They had made an incredible journey in eleven days of non-stop travel, pursued by Indians in territory that was often nearly trackless and that challenged them at every dangerous step. One of the eleven days had been taken up crossing the Great Swamp, another had been spent passing over the flooded Ochali River which was beset with Indians. Out of the thirty horses that started the trip none died, even Cacho's weary mount being brought in three days later by Indians. On the return trip to de Soto, de Silvestre's horse died, struck down by charging Indians, and Garcilaso recounts that the army mourned him as the best horse in all the Indies.

From such stock the present-day American mustang draws its earliest blood, and from the expertise and methods brought in by those long ago adventurers stems much of the rich tradition of the American West and its rightly famed horses.

5 Bitter warfare of the nineteenth century

The Corunna campaign

At his apogee Napoleon Bonaparte was the acknowledged master of Europe, extending French dominion on an ever-increasing scale. He had yet to turn his army's steps towards Russia, but in 1808, during the Peninsular War, Spain was held in the French grip. It was first infiltrated schematically and then nakedly and aggressively occupied by a foreign power. Across the Channel Britain chafed as Napoleon tried imposing a blockade, choking her seaborne trade routes. In an effort to loosen the blockade and to keep her sea lanes open Britain supplied munitions, equipment and vital cash to Spanish guerrillas, and on 19 July 1808 the guerrillas, aided by a British force under Sir Arthur Wellesley, scored the first victory at Boylen against the French, who were under the command of Marshal Soult. Further, in September of the same year a British force augmented by 125,000 Spanish irregulars drove the French, under Marshals Junot and Murat, back to the River Ebro. Alarmed, Napoleon hurried to Spain where he joined his army on 5 November, losing no time in capturing Madrid. Meanwhile under Sir John Moore the English were advancing from Corunna to join in battle with the Corsican's army, forcing Napoleon to divert from Madrid in order to engage the British.

The British force was to be augmented by the crack cavalry of the 15th Hussars, whose Lieutenant and Adjutant C. Jones has left a diary of the campaign – cryptic, pared to essential notes, but clear, written day by day in bivouacs throughout the bitter cold of Spain's winter, in which men and horses suffered abominably on the 200-mile probe into the French-riddled Spanish interior.

The Hussars embarked at Portsmouth on 28 October 1808, the troops and horses enduring more than two weeks of storm-tossed conditions crossing the infamous Bay of Biscay before disembarking at Corunna on 15 November and heading for a proposed merger with Sir John Moore's forces. Five weeks of marches through deepening winter weather and across bitter mountain ranges faced them – horses that were used to the regimented life of cavalry care and largesse now living off a land already stripped, the troopers in constant fear of apprehension by patrolling French. Bivouacs were bad, food short, fodder often non-existent. Wrenched from comfortable cavalry stables the horses quickly became debilitated, one dying early en route, yet the Hussars rode onwards, carving through increasingly hostile territory as the relative safety of the coast dropped further and further behind.

From Corunna they rode inland to Betanzos, Lugo and Constantin, where the road was littered with dead horses, witness to earlier engagements. From Constantin they dragged on to Nogales, then Travatillo, where the entry recorded a 30-mile mountain march in ever-worsening conditions. Via Benbiere, La Baneza, Benevente, Zamora and on to Toro where they almost cut back on themselves to Morales and Mayorgo. Here another 30-mile march was hampered by a raging snowstorm, until on 20 December they arrived at their penultimate bivouac.

They had been lucky so far. Secrecy of movements had been maintained, no doubt because of the atrocious conditions. No enemy had been encountered en route, but at Sahagun on 21 December their luck ran out, as an unexpected force of French – the 11th Cuirassiers and the 8th Regiment of Chasseurs under the nephew of Madame Bonaparte – materialized. Both sides were caught by surprise and the French gave battle in the mistaken assumption that it was a force of Spanish irregulars facing them. Too late, they realized it

41

was a troop of the feared British Cavalry. In the ensuing skirmish Cuirassiers and Chasseurs disintegrated, thoroughly demoralized and 'every man for himself', as Lieutenant Jones noted, breaking off the engagement inconclusively. British casualties were light – two dead, four wounded, ten missing – but the penalty for war in hostile territory amongst the now alerted enemy forced the Hussars to destroy many of the remaining horses to save them from falling to the French. With little enough time to recoup and recover Lieutenant Jones' diary records that the retreat from Sahagun began on New Year's day 1809, with debilitated, starving horses, while all the time the French harried their rear.

Their retreat through 200 miles of hostile terrain, mountainous, foodless, and endlessly wearing in worsening weather, was conducted skilfully under Sir John Moore. At Nogales Mountain conditions were so bad that many men froze to death when night-time temperatures plummeted. The horses had deteriorated so badly that many were destroyed. By the time they reached Lugo the British Cavalry had become totally unfit. Fifty miles later they reached Corunna on 11 January, to find that the hoped for succour had not arrived. The sea roads were empty. There followed five days of suspense. The French were closing the gap with fresher men and well-fed chargers. To minimize casualties and leave nothing for the approaching French the magazine was blown up, and finally on 16 January Sir John Moore also reached the coast, joining the advance party of Hussars. The ships arrived, but too late to avoid battle. Although ranked as a British victory it was hard won, Sir John bringing 15,000 safely to embarkation but dying in the attempt. The toll in horseflesh was horrific. The transports were insufficient, only thirty horses per regiment out of the thousands originally embarked being given passage back. Hundreds were despatched on the beaches, the tides doing their grisly but cleansing work, until on the 17th the remnants set sail for England, reaching Portsmouth on 26 January.

It was said that Napoleon claimed he 'had driven the easily defeated English into the sea', yet he would meet those same English again on the field of Waterloo. We know of the famous Marengo, Napoleon's grey Arabian charger, and Copenhagen, Wellington's favourite chestnut stallion, but for a troop of Hussars infiltrating 200 miles deep into war-torn Spain all trace of their beloved chargers was washed from memory by the tides, save for brief references in a little-known war diary relating a bitter campaign that was even costlier in equine than in human life.

'Theirs is not to reason why'

A twenty-minute cavalry engagement on 25 October 1854 when the brilliant Light Brigade, led by the irascible Earl of Cardigan, charged Russian guns head on in the valley north of Balaclava marked the culmination of a campaign of disaster and unparalleled endurance by British cavalry. [This section draws heavily on the authoritative work by Cecil Woodham-Smith, *The Reason Why* (Constable, 1953); quote from Tennyson.]

The carnage of the famed charge into the Valley of Death was the final milestone for 500 erstwhile sleek horses on an endurance trail that had started in January when the Crimean War became inevitable. Britain's Turkish allies had had their navy annihilated by the Russians, and Britain ostensibly armed to protect them in the Danube provinces. However, the real aim was openly avowed to be termination of Russian naval power in the Mediterranean. To do that Sebastopol, the Russian base, had to be crushed.

Right at the outset that old bogy 'class' dictated cavalry leadership. The cavalry had an inborn belief in their own superiority. Their blood horses and their men were superior; their officers in the main were not, in spite of their own good opinion of themselves. As the renowned French cavalry commander, Excelmann, commented after praising the horses and men: 'The British cavalry officer seems to be impressed by the conviction that he can dash or ride over everything; as if the art of war were precisely the same as that of foxhunting.'

Three such officers were appointed to command: Lord Raglan as Commander in Chief; Lord Lucan as Commander of the Cavalry Division; and Lord Cardigan as Brigadier General in command of the Light Brigade. The Heavy Brigade was given to Colonel James Scarlett, the only cavalry commander who had enough sense to realize he was new to actual warfare and to equip his brigade with battle-experienced officers from the Indian campaigns. With the exception of a quarter-century-old engagement credited to Lord Lucan, none of the others had experience of warfare. The irony was that there were cavalry officers with vital experience, but all were from the Indian regiments. 'Class' dictated that they were inferior, so they cooled their heels in England.

The journey to the Crimea was horrific for the horses. Notoriously bad sea travellers, as many as eighty-five at a time were crowded into small sailing ships to endure nearly two months of fetid conditions below decks, the storms in the Bay of Biscay sending the horses cannoning across the hold every time the ship rolled and heaved. Crossing the Mediterranean the temperatures soared. Confined in their below-deck hellhole several horses went beserk and had to be destroyed. Better and quicker passage could have been made in steamships had the command planned ahead. Lord Cardigan travelled independently and comfortably to Scutari.

Many horses were injured during the landing. Insufficient feed and water were available. It was sweltering summer. Cholera raged amongst the men. Horses were increasingly debilitated, hungry and dehydrated.

Both Lord Cardigan and Lord Lucan were impatient to engage the enemy, but Silistria had been relieved without the cavalry's involvement, the Turks aided by British officers from the Indian Army. Lord Cardigan angered his superior, Lord Lucan, by going over his head and consulting directly with Lord Raglan, and was sent on a reconnaissance mission to see where the Russians were. He took 196 horses into a baking interior, travelling light and hard for four days, covering over 200 miles to the Danube, constantly on the alert. The Russians had crossed the Danube, and for days the cavalry patrolled the river banks before heading back for base at Varna. Horses and riders arrived in a terrible state seventeen days after setting out, the horses exhausted and under great

stress from the forced pace, heat, hunger and thirst. Many were so exhausted they had to be forcibly driven into camp where over seventy-five died and others were rendered permanently unfit. Of the original 196 horses, less than half were left for active service. The utter stupidity of the action was revealed when Lord Cardigan brought back no information about enemy positions or strength.

Lord Cardigan was totally immune to the sufferings of both his men and his horses, drilling them incessantly under burning skies, insisting on Parade Ground turnout, playing at war. When they removed to a new camp hoping to outdistance the cholera which was decimating the troops, he selfishly secured the only shade and water for himself and his luxurious equippage. The men had to tramp nearly a mile over a pitiless plain for water, dragging animals with them.

So far Lord Lucan had been denied any action, even of a reconnoitring type, and he was fuming, angered by Lord Cardigan's behaviour. When orders came early in September to board ship for the Crimea he resolved to place Lord Cardigan firmly under his command.

The situation in regard to horses and pack animals was chaotic, as transport was inadequate. Over 6000 horses and pack animals were left behind in corrals to die of starvation. At Varna the waters were crammed with vessels around which bobbed the decomposing corpses of cholera victims. At Balchik Bay the horrendous sights were repeated. Embarkation at Varna, rendezvous with the fleet at Balchik Bay, and sailing spanned a week, during which time horses stifled and sweated in fear below decks. Storms broke out in crossing the Black Sea to Eupatoria, the port of disembarkation in the Crimea. On one ship, out of a complement of 100 horses packed into the space for half that number, seventy-five animals died. For some a three-day journey spun out into seventeen days of hellish torment.

Before embarkation General Richard Airey was appointed to Lord Raglan's staff. He brought with him Captain Nolan, a man devoted to horses and cavalry; a horseman famed for his revolutionary approach to training horses by the 'softly' method we recognize today. He was also the catalyst for the charge immortalized by Tennyson.

On 13 September the fleet anchored off Russian-held Eupatoria which surrendered, its whole garrison consisting of invalids. The fleet then sailed into Calamita Bay where disembarkation started on the 14th, Lord Cardigan complaining of the horses' bad condition. Notwithstanding this, the Commander in Chief ordered an immediate reconnaissance with a combined cavalry and infantry force. It was a disaster: men collapsed, horses returned hardly able to stand. Due to severe debilitation the Light Brigade could neither function as scouts nor find provisions. Lack of planning put the army in a parlous state – without food, water, forage; indeed with insufficient supplies of any kind. Rations were disgusting – biscuit and salt pork in a climate guaranteed to turn such meat rancid.

The Crimea offered ideal cavalry terrain, yet the British had brought only one division. Lord Raglan had refused to allow Indian officers to raise local cavalry, his personal dislikes extending both to Turks and to English officers who had served in India, yet the army was soon to face Russian hordes on their way to Sebastopol.

The army toiled on under relentless heat, maddened with thirst, until cresting a rise they saw the River Bulganek below. Caution and restraint dissolved in a wild rush into the valley. Cossack scouts suddenly appeared and disappeared on the heights across the valley. Four squadrons of cavalry were sent to reconnoitre. Lords Lucan and Cardigan were at last on the edge of action, with 2000 Russian cavalry facing them on the opposite slope of the valley. From his vantage point above the valley Lord Raglan now saw what they had been dreading – the massive Russian host of 60,000 infantry and a dense mass of Russian cavalry and Cossacks. His cavalry must be protected. It was too precious to lose in a senseless engagement. Reinforcements were sent in. The Parade Ground earls were forced to retreat to the jeers of the Russians. Now nerves were on edge. An attack was imminent, but nothing happened. The Russian base was in an unassailable position 6 miles away. The British would beat themselves out at the foot of the

impregnable heights overlooking the River Alma. But by a string of incredible tactical errors what should have been an overwhelming Russian victory turned into a rout. Due to an equally incredible blunder Lord Raglan refused to allow the seething cavalry to pursue the fleeing enemy. The whole Crimean campaign from start to finish was a mass of stupid errors, not least of which was failure to consolidate gains.

The site of the Battle of Balaclava was a plain to the northeast of Balaclava. This 2 by 3 mile area was bisected by a ridge. Russian forces deployed in the northern valley backed by the Fedoukine Hills; the British deployed in the southern half. A battery of Russian guns was sited at the eastern end of the valley. To the south were stationed the Highlanders of the 93rd Argyle and Sutherland Regiments. To the west were the heights on which the British Commander in Chief and his staff overlooked the valley. South of these heights was the fateful gap through which the bravest and the most wasteful act of the whole campaign was to erupt.

Balaclava was to see two major cavalry engagements. Both have gone down in history: the charge of the Heavy Brigade under General Scarlett for the sheer valour of British cavalry against overwhelming odds, and the fatal charge of the Light Brigade.

Fighting was fierce, and superior Russian numbers told, the British losing their redoubts to Russians. Russian cavalry stationed in the northern valley massed in solid formation and came at a steady trot, crossing the ridge and overrunning the British. All that stood between the Russians and Balaclava were the Highlanders and the Light Brigade guarding the approach to the town. The Highlanders had been told to lie flat and as the Russians confidently advanced they rose and fired. Three withering salvoes tore into the Russian cavalry who turned tail and fled. Four thousand Russian horse were bearing down the ridge towards the meagre numbers of the Heavy Brigade who were calmly dressing ranks and waiting to receive the onslaught. Then unaccountably the Russian line wavered and halted, and Colonel Scarlett launched his charge uphill. In a frenzy the first line of 300 Scots Greys and the Inniskillings tore into the Russians to be lost in their midst, only bright specks of red telling the Commander in Chief on the heights that the Heavies were taking toll of the grey mass of Russians. Then the second line launched, the second squadron of Inniskillings, 5th Dragoons, and Royals. The mass boiled, surged, and still the embattled few fought on, hacking and carving their way through the Russians.

Unbelievably the Light Brigade, a scant quarter mile away, remained motionless. No orders had been received. They were to guard the route to Balaclava. Then Lord Lucan sent in the 4th Dragoon Guards, and incredibly the mass of Russians wavered, rallied, wavered, and fled. The Light Brigade under Lord Cardigan were livid. Denied the chance to prove themselves they felt their honour was at stake.

With the Russians retreating up the ridge the north valley was clear of enemy, though they still held the Fedoukine Hills. Lord Raglan decided on desperate measures and issued orders for the Light Brigade to charge down the northern valley and retake the redoubts. Captain Nolan risked his and his horse's life careering full gallop 700 feet down from the heights carrying the directive from Lord Raglan to order the Brigade to charge immediately. The wording was ambiguous. Lord Raglan said the charge would be backed by infantry which had been ordered down. Lord Lucan understood it to mean to charge when the infantry arrived. He knew that riding into that valley meant annihilation and questioned his target. Nolan emphatically gestured towards the Russian guns at the eastern end of the valley and reiterated the order. Lord Lucan was tied. Queen's Regulations specifically stated that aides carrying orders were to be obeyed without question. At last Lord Cardigan, who commanded the Light Brigade, would have his moment of glory. Lord Lucan was to back up the Light with the Heavy Brigade.

Riding his favourite charger Ronald, a chestnut Thoroughbred, Lord Cardigan rode ramrod straight at the head of his 700 men. Iron discipline maintained a steady trot, even as horses and men fell rapidly in a withering crossfire from the ridge to their right and the Fedoukine Hills to their left.

Gaps opened and immediately closed, ranks redressing as steadily the Brigade shrank. Maimed and riderless horses charged into the Brigade causing havoc, desperately seeking the safety of their own kind. Pressed from behind Lord Cardigan angrily maintained his leader's position, even laying the flat of his sword against the chest of an eager Captain. Eight minutes had passed. Troopers being mown down from both sides could be held back no longer and broke to a gallop, carrying the charge towards the Russian battery hidden in a pall of smoke. Eighty yards from the guns a salvo exploded and the front line of the 17th Lancers and 13th Light Dragoons disappeared, mown down, as grape, shells and round shot poured from the battery. The Light Brigade was being destroyed, not by ones and twos, but in whole sections which shattered under fire from three sides. Wearied from their earlier punishing engagement, the slower Heavy Brigade bringing up the rear were checked, Lord Lucan calling a halt, exclaiming: 'They have sacrificed the Light Brigade; they shall not the Heavy, if I can help it.'

Alone the remnants of the Light Brigade charged into the mouth of the Russian battery. Lord Cardigan, with horses falling screaming around him, was the first at the guns. Only fifty of the hundreds in the first line survived. The second line of 4th Light Dragoons, 11th Hussars, and 8th Hussars charged on. Fighting to secure the guns the Brigade Major, Colonel Mayow, looked up to see a mass of Russian cavalry bearing down, and gathering the remnants of the first line charged the Russians, putting them to flight. Meanwhile the second line poured in. The 11th Hussars, after successfully despatching a body of Russian lancers, found themselves face to face with the bulk of the enemy cavalry and infantry and were forced to retreat, tangling with the 4th Dragoons who were advancing after securing the guns. They were in an impasse. Facing them was the mass of the Russian cavalry. Behind, their retreat down the valley was cut off by a troop of Russian lancers. Lord Cardigan, the Brigade's commander, had disappeared. Incredibly, feeling his job of leading the charge to the guns to be over he had ridden off the field of battle, and even more incredibly he emerged almost unscathed, even passing close by a band of Cossacks who let him go.

Meanwhile without their commander the remnants of the Brigade sold their lives dear, charging the Lancers, spurring their exhausted horses into a last desperate gallop. Again, unaccountably, the Russian line gave. Lord George Paget noticed them waver indecisively as they had done earlier, and with no more than a few jabs allow the few survivors to pass unhindered.

The retreat stumbled back down the valley, broken horses and wounded men dragging painfully along, troopers refusing to abandon their beloved chargers. The few capable of being ridden carried wounded. The Russian lancers harried their rear until they too fell back, succumbing to shots from their own riflemen on the heights who were picking off the straggling remnants of the once glorious Brigade.

Limping up the valley 195 men returned from the 700 who had entered it twenty minutes earlier. Five hundred of their gallant chargers lay shot to pieces on the valley floor.

In the aftermath there were recriminations: Lord Raglan blamed Lord Lucan for attacking; Lord Lucan averred that he had been ordered to do so; Lord Cardigan arrogantly explained his early retreat from the battlefield by saying that it was not his duty to fight among privates. He had discharged his duty by leading the charge.

And the horses and their riders – in the ranks Sergeant Major Loy Smith of the 11th Hussars was 'moved to tears when I thought of my beautiful horse; she was a light bay, nearly thoroughbred, I became her master nearly three years before'. Five hundred beautiful horses lay on that battlefield, at the end of a reckless campaign where position in the army was gained by purchase, by class, by influence, but nowhere by experience. From start to finish the ranks and the horses suffered privation, heat, parching thirst, hunger, and for the remnants of Balaclava it was not yet over. Far from honourable retirement the chargers suffered a bitter Crimean winter in starving conditions so bad that they ate their halters, their saddle flaps, and each others' tails. When it was suggested to Lord Cardigan that the horses should be sent to Balacla-

va where there was limited forage he refused, saying they were needed at the camp base in case of another attack. Only maimed horses were allowed to be destroyed. Those in their agony of starvation suffered until the end, while Lord Cardigan slept in comfort aboard his yacht.

The flight of the Nez Percé Indians

They made us many promises, more than I can remember, but they never kept but one; they promised to take our land, and they took it.
Red Cloud of the Oglala Teton Sioux

[Quoted in Dee Brown, *Bury My Heart at Wounded Knee* (Barrie and Jenkins, 1970), from which this section draws.]

Red Cloud's terrible indictment against a people living in 'the land of the free' was repeatedly justified as these freedom-loving settlers carved their homesteads out of Indian territory. Early in the nineteenth century Washington bureaucrats coined a pseudo-legal sounding phrase. They called it 'Manifest Destiny', its arrogant interpretation the white man's assumption that he was destined to rule the Indians. Coupled with the assumption went the implied right to appropriate the Indians' heritage – their ancient homelands. The settlers showed themselves to be inheritors of the Assyrians, who were the first to practise mass deportations, as well as precursors of the twentieth-century racists whose tenet is that white is supreme.

One Indian tribe to suffer depredations was the peaceful Nez Percé living in the Columbia Basin in Washington Territory. The tribe's acquisition of the horse in the early eighteenth century gradually changed their culture from sedentary fishermen and cultivators to a nomadic existence, enabling them to range far and wide in pursuit of buffalo. By the time the white settlers had laid covetous eyes on their territory they had become famed for the quality of their horses. Where other tribes acquired their horses by raiding or as the spoils of war, the Nez Percé followed a breeding policy, constantly improving stock, gelding undesirable colts, culling all but the best. Their herds numbered in the thousands and were of a type unusual in Indian culture; they were larger, standing 15 hands and better, and of a heavier build but with the elegant characteristics that denote well-bred stock as we understand the term. It was on this wealth of well-bred horses, of both solid and Appaloosa colouring, that the Nez Percé were to make their bitter ride over 1300 miles of rough mountains and steep valleys, harried by the cavalry throughout three and a half months of a desperate fight in the summer and autumn of 1877 to retain their personal freedom.

White acquisitiveness had surfaced more than twenty years before when the Governor of Washington Territory informed the Nez Percé chieftain, Tuekakas, that the government required the white man and Indian to have separate territories and demanded the chief's signature on a 'treaty'. The old chief refused, but some of the lesser chiefs were persuaded by the promise of presents, though Tuekakas warned that taking presents of any sort implied acquiescence. Repeatedly over the next few years other 'treaties' were enforced, the Nez Percé homelands shrinking at each signing. In 1871 when Tuekakas died his son Heinmot Tooyalaket, known to us as Chief Joseph, succeeded to the chieftainship, and so began the final phase of disinheritance. Chief Joseph refused to move his tribe to the Lapwai Reservation, requesting the Great Father, President Ulysses Grant, to allow the Nez Percé to remain in their Wallowa Valley homelands, and receiving the president's promise to bar the valley to settlers. In 1875, only two years later, the promise was broken and settlers allowed in, while the tribe was ordered on to the Reservation. For two years longer Chief Joseph's people held out, until General Oliver Howard arrived with an ultimatum in May 1877, giving them one month to comply or be forcibly deported. With the courage of a man making an unavoidable decision, and in opposition to the tribe's other leaders who counselled war, Chief Joseph assented but asked for time to gather the herds of valuable horses and cross the Snake River when its spring spate was over. To no avail; General Howard was adamant.

So began the long march – 100 warriors with the old folk, women and children, and 2000 head of prime horseflesh: stallions, mares in foal, youngstock, warhorses. They crossed the raging Snake safely, men riding across, the women and children crossing on hide rafts hitched to more horses, but in the boiling waters many horses were swept downstream, and gutted on submerged rocks.

Furious at seeing their precious horses lost Chiefs White Bird, Ollokot, and Toohoolhoolzote called a halt in Rocky Canyon and demanded war, while Chief Joseph counselled peace, knowing their numbers were too small to stand against the might of the army.

The Nez Percé had lived at peace with the white men, but that night a band of warriors broke away, killing white settlers in revenge for land and stock seizure. Still hoping to get his people away to Montana and thence across the Canadian border to safety, Joseph led them 16 miles on to White Bird Creek to collect the remainder of their stock. There the cavalry attacked, with the odds two to one against the Indians. Desperate, the Nez Percé fought back, inflicting heavy casualties on the Bluecoats and putting them to flight. So started months of harrying, the army being constantly reinforced, while the Nez Percé were driven relentlessly right across Idaho to the Clearwater River and a meeting with Chief Looking Glass.

The Nez Percé now numbered 700, of whom 250 were warriors. Their objective was the Bitterroot Mountains and the Lolo Pass into Montana. Even burdened with non-combatants, baggage and herds of 2000 horses, their knowledge of terrain and the speed of their horses enabled them to outmanoeuvre and outmarch the soldiers, but at Lolo Pass their scouts found their way blocked by a log barricade. Under a truce flag Chief Joseph asked for a peaceful passage. Demands to give up the tribe's arms in return were refused. After days of the soldiers' delaying talk tactics while they waited for reinforcements the Nez Percé moved into action. Looking Glass stationed warriors amongst trees overlooking the soldiers at the barricade, while Joseph, using his knowledge of terrain, took the women, children and stock up a gully and was around the barricade before the soldiers knew what was happening. Looking Glass's warriors protected the rear from a belated Bluecoat sortie.

Relieved, and thinking themselves safe, the Indians turned southwards to their hunting ground at Big Hole over 100 miles away. They had already covered several hundred miles and they needed to hunt for food and rest their horses. Relentlessly Colonel Gibbon, who should have been at Lolo Pass, pursued them and finally burst in on a sleeping camp at dawn with orders to take no prisoners. In the ensuing carnage eighty Nez Percé were slaughtered – men, women, children – before White Bird could form a rearguard action to enable Joseph to get the rest away. More soldiers' reinforcements were coming up and harried the Nez Percé for six days and over 200 miles toward Yellowstone. Finally the Indians turned and struck back, pinning down the army and capturing all their baggage animals together with the ammunition they were carrying.

They crossed into the newly formed National Park on 22 August at Targhee Pass. One of the park's earliest visitors was General Sherman, out from Washington DC to see just why the whole of the United States' army was unable to contain less than 300 Nez Percé warriors.

By now the Seventh Cavalry was on their heels, and their flight from Yellowstone heading north for Canada and freedom was a continuous rearguard battle day after day. They were now well into September, the weather was deteriorating steadily, their horses ground down, and they needed food. After shaking the Seventh and not sighting any enemy for three days they felt safe enough to camp, rest their horses, and hunt. They were within a long day's march of Canadian safety, and the Seventh was two days' march away from their camp in Bear Paw Mountains. But unknown to them the new telegraph system had been able to summon the cavalry officer Bear Coat Miles from east of their line of retreat. At dawn on the morning of 30 September 600 cavalrymen descended on the camp at the gallop, guided in by turncoat Sioux and Cheyenne. The Nez Percé fought desperately. Deadly shots, they mowed the soldiers down, captured their ammunition, and at night tried to slip quietly away for the border, only to find themselves hemmed in by Miles' cordon of sentries. Trapped, they waited for morning and renewed attack, but instead under a truce flag a soldier carried a demand for surrender.

Constant fast travel across 1300 miles, fighting repeated engagements against overwhelming odds and being constantly harried had taken its toll. After five days Chief Joseph surrendered on the promise of safe conduct back to the small Lapwai Reservation in Idaho.

Beaten, the Nez Percé were to be ground down still further. Prating missionaries and government officials ensured that they never fought again. They were to be forced into farming. Their arms were confiscated, and the bitterest blow struck – their horses were stolen from them, hundreds of beautiful animals being shot in a canyon with orders to let not one come out alive. Others were sold to anyone who had the price. What few they were permitted to keep were crossbred with common draught animals to downgrade the stock so that the Nez Percé would never again be a mounted threat.

The herds that had taken over a century to bring to perfection were almost wiped out in savage reprisals, but not quite. Some few had remained in their old homelands when time to gather the herds had been denied. Of the solid coloured stock no record has come down. But of the others, the highly coloured, incredibly tough spotted horse? They carried their record with them into successive generations until eventually, many decades later, they served as foundation stock for America's modern Appaloosa horse, still a tough contender whenever great distances have to be covered on both sides of the Atlantic and in Australia and New Zealand.

Chief Joseph never did see his homeland again. Once more the government broke its promise, shunting him from one reservation to another, from malarial Fort Leavenworth to bleak Indian Territory, and finally, as an Indian too dangerous to allow back to Lapwai, to the Colville Reservation in Washington where he died in 1904, as the Reservation physician noted 'of a broken heart'.

6 Communications across the ages

Messengers in the ancient world

Across the centuries the horse has been indispensable in the area of communications. Earliest transport of news was, and remained for thousands of years, in the hands of itinerant merchants travelling from market to market, country to country. Prompt delivery depended on the speed of the donkey or mule that carried them along the trade network. For a price tablets and later letters were carried in this time-honoured but inevitably slow fashion.

As shock strike forces of conquering armies became horseborne and cavalry a major weapon of war, ambling donkeys and plodding mules were no longer adequate. Thus the first fast mounted courier service was born.

Credit has usually been given to the Persians for this development but they were in fact the inheritors of the Assyrians who, by the eighth century BC, had developed their own royal postal system known as and carrying the Amat Shurri – the King's Word. We know from the amazing legacy of tablets, records of every miniscule part of Assyrian life, that highways were maintained throughout the kingdom. Assyrian kings delighted in having their deeds struck on clay and baked for posterity. Tukulti-Ninurti I (1244–1208 BC) boasted of construction in eastern Turkey: 'I cut into their mountains with copper picks and widened their unopened paths', and 200 years later in 1100 Tiglath Pileser I (1115–1077) proudly claims: 'I hacked a troublesome mountain and difficult tracks with copper picks and made the road good for the passage of my chariots and troops.'

Roads were developed and lengthened, expanded from earliest trade routes with Cappadocia (Turkey) and Anatolia until a network covered both nuclear and 'acquired and conquered' Assyria, stretching clear across the country's 1000-mile length and breadth from Egypt to Iran, southwards to the Persian Gulf, northwards into Urartu (Armenia) and to the fringes of the Steppes. Along these highways sped fast posthorses, mainly of the breed of Koa imported from Cilicia. Posting stations were maintained at regular intervals, and with the exception of the Sinai Desert which needed camel transport and Bedouin guides, the king and his generals could send vital messages anywhere in the kingdom and receive a reply within a week. Considering the extreme aridity of vast stretches and the swampy riverine areas with high humidity, the horses must have been incredibly fit and tough as both climatic conditions are ones which today's endurance riders know only too well as prime toll takers in competition.

Nothing was left to chance. Where mountain tracks made it too dangerous and time consuming to trust horses, surer-footed mules and riding donkeys were used. Here it should be stressed that the donkeys used were not necessarily the little grey or piebald burros, but larger and better-bred donkeys, the descendants of which are still prized as mounts in the Middle East today.

At the end of the eighth century BC when Assyria was at its zenith the Medes were waiting in the wings. They constantly chipped away at Assyrian territories, absorbing and learning so that when the Assyrian might grew so great that it outstripped its own strength they were ready to adopt and adapt the best of the older culture, not least of which was a rapid communications system.

Though the Assyrian Empire was large by the standards of the first millennium BC, that of their Persian inheritors was gigantic. From its heart at Susa it stretched westwards to the Nile and beyond into the deserts of Put (Libya); eastwards to the Indus; northwards to the Caspian and further to the Aral Sea; northwest to Greece, Cappadocia

(Turkey) and beyond to the Black Sea and the land of the Sakae (Scythia) – a vast tract of many lands some 3000 miles by 1500, all under the sway of Persia's Great King.

Persia's great Royal Road was built under the Achaemenids. Constructed for all-weather travel, it started from Sardis in Lydia and stretched for 1600 miles to Susa in Elam, its extension going further south to Persepolis. Other great roads were built linking the empire's nodal points, but it is about the Susa/Sardis road that we have the most detailed description from Herodotus. About the horses used we can only surmise, but the road ran through the main horsebreeding centres of the Persian Empire – Cappadocia, Cilicia, Armenia, Media. The Lydians, where the road started, were famed for the quality of their cavalry, and the Assyrians already knew the value of the Koan horses of Cilicia. Speed and toughness were definitely two of their attributes because according to Herodotus nothing travelled faster than the Persian Angaros (messenger) on the king's business. His actual words, 'neither snow nor rainstorm nor heat nor night prevents his passage', became the motto for America's modern postal system.

As with much of the ancient world, what we know of the physique of men and animals comes from the vast treasure of carvings in the round for Greece and Rome, and in relief for Assyria and Persia. From the Persepolis friezes we get an idea of many of the horses in use in ancient Persia, and on two counts the horses of Media would be ruled out as speedy carriers of king's mail, being too heavy and for the period extremely large. From literature we learn they were for the most part reserved for nobility and warfare. The other horsebreeding centres, already used to paying massive tribute in horses, must have continued to provide the speed machines needed for the courier service.

The Royal Road's 1600 miles was split into 111 divisions. The unit of measurement was the parasang, which was approximately 3¾ miles. Fresh horses were available every 15 miles or so, with each staging post being at roughly a normal days' travel apart – normal, that is, for the incredibly slow trade caravans that formed the bulk of the highway traffic. The average time for a merchant to travel the route would be about three months, but the Angaros, using fast horses, was expected to achieve a true endurance feat, galloping the 1600 miles in barely a week's time. Even with fresh relays of horses and riders it was stretching the powers of man and beast. The climate could be hostile in the extreme, Elamite Susa being flat, torrid and windless, while the stretch through the Mesopotamian flatlands was hot and humid, with miasmic marshes bounding the Tigris. On the credit side the Angaros could travel alone and safely, as the whole of this particular route ran through well-populated areas. He had nothing to fear from the bandits that frequented the other less heavily travelled routes that criss-crossed the empire. From the one main trunk route many other major cities of the empire could be connected with, so that Babylon, Ecbatana, Arbela, and even Bactra in far-off, mountainous Bactria could have been in constant touch and the Great King kept well advised. In hostile territory on the fringes of the empire where petty revolts and uprisings constantly erupted the Angaros might ride in fear of his life from bandits, though when apprehended bandits could expect no mercy, blinding being a common punishment for highway robbery. About communications from Egypt the annals are silent, but speedy crossing of the Arabian desert to the east would be impossible with horses, so the most likely route would be through the Abarnahara Satrapy (Syria) until it joined with the main route.

One intriguing journey is worthy of note for its speed and its relation to concepts of endurance riding. By no means carrying the Royal Mails, the traveller was a respected banker named Itti Marduk-Balatu, head of the firm of the Babylonian House of Egibi Sons. The tale of his many journeys on behalf of his firm are related in a group of Akkadian tablets. He had travelled from a town called Humadeshu to Babylon, and the intriguing point is the argument between two historians as to where Humadeshu was. One, Hallock, says it was a suburb of Persepolis, equating Humadeshu with Uwadaichaya, a town mentioned in the tablets identified by a historian called Zadok, but not located. Zadok and Hallock disagree on the town's location, Zadok maintaining it would have been impossible for the banker to travel the 600 miles between Humadeshu near Persepolis to Babylon in the fifteen days mentioned. However, given an Angaros' travel time of in excess of 200 miles a day, even an elderly banker (and there is nothing to suggest that Itti Marduk-Balatu was elderly) who was fit enough to ride his routes could manage 600 miles if not with ease, certainly with determination if pecuniary matters were pressing. In modern Competitive Trail Rides a 40-mile daily stint is covered in six to seven hours. Even lacking modern comfortable saddlery such a feat would not be impossible. An ambling mule or plodding horse might be slower, but bearing in mind that fresh mounts were available for authorized travellers with a firman at frequent posting stations, 40 miles a day is perfectly reasonable, especially with the spur of profit to urge the rider on.

One point that has struck me in delving into the past is that modern historians seem almost totally unacquainted with the actual capabilities of both horses and riders. Indeed, not only historians, but even many of today's horsemen, other than endurance riders, seem amazed when one talks of rides of 20 miles and over, and the usual query as to having done a 100-mile ride is 'how many days did it take you?'

The picture we receive of the past is of infinite slowness, but I do not think individual travellers of old would have moved at the snail's pace we are constantly expected to accept. Then as now people were in a hurry – time was money, and with its attendant discomfort, and frequent danger, in former times travel was best despatched as fast as possible.

Posts of the Roman Empire

Rome might not have been at her most brilliant in operating cavalry, but when it came to communications she showed her organizational ability at its best. Inseparably linked with her legions' movements was the vast network of Imperial post roads. In Asia Minor the already known trade routes quickly became military roads, and from Republican times onward as new and 'barbarian' territories

fell under the Roman *caligulae* (marching boots) the roads expanded and lengthened, the legionaries themselves carving out new routes as they marched forward, each soldier carrying in his 70 lb pack road-making tools. On these old and new roads in the early empire Augustus (27 BC–AD 14) created the Cursus Publicus, down which the official communications system sped, along with the multitudinous traffic of the mushrooming empire.

At Rome's greatest extent the main roads alone amounted to 53,638 miles of highway. At strategic points along these highways posting stations were built, varying in size and importance from the Stationes where soldiers were stationed, to Mansiones, which were overnight stops, and Mutationes, which were just relay changeovers. At all stations there would be fresh mounts and harness animals available, the smaller establishments mustering only about ten horses and thirty mules, while the larger overnight places had up to forty horses and correspondingly more mules.

At first the Cursus was a civilian organization, but later when it came under the Imperial aegis the stock was provided from large state studs. The Elder Pliny tells us that Italy bred a Reatine mule (modern Rieti), whereas Greece's breed was the Arcadian. He also reports that she-asses were exceptionally valuable, and that mules had the great endurance feat of being endowed with an eighty-year lifespan, and that to stop them kicking, which would have been disastrous when loaded with heavy baggage or hitched to a vehicle, it was recommended to give them wine to drink. Maybe drunk they lost aggressive motivation and became docile! Horses were bred in Italy mainly in Apulia and Lucania – who knows but that Offonius Tigellinus might have had a profitable contract to supply both army and post horses to the state as well as to the Circus before he latched on to more profitable and nefarious means of advancement in Nero's reign. Macedonia, Numidia, Spain, Gaul, all supplied stock, and the Cursus must have had a very cosmopolitan look to its equine travellers.

Main stations were provided with a farrier and a mulomedicus (vet) plus grooms in the ratio of three animals under the care of one man. The outlying countryside was bound to supply necessary fodder for the stock. Other personnel included a carpenter for repair and maintenance of the variety of carriages that were used on the Cursus in an official capacity. Possibly the farrier would be more used to welding wheel rims than attending to horses hooves other than trimming, as the hipposandal was still in use. This was a detachable shoe strapped to the hoof, similar to today's 'easy-boot' and with much the same function, even to being used for veterinary reasons.

Augustus initially directed that the Imperial Post was to be carried by relays of riders, but later switched the system to one courier going the whole way in a light carriage. When carrying bulletins of military engagements the courier gave advance warning of the content of his despatch by carrying a spear tipped with laurel denoting victory, or a feather warning of a defeat. The Romans, particularly in times of peace, were more interested in the reliability of the postal service than its speed, but nevertheless couriers still did a daily stint of between five and eight stages at an average speed of 5 mph, covering a minimum of 41 and a maximum of 67 Roman miles. In disturbed periods when speed was essential despatch riders would forsake the slow-moving raeda (four-wheeled official postal vehicle) and take a swift horse covering up to 160 Roman miles a day. [A Roman mile is only marginally shorter than an English mile, 1611 yd as opposed to the English 1760 yd.]

Even in a raeda travel could be fairly rapid provided passengers were prepared to put up with the constant jolting. It must have taken more in endurance from the occupant than the mules or horses when Julius Caesar chose this means of travel for a 100-mile stint, but then as Suetonius tells us he took his secretaries along with him, not wanting to waste precious time en route.

There are many instances of rapid travel down the Cursus when danger threatened, and some remarkable rides were recorded. That of Tiberius surely heads the list. He rode 200 miles in one day from Ticinus in Italy to be at his brother Drusus' deathbed in Germany, exhausting several horses en route.

Tacitus tells us of a real endurance feat ridden in the depths of Gallic winter. The year AD 69, known

as the year of the four Emperors, started with a revolt in Germany against the Emperor Galba by the IV and XXII Legions stationed in winter quarters at Mogontiacum (Mainz). On 1 January a standardbearer of the IV Legion carried a message of the revolt to Vitellius, who was stationed in Cologne 108 miles away, galloping through day and night and covering the distance in just over twelve hours. From amongst those few remaining loyal to Galba one got away from Mogontiacum, galloping the 200 miles along the Cursus to Rheims to warn Pompeius Propinquus, Procurator of Belgica. Alerted, Pompeius Propinquus despatched word to Rome, routing the courier via Lugdunum (Lyon), Vienne, Mediolanum (Milan) and Durocortorum. History is silent as to whether the courier galloped into Italy via the Graian Alps or the Cottian Alps, but the latter is the obvious choice: it was the depths of winter and the Cottian Alps with Mont Genevre Pass, although the longer route by over 100 miles, was the easier. Regardless, the minimum distance covered by the despatch rider, running ahead of the Vitellian troops, was 1440 miles, covered in nine days. In Rome a panic-stricken Galba tried to mend his fences and strengthen his position, only to have internal strife culminate in his murder. Otho was proclaimed Princeps and marched straight from Rome (at the beginning of his three-month reign) to war with Vitellius. Vitellius triumphed, but his reign lasted only eight months and he was succeeded by Vespasian, whose rule restored order.

Throughout the empire the Cursus must have rung to the beat of hooves. Rome never had enough, constantly marching her legions from freshly conquered territory to new vistas, and the battles both large and small, the campaigns mounted against new enemies, the insurrections and so on must have kept the couriers and horses in a constant state of emergency, carrying orders from Rome, the empire's heart.

Down these highways a legacy travelled which persists in Europe and England right up until today. Instead of the racing courier and his labouring horse, or the heavy cavalry cataphracts pounding along, today's diesel-belching juggernauts still benefit from the sweat shed by earlier legionaries in laying the foundations of what is the basis of much of our modern road system.

The Korean and Mongolian mails

The early Asiatic peoples became excellent horsemen. The rugged steppe ponies ranged over vast wastes of land affording only hard-won forage, so that toughness became inherent in their makeup, weaklings not surviving such harsh conditions. Such ponies provided the basis for rapid transport in the spreading empires of China, Mongolia, Manchuria and its neighbour Chosĕn (Korea).

In the late fifth century AD the Korean king So Chi founded the precursor of the later Mongol postal system. Small in comparison to Mongolia, and the even larger China, Korea nevertheless was very well served by this early system which was used exclusively by nobility and government throughout the kingdom. In AD 935 when Korea finally came under the overlordship of the Silla dynasty, the system was enlarged but was still reserved for military and government usage. When the Mongols swept out of the Gobi Desert encompassing all the neighbouring countries they imposed their own improvement on the Korean system, but when their power finally outgrew itself, fracturing as a result of internal dissent, the whole service deteriorated.

For two and a half centuries the communications system was in confusion, until in the late sixteenth century King Song Jong revitalized the ancient routes, building staging posts every 50 miles equipped with at least five horses and enough men to run it. The post rider's insignia was a Mae-Pae, a horse badge which designated the bearer's rank, five horses denoting officials of the highest order down through the grades to a one-horse Mae-Pae. High-ranking officials could commandeer two horses, riding one and changing about when the first tired. If the horses could not make the 50-mile stretch between posts he could demand a mount from travellers on the road or from habitations he passed en route. Payment was guaranteed by the Korean Ministry of Finance, and should an official be caught profiteering in his post death was the penalty.

Today Korea remembers her ancient postal system by stamp issues bearing the Mae-Pae insignia, much in the same way as the US Postal System has a Pony Express rider for its insignia.

From the relatively small communications system maintained by the Korean Royal House, the Mongols under Chingis Khagan took a massive step forward and organized the most renowned system the world had yet known, or was to know until modern mechanical means enabled rapid transport of mail. (Even then the absolute reliability of the Mongol system makes me doubt that modern postal services could do better or even as well, with their constant goings astray or 'lost in the post' excuses for non-delivery.)

Reliability and speed stamped the Mongolian Yam: the first as a result of the meticulous organization and the authority vested in Yam riders to commandeer transport en route at need; the second as a result of the fitness and endurance of both rider and horse. At its height the Mongolian Empire encompassed two-thirds of the then known world. East of Mongolia it reached Manchuria and Korea; southwards it swept into China, Kublai Khan at one time making Peking, or as the Mongolians called it Khan Balik, his capital; north into Russian steppelands, and ever westwards – Persia, Armenia, Syria, Khwarizm, and into the borderlands of a trembling Europe. It vast network of trade routes and military roads surpassed even the 85,000 km of Roman roads recorded in the Emperor Diocletion's day. Sound horses guaranteed reliability, and no part of the Mongolian system needed to trust to fickle sea weather and even more uncertain sea transport.

The network backing this vast enterprise was organized down to the last detail. As many as 300,000 horses were kept in readiness, distributed in herds of anything from 200 to 400 head between the more than 10,000 stations throughout the empire. Maintenance of these herds was a charge on the local populace, the horses receiving good care and feeding. As the empire expanded, contrary to the accepted image of a Mongolian mount these were not solely of the common cold-blooded Mongolian type of pony, as the favourite tribute laid on subject nations was a levy of horses, the best the conquered country could supply. The Great Khan numbered the finest horsebreeding countries amongst his conquests. In contrast with the flying riders of the later American Pony Express the Mongolian courier rode at a steady trot, acknowledged by good distance riders to be the best pace for clipping off a steady mileage. Naturally in military emergencies record times would be set, but even the daily norm was impressive.

Stations in populous areas were approximately 18 miles apart, and in less habited areas as much as 40 miles apart. Each Yam rider covered between 50 and 70 miles a day, upping this to 120 miles in times of need. Night-riding couriers would be accompanied by a guide on foot through the darkest hours, slowing the speed. When carrying vital military information where speed was essential the riders bound their heads, chests and stomachs tightly to withstand the constant pounding of a hard gallop. In such cases these riders would cover up to 300 miles at a stretch. Again, unlike the Pony Express but in keeping with the Roman system, one rider completed the whole distance, carrying the 'gerfalcon' insignia denoting top priority and the authority to commandeer a passing traveller's mount if need be, the stranded rider being powerless to resist upon pain of death.

In summer the roads were choked with blinding dust and desiccating sands of desert and plains. In winter withering winds whipped down from mountains across freezing steppes, but like the Mongolian soldier Yam riders were inured to hardship. In Timur-i-Leng's day the already vast network was extended and improved, and maintenance was kept at a high level even to clearing snow drifts in bad winter weather.

Had the courier carrying the gerfalcon tablet and the news that saved Europe been a contender for any endurance award he surely would have been hailed a World Champion, pounding the 6000 miles from Karakorum, the administrative centre, carrying news of Chingis Khagan's death to Batu Khan poised to scourge a quaking Europe. As it was he unwittingly gave Europe a reprieve, for the missive recalled all Khans to Karakorum to elect the great Chingis' successor.

Posthorse and mail coach in Britain

The picture which springs to mind of Britain's postal system is the Christmas card mail coach drawn by a spanking team of four matched horses rocketing along at breakneck gallop or flying trot, the coachman's horn trumpeting his arrival at a festive inn, romanticizing the age of Turnpike and Toll. The inside story was something different: far removed from the earlier super-efficient Roman post routes, and the unsurpassed Mongolian system. Yet the British communications system had many echoes from the ancient past.

Unlike the ancient military postal systems which were run to a high degree of proficiency, Britain's and Europe's post roads had largely fallen into disuse, and definitely into disrepair, once the all-pervading impact of Rome's presence was no longer felt. By the Middle Ages the roads had disintegrated into winter quagmires and summer ruts, maintenance lying in the hands of the church whose pilgrims, trudging along the highways to the innumerable holy shrines, did so at peril of their lives and in extreme discomfort either on foot or aboard horses and mules. The Statute of Winchester whereby roads had to be cleared to the depth of a bowshot to allow safe passage for travellers was honoured more in the breach, as there was no legal system to undertake its enforcement. Further Highway Acts continued to be ignored. Travel on any routes crisscrossing Britain was a feat of endurance for both man and horse.

As in the ancient world the services of packmen and merchants were used to send what few letters went outside the privileged system of Royal and Ecclesiastical messengers.

Henry VIII created the office of Master of the Postes, the Royal Mail operating from London to Dover, Plymouth, Chester and Scotland. As Henry VIII had also been the instrument for widespread destruction of any but the lumbering 'great horses' only afforded by wealthy nobles, the requisitioning officials must have been hard put to it to obtain horses with sufficient speed to ensure rapid transit along the Royal Highways. By Elizabeth I's time the system had become sufficiently entrenched to have acquired its own built-in system of abuses, travellers purporting to be on royal business arrogating posthorses to their own use. However, the type of horse used must have been greatly improved as, using posthorses, Robert Cary, later the Earl of Monmouth, was able to execute a remarkable endurance ride of 401 miles in three days, carrying word of Elizabeth I's death to Scotland and a waiting James VI (of Scotland) and I (of England), Elizabeth having left it until her deathbed to name her heir. The rewards of being the first to do homage to the new sovereign were worth suffering the appalling March mire through which he had to batter his way.

Two measures enacted in James I's day reflect the ancient system: as with the Romans, James insisted that posthorses were only to be hired to those with the requisite signed pass; and, echoing the Mongolian system, if the post stations could not supply mounts they could be commandeered by royal officials from private owners.

The system of riding post continued until well into the eighteenth century, having become a solely government monopoly by the mid-1600s, although private enterprise for the carrying of mail still flourished, albeit illegally. It was only in the late eighteenth century and coaching's heyday that the Royal Mail became almost exclusively carriage borne. As the Mails rumbled their way along the extensive maze of Britain's post roads, the feats of competitive coachmen squeezing the last ounce of endurance out of their four-horse teams became legendary. Carrying the Mails, the faster the better, became big business, and to that end thousands of well-bred horses were regularly in harness, lunging under the crack of the coachmen's whips.

A coach-horse's life was arduous, his endurance measured not in miles but in the severity of the conditions he laboured under. It is from this era that the common phrase 'to die in harness' derives: whereas it now denotes an accolade to a man or woman's tenacity and dedication to work, in the coaching era it meant exactly what it said. The toll in horseflesh was enormous, the labours frequently beyond the strength of even a six- or four-horse team. To get the mails through was the prime concern, the conservation of the poor brutes in

harness not weighed in the balance. It was a common occurrence for horses to founder en route, break limbs in diabolical road conditions, or merely drop dead from over-exertion. On one coach route alone in a twelve-month period no less than twenty horses just dropped dead, and this did not take account of deaths from other causes.

Roads were often little more than mired ruts carving their way into the countryside, all attempts at surfacing stopping at the edge of towns. To add to the mud and holes, the loose stones and rocks, which on occasion would cause horrendous accidents to the horses, there were the added hazards of coaches weakened by constant strains of travelling the highways. Breakdowns were all too common, wheels shattering, harness ripping, and on top of all the threat in the open from the Gentlemen of the Road ready to relieve travellers of their valuables. No wonder the coachmen laid on with their whips.

Initially the same horses pulled the coaches throughout the journey, but as the need for speed increased stages were introduced at 20-mile intervals, contracting to 10 miles as improved roads permitted even faster speeds to be maintained.

In the early days of coaching a horse was lucky to last longer than three years in harness, being sold if he was fortunate into less strenuous work. The coaches could weigh as much as three tons, with added freight and passengers, and although the stages were relatively short, around 10 miles for a one-day stint, or 6 if the same horses were to do the out and back journey in one day, they had to maintain a speed in excess of 8 mph to keep the Mail Service's schedule. This included stops, and horse changeovers, at every staging post, and was adhered to in both summer and winter. Some examples of speeds are the 116-mile run from London to Bath in sixteen hours; and 186 miles from London to Manchester in thirty-six hours. Many a speed rider today would come home with a well-earned trophy for such a ride, yet the coach-horses would be pulling their hearts out in hock-deep mud, or floundering in drifting snow, or sometimes somewhat luckier in summer weather pounding the dusty rutted roads.

As roads improved, marginally to our modern

55

concept of roadbuilding, travel increased and in addition to the Royal Mails there was a plethora of coaches plying the road network. In major towns, inns and livery yards would house hundreds of horses at a time, one coaching entrepreneur having 1800 head in harness at one time in the mid nineteenth century. With expansion came competition for faster and faster sevices, the average speed rising from the Mails' 8 mph to over 11 mph on the London to Shrewsbury run, the even longer route from London to Exeter (176 miles) being covered in sixteen and a half hours. Yet on occasion the horses' endurance was pushed beyond the bounds of tolerance and some of the feats make unpleasant reading, such as the pace being so forced in a 7-mile stage from Great Smeaton to Northallerton that three of the four horses were killed by the reckless driving of a coachman named Ralph Soulsey, the lone survivor bringing in the coach in a solo finale.

To the hard-driving professional coachmen were added the elite of the amateurs, the Regency Bucks and Victorian Dandies who saw themselves cutting a dash with a smart four in hand. The acquisitive and reckless amongst the professionals, although prohibited under pain of instant dismissal, nevertheless chanced their luck for the opportunity to boost their earnings by putting the young blades under their tutelage, sacrificing the horses and terrorizing the passengers who suffered the joltings and strains of a coach hurtling along the highways at speeds in excess of 20 mph.

No wonder the working life of a coach-horse was both harsh and short, though as time progressed roads improved and vehicles benefited from less weight and better design. The horses' lot improved also, their working life lengthening to an average of four years on the fast routes, and as much as seven years on the shorter-haul, slower journeys.

The Pony Express

From the Middle East and its ancient highways, the Roman Cursus and the Mongolian Yam, and the heart of Europe in the Old World, a great ocean separated the beckoning New World and the burgeoning nation that was early America. Seaborne traffic carried immigrants to her shores and colonization invested her eastern seaboard, gradually expanding westwards. Settling on the western coast meant an extremely hazardous journey into the unknown middle of the continent, or a long and difficult journey around the coast, over the Isthmus of Panama and thence by ship to the west coast, or an even longer and far more dangerous trip rounding the Horn at the tip of South America through the Roaring Forties and the icy conditions off Tierra del Fuego, then the long haul up the western coast – a journey that could take five months or more, if the ship did not founder.

Any mail carried via Panama had to go at the rate imposed by the New Granada government of 12 cents a pound for its Isthmus transit. With the acquisition of California in 1848, and the opening up of vast new territories, people needed to be in communication with the east and the government far faster than trade winds permitted.

In 1851 the first overland mail service began, the contract being between Sacramento and Independence, Missouri. The first section, Sacramento to Salt Lake City, was supposed to take thirty days by mule carrier but ended up being almost twice as long due to bad weather. Seven years later the Post Office contracted with the Butterfield Overland Mail Company and mail coaches plied between St Louis, Missouri and San Francisco, California. The first run over 2700 miles took twenty-three days, two days ahead of contract time. The next year three entrepreneurs took over an existing freighting concern which had a government mail contract and renamed it the Central Overland California and Pike's Peak Express Company. The new company was set to run over the shorter central route and the most ambitious of the partners, William H. Russell, had an even more exciting project. He planned to cut the time taken to deliver mail by coach by more than half using a series of superbly mounted, lightweight riders who had the courage to go it alone through rough, dangerous country, taking a maximum of ten days for the 1966 miles of the shorter route.

The planning of this venture was enormous but

was accomplished in three short months. Five hundred horses were purchased at the then high price of between $150 and $200 each, soundness and speed being the prime requirements. The eastern section of the route was the least hazardous with easier terrain and for this Kentucky horses were used. For the rugged western half nimble, sure-footed, fleet mustangs were purchased. There were already staging posts along the route every 25 to 30 miles, but before the Express opened additional intervening posts were set up, each holding three or four horses and primitive quarters for the riders and horse tenders. In all, 190 changeover posts were incorporated into the route.

The riders recruited had to be young, lightweight, have no family commitments, be excellent horsemen, abstain from drink and foul language, and be considerate to their mounts. If they infringed these last three rules they would be dismissed without pay, having sworn on a bible to keep the Pony Express Commandments. They also had to be supremely fit, as their job meant riding a 75- to 100-mile stretch with up to eight changes of horses and no rest in between, and maintaining an average of 12½ mph no matter what, even if attacked by Indians, many instances of which are recorded. For risking life and limb they earned $50 a month. Though not a princely sum it was much above average for most, especially for teenagers. Riders were supposed to be at least twenty but there are several instances of much younger lads riding the route, the youngest being just fourteen years of age. In general, candidates were drawn from the locality in which they were to ride, so that they knew conditions in that particular area. Those at the eastern end definitely had an easier time of it than their westerly colleagues.

It was on an eastern rider, Johnson William Richardson, that first honours fell as he swung aboard a light bay in front of Patee House in St Joseph, Missouri, at 7.15 in the evening on 3 April 1860, to start one of the outstanding endurance feats for men and horses in American history. The 1966-mile route would test the sinew and muscle of countless horses in the Pony Express's eighteen-month history, as well as the bravery of many of the youngsters who rode into American legend. It was

a time of great unrest amongst the Indian tribes, and much of the route ran through disputed Indian territories, but as the first rider flew down the track into the night it was to acclaim and a future that protagonist William Russell was convinced would make history.

Right at the outset riders had to push their ponies to maintain a rigid schedule. The first section east of St Joseph to Fort Kearney, Nebraska, was fast country, mostly well-watered prairie. From Fort Kearney on to South Pass, Wyoming, the land became dreary desert, green only at river bottoms. Then on into Utah and to Salt Lake City it was mostly arid, rocky and barren with speed cut down as the route climbed towards the Rockies. The last section from Salt Lake City to Carson City, Nevada, was through the worst stretch of desert – burning in summer, icy in winter, and at all times utterly lonely except for roaming bands of renegade Indians. Once past Carson City on the final run into Sacramento the rider could feel safe once more.

With the target set for a ten-day delivery every rider was primed. Changeover every 10 to 15 miles was rapid, with no saddle change but a quick movement as the rider dismounted, whipping a specially designed saddle cover off and flinging it across the saddle of a fresh pony waiting to gallop. Called a *mochila* this cover had four integral pouches, a hole for the saddle horn, and a slit for the cantle, and was impossible to dislodge while the rider remained mounted. Three of the four pouches were padlocked at one end of the route, to be unlocked on delivery. The fourth was unsealed so that telegrams and letters could be added en route. A half ounce letter cost $5 to send, cheap considering the delivery hazards. In the whole history of the Express, during which time a total of 616 runs were made, only one *mochila* was lost, a tribute to the skill of riders able to negotiate any and all conditions no matter what the hazards from route, weather, or Indians. Contrary to predictions the Express ran through the foulest winter weather and right through the period when the Pah Utes were on the warpath in western Nevada.

The records of the Pony Express are full of tales of human and equine valour and endurance. The initial decision to purchase only the best in horse-flesh paid off. Well fed, the Kentucky thorough-breds and wiry mustangs were ready to run for their lives, and frequently did so.

Sioux were on the warpath in Wyoming in 1861, lurking in the vicinity of the Pony Express route, and it took a deal of courage to ride on alone. Henry Avis did. His stretch ran from Mud Springs, Nebraska, to Horseshoe Station in Wyoming, where he was due to hand over to the next rider going west, but word had reached Horseshoe Station that warring Sioux were near Deer Creek Station and the westbound rider refused to take the risk. Avis took up the challenge and plunged on-wards, to find that the war party had attacked the station, running all the Deer Creek horses off. When the eastbound rider arrived he also refused to go any further, so Avis turned about and gal-loped back along the route, drawing rein at Horseshoe Station after a non-stop, flat-out ride of 220 miles, changing horses where he could, but at Deer Creek having to push his tired horse into further effort to retrace his steps until the next changeover. His speed can only be guessed at but surely the regulation 12 mph was well surpassed.

One of the riders who became a legend in his own lifetime was William Frederick Cody, later known as Buffalo Bill, and the subject of famous equestrian French painter Rosa Bonheur, who pictured him riding a grey-flecked Arabian. A classical rider commented that Cody was 'the closest thing to a centaur in nature'. This ability to get inside the skin of his mount enabled him to make the longest Pony Express ride on record. Again it was in the dangerous Horseshoe Station section. Joining the Pony Express at fifteen years of age he was soon sent to ride the most hazardous section of all, 116 miles of Indian-infested territory in Wyoming between Red Buttes and Three Cros-sings. On one run he arrived at the Three Cros-sings post to find the next rider had been killed by Indians the night before, so without pause he changed horses and raced on a further 76 miles westward to Rocky Ridge, and because he was needed back at his home base of Red Buttes he turned about and raced back along the trail. Cover-ing the ground meant to be traversed by two riders

with a break between their stints he made an un-broken ride of four stages across a total distance of 384 miles without stopping. Greater distances have been covered by record seekers, but it is a safe bet that none faced the challenge of running the gamut of possible Indian attack while piling on the miles.

Not all the marathon rides were made outdis-tancing Indians or running before a storm. One undertaken by Richard Egan was made to help a friend keep a tryst with his girlfriend who lived in Salt Lake City, the depot Egan should have been returning to. Instead of changing the *mochila* on to the next eastward-bound horse at the end of his stint he rode on, covering 165 miles without stop-ping, and in order not to throw the works out of kilter he had to turn about and retrace the route, running up a mileage that for many today is a full season's competition total.

Speed quickly became a byword for the Pony Express, but it outdid even its own records when riders were primed to carry President Lincoln's historic first speech to Congress. A 15 mph aver-age was demanded and in a blinding succession of fleet ponies the precious speech was flashed across the continent in seven days, cutting three days off an already rapid service. During this epic run what must be an all-time speed record was performed by Joseph Wintle, who covered his 110-mile section between Fort Kearney to Cottonwood Springs in a flat five hours, changing horses ten times.

Today's endurance riders are doing fantastic feats with their own horses, bringing them through with flying colours and fit for more. Their need to beat the clock is for personal achievement and a love of sport. The Pony Express riders, using fast relays of horses, often ran with the Indians on their tails, trusting their fit, grain-fed horses to outdis-tance their pursuers. Additionally they rode the route year round, coping with boggy trails, quick-sands, torrents in spate, or blinding snowstorms, keeping to the route by the line of weedtops spiking through the drifts, and at checkpoints arriving to find that their remount had been driven off and having to push a tired horse even harder to the next station, not knowing what they would find on arriv-al. Many tales are told of narrow escapes.

Considering the odds against their safety it is remarkable that in the eighteen months it ran only one rider was killed. Many station keepers and horse handlers lost their lives in Indian attacks, as the route ran directly through Indian territory and 1860 was a time of dreadful reprisals and continued unrest. Most of the epic runs were due to depredations on the forts. A rider rivalling Buffalo Bill for top honours in the distance stakes was 'Pony Bob' Haslam, who rode a Nevada section. At relay stations horses had either been run off or were commandeered to chase Pah Utes and he had to push his tired horse on. At his first rest stop the waiting rider refused to continue, so Haslam felt duty bound to step into the breach and ride an additional section. When he pulled into Smith's Creek he had ridden 190 miles non-stop, and with a rest of only eight hours he turned about and galloped back westwards with the incoming mail from the east. En route he found stations burnt, stock run off, and stations barricaded against Indian attack. Plunging on he finished his return 190 miles, and in spite of a lack of fresh horses and holdups en route he pulled in only three and a half hours behind schedule. Only a crazy type of courage and sense of loyalty and duty could have induced him to continue in the face of such hazards.

Those dangerous months of May to July 1861

with the Pah Utes scourging the deserts and plains were a forging ground for courage and it was a rare rider that failed to bring the *mochila* through on time. But with the Civil War looming the pressure was on, and the service went from a weekly to a twice-weekly run. It had been foreseen even before the first pony had left St Joseph that the service would be superseded by rail, but well before that came the telegraph, the talking wires. With the race to get the east and west sections of wire to a meeting point the days of the Express were numbered. By 24 October 1861 the two wires were joined and two days later the official closure of the Pony Express ended one of the most stirring episodes of pioneering days, out of which would grow a host of legends and a modern desire in endurance riders to emulate the feats of the youngsters who joined east to west.

Thus a new commemorative race is planned for Labor Day, 1988, with an estimated field of 2500 horses racing for California and competing for a total purse of $2,500,000, more than the total cost of running the whole venture over a century and a quarter ago. Indeed, the Express was judged a winner in all respects but finance, one of the partners in the firm operating the Express admitting the loss was 'several hundred thousand dollars'.

7 Expeditions and everyday life in the early 1900s

Scott of the Antarctic

Setting sail on a barque-rigged, converted wooden whaler in New Zealand's Lyttleton Bay is a strange start for one of the toughest endurance challenges any equine has had to meet, yet at the end of November 1910 it was only a way-station on the journey of nineteen Siberian ponies who exchanged the Russian steppes for the icy wastes of sub-zero Antarctica. Selected by Cecil Meares who initially shipped them out from Vladivostock, accompanied by a Russian groom, Anton Omelchenko, they were bad sea travellers, and suffered tremendously during their five-week incarceration in cramped quarters aboard the *Terra Nova*. Two died en route during a pounding storm that had the ship rolling and shipping water. The seventeen temporary survivors finally felt firm ground under their hooves in early January 1911, and rapidly set to rolling and generally kicking the stiffness out of their limbs before pulling sled loads of 700 to 1000 lb of ship's stores to the camp which was to be the base for Captain Scott's expedition to the South Pole.

The ponies themselves, under the care of Captain Lawrence Oates, quickly showed their own individuality. Some of them were intractable, to say the least, bolting at every opportunity. One named Weary Willie showed less than enthusiasm when harnessed; two proved too old for the demands – an oversight hard to understand when age should have been checked before purchase.

An early disaster had been the loading of insufficient fodder. Arguments had developed between Captain Scott and Captain Oates, who pressed for extra rations, finally taking it on himself surreptitiously to up the tonnage, which still proved inadequate. At that time equine nutrition did not have the available benefits that horses under stress can enjoy today. Though known for their toughness, and picked for their home climate's harshness, even these Siberian ponies were unequal to the task, attrition starting almost immediately. The distances they covered under the most extreme conditions of weather, winds, and inadequate fodder were remarkable. Much of their energy must have been eroded in maintaining their own body heat, let alone in the enormous exertions to come.

On 2 February 1911, soon after sledding the ship's stores to Base Camp at Cape Skuary (renamed for Lieutenant Edward Evans as Cape Evans), eight of the ponies were harnessed up to sled one ton of stores to a depot to be located approximately 140 miles from Base Camp. Additional weight was made up from five weeks' provisions for the teams of thirteen men, eight ponies and the full complement of thirty-three dogs, one having died on board ship during the storm. The appalling conditions where the ponies' small hooves cleft through the soft snow at every step, exhausting them as they plunged and foundered forward, made the daily average of 10 or 11 miles a nightmare. Lamentably all but one set of pony snowshoes had been left back at Base Camp. Three exhausted ponies were sent back to Base Camp, two succumbing on the way, and the human complement was reduced by five, two who had been left behind at an earlier camp, and the three pony handlers. Weather conditions had worsened. Already there had been a three-day hold-up in their first blizzard. Days were shortening and temperatures falling rapidly. With the diminished number of ponies now pulling more poundage each the animals began to weaken further. Sensing that Weary Willie was the weakest, the sled dogs turned wolf and savagely attacked the pony, severely biting him before they were thrashed off. His load was then dragged by four of the men, which made Scott record his realization of the ponies'

60

daunting task. Weakening visibly the remaining five ponies made it back to Safety Camp, just over 20 miles from Cape Evans Base, but all were now in a terribly emaciated condition. The final miles to Base were across sea ice which was not yet sufficiently hardened, but the alternative route was too difficult for exhausted animals and so the chance was taken. Weary Willie had hardly begun the final stage when he collapsed, thus halting the party for the night during which he died.

With the initial eight now reduced to four worse was yet to come. Three ponies, accompanied by Bowers, Cherry Garrard and Crean, set off ahead of Scott and Oates who had stayed behind with the dying pony, dropping down off the Barrier on to the supposed safer route across sea ice. Mist shrouded their way round Cape Armitage; the sea ice was not yet sufficiently hardened and started to break up. Turning back they camped on a 'safe' stretch of ice, only to find come morning that one pony had gone. Their 'safe' ice was rapidly disintegrating and the only means to safety was by a series of jumps from floe to floe. Initially the ponies jumped, but then an insurmountable obstacle of water separated them from the safety of the Barrier, which reared twenty feet up. This water was filled with hopefully cruising killer whales. Nimbly tackling the patches of ice Crean managed to reach the Barrier. The ponies and handlers had already spent a night and a day on their floating hell by the time the rest of the party caught up, with Scott concerned for the men's safety and Bowers stubbornly holding out for the ponies' too. While Oates was feverishly building an escape ramp for the ponies the ice shifted and drifted, leaving the ponies stranded for the night. By morning the floe had drifted back inwards and rescue was underway but at further cost, one pony balking at the cracks and falling into the water, to be finished off by a merciful blow from Oates' pick before the whales scented blood. Only two ponies remained – Uncle Bill and Nobby – and of these only Nobby reached safety, Uncle Bill slipping and also having to be despatched before the whales reached him. From eight ponies only two survived this first trip – Nobby and James Pigg, the only survivor of the three that had been returned to Base Camp earlier.

It was now early March and they had to wait at Hut Point a further five weeks before the winter clamped down, freezing the sea ice to safety point for the final trek back to Base 15 miles away. Temperatures were now at −40 °F. Arriving, they found that one more pony had died at Base, reducing the original nineteen to ten. By the third week in April perpetual night set in, the sun not appearing until 26 August. The ten ponies came through the winter but not without cost, the two who were too old for the job being weakened by sub-zero conditions. The sun's return meant daily exercise again and increased feeding, plus a daily battle with the vicious and totally intractable Christopher, who seemed more of a hindrance than help being unwilling to co-operate in the slightest.

The unsuitability of ponies for the Antarctic expedition was one cause of the late start of the next season's final assault on the Pole, the ponies being infinitely slower than dogs, and much time was lost trying to alleviate their suffering. On 1 November the ten were harnessed up for the final trek. The Pole was nearly 900 miles away and the journey forward was waymarked by successive camps with food caches for the return journey marked by flags. On 24 November the first of the ponies was shot, and successive daily treks were in turn the final journey for ponies who had reached the end of their march, until on 10 December the last five were despatched.

These hardy hauliers had come 500 miles across the most inhospitable terrain known to man. They had endured deprivation and cold of an unbelievable nature, with temperatures in the winter falling to −79 °F. Even in the height of Antarctic summer the temperature rarely rose above freezing in the daytime, dropping to energy-consuming lows at night. It was recorded that even in the last trek done in the summer not only did the temperature never rise above freezing but rarely above 0 °F, except on the one instance when a clammy wet blizzard halted the team for five snowbound days. With the rise to just over freezing thaw set in, making the snow incapable of supporting the weight of the remaining ponies who floundered and sank continually up to their bellies, exhausting themselves totally so that the final pony camp where the remaining five were shot was aptly named Shambles Camp. [In medieval terminology, a shambles was a place of butchery.]

These ponies had earlier been described by Captain Oates, who had done everything in his power to make their lot easier, as 'the most unsuitable scrap-heap crowd of unfit creatures that could possibly be got together', yet this scrap-heap of ponies must surely be ranked among the most enduring of all time, and also as the most unacclaimed in modern feats of equine fame.

Fenland flyers

To the general public, and even to the majority of horseriders, a 20- or 30-mile ride is cause for comment these days, but it was not so very long ago that double or treble that distance would not only go unremarked but be part of the daily routine. This was never more so than in the flat, watery wastes of East Anglia's Fenlands. Tony Brundle, a typical modern Fenland horseman who is well known in the British show pony world, draws a fascinating, and often humorous, picture of turn-of-the-century Fenland as lived by grandfather Albert.

Albert Brundle was born in 1897 at Denver, a small Norfolk village. His father was a publican and small farmer with an agistment on the nearby marshes where he ran cattle and ponies. In 1901 the River Ouse/Wissey burst its banks and flooded the surrounding countryside, drowning the pastured animals. For the Brundles it was devastating. Bankrupted, Albert's father lost his pub and his living and went into the employ of the Walker family as stockman on their Long Sutton, Lincolnshire, farm. It was here as a twelve year old that Albert and his brother Charles started work as stable boys for the princely sum of one shilling a week. For this they worked Monday to Saturday from 5.30 a.m. to 6 p.m., and on Sundays from 8 a.m. to 12 noon, and there were no annual holidays. There was a plenitude of hard graft and Albert soon learnt to ride by 'the seat of his pants', they being in fairly constant contact with the farm cob, as one of his regular tasks was checking the herds and flocks. Not a saunter around the home farm field, but a trek to the Walker pastures at Crowland 18 miles away, slip in a 10-mile 'rekky' on the livestock, and back by midday to catch a 'dockey' (lunch snap) and be ready for the afternoon's chores.

From the time he was old enough to work until he was drafted for World War I Albert absorbed horselore. Indeed, the tenor of farm life revolved around it. It was his responsibility to keep Boss Walker's horses up to the mark, as in common with other Fenland farmers he relied on the drive-and-ride cob for work and transport. The Walker family had many landholdings, one branch living at Fransham, Norfolk, and visiting combined with a spot of business often took place. Long Sutton Walker would drive the 45 miles to the Fransham Walker, stay overnight and drive the 20 miles into Norwich for the morning market, putting the horse up at a town pub for a few hours and a feed while he dickered and traded, then drive back to Fransham, take a short break and drive home late the same night, covering 85 miles in the day preceded by 45 miles the day before.

Spruced up, the Walker cobs were truly all around horses: market hauliers one day; 'Sunday go to Meeting' another; and on a Saturday they took the master courting, the Fransham Walker courting his lady love, a Miss Kilham, 45 miles away at Tydd St Mary, arriving on the Saturday evening, stopping over and being whisked back the following day. Courting came hard, but I suspect none the less rewarding, for a 90-mile drive – at least from the driver's standpoint. Farm cobs did not get Sundays off any more than farm stable hands.

After the Armistice, Albert went into business for himself equipped with horselore culled from caring for a variety of equines: from the adaptable drive-and-ride trap horse to the elegant 16-hand hunters usually sired by the local travelling Thoroughbred stallion. Amongst the stable inmates he also cared for carty vanners used for general farm work, and the heavy horses used for haulage and deep ploughing – indeed the Fens around Wisbech, Cambridgeshire, are still noted for their world-class Shires, many good specimens finding homes as far away as Australia and America.

In his own farming and general livestock dealing Albert relied heavily on the drive/ride horse. This type was common in the Fens in the early part of this century, and many were descended from the famous Marshland Shales, a local horse foaled at Terrington St John. They were hardy horses standing around 15 to 15.2 hh, clean legged with very little feather, and capable of a spanking 15 mph trot which was used to devastating effect in spur-of-the-moment trotting races. Compared to today's horses they resembled the refined type of English cob or the American Quarter Horse of the heavier sort used for roping.

Coupled with the old type of horse, proven in a century of farm living and countrywide driving since 1802 when Marshland Shales was foaled, went the old ways of care and feeding. None of the modern-day additives that line the manufacturers' bank accounts so well; the farm cob thrived on good old oat chaff, plenty of prime oats, mixed with a generous helping of linseed cake prepared in the Fen 'slap tub' manner, a weekly dose of 'blood powders' (similar to today's Kossolian) and rainwater drawn from a well (tapwater was not so readily available and all the roof run-offs were stored in vast underground cisterns). On this regime Albert Brundle expected and got a thoroughly honest outpouring of horsepower, particularly with his favourite gelding Magic.

A typical week's work for Magic would start with an easy day on Monday, which was occupied with general farm work and shepherding duties, with maybe a round trip to the second farm 5 miles away. Every Tuesday was King's Lynn Market and Magic would be 'put to' at 6 a.m. to drive the 14 miles with a load of six to eight fat 200 lb pigs on the float. The 14 miles would be clipped off in around an hour and a half. After half an hour to unload the stock Magic would fly back at a rattling 12 mph trot for another load – farm produce to sell, or even a second load of stock, possibly weaner pigs – returning to King's Lynn by 11 a.m. After the morning market and all farming business had been concluded in the 'Bird in Hand' bar came the final leg of the day's trip back to the farm. By lunchtime the horse would have covered a smart 56 miles, ready for his oats, a night's rest, and the next day's

jaunt. Wednesday was Boston, Lincolnshire, cattle market and he would be ridden the 27 miles, catch a feed at a pub while Albert did his dealings, and hie back in time for afternoon milking, another 50-odd miles under his girth. Thursday and Friday were in the nature of easy days – only 10 or 20 miles of shepherding and visiting outlying farms with any other farm-connected business thrown in. Saturday was market day for the whole family, a round trip of 22 miles to Wisbech for supplies and the weekly social gatherings. So to Sunday, the one blessed day when work ceased for Albert. Not so for Magic. Family lunch at Gedney Drove End 8 miles away meant a smart trot with all the family aboard, a swift post-prandial turnabout under saddle back to the farm so chores could be done, and return to pull the family home in the evening. Holidays for humans meant double work for the trap horse, as visiting for Christmas and Boxing Day was a hallowed event. Just occasionally Boston would be visited twice in the week – market on Wednesday and a brotherly visit on Sunday, the 54-mile round trip completed by 3.30 in the afternoon with visiting sandwiched in between.

All in all the farm cob's working week easily exceeded that of even the hardest-working and longest-ridden endurance horse of modern times, with an average of upwards of 170 miles for an easy week to well over 225 miles if the visiting urge came on Albert. The Marshland Shales' strain must have passed on very strong genes in the endurance department.

It certainly passed on its speed genes. Not content with merely getting to and from the markets, the roadways were turned racetrack for hair-raising contests along the stretch from Long Sutton to King's Lynn with Albert and his arch, but friendly, rival Harry Skate trying to prove who was the better whip. Usually a tit-for-tat race, on one occasion such a furious pace was set that Albert's gig overturned in a ditch on the outward journey, giving Harry the edge and a win, but Albert turned the tables on the homeward stretch, scorching ahead a clear winner. Modern sulky races are exciting, but a 14-mile trot down the main highway must have been some spectacle!

Even more of a spectacle, but not for the poor

driver, was the time a local farmer who was completely 'Brahms and Lizt' [Cockney rhyming slang] was rescued by Albert, who kindly led the farmer's cob home, drove it inside, unyoked it, led it back outside, carefully closing the gate, and very thoughtfully 'put it to' again. The air was no doubt highly coloured when the farmer recovered his wits and realized what had happened as he tried to drive away!

The steady round of farm life was frequently enlivened with a spot of horsetrading. No such luxury in those days as boxing the horse home from auction. After paying 47 guineas, a high price in those days, for 'a good nag to ride or drive' and trusting the warranty, Albert rode it the 45 miles back from Cambridge to Long Sutton. Knowing a little about current horse auctions on both sides of the Atlantic I would not like to be forced to ride a horse so acquired any such distance, let alone in the pitch dark on roads unknown to it. Evidently in those days auction horses did not carry the present-day connotations of suspicion.

Most of the farm drive/ride cobs would be bought as three year olds, many at Holbeach May Fair, and a good colt fetched £30. Kept a year it could be sold on for a handsome profit at £100 if it was 'warranted quiet in all gears', which meant it could be ridden, driven, hitched to a harrow, and on occasion to a light plough. Of course if it was really excellent Albert would keep his newest acquisition and sell what he already had. However, one youngster better for passing on was Darkie, who found a new home with the local milkman. The milkman was soon complaining that Darkie had dashed his milkcart in, only to be informed with typical horsetrader's nonchalance that he had not kicked Albert's in, with no mention of the fact that Albert did not possess one. Maybe then as now some horsebuyers were gullible and maybe even deserved to be labelled the 'local yokel'.

Nowadays the roads are rarely graced with harness horses. The highways are far too dangerous with the heavy traffic and the hard metalled surfaces. Even so there is a revival of carriage driving and with it the resurgence of breeding the 'right sort of cob'. Indeed Red Shales, a descendant of Marshland Shales, stands at a famous showjump-

ing stud in Buckinghamshire passing on the Shales blood into future generations of British showjumpers. But the sight of the flying trotter belongs to the past, along with the country characters, as well as much of the ancient horselore that our forebears took for granted. In its place we think we are finding much new about the working and training of our long-distance horses, when in reality none of it is as new as we think, only re-vamped and put to pleasurable use, rather than the grind of the old-time farm routine.

Yesteryear's cob trotted up a storm on the Fenland highways, while today's rider sets new records in 100 milers; both have Fenland representatives – the old and the new both come from Brundle territory (for a Fenland representative in modern competition see p. 162).

Buenos Aires to New York

Many of history's horses have had illustrious careers. Many, especially those who have been man's companions in epic endurance campaigns, have gone unmarked down a harrowing trail, any blaze of glory an aureole round their masters' names. Not so the trio who set out in the mid 1920s from Buenos Aires in Argentina to New York, a journey of more than 10,000 miles, taking two and a half years, and covering eleven countries en route.

The challenge of plain, jungle, desert and mountain had been calling to Swiss schoolteacher Aimé Felix Tschiffely for many years, and in 1925 he left the quiet halls of academe for a journey of adventure and hazard, but, for a change, one with a happy ending. His companions for the trail were two Argentinian Criollo geldings: Mancha, a sixteen-year-old red and white overo, and Gato, a fifteen-year-old buckskin.

Tschiffely has written an incident-packed account of equestrian, topographical, and anthropological interest in his *Southern Cross to Pole Star*. In it he relates the many dangers and hardships he, Mancha and Gato endured throughout the 10,000 miles, as well as the joys and hospitality he received. Leaving the civilization of a capital city the horses carried him through as wide a variation of terrain and climate as it could be possible to en-counter. They did it alone, with no back-up crews tailing them with creature comforts for man or horse; with little in the way of communications available once away from the well-used tracks and into almost unmapped wildernesses that made up much of their route. Then there were many regions still unexplored, or relatively little known. Though not so very long ago it was a totally different age, especially in the primitive areas of the South and Central American countries the trio traversed and which comprised the bulk of the epic journey.

The horses used came originally from the Patagonian pampas. Of the renowned tough Criol-lo breed, they were hardly what today one looks for in an endurance horse where toughness has to be allied with speed to be in with a chance. But the chance they were taking was one for mere survival. Tschiffely had the faith in, and the wish to prove, Criollo supremacy in continuous work under harsh conditions. This he did while carving a niche in equestrian history for the triple partnership.

Across eleven countries he met with everything bar arctic conditions, and even these were well simulated at elevations of over 16,000 feet in the Andes. In Argentina, his first leg of the journey was well over 1000 miles and he headed in a north-westerly direction, across rolling pampas, arid de-sert, and fertile regions, climbing to cross into Bolivia at Le Quiaca, 11,000 feet of cold, windy mountains. A change came with the canefields in sultry lowlands, before climbing again to Peru to where the highest-known navigable stretch of wa-ter lies at Lake Titicaca at 11,400 feet. Higher still were the Cerro de Pasco mines at 17,000 feet. Dropping from the icy Andean heights to sea-level Lima, hundreds of miles of a scorching inferno of coastal desert stretched before them to Ecuador and Colombia and more mountains.

Since Bolivia the scarcely broken Criollos had been developing a rapport with their rider, and suffered along with Tschiffely extremes of climate and erratic feeding. Sometimes in fertile regions they feasted on alfafa; in the poverty-ridden Indian mountain villages they were lucky to get an armful of cut grass, and sometimes went hungry with no food at all. They became used to eating, if not with relish, a weird variety of foods including sugar cane, bamboo, bananas, yucca and tobacco leaves. And on this they never became sick or sorry, main-taining flesh relatively easily – better by far than finer-bred horses would have done. They became trail-clever, too. Bred almost wild they retained an inborn sense of self-preservation and Tschiffely learnt to respect his horses' judgement of safety, especially after Gato saved them all from miring in a quicksand. In dry regions they gave advance warning of water ahead.

As well as normal trail hazards there were a legion of others – insects, both biting and parasitic, and vampire bats which often attacked the horses at night, mainly in the saddle region. Being before the days of modern veterinary science old-time herbal remedies proved sovereign, and one item in Tschiffely's pharmacopoeia was garlic. Used crushed with Indian pepper it was reputed to keep the bats away; crushed with alcohol it was a remedy against mountain sickness; and by itself, again crushed, it was supposed to be so noxious to snakes that they would stay away. All three were hazards at differing stages of the journey and likely to bother men and horses.

To the lack of horse fodder and poor food were added the very primitive and unsanitary conditions for both horses and rider. It was a relief on coming to a modern town to exchange the rough for the civilized: cleanliness and good food, and clean fields and pure water for the horses – at times, where water was polluted Tschiffely disinfected both his and the horses' water.

Throughout his tale Tschiffely pays tribute to Mancha and Gato, their courage and sagacity; the sheer doggedness displayed in conditions more often than not adverse. Not intended as a ride to break any speed records, even had it been it was doomed to failure in that respect. In every major town the trio were fêted, loaded with days and even weeks of hospitality; then once embarked en route again they returned to the hinterlands and priva-tion, yet in all the mileage and the yo-yo of hunger and surfeit they pulled through in superb condi-tion.

On reaching Mexico two-thirds of the journey was behind them, with the easiest stretch to come, though not easy by today's reckoning of endurance rides. Banditry there certainly was, but not on the level of some of the Southern American countries already traversed. Indeed after having crossed the swamplands and jungles of Panama and Costa Rica they were advised to delete Nicaragua from the itinerary, taking a sea route to San Salvador, to avoid getting trapped in the revolution taking place. Guatemala was crossed with trepidation. Law was marked by its absence, Tschiffely being warned against murderous bandits, so it was almost a relief to cross into Mexico. But in Mexico lawlessness caught up with them as here too one of the periodic upsets was occuring, and it was only when the American border was crossed and arms surrendered to border officials that the journey was in guaranteed safe territory.

On arriving after 2000 miles of transcontinental riding from Laredo, Texas, Tschiffely and Mancha were fêted in Washington and New York, Gato having been left behind in St Louis because of the increasing danger of leading a horse in the many traffic-crowded towns through which the final part of the journey was routed. Still not entirely domesticated, even after traversing eleven countries in 504 days of actual travel, Mancha was prone to rodeo displays, especially if a strange rider dared step aboard. The two geldings were re-turned to Argentina and the rolling pampas rather than subject them to incarceration in a public park as tourist attractions, as was one insensitive suggestion.

Many long-distance treks, some races of prodigious length, have been achieved since Tschiffely's ride, but none has captured the imagination of so many nations; none lived as a legend; and no one I warrant has voluntarily undergone so many hazards, discomforts, and privations. Indeed with the constant South and Central American unrest today it would take an even more intrepid voyager to clear the hassle of paperwork, visas and permits, and inter-country vaccinations for the horses. Some things are easier, but danger there still is, particularly as half of those eleven countries live in a state of perpetual ferment.

A lot was asked of two chunky pampas horses and they gave in generous measure, proving beyond doubt all that is claimed for them by Criollo afficionados. I can think of only one other breed that truly meets the claims to excellence made for it, and that is the Arabian, who along with the Barb in the distant days of the Spanish Conquest laid some of the strains of the present-day Criollo.

It would take nearly sixty years and a far-sighted Frenchman before there was an attempt to break Aimé Felix Tschiffely's world distance record.

8   The twentieth-century horse in war

Not all of the endurance feats of the mid twentieth century have been of a sporting nature, or undertaken for pleasure, to raise money for charity, or to test the capabilities of horse and rider.

Some rides by their very nature hearken back to previous centuries when the horse was still embroiled in the horrors of war and was often his rider's only means to safety, so before we forget his courage in the face of hardship let us take a look at just a few of our modern mechanical world's heroic horses.

Some experiences from the Middle East

Though the world had almost completely gone over to mechanization in World War II there were still a very great number of horses and mules in cavalry divisions used both as mounts and pack animals.

Shortly before that war the British Army still used horses to patrol in both Palestine and Egypt, and an old-time farrier, Harold Parr, AFCL, who used to shoe my endurance horses some years ago, told me of one such trip when he was a trooper in the 14/20th King's Hussars Regiment stationed in Egypt in the early 1930s. War Office orders came through for the regiment to prepare for an endurance march, and in temperatures we would consider sufficient to cancel a ride, lower speeds or extend recovery limits. Each troop took three days to do a 90-mile trek across the desert from Cairo to Wadi le Truni, being allowed a twenty-four hour break before the forced return march started: a 90-mile trek in twelve hours starting at 4 a.m. and arriving back at the Pyramids at 4 p.m., reaching a speed that many a 100-mile winner today would not be ashamed of, yet scarcely under favourable conditions. Each horse carried over 300 lb and proceeded at walk, trot and canter for five-minute intervals repeated throughout the distance, every horse, due to sound management and horsemanship, arriving in good condition.

Similar desert conditions were experienced by Noel Carney, whose son John related his father's experiences as a cavalry trooper. After two years in the Queen's Bays in the late 1920s he was transferred to the Middlesex Yeomanry, and in the early days of the last world war found himself stationed in Palestine when the whole regiment, complete with horses, was shipped in for police duties, trying to keep the Zionists and the Palestinians from their interminable internecine warfare. They were stationed in the desolate barren Dead Sea area where the searing heat evaporated every vestige of moisture from the forbidding land, sucking up the chemical-laden sea waters into the choking air. It was hardly an area suited to the health of any horse, let alone the hunter types the troopers rode. Such horses are ill suited to extremes of climate, having been raised in temperate and lush surroundings, yet it was in these conditions that they operated on arduous desert patrols. There were frequent emergency dashes to towns flaring with hatred and discord. On occasions they resorted to encircling townships and tightening the grip with sabres drawn till some sort of temporary peace ensued. The task of the Cavalry colonel was made all the harder as the replacement troopers lacked military bearing, being drafted from amongst conscientious objectors who bypassed the dangers of the front line. Even the officering at times left much to be desired, one incident illustrating the almost total lack of discipline, though it had a salutary effect, and at this far-removed date a rather amusing sequence.

On forced route marches each trooper's horse carried a full complement of arms strapped to the saddle. Units were frequently called out to restore peace, often riding through terrain where they never knew when a sniper's bullet might reach them. On one such march under the 'control' of a young Lieutenant the column halted to water their parched horses at a desert rill, troopers taking the chance to relax and stretch their legs after hours in the saddle, when shots rang out close by. The cavalry chargers bolted en masse, fully accoutred and with rifles still in the saddle scabbards, leaving the troopers stranded on foot and the officer in charge facing shipment home and a dreaded court-martial.

For weeks thereafter the desert Arabs proudly paraded on captured chargers resplendent in full military equipment, their new 'owners' brandishing weapons. To the Arabs no doubt it was a successful razzia with valuable booty of trained chargers and accurate modern rifles to boost their collection of antique weaponry.

The retreat from Moscow: a soldier's story

While British hunters were acclimatizing to the desert aridity and sharing the harsh life associated with Arab culture and a people in perpetual ferment, thousands of miles away in the frozen wastes of Russia it was a far grimmer scenario.

During January 1986 when Britain froze in a Siberian grip and temperatures dropped to new record lows, I met Gustav Lodderstedt, who as an eighteen-year-old private in the German Cavalry had been in the retreat from Moscow in the last days of December 1941.

As a sixteen-year-old farmboy whose life revolved around horses he was conscripted into the 39th Cavalry Regiment and spent two years in cavalry and weapons training. Among the cavalry duties was the early training of horses destined for the front, and he recalls long hours working the Hannoverian and Trakehners that had been mustered from the German State Studs.

Early in 1941 he was transferred to the Heavy Machine Gun Regiment. Suddenly the tempo of war increased, and at 3 a.m. one May morning a despatch rider galloped into their headquarters with orders to move. Thirty minutes later they mobilized for the Russian front, horses and men being transported by rail as far as Radom in central Poland. From there on it was an eight months' constant trek – north of Radom to Warsaw, then to a border crossing in southeast Poland to Russia. Once across the River Bug they headed north again to Smolensk and thence to Moscow, only halting 60 km outside Moscow itself – 2000 miles of riding, fighting, foraging, scouting, through hostile territory, inching forward with the odds stacked against them.

However blame is apportioned in any war the general rank and file, apart from national pride and loyalty to their country, have no especial hatred of a collective enemy. They are conscripted, they serve, they kill, and they hope to survive. In the conditions that Gustav Lodderstedt rode into many did not survive, and among reminiscences called up from over forty-five years ago foremost in his mind was the debt they owed to their horses. Without the horses, he said, the German army could not have functioned. Many hundreds of thousands of them took a one-way trip from Germany: most never returned. Equally the Russians too depended on horses for survival and continued operation. It came as a surprise to me to have it categorically stated that, although there were the tanks, the guns, the heavy equipment on both sides, it was still the horse that was a vital element in those not so far off days of our twentieth century.

Heavy armaments were pulled by horses. Two horses were hitched to each limber transporting a double machine gun, the MJ 42, capable of firing 300 rounds a minute. In Gustav's regiment there were in excess of 400 horses, and with other similar regiments the total in that one small section came to 2000 horses deployed in moving armaments through very hostile country.

Logistically the horse was essential to the German army. Supplies depended on him, and the State Studs had been drained of available horse-flesh – Mecklenburgs, Oldenburgs, even massive heavy draft horses, but the latter soon proved to lack the stamina of the lighter breeds. Even laying cable for communications was done from horseback. Constant horse reinforcements were sent eastwards into the Russian wastes. Gustav himself rode a Trakehner mare who exhibited all the toughness and durability of her breed. She needed it because at over six feet tall Gustav was no lightweight, weighing around 200 lb, to which was added at least 60 lb of equipment: saddle, leather saddle bags, replacement horseshoes, arms, food for horse and rider, heavy trench coat and blankets for both man and horse.

Gustav's main duties were to scout around and far ahead for Russian troops, and bring back vital information on their movements. Scouting entailed forced marches of 80 to 90 km a day, and there were many times when he recalls being in the saddle for eighteen hours at a stretch, the longest being a 5 a.m. pre-dawn mission that saw him still mounted on a very weary horse at midnight. Often he and his fellow scouts lost the element of surprise and had to make a run for it, on horses that frequently had upwards of 50 miles under their hooves that day. All the horses were used to gunfire and in addition to his rifle he also carried and used a machine gun.

Quizzed on terrain he told me it ranged from open plain to dense forests, to boggy treacherous quakes where horses mired to their bellies, the only safe way to cross being to lay solid materials such as planking and brushwood across the sucking mire.

They deployed ever deeper, leaving Poland and marauding into Russia as the year wore on. Unlike film presentation of famous set piece battles he said it was more like a jigsaw puzzle. Pockets of Germans and pockets of Russians continually engaged, the night forays being the worst. During one night alone in his troop of 120 eight horses were killed, some from wounds, others shot outright, yet others dying from sheer exhaustion. Equine losses were continually heavy. The further into Russia they drove the more erratic were supplies. Foraging was difficult. Once summer passed horses often went hungry. Replacements were commandeered from amongst the Russian horses – either captured or sequestered; he does recall one Akhal-Teke, not for the breed's noted endurance but for its evil manner and the efficient way it used teeth and heels.

He lost his original mare and the replacement,

also a Trakehner, carried him into the worst winter he can ever recall. Himself coming from East Prussia, the horseman's paradise, he was used to their cold winters, but what faced him now was beyond belief. In September the bad weather set in; until October he recalls that it was wet – insidious, incessant, debilitating. By November the Russian winter had clamped down, and used as he was to the cold of East Prussia he endured the snow, the cold, the ice. It was in these conditions that they had to cope with the Cossacks. Dressed in masking winter white they would appear silently, ghostlike out of nowhere, horses seemingly riderless silhouetted black against the frozen background. Germans would be cut down, their horses the first target, men the second, the withering fire coming from Cossacks hanging on to the side of their own horses and exposing no target for retaliation. Then using the element of surprise Cossacks would bear down, now upright in the saddle, lances couched or swords cleaving. They gave no quarter and seemed to come scything down from an earlier savage century. Of all the Russian troops Gustav said they feared the Cossacks most, but admitted to admiration for their incomparable horsemanship and the stealth used to creep up unawares.

Into this bitter winter came a sudden thaw and the horses were in horrendous conditions, mired to their bellies in mud as they stood in camp, and the constantly sodden clothes rotted off the soldiers' backs. They had cut their hazardous way right to the environs of Moscow and were camped on one side of the Moskva River. Across the river the Russians faced them. By now it was late December and the weather turned viciously: ice and snow, raging blizzards, and temperatures plummeting to −20 °C overnight. Horses mired in holding mud were now frozen solid in ice. Men were freezing, Gustav himself being one to suffer from frostbite in feet and hands. They had to fight for survival alone.

Over the next two days the temperature sank to −40 °C. Across the now frozen river the Russians waited. Used to their hostile winter climate they were prepared. The Germans were not. The oil in their guns froze, jamming the mechanism, and taking them completely by surprise; no precautions had been taken against their armaments freezing.

The Russians poured across the river and the German advance turned to flight. Gustav recalls his unit's flight; the punishing ride – 300 km (close to 200 miles) in two days, riding all the first night, the next day, the following night, and part of the next day, with the elements hurtling into their faces, blinding snow, and the ice-laden wind. Across frozen wastes the horses ploughed remorselessly on, sometimes stumbling into ditches where equipment would be burnt to save it falling to the pursuers. At times the Russians were less than 200 yards away, and in some cases only a frozen river would separate them. Lacking any means of defence with all guns frozen, the only device left to delay pursuit and capture was to throw a bomb made of six grenades lashed together on to the ice, exploding it into lethal shards. Delayed, but fording lower down, the Russians would close again. Gustav had one horse shot from under him, commandeering another from a fallen mate, until at the end of two days they had outdistanced the Russians and fallen back into the temporary safety of the German lines. But the cost had been high. Out of 120 men and horses in the troop only 60 survived, and those were in a sorry state. Gustav's feet and hands were badly frostbitten and he was shipped to hospital in Czechoslovakia. He remembers seeing the gruesome results of soldiers less fortunate than he whose frostbitten extremities had been eroded to the bone. Horses too had suffered, and such was the state of supplies that dead horses were consumed to keep starvation at bay.

He recounted one poignant story, the like of which is usually associated with dogs. Each rider naturally grew fond of his own mount and the maxim of horses first, men second was imbued in them. Heavy horse losses hit hard and sundered partnerships that had endured for countless frozen miles and months. On one march in forested country he recalls hearing a whinny coming from the woods through which the troop was passing, and on tracing the source they came upon a charger almost frozen stiff, lying on the ground next to his rider who had been shot. The rider was beyond help but the bond forged had kept the horse by his side until help arrived.

Losses were so heavy that Gustav's regiment was disbanded and after hospitalization he found himself in the 23rd Infantry, the Hindenberg Regiment. His days with the cavalry, apart from escorting a shipment of 500 new horses to the lines, were over. Later he was captured and sent to a POW camp in America in August of 1944. Now he lives in retirement only a scant 6 miles from me. He is filled with memories, one in particular of a Polish prisoner who fell to the Germans and who earlier had been present at the Battle of Warsaw and Kutno-Lódź when in 1939 Walther von Reichenau's 10th Army waged a *blitzkrieg*, annihilating the Polish forces. It was in this battle that the ill-fated Polish cavalry charge took place, with men and horses pitted against heavy armoured tanks. Gustav related how this Polish prisoner said that the Poles had been told the German tanks were a bluff, made of wood and mounted on flimsy wheels, and the cavalry had charged with lance and sword. Many years ago when I worked in Warsaw for the British Embassy I was told a similar story by a Polish *pani* (the name we used for the charwoman) who worked in the American Embassy. She said that the Poles, through German disinformation, had learnt that the tanks were fabricated from papier mâché and would disintegrate under a charge and fire.

Of the prisoners from both sides Gustav said that in the theatre of war they were well treated, and it was only as they retreated further from their capture point that maltreatment would begin. The front line soldier had no personal hatred, he was merely doing his job for his country. Of the repatriated horses many were sent to France to be cared for in the veterinary hospitals especially set up for injured horses, others to depots in Germany.

The flight of the Trakehners

When the maps were redrawn after World War II Trakehnen was lost to that famous breed of horse for ever, and the nucleus of horses that survived were resettled in a diversity of new homes, scattered throughout the New Germany.

Survival and endurance have stamped this erstwhile East Prussian breed no less strongly than their seven-branched Elkhorn brand. They are now known worldwide as successful horses in many spheres, even into the ranks of modern endurance riding, not only in the land of their birth but in England too (see p. 161). But it is an older and infinitely bitter feat of endurance that won the Trakehners through and gave the world its so resilient descendants.

The evolving of a new breed takes several lifetimes, and with the Trakehner it took the best part of two centuries until East Prussia had one of the best warmblood light horses in the world. They were used extensively as both saddle and work horses, cavalry remounts, and elegant carriage horses, and the wide reaches of pre-war East Prussia were imbued with every facet of horse rearing and training. Trakehners were raised in ideal surroundings, either at the large State Studs or in the many hundreds of smallholdings and farms that made up the highly successful agrarian economy. Then in October 1944 the centuries' old peaceful existence was shattered.

Germany had cut deep into Russia and as the tide of war turned it suffered crippling losses and was relentlessly driven back. Trakehnen is so close to the Russian border that gunfire could be heard booming and fire flashes were seen horribly close. The Stud Director's repeated requests to the Nazi administration to evacuate the horses were denied on the premise that Germany would withstand and triumph, and if she did not then all would go down to perdition. At last when it was clear that the Russians were on the point of crossing into Germany the order to evacuate came through and the long trek to West Germany began.

With younger men conscripted it was left to old men, women and children to hustle the 1200 horses – stallions, in-foal mares, youngstock, and even foals – along the first stages of their 900-mile bid for freedom. The first stage covered 70 km and the few mounted drovers kept the bands moving at a trot, passing crowds of fleeing refugees with their few possessions. Many smallholders were driving their prized Trakehner mares hitched to heavily loaded wagons. The first objective was to take refuge in the western part of the East Prussian Province and then return once the Russians were beaten, but by the end of January 1945 it was clear

that further flight was imperative. Russian tanks were bulldozing their way steadily into the Province in a remorseless advance. By now a vicious winter had clamped down, snow piling deep and rivers frozen, tracks rutted hard, and temperatures plummeting to twenty degrees of frost. Only a small gap was left through which to force exit from the Province, which was by now slowly being throttled by Russian troops. This avenue, an ice-locked inlet from the Baltic Sea known as the Frisches Haff, was 30 km long and treacherous with suddenly thawing ice. In haste born of fear many drivers pressed too close on the leaders, and wagons and horses were lost in the churning waters. Many of the fleeing horses stood harnessed for weeks at a time, drivers not daring to unhitch. Mares heavy in foal were miscarrying as conditions worsened. Fodder was disappearing fast, the supplies carried diminishing and the land they trekked through desolate and offering little sustenance. Harvests had not been cut; whole villages were empty save for scavenging pigs and scrawny cats left behind. Rations for the horses were cut to 6 lb of oats a day, and then to 3 lb, and sometimes none at all. If they were lucky they might find straw or a little hay at nighttime stopping places where they stood to in harness outside, weathering wind and snowstorms. Many horses were footsore with hooves worn to the quick, yet they were pulling heavy loads in a half-starved condition, heavy in foal, for distances ranging from a normal daily stint of 30 km to sometimes as much as 50 km. In certain instances families would force the march for 120 km (75 miles) when hard pressed.

Along the route horses succumbed to deprivation. Many foals were born perfectly formed but dead at birth from starvation in utero. When the trek was halted for weeks at a time the horses, weakened as they were, were conscripted for work on the land, and then resumed the march until nine weeks later they shook free of the Russian grip, dispersing into an occupied Germany but under the less stringent conditions of the Allied forces. For the people it was a haven, but a harsh one. Homeless, and with few possessions, they tried desperately to hang on to their beloved Trakehner horses. The horses, particularly the mares, having come through 900 miles of unbelievably bad conditions and though grossly debilitated, still struggled for survival as they were immediately forced on to the land to till the soil in an attempt to feed the swollen population. Impoverished owners were forced to part with many mares, making those grimly retained all the more precious. Some had not survived the vicious journey, others had not outdistanced encroaching Soviets and had been shipped into the wastes of Russia, along with many refugees who could not make enough speed in flight. Yet others, after successfully outdistancing the Russians, were simply handed over to them when Germany was partitioned.

The numbers of state-owned horses from the Trakehnen stud had been sadly diminished, largely due to partitioning and falling to Russian exploitation. Some few dozen out of the hundreds that started the trek found haven in the West and from these, and from the gallant remnants in private ownership, the new twentieth-century Trakehners descend. Over forty years later the Trakehner Society is thriving and the horses are in demand worldwide, yet from the destruction of the flight few foals survived. Breeding ceased for two whole seasons – the horses were too debilitated and their owners' future so uncertain that it took reassurance that they would not be returned to Russian-dominated East Prussia. The breed was held in suspension.

In 1948 sufficient confidence and a measure of stability for the owners, and new health for the horses, resulted in a crop of foals in 1949. Since then the breed has prospered, and from horses who have truly been tried and tested for endurance in a way no organized system can possibly devise, these descendants have inherited ingrained toughness that was without parallel in the closing days of World War II. Without these Trakehner horses, and the thousands of others that ground through the 1945 winter, many more refugees would never have made it to the West, safety, and personal freedom.

Guerrilla warfare in Afghanistan today

Right up until the present day in Afghanistan horses and donkeys too play their part in the Jihad, or Holy War, being waged by the Mujahideen against the enforced Russian occupation. Led by Ahmadshah Massoud, a Tadzhik who is fast becoming a legend in Afghanistan, the Mujahideen fight a guerrilla war with headquarters in the mountainous wilderness of the Panjsher Valley. Constantly on the move their leader never spent more than a night in the same place, and as the living legend grew he moved from camp to camp astride the black horse presented to him by grateful villagers. Yet it is the packhorses and donkeys that are earning themselves a small place in history. Crossing the Durand Line separating Pakistan from Afghanistan, they regularly make the 200 mile trip from the Line to the Panjsher weighted down with 154 lb (70 kg) of arms and ammunition and are constantly under threat of attack from ripping bullets or strafing machine guns. They are tough little horses of about 14 to 15 hands, and for all their narrowness and lean condition they have the wiry frame that denotes great strength and resilience.

From their appearance these horses appear to be Kathiawaris, a breed native to India with a lot of Arab blood in its makeup. [I am indebted to Sandy Gall of Independent Television News for answering a few questions about these horses, though he was unable to confirm their breeding.] Their resilience is much needed because the 200-mile inward trek packing a heavy load is travelled over very rough going, climbing the Hindu Kush to passes at over 12,000 feet with all that high altitude brings: rarified air, mountain torrents, bitter cold and high winds. Yet these little horses are on a regular trip – two weeks in and two weeks out carrying their return load of precious lapis lazuli, which is mined in the mountains of Afghanistan from the same mines that produced it 2500 years ago for the Achaemenids (Persian royal line) when the area was known as Gandara, one of the northernmost Persian satrapies.

Each horse is privately owned, shod, and fed barley and a little hay en route – hardly the generous diet our own endurance horses are used to. The Mujahideen levy a tax on outgoing lapis lazuli of 5 to 10 per cent, raising a £75,000 yearly income:

on the emeralds coming through the Panjsher they do even better with a £150,000 tribute, all of which is turned to good account in exchange for the horses' return burden of armaments, including rockets and BM 12 rocket launchers.

These little Kathiawaris must surely be the last horses still being used in a theatre of war in this supposedly enlightened age of the late 1980s.

Mongolia, twentieth-century style

Earlier in this book we met the Mongol horsemen, coming out of the wastes of the Gobi desert on their shaggy little horses to sweep their way 6000 miles into a terrified Europe.

Today's Mongol still depends to a large extent on his horse, the same type of animal that carried the earlier conquerors, for transport. I am indebted to a good friend, Lieutenant Colonel Stephen Jenkins, TD, who was sent in the 1960s by the Arts Council to fill a teaching post in Ulaanbaatar, the Mongolian capital, for glimpses of the still enduring horsemen of twentieth-century Mongolia.

Mongolia itself encompasses an area comparable to France, West Germany, Spain and Portugal put together, added to which are the territories of Inner Mongolia inside China and Buriat Mongolia inside the USSR. Additionally there is a considerable Mongolian population within the confines of Manchuria. The horse is still vital to all these peoples in their everyday lives. With rare exceptions related below, it is not an animal used for sport. Consequently, used as an everyday conveyance, there is no body of literature about the horse as has arisen in countries where every aspect of equine sporting activity is studied in great detail.

Still remaining largely a pastoral nation, Mongolians look with equal value on horses, cattle, camels, sheep and goats, due recognition being given to all as symbols on their coinage. Within herds of cattle, sheep, goats, and so on, individuals have no names, and so it is with the horse, any Mongolian finding our attitude to individuals strange: 'You don't name sheep, do you?' asked one. Horses are just an intrinsic part of the day-to-day life of a pastoral people. Consequently there are no feats of endurance that would normally gain recognition in equestrian journals, and admiration from riders acknowledging such feats finds no echo in the Mongolian horseman's life.

It is still common, more so than the motor vehicle, to find horses used for transport even in Ulaanbaatar itself. Much of Mongolia is without metalled roads, these being reserved for the closer environs of major towns. The people still camp in large spaces that are often palisaded, and within towns themselves there are vast tracts given to encampments with their accretions of horses, sheep and cattle. In the outlying districts herds of horses and cattle are extensive, running from small units of maybe 100 or so animals up to larger 1000-strong concentrations. In travelling the great distances within a largely unpopulated country it is quite common to exchange the current ridden horse for one from any herd the rider may be passing. The environment is somewhat hostile compared to the lushness that Europeans consider normal grazing, and chill at an altitude of 4000 feet above sea level. The ponies and other animals scratch a living from vast stretches of sparsely vegetated steppe. Summers are short and hot, scorching the scant grazing so that the sudden April flush is short lived, and by early October a thin dry snow is falling. The air is largely windless, thus fooling an outlander that temperatures are higher in winter than the actual average of $-35\,°C$. It has been known for a horse, hobbled for the night by being restrained by both front feet and one hind strapped to the front, to be frozen to death next morning after a nighttime plunge to $-60\,°C$. No wonder that the Mongol ponies of the Golden Horde were able to survive what to them must have seemed Europe's succulent forage and beneficent climate.

The pastoral way of Mongolian life means that herdsmen travel from waterhole to waterhole, especially once inside the Gobi itself, which, contrary to the belief I and no doubt others hitherto

3 A schoolboy takes his turn at horse herding in Mongolia today. (Mongolian Embassy, London)

held, is not a sandy treeless waste but is clothed with scrub and scant vegetation, sufficient to support the ranging herds on a borderline diet. Children in Mongolia are used to riding early, from the age of eighteen months when they are first introduced to the horse.

Though definitely not a horseman, only once having tried his luck aboard a gentle grey Mongolian pony, Lieutenant Colonel Jenkins met many of the herdsmen during his tour of duty, in particular one civil servant named Adalbish who on his month's annual holiday trekked the 1200 miles from Ulaanbaatar to the Russian border and back, crossing the Hangai Mountains en route. Temperatures were good, averaging around 75 °F. Mounts, as was the custom, were exchanged en route at need. This feat, accomplished as a holiday jaunt in a month, occasioned no acclaim, and to boot was undertaken by a man not in the daily habit of riding 50 miles, as he was deskbound for the rest of the year in the capital.

A trek of a different nature and unwelcome at

that entailed a three-day chase after a loose horse that was last seen heading towards China. Fanciful but true, and the culprit was a young Mongolian lad lucky enough to gain himself a place at Leningrad University. On vacation he visited his grandfather who was still living a herdsman's life and at the time was bivouacked in a treeless encampment. City life had so completely overtaken the lad that when he dismounted after a ride, on being told to 'pat the horse's shoulder and let him go' he did just that, to the chagrin of his grandfather who had merely been using the normal Mongol idiom for hobbling a horse.

On one occasion while travelling in January Lieutenant Colonel Jenkins came up with a string of camels loaded with firewood and herded by drivers on tough Mongolian ponies. They had been crossing the mountains northeast of Ulaanbaatar for three weeks in temperatures that rose to −35 °C from a nighttime low of −60. Endurance would not be the word coming to most people's minds of trips taken under such conditions, yet these pack trips are a common occurrence in this modern age. Indeed, much of Mongolian life consists of tough, enduring feats, pack ponies and camels being the usual means of transport over rough terrain. Transporting staples such as rice from the Chinese border which is a mere 300 or 400 miles away is undertaken by animals in a largely roadless country.

Even the rare occasions when horses and ponies are used for sport are of an enduring nature, though compared with the normal distances travelled the endurance this time goes more to the credit of the young riders. Once a year the Naadam takes place. These are the annual games held in the capital and the three events are archery, wrestling and horse-racing, the last-named being restricted to children between three and ten years of age. The distance they race is 30 km and the course is set through the rolling scarps of the Altai Mountains. It seems that it is not only the Mongolian pony that deserves the accolade of toughness.

The horse remains an integral part from childhood onwards of the modern Mongolian's life, even for the country's high officials who ride to their appointments much as an old-time circuit judge would travel in an England or America of previous centuries.

Ganador

Winning a scholarship to study under Joaquin Rodriguez de la Villa, one of Spain's leading High School and classical trainers, was the first step on the road to Rebecca Howell's acquaintance with Ganador, a grey eight-year-old Hispano-Arab gelding. He was to carry her on her treasured trip through La Mancha, following the legendary Don Quixote. At first it was an inauspicious introduction to Ganador, a name prophetically meaning money winner, who arrived as a replacement for a dressage horse gone lame. Stepping down from a tipper truck Ganador, though accomplished in the showjumping arena and in the bullring from whence he had been seconded, turned out to have no dressage training. With a scant forty-eight hours to go until the dressage event, Rebecca soon 'clicked' with the gelding. He was willing and quick

4 Ganador and Rebecca Howell.

to learn, and notched up a third place in the competition. Small beginnings, but by then Rebecca decided he had to be hers and a deal was struck.

She had her partner for the 250-mile route from Albacete to Altea, a ride she had long wanted to make. As the crow flies the distance is roughly 100 miles, but the peregrinations of the route extend it to 250 miles – a fair distance for any ride, though Ganador's claim to be an endurance horse does not rest on this trip alone, as he took fourteen days to complete it. The daily average was small, but throughout there were many distractions, not least the extended hospitality received by both horse and rider along the route, so that with days out for visits Ganador was in fact approaching a respectable distance each day. Packing in excess of sixteen stone (225 lb) with rider, Portuguese saddle, grain and related gear, not much of the horse was visible from the saddle except his ears. Daily rides averaged between five and six hours, on occasion extending to as many as fourteen hours. Much of the route was through roadside caminos (dirt tracks), some along busy highways, but at times when these petered out it was find as find can. Carrying sixteen stone up a sheer climb and down a dizzying mountain the other side to pick up the track was par for the course. Temperatures fluctuated from below zero at night to 110 in the non-existent shade by day in an arid zone.

The last day of the journey to Altea was over 50 miles and was immediately followed by a three-day pack trip in the mountains, climbing to 6000 feet and into the beginnings of rarified air, passing en route an ancient ice house built by the Moors more than 600 years ago. To be sure, the endurance in the latter stages was the rider's, as an onset of bronchitis turned rapidly to pneumonia.

Following the ride and the end of the scholarship period Ganador accompanied Rebecca to England, where the Spanish prelude was followed by two fund-raising rides in England of 100 miles each, the aim being to swell the Cancer Research Fund. This was achieved beyond all expectations and cheques totalling £14,000 were presented at Olympia Horse of the Year Show in 1983 and 1984.

There is nothing very remarkable these days about a 250-mile jaunt on horseback, taking one's time, followed by two 100-mile rides, again not against the clock or other competitors. But Ganador must be reckoned one of those uncrowned champions when it is realized that he did all this under severe handicaps himself.

On coming back to England a peculiar condition manifested itself, at first mystifying the veterinary profession but later recognized as equine diabetes. Treated and kept in check by rigorous diet of plain oats and hay, he got fitter and fitter on the oats, needing more and more exercise, thus suggesting that he was fit enough to do the fund-raising 100 milers. Then disaster struck, not once but twice. He broke his near foreleg – three breaks in the knee joint and the shaft of cannon – and when it mended it mended rigid, necessitating magneto-pulse treatment for six weeks to bring him to soundness again. A tremendous recovery, but more was yet to come when Ganador himself was

found to be suffering from cancerous tumours with lesions on the liver and pancreas and a brain tumour that occasionally flared, giving Rebecca some worrying moments when for safety she had to bale out of the saddle in a hurry. All his exploits were guided by veterinary advice.

It is that which sets Ganador firmly among the cohorts of endurance champions. A courageous horse battling through his pain, a dedicated rider, and skilled veterinary care: these keep an active horse able to remain undefeated. Indeed were he not named Money Winner he could well deserve the title Invicta.

The Trans Moyen Orient Ride

On 13 February 1982, two riders on Arabian stallions set out from France to break the world endurance ride record of 16,093 km held by Aimé Felix Tschiffely on his historic ride from Buenos Aires to New York. Over two years later they returned to Paris, having covered more than 21,000 km travelling to the heart of Saudi Arabia and back, breaking the record, and fulfilling the dream of Josain Valette, the owner and breeder of high-class Arabians at the Haras de Gardelle in the Gascogne area of southwest France.

Monsieur Valette had dedicated his life to breeding purebred Arabians and to proving that they were truly the world's most versatile horse, inheriting in full measure the strength and endurance of their desert forebears. In his two protégés, Pascale Franconie, an arts student, and Jean-Claude Cazade, an ex-military rider who had an early acquaintance with desert-bred Arabs at Djibouti, he had ideal partners for the adventure. He provided them with two young Gardelle-bred Arabian stallions, El Merindian and El Mzuine, who were sired by the versatile Gardelle-bred champion Al-Drif and out of two imported English mares. Both colts had been raised together, running out on the Gardelle pastures until the time came for their training.

It took a year to turn them from unbroken colts into super-fit athletes ready to take on the Trans Moyen Orient Ride challenge, a year that had been filled with pre-planning on the stud's part, arranging all the vast amount of documentation needed nowadays to travel, particularly in the danger zones of the Middle East. At the end of their training the stallions were putting in a daily six-hour stretch carrying a full complement of 120 kg (264 lb). Equipment had been planned down to the last detail – medicines for horses and humans; shoeing equipment; clothing; sleeping bags; staple rations; repair kit for clothing and tack; photographic equipment; maps, and considering their Islamic destination a tri-lingual Peace Message transcribed from the Koran. Spare equipment and changes of tack had been sent on ahead to the various ambassadors of countries they were to travel through. The riders had also attended various courses: in veterinary care to give them the confidence and ability to attend to the stallions with on-the-spot treatment should it be needed; and in shoeing so they could cope with regular hoof care. The horses' shoes varied from normal keg shoes to solid iron tipped with tungsten, and in the desert area the regular shoes were borium clad, which lasted them for 1800 km before new ones were needed.

The first stages of their journey, ridden in winter mists and cold rains, took them through Southern France and the Camargue marshes, over a variety of tracks from verges alongside metalled roads to the narrow sheep and goat tracks as they went deeper into sparsely populated countryside. Hospitality was sporadic, at some places the quartet being turned away and at others welcomed, the horses given warm stabling and food and the riders a roof over their heads. At first the horses frisked and were too eager but soon learnt to conserve their energy, which was to be sorely tried. Six weeks after starting and with spring coming into the lowlands they began climbing to the Mont Genevre Pass in the Cottian Alps, the old Roman Route from Gaul to Italy and Rome. They opted for this difficult route to avoid a dangerous tunnel that would have terrified the horses, and at the pass they met snow for the first time along with a maze of ski lifts and tows. Then the long descent into the industrialized north of Italy began.

Italy proved hazardous in more ways than one – dangerous roads; speeding trucks and cars; in-

accurate maps; isolation, several days at a time passing without them seeing a soul. Then disaster struck, not once but three times – their saddles were stolen, but luckily replacements had them on the road again quickly; then El Merindian injured himself going through a narrow gate; and finally El Mzuina was poisoned after eating roadside grass that had been sprayed with weedkiller. They were held up for a week while the stallions recovered, and then ten days later crossed the border into Yugoslavia where at last they began to make very good time, covering the next 500 km, much of it roadwork, in eleven days.

Throughout the journey the horses ate whatever was available, and it says much for their really tough constitution and preconditioning that they survived the constant changes in diet and the haphazard feast or famine pattern they endured.

It was definitely famine in the later stages through Yugoslavia. From the bounty of barley, oats and maize throughout France and Italy, they went down to a daily ration of a couple of pounds of corn, rice and finally millet. During the month it took them to travel through Yugoslavia's plains, mountains and valleys this pattern continued – 1500 km of little to eat and scratching for grazing. They lost weight but not heart; learnt to appreciate a human diet, relishing anything they could share with Pascale and Jean-Claude; and they became thoroughly trailwise, even to river crossings via a tiny ferry – or at least El Mzuina did, El Merindian taking fright and falling overboard, but at least he learnt to swim.

By the time they hit the Greek border they had 4000 km under their girths with no rest period, and thankfully food proved less of a problem. However, their arrival in early June co-incided with a bank strike and they were grateful for a short rest until they could change their currency, as well as being able to enjoy Greek hospitality, the media having already broadcast their coming.

Refreshed after their enforced wait they encountered real thirst for the first time, the most dangerous element of any endurance ride for human or horse. Looking for a hidden Greek village kept them in the saddle for close to 100 miles. Some of the Greek route proving trackless, in any case in the direction in which they were headed, they rode by compass to their next destination, Turkey, where they had their first desert vistas. It had taken them just over two weeks to cross Greece and reach that next frontier crossing into Turkey, and at Istanbul they took a much needed and deserved rest before tackling the arid countryside en route to Syria.

Eight weeks later they met the first real hold-up with officialdom, as it seemed that the Syrians were not sure of the legal niceties for allowing riders and horses through the frontier, and it was not until 10 August that Pascale and Jean-Claude crossed into the last but one country before their Saudi Arabian goal. Here the unbalanced and insufficient diet caught up with the horses and they took an enforced rest at a riding club at Aleppo where, although the club horses were also Arabian, El Merindian and El Mzuina aroused much interest. The riders were presented with beautifully crafted colourful Arabian bridles made from softest camelskin that could not possibly chafe. In turn the two stallions made their own bequests, eagerly 'honouring', as the French put it, several mares belonging to local Bedouin. They had the pleasure of a continual 'honouring' throughout the whole of the Saudi Arabian part of the journey in what must be the most unusual return to the old-time 'travelling stallion' system on record.

Travelling through the steadily increasing heat and desert conditions they made their way towards the Jordanian border, but not without incident or excitement. On one occasion an attempt to kidnap them was made, thinly disguised as an identity check, but fortunately this time officialdom worked to their advantage and thereafter they were assisted throughout the rest of their Syrian journey, and lionized by both press and television.

Once in Jordan the first major wait for documents forced them into a month-long rest until

5 El Merindian and El Mzuina on their first day in the Saudi Arabian desert.

their visas for Saudi Arabia came through. During this time El Merindian and El Mzuina were kept fit by regular 30 km rides around Amman. They had time to recover condition and Pascale and Jean-Claude were surprised by the speed at which they regained their lost weight once their diet was regularized and improved in quality and quantity. With help from the Jordanian Royal House their visas came through and eight and a half arduous months after leaving Gardelle they headed out over high ground on the last few hundred miles before the Saudi Arabian border. Riding through one of the hottest places on earth they were within sight of the Dead Sea.

Finally crossing the Saudi border they had reached their goal – to ride two modern Arabians back to the cradle of the breed. Before them stretched 6000 km and six months of the toughest travel imaginable, a furnace by day, bitter by night, but throughout their Saudi Arabian adventure they

were made welcome. Presents and hospitality were heaped upon them, the value of their mission truly appreciated, particularly by the older Bedouin who still recalled the intrinsic part their own Arabian horses had played in their restless, nomadic lives. In the desert where the sand offered firm footing they made between 60 and 80 km a day, but in shifting dune country they could scarcely make 3 km an hour, and much of the time the riders walked alongside the stallions. During the heat of the day it proved too hot to travel. Saudi hospitality extended to protection against desert bandits and the various sheikhs provided them with official guards.

Half way through their Arabian sojourn they rested the horses again. The Saudi Crown Prince arranged for his own veterinary surgeon to treat the horses, and replenished the supply of vitamins and minerals the riders carried with them. It was in the Saudi Arabian desert where, revitalized by the lush

6 Pascale Franconie with the two Arab stallions in the snows of Yugoslavia.

feeding from the Riyadh farms, the stallions came into their own, covering mares at every stud they stayed at, providing a valued outcross of blood that will certainly be of greater value being from tested stallions than from a prizewinning show ring beauty.

At last they turned for home. They had covered 14,000 km in thirteen months – not far short of the total record they had set out to challenge. They had nearly 8000 km left to cover, and on the year-long return trip they came from scorching desert into the winter snows of Yugoslavia. Fortunately most of the journey was covered at a more leisurely pace, much of it in the good season when feed was plentiful. In the poorer areas, where they had earlier gone hungry, there was still sufficient in the granaries to spare some extra for passing travellers. In Yugoslavia they rested and awaited the results of a blood test that had been forwarded to the Pasteur Institute in Paris. Had they contracted African Horse Sickness their re-entry would have been barred, but once cleared they set off back over the Alps and into their homeland.

On 5 April 1984 they reached Paris to well-deserved acclaim and the French press crowding around. Josain Valette's breeding programme had been well and truly vindicated, and he had proved without a doubt that the Arabian breed, and his own two stallions especially, were indeed more than toys for the rich. The horses' condition at the finish of their epic trek was superb.

In a most generous act, instead of capitalizing on the fame and stud value of two such proven stallions, El Merindian and El Mzuina changed owners in a deed of gift to their partners of the past two years, Pascale Franconie and Jean-Claude Cazade.

PART TWO

THE PRACTICAL SIDE

Though a relative newcomer as an organized equestrian discipline, long distance riding, and its main branches Endurance, Competitive Trail and Pleasure Riding, has an age-old history dating from the time when it was performed out of necessity. Nowadays as a sport it is gaining popularity at a tremendous rate in many countries around the world. Happily the horse is now accorded more humane treatment than in the periods covered in Part One of this book. The reasons for this are manifold, but of prime consideration in this day of more leisure with less cash to enjoy it must be the fact that it is not absolutely vital to have a specialist horse for the job, unlike in the showing, jumping, eventing or Western scenario. Naturally the more one becomes involved in the sport the more one asks of one's mount, and the more careful one needs to be in the selection of the right horse for the course. When a rider becomes really ambitious in length and number of rides entered it must be realized that the really tough endurance rides do demand very careful selection of the right horse.

Types of ride

However, to enjoy our sport any healthy, well-conditioned horse should be able to cope with all but the most specialized rides, particularly if completion rather than winning is the prime objective. The following are noted as being the types of ride most likely to be encountered in the ever-expanding worldwide sport of endurance riding.

Pleasure Rides

No placing, grading or winner, but used as introductions to the sport.

Novice Competitive Trail Rides

Shorter-distanced (around 25 miles) rides judged on a time plus condition basis. Awards either of a graded nature or in some cases placings in order of merit.

Open Competitive Trail Rides

Longer rides with distances ranging from 25 to 60 miles in one day and judged on a similar basis to the Novice Rides, but open to any horse that has reached the age required in the stated rules.

Competitive Trail Rides spaced over two or more days

These are usually of 100 miles' (160 km) duration and represent a tougher challenge to riders and horses, but judging is broadly the same as in other Competitive Trail Rides.

Endurance Rides

These normally range from the 50-mile lower level on up to 100 miles in one day. In most countries horses are required to be older to enter Endurance Rides, particularly the 100-mile event, than they need to be to enter Competitive Trail Rides.

Two-day (or longer) Endurance Rides

A smaller number of events are run where the judging is of Endurance nature with the fastest fit horse winning, but the ride is run over two or more stages, the times being added together at the end to decide the winner.

Qualifying Rides

These are run specifically in Britain by the British Horse Society and horses satisfying the veterinary judges are then entitled to enter other more stringent rides.

There are, of course, variations on the main themes in different parts of the world, and individual national associations have their own structure of rides, but the above are the broad headings under which endurance riding is operated.

To avoid either physically or mentally overtaxing both horse and rider preparation should be undertaken over a lengthy period. The sport offers a tremendous sense of personal achievement, as all training should be done by the person who intends competing in the rides.

Although any form of competition with horses these days involves considerable expense, endurance riding and its allied events compare very favourably with other equestrian spheres. Currently the major expense is that of transport, but that also applies to any other equestrian event that entails travelling to a venue. On the bonus side is the fact that specialist clothing, other than serviceable and comfortable gear, is unnecessary; tack requirements are modest; and training ground, of necessity, has to be what the locality has to offer. Of course these are the bare bones of the facilities and props that one needs to contemplate involvement.

7 Some of the rewards of endurance riding, where completion is as important as a win. The winnings of Australia's Andarra Shareef.

For countries and associations with scaled distances for novice and/or young horses, or for riders who wish to compete but not in the longer rides, costs can be kept to a minimum. When enthusiasm escalates, and the greater capabilities of one's mount become apparent, it is time to decide whether you can or should afford the greater expense in time and cash that a more taxing yearly schedule will need.

Competitions are attractive because they are run over different parts of very beautiful and varied countryside. This gives a welcome change of scene to both horse and rider, and a mental fillip in a training schedule that can become somewhat dull when always done in the same surroundings, particularly for those not blessed with variety in their home territory.

Although competitive, the main object is to finish the course, placing or scaled awards being of secondary importance. This considerably alleviates competition tension. It also makes for a very friendly and informal atmosphere amongst competitors who usually look upon rides as chances to meet friends made over previous seasons. Newcomers are given the chance, and often help from seasoned riders, to enter an entirely new world of equine competition. It is very difficult to remain tense over a lengthy course and once en route riders relax and settle down to the enjoyment of a powerful, rhythmically striding horse, constantly changing and challenging scenery, and the companionship of fellow enthusiasts.

Judging of equine events always gives rise to speculation on the winner's merits, and to the preference of those who adjudicate. There are inevitable disappointments, often blamed on inadequacy, bias or ignorance – mostly unfounded and sour grapes, but there all the same. Fortunately, judging in this sport is done purely on a horse's fitness and ability to cover ground at a fair, required speed in Competitive Trail, and on speed and ability to continue in Endurance Rides.

'Judging' is simply the team of veterinary surgeons' findings about each animal's capabilities as detailed on the veterinary score sheet. Most societies return a copy to the rider at the end of the event for information and future assistance. There is absolutely no preference as to breed, conformation or action. Everything revolves around the horse's ability to perform, regardless of other criteria. Where these criteria do become relevant is that the horse best suited to, and best conditioned for, the job inevitably has a higher success rate than his cousin hampered by deficiencies in build, gait or preparation.

Choosing a horse for the purpose has changed little. The Greek Cavalry Commander Xenophon's advice, written 2400 years ago not long after the Peloponnesian Wars, still holds good today; in particular several of his recommendations are very apt to the endurance rider's horse: 'The bones above the hoofs and below the fetlocks should not be very straight up and down, like the goat's; for if they have no spring, they jar the rider, and such legs are apt to get inflamed. These bones should not come down very low, either, else the horse might get his fetlocks stripped of hair and torn over heavy ground over stones.' So much for the ideal pastern. 'Wide nostrils mean freer breathing than close ones', vital for good oxygen intake. In Xenophon's time horses were used primarily for war, and with bad terrain, climatic variations, incessant travel, and often lack of adequate fodder and water only the toughest animals survived. Most of these warhorses of ancient times were of eastern origin, giving a tenuous link with the modern equine. It is very much the type of mount that today still comes up trumps in the far easier field of endurance riding.

It has taken the rise of technology to free the horse from being a beast of burden and subject to the inherent cruelty that the warhorse and old-time charger were heir to. Nowadays we use the horse for pleasure, albeit often competitively. This in itself has produced the need to safeguard our beloved equines against unwitting cruelty and the hazards of tough competition. All associations make safeguarding the health of the endurance horse their foremost aim. At the same time they promote the sport and seek to find just what the modern pleasure horse is capable of in terms of stress, endurance and ultimate performance on the trail.

The following section of the book is intended as a guide for riders interested in participating in the very varied sport of long distance riding. Wherever a rider competes in this 'endurance riding world' the hardcore of endurance knowhow will be basically the same. What a rider requires from his horse and the judging criteria will differ very little from country to country. Indeed the bigger the sport grows the smaller its variations, as international participation becomes more and more popular and possible. The chapters incorporate a body of information as well as guides for both the novice and the more experienced trail rider, plus information for the ambitious endurance rider.

These notes, hints and guidelines have been culled from experience gained over a period of more than twenty years as a rider, organizer, writer and researcher, and from both Competitive Trail and Endurance Rides in the USA, Britain, Australia and Germany, and on the backs of a variety of mounts from the purpose-bred Arabian, a great-hearted Standardbred, several Quarter Horses, partbred Arabians, and a Heinz 57 toughie.

11 Choosing the right horse

Having decided that endurance riding definitely appeals to you, the first step is choosing your competitive horse.

Although it is rather a chicken and egg situation in that until you have tried the sport and become involved at a competitive level you will not be absolutely sure how far you want to involve yourself, it will pay dividends if, at the outset, you have a clear idea of what you are ultimately going to aim for. This is very important, as the choice of horse depends in large measure on the level of event you wish to aim for.

As a horse is not just a vehicle of conveyance but, to most people who own them, a personal friend and companion with whom you will form a strong and emotional bond, it is very relevant to choose the horse that will carry you right to the top echelons of the sport. Unless, that is, you either have the finances and facilities for more than one horse, or do not form the strong bond that most riders achieve with their personal mount, and can readily exchange horses when the time is right. From personal experience I know that even with a choice of horses I have not always ridden the one that was best suited to the specific event, but have been content with a lower placing in order to ride my favourite while 'superhorse' stayed untested. I could cite several instances of well-known riders doing the same.

Basically any sound, fit horse or pony should be capable of performing creditably on pleasure rides and lower distance one-day Competitive Trail Rides, which are usually run at approximately 7 mph and over distances ranging from 20 to 40 miles without any mandatory stops. At less than 25 miles, under Competitive Trail Ride conditions stress symptoms rarely show with a fit horse, and between 25 and 40 miles the stresses should only be sufficient to sort the very fit from the fit without

any damaging effect to the horses. It is when contemplating deeper involvement that selection of one's mount becomes of greater importance.

Beyond 40 miles a day, or at a lower mileage but coping with the increased stress conditions of the fast Competitive Trail Rides that some societies offer, the choice of the 'best for the job' narrows. I expect that many readers will feel that asking an additional one or two miles an hour from a horse is no great thing. That would be true over a very short distance, but when you start training you will realize that to average even 7 mph means that considerable stretches have to be covered at far greater speeds. Momentary stoppages, or small sections needing slower negotiation, can markedly affect an average. Upping the average to even 8 mph is quite taxing. Later when entering the realm of Endurance Rides, with 50 miles minimum done at sustained speed, it follows that the choice of mount narrows yet again. This is not alarmist, but plain commonsense. It does not mean, either, that only a certain type of horse can successfully complete a ride, but that to have the best chance of reaching the top it is sensible to get as near perfect a mount as possible.

There are three methods open to riders embarking on their distance career. These are:

(1) selecting the suitable horse;
(2) using the one you already have which seems a likely candidate;
(3) if you have the enthusiasm, foresight and patience to wait (preferably while using another horse to teach yourself the ropes), breeding your own or purchasing a youngster from proven stock.

The latter course is now far more feasible as with several decades of organized endurance competitions certain patterns of breed and type have stood out in the forefront of success. Naturally each country has its own 'national' breeds in addition to 'universal' breeds, but certain horses will have proved themselves incontrovertibly, and either they, in the case of stallions and mares, or in the case of geldings their close relatives can be used to produce suitable potential endurance horses.

Breeds

In choosing a prospective endurance horse the first thing to consider is his breeding. Study of long distance rides in Britain, the USA and Australia – three countries where the sport is very progressive and has been for several decades – and more recently France and Germany shows the highest percentage of major successes have been achieved by horses of either pure or part Arabian blood. This is not chance, but a realization that this is the breed best suited to the work. The Arab has been bred for centuries under what is considered by the majority of horsemen to be far from ideal raising conditions. He has had to endure extremes of climate, short rations in both feed and water, and tough going – either holding sand or sharp rocky footing. Being a horse that was originally a necessity rather than a luxury to the nomad Bedouin tribes as a conveyance in both war and travel, stamina, courage and speed were the essentials looked for in his makeup, as well as freedom from leg troubles and a disposition that had fire but was withal amenable. These attributes have combined in producing the endurance horse *par excellence*, because what he is now asked to do for his rider's pleasure and sport he once did from sheer necessity, and with scant attention to his wellbeing.

In recommending the Arabian, or his partbred cousin, I do not do so from sheer breed bias, though I admit to the breed being my favourite for many reasons. In any equine sport a certain breed will usually excel, and this excellence is derived by narrowing the selection from amongst horses that consistently turn in better performances than their able, but not so successful kin. The Arabian is a natural because his environmental history is centred around survival and endurance in his native lands.

Owing to this heritage Arabians are tough, courageously willing but innately sensible, not wasting precious energy in frivolity when really working; they have a denser but finer bone and are not as prone to as many leg troubles as other breeds. They can also take tremendous strain with no apparent ill effects. Their strength in ratio to size is outstanding, in that because of their compact build (they have less vertebrae than other breeds) they can carry more weight than the same sized horse of a different breed, even though that build is often of an ethereal quality. I recall one very fit, compact, purebred Arabian in one of the Florida, USA 100 milers successfully carrying 240 lb – a six-foot-four rider plus heavy Western saddle.

It is worth mentioning that in England especially it has been a concept that the tall and/or heavy person needed a correspondingly taller and/or heavier horse. This also pertains to some European countries. Purely from the visual aspect this may be so, but from the performance side it does not follow. England has a wealth of very strong, sturdy native breeds capable of carrying weight disproportionate to their size. The Arabian, for all his dainty looks, is anything but fragile, combining strength with a weight-carrying capacity not related to his own bulk, with added bonuses of speed and stamina. In countries where horses are still used for work, especially on ranches, smaller, more compact animals are found best suited to the work, being both tougher and handier.

Therefore I would recommend the Arabian which today is a very economically priced horse within most riders' financial reach. It should be realized, however, that the Arabian is not the complete passport to success, but with a good Arabian, well trained and conditioned, half the battle is won.

Unfortunately, and as a cautionary tale, purchasing a purebred Arabian mare from an endurance family did not give one expectant new owner 'instant' success. The horse was ideal. The overtraining and overriding and bad horsemastership were not. Even an Arabian needs knowledgeable preparation.

The partbred Arabian, especially when crossed with one of the larger British native ponies such as the New Forest, Highland, Welsh Cob or Connemara, makes a tough prospect that also gives a bit of scope in size, generally producing animals from 14 to 15 hands which is ideal for such work. [These British native ponies are now exported to most countries, including the majority of endurance riding ones.] Failing either the pure or partbred Arabian, select a horse with a Thoroughbred cross, but preferably not a full-blooded Thoroughbred as these often have unsuitable temperaments for endurance work, even though much temperamental unsuitability in horses is man-induced and with the right handling could be channelled productively. Thoroughbreds frequently find their way into general riding via the racecourse, where they have either been not too successful or have broken down. If such a breed is your choice be very careful to acquaint yourself with your particular Thoroughbred's previous history. As with all exceptions to rules, many Thoroughbreds have done extremely well in endurance competitions.

An admixture of Thoroughbred blood often gives the needed verve and punch to some of the heavier, slower breeds that, though all right in the hunting field or as general pleasure horses, are not best suited to endurance work. Again the choice of one of the larger British native breeds crossed with Thoroughbred is very good as the mixture will produce a horse with enough speed, courage, stamina and hardiness.

The Appaloosa horse has a strong reputation for being an extremely tough, hardy mount. Primarily used today for racing, ranchwork and showing, many have also excelled in endurance work. Their American heritage stems from the type of horse found around the Palouse River in Idaho and recognized by the Nez Percé Indians for its qualities of toughness. Initially an American breed it is now to be found in many other countries, considerable numbers being found in Australia, Britain and Germany among others.

Britain has a very good example of the toughness of this breed with Mrs Judy Beaumont's Fforest Orchid, a true Appaloosa that has done exceptionally well in our 100 milers plus winning the European Championship in recent years. For those leaning towards this breed care should be taken not to confuse the less hardy other spotted horses, for instance the cobby British Spotted Horse and heavier European Spotted Horses, with the true Appaloosa. The Appaloosa has many other breed characteristics stamping him, as well as the distinctive coat colourings. If in doubt demand to see the registration papers.

The American Quarter Horse is a breed that has become fairly widespread worldwide in the last twenty years. Britain and many European countries, particularly France, Germany and Italy, now have strong nuclei from which to choose, and New Zealand and Australia also have progressive Quarter Horse breeding programmes.

It is a compact horse standing in the region of 15.1 hands and generally speaking with a calm disposition, so important for good pulse and respiration recovery and for not fretting energy away. If any enthusiasts of the breed wish to campaign Quarter Horses be careful to choose the right horse for the job. I would recommend one of the lighter-framed types, preferably with Thoroughbred blood close in the pedigree, or an admixture of Quarter Horse and Arabian or Thoroughbred. Avoid the heavily muscled, very chunky type, unless lower level speed Competitive Trail Rides are your forte, as these are better suited to sustained work at a moderate pace. Again, if the horse has been to the track at an early age it is better avoided. Too much stress will have been put on limbs and joints far too early in his life. Unfortunately for the Quarter Horse he *appears* mature at a younger age than other breeds, and this trait is often capitalized on by riders not wishing to bide their time and give the horse a chance really to mature.

The National Harness Racing Club governs all official racing concerning the Trotting Horse in Britain, and in America the sister body is the United States Trotting Association. At first glance you may ask what this has to do with endurance riding. The breed of trotters most generally found in Britain is the Standardbred Trotter or Pacer. There are also French and Russian breeds used in addition to the Standardbred, though both these countries have used infusions of Standardbred blood. From my own experience the Standardbred Trotter has proved itself eminently suitable in endurance riding, my own Magnet Regent giving me my introduction to 100-mile riding and endurance racing in America, and since living in Britain producing excellent endurance horses when covered with my Arabian stallion Nizzolan. One of their offspring, Zoltan, has been the French Champion, and another shows every indication of being equally as good. Two others have been a credit to both parents in shorter-distanced rides in Britain.

In America and in Australia the Standardbred is frequently found in the top echelons of the sport, and in America the Arabian cross Standardbred has come to the forefront. It is a breed not generally realized as being available in Britain or Europe, but it is there and it is worth investigating. A horse that does not make the grade in racing, provided it merely lacks speed and has not broken down or developed leg blemishes and unsoundness, could be the ideal endurance prospect.

The Anglo-Trakehner, a horse of Germanic descent and allied in Britain with Thoroughbred blood, has recently come on to the British equine scene. There is not much recorded in Britain for these horses in endurance, with one notable exception (see p. 161 below), but in Germany the Trakehner is one of the successful breeds used in their expanding sport.

The Morgan Horse is again a horse from the USA that has started to make an impact outside its native land. In America this breed is one of the toughest imaginable, stemming from a horse called Traveller, and renamed after his owner Justin Morgan. It is a horse of smallish stature, very similar in appearance to a slightly heavier set Arabian. Physically very compact, strong, but refined, it has a deal of fire and a lot of toughness, stamina being the most prized attribute of a good Morgan.

Many substantial riding horses, particularly those in Britain, have infusions of common or carty blood and, although undoubtedly weight carriers, they are not ideal mounts for endurance work unless crossed with a lighter breed. Avoid any horse with too coarse a conformation; heavy rounded bone (not to be confused with good dense bone); or heavy, ploddy or trappy gaits. These will tire easily, wearying themselves and their riders, and a tired rider tends to ride heavily, which in turn results in back problems for the horse.

While on the subject of bone I must also say something regarding physical condition carried. There are three basic types of horse: the heavy-boned horse carrying gross flesh; the middle of the road type carrying sufficient condition and which, even when out of work, does not run to fat; and the greyhound type, that, try as you may, you cannot induce to carry any appreciable condition. The middle of the road type is preferable as he has a reserve of condition without carrying too much bulk of bone and fat in the first place which would put excessive strain on heart, lungs and limbs. The greyhound variety often goes with a fretful disposition and/or unsuitable conformation.

The foregoing is a general outline of breed suitability and a small selection of what is available. There are exceptions to every rule, as the horse world frequently proves in many of its sporting divisions.

Conformation

The ideal endurance horse should be fairly small, at least compared to the general conception of size as understood in Britain and much of Europe where many riders tend to ride a larger horse than is necessary. Height should be in the order of 15 hands or an inch or so either way. Weight should be in proportion to height, if anything leaning towards the lighter than the heavier side. It has been found in the USA, where statistics are often taken into account in order to facilitate later choice, that an ideal weight in the above height range would be around 800 to 950 lb. I always prefer to know my horse's approximate weight, as merely saying a 14.3 or a 16 hand horse does not convey the necessary mental picture to anyone. The horse should be of compact build, as such compactness will indicate greater strength than the strung-out horse with an exceptionally long back and frequently weak loin area.

The horse should be deep through the heart, with a well developed chest. Ribs should be well sprung and loins strong. Shoulder, pasterns and hooves should slope as close as possible to 45 degrees for a smooth ride and minimal leg concussion. Pasterns should be neither too short, which could result in a jarring ride and leg concussion, nor should they be disproportionately long with the often inherent weakness this brings. Throatlatch should be clean and wide giving good wind passage. This will be especially important in endurance riding where continued high speed over extended mileage will necessitate very efficient lungs and breathing apparatus. Hooves should have good quality horn as dry, splitty hooves cannot hold shoes nearly as well, lack resilience, and are prone to sand crack, quarter crack and so on, which in extreme cases can cause lameness. Heels should be wide, not pinched in, and the frogs healthy so that they can do their special job of shock absorbing. More about hooves and shoeing is given later as I consider the construction and care of the endurance horse's hoof to be of prime importance.

Quarters should be strong and muscular, because from this section of the horse comes the driving power essential to effortless, rhythmic stride. Legs should be of good strong bone, with muscular forearms, large flat knees, and short strong cannon bones, with tendons clearly defined and not fleshy, which could indicate a weakness. Hocks should be well let down, again giving short cannon bones behind. Look for straight hocks, not ones carried too far under or too close together. Another fault in hocks is the type known as 'camped out' – that is, hocks too far away from the quarters as opposed to being set too far under. Neither do you want a horse standing so wide behind that half his force is spent motivating his legs under him before any forward propulsion is gained. All these faults could lead to weakness and result in too much strain over a gruelling course. In shorter-distanced and slower Competitive Trial Rides many of these faults can be tolerated as the stresses are not sufficient to aggravate problems, but as the mileage, speeds and stresses escalate any weakness will rear up to plague the horse and lead to possible elimination, or curtail the rider's following a progressively more demanding regime.

In the front leg department, as well as the basic good bone and musculature, the actual leg formation should be closely examined. Ideally the forearm should enter the knee area in the same plane as the cannon bone leaves it. Too often faults in this area are seen – legs are crooked, pasterns frequently so. All this means that ugly phrase 'strain and stress' when least needed. Neither front nor back hooves should stand too close together – these faults predispose a horse, especially a tiring horse, to inflict damage on himself. Set too wide apart, excess strain is more than likely.

Having satisfied yourself that the physical requirements are present take a good look at the horse's head; not for mere beauty but as a guide to his temperament and also to his forward propulsion, odd as it may sound. A large, expressive eye will give you a pretty good lead to the horse's temperament. A neat, dry head, coupled with that good alert eye will indicate breeding, intelligence and, very important, the ability to have his balance right. A heavy coarse head frequently indicates that the horse could travel poorly, head low, and gait therefore hampered by too much weight on the forehand. Look about you at other horses. Note the build and natural carriage: light and well formed – a free airy movement; heavy, coarse – frequently lumbering, ungainly and energy consuming.

While checking the outward conformation do not forget to make sure his teeth are in good condition and that the bite enables him to chew his food properly, as a horse getting less than the best from his rations will not carry the condition or give the output necessary for the work demanded of him. Not for nothing did the British Ministry of Agriculture, Fisheries and Food refuse to grant stallion licences to horses with the 'parrot mouth' defect. Regular veterinary attention is necessary if the teeth are suspect, as rasping can improve their efficiency. Grain being passed in the droppings in any appreciable quantity is a warning that teeth need attention.

Temperament

The temperament should be generous, lively, but amenable. Frequently horses with other than ideal temperaments do perform superbly, but how much better it is to have your endurance horse's moods dovetailing with your own. Where so many hours are spent working together, the bond between horse and rider can become a true fusion of effort and will. While on this point it is worth a few lines to return to the breed of horse you will choose. Some breeds do excel at distance work; others are efficient but lack that necessary fillip; yet others are extremely dull to work with though adequate otherwise. When choosing your horse, unless you are totally dedicated to winning, do choose the horse you can work happily with, even if it is not the absolute tops. I would rather take a horse that was good, very good in fact, if I liked the horse and/or his breed, than the excellent to superb specimen if I found I could not work up a rapport with this Supremo. If you have even a suspicion of dissatisfaction with your chosen mount training can become a chore rather than a shared pleasure, and you will be tempted to curtail workouts. In the end, Supremo could fail from not having sufficient preparation.

My own ideal is a horse that is itching to give a lot more than he is asked for, but is mannerly enough to accept restraint without fretting and in so doing using precious physical and mental energy. I have been very fortunate in owning several such horses both in the past and currently. In the USA I had an Arabian stallion and a Standardbred mare, Magnet Regent, who introduced me to 100 miling. In England my best horse to date has been Nizzolan, who achieved many of Britain's top awards including three Golden Horseshoes and a 100 mile win. His endurance companions have been his son Zoltan, now exported to France where he has become a champion, and a Heinz 57 called Katchina. In Australia I rode Faraway Lutana bred by Mrs Betty Serpell who is one of Australia's best-known 100-mile buckle winners. Lutana was a very game 14.1 hand partbred Arabian mare who carried me on their famous Quilty ride. I still have Nizzolan and Katchina, both old-age pensioners. The future for me lies with a purebred Arabian mare, Harmony's Legacy, who had a good novice season, and what I feel could be the best yet, Granicus, a son of Magnet Regent and Nizzolan.

Another aspect of the horse's temperament connects with the condition the horse should carry. I once had a mare for whom I entertained great hopes. She was a partbred Arabian, very fast, inexhaustible, clean legged and great hearted. In fact she was everything a good endurance horse should be with one exception, which became apparent on her first trip away from home. She refused to eat, sulking all the time and fretting. Not the ideal horse. I did not pursue her distance work as I could not chance all the training being brought to a fat zero with the horse stressed, fretting and not eating.

Gaits

Gaits are inseparably linked to conformation. Good gaits usually go with good conformation, and if these meld with the right disposition the result should be an excellent prospect.

Endurance horses, especially those destined for the really long, fast rides, should possess a long, free elastic stride, and be equally comfortable on both diagonals at the trot and leads at the canter, for minimal fatigue to rider and horse. Horses with the right conformation and basically good strides should be schooled to get the maximum efficiency from their gaits. This will be dealt with in a short chapter on basic schooling for endurance work. Rough diagonals could be the result of faulty hoof trimmings. This was proved to me with my Standardbred mare in Florida. Bill Tobin, a noted farrier of Standardbred racehorses and acting as official farrier to the Florida 100, took one look at her hooves, brought out his hoof leveller and found that the angle of one hoof differed five degrees from its mate. He corrected the hoof and the problem corrected itself.

Any irregularity in a horse's gait could be tiring for him, and/or put undue strain on his normal self. The longer the ride the greater this strain will be. Not to be confused with irregularities that hinder, such as winging or hitching, are the gaits that are perfectly normal to one horse yet abnormal in another. I again illustrate this point with my Standardbred (and her offspring by Nizzolan), who when at extended trot brings her hind hooves out and in front of her front hooves by a couple of feet. This gives a very wide track behind and a tremendous stride, but by such width she avoids any possibility of over-reach. It is normal for her, and others of her breed, when speed is called for as otherwise she would end up in a tangle of legs, but in some horses with too wide a leg placement it could prove very tiring. Arabians also widen their hind leg track markedly when in high gear at trot without undue stress.

Although some gaits are peculiar to some American breeds such as the rack, pace, singlefoot, or running walk, it is also worth noting that some horses not supposed to have 'peculiarities' according to breed characteristics nevertheless exhibit a variance to the accepted norm. Katchina, my Heinz 57 and purely British bred, proved both to pace and to rack at slow speeds. If you are riding in a country where gaits other than walk, trot, canter or gallop are not usual, declare any such differences at ride vettings. I was warned by my own vet who was used to seeing my horses that some vets could confuse it with lameness. In the country of origin of such horses vets see it all the time and so do not get confused.

Horses that do have a tendency to over-reach, forge, brush, knock themselves and so on should be avoided, as the gamble is too great and disappointments too bitter. A horse with these tendencies, even when fit, is in danger of damaging himself when he is stressed at consistent high speed. Many interferences occur when a horse is beginning to tire, so do not select a mount with these deficiencies.

Some ride rules do not permit protective equipment. Yet other rules have no restrictions. Others permit certain latitude. Check carefully to see what is and what is not permitted. Some societies allow leather soles, some do not, but with protective soles grit can work in and lame a horse, so it is better to choose a very tough-footed horse rather than one that needs protection. A horse on a 100 miler I was on in North Carolina had been champion on several previous 100 milers, but because the Asheville ride was a mountain ride with stony going she was shod with protective soles. She paid the penalty, being lamed by a miniscule piece of trapped grit. The lameness was so very slight it took the judges some time to establish it, but it was there and she was eliminated.

The points discussed in choosing your mount are also relevant if you decide to breed your own future distance horse. With care in choosing the right mare and stallion the chances are very good that your ideal distance horse will result, but it does not always follow, genetics being occasionally very haphazard in the gifts they confer. A young foal or yearling with the right breeding can be purchased. The raising and conditioning of the resulting youngster will be in your own hands.

Many horses are subjected to work too young. Some, although appearing in top condition at time of purchase, may have had a bad patch in growth or feeding levels some time in their formative years. Also disposition may have some undesirable quirk not immediately apparent. By breeding your own horse most of these pitfalls can be avoided.

The most likely situation will be the mare owner who is going to raise a foal with endurance riding as the long-term view, particularly if he already has a mount and needs a youngster coming on. Decide if the mare has all or most of the necessary qualities, then send her to a stallion, who, if possible, has already proved himself in distance work or other stress fields. Be careful in this case though, as lost veterinary marks are not always the horse's fault. Do not go on the results of one or two rides, but use a horse that has been campaigned over several seasons.

Only use a mare and a stallion that are free from a history of breakdowns of any sort, other than outright injury, resulting in unsoundness. If you cannot find such a suitable stallion use one whose close relatives have proved themselves in stress fields – endurance, eventing, hunting, polo. Show ring successes are not indicative of suitability as judgement is of outward appearance, and the animal is required to perform nothing other than mincing around an arena, usually in gross condition which hides a multitude of conformation faults at first glance. Show ring beauties have rarely had the chance to prove their disposition under ride conditions. I am not saying that a show horse could not make a good distance mount, but his show ring wins indicate nothing helpful. I know of one horse that had a highly successful show ring career and was bought at a premium because of it, but in endurance riding continually came up lame due to a very bad set of front legs that just could not take the strain. How the judges of conformation could have missed these defects I do not know, as they were glaring faults.

The most common choice of mount will be the horse you already own, at least when initially entering the sport. Increasing enthusiasm may spur many riders to search for the 'horse for the course'. If you intend using your current horse it is absolutely vital at the outset of training to overcome any tendency to stable blindness and make an honest and strict assessment of any drawbacks and limitations your horse has. If such drawbacks are admitted to, many can be either overcome or minimized with judicious training and riding.

For instance, imagine what damage could be done to a horse with a tendency to even minor leg troubles, such as puffy or slightly strained tendons, filling, stocking up, sprains, or fever in the limbs through stress. If any of these were unsuspected, as they could well be in the very early stages when hardly or not noticeable, lameness could follow. If you are aware of pitfalls caution is indicated and much future trouble avoided. In minor cases correct training can strengthen legs and overcome these defects, where injudicious use could cause irreparable harm. Constant awareness of any possible weak areas throughout training can eliminate and/or reduce problems, and veterinary advice should be sought when needed, not when the damage has gone too far.

When putting your horse into training bear in mind his type with regard to distance and speed requirements and do not attempt more than you know he is really capable of. Feel your way into the sport. Use your first season to explore the possibilities and content yourself with completions, treating higher awards as wonderful bonuses.

If you are at all unsure about your horse's suitability, whether it be a purchased prospect, a horse you want to breed from, or one you already have, get the advice of a good veterinary surgeon, preferably one who has been involved in veterinary judging at many rides. It is worth the extra cost. It could save you a mint in the future.

A word on the cost of horses. It is a funny quirk of many British riders (and maybe also other nationalities) that they will look for the cheapest horse for the job, and nowhere more so than in the distance riding field. In the middle to upper range of tough competition it has become a very specialized sport. Therefore when leaving the 'trial' period and having decided after a season or so that total involvement and high-level performance is for you it is a specialist, a superb athlete, that is needed. Extra money spent on the right horse at the outset can save you a great deal later – vets' bills; wasted entry fees; haulage costs; general dissatisfaction; feeding the wrong animal; and time wasted on a horse that will never make the grade. A bargain at the outset may be the worst economy you ever make. The fact that a pleasure horse, a hunter, or a jumper can be bought for less than is being asked for a distance horse is just not relevant to the distance horse's price, though that argument has been offered to try to bring the distance horse's price down. The hunter, whatever his price, may be too expensive if he is no good. A horse placed in his wrong *métier* is too expensive a horse for the job. Naturally horses intended for general long distance work at lower mileages would not be as valuable as those intended for true endurance work. The price asked and paid should reflect the horse's potential and include a fair margin for the breeder's profit.

95

12 Hooves and shoeing

Thick horn is a much better mark of good feet than thin. Again, one should not fail to note whether the hoofs at toe and heel come up high or lie low. High ones keep what is called the frog well off the ground, while horses with low hoofs walk with the hardest and softest part of the foot at once ... for a hollow hoof resounds like a cymbal as it strikes the ground.

Xenophon, Greek Cavalry Commander (430–355 BC)

Apart from the comment about the frog there is still good reason to follow Xenophon's advice thousands of years after it was written, and his tenets can be summed up in the old saw 'no hoof, no horse'. This is particularly true of the endurance horse, because he will be subject to great stresses and strains, all directly bearing on his hooves.

Racehorses are subjected to severe strains, as are jumpers, eventers and polo ponies, but all these travel over ground that yields to the hoof, offering no obstructions to impede forward movement, with the exception of course of conditions brought on by prevailing weather which can affect going, making it firm, hard, yielding or heavy. The endurance horse must be prepared to cover absolutely any type of terrain since the course, to offer a true test of a horse's ability to endure, will be set out over as much variety of ground as ride locality allows.

During competitive rides the types of ground I have encountered have ranged from and included sandy firm going; sandy, shifting, heavy going with sand eighteen inches deep in places for considerable stretches; slick grass with no bite to it as the undersoil was baked hard; gravelly tracks with small-size stones. Further up the scale are tracks constructed almost solely of flints, many of which had sharp edges protruding; slippery shale; rock,

heavy mud and sucking clay; freshly turned, holding plough; and happily the rider's dream of good going, where time lost on footing needing careful and somewhat slower negotiation can be made up. In Britain and in some parts of densely populated Europe there is a considerable amount of roadwork with its concussive effects, not to mention slipperiness, and the bugbear of heavy traffic.

From this overall picture of the conditions a rider can expect to meet, if not all in one competition at least during a competitive year if he plans on doing several rides, it will be understood that the hoof, its construction and care are extremely important.

From the types of going described several points relating to hooves are apparent. Sandy soil means minimal shoe wear, but if a shoe is loose particles can abrade between metal and hoof, or work into cracks. Heavy sand, mud or clay, as well as pulling on tendons and muscles, sucks on the shoe loosening it if clenches are risen. Slick grass on a worn shoe can up-end a horse or cause him to slip with resultant strain. Gravel can pinprick a thin sole or work into crevices, and between a loose shoe and the hoof. Flints and sharp stones may bruise soles. Shale and roadwork need shoes with a good bite, meaning freshly shod hooves with nail grip.

When selecting and conditioning your endurance horse, the first thing to look for is the general structure of the hooves, which should be wide, without the excessive size that comes under the descriptive heading of 'dinner plate feet'. Such feet are usually very shallow in construction and frequently of a very soft consistency.

On examining the feet, particular attention should be paid to the underparts of the hoof as these are abused by terrain. The sole should be arched or concave, not flat or dropped which brings it into contact or too close a proximity to the ground. The frog should be deep, wide at the heel and resilient to absorb shock. The wall should be thick, with the ideal minimum measurements being a quarter inch wide at the heel increasing to half an inch at the toe. The ideal angle of the hoof from coronet to ground should be 45 degrees. If the slope is too shallow excessive strain will be put on pasterns and limbs; if too upright concussion will result. The hoof angle is also normally repeated in the slope of pastern and shoulder so the workings of hooves, shoulder and legs are closely interrelated.

Naturally, even the best of feet will not remain so unless adequate professional care is taken of them. When the horse is subjected to excessive work while still too young constant pressure will cause too great an expansion, resulting in shallow hooves and later problems.

A healthy, strong hoof will grow between a quarter and five-eighths of an inch a month. Monthly, or at most six-weekly, intervals between visits to the farrier are necessary, for either new shoes or a reset of the old ones. Neglect of hoof length can cause strain and general breakdown of laminae, and risen clenches are a cutting hazard standing proud above the hoof.

If the hoof is allowed to grow too long, the horse's angle of placement changes. As the toe grows outward and forward more pressure comes to bear on the heel. The old shoe becomes embedded in the hoof as new growth progresses, causing pressure in the wrong place all around, especially at the heel where corns may set in. As new, untended hoof grows, there will be a gradual splitting and weakening of the wall as old hoof separates and grows over and around the shoe. Hooves neglected in winter lay-off months may be in bad shape for summer and spring conditioning, therefore hindering action, suitability, and ability to work to full capacity.

With the normal hoof and normal action, the best shoe for endurance work is the concave fullered type not less than five-eighths of an inch in width (web) and not less than seven-sixteenths of an inch thick. The fullered shoe offers more grip and, because of the air pocket, retraction is made easier, especially in holding going, resulting in less physical strain on tendons, legs and body. With less pull on the shoe itself clenches will stay tight longer, minimizing the possibility of thrown shoes.

There are several points worth mentioning over the actual shoeing of any horse. One is to beware of having shoes burnt on to see if they fit. Once may not affect hooves, but repeated burnings will tend to dry hooves and reduce resilience. Burning the shoe on to ascertain fit, and to obtain a good seating, is the old-fashioned method and many farriers argue for the practice of continuing it. In effect it gives the farrier a guide to placement, saves time and facilitates his work, but it is not in the horse's best interests. You are paying the bill. You decide if you are prepared to accept this practice. By avoiding this practice I have never had a horse with brittle feet. The best farrier I ever had, Charlie Hutchings, who was one of the old-time craftsmen, never used this method and his shoeing was absolutely superb. Another of the old school cooled his hot shoe in water before trying for fit, reheating if necessary. Both were more concerned with good shoeing than fast work. Also neither rasped the foot excessively after nailing on – another current bad practice which takes much of the protective outer layer from the hoof surface. A hoof should not have too many nail holes in at, as an excessive number tends to weaken the wall. If you do have any special requests to make of your farrier do so with great tact, as good farriers are at a premium and often have an ingrained feeling that the owner, while knowing a great deal about the physical attributes of his horse, knows nothing about its hooves.

Another practice I dislike is that of paring the sole excessively while preparing the hoof for shoeing. Many farriers are knife happy, leaving the sole with no protective cushion to ward off the effects of sharp stones, flints, and so on. Many horses, particularly Arabs, grow a double sole at times. The dead sole will slough off, and if very thick can be pared lightly, but generally speaking I prefer the soles left as they are. Mr Hutchings also advised this.

Endurance horses have to contend with such a variety of terrain, some of it very slippery, that even with the ideal hoof problems do arise. There are additional aids to shoeing to counteract rapid wear or to aid traction.

Extended shoe life can be obtained by welding either hardened metal (trade name in Britain 'Stalite') or borium, a metal rod incorporating carborundum crystals, on to the toe and both heels of the shoe. Stalite affords no extra grip. Borium affords both grip and long life but has the disadvantage of inhibiting natural slide action of hoof placement and thereby causing a more jarring action. Weigh the advantages and disadvantages well. In an area with excessive and slippery roads I would use borium but limit fast travel on road surfaces – that is, no hammering trotting.

Studs can help give extra grip but may result in throwing the horse's weight too far forward and putting a strain on the tendons. If they must be used fit them early in training so the horse becomes used to them and no sudden strain is there immediately prior to competition. Jumping studs are unsuitable. Road studs will afford adequate grip but may impede going on soft ground. Plug studs set into the shoe afford grip in slippery conditions but on natural surfaces do not impede movement, so if you must use studs these are preferable.

Calkins afford extra grip but should be used in conjunction with rolled toes, otherwise tendons will jar causing stresses that under hard use could result in lameness, because the toe bears the brunt of hoof placement as the heel is raised, distorting normal weight displacement.

If a horse's hoof growth is poor it could be a deficient diet which will be reflected in levels of hoof growth. If this is the problem attention to his diet can rectify the problem, though it will take some time to filter through as hoof growth is slow. Various proprietary brands of hoof supplement are available to help improve growth and consistency; look for the ingredients 'biotin' and 'D.L. Methionine' in the descriptive small print. Growth can be stimulated by a mild blister to the coronary band, but care should be taken not to blister to excess as this weakens the growth. It is no good applying salves to the hoof itself as that is purely cosmetic, and I dislike oiling feet as oil forms a seal. Moisture cannot get in, a fact largely ignored by the oil buffs who think to preserve the moisture con-

tent. This is taken in from the frog but as the whole hoof is a living organism, other than the bit that gets pared away, there should not be an unnatural seal applied to interfere with nature's work.

When having your horse shod for the first time ask the farrier to watch him track up so adjustments can be made to permit optimum performance. Some horses are not equipped with the ideal, but are still able to perform very well, particularly if the less than desirable construction is helped in one of the many ways open to the owner. A good farrier can always advise his customer on what will minimize such defects and with good care in the future many defects will be counteracted and may in time, if they are minimal, disappear,

The two main categories of undesirable hooves are the shallow and the boxy types. Shallow hooves are usually also very wide and bring the sole too close to the ground, predisposing the horse to sole bruising. For an endurance horse this could spell the finish of competitive hopes as at least some of the year's rides will be run over stony ground. Thin walls often go with shallow feet which means extra pressure on a more limited surface depth area, which may result in corns. Too thin a wall leaves less area for the nails to be inserted with more likelihood of nail binding. In addition a thin wall can lead to over-expansion of the hoof because it is not strong enough to withstand both the weight to be carried and the strains of very hard work. In the case of a thin wall correspondingly thin nails should be used to reduce hoof splitting.

Although thin walls are often weaker in construction this is not invariably the case as some thin walls are also very strong. But, on the whole, it is better to avoid choosing a horse with these, as weaknesses will not become immediately apparent and much time and your investment will be at risk.

Boxy hooves are usually very deep and narrow and frequently have contracted heels. One of the hazards of such hooves is the strain put on the tendons, and because of the upright construction of the hoof there will be jarring in both pastern and shoulder, resulting in concussion. The horse with boxy hoofs, and frequently an upright shoulder, will also probably have a shorter stride and a more tiring ride.

Boxy hooves are frequently caused by dumping – setting the shoe back and filing the hoof to fit it. Contracted heels are often the result of using too narrow a set of shoes over a long period of time. If both these cases apply the state can be rectified by remedial shoeing, and an indication of whether it is natural or manmade can be gathered by comparing hoof angle to pastern and shoulder angle. If they are the same it is natural. If they differ bad shoeing is probably the cause. To correct it, the farrier will probably cut the heels low to the ground, taking care not to put too much strain on flexor tendons. Then the frog can be used correctly and with the correct shoe the hoof should be able to expand and regain a better shape.

Any change in hoof angle should be done gradually, as too sudden a change can strain tendons, causing temporary lameness. Over-reach can be helped by dropping the shoe behind the toe and leaving the toe quarter of an inch over the shoe edge. Should the horse still strike himself damage will not be as severe, but with the weight of the shoe set slightly back over-reach may be counteracted. Brushing can be minimized according to its severity by using a feather edged shoe and setting the shoe in a fraction, so that the inside edge of the hoof carries no metal. However, constant use will sharpen even the feather edged shoe, so carry an old rasp in your grooming gear and then where possible at checkpoints the shoe edge can be bevelled.

Rolled toe shoes can help both the horse that has excessive wear at the toes and also a horse that drags his toes. If the dragging is very bad it helps to draw the metal upwards to give more protection to the hoof. However, rolled toes or flat shoeing with-

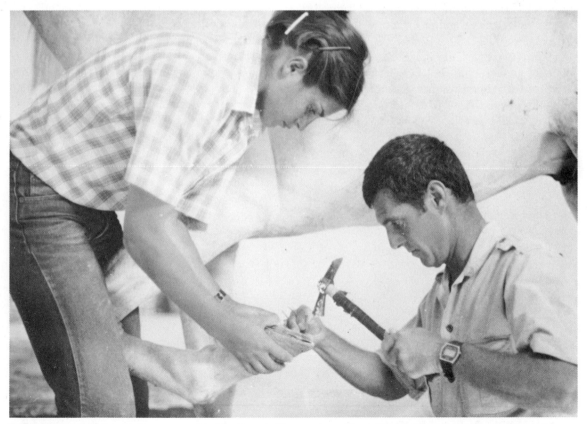

8 Attention to the feet in the course of a ride. Pascale Franconie and Jean-Claude Cazade during the Trans Moyen Orient Ride.

99

out clips is not ideal in hilly country, as the clips do help keep a shoe in place.

If a horse is heavy on one side of his shoe it may be indicative of uneven trimming which can be rectified, or it may be the result of uneven action. More seriously it could be a sign of lameness as well. To help counteract uneven wear the side that wears most should be made of a wider web than the normal wear size. Close liaison with the farrier is necessary as most use either ready-made shoes, or already fullered metal of even width, and rarely make the whole shoe from start to finish, only adjusting each set to individual horses.

A young horse that has very minor problems of occasional brushing may outgrow them with maturity and development of muscle, particularly the inner thigh muscle. This was the case with my Nizzolan, who as a five year old occasionally brushed. From six years onwards he did not, and the change came as he muscled up and developed a slightly wider track behind to accommodate his extra muscle bulk.

In purchasing a horse watch his action both mounted and in hand to see if he has any such discrepancies. Going away reveals more than coming towards you, but you should watch from all angles – coming at you, going away, and sideways on from both sides.

Shallow feet with dropped soles can be pro-tected by the fitting of a metal plate between shoe and hoof. Leather is commonly used for this but it has the disadvantage that when it gets wet it swells, pulling on clenches, and when it subsequently dries out the shoe is found prematurely loose. All pads, whether leather or metal, should be packed with Stockholm tar and tow, otherwise foreign matter can enter at the frog. Pads of any sort should only be used on a temporary basis if indicated in order to keep a horse in work, should he have bruised a sole, for instance. Remember that some ride rules forbid pads in actual competition.

If a horse does have soft soles they can be toughened a little by a gradual process of riding him over increasingly stony ground. Horses used only on soft going will not develop tough feet, whereas it is widely acknowledged than in the wild or semi-wild state horses that do cover rocky and stony ground develop amazingly tough hooves. But do be extremely cautious. Climate dictates the consistency of hooves to a great extent. Soggy, wet conditions as experienced for months at a time in England mean considerably softer hooves than would be the case in drier zones. Two horses I had in the USA and rode unshod needed constant shoeing under English conditions.

Of all the aspects of a horse's conformation the hoof is one of the most, if not the most, important when that horse is to be used for endurance riding.

13   Basic schooling

Although this is not intended as an equestrian manual I feel a few words on elementary schooling are in order before progressing to specific long distance work.

A few years ago when the sport was in its relative infancy many riders felt that long distance riding was easily undertaken. One did not need any special horse, and that non-special horse certainly did not need any refinements in schooling. Just to get from A to B was sufficient. Unfortunately this opinion is still held by some and was brought home to me very sharply by a comment from a supposedly educated horsewoman who is prominent in another field. When discussing a certain versatility award given by a breed society in which endurance riding at that time was allocated considerably more points than, for instance, showing or hunter trialing, the opinion was tendered that 'of course an endurance horse only has to put one foot in front of another and certainly does not merit any extra points for such an achievement'. Only when actually undertaking the sport does it become very apparent that the well-schooled horse tires himself and the rider far less. Any good endurance rider, if he does not know at the outset, quickly finds out that the sport entails far more than 'putting one foot in front of another'.

All work, whether it be on the lunge, on the lead rein, in the manège, or on the trail can be used to get an endurance horse fit. All four elements have their right place in the endurance horse's training, the last named of course forming the bulk of his regime. It will help if each of the four is taken separately.

Lungeing can be a very useful exercise. When the horse is soft it can be used to tone his muscles, teach him to regulate his stride at all paces, get him supple, and take the kinks out of a too lively mount. It should be remembered that lungeing is harder work than work on the straight, and more pressure is borne on the inside of the legs and hooves than on the outside, so rein reversal is important, doing half the work on one rein, half on the other, unless at the outset more work is indicated to achieve suppleness on a stiff side. The horse should also use himself efficiently. The exercise is not going around on a piece of rope in an undisciplined manner. It is rating his gait, listening to commands, and working strongly from the quarters with the hind leg placement coming well underneath and indicating that the horse is pushing forward, not diddering along in a purposeless manner.

Initially with a soft horse I would not lunge more than about twenty minutes and at moderate pace; later when fitter half an hour to a maximum of forty minutes at a working pace would be in order. However, this is only as part of a training programme, to be used sparingly and not as a substitute for ridden work. Examples of when lungeing can be used effectively are: as part of a programme; when the rider for various reasons has not got the time for a day or so to do a lengthy ride, and in this case lungeing can achieve more output in half an hour or forty minutes than riding can for twice that time; when a shoe is cast and it is impossible to get the farrier for a day or so, but you don't want to curtail training; if the horse has a girth or back lesion which precludes ridden work for a short spell; and finally if trail or roadwork is made dangerous through either fog or ice.

Leading from the back of another horse is very useful if you have more than one horse to get fit, but be careful to do it only as often as lack of time dictates. Many horses can be got fit by the ride one day, lead the next system. Again should there be any reason such as girth galling, leading can help keep the horse ticking over.

With manège work we come to the core of the

endurance horse's performance. Many horses are very keen and adore going for exciting trail rides, but their actual work leaves a lot to be desired. A great percentage only receive decent schooling at the outset of their ridden lives and are considered schooled for ever after. Would you consider a child had received enough schooling by the time he or she was nine years old?

The most important thing in schooling is to get the horse responsive both in upward and downward transitions. Once this is achieved he can be taught to use himself and give a long, strong stride at whatever gait is required. Once in a chosen gait he should stick to the required speed and manner of achieving it until the rider dictates otherwise. It is also a good thing to teach the horse to go on a very loose rein at all gaits and speeds without hotting up, as it is important that an endurance horse have freedom of head and neck. His balance will improve and his breathing will be more efficient if he is not over-restricted by rein restraint. Work frequently on the circle with emphasis on correct bending at all stages to enhance his suppleness. Another point is to make sure the horse is taught to stand stock still for mounting and dismounting and while you open and close gates. Considerable time can be lost if the horse is fidgeting about all over the place. This leads to lateral work. It is important to make sure he moves away from hand and leg, and is capable of turns on haunches and forehand. All these manoeuvres help when manipulating gates, particularly on rides where there are an inordinate number.

While you are out trail riding continue the manège work. It is no good allowing the horse to become dilatory just because you are away from the arena. The whole idea of schooling is to fit him for the trail and his, or rather the rider's chosen *métier*. It will pay dividends in energy saved for both horse and rider, and more pleasure for both will be achieved.

14 General conditioning

The training programme must be well thought out and, once started, must be adhered to. To keep the horse interested and keen and giving his best a flexible programme tailored to the nature of the work involved is essential. Not all horses need the same length of preparation, nor identical workouts. Their physical and mental makeup will dictate to a large extent the type of conditioning necessary, but skimping must be resisted.

There are no short cuts to fitness. A hurried programme will subject the horse to too great a stress load and possible physical breakdown during a hard ride, or to a complete breakdown after competition stresses have ceased.

Quite often a visit to the stabling at a ride reveals a totally different scene to that shown during the ride where some apparently fighting fit horses exhibit fatigue and stress later on, while other seemingly moderate performers prove to have suffered no setbacks, being calm, relaxed and quite obviously ready for more.

Training should place no undue stress on the horse. It is important that all training be done by the rider who is to compete. The prime reason for this is that an unfit rider would hinder the horse, especially as the rider tires and sits more heavily, possibly giving rise to either bruising or back lesions under the saddle, at the same time interfering with an economical expenditure of the horse's energy.

During training the rider should come to recognize every subtle indication as to how the horse is feeling and using himself, so he can immediately sense adverse symptoms and ease up momentarily to conserve energy and avoid a relentless push in the last stages of a ride. Over-stressing the horse's organs and limbs denies him an adequate chance of recovery. Unless the rider also does the training he will not know how to pace a ride. He risks burning the horse out too soon, or dropping too far

behind schedule and in the rush to finish on time jeopardizing the chances of the horse passing the veterinary check.

Before embarking on any training programme ensure that the horse is in good physical condition, has been recently wormed, and, particularly if he is an older horse, has had his teeth checked by the vet. If he has been purchased for endurance riding have him thoroughly examined for suitability to the work involved before paying for him. As you know the horse will be covering greater mileage, make prior and regular bookings with your farrier. Training interrupted for days at a time because you forgot to book an appointment is frustrating and not fair to the horse.

At the outset the horse should be carrying sufficient flesh so he does not whittle away in early training. Once fit he should be very hard, with no excess soft fat to impede him, but still carrying a little reserve condition. I see too many horses that have been overtrained and look scrawny rather than fit.

I prefer working with a horse that does not run to fat, and which even when resting maintains considerable muscle tone. This type frequently possesses a keen but equable disposition. If the horse is straight off grass, grossly overweight, or a very young animal, be very conservative in the early stages of training as pressure early in work could have adverse effects, whereas a mature, fit animal could cope easily.

Ensure that the endurance horse uses himself adequately at all times. Demand free forward movement with all impulsion coming from behind. If he is on the forehand he will probably hang on your hands – it will feel as if should you relax the reins the horse will fall flat on his face. Pounding along on the forehand will make his front limbs more susceptible to ailments.

School the horse to give a light mannerly ride

both in company and by himself. He must be relaxed but alert enough to obey immediately. A tense horse wastes precious energy and a lazy animal tires his rider. Of the two I would rather have the tense horse as proper schooling can nearly always induce relaxation, but a really lazy horse is about the most unpleasant animal to ride and too discouraging to have to prod into some semblance of awareness. On the other hand many apparently lazy beasts are merely unschooled, have never had to exert themselves, or their senses have become dulled by routine. A good positive rider can often persuade these dullards to wake their ideas up.

Horses suffering from flightiness, tension, lack of concentration, playful shying or just plain boredom are often completely changed by a challenging season. During this time they come to realize they have a job to do and need to concentrate all their energies into producing maximum effort with minimum fatigue. Work is also an anodyne for some really nervous horses who unwind as the miles reel out.

The trot will be the main gait used as it is both ground covering and spreads the work load evenly. Make sure you change the diagonal frequently to give each pair of legs equal work. Some but not all horses react to continuous use of one diagonal by stiffening on the load-carrying legs. This does not normally show until the horse has rested, and in very long rides could prevent a perfect veterinary score or cause elimination. The same applies to cantering. Continuous use of the same lead puts stress on that lead and set of muscles. It is the rider who changes the diagonal, the horse the lead.

Most endurance riding countries have their main events scheduled for spring, summer and autumn. Australia, where the summer climate is adverse, has its main rides in winter, though their winter is nothing like the winters experienced in Europe or some parts of the USA.

I dislike the too rigid system of training incorporating week one, two, three, and so on with exact times and mileages laid down. Have a skeleton routine but be prepared to change it according to the way the horse reacts. Terrain itself will dictate much of the work and speed, and the more diverse the route the fresher and keener the horse will stay,

and his legs will toughen better if underfoot conditions are varied.

Many riders worry if their home territory does not offer enough variety and challenge, particularly in regard to hill work, or to work in very holding conditions. Although it is advantageous to have ideal facilities it does not necessarily follow that only horses trained on them will be successful. One of our British 100-mile winners trains exclusively in the totally flat and extremely dull Fens of Cambridgeshire, yet has won awards in the toughest areas the rides are set over (see p. 162).

I once lived in a completely flat area of the USA and training ground was almost totally of hard-packed sand roads and looser sandy woodland trails, yet the Standardbred mare, and later an Arabian stallion, coped very well with holding sand, hills, and even later on mountains and steep climbs up rocky tracks.

Where it is practicable transport your horse to a change of terrain. However, I realize that for many, if not most, that is impracticable either because of cost or, in some areas, because the countryside stays the same for vast stretches.

During a British season rides spread right throughout the country. Horses are expected to cope with a great variety of routes. There are deceptively easy flat rides where the temptation is to go too fast; the hill rides with resultant drag on muscles and tendons; mixed rides with both hill and flat work; prevalent road work with its concussive effects; the heavy holding going of early spring and late autumn sandwiching the iron hard conditions of a baking summer (on the rare occasions we get a summer in Britain). Underfoot it can be smooth, slippery, gravelly, rocky, and sometimes, thank heavens, just perfect. In no other country are there the peculiar climatic conditions to contend with. British horses do not have time to acclimatize to seasonal norms as we can have icy winds and very cold rainy days followed next day by an exceedingly hot and humid change to the high 70s.

Most serious competitors will, in the course of a season, travel to parts of their country, or to venues abroad, that are totally different to 'home base', and will meet with a considerable variety of going as we do in Britain, but probably without the added hazard of peculiar weather. It could well be that the constant variation in going and climate is one of the many reasons why British horses do so consistently well in events abroad.

Early training calls for plenty of walking with the horse striding out, and steady trotting to strengthen legs, tone muscles, and stabilize the horse so that he does not get the idea that long rides mean an undisciplined scamper to eat up the miles. That would risk whittling his condition, overtaxing his as yet underconditioned frame, and encouraging him to become uncontrollable in fast-moving company.

Initially while stepping up both time and mileage do no speed work at all, other than an occasional sharp canter to vary routine and keep him in-terested. If he gets bored he could become lethargic, or the reverse, constantly looking for stupid games which could turn into dangerous vices.

Today's riders are also busy people with riding having to be sandwiched into a tight schedule except at weekends. Many have a nine to five job with travel time tacked on to each end of the working day. However, with dedication, dual fitness of horse and rider can be achieved provided the rider realizes it will not be reached as early as those with a more generous amount of time available. Use every weekend for longer rides for the first two months of the training schedule, and it should be possible with some sacrifice to manage the other three days' necessary work by manège schooling,

9 Many endurance rides throughout the world have large sections run in total darkness. Terry Woods and Andarra Shareef in the 1985 Australian Quilty. (Andrew Roberts Photographics)

lungeing, and riding out for short periods if daylight is sufficient. If you are forced to ride in the dark use a fluorescent jacket and a stirrup light and stay off busy roads. If you have good riding country the safety situation will be eased, though you will have to get used to riding slowly in the dark. Many endurance rides throughout the world have large sections run in total darkness, a facet of the ride I dislike, but which is necessary to get the distance in with ride time rules. Take advantage of an indoor school. Many areas that have less than ideal riding country do have a horse-orientated population with equestrian centres whose covered schools are open to outside hire. Team up with others for this if possible to share costs.

Taking a completely idle horse, a couple of weeks of daily riding starting with an hour a day should set him fair to being put into more exacting work. By the end of a two-week period he should be able to cover a 15-mile stint in about three hours or less. Do remember throughout training that the horse is not delicate. He is a work animal, though this fact has largely been forgotten now he is used almost exclusively for pleasure. But care should be taken to toughen the skin under saddle and girth. On an unfit horse soft skin can chafe very easily. Either surgical spirits or methylated spirits have proved useful.

Although there will be some days when the rider's schedule has to be interrupted for valid reasons it is all too easy to find excuses to defer training. To be fair to both horse and rider a tight check should be kept on such tendencies or true fitness will not be achieved. If such lapses occur later on in training the horse will not maintain peak condition.

The rider who trains mostly alone should try riding with others occasionally, as the solitary horse that has gone stale often finds new energy in company which sparks his competitive spirit and keeps his interest keen. Conversely, if you normally ride in company occasionally ride alone as there will be times on competitive rides when you will definitely be going solo.

In competition do not impose your company on another. His or her horse may go better alone, but there are occasions when a tiring horse can chalk his completion up to teaming up with a fresher horse and being 'towed' in. However, consideration *must* be given to the other rider's wishes.

On one competitive ride I rode with a friend. Both our mares were similar as regards speed and keen dispositions and we overtook a very slow cobby gelding. Later when we slowed down along came the cob to join us, which was in order. Thereafter each time we put a spurt on so did the cob, only slowing down when we did but doing so in front of our horses. He got progressively slower and when we made a move to pull out and overtake he speeded up just enough to overtake us, and then crawled once more. This was fraying our horses' and our own tempers, forcing us to such a hot pace that the cob was thankfully at last outridden. I can well imagine that if an endurance rider got hampered in such a way at a crucial point he may well indulge in a 'Harvey Smith sign' and be understandably forgiven for so doing.

It is unwise and inconsiderate to team up with horses who are not comparable in stride and speed. It could make a keen horse fret precious energy away being restrained, and a slower horse overtax himself, burning out his energy reserves.

It is important to know your speed and a help is to have a car alongside over ground suitable to both. Consistent riding where the horse has become stabilized in his gaits will enable you to dictate and maintain speeds for a considerable time, certainly long enough to correlate them over a measured distance with your car pacemaker, and thereafter translate them over any going. The endurance horse should maintain an 8 or 10 mph trot, holding it until geared up to greater speed. Later as he progresses the trot will develop into a longer-striding and faster gait that outpaces the canter. The flying trot of an endurance horse can reach speeds well in excess of 16 mph, while the canter should be a rolling, relaxing 12 to 14 mph.

A specific gait should be maintained for appreciable distances so fitness, muscling and conditioning progress, allied to improving the horse's wind by getting him to use his lungs to capacity. Consistency in riding will save energy and maintain a strong, almost machine-like rhythmic stride which is the hallmark of the experienced animal.

To help toughen the horse's legs and feet work him on as varied going as possible. In competition you could meet hard, flinty going ranging through to the other extreme of heavy, holding ground. Conditioned tendons and ligaments will stay clean, hooves be tougher, and concussion less of a problem.

Varied terrain teaches a horse to look where he is going. Some horses have a natural gift for being clever on their feet. Others think the rider is there to support them over every little hillock and depression. I have owned both types. Katchina and Jacobite were naturally well balanced and never took a wrong step. Nizzolan in his early years and later when a very keen endurance horse treated short rides with disdain and accompanying clumsiness if he estimated I should be pushing him on and I was going too slow for his liking. This was very costly on one occasion, Britain's 1977 100 miler, where he was totally bored at 40 miles. He repeatedly ignored calls to attention until he literally tripped over nothing, and this a horse who had tackled rough stuff beautifully. It caused no apparent damage, until at 88 miles he came in sound, was rested up and re-presented to the vets fifteen minutes later fractionally lame, going sound again within the hour. Such is the hairline difference between success and costly failure. Needless to say I was not best pleased with his earlier attitude.

With the type of horse that just will not look for himself through sheer bloody-minded laziness I have taken drastic measures. Though in no way an endurance horse but a livery who came in to be schooled, I once had a Quarter Horse that hailed from the flat Fens in Cambridgeshire. He was terrible to ride out, constantly tripping and stumbling, just refusing to look where he was going – until the day I purposely rode him with no help, but going quite fast. He landed flat on his face in soft sand, but thereafter minded his manners and became a safer ride.

Once the horse is fit, demand the best from him in the form of very active rides of 25 miles and over with the greater part of the mileage done at ground-eating trot, interspersed with strong canters. Ride on a loose rein where possible, especially at the walk as this will enable him to stretch his neck muscles and refresh himself, as well as permitting a degree of relaxation. His breathing will also be more efficient if he is not held in a restricted arc.

I have not stipulated time or distance. Each horse varies, but broadly the horse's working week should be five days on and two off, particularly when really fit. Initially one day a week off is all right, but the really fit animal needs keeping so, not getting to that stage, therefore the extra day to himself. If aiming for the really tough rides, or contemplating keeping a horse competitively fit for the whole season, a different work spacing will be beneficial, but that is dealt with later.

Whatever length of ride you intend tackling make sure in advance that your horse is really up to it. I like to put him to the test by doing a ride about two-thirds to three-quarters of the forthcoming event's total distance prior to the ride itself. How close to the event this is depends on the event itself. Again this subject is developed later.

One point all distance riders must bear in mind is that they must not bring their mount to the start past his peak. Many riders, especially novices, overtrain particularly in the penultimate phase and bring a horse to the event jaded and leg weary. Prior to any event ease up in the final days. The horse's whole physical and mental outlook will be brighter.

15 Specific conditioning

The following notes are on how to vary programmes according to which rides you will be tackling. Obviously length of ride will affect amount and type of training. Overconditioning stresses a horse, leaving no reserve to call on. Underconditioning is the prime reason for most attrition in longer rides, giving rise to various types of breakdown. Basic Competitive Trail Ride (CTR) training will give a good base on which to rest Endurance work. Sometimes it is the pleasure gained from a fun ride that spurs the rider on to tackling competitive events, and this is the time to have a rethink.

It will help you stick to a routine if you decide what you are aiming for before designing training and competitive programmes. The race element of Endurance Rides (ERs) is unnecessary in training, though there will be times in later training when the horse should be put under stress to see how he copes and to give you time to adjust if necessary.

The following is a guide to *approximate* times needed for conditioning to various levels and is taken from the standpoint of the horse coming in to work after a two-month layoff. This rest is very important for a distance horse, particularly those destined for, or recovering from, a season of tough rides. The harder an animal's work the more he needs that complete physical and mental break, particularly as most competitive seasons run for between eight and ten months out of the year. If you only do infrequent and short distanced rides then the rest is not so vital. The more you demand from your horse the greater the chance for error, and the narrower the limits for luck baling you out of an emergency. A finely tuned instrument needs more efficient handling than a very simple device. So it is with the horse.

This chapter outlines an approximate training guide for the following goals:

(1) Pleasure rides and 25-mile CTRs at lower speeds; minimum training should be around six weeks.
(2) CTRs with 40-mile maximum and at lower speeds; minimum of two months, preferably two and a half months of steady training.
(3) Fast CTRs and lower level of ERs of 50 miles; a minimum of three months, preferably a little more.
(4) CTRs and ERs covering 100 miles and spread over two or three days; minimum of three, but preferably four months.
(5) ERs 75–100 miles in one day; four months minimum for 75 milers, and a full six months for 100 milers.

I re-iterate *approximate* duration because some horses take a little longer, but no horse, except for the shorter pleasure rides, should be given any less than the minimum time. To do so will incur a debt that, believe me, you will be called on to pay at some future date. You may get away with cheating time (or the lack of it in preparation) for a season or two, but the successful ER horse is a campaigner that wears well season after season.

The final work for one level carries well into the middle level of the next strata, with the exception of the really long endurance rides where I prefer to have a slower build up, still doing long rides, but postponing any speed work until a little later in the programme.

Pleasure rides and lower-distanced and slow CTRs

Pleasure rides are more usually run in Great Britain, but clubs the riding world over have 'unofficial' pleasure rides and horses should be adequately prepared for these.

Pleasure rides vary from 15 to 25 miles in length. Most do not specify speed. Some require a 5 mph minimum. In practice they will average about 6 to 7 mph unless you get that most unwelcome cavalry charge of inconsiderate riders thinking the word 'pleasure' means theirs only. Considerately paced rides are good for introducing young and/or novice horses. For the lower distance a horse needs only moderate preparation and, unless he is destined for later endurance work and starting from a layoff, will probably be in regular if light work already and used to doing 6 to 10 miles at a stretch. An extra two weeks in which the rides are lengthened a couple of times a week will set him fair to coping well.

Once over 20 miles, training for longer pleasure rides and short CTRs can dovetail. Stress should not have been apparent in a healthy horse at 20 miles. Riding several times a week has toned muscles, strengthened legs, and toughened skin over the horse's back and around the girth.

Progression from 20 to 30 miles and into competition status means generally lengthening the distance travelled on the longer rides, and incorporating into such rides several miles of uninterrupted steady trotting at around 8 to 9 mph, interspersed with the odd sharp canter of about a mile or so. Stress should still be absent if training is progressive, not rushing one day, dawdling the next. Occasionally work out your average speed so you begin to ride to a 'ride time limit'.

The time taken from ordinary light riding fitness up to being able to tackle 25 or 30 milers at lower speeds should fit very well into the suggested six weeks. This type of ride has the advantage of being highly suitable for those with limited time, as the schedule is not so severe or time-consuming as that for longer and/or tougher rides.

While working towards pleasure rides daily riding is not necessary, but for CTRs up to 30 miles five days a week out of which two days include longish rides should be the pattern. Longer rides should be more leisurely, and the shorter rides of sharper consistency. Let the horse warm up adequately first.

A rough work guide of a 25- or 30-mile CTR could be: easy day of 6 miles walking and trotting; rest day; day of 10 miles in one and a half hours; two-hour day done steadily but with 2 miles of sharpish travel incorporated; rest day; then a weekend of two long rides of say 15 miles one day and 20 the next in the last couple of weeks of training.

Lower-speed 40 to 50 milers

This section is worked around British rides which have an overall higher speed than American CTRs. For the latter a slightly more relaxed training speed can be used.

With the horse fit for a 30 miler after being in work approximately six weeks you now have one month to tighten up his schedule for 40 miles in a day, still at moderate speed. The 20- to 25-mile training stint needs to be a regular feature and in the last month before a 40 miler I like to fit in at least two long rides a week. I also like to increase the overall speed of at least half of my longer rides to at least one mile per hour above the speed that will be required in competition.

For a programme of 40 milers, which is the fringe of endurance work, this is where I would suggest keeping a work log and regulating mileage by the week, with maybe a twenty-minute session on the lunge on one of the other two days if you feel the horse must be exercised – for example, if he has no pasture and gets fractious being in a stable too long.

Not only will the horse be covering more miles at a go, but he will be carrying weight for another two hours or thereabouts. This in itself is stressful, so he must be conditioned by a combination of long slow rides for the weight-carrying part, and long speedier rides for leg, lung and heart capacities to be tested.

For the first half of the last month I would recommend out of the five-day working week: easy let-down day of 6 to 8 miles; rest day; two hours steady; 15 miles done at approx $7\frac{1}{2}$ mph; rest day; 15 miles steady; 20 miles at 8 mph. As the last two weeks prior to the event arrive, step up demands on at least one weekend day. No less than one week prior to the event I would want to feel happy with my horse doing 32 miles in approximately three

	25–30 CTR	40 CTR (lower speed)	40–50 fast CTR/ER
Mon	6 m walk/trot	6–8 m easy	6 m easy
Tue	rest	rest	rest
Wed	10 m in 1½ hr	2 hr steady	12 m steady (1½ hr)
Thu	2 hr steady with 2 m sharp	15 m at 7½ mph	rest
Fri	rest	rest	12 m steady (2 hr)
Sat }	longer rides; last	15 m steady	20 m fast (2 hr)
Sun }	two weeks 15 m and 20 m	20 m at 8 mph	25 m hard (3 hr)
Total time 6 weeks		Additional 4 weeks	Additional 4–6 weeks

Suggested programme for rides up to 50 miles. See text for explanation.

hours and forty minutes – just under 9 mph. He can then do 40 miles easily between 7 and 8 mph CTR speed.

When planning to enter 50-mile CTRs an extra two weeks should be allocated, distances amended, and at least one training ride of 35 miles plus undertaken on the same lines as above. I must reiterate that all suggestions both above and to follow are *guides* only. Some horses need more, some less, some slower, others moderately faster work according to their natures and build. The two points to be alert for are *underdoing* or *overdoing* work. The first is cheating the horse, and the second is too common; it stems from thinking endurance riding means the poor horse really has to endure his working life with continual hard grind, and eventually will result in a shorter working life for him. Training fits him to endure occasional testing periods. Do not make his working life a continually stressful, and ultimately unpleasant, effort.

The rider must pay particular attention to rating his horse, and it is worth experimentation with speeds and distances until you easily recognize at approximately what speed your horse is travelling. This will be a much better guide than constant map reference.

In preparing horses I have worked considerable mileage at the strong trot *averaging* around 10 mph, which gives some leeway for relaxing travel when the horse can recoup energy. Where going permits I switch to the canter, alternating leads.

The means of telling what reserve a horse has left is gained by experience. This is one of the many reasons you should ease into the sport, giving yourself time to become educated to the sport's demands. A good guide to this reserve is how the horse actually feels. Does he still respond to the leg as quickly? If in company is he still competitive? His eye will also give an indication – if it is still wide open and alert, albeit calm he is feeling great. If on being asked to move on it looks relatively dull then fatigue could be setting in. Head carriage is another guide. When a normally gay head carriage lowers it could be a sign of tiredness, and if a horse has a normally low head carriage he may indicate fatigue by leaning on the rider's hands. Some horses get clumsy when tired, tripping and stumbling; others tend to damage themselves by hoof interference, this in particular being a sign of muscle fatigue.

Each rider will know his own horse's normal bright attitude and, paying attention to this, be able to detect when something is not quite right. The best guides of all to fatigue are heart and respiration rates. The latter is visible and can easily be checked en route. If the heart rate is really accelerated you can actually hear (and see) it by listening close to the girth, or, provided you have sensitive finger tips, you can place your fingers over a pulse spot and count. Both heart and respiration rates should drop very rapidly as soon as work ceases, and after a ten-minute break should be coming somewhere near the normal count. Both rates drop quickest in the first few minutes, thereafter rate of decrease slows down, and after thirty minutes, which is the time given on most rides between finish and vetting, they should be almost back to starting rate. Naturally the tougher the ride the more fatigued the horse and the higher the final count will be. All endurance riding countries have a heart-rate rule and no horse may proceed with heart rate in excess of maximum allowed. If recovery is insufficient the horse is eliminated.

Invest in a stethoscope so you can monitor heart rates. This should be done when the horse is at ease in his stable. Some horses show alarm and the rate will rise when first taken, but if it becomes a regular thing he will ignore it and the rate will stay constant. It will pay to get the horse accustomed to this well in advance of any competitive ride, as his heart rate taken on the ride will be a true indication of his fitness, and no allowance will need to be made for 'nerves'.

Make a practice of taking heart rate as soon as you finish a strenuous workout and again thirty minutes later. If it has not dropped back to normal or near normal considerable conditioning is still needed.

The method of taking heart rate is to place the stethoscope in the region of the girth just below the elbow. At first the right spot may take a bit of finding. Once located you will hear a steady two-part beat, the first part lighter, the second more positive, repeated rhythmically. Some horses seem to have a very loud beat, others are rather quieter, and it is just a matter of differences. It is easier to locate the beat on a fit horse as gross animals have a layer of fat muffling the sound. If you only do a fifteen-second count you could be off by several beats a minute. On training rides, though, the ten- or fifteen-second count can be used as a quick monitor.

Actual readings vary from horse to horse, but the average horse has a reading of around forty per minute, take or give a couple. When very fit he may get into the low thirties. At ride venues such low rates are unusual because the peripheral activity will serve to raise rates just a fraction, unless he is like my Nizzolan and Margaret Montgomerie's Tarquin who were always so relaxed that they gave very low readings. This is not very helpful at all when you want the readings after exertion of maybe 50-plus miles to return as close as possible to normal. After a tough test, no matter how fit the horse is, heart rates will not return to low thirties. Therefore horses who have venue exciteability even to a minor degree have an advantage, because that excitability will have definitely disappeared

after 50 miles and their readings be true, but they will have that initial slight advantage.

In actual work the horse's heart rate will accelerate tremendously and if a vet could actually take it while he was in motion at gallop the rate would sound alarming, but for practical purposes a check immediately on pulling up from an extended session of fast trot could easily be into the eighties, and after a gallop well over 100. This will drop very rapidly, being back below sixty in a very few minutes. If the horse's heart shows excellent recovery one day and not the next look for some other cause. He may be very slightly lame, or feeling discomfort in some area. In any case it will be a warning that something is wrong, probably not much, but the warning should not be ignored.

You can monitor respiration count two ways. A very quick way is to place a hand over the horse's nostrils and literally count the exhalations. It is not the most accurate method as some horses sniff a few extra at the smell of your hand, but it could do as a rough guide. The best way is to train yourself to watch his flanks and watch the in and out of each breath. After great exertion it will be easy, but at rest in the stable it can be difficult, particularly with a very relaxed horse. Normal respiration varies from about eight per minute up to twelve or fourteen depending on the horse, but ten to twelve is average. Some go lower than eight when very fit. Venue activity can slightly elevate rates with excitable horses, as can hot humid weather.

Currently a horse's respiration rate does not figure in *most* ride rules as far as judging goes, unless it indicates something is wrong, but it is as well to understand the system. In work the rate will approximately triple, except under great exertion when it will escalate even further. It should decelerate as soon as work ceases. High humidity with heat can cause respiration rates to stay somewhat higher than they would on days with normal atmospheric conditions. This should not alarm you as it is nature's way of coping.

If the horse's respiration does not drop satisfactorily he is not fit enough. If it stays close to the heart rate, or becomes inverted, after the thirty minutes have elapsed the vets will eliminate the horse. If this happens on rides at home consult your own vet as trouble could be brewing, and it is no time to count cost.

Fast CTRs and lower-level ERs of 40 to 50 miles

I have put these two together because fast CTRs, British Horse Society Qualifying Rides and shorter ERs are all run at relatively high average speeds. A rider going out and out for a win in a 50-mile ER will notch up a really fast time, but a rider going to complete or place (with a win a bonus) will be travelling at about Qualifying or fast CTR speed, and though the distance may not be of epic length the performance is very stressful. Bear in mind that on routes with roadwork, and few rides are completely free of this, speeds will be curtailed for part of the route, thereby forcing a very high speed for the remainder of the distance.

I am a great believer in a system with a great deal of build-up work before introducing speed. This gives a firm base to support stresses of speed work. Whereas at speed a tired horse damages himself, going slowly he can usually continue without risk.

In British ERs, other than 100 milers, there is a minimum speed of 7 mph so it is quite possible, though not if going for a placing award, to do the ERs slower than the fast CTRs by quite a few miles an hour. Also on ERs there are mandatory stops for rest and veterinary checks. On CTRs there are no stops.

In a 40- to 50-mile CTR, time taken to ride the route is in the region of five and threequarter to seven hours (see table). In a fast CTR of 35 miles, only 5 miles less, or less than an hour shorter at ordinary speeds, the distance will be clipped off in approximately four hours, and the top winning times in 50-mile ERs are in the region of four and a half to five hours, so you can readily see that a great deal more stress is involved in rides of this nature.

Once your horse is fit for a 40 miler at normal speeds you can begin to introduce speed work. For fast CTRs the mileage you will be covering need not be altered, just the manner of tackling a portion of it. For 50-mile ERs naturally the mileage will increase. Up to now speed has been absent from training. Introduce it gradually and do not make the mistake of thinking you need to do every workout at a high pitch. That way you risk breakdown. With a total programme of three to three and a half months' preparation you have four to six weeks to introduce the speed. Your total weekly mileage will be in the region of 70 to 80, still with two days off. That gives an average of 14 to 16 miles a day. Still pull two long rides a week totalling just over half the weekly average, and use one for a speed workout. The other three days can be split at your convenience. You have the horse fit now; he can be kept ticking over on the lower-distanced days with extra effort on only two days.

A rough guide could be: easy day of about 6 miles; rest day; 12 miles steady (one and a half

| Distance | Lapsed time (hours, minutes, seconds) | | | | | |
	5 mph	6 mph	7 mph	8 mph	9 mph	10 mph
1 mile	12 m	10 m	8 m 36 s	7 m 30 s	6 m 40 s	6 m
5 miles	1 h	50 m	43 m	37 m 30 s	33 m 20 s	30 m
10 miles	2 h	1 h 40 m	1 h 26 m	1 h 15 m	1 h 6 m 40 s	1 h
20 miles	4 h	3 h 20 m	2 h 52 m	2 h 30 m	2 h 13 m 20 s	2 h
25 miles	5 h	4 h 10 m	3 h 33 m 44 s	3 h 7 m 30 s	2 h 46 m 40 s	2 h 30 m
30 miles	6 h	5 h	4 h 17 m 12 s	3 h 45 m	3 h 20 m	3 h
35 miles	7 h	5 h 50 m	5 h	4 h 22 m 30 s	3 h 53 m 20 s	3 h 30 m
40 miles	8 h	6 h 40 m	5 h 43 m	5 h	4 h 26 m 40 s	4 h
50 miles	10 h	8 h 20 m	7 h 8 m 36 s	6 h 15 m	5 h 33 m 20 s	5 h
75 miles	15 h	12 h 30 m	10 h 43 m	9 h 22 m 30 s	8 h 20 m	7 h 30 m
100 miles	20 h	16 h 40 m	14 h 17 m 12 s	12 h 30 m	11 h 6 m 40 s	10 h

Speed and distance as measured by lapsed time

These times are to the nearest second and do not allow for any mandatory stops, time taken for these having to be added to the total.

hours); rest day; 12 miles steady (two hours); 20 miles fast (two hours); 25 miles hard (three hours) – week's total 75 miles.

As you get closer to the actual event of, say, the 50-mile ER, do a simulated fast 35 miler, or a competition if available, averaging about 10 mph. Do it at least ten days away from the event. Monitor your horse's attitude, recovery, legs for any heat or swellings, body weight, dehydration, pulse and respiration, and his ability to bounce back and be ready for more.

If he answers all these criteria with a green light he is fit. In the final week ease up considerably. Only include one long ride at speed; use the others to keep him fresh and do at least two easy days with just enough mileage to exercise him. You want that reserve to build up. For the first four of the last six weeks' training include two speed rides a week. The fifth week is when you test him out, and the sixth week you keep him ticking over, ready, as it were, to come out of the starting stalls.

In the fast training check his attitude to greater sustained speed. The way he reacts will tell you if he is going to make winning or high-placing endurance material. If he relishes the extra demands and is not unduly stressed at any stage you have a very good prospect. If he is willing but slightly stressed it is a warning. He needs more conditioning. If he is still young, and in endurance terms that means eight years old or younger, he needs another season at lower speeds. Be careful in this area. It would be so easy to overtax the horse just because he is willing. Endurance horses do take time, several seasons, to get to their best. He must continue to enjoy his work, not dread the effort he knows is going to be demanded.

If there is no improvement after either a rest, more conditioning, or another season with a youngster, settle for what he is happy and successful in. He could well go on to Endurance Rides for good completions, which are what you should initially aim for. If he finds fast CTRs, which need similar speeds to Endurance Rides, a constant effort, re-assess the horse and re-design your programme.

Two- and three-day rides

Many national associations hold either CTRs or ERs spread out over two or three days. The CTRs are judged on a time plus condition basis, while the Endurance Rides are on a total time taken for the whole ride, so that the leader on day one is not necessarily the leader at the finish. The total mileage of these rides is usually 100 miles, although some countries have longer rides of Endurance type.

To do well in these events the horse must be super fit and able to pull out the next day not just sound and moving well but with plenty of energy for one or more days' extra work.

Basic conditioning will not vary much from that of getting any horse fit for long distance, but this type of ride does have built-in danger areas, and its own special type of hazard. It needs a better overall strategy and a stronger determination not to be influenced by what other competitors are doing. The type of horse needs a more durable temperament – one that will happily pull out and do a repeat of the day before with the same amount of energy. He also needs a rather more relaxed attitude, as energy wasted fighting to get ahead on day one may not show a deficit until day two. Overall weekly mileage will not need to alter from that done to achieve fitness for the 50-mile Endurance Rides, that is about 75 miles per week, but as you approach the last few weeks prior to the ride date the break up of the mileage will need to change. At least twice during the later training stages try to fit in a two- or three-day stint (depending on your competition aims) when successive daily mileages approach actual ride demands. If your horse can do a 30–30–10 or a 35–35-mile session at ride speeds adequately he will cope with the added extra in competition.

After such a workout do not just lay the horse off with the weekly mileage completed, but give him an easy day to unwind, followed by a couple of days off and an easy day to follow where limbering up is the aim. He is already fit. Care has to be taken not to overdo the strenuous distances, so strike a medium between trials and ticking over work. The stresses involved in doing successive long distances are just as relevant as doing an all-out race, though slightly different. The horse for the out-and-out endurance needs to be a speedier animal in the final analysis, as well as having all the other attributes. In the 'spread-over-days' ride the equally good but maybe slower horse can just as easily come up a winner. Tactics, because they are spread over several days, need to be that little bit cleverer.

Endurance Rides of 75 to 100 miles

These really should not be attempted by either a rider or a horse in his first season of distance work. Both need time to learn what the demands of the sport are, and the rider will need at least a season to accurately 'read' his horse. There is no other equestrian activity that will give him this feeling, as distance riding at the higher levels is the only sport that has such a tremendous continued demand on both horse and rider. The horse too will need at least a season to get used to giving an ever-increasing optimum performance. To demand too much too early will mean the horse will never reach his real potential, as the guts will be worked out of him before he has had time to develop all systems to maximum capacity. Horses, particularly Arabians, do not mature until late in life, and though five years of age is when a horse is considered mature it really is the age at which his best years are just starting. He is not mature in terms of ability to perform to his lifetime's best. For that he needs a couple of years more. It also takes him time to learn how to use himself efficiently and economically, two facets of performance vital in top distances of endurance riding.

When you enter 75 or 100 milers the horse will be tuned to such a peak of fitness that there is really no margin for error, particularly if placing awards are your real aim. The *absolute minimum* for training should be four and a half and six months respectively, erring on the generous side. Doing a season or two of prior competitions will also enable you to plot your 100-miler year to a much better degree. Many of your really long workouts will take the form of actual competitions. Take advantage of as many 40-mile-plus CTRs and 50-mile ERs as you can afford financially and timewise. Training

at home is excellent, but there is something special about the atmosphere at a competition that brings out the best in the horse. It also keeps him interested and gives him a chance to be so accustomed to away-from-home venues and strange footing that whatever is thrown at him in a 100 miler will not ruffle his equilibrium, and he will be able to concentrate all his energy on producing that forward drive to the finish post.

While recommending as many competitions as possible I do not mean one a week, but you should practice common sense and moderation in asking maximum output from your horse. Five really long rides in competition as well as your elevated training should see you fairly confident the horse will go the distance on the day.

Your elevated training should include at least two 60-mile (or thereabouts) stints done within the last month of training, the final one only two weeks to ten days before the actual event. If there are suitable competitions near that distance use them. If you have very easy going in your area it would be worth going away for at least one of these stints to a district with the same, or similar, terrain as that over which the 100 is to be run.

Having mentioned easy going it is important to realize that a horse can be got fit for a tough ride in relatively easy going. What must be realized, though, is that a 20-mile ride in tough going could well use up the energy that a 30 or 35 miler would take on easy ground. Hilly ground will put extra stresses on leg muscles and on the heart and lungs.

When I lived in the USA my 'territory' was so flat that when the farmer we rented grazing from referred to 'that hill over there' I couldn't see anything resembling even a slight mound, let alone a hill. He was referring to a minimal rise in a patch of field, yet in this type of going I produced horses for both Florida and Asheville 100s, the former being relatively flat country with very holding going, the latter having mountains and long pulls up the hill roads. The horses responded well but I had not taken chances at home and at that time there was virtually no written information to help newcomers to the sport.

If you have access to some holding ground use it, but only when the horse is already fit. The muscles and tendons will be worked albeit in a pulling rather than a pushing manner, but the horse will have a chance to know what stress in the limbs is and get toughened to it. The thing to remember is that a flatland horse fit for a 100 in his own territory may well not be fit for the same distance in rough going. Away-from-home events will clue you in to this aspect and show you what tightening up in your schedule is needed. Conversely, a rider used to piloting a horse in rough going where speeds are necessarily somewhat curtailed may be tempted to do a rush job in the deceptively easy flatland rides.

To complete a 100 miler is a tremendous achievement, and for the first time or so of trying, particularly if it is also the horse's first time, be content with piloting him safely around without the element of 'getting the edge on so and so's horse'. Do not allow yourself to be pushed into a mad dash by other competitors. Some people ride conservatively, some aggressively. You do what you feel is right for your horse. Make a pre-ride plan with your 'crew' and stick to it. Your 'crew' will be able to report on who's where and doing what in the field, and you can thereby monitor other's progress and use that knowledge to your advantage if opportunity presents itself. I am not a gambler risking elimination for a win, yet a fair number of successes have come my way over the years. My stallion Nizzolan's 1975 100-mile win was a bonus and I stuck rigidly to the pre-plan. It was his first and Britain's first 100 miler, and a completion was very important. Later on when Margaret Montgomerie and I rode the German 100 we followed a pre-plan and it worked for us as a team.

In doing the Australian Quilty I was urged to put a spurt on so that the mare I was riding could gain an extra award for coming in under fifteen hours, but I 'just didn't hear' the admonitions as I felt she did not have the reserve left to go a notch faster. I am glad I resisted the call to hurry, as I know I would not have got through the final check.

I only make the above observations to illustrate that in a ride of such a nature it is definitely best to ride within your horse's capacity. There are too many variables and chances of horses being eliminated to worry about being faster than a certain competitor. There have been times when that dash for the finish line has resulted in eliminations, allowing a much slower horse ridden within its known limits to come in quietly to a 100-mile win.

A similar situation occurred in the 1976 Hamburg to Hannover 100 miler with Tarquin and Nizzolan. When we reached the first veterinary check at around 25 miles the stewards had already left, thinking we were not coming. Yet we had held a speed of 8 mph and over throughout, which was what we had decided on prior to the ride. The other competitors had come through with a rush and were long gone. However, at the 40-mile mark we steadily overhauled horse after horse and gave Britain her first European triumph, in spite of going off course and having to find a 'mislaid' marker which cost us an hour and many extra miles backtracking, as well as never having an accurate translation of the rules.

Keep a meticulous '100-mile log' noting each day's work, manner and content of same, any unusual weather conditions, occasional pulse and respiration readings, general escalation of distance and speed and how the horse responds. Do this month by month with a running total and then you can watch that you are not underdoing or overdoing training. It is very difficult in early May to remember exactly what you were doing in mid January, and a log can definitely be of great help.

As well as the day-to-day log make a very detailed projected ride plan for the actual competition, with the earliest and latest times of expected arrival at each checkpoint. This way you can check on your steady progress throughout the ride. Do not bother about what anyone else is doing around you on the day.

Next in preparation for the 100 (or any major ride) comes the list of items needed and their location in the back-up vehicle. Time will be saved at those too short mandatory stops if you know exactly where to find each item, and if they are returned to their exact slot, not just slung down when used.

I have dealt with 100 miling first as more and more countries are offering that distance for their international events. Naturally, 75-mile ERs need to be pitched between the 50- and 100-mile levels when it comes to training. With the proliferation of rides in almost all countries the days have gone when all yearly events for each society or association were progressive, with shortest rides early in the season and the longest finishing the season. Now 100 milers, 75 milers and 50 milers are dotted throughout the calendar, and as the sport becomes international, particularly on the European scene, most go for the 100s and in working towards these 75-mile fitness is incorporated.

A point that has not been mentioned before: if you are training for one ride of moderate length the conditioning is totally progressive. If you are doing a season in which there are several really long tough rides you must incorporate frequent mini-breaks for the horse. The recommended *guide* has been on a weekly cum monthly basis, but going by the feel of your horse and by the season's ride plan do insert occasional three- or four-day breaks once the horse is really fit. It will stop him going over the top and getting stale, and/or grinding him down by incessant demands. After a 100, give him a couple of weeks off with only a light limber-up ride. Remember the recommendations are just that. It is up to your skill as a horseman/woman to be able to use a guide plan and then formulate one tailored to your own individual circumstances and your own very special equine.

16 Crewing on a ride

At some time during a season of competitive rides you will probably need the luxury of having a crew, support team, or as the Australians call it a 'strapper'. It is possible to dispense with this on shorter rides, particularly those coming back to base for all major checks and mandatory stops. If you have to go it alone be very, very organized in preparing your vehicle with all the things you may need. On endurance rides, particularly those with linear routes, it will be vital to have someone to assist you at stops. Certain ride rules make having a 'crew' mandatory, so do check the small print.

There are a few tips that may be helpful in this direction. When arranging details with your assistant have your ride planned beforehand, making allowances for early and late arrival at stops. Riders should definitely not have to worry about the route, but unfortunately some rides are not marked as well as they should be. Markers are also a target for removal by vandals in some popular regions where rides cross tourist areas. The support crew will need a map of the course. Sometimes they will have to drive considerably more miles than you will have to ride. Make sure all access points for a vehicle are noted and plan your ride around these.

One point to make very clear at the outset is that the crew must stick to what the rider wants done for the horse, even if it may not be what they themselves might do. Once, many years ago at a Golden Horseshoe final, there was a great amount of attrition due to the fact that crews had not been briefed. Colics resulted when horses swilled excessive amounts of cold water while their body temperatures were very high. The reverse happened in Australia. As the little horse I was riding was the substitute's substitute and not initially designed or trained for a 100 miler, a lot of her success was directly attributable to her strapper, Ernie Sinfield, and his helpers. Throughout and at the finish Ernie followed instructions to the absolute letter, despite what he may have felt himself, and he was a very experienced strapper. The horse passed with flying colours. This point is made because it is the rider's responsibility for getting the horse through. If he succeeds there is the satisfaction of having done a job well, and being thankful to an expert crew. If the horse fails to pass the vet no crew should have the onus placed on them, yet mistakes can occur if instructions from the rider are not absolutely clear. Anyone offering assistance as 'crew' must also be able to take orders, even if they do not agree with them. A person crewing must be very tolerant, because as a very long ride progresses the rider is coming under increasing strain and the effects of tiredness, and may not always be his or her normal, polite self, perhaps being a little peremptory in requests that come out as orders, or maybe he or she will be a little irritable – all without realizing it.

The crew should have everything ready before the horse arrives at each stop. They should attend to the horse in a very unhurried calm manner. Go through routines for the respective stops well beforehand. Be prepared to make sudden changes, and also be prepared to lend a hand to other riders whose crews may have got lost, or whatever, en route. I know Major Broun and Angela Holden, who crewed for me and Nizzolan, were an absolute godsend to others, having plenty of water always available. *But do remember* when you are crewing that your particular horse is of paramount importance and must claim your attention as soon as he hoves into sight.

I always prefer to do any tack changes myself, but if the crew has to attend to that department they must be very sure the horse is tacked up exactly as the rider wants. Again, a pre-ride dry run is advisable. At ride end I feel the rider should attend as

10 The importance of good crewing: they should attend to the horse in a very unhurried calm manner. Rufus in the EHPS Summer Solstice.

much as possible to the horse himself, even after a 100 miler. The rider will know from feel exactly what the horse is in need of, but the crew should be able to take over completely and efficiently if necessary. Details in the next chapter apply equally to rider or crew.

A greater percentage of success is attributable to good crewing than is generally realized, and for the most part these vital helpers rarely receive their highly deserved recognition.

Common sense must be used in preparing the horse for his work with a sensible routine regarding feeding, not feeding at dawn one day and 10 a.m. the next, although I do not think it necessary to be absolutely punctilious about feeding times. If the horse expects his oats on the dot he may start pawing or door banging if he is not appeased with his full bucket.

I once had a favourite character who started the caper of rattling his snap chain (without it he excused himself from stables) accompanied by hoof scrapings at dawn. The stables were adjacent to and within earshot of the house. Verbal reprimands gave only momentary relief, so one morning he had the wrong type of attention from his point of view and no breakfast. Future dawns were quieter and he had his feed at a more reasonable hour.

Throughout training, allow the horse freedom to roam his pasture for most of the day. In summer heat reverse this, letting him out at night to avoid flies. Particularly when turning out at night make sure all fences are safe and that there are no bullies in the field. What a waste of time and what a disappointment if your distance horse is lamed by a kick from another horse, or driven into a corner of the field. I prefer not to have corners where the horses can be boxed and if possible arrange the fencing so no acute or 90 degree angles exist. This makes entrapment more difficult.

If your pasture has lush grazing you will have to limit the horse's time on it. If it is sparse and of poor nutritional quality the horse can remain out for longer at a time. Some horses blow up into fat-stock (Smithfield) proportions. Not only will they be softer and have to work all systems harder, but they will not eat their proper rations, unless they are compulsive eaters, and then they will run the risk of other disorders associated with over-feeding. If at all possible, particularly with a horse

in very strict training, try to provide a sparse, even an overgrazed, paddock. Maintain a clean field by removing droppings. Harrowing or scattering is not adequate; it just spreads the problem. It is important for the overall wellbeing of the horse to have a certain amount of freedom, which provides the gentle but constant exercise that prevents an endurance horse from stiffening. I also recommend turning the horse out immediately he returns from a stiff competition. Stabled he will stiffen; pastured he will slowly unwind and relax.

Grooming should be thorough, especially where tack touches the skin. A chafe on an endurance horse can curtail training at a vital point. Saddle pads and girths should be kept very clean.

If the horse has a heavy coat, even in summer, clip him. It will be easier to keep flesh on him as clammy hair acts like a Turkish bath when he is hot, and a dangerous chiller when he is cold. In hot weather sponge down with lukewarm water. It makes the horse feel good and gets rid of clogging and sticky grime and sweat.

Preparing for the ride

If you are entering rides away from home stabling do a trial period to see the horse's reactions. I have known horses to become frantic away from home and normal companions, and this condition can result in distress, wasted energy and in extreme cases colic, and it could entail withdrawal from the competition.

You may find the first time or two away from home the horse goes off his feed and water, so it is well worth the added expense in the first year of competition to do a couple of these away-from-home sessions, either at rides, where you are more concerned with getting the horse used to his new role, or just as a practice session. I have known

Leave at ride stable	In vehicle with crew	With horse/rider
Feed and hay	Small feed and haynet	Extra hoofpick
Sawdust	Small bag sawdust	Bandage
Shovel and rake	Water containers	Small sterile pad
Claw hammer and nails	Loose salt	String
	Electrolytes	Change for telephone
	Grooming kit	Sponge
	Spare set horseshoes and nails	Gloves
	Hoof rasp and hammer	Chaps
	Three clean saddle pads and washable girths	Hard hat
	Spare stirrups and leathers	
	Spare bridle and reins	
	Light rug	
	Two coolers (one lighter, one heavier)	
	Needle and strong thread for tack	
	Tack-cleaning gear	
	Extra buckets	
	Antiseptic lotion	
	Wound ointment	
	Antiseptic dusting powder	
	Complete change of clothes	
	Light walking shoes	
	Insect repellent	

Equipment to take on ride

some horses to ignore water in their stable if it tastes strange. Fortunately this is not usual but be alert for it. As a precaution take several full water containers so he can have his own until he settles. When he is thirsty during the ride itself he will drink, and provided he is used to them electrolytes can be added to his water. It is important that he has been got used to these earlier, so that under ride conditions when he is in real need of their help he does not refuse to drink electrolyte-laced water. If you skimp on the try-outs with a horse known to be distressed in strange surroundings you are wasting time, effort and expenditure. Where you could perhaps have got a high place, you may be lucky to get a completion, or if the distress is really bad you might have to withdraw the horse.

Prior to packing for rides I make lists, checking off items as they are loaded. All feed and hay should be taken, as sudden changes in diet can be disastrous. Allow extra in case the return is delayed. I also take a jar of loose salt; regular grooming kit; shovel and rake; a spare set of shoes for the horse; spare hoof pick to tie to the saddle; rasp for bevelling sharp edges that wear on his shoes; at

least three clean saddle pads and washable girths; spare stirrups and leathers; spare bridle or reins; a light rug and two coolers (in case it is raining and one gets wet at an early checkpoint); needle and strong thread for quick tack repairs and also for braiding the horse's tail if it should be very muddy – it is uncomfortable for him to have it clinging wetly around his legs; tack-cleaning gear; extra buckets; antiseptic lotion; wound ointment and antiseptic dusting powder in case a chafe occurs; a bandage and a clean handkerchief, string, and loose change for a telephone call (this may sound wishful thinking but it is best to be prepared). Check the rules with regard to external medications. Some rides permit them, some do not.

My own equipment includes a complete change of everything because of weather unpredictability, and a light pair of shoes suitable for gripping slippery surfaces. I have found I can make better time on foot leading the horse down tarmacked roads or over slick patches. Without my weight on his back he is better balanced. Check the ride rules to ascertain if forward movement is permitted while dismounted.

11 Leading your horse. Richard Barsaleau and Good Trip in the 1978 Tevis Cup Ride. (Charles Barrieau)

By all means be neat, but also be practical. I am more comfortable riding in a sweater and loose jeans than in jodhpurs and jacket. Gloves can be necessary in case weather turns wet and makes reins slippery. Hard hats are compulsory on some rides. Leather chaps afford considerable grip and are very comfortable and warm as well as providing a certain amount of weather-proofing. Very few societies impose any clothing restrictions on riders, but do check the small print. Insect repellent is useful for both horses and riders and affords a degree of personal comfort for both.

If the ride is fairly close it is in order to travel the day of the ride, but if it is a good distance away travel the night before either to the venue or to stables close by. A three- or four-hour journey, plus a 50-mile ride, followed by the return journey is too much for both horse and rider. The horse will not be as fresh as he should be, and returning home the rider could be fatigued with resultant road risk. If the horse suffers various bad effects from a long trip he will be able to recover and to rest prior to the ride. Some horses become very distressed, sweat up, and use a lot of energy travelling, others have filled legs, others get congested lungs. All these symptoms will have disappeared if you can manage an overnight stay.

If your horse is a bed-eater request some other bedding than straw when booking stabling. Most organizers do make provision for this. If not, be prepared to carry a bale of sawdust or peat with you as part of your ride equipment and dampen it if necessary. When your horse is in his temporary surroundings do not keep fussing around him.

Attend to him normally and let him alone. Just the fact you are there is reassuring.

Most major national rides have centralized base stables. Other smaller ones have horses stabled close by. When booking in tell the Ride Secretary if there is anything he/she should know about your horse: for example, a stallion that needs solid stabling; a mare that could be in oestrus (so she will not be stabled next to a stallion); if you require your horse to be stabled next to his travelling companion; and so on.

It is a good idea to have a claw hammer and a few nails amongst your gear. I always make a routine check of any box and immediately remove or flatten any projecting nails. It is really amazing how many stables do have a quota of these and get away without injury to their own horses. There should be no gap between wall and floor that can trap a hoof when the horse is rolling. If there is, tactfully ask for a board to be fixed there, even if you have to say your horse is prone to damaging himself. If the hayring is too low do not use it. For once, waste some hay and feed off the floor rather than risk a hung hoof. If your horse chews wood, or kicks causing damage, offer to pay for it. It is not included in the entry fee.

If you are not staying at ride base leave the address and telephone number of where you can be contacted with the Ride Secretary.

The ride

All rides have pre-ride veterinary checks. Make sure you declare any peculiarities in gait; fresh cuts or bruises such as an interference mark on legs or hooves; tendency to sweat very freely. Sometimes a vet will find things you did not even know were there, which serves to help for future declarations or pre-ride precautions.

Study ride details and note route warnings. Stick to the marked trail. Accidents have happened to riders who diverge and organizers have enough to do without the added burden of lost and/or injured horses and riders. All ride routes are checked and where the path is indicated it is safe to go, even if a bit poached in places. However, sometimes markers are shifted by pranksters, so riders do beware.

(This is usually reported back to base and organizers are very prompt in rectifying deviations.) Take note of vegetation and colour of grasses. Where there is sudden lush green amidst rather sere surroundings it probably means bog. Unsafe patches sometimes appear in the middle of a hillside and will be indicated by sharply contrasting natural bright growth amidst drier fern and heather coverings. Merely because it is on a hill is no surety of dryness. Often subsoil structure changes abruptly, causing dangerous mire pockets. Where there is a sudden appearance of thick yellow or grey clay go slowly. It can drag a horse down, or cause one to somersault, particularly if ridden into at speed. Gravelly streams are safe. Unclear murky streams that have a poached approach may not be safe for a horse with the added weight of a rider aboard.

On ride day I like to feed about three hours before my scheduled start. Then just about an hour before I offer a tiny feed of about 1 lb. Groom thoroughly and saddle up very carefully, paying particular attention to placing the saddle pad, if used, and to the girth, making sure there are no skin wrinkles that could chafe.

In my pocket I carry a piece of string; telephone money; bandage and sterile pad (in a plastic bag) in case of emergency. I have not needed the latter but a rider without it but with an injured horse was glad of it on one occasion. I know it sounds a lot of bits and pieces but packed efficiently it is minimal. Also tie the spare hoof pick on the saddle.

The vehicle is ready packed for my crew to drive to checkpoints. Contents comprise all the things in the table (p. 120) leaving behind the feed and mucking out tools. If it is a cold day the water container could travel in the front passenger well where the vehicle heater and engine will serve to take the chill off the water.

At the start of the ride give yourself plenty of time to check in so that there is not a last minute rush. On rides I travel to on ride day I like to have at least one full hour at ride base before veterinary check is called. The early arrivals always get the best parking places, and it is surprising how quickly an hour will flash by with parking; getting your number; laying gear out ready to tack up; and then unloading your horse and getting him ready.

12 Allow the horse as many drinks as possible en route from streams and clean puddles. A group of 100 milers half way through their ride. (Dr R. Marshall)

I do these things in that order, finding it more efficient.

Once started there is no need to charge forward as so many riders seem to. Let the horse set out at a moderate trot for the first few minutes until he is warmed up and in his stride, and then he can move on more strongly, settling to concentrate on pacing according to the terrain. Studying contour lines on the map will warn you in advance of where the route climbs or where it is fairly level if you are in a strange area.

During the ride I allow the horse as many drinks as possible en route from streams and clean puddles. This way he can keep his fluid level up. Make sure he learns to do this in training. Do not expect him to oblige for the first time on a ride. If he has frequent drinks he need not be rationed as to intake, but do give him a little stretch of easy

work so he does not surge forward with a lot of fluid sloshing around inside him. You do not want to risk colic. One word of warning for people where rides are run in agricultural areas. If ditches and dykes border croplands be careful. The water may be polluted with chemical run-off from the fertilizers used on the crops.

If for any unforeseen reason – either your crew cannot get to you; it is a dry spell; the route has no streams; or the above 'chemical' hazard – your horse has not had frequent and sufficient access to water, when he finally gets it be careful and sparing about his intake. Allow him about six swallows, wait for a few minutes and repeat. Do not allow him to gorge. If he is extra thirsty it would be worth the time taken in delaying restarting, if you have taken time out on a CTR. On an ER there will be ample time at the mandatory stops for topping up fluid level with a horse that is merely thirsty, not one suffering from serious fluid depletion.

Before arriving at mandatory stops slow down so the horse's heart rate is also slowing down, and he comes in with a gradual lessening of bodily activity. The sudden change from movement to standing to be checked and worked over is then not so drastic. By all means have him come in looking as if he is ready for more. Visual impressions do count.

During the lay-over sponge the face around nostrils, mouth and eyes to refresh him. Get a cooler on immediately, but leave the saddle on, relaxing the girth gradually. Whip out the wet saddle pad and slip a clean dry one in once the initial maximum pressure has been released over the back. The reason I leave the saddle on and girthed is so that pressure is not released too suddenly. If a horse's back has had a considerable weight on it for several hours the saddle is in close pressured contact at some points. If pressure is released suddenly it *may* cause pressure bumps to flare up as the blood rushes into the capillaries. Not all horses' backs react this way but some definitely do, and it does not necessarily mean the saddle is ill fitting. It could be the way the rider sits, and there are very few riders who do sit absolutely central and distribute weight perfectly. This is again not due to bad riding but to deviations from perfect in the rider's anatomy.

If you do get pressure areas ice will help reduce them. If, however, rules preclude use of this, bumps can be reduced by very careful massaging, but be careful not to abstract hairs and create another problem. Another tip is to girth up incredibly tightly for a considerable period after the ride, putting a lot of pressure in this area but without the weight. It does work.

At mandatory halts there is little enough time to see to watering, cleaning up, checking for minor galls and hoof interferences, and changing wet gear, let alone taking the bridle off, haltering, and later re-bridling. This is fine at the finish or on the 100 miler hour lay-over, but best left alone in thirty-minute halts as time can be more advantageously spent on other things. Be very careful when regirthing not to pinch the skin.

Ride successive sections as carefully as the first,

slowing down in the final mile or so, unless it is a close call with a racing finish and a win depending on it.

After the ride

In ERs, particularly 100 milers, where there is a best condition award the next day, the real work sets in and it is back in the stables that the horse's true condition will show itself. He has been subjected to extreme stress, particularly if aiming at high speed, and once movement has ceased he should relax, but if he is overtired he will not.

A sensibly ridden ride will make sure the horse does relax. A stupidly ridden one, where excessive speeds have been asked for, will ensure a bad recovery, and in many cases horses so ridden have colicked severely or had frighteningly bad heart rates; some have never been completely fit again. Proper conditioning and sensible competing in most cases where this happened was lacking.

If he has had plenty of chances to drink en route the horse can have a reasonably liberal amount of water; if he has been restricted for any reason get the fluids into him gradually. Walk him slowly so his muscles start to unwind. If you put him away immediately he will stiffen and not move freely when run up next morning for best condition. According to the day's temperature put a cooler on: a very hot day – none; warm but a slight breeze – a light one; chilly – his heavier one. If it is very sharp I would take longer on the walking out as muscles will stiffen just that much more quickly in low temperatures after high exertion. Once he has been returned to his box allow him hay to nibble, but unless he has stopped craving water keep it out of his stable. Keep offering it to him frequently, and when he has stopped craving it then put a full bucket of tepid water in his stable. While he still wants water badly I put a couple of ounces of salt in his water as he will be thirsty enough to drink and replace salts. Any excess he gets will be excreted. If it is put in his feed and he is a horse that dislikes it he will not eat.

Once he has cooled down he can have the cooler taken off and then he will probably roll to scratch his hide. I do not clean the horse as soon as he is put into his stable. If he has a great amount of mud on him remove the worst, but other than that let him alone to rest as that is the most important thing in the first hour after he goes into his box.

If it is a blistering hot day and the air is still very warm after the ride the horse can be sponged down with warm water. Cold water causes muscular contraction just as in humans. The heat will have made him sweat more profusely and he will feel better for a good wash, and he will pick up more quickly if he feels good. As the sponging takes less time than grooming it can be done before he is left to rest. If it is excessively hot without a breeze he will not need the cooler, which will hinder ventilation under these conditions.

His hard feed quota will be about 15 lb at this stage, and he will have about a third of that in the morning over the normal and tiny feeds. He may have had time to eat a few mouthfuls at major lay-overs, but I feel it best not to offer it even then. That leaves 10 lb of his daily ration. It would be very stupid to try to get all that into a tired horse. It is better to cut his amount for just that one day, rather than overload his stomach and risk colic.

His feeding will need to be drastically altered in timing after a strenuous ride, so forget about normal feeding times. About two hours after the finish I give a small feed of about 1 lb, and then over the remainder of the evening get the balance into him, feeding the last amount around 11 o'clock. I aim to get at least 7 of the 10 lb balance into him and to that end split it up into four feeds, one of 1 lb and 2 lb for the others – these last three given at two-hourly intervals. At no time is his stomach overloaded and digestion will not be strained. If he is too tired to eat do not just pile one feed on top of the other, but see what he will clean up, and before going to bed leave about 2 lb in his feed bucket for him to pick at.

When he has eaten his first feed and is comfortably chewing on his hay groom thoroughly, but do not take more time than is absolutely necessary. I find a tired horse gets a bit cranky and is entitled to for once. Do the job and leave him alone, checking over the stable door periodically to see everything is all right.

If there is a hint of coolness in the air put a light blanket on him to stop his muscles tightening. It will pay off in extra suppleness the following morning. I make a final check about midnight, just looking in and not disturbing the horse. But between returning the horse to his box and that final check take him out two or three times for a very short walk to keep him supple.

At 100 milers when preparing for veterinary check the morning after, the stable routine should include some slow walking to limber up and then when asked to move out he will do so more freely.

The above systems relating to stable and grooming care have worked well under the conditions prevailing at British rides, and with the variable but withal temperate British climate. In other countries where different conditions occur, such as ride venues without box stabling, accommodations to the differences will have to be worked out. Also many endurance riding countries have what to us in Britain seem excessively hot climates where horses' temperatures can soar, and there cold water is used to advantage in reducing body heat.

18 Feeding

Maximum effort needs massive energy. A good feeding programme provides this, and in order to get continued top results the horse must have the best feeds available in the right quantity. It is no good trying to economize on grains and hays as the horse's condition will deteriorate, and he will be working off his built-up reserves which he will need for the all-out effort of a season of sustained endurance work.

At his peak output periods the horse cannot actually eat enough to replace the energy expended in, say, a ride of 75 miles or more. Therefore he relies on his reserve to supplement his normal rations. If he is really fit his weight loss should be minimal and replaced within a very few days.

Careful feeding of the right rations will enable the horse to withstand the strain, whereas poor quality feed, even in greater quantity, will not give adequate nourishment.

At the beginning of training the horse will be in relatively soft condition. Each owner will know which category his particular mount falls into: the easy keeper; the moderate; or the real hay and oat burner. Whatever his type the same, or basically the same, feeding methods should apply. A soft horse in light work will not burn up so much energy as the fitter animal in a further stage of training. It follows that feeding will have to be geared to physical output. At first go easy on the grain, offering all the hay the horse will eat.

A very broad guide to feeding, for an average 1000 lb horse which will be of medium build and around 15 hands or a little over, is shown in the table. Rations are expressed per 100 lb of body weight. It is only a very broad outline as each horse is, and should be treated as, an individual. This feed basis is for the horse that is a relatively easy keeper, but not the type that lives on the smell of an oily rag.

With horses that have a higher metabolic rate the grain ration will need adjusting upwards, and in that case I allow them all the hay they will eat, as, unless they are absolutely compulsive eaters, they will quit when they have had enough. I do ration compulsive eaters with the suggested ration for medium keepers, fractionally more for horses with higher metabolism. Many feed charts cut hay considerably for horses in hard work, but I have never found this to be necessary.

As well as the amount of feed, the types need to be thought about. With hay, a good timothy or timothy and clover mix is good as is quality lucerne (alfafa). The latter is high in protein and if very good can serve to cut the grain ration a little. Mix lucerne with another hay as it can make the droppings loose with some horses if used to excess. Most horses find it far more palatable than other hays and may waste other good hay if given both at the same time. Try and get first-cut hay, cropped before it goes to seed as the nutritional value is at its highest when in leaf.

With grains it is a matter of personal preference and individual horses whether you feed entirely one or mix several types. A mixture is a good insurance, as should the grains come from a feed merchant you have no knowledge of their source, and in using a mixture you do guard against a deficiency by 'hedging your bet' as to the content. If your basic ration is oats they should be plump and clean, weighing more pounds to the bushel. The heavier the oat the better – not so much is wasted in non-nutritional husk. I like oats crushed, but if you have to store them for any length of time they lose some nutrients. Bruised or crimped, they lose less in the process. Crushed oats are less likely to pass through the digestive tract. If this happens have the horse's teeth checked. Good oats have a protein content of between 11 and 13 per cent.

	Grain (lb)	Hay (lb)
Maintenance or light work up to 1 hour a day	0.50	1.50
2 hours average work	0.80	1.50
3 to 4 hours average work or 2 hours hard work	1.00	1.50
Medium hard work up to 6 hours steady, or 3 hours hard work	1.25	1.25
Later stages of training when pressure mounts	1.50	1.25

Feeding guide per 100 lb bodyweight

If a horse is a little on the racy side, or not particularly thrifty, I feed a certain amount of barley, but not too much at one feeding because of overloading the stomach. Barley has a similar protein content to oats and a higher starch content, and I find it a very good feed indeed, being able to feed less poundage with the same result. In calorie content, 1 lb barley equals 1 1/4 lb oats. With a horse in CTR training that needs less food than an endurance horse and is not going to be worked at such a high speed, barley could, if it suits your horse's digestion, substitute for oats. I have had crushed barley from the same source for years with good results. I feel that boiling the stuff, or paying extra for a fancy preparation, is not cost effective in time or money. However, if you have just the one horse you may indulge yourself in the wide variety of prepared grains and mixes available, some of which are undoubtedly first class. Nowadays there are so many feeds recommended for the top competition horse that it is a veritable maze to find one's way through, and I do not propose to elaborate. Each company will be more than pleased to 'explain their product's advantages'. They of course have 'no disadvantages'!

Cubes of the various varieties with their stated contents can be used, but apart from the racehorse variety which may be given as either an additional feed or a complete short feed I have not used them to any great extent. (When I did do a complete trial long ago the pony went crazy for just any 'real food', like a dieter denied favourite dishes!) There are some brands specifically formulated for horses in hard work and if it is impossible to get the top quality grain necessary I would rather use cubes because they do keep to a given standard. However, I do not like using the type that enables you to dispense with hay as the horse becomes bored and will inevitably supplement his feed with part of his stable.

Flaked maize is useful and is comparable in nutrition to barley. Never feed it whole, as it is too hard to grind efficiently. Bran used to be thought indispensable in feeding systems, particularly allied with oats. Research has proved that the two are not such good partners. Oats are relatively low in calcium while bran is high in phosphorus. You do not do the horse a service to get his trace minerals out of kilter. Chaff can bulk the feed of a horse that gobbles. And if a horse really bolts his feed try a few large stones in the feed trough so he will have to eat slowly around them to get all his ration. Molassine meal is a good additive for palatability and the trace minerals it contains. Salt is one of the most important staples for a horse in hard training, and although regular feeds and hays contain a certain amount of natural salts the horse will sweat out more than these provide when he is really working. Either mineral or plain salt can be used. Electrolytes also are a boost and safeguard against deficiencies, and there are many proprietary brands on the market. For a horse in training for really tough rides they should form part of his diet.

Taking the average horse that is receiving the 10 lb grain allowance a day I would work his feed roughly as follows: 4 lb oats, 4 lb barley, 2 lb high protein cubes. If you use molassine meal either add a handful morning and night, or add a pound every other day with the feed. I use well-soaked sugar beet pulp as a moistener. It is succulent, bulks the feed, is palatable and binds the grains together and helps prevent loss by an untidy eater. If you are going to use it go sparingly with it for a horse in very hard work, as it is rather like suet pudding in the stomach. When a horse is not in work, or in the early stages of training, I will use a couple of pounds dry weight a day; as his work increases the amount of beet pulp decreases. It can tempt a shy feeder, and it can help a horse flesh out. When a horse is in racing fettle only use a handful to moisten feeds. I find it useful to get salt into a horse by soaking it in salty water. Some horses will take salt readily; others ignore their salt licks; others grind them into their beds (the holders do not work adequately). Do not overdo the concentration of salt or the horse will refuse his feed.

On a horse's day off when he is in hard training and at high levels of feeding, cut his hard rations drastically. It will help him rest internally, help prevent azoturia, and sharpen his appetite for resumed full feeds. Some horses on a very high ration do sometimes go off their feed. I do not recommend the old-fashioned advice to remove all that is uneaten after thirty minutes. I have had horses that will pick away all night. Provided the feed is eventually cleaned up that is all right. However, do not put fresh feed on top of old as souring and fermentation will occur and possibly colic, or rejection of all feed. Occasionally, if a horse continues to eat badly, let him miss a meal or two, but use common sense and do not do this when energy output is at its highest.

The number of feeds per day varies according to amount fed and degree of training. With a full-time job it is not always possible to stick to the old-time best feeding schedule. In early training when the horse is not getting much grain I feed morning and evening with all the hay at night as he is out in the day. Later as feed increases I include a mid-day feed, again haying only at night. In the last stages when he really gets a tremendous amount of grain I feed four times, the last feed just before I go to bed. The mid-day feed is always the smallest.

One point to remember and one that is not generally thought about is that although a feed or grain may state protein content of say 13 per cent, this protein is not the actual amount available to the horse. The total digestible nutrient (TDN) is somewhere about half or a little over of the stated content. You can see why it is important to give the horse only the best hay and grain, as during extremely hard work he will need the protein to repair body tissues.

If you cannot get the quality feeds you would like, although this is unlikely as horse nutrition these days is being catered for far better, be advised by your vet as to a good supplement. I feel good quality feeds in sufficient quantity and variety will supply the horse's needs. Supplements may be good; many will sound marvellous; and many will be wasted on your horse but will convince you he is having the best. By and large they are not vital to his wellbeing. If you have difficulty in getting very good hay see if you can get grass pellets, or lucerne (alfafa) pellets. These are merely dried, compressed grass of excellent quality cut at its nutritional best, and could serve to make sure your horse has the nutrient in the hay department that he needs. He can still be fed some long feed to keep him amused. Oat straw in that case will be just as good or better than poor hay, being freer of dust. If using grass pellets you will not need to feed the full weight plus the full weight of grain plus the long feed. Use common sense in balancing the feeds out. The pellets could be used as a complete food for resting or lightly working horses. A packaged hay, such as the British product HorseHage, is really super feeding value, is totally free of dust, but has two disadvantages. It has to be used within a very short time of breaking the seal on the airtight packaging. Because of this, unless you have more than one horse, it is too expensive to use, as at present the bales only come in approximately half hundredweight sizes which is too much for their limited lifespan after opening and before fermenting.

A last word in this chapter, and one directly related to feeding. Make sure you have a regular worming programme, and do pick dung up from fields. It will lessen the worm burden, improve grazing, and allow your horse to get more value from his feed, not having to share his intake with so many parasites.

19 Tack and saddlery

No matter what equipment you use in any riding activity it should be correctly fitted to the horse, kept in good repair, and clean, particularly the parts in contact with the horse's hide. An endurance horse wearing tack for very long periods is extremely active, which means that constant movement of muscles over the back area will need a supremely well-fitting saddle.

When choosing the ideal saddle several points must be considered. It should be contoured to the horse's back so that correct fit is achieved. The front arch should be clear of the withers by a minimum of two and a maximum of three and half fingers' depth, when the rider is in the saddle. If a saddle is too wide in the gullet it will drop down and the spine will bear the pressure that should be carried by the bars of the saddle. If too narrow it will sit too high, affect the rider's position, and result in the side of the withers and the top of the shoulders being pinched and bruised.

The stuffing should be properly proportioned. Too much in the rear will tip the rider forward, and although weight should be carried over the shoulder section and forehand, too disproportionate a weight there could dig in over the shoulders impeding proper shoulder movement, which in turn could hinder front legs and possibly result in strain. It may also result in pressure over withers causing heat, soreness, friction and so on. Too much stuffing in the front will send the rider back on the cantle, thus putting undue weight over the kidney and loin area which is the weakest part of the horse's anatomy. It will also affect his propulsion.

An incorrectly stuffed saddle could result in saddle movement which will gall a horse. Slight incorrect stuffing is not always at first apparent, as I once learnt to my cost with a saddle that appeared perfect when used in flat country, but on hills the front arch was seen to rock, causing minor chafing over the lower wither and shoulder region. Hill work often reveals inadequacies in saddles, and many of the white patches horses have in the wither area are caused by imperfectly fitting tack when used in constant hill work. This is where a breast-collar is very useful.

During the horse's progressive training period, when he will go from soft to moderate to really hard condition, his wither, shoulder and back areas will show a marked change of shape. The withers will become more prominent as fat fines down. Shoulders will reduce in fat and build up in muscle, and over the back fat too will disappear and muscles become strong and elastic, showing considerable movement under the skin. The saddle that fits at the outset of training may well need adjustment during training. It is useless just to request a re-stuffing or additional stuffing. It is worth paying a little extra and have the saddler come out to see the horse, or take the horse to the saddler.

When asking for a saddle to be *re*stuffed stipulate that you want exactly that, not just packing in additional material jammed in so hard and lumpily it could start pressure bumps on the horse's back. A soft, even-textured material should be used – layered lambswool is recommended by a top saddler, not the mess of carpet fillings that was abstracted from an almost new saddle I had sent in for attention. A saddle should not be stuffed to maximum capacity as this prevents contouring to the horse's back. Preferably the saddle should be used on only one horse, to retain ideal fit. Not only should the saddle fit the horse, but it should be comfortable for the rider and as far as possible aid in maintaining the rider's position.

A rigid tree saddle is stronger than a spring tree, and the bars have a wider bearing surface thus spreading the load better. The thinner width of the spring tree bars are subject to both normal stresses and metal fatigue which could result in a fissure, most often in the front arch, necessitating costly repairs, and in the interim maybe causing damage to the horse's back.

These days very few riders ride without using a saddle pad. These should not be used merely to alleviate pressures of an ill-fitting saddle. Unless the padding is very thick this will not be achieved, and if excessively thick padding is used it may have the effect of forcing the bars apart and thus lowering the saddle on to the horse's spine.

There are many types of pads on the market, with one of the best being dense, cushioned double-pile acrylic fibre with very absorbent qualities. The types with thick foam between cotton twill or mock fleece are not suitable. They are not absorbent and sometimes make the saddle roll. The variety known as 'cool back' pads are specially designed for the job, being highly absorbent and living up to their name. Sheepskin is absorbent, provides fair cushioning, but is difficult to keep clean, as washing can harden the skin and constant use tends to mat the wool into a lumpy texture. Modern techniques are constantly improving and sheepskins are now available that can be washed normally and retain initial qualities, but they are pricey. Nylon, while looking neat and being easily washable, slips and draws the back, allowing no absorption of sweat. Natural wool folded into several thicknesses is very good. The Western saddle padding of felt and hair with a wool blanket over it that can also be used under an English saddle is adequate, absorbent, non-slip and non-drawing, but care should be taken that it is not too thick and that it does not wander under the saddle.

All padding should be kept scrupulously clean. When *in situ* it should be pulled into the arch or gullet so it does not cause pressure on the withers. Natural fibres tend to grip the horse, staying where they are placed. Artificial fibres need fixing methods and the most suitable are velcro fastenings as they stay put.

Very popular in its home in the USA, the Western saddle is also frequently seen on endurance rides in Britain and to some extent in Europe. The previous comments about fitting a saddle to the horse apply. The type of saddle preferred is indi-

vidual, but the tree again falls into three basic types: wide, narrow, or medium gulleted. The bars are of a different shape – more of the back is covered and the weight-carrying surface is spread over a wider area, which is a definite bonus.

All Western saddles should be used with blankets and pads. A thin blanket is insufficient as it will twist and slip. The Western variety of 'cool back' pad is ideal. Also adequate are the felt pads, Navajo blankets, or wool blankets folded to sufficient thickness. The artificial fibre ones are not to be recommended. Keeping most Western pads clean is more difficult than the English variety, as apart from the 'cool back' pads they are not so easily washable, and so great care must be taken in this department.

Points to watch on a Western saddle are that the sheepskin lining of the saddle does not become worn. The saddle strings are fixed through leather conchos into the saddle tree and these, though usually covered by a thin layer of sheepskin (or simulated sheepskin) can cause pressure points on the horse's back if it is a cheaper type of saddle. Some horses tend to be rubbed behind the cantle where the saddle pad moves slightly, usually when the saddle does not fit perfectly and moves across the loin area.

The advantage of a Western saddle is that weight is better distributed. The disadvantages are greater weight and the fact that little air passes through the gullet, as the rear housing is flush with the horse's back. With a horse prone to pressure problems I would accept the extra weight if switching saddles averts the problem.

Some English saddles, when used in steep hill country, rock when going up and down hills. The upward climb sometimes results in the front arch rising while the cantle dips. Going downhill the reverse works. The Western saddle tends to remain in place better over the shoulder, not altering pressures.

Bridles used on endurance horses should be as simple as possible, with a bit that is comfortable and preferably of thick construction, as thin bits can cut, cause abrasions, deaden nerves, and cause tensions which will be reflected in the horse's performance. If fitted too loosely the leather parts of a bridle can chafe, as well as causing the bit to be incorrectly placed in the horse's mouth. If too tight pinching occurs.

An endurance horse will travel differently from others because collection, as basically understood, will be absent. He will be more inclined to reach with head and neck, and there will be great distension of nostrils and windpipe which 'normal collection' can hinder. Particular attention should be paid to noseband and throatlatch so that no constriction is present. These comments do not apply to the horse needing corrective bits or nosebands, as the rider will have to arrive at the solution whereby the horse is under control but not hampered in performance.

Although martingales are used only as corrective measures, mainly on the headcarriage of the horse, I find them handy on a horse that sometimes raises his head in resistance against control. A running martingale prevents this with no fretting on the horse's part. Should a horse get his head too high I find he is far more prone to trip through imbalance than a horse with a lower head carriage.

Breastcollars are very useful and nearly all endurance horses will need one at some time in their competitive careers. They prevent saddles slipping back on steep inclines, as even the best saddle will do if the going is steep enough. There are several types to choose from, and with English equipment the best is the hunting breastcollar which is shaped to the horse, thus preventing breathing restrictions. It also holds its place better. Choose one that has shoulder straps in rounded leather as with these there are no edges to cut or chafe the skin.

They are more expensive than the normal flat variety but well worth the extra cost.

The best Western breastcollars are those that have a slight 'V' at the chest, being contoured to the horse's shape. They should be of reasonable width and lined to soften contact and distribute pressure better when in hill work. The 'V' prevents pressure on the windpipe and allows unimpeded movement. Restriction there could restrict breathing, raise headcarriage, and thus affect the way the horse moves.

The other main pieces of equipment likely to be used in general riding are one of the many types of protective boots – for the hoof, the fetlock, the cannon. Some rules do not permit them, others do, so check the small print. A horse that damages himself badly enough to need protection is not really suitable for the job. Slight brushing can be overcome by the blacksmith, or by muscling up as condition improves. Protective equipment invites the additional hazard of mud or small pieces of grit working between boot and hide, causing friction resulting in penalties and soreness for the horse. If you do use brushing boots do not use felt ones. Almost certainly there will be water to cross en route, and briars will catch more easily on material. Much the same comments apply to horses needing over-reach boots as to those needing brushing boots.

Keep all tack clean, supple, and checked for wear. Bits should be looked to occasionally to make sure no joints are wearing thin and that no movable pieces in contact with the horse are burring against each other, causing sharp edges.

20 The moral issue

Is it right to push our endurance horses to better and faster performances to gratify owners' need to excel, albeit by their horses' ability and willingness to endure stress?

Sport by its very nature is competitive. Even when undertaken by those whose prime aim is just to become proficient and enjoy the stimulus of getting their own body to respond to physical and mental demands, it still has that element of competition because the 'win factor' is how a sportsman's real success is evaluated. This is true whether the sportsman is pitted against other humans or against a set of criteria to aim for. Does he beat his human rivals, or does he lower the score needed to achieve, say, a good round at golf, or stretch his capabilities to their utmost in marathon running, and succeed by crossing that elusive finishing line?

It is only to be expected then that any sport undertaken with horses also becomes competitive, with the horse being the instrument by which the rider either wins or fails. The question at stake is 'Is it right to subject the horse to stress of any sort to fulfil personal ambition?' There will always be a body of people who spend considerable time and energy campaigning for animal rights. Some of these people are doing a very worthwhile job, while others are concerning themselves with issues about which they have only a very sketchy knowledge and therefore are not in a position to criticize or offer valid judgement. Some indeed criticize from the standpoint of complete ignorance!

In the case of the endurance horse it would be a good idea and instructive to lay before the public the arguments for entering our horses into this very demanding sport, and to point out the very many safeguards for their health and wellbeing. Throughout this book there are stories of feats of endurance. All of them show the courage of the horses; some from ancient history have had to show the darker side of the picture, yet others show the bright side of fit healthy horses excelling in a sport which they quite clearly enjoy.

By the category into which it falls – that of sport – endurance riding and its related activities has a prime safeguard. The horse is not expendable, for to succeed the horse must be in good condition and not suffering from undue stress, as the existence of the second condition would be a contradiction of the first. Now I am aware that someone is bound to ask 'What about those horses that do suffer undue stress and thereby do not succeed?' This is a valid question but one that can be more than adequately answered by the fact that the rules under which a horse competes in endurance riding are so structured that from start to finish the horse is monitored by a team of very skilled veterinary surgeons trained to spot incipient stress and to terminate that horse's participation before stress becomes of the 'undue' variety. Stress in itself is not bad. It is merely the term for stretching the limits of physical performance. Every time a human or a horse achieves just that little bit more he has stressed himself just that little bit to achieve the extra.

In the past when horses were used to further man's needs there were undoubtedly instances where cruelty was an inherent part of the process. In general it was not intentional, but of the nature of the undertaking. The horse was necessary to the function, or considered to be so, and because he was necessary he was expendable. Morality did not enter into the issue. When man went to war he was laying his life on the line, and if he was prepared to do so then by implication so was his horse. Man had no other means of transport, and however he must have felt about his horse it was part and parcel of how things were conducted. The rights and wrongs of this use were not considered of paramount importance. Exploration meant furthering man's knowledge of the known world, and new knowledge meant benefits of many kinds to man as a whole – if not material benefits, then more aesthetic ones! Knowledge for the sake of knowledge. Horses would be employed where today mechanical traction or loading capacity would be used. Horses could also go into some geographical situations where early machines lacked the capacity to operate. Again there was no intentional cruelty, even if in the end the result was the same – suffering for man and beast alike.

However, with the rise of modern technology – machinery in all its various permutations from munitions capable of great slaughter but at a distance, to all manner of vehicles capable of operating under almost any conditions – the horse became obsolete in the arenas where he had earlier suffered. Because of technology the horse's future, though thankfully diminished in scope, was a far happier one. The rise of technology had other implications. Much of the drudgery was taken out of everyday life and this affected man and horse. Machines did the work hitherto done by man. The horse was no longer needed for the bone-jarring haulage work in city streets. From being a necessity to the drayman he became a status symbol, a form of advertising and as such shown at his best, and to do this he was kept at his luxurious best. Apart from the dray horses used by the brewery trade and police horses, the horse has almost disappeared from city life.

Technology not only took drudgery out of everyday living, but it permitted the quality of life to improve and the standard of living to rise. In the so-called affluent nations amongst which we must include the major endurance riding countries – the USA, Australia, Great Britain, Germany and France – the rise in living conditions meant that the general populace had both more time and, more importantly, more money to enjoy the increased leisure, never more so than in the last twenty years which is where we come to the emergence of endurance riding as a major sport.

Where man is not crushed by the very struggle for existence, as unhappily still occurs in some underdeveloped countries, the natural instincts of a human being can emerge, and happily one of these is a love of animals. One has only to look at any random group of households and the welfare, and downright spoiling, of the animal inhabitants is very evident. I could give innumerable instances, starting right here at home, where the family pet could quite as easily be called the family tyrant such is the force of the canine, feline, avian or equine personality that is imprinted on the family. The dog must be walked; the cat made comfortable; the bird allowed his freedom-fly of the house; the horse must be fed, exercised, rugged, mucked out; only then may the family's wants be attended to!

Care is the pledge of all but a very few animal owners, and these latter are to be found in any walk of life. Fewest of any will be found in the sphere of endurance riding. The reason? To succeed, not only must the rider have an abiding rapport and consideration, if not love, for his horse, but he must at all times conduct his sport within the horse's capabilities. If any equine sport is lacking in cause for adverse comment, then endurance riding is it. Even training at home must be conducted at such a pitch that the horse has plenty of reserve left in him for competition. With such 'plenty' still available the stress boundaries will not even have been touched upon. In the early days of competition there were undoubted cases of overstressing, but mostly because physiological makeup of the horse under stress was not fully understood. But, right at its modern outset, as outlined in Chapter 21 below, competitors were fully aware that veterinary control was vital. Stress was limited, and in endurance riding there is far less wastage of good horses than in other equine stress sports.

The biggest plus is undoubtedly the veterinary supervision. In one major ride, such as the worldwide 100 milers, a competing horse is likely to receive more expert veterinary examinations and control than the 'backyard horse' will receive in a lifetime. The pre-ride examinations are so detailed that a complete picture of the external and internal horse is logged on the horse's own chart. Throughout any ride there is a constant overseeing of horses. Frequent mandatory stops where horses are checked for stress symptoms, lameness and so on, and given an enforced rest period are part and parcel of any endurance ride. Additionally, roving veterinary surgeons will patrol the course, especially in the later stages of a tough ride. Advice is frequently given by a monitoring veterinary surgeon of the order: 'I would advise dropping your speed and bringing the horse in slowly.' What he is in effect saying is 'do so or I will pull your horse'. The experienced rider knows he had better take the advice. The inexperienced rider does not have a chance to go counter to the advice as he finds it enforced with elimination. Result – undue stress avoided.

Other rules also govern the safety for competing horses. Animals must be of a minimum age – usually five years old before being allowed to compete in the first low mileage events. Riders are not allowed to subject their horses to the rigours of a ride until the horses have had time to mature. Racehorses are not so lucky. Drugs of any nature are absolutely forbidden. The horse must compete 'unaided', if that is the correct word. If there is a weakness the veterinary surgeons want it to show in order to save the horse further stress. Showjumpers on phenylbutazone are not so lucky. Throughout the ride, with the 'spot checks', veterinary surgeons can pinpoint incipient trouble and withdraw a horse. Even eventing, a well-monitored sport in the veterinary department, is not so meticulous. Once passed and committed to a very demanding course there is no official brake on competitors. The eventer goes on to the finish however much stress he is undergoing, and it is only the rider that can pull up if he feels it wise. The showjumper always aims higher and higher, and, although most horses love it, there is nothing official to stop them if they are about to be overfaced, other than a considerate rider. Racing, being an industry, has a tremendous wastage in stressed limbs on very young horses, most being 'past it' when their endurance contemporaries are only just starting their own education, let alone competition, at three and four years of age.

I think that anyone questioning the moral aspect of the sport of endurance riding, once apprised of the facts, can rest assured that in this sport the horse's safety is of paramount importance, and whereas there may be good supervision in other equine sports, in endurance riding there is a double insurance: the love of the rider for his horse, to whom he accords consideration coupled with demands, and the intensive veterinary supervision under which all endurance rides are held.

As a final thought on the morality of the sport you may say: 'But the horse has no choice!' Indirectly he has a considerable influence on whether or not he competes. The good endurance horse has what a good friend, long-time endurance rider and medical doctor calls 'inherited competitive instinct'. Such horses love the action, the tougher the better. Riders owning horses that lack this attribute very quickly settle for either completions, or get a horse that enters into the spirit of the event. It must be remembered that the majority of riders who participate do so because they love the challenge and the companionship. They know only the best are going to be the big winners, but they are content to let their success be decided by whether they have put enough into their horse to get enough out of him just to complete.

The slogan 'To complete is to win', upheld by many of the world's endurance associations, is appropriate. In what other competitive equine sport can success be so measured?

21 Veterinary considerations

As with most equestrian sports endurance riding has changed markedly from its earliest beginnings. The horse, once man's means of transport whether under saddle or harnessed, particularly in the last half century has become man's means of recreation. Along with the pure pleasure of owning a horse and the companionship derived in his company has gone *pride* of ownership. The logical consequence of pride of ownership has been the rise of many forms of equestrian sport to prove 'which is best'.

Endurance and Competitive Trail Riding has had no one birthplace. Many countries have at some stage in their peacetime pursuits staged rides of varying lengths. In the 1930s Britain saw the Country Life 100 mile rides, and as far back as the 1920s the Arab Horse Society was putting their famed horses to the long-distance test. Cavalry of many nations has always put a premium on durability and the endurance factor for its horses, and many breed associations, particularly those in Europe, test their young stallions well and truly in stressful conditions before allowing them to stand at stud. But I think if there is a waymark in time for the emergence of endurance riding as a sport it must be that blazoned by the very first Tevis Cup Ride from Tahoe City to Auburn, California. Pioneered by the late and famous Wendell Robie the first 100-mile Endurance Ride, patterned on the Pony Express feats of yesteryear, was inaugurated on 8 August 1955 under the stringent controls of veterinary surgeon Dr Wheat of the University of California Veterinary School of Medicine.

Under the care of Dr Wheat none of the five horses tackling this first 100 miler suffered undue stress or discomfort, and the pattern was set for future veterinary care on rides in America and subsequently round the world.

The primary aim in any endurance ride is to finish, and to do this the horse must satisfy the veterinary criteria. If at any stage in the event he fails to maintain satisfactory condition the veterinary surgeon will 'pull' the horse in question. He does not wait until the horse is past the point of no return. This has led to endurance riding being regarded as a very safe sport for the horses involved. There are far fewer accidents in endurance riding than in many other equestrian sports where the danger element is present. The rides are tough and challenging, but overall within the capability of horses entered. Some countries have a grading system whereby horses may not attempt the longer rides until they have proved themselves at shorter distances. No country permits entry of immature animals into situations too stressful for their development to bear. Most countries require a horse to be five years of age to compete even in the lower echelons of the sport, and for the longer rides a minimum of six years is necessary. Britain in particular requires 100-mile entrants to be seven years old.

Many factors determine the suitability of a horse for endurance riding and a correspondingly long list of criteria determine how the veterinary judging goes, but the prime factors in assessing a competing horse's ability to start, continue, and receive his eventual completion award are governed by his achieving a satisfactory heart-rate reading and by his locomotor function being adequate, or sound. Respiratory function is high on the list of criteria, as is temperature in climates where this can become more relevant than in temperate or cool areas. In addition trauma, or wounds, stiffness, state of hydration, equipment lesions or abrasions, and fatigue all have their place in assessing whether an endurance horse is fit. In the evaluation of a Competitive Trail horse they determine not only

13 The horse must achieve a satisfactory heart-rate reading to be allowed to continue. Sally Scorey's Squire Tebeldi at a vet check.

whether he is fit to continue but what place he shall eventually take in the final order of finishers.

In 1955 and for many years after, though stringent in their application the criteria were merely that. They kept the sports geared to the horses' welfare and prevented adverse situations developing. Riders knew that to win they had not only to produce a fit horse to start with, but to ride it with extreme consideration throughout if they expected to get past the finish line.

The first Tevis Cup sparked off great interest in the sport and from that date in 1955 it has never looked back. It caught the imagination of the rider who was not interested in the 'formal' aspects of competition but nevertheless wanted to test his horse both against the conditions of the ride and against those of other competitors. It also presented the veterinary profession with the perfect gift – horses performing under maximum stress in

increasing numbers, while at the same time being safeguarded from overexertion and abuse. As one veterinary surgeon friend put it to me, it was 'the opportunity of seeing fit and healthy animals, not the sick ones we usually see'. Study into the physiology of the endurance horse naturally followed.

Though the ultimate responsibility lies with the rider veterinary surgeons were quick to act in horses' interests, but inevitably in feats of endurance various deleterious syndromes became apparent while the horses were under stress. The main plus factor was that being under monitored conditions the stresses could be ameliorated by veterinary intervention in pulling horses. The other advantage was that veterinary surgeons became increasingly interested in how to enhance the horses' chances of success. This led to further research into various elements used in the evaluation criteria of a fit or unfit endurance horse.

With the research came the knowledge that to-day's endurance rider finds so invaluable. It is no longer enough to have a horse that is fit and eager. Today's rider can not only make a study of how to train his horse to maximum fitness and efficiency, but he can understand what actually affects his horse for either good or bad. This has led to better performances with new records for tough rides constantly being set, at the same time without hazarding the horses' health.

The main areas where knowledge is now more freely available to the rider is in the various criteria used in the veterinary examinations that are part of every competitive ride. Along with knowing more about what makes an endurance horse tick, treatment of fatigued horses has greatly improved. Veterinary surgeons can now more readily recognize imminent danger and treat horses on the spot. From the riders' stance, training can now be undertaken in a more systematic manner with the riders knowing what clinical effect such training can have. Also through research, particularly into the use of electrolytes, the horse's diet can be better geared to his energy expenditure requirements, and to the absorption or, when depleted, the replacement of valuable trace elements in a balanced manner.

The United States of America has undoubtedly led the field in research into the endurance horse's performance – a natural succession in a country where the sport is of really outstanding proportions, both quantitive and qualitative. Australia follows hard on its heels. There the number of rides may not be as great – their much smaller population would hardly sustain the American involvement – but the nature of some of their rides is certainly of equal standard in both severity and quality of horses entered. Britain, where the sport took much longer to catch on but where it is now one of the major equestrian disciplines, has a continuing research programme in several areas connected with endurance riding. It is thanks to the help of Dr David Snow, BSc, BVSc, PhD, MRCVS, from the Newmarket Equine Research Station of the Animal Health Trust that some of the most up-to-date papers on subjects related to the endurance horse have been made available to me.

The veterinary control at rides

Over the years it has always been necessary for a team of veterinary surgeons to be present at long distance rides of any competitive nature. Initially it was on a less formal basis, but experience has taught that running a very tight veterinary ship is absolutely vital. I do not think the veterinary recommendations of James H. Steere, DVM, MS, Hyg., of Novato, California, can be bettered. He has looked at every angle of the veterinary side of endurance riding and written very concise requirements for the successful running of a good ride.

His advice to a Head Ride Veterinarian includes undertaking the selection of the other veterinary surgeons oneself, and giving them plenty of warning of date, type of event, drugs and equipment necessary. A contract setting out the terms of their employment, duties, fees and so on is included when they are first asked to officiate. He recommends that the Head Veterinarian involve himself with ride management in all phases of the ride where health and safety of horses is indicated, and to that end advises him to check the venue personally and to ensure that water, and a safe area for the start, are provided. Best placement for en route veterinarians is his responsibility, as is familiarizing himself with the route, which he should reconnoitre on horseback or by vehicle. He also ensures adequate water is available for horses at every checkpoint. A Head Ride Veterinary Surgeon is responsible for briefing assistant veterinary surgeons and student veterinary surgeons as to ride procedure, and in the case of students making sure they are capable of the job they are to perform, though they are at the rides only in an assisting capacity and no final decisions will be taken by them. It is one way in which the rides can pay back a little to the veterinary profession by giving students on-the-spot field experience. He also makes sure that transport and well-oriented drivers are available to get veterinary surgeons to vital checkpoints, as in the past this has been found somewhat of a hazard.

Before the ride the Head Veterinarian also briefs the competitors, introducing the veterinary surgeons and students; warns of any trail hazards;

explains the veterinary examination and recovery criteria, and the final assessment of the horse's ability to proceed. He will explain his duties in relation to caring for the horses, but makes it crystal clear that the onus is on the rider to ride with care and consideration for his/her mount bearing in mind the terrain, the ambient temperature and the humidity. Advice is given on lay-over care at each checkpoint, and a caution issued to riders not to try to confuse the veterinary surgeon, if in his opinion the horse is under stress, by denying it and claiming it to be the horse's natural attitude. He reassures contestants that it is the veterinary surgeon's aim to get all horses through, but that failing condition will ensure elimination as will definite lameness. Suspect lameness will not, unless confirmed later. Advice is also given on how to cope in the event of trouble arising during the ride and out on the trail.

Much of the veterinary side of the ride consists of meticulous attention to pre-ride detail, especially to organizing and distributing a chart to all participating veterinary surgeons and ride management showing where and when each veterinary surgeon will be throughout the ride with due allowances made for a spread of time between expected time of arrival and actual time of arrival and departure. Veterinary surgeons are instructed on examination procedure and given a complete list of essential equipment to carry with them during the ride itself.

Dr Steere leaves nothing to chance and the very fact that such meticulous preparation is adhered to by the veterinary profession should give all riders a great sense of security.

Fatigue

[This section draws on work by Prof. G. P. Carlson.] From among many aspects of what makes the endurance equine perform to optimum standard various clinical states have been observed and studied. A general term for one of the most common disorders seen on endurance rides is that named 'Exhaustive Disease Complex'. Under this general heading come several individual disorders, some of which are closely linked. They include depression, dehydration, lack of interest in food or water, muscle cramps, shallow respiration, colic, and various cardiac and respiratory problems which include synchronous diaphragmatic flutter, or thumps.

Dehydration occurs when the horse sweats excessively, and along with the fluid loss goes loss of important electrolytes and a subsequent imbalance of the finely tuned proportions of these electrolytes, namely sodium, chloride, potassium, calcium and magnesium. According to the severity of the loss the exhaustive condition becomes apparent in escalating degrees, but owing to the nature of the veterinary control on endurance rides it is rare for horses to reach an advanced stage of exhaustion, the veterinary surgeon being aware of the problem in its early stages. An early warning sign to the rider is a combination of delayed capillary refill time (pinch test), and high heart and respiratory rates with a refusal of the rates to decrease rapidly on cessation of work. It has been found that though all horses sweat, other than those suffering from anhydrosis or the inability to sweat, the further into fluid deficit they go the greater the manifestations.

In early stages the officiating veterinary surgeon will hold horses up until pulse, respiration, and temperature have decreased and then allow the competitor to proceed with a caution to watch for any recurring signs. If the horse in question does not respond to rest, liquid and food, but maintains elevated rates, and additionally appears depressed and uninterested in either food or water, he is in need of treatment. All endurance ride veterinary surgeons now carry the necessary equipment to administer either stomach or intravenous fluid and electrolyte replacement. The most severe depletion is usually that of water and sodium, and rapid replacement is called for of plasma and extracellular fluid volume. The most favoured remedy is Ringer's Lactate Solution to which potassium is added. With horses with low blood sugar glucose can also be added to the intravenous fluid. Response in most cases is rapid and evidenced by accelerated capillary refill time, and lowering of pulse and respiration rates. If the horse is in an advanced state of exhaustion and provided signs do not indicate imminent colic, the same solution via stomach tube may be given. As therapy proceeds the packed cell volume and the total plasma protein concentrations reduce to normal, but sodium usually remains unaltered. Depression lifts and normal eating and drinking usually follow, succeeded by urinating as the fluid content becomes adequate. Once the horse is out of the exhausted state he can bring the balance of his electrolyte level back to normal by adequate eating, obtaining the needed elements from his rations. The addition of dextrose in the solution will raise the blood glucose to normal, thus supplying the brain and other glucose-dependent organs adequately, but it will not replace the energy that has been totally depleted.

Synchronous diaphragmatic flutter (SDF)

[This section draws on work by R. J. Rose.] SDF is seen fairly frequently in endurance horses, more so in those performing in very hot climates. It is the result of contraction of the diaphragm synchronous with the heartbeat. It manifests itself by a tic in the horse's flank, but is not related to the horse's respiration. Although by itself SDF is not considered dangerous it is indicative of, and in fact often goes with, electrolyte imbalance and the fatigue syndrome. Consequently if apparent during a ride at any of the mandatory stops en route the veterinary surgeon will feel it wise to pull the horse from the competition. SDF also occurs in horses not showing any signs of fatigue and in this case most commonly when the horse has finished the ride and is being cooled out.

The disorder can be readily treated by fluid given intravenously and containing the depleted electrolytes associated with the condition, such as calcium, magnesium, phosphate and glucose. Diluted with saline or dextrose the intravenous fluid can be more rapidly and safely given.

Unfortunately some horses are more affected by SDF than others, and the condition shows itself whenever the horse is put under stress – in this I am thinking of horses known to me who appear to be good endurance prospects in all other aspects but on many occasions, while passing all other criteria, are frequently eliminated on this one

count alone. Giving an electrolyte supplement containing chloride, potassium and sodium during the ride will help prevent a major electrolyte imbalance. Some horses also benefit from addition of calcium and magnesium. It is thought that a diet high in calcium predisposes some horses to SDF. They become reliant on calcium being rapidly absorbed through diet and made readily available. Under stress conditions the intake is non-existent and the stress-associated release of adrenal hormones blocks calcium mobilization from that stored in the bone. Thus denied the horse quickly goes into calcium deficit. It has been recommended that horses with a recurring SDF problem should not be fed a diet high in calcium just prior to a ride, thus forcing the body to call on the reserves before the stress suppresses the source. Therefore if they cease to be so dependent on intake of calcium it is hoped that the problem will be avoided or at least curtailed.

Muscle fatigue

Muscle fatigue is the most common cause of 'running out of steam' in most endurance horses, and much research has been done in this field, in particular in Britain by Dr David Snow from the Equine Research Station at Newmarket. Muscle fibre types have a direct bearing on the performance ability of a horse, and it is considered that they are genetically inherited. Unfortunately it is not, at this stage, possible to pick a winner solely by considering the structure of his muscle fibres, although some indication of potential could certainly be given.

There are basically two main types of muscle fibre, the slow contracting (slow twitch) and the fast contracting (fast twitch), and each muscle has these types of fibre in varying degrees.

The proportion of these two fibres is important in determining the force and frequency of limb movement. However, to maintain repeated contraction of these fibres the ability to utilize oxygen is very important. This is because when fuels are burnt to provide energy, in the presence of oxygen water and carbon dioxide are produced, while in the absence of oxygen lactic acid, which when it builds up is toxic to the cell, is produced. Normally all slow twitch fibres have a high capacity to utilize oxygen, thus making them very fatigue-resistant and able to continue contracting for long periods of time. On the other hand the fast twitch fibres have a varying capacity to utilize oxygen, some being nearly as fatigue-resistant as the slow twitch, others with low oxidative capacity being rapidly tired when used. The proportion of slow to fast twitch fibres is essentially genetically determined, whereas the ability to utilize oxygen is greatly influenced by training. It has been found that the best endurance horses have a higher proportion of slow twitch fibres than, say, sprinting Thoroughbreds. They have also developed a high oxidative capacity in both slow and fast twitch fibres. These characteristics thus bestow on them the ability to maintain fairly high speeds, although lower than those breeds having other fibre characteristics important for power development such as animals under track racing conditions.

When muscles contract they utilize fuels to produce the required energy. In the horse the two main fuels are glucose and fatty acids. The former comes from the glycogen stored within the muscle fibres themselves, and also that brought by the blood from the liver. The latter is mainly derived from the fat stores located throughout the body. From there the fatty acids are released and transported to working muscles. The proportion of glucose and fatty acids used by the muscle varies according to speed and fitness. The utilization of fuels is very important in considering the prime cause of fatigue in endurance animals. In the well-trained horse, fatigue should not come about by the production of lactic acid but rather the loss of glycogen within muscle fibres. This then leaves some of the fibres without adequate fuel to provide sufficient energy for contraction, which results in the horse having to reduce speed.

Proper training leading to improved fitness should enhance the ability of the muscle fibres to utilize oxygen, and therefore allow more muscle fibres to be used without producing lactic acid. Another very favourable effect is to increase the muscles' ability to burn fatty acids to produce energy. This leads to what is referred to as a 'glycogen sparing effect' and allows the horse to work at the same speed for a longer period of time than before it was well trained.

An endurance horse extraordinaire

Kansas State University Veterinary School has set up an exercise physiology programme to determine what makes super equines perform to such high standards. The main prop for this programme is a Sato high-speed treadmill, made in Sweden, and capable of making horses produce speeds of over 30 mph. Though racehorses, especially Quarter Horse sprinters, had been tested, a remarkable ten-year-old purebred Arabian called Dana's North Lite, owned by Mary Koefed, was its first endurance guinea pig. [Experiments reported by E. Kilby in *Equus Magazine*, August 1986.]

Using the treadmill it is possible to make cardiovascular studies of horses under stress and Dana's North Lite had a history of excellence in 50- and 100-mile rides, being able to clip off 50 in less than three hours and 100 in under eight and a half. It was hoped to find out what made him tick.

The main benefits of work on the treadmill are that biochemical changes can be registered while they are happening, not immediately after movement has ceased, enabling pertinent data to be collated. Electrodes glued to the head, withers and girth line picked up electrical impulses that triggered the heart's mechanism and in turn transmitted them to the electronic data recorder. Nearly continuous blood sampling was made available by a catheter with its tip placed in the jugular vein at the right atrium, where blood returning from the head and body enter the heart. Blood temperature was recorded by another catheter in the jugular vein just above the heart. This held a thermistor and wire leading back to the recorder. Right at the outset it appeared that the Arabian generated less heat while under stress than other animals previously tested. The treadmill test, devised to simulate racing conditions, involved putting the horse on the treadmill for two minutes at two metres per second (approx 4½ mph or walking pace), then elevating the speed to 10 metres per second and maintaining that for two minutes (21½ mph or a strong gallop). Blood was taken before, during and after exercise.

Following on the treadmill tests and sampling, the Arabian was then tested in the field over a ten-mile distance at a gallop, regulating the gallop to the desired heart rate. Prior to and immediately after the gallop was completed temperature, heart rate, respiration rate, blood samples and muscle biopsies were taken. The latter especially would determine how much his fuel supply had been eroded and how well the muscles had utilized the oxygen and glycogen.

It was hoped that the results of the laboratory and field tests would show why the Arabian was such a super endurance horse.

Taking it as normal that such an athlete was operating efficiently, with sufficient oxygen being transported by healthy lungs, it was determined that the main elements of the sustained aerobic work were his cardiovascular system, his muscles, and his ability to eliminate waste. To have some means of comparison two other horses, both Arabians, were also monitored throughout. They were both endurance horses – one past and one novice, but nevertheless suitable for comparison. When correlating data it was found that Dana's North Lite was not markedly different to the others, only ahead by a few per cent here and there, but the sum total did add up to a considerable benefit that showed his superiority.

On the treadmill at maximum output Dana's North Lite's heart registered 218 beats per minute whereas the other horses' hearts registered 200. At first glance this could be interpreted as his heart being less efficient than the others, but owing to the exceptional facility for recording data it was found that Dana's North Lite's heart muscles became markedly thicker than those of the other horses. During the systolic phase the contracting muscle showed marked increase in thickness and squeezed down to almost zero, whereas in comparison the others did not show nearly so great a change. Dana's North Lite's heart was much more powerful in ejecting the blood to the system. Also the duration of each pumping contraction indicated that a great supply of blood was getting through. What emerged from the tests was that the top endurance horse will have an extremely muscular heart of normal size with exceptional contractility, prolonged stroke and a relatively high rate. Although appearing to break the rule of thumb that slow and larger is better, it showed that the better ejection effect allied to faster rate gave greater volume than a less efficient heart. In the recovery phase Dana's North Lite also showed superiority. The inherited mechanism is enhanced by a tough but safe training regime.

The next consideration and comparison was the supply of oxygen transported in the blood via the red blood cells. Although the other horses used in the test had a larger volume of red blood cells than Dana's North Lite, he for his part showed a greater haemoglobin content to each red cell thus enabling more oxygen to be transported. Additionally the plasma volume in Dana's North Lite's blood exceeded that of the other tested horses, making for a thinner consistency and therefore an easier flow carrying the vital oxygen around the body. It also meant that Dana's North Lite could lose more fluid in sweat before blood viscosity impaired performance. Dehydration effects would be delayed for many miles. At start of work Dana's North Lite needed fewer red cells in circulation, and though increased activity demanded higher concentration, cessation of work saw his recovery to be far more rapid than the horses with lower haemoglobin content in the red cells. Conclusions were that his better performance in the oxygen department came from enhanced blood volume with increased plasma giving a thinner mix and therefore delaying the onset of dehydration; a higher haemoglobin content in the red blood cells, and fewer red cells needed to supply less stressful work, and a more rapid recovery when the workload decreased. Heredity determines blood composition with training enhancing the use the horse is able to make of it.

In the muscle or power department it was found that Dana's North Lite had a greater percentage of slow twitch oxygen-using fibres than the other horses tested, predisposing him to superior endurance powers. Though his sprint muscles were on the low side they were sufficient to power a dash for the line at the end of a prolonged race. Again heredity had well endowed Dana's North Lite. Throughout the tests the lactic acid build up in Dana's North Lite was far less than in the other Arabians involved, and very much less than Quarter Horses previously tested. His ability to eliminate wastes so efficiently was the result of training, as was the ability to utilize to maximum efficiency all the inherited factors – a more efficient heart, better blood composition, endurance-oriented muscle fibre mix. Dana's North Lite was an athlete waiting to be found. His fortune was to be owned and trained by a person dedicated to a sport he was to excel in.

Though horsemen have long recognized when they have 'a good 'un', it is only with research into the physiology of the endurance horse that we are beginning to understand why these 'good 'uns' are such athletes. As the sport gets more demanding and interest grows apace, it is imperative that right selection allied to right training are aimed at from the start. Medical science can offer an insurance policy. It is up to the rider to pay the premium of careful choice, right diet, methodical training and calculatedly careful competition.

Thou, Oh Nashuan, were irreproachable, and without reproach has past away to those already gone.

By thy generous nature thou hast endured every test, for endurance is the test of generosity.

The poet Abu Bekr (early fourteenth century) on a favourite Arab horse

Sentiments expressed more than 600 years ago are still relevant today. Abu Bekr's succinct description of the endurance of his favourite Arab steed is also one that epitomizes the modern picture of the Arabian endurance horse all over the world today.

Throughout the centuries, wherever toughness of body and spirit of mind have been sought, the Arabian has been the choice of countless riders – military men equipping their forces with remounts; talent scouts searching for that racing certainty for the Roman Circus; emissaries seeking to please potentates; travellers needing a surefooted, durable companion. Tribute to the Arabian has been paid in poetry, military acclaim, sculpture, art. He has touched the emotions more than any other breed, for the Arabian combines beauty, speed, intelligence, durability, and force of character in larger measure than, in this author's opinion, any other breed alive. I know that a similar opinion is also held by a very large proportion of the world's endurance riders, and frequently by panels of veterinary surgeons who have learnt that the tough little desert descendant is more than likely going to be their choice of the day.

This opinion was also held by the forerunners of today's endurance riders, because in both America and England there have been precedents for Arabian supremacy.

In Britain in the years 1920–2 the Arab Horse Society held 300-mile endurance rides. Spaced out over five days the horses covered 60 miles on consecutive days. In the three years of the race two horses especially distinguished themselves. Shazada, initially owned by C. Edmunds and subsequently by S. C. Hough, won the race in 1920 and 1922, and in the intervening year was second to the grey mare Belka, who had been third in 1920. In her winning year Belka turned in a cumulative time many hours ahead of her rival. Shazada proved that a performance horse is also deserving of high show honours, as in his later years he repeatedly won the Arabian Championships in Sydney, Australia. I wonder how many of Australia's present-day endurance Arabians can trace their pedigree back to this superb horse who now has a similar five-day, 250-mile ride commemorating his earlier English victories.

Similar endurance races were being held in America and one of the two outstanding horses of the era was Ramla, a mare bred at the famous Crabbet Stud, who won her American race of 310 miles carrying 14½ stone (203 lb). (In the 'pedigree game' I have been able to trace my own Nizzolan back and he carries crosses to the same lines as Ramla through Astraled on both sire and dam's sides, so his long-distance career was a case of the right horse waiting for the opportunity to happen!) The other was another Crabbet horse named for the stud he came from. Crabbet had a long string of successes in endurance races, including one of 98 and another of 100 miles in 1918 carrying 14½ stone, and in 1921 he won the 310 mile race carrying a record weight of 17½ stone (245 lb). After Crabbet's win he was denied entry the next year, with the humiliating experience for the other entrants and the organizers who failed to achieve a single finisher. Eventually the race was discontinued as being too severe. For many years the

143

14 Belka, winner of the 1921 300–mile endurance ride. (Arab Horse Society Trust Collection)

sport of endurance riding lay dormant. Arabians had classed themselves out of competition, others not being willing to pit their less enduring talents against them. A point well worth noting, particularly in relation to Britain where the lightweight versus heavyweight capabilities of horses raged far too long, is that each horse in these truly epic races carried far in excess of what is even nowadays considered the heavyweight division.

Portugal claims the longest pre-modern endurance era race on record of 1200 miles, and this was won by Emir, a partbred Arabian bred by Ruy Andrade. Emir's sire was from the Blunt stock and he came from their stud maintained near Cairo in Egypt.

In the reference section of this book where each country's greats are depicted, the selection of

horses is not biased because of the author's personal choice. The fact that again and again nations' top endurance horses are representatives of the Arabian breed – mostly purebreds, followed by a host of able partbred Arabians and Anglo-Arabs – is no mistake either. Nor is it a chance happening because this horse, more than any other, has at last found his proper niche in the world of modern equine sports competition. He can finally be accorded the triumphs he deserves in open competition because winners are judged solely on capability, and no preference as to type, looks or conformation is allowed to influence a judge's choice in Competitive Trail Riding. In Endurance Riding the results speak for themselves.

I have owned (or been owned by!) Arabians for more than twenty years, starting off as so many do with a super partbred from whom I caught the disease of Arabitis. The cure was a stronger dose of owning purebreds, and it was while finding my way into the long-distance riding scene in the American East Coast 100 milers that I became more aware of how right it was that I had opted for full commitment. Repeatedly, no matter what weight they were carrying, and some carried well into the 225 lb plus category; what countryside they traversed; nor what level of experience their riders had in the sport, Arabians were filling the majority of available places and frequently earning ride championship honours. As I said, I was only starting out in the sport and the Florida Ride of 1967 was my penultimate American 100 miler before I returned to England, and my little Arab stallion Royal Command gave me my first 100-mile placing award. Out of twelve places (six each in the lightweight and heavyweight divisions), seven were filled by pure Arabs, and one by a partbred Arab, with championship and reserve championship going to the partbred and a purebred respectively.

On returning to England it was to find that the sport that was already flourishing in America was only in its infancy in England, and in those early days not very much was known about it. With only a meagre handful of 40-mile qualifiers and one 75-mile final Golden Horseshoe Ride a year, there was insufficient evidence to point to any particular trend in the British side of the sport. However, by the time the yearling Arabian colt I had brought with me had grown up and was old enough to participate in his first Golden Horseshoe in 1972, the picture was rapidly changing. A brief look at the results from the years 1972 to 1975 will give some idea of how the Arabian was doing in this by now prestigious event, both as an individual and taken alongside other breeds.

The 1972 ride drew seventy starters, of which thirty-eight finished; of the four gold awards three went to purebred Arabs; of the twenty silver, six went to Arabs and partbreds, and out of the thirteen bronze awards one went to a partbred. More important from a statistical viewpoint is that out of the thirty horses who were eliminated for a variety of reasons, only five carried Arabian blood. In 1973 forty-one horses were presented, seven golds

awarded, thirteen silver and five bronze, and thirteen horses eliminated. Others went for the completion only rosette. Arabs won five golds and two silvers. Out of the thirteen eliminated none carried Arabian blood. In 1974 forty started, with eleven golds, eight silvers, five bronzes and sixteen eliminations. Arabs won six golds, two silvers, one bronze, and only one Arabian was eliminated. In 1975 the field was the biggest ever, with twenty-five golds awarded. However, the programme for this year did not list the horses' breeding, but out of the twenty-five golds I know at least eight were Arabian, and out of the eleven silver at least five were of Arabian blood. This itself is not too indicative of the superiority of the Arabian breed, but since then in Britain they have continued to prove themselves. They show remarkable consistency with a very high percentage of wins, and always feature in Britain's two endurance riding societies' table of top horses.

When the Endurance Horse and Pony Society (EHPS) of Great Britain was formed it grew very rapidly. So much so that by its second full year it instituted a Leading Horse Championship, the Manar Trophy, and by its fourth year it also had a Novice Championship, the Goodwood Trophy. In addition to the plethora of trophies offered to just about all levels of distance ride achievements, the other two most important trophies are the Jasper Trophy for the Leading Competitive Trail Horse of the Year, and the Adonis Trophy for the Leading Endurance Horse of the Year. Both these trophies count the best three scores of entered horses. Both are named for partbred Arabians who were themselves top flight endurance horses owned by the Nicholson family who did so much in the early years to promote British endurance riding.

Arabian successes in these four categories have been:

In thirteen years of the Open Championship, seven wins and four reserves.

In eleven years of the Novice Championship, eight wins and seven reserves.

In eleven years of the Competitive Trail Horse trophy, seven wins.

In ten years of the Endurance Horse trophy, seven wins.

These results are from literally hundreds of horses entered in the rides through each competitive season. There are years when Arabians and their kin do not win and others take centre stage for a deserved share of the limelight – great horses such as Tarquin and Nimrodel – but over the years it is unusual not to see the name of Arabians featured strongly in the major awards at the end of each year.

When it comes to Britain's 100 milers, whether the one, two, or three day variety, Arabians have inevitably led the way. Nizzolan, the only purebred Arabian entered in Britain's first 100 miler in 1975, set the ball rolling, and of the other five places behind him the second and fourth places were filled by a partbred and an Anglo-Arab respectively. Nizzolan held the record for nine years until it was broken by another Arabian, the superb little chestnut from Wales, Tarim, who clipped his 100 off in nine hours and forty-nine minutes.

From the records of the first eight seasons of the EHPS the society's archivist, the late Robin Nicholson, published a table giving mileages and placings. Out of the top thirty horses, nine were of pure and ten were of part and Anglo-Arab breeding.

Though for the most part gaining the bulk of my long distance riding experience in Britain I was fortunate to start in America which holds world supremacy, mainly I think because of their lack of strict formality coupled with the need still to use and therefore appreciate the working horse. Hard on their heels comes Australia, which also still uses horses in a real work sense and is blessed by a similar lack of conservative narrowness. There the Arabian quickly came into his own, his rider untrammelled by external niggling rules, and where it is truly what your horse does that is the sole criteria.

At home in Britain and when talking or writing to long-distance riders their most frequent choice is the Arabian. Maybe they have a partbred Arabian and see their successful future aboard a purebred; or admiration of the effortless ease which Arabians possess while turning in winning performances influences their choice. The comfort; inherent soundness; plus the bonus of the 'Hey! Look at me. Aren't I great?' attitude of Arabians at work all go to mark the breed as the horse for the job. Records in England speak for themselves. Britain loves its partbreds of any breed; its unregistered animals; its tough native ponies and their various crosses. For a great many riders these are the stepping stones to the longed-for Arabian. Whatever the distance Arabians seem to do well, but the further they are stretched the more they seem capable of – one reason they seem to shine in the longer, faster endurance rides.

Long treated as 'pretty faces' they came late in our century to their deserved rank. For too long their beauty was paraded here in Britain as their *raison d'être*; in America too to some extent, although there they achieved recognition somewhat earlier. In Britain they were prevented from really showing their class by two main factors. The majority of riders who merely wanted a horse to ride just could not afford the Arabian, much as they might desire him. For a long time he was priced out of sight for the weekend or trail rider. Then there was prejudice – unfortunately it was there, and still is in remaining unenlightened quarters. The vast majority of the ultra-conservative hunting and showing fraternity would tag the breed as those 'pretty and silly Arabs'. On occasions when an Arabian challenged their 'set beliefs' the comment would be 'Oh, well he's an exception, isn't he?' It was a phrase I was to hear many many times, and no doubt others can echo my experiences.

I know when I brought Nizzolan home to England as a yearling in 1968 and later started riding and competing with him in open competition there were some very odd comments passed. One that does stick in my mind was from a Thoroughbred breeder who was judging a riding horse class. After putting Nizzolan first, she passed the sour comment: 'I had to place him first because he did everything I asked, but I don't consider you can ride an Arab all day!!!' It was also found very strange that a stallion standing at stud with a full book of mares would also engage in a very full round of ridden activities. It is still difficult to succeed with an Arabian in open showing competition, except under totally unbiased and unprejudiced judges. Erroneous ideas die hard and in some quarters the Arabian still carries the tag of 'pretty face'. At the root is often a hint of jealousy that the 'pretty face' is also a very good performer and certainly representative of a whole breed.

Fortunately in Britain, and concurrently in other countries with their own Arab Horse Societies, our Arab Horse Society has done a lot to dispel false notions and an equal amount of promotion of their special horse into the world of true performance. They were jointly responsible for many of the earlier Golden Horseshoe Rides and alongside their show shop window have also instituted areas where they actively encourage their breed as a tough, fast distance campaigner. At every major ride some member of the AHS hierarchy can be seen encouraging the Arabian owners. They have taken a very active part in promoting the sport of long distance riding. Ronald Kydd, three times President of the Arab Horse Society, was a long-standing member of the EHPS Committee and since 1982 has been the Vice Chairman of the European Long Distance Rides Conference (ELDRIC). He also chaired the joint AHS/British Horse Society Golden Horseshoe Ride Committee and his wife Rachel has a wealth of knowledge on Arabians in endurance riding, a knowledge she regularly shares in literary works.

Additionally the AHS also runs annual long-distance events – their highly acclaimed Marathon Ride held in the autumn at a changing venue is always run at a high rate of knots. The winners turn in times of just over an hour and a half for the twenty-six miles, even when it is run in conditions such as the treacherous combes, bogs and tracks of Exmoor and often in a deluge of rain, wind and holding mud – it does not seem blessed with the somewhat better weather of mid-season's events. Their other venture has been the exciting Ride and Tie race – a relative newcomer to Britain but one that raised considerable support, though here I do not think it depends so much on the Arabians' endurance as those of the runners/riders, particularly the former.

There have been many other factors going to make up the present-day platform for Arabian acceptance and integration into the general riding fraternity, and one of the most important is that financial rewards for the 'man in the street' wage-earner are infinitely better than a couple of decades ago. The formation of societies specifically geared to long distance riding has come about, in Britain at least, because the trail rider wanted such societies, and their rapid growth from a few dozen members to four-figure participation in a decade shows that the powers that be have finally realized, even in our conservative society, that riders must have outlets for activities they wish to pursue, rather than be fobbed off with what is available. With the new outlets and the increasing amount of leisure and money to go with it the average rider who dreamed of his purebred Arabian can now own one, particularly as there has been a welcome levelling of prices so that the Arabian is now just as available and at a price comparable to that asked for any other breed.

When Britain sends a team abroad to compete in the European Distance Rides there is nearly always a preponderance of Arabians or part Arabians making up the team. And for that matter in Europe as a whole Arabians again and again come up trumps in the various national ratings. To illustrate this very briefly what better than to take the very first 1986 world championships, with a look at the top ten placings and the team awards. Gold and silver medal winners were the Americans, Cassandra Schuler and Jeanne Waldron, riding two Arabians, Shiko's Omar and Cher Abu. Third was Drago, the unregistered German horse ridden by Bernhard Dornsiepen, fourth was Val Long riding her Arabian stallion Tarim. Of the teams, Britain took gold with three out of the four team members on Arabians. America took silver, again with Arabians, and France bronze with Kamir, ridden by Francoise Rimbaud, and Melik, ridden by Michel Laracine, both Arabians. Out of the top ten, six were Arabians.

It was no surprise that America fielded Arabians because their national ratings are dominated by the breed. One of their national greats (see p. 258) is Witezarif ridden by Donna Fitzgerald, whose partnership as multiple winners of the Tevis Cup will surely be unassailable for many years. The Tevis Cup itself in all the years since its first run in 1955 has only been won by non-Arabians twice.

The same pattern occurs 'down under' and I am

15 Ride and Tie. Nigel Clarke and Steve Sowerby winning the AHS Levi competition with Shaaban in 1981. (Peter R. Sweet)

indebted to Patsie Sinfield who furnished me with details of Australia's top ten. Out of that number, seven carried Arabian blood, mostly being part-breds, including the leader in competitive miles covered which is her own mule Juanita who is out of a partbred Arabian mare. Again the selection was not random or biased but taken from those equines achieving the highest honours in Australia.

South Africa also follows a similar pattern, her endurance riding history being strong in the numbers of top Arabians competing. Her current results lists show a preponderance of Arabians leading the field, with nine out of the top ten in their latest National Championship Fauresmith Ride being of Arab blood, while the Best Condition awards on a nationwide ride basis again prove Arabian ability.

Europe, or the ELDRIC which is the governing European distance riding organization, has a majority of Arabians in their International Awards each year. The European Championships have been awarded since 1980 and initially Arabians did not feature too strongly in the list of winners, largely due to that tough little British Appaloosa Fforest Orchid who swept the board for two years. In the first three years Arabians achieved only two third places, but now with more and more countries joining the ELDRIC there is a growing number of riders and horses eligible for international honours. Considering the very large number of breeds taking part in the expanding European scene it is to the Arabian's credit that he is taking an ever-larger share of the limelight – or is it that riders are feeling 'If you can't beat them get one?' In 1983 an Arabian

was equal first for the European Championship; in 1984 only a third place was achieved; but in 1985 Arabians took second and third places, and in 1986 they had a clean sweep of the first three places. The ratings go considerably lower than the first three places and among the minor placings approximately 50 per cent carry varying degrees of Arabian blood.

So it seems that from amongst the dozens of breeds available, particularly in Europe, the Arabian and his part and Anglo brethren are the most sought after mounts, whether it is for the highly competitive field of Endurance or Competitive Trail riding, for pleasure, for the hazards of a fast-paced marathon, or indeed for the steady trek of fund raising. When sheer adventure is the goal Arabians are the number one choice. There have been many long-distance endurance feats undertaken and the most challenging of all and one which created a new world record is dealt with separately (see pp. 77–81).

The Arabian is not the total answer to success as I know from some less happy experiences, where people have considered all they have to do is purchase an Arabian from a proven long-distance line and success is theirs. But take the good Arabian, ally it with sensitive and dedicated management and training, and success will definitely follow – not necessarily in a string of first place awards, but in the tremendous feeling of partnership with one's mount; and, as Abu Bekr said, knowing that there is supreme generosity and endurance there for the asking.

PART THREE

NATIONS' REFERENCE

23 Introduction

The years since 1955 when the very first Tevis Cup was run have seen the sport of Endurance Riding and its related activities of Competitive Trail, Long Distance, and Pleasure Riding escalate into one of the major equestrian disciplines. It is also the one by far the most suited to the everyday rider who enjoys the triple pleasure of achievement, relaxation, and the natural resources of untrammelled countryside.

From its beginnings as a recognized sport in the United States it spread, and not so slowly, to Great Britain where the Arab Horse Society and the British Horse Society jointly backed the earliest Golden Horseshoe rides; and to Australia and the very tough challenge of the Quilty 100. By the mid 1960s endurance riding was an ever-widening sport in these three countries, soon to be followed by South Africa with their 130 mile (210 km) Fauresmith National Endurance Event in the 1970s. Europe was next, with Germany and France pioneering the European involvement. Now the sport is truly international, many nations listing endurance riding as one of the fastest-growing sections in their calendar of equestrian events.

Each year there are many newcomers to the sport who are welcomed into the many associations devoted to promoting both the sport and the welfare of the horses who compete for endurance riding laurels.

From being originally an insular sport where each country 'did its own thing' it has now become very international indeed. Quite early in the sport's 'world' life, American riders competed in Australia and vice versa. One of the first, if not the first American rider to compete in Britain was Sharon Saare, riding my own unregistered gelding Katchina way back in 1976. Germany sent a team to Britain's first 100 miler in 1975, and in the follow-ing year Margaret Montgomerie and I, riding Tarquin and Nizzolan, reciprocated, being the first of Britain's riders to compete abroad officially. I was lucky enough to be invited to ride in the Australian Quilty, Mrs Betty Serpell loaning me a partbred Arab mare, Faraway Lutana, with whom I achieved a treasured Quilty buckle. The same year Dr Barsaleau from the USA rode one of R. M. Williams' Rockybar Arabians – Samal – to first place in the Quilty Heavyweight Division. American Pat Fitzgerald has also twice ridden the Quilty 100.

In the last few years international participation has changed from a rare occurrence to being a very regular event. Great Britain frequently sends teams to the Continent with a great deal of success. France has representatives ride in Britain and in many other European countries. Riders from many countries ride on loaned horses where transport of their own mounts is too costly, and in 1986 the Americans made the breakthrough in flying a full team to Italy for the very first World Championships, with spectacular but, I suspect, expected results.

In the following section of the book the growth of many of the endurance riding societies of the world is charted: an outline is given of their activities; types of ride offered; scope of events; general rules, and so on. I am indebted to the Secretaries of the societies who have answered my detailed queries about their national associations, and to the riders who have not only supplied information regarding their horses, but in many cases photographs as well. Where it has proved impossible to get first-hand information I have been assisted by friends in the expanding endurance riding world. At the end of each association's résumé cameos of the top horses are drawn – not only the current winners, but the horses and riders who have earned a place in endurance riding history; horses and riders who have campaigned successfully for season after season. Some of these are not the big prizewinners, but the horses that do consistently well year after year. In my opinion, and in that of many well-known endurance riders, the truly successful Endurance or Competitive Trail horse is not the horse that carries all before him for a season and disappears into limbo, but the stalwart who remains sound year after year and in a quiet way racks up the miles. Many associations have now recognized these quiet performers with high mileage awards. There are a few equines who have massive mileage: Juanita, an Australian mule; Tarquin, an Irish cob; Smokey Killen's Bandit, with an incredible score of over 13,000 miles. In the following pages you will meet many of these, some champions, some just tough old campaigners.

Fortunately the main achievement for the greater proportion of entrants is to finish a ride with the horse sound and merit the completion award. The win or place is a bonus. Some riders are especially competitive, but the bedrock of the sport is the wide base of competitors who ride for the pure pleasure and stimulus achieved, and gratification gained, when their horse passes a tough test with honours. It is this larger number of horse lovers who are content with achieving a modicum of success allied to the greater pleasure of partnership with a good horse, who both provide and fund the upper reaches for highly competitive endurance riders.

In this encompassing sport of endurance riding there is something for everyone – from the tyros just starting out, right through to the ultra keen, determined to add 100-miling laurels to their own and their horse's credit.

To start the survey of world associations I shall begin at home with a country and a society that caters for every level of horse and rider.

Dare I say it? Great Britain is the most prestigious nation in the equestrian honours list! A country from whence many nations draw foundation stock and new infusions of blood to many well-known breeds. A country with a very long history in racing, eventing, showjumping, hunting – in fact all the many aspects that make up the world equestrian scene. Also one that has a thriving endurance horse scene, and which produced the winners of the very first team gold medal in the first world championships held in Italy in September of 1986. Britain is fortunate in having two societies that promote the horse in the field of endurance endeavour, each running its own series of rides of differing types. A Highland group has also recently begun.

The Endurance Horse and Pony Society of Great Britain

The EHPS of GB was founded early in 1973 by two people: the then Fleet Street journalist and proprietor of Farming and Equestrian Magazines, Alan Exley, who was the society's first Chairman; and myself, who while living in the United States had been very impressed with the sport of Competitive Trail Riding.

Growing from an initial small group of a dozen endurance enthusiasts the society managed a short fixture list of two competitive and a fistful of pleasure rides in its first year. Growth was extremely rapid. By 1975 the EHPS felt confident enough to take a momentous step forward by running England's first 100 miler in a day, backed by the financial sponsorship of Messrs Spillers, the horse feed manufacturer, and the team of very hardworking, behind-the-scenes organizers headed by Major Michael Lewins, who continues even today to be one of Britain's top ride and seminar organizers. Veterinary supervision was exceptionally tight and led by the society's panel of veterinary advisers, the late Peter Hall-Patch, MRCVS, John Sampson, MRCVS, and Dick Orton, MRCVS. The society, and the sport in general in Britain, owes a tremendous debt to Dick Orton for his unstinting generosity in the amount of time and advice he gave to the sport in its early years, when he worked very closely with me as society secretary. From a field of over twenty entered in the 100 miler six horses finished, the winner being the American-bred eight-year-old Arabian stallion, Nizzolan, owned and bred by myself, with a partbred Arabian Wootton Jasper second, and the indefatigable Tarquin (see p. 170) third. The main thing about that first British 100 miler was that it was the most important British milestone in the sport to date. It set the standard for the future. Though the number of finishers was small it was a first. Veterinary supervision was exceptionally strict, as the panel was determined that nothing would go wrong. Not one horse was ill or ailing after the ride, and since becoming a yearly fixture hotly contended by an increasing number of very successful horses that '100 per cent well' standard has been maintained.

Over the years since 1973 there has been a steady stream of really tough campaigners, both equine and human, the most outstanding of which are 'cameoed' below. Because of stringent veterinary conditions, not once has there been a really sick or sorry horse in EHPS rides, and no fatalities, which should set the minds at ease of people who worry about subjecting horses to undue stresses. Our present long-time veterinary adviser is Jim Kerr, MRCVS, who is also on the International Veterinary Panel (see p. 157).

Membership of EHPS stands at close to 1000, the greater part of whom are riders in one of the many levels of competition offered to members. Some are non-riding members who give valuable time and assistance at rides, enabling the riding members really to benefit from the society's events.

Without a doubt the EHPS has the widest choice of rides available, not only in Great Britain, but anywhere in the world. It offers three distinct types of ride.

Pleasure Rides

They are run purely, as the title indicates, for pleasure and to introduce novice horses and riders to long distance riding. Distances range from 15 to 25 miles and though there is no speed element there is usually a lower limit of 5 mph (8 kph) so that stewards and organizers are not kept waiting about for too long.

Competitive Trail Rides (CTR)

They are run on a very similar pattern to those run in the USA. These rides are of varying length, and are usually of only one day's duration, although occasionally a 100 miler may be run over two or three days according to the organizers' available time. The minimum distance for a one-day CTR is 25 miles, the maximum 60 miles. However, novice CTRs may be of 20 miles only, but usually follow the 25-mile distance. It is the horse that is classified a novice in British rides, whereas in the USA novice can denote the rider new to the sport. Judging is done on a time plus condition basis. Ride category determines the speed, with novice horses travelling between 6 and 7 mph; junior riders (seventeen years and under) between 6 and 8 mph; and open horses between 7 and 8 mph. There are also fast CTRs of 25 to 35 miles with speeds approximately 1 mph faster than the other open classes. Penalties are allocated for being outside the time bracket either way. Veterinary penalties are also allocated in both the pulse and trauma departments. There are no degrees of lameness: the horse is either sound or not. There are no mandatory halts on CTRs but there are spot veterinary checks on the longer rides. The distances most commonly offered in CTRs are 25, 40 and 50 miles. This enables a rider to take his horse through the range gradually and find out his real potential. No horse may start CTRs before he is five years old, with the exception of riding for completion only as a novice four year old. Older horses in their first competitive year are also eligible for novice classes, but may grade up within the same year to open. Open horses must be a minimum of five years of age. Awards in CTRs are in escalating grades – completion only, grade 4 up to grade 1. Grade 1 must not have any penalties whatsoever. Grade 2 only allows for a meagre two-point penalty.

Endurance Rides

They are run on the same principle as Endurance Rides the world over, with the fastest horse that is also fit to proceed being the winner. Horses must be a minimum of six years old to enter EHPS Endurance Rides, and also have achieved a grading in at least two CTRs of 40 miles or more. To enter the 100 miler in one day horses must be a minimum of seven years of age, and they must also qualify by completing an Endurance Ride or a CTR of 50 miles, or a BHS Golden Horseshoe at a minimum speed of 7 mph, plus the earlier qualification of two 40-mile CTRs with gradings. Distances for Endurance Rides in the EHPS are a minimum of 40 miles with a current maximum of 100 miles in one day. Several 50 and 75 milers are offered in each season, but at present only one one-day 100 miler. Speeds on an Endurance Ride are a minimum of 7 mph to merit a placing, and 5 mph if only completion is being ridden for. On a 100 miler in one day, however, the average minimum speed permitted is 5 mph.

An unusual feature of EHPS competitions is that each event has a multiple offering of rides with up to six, and sometimes more, classes held, so that just about every level of fitness and experience is catered for. All events include at least one novice, one junior, and one open class in the CTR category. Endurance Rides are always run with supporting CTR classes, but the reverse is not always so.

There is absolutely no financial inducement. Prizes are purely of token value – trophies, rosettes and plaques, or occasionally something for the horse such as electrolytes or feed, particularly if some advertising sponsorship has been gained.

Riders may enter their horses for a truly glittering array of end of season high point awards. There are also prestigious mileage awards with gradations from 500 to 1000, 1500, 2000 and so on. To date, only one horse has achieved over 3000 in EHPS rides and that is Margaret Montgomerie's Tarquin, still competing at a ripe twenty-four years of age.

As with all sports societies the competitors and their horses are only a part of the picture. In the background are the many who make it all possible, especially the organizers. EHPS has many area groups. They adhere to the main society's policy but give their area members the added incentive of competing for area trophies and also offer a range of rides closer to home for those unable to travel to events further afield.

Thoughts from W. J. Kerr MRCVS

Jim Kerr, veterinary adviser to the EHPS and a member of the international panel, feels that distance riding in Britain differs from distance riding on the Continent of Europe, not least in the temperament of the rider. He offers the following observations.

In Britain, the CTR and Bronze or Silver qualifiers over comparatively short distances and at comparatively slow speeds are the most popular rides. Endurance Rides (minimum of 40 miles) are not so well supported, although more riders are being tempted to try.

Not long ago, veterinary judges were expected to place entrants in order of merit after, for instance, a ride of 25 miles over a flat course at speeds as low as 6 mph. The easily measured parameters (heart and respiratory rate) had in a great many cases returned to normal thirty minutes after the ride, so that other subjective and possibly unreliable parameters had to be used, and I am quite sure a number of decisions were, to say the least, open to discussion.

The EHPS of GB now adopts a grading system, which allows for any number of equal firsts, seconds and so on. Before the ride, a veterinary judge is required to take the heart rate and make a physical examination of each animal, paying particular attention to mouth, limbs and those parts of the body in contact with the saddlery. He must also see the animal move at walk and trot to make sure that it is fit to take part in the class in which it is entered. This examination is repeated thirty minutes after the ride and penalty points awarded. There should be very few veterinary problems on shorter rides, even at speeds up to 9 mph. When the distance goes up and, in Endurance Rides, the speed as well, then obviously problems do occur, and this is when experience is required from the veterinary judges. At checks during the ride he must decide whether the horse should be allowed to continue, eliminated or recommended to retire.

In some countries lameness is graded and animals with grade 1 or 2 lameness are allowed to continue. There is a suggestion that this should be allowed in Britain, and at the highest level in the sport. I feel this must be resisted and not incorporated in the rules. Where experienced veterinary judges are used, they alone should make the necessary decisions to ensure the welfare of the animals concerned.

The 100 milers

By far the most prestigious ride in the British endurance ride calendar is the Summer Solstice 100 miler, so named because the very first time it was run it fell on 21 June. To date it has been run nine times, and seven horses have been ridden to victory. It has been won by Arabians three times, an Anglo-Arab once, an Appaloosa once, a Thoroughbred with some Arab and other unknown blood once, and twice by an unregistered mare with Thoroughbred, Trakehner and Welsh Cob in her 'pedigree'. The 1987 winner was an unregistered Arab-cross gelding.

The clutch of cameos deservedly starts off with a brief look at all seven 100-mile winners. Some of them have offspring waiting in the wings to take up the endurance challenge, others already have winning progeny.

Nizzolan

Nizzolan is the grey 15 hand Arabian stallion of 75 per cent Crabbet breeding that I brought back from the USA when I returned to England in 1968.

16 Nizzolan (left), first Summer Solstice winner and twice Manar Trophy winner, here with his stable companion Katchina. (Eastern Daily Press)

He was the first 100-mile winner in a time of twelve hours, one minute back in 1975. As early as his yearling days I had endurance riding in mind for him. In fact his close relation, Pazzam, was an East Coast 100 Mile Champion in the USA. Definitely not a horse to be led around a show ring in hand he revelled in work and variety – the harder the work the better he liked it, combining stud duties with endurance work as well as the occasional ridden class at shows. He was a super hunter and adept at working cattle, either rounding them up or cutting an individual from the herd – a talent appreciated at cattle drift time in the New Forest. His long distance career started as a five year old where in his first big event, the British Horse Society Golden Horseshoe Ride, he gained a silver award, and subsequently won three successive gold

awards. In all his four Golden Horseshoes he never acquired a veterinary penalty. In 1973 the EHPS started holding a series of rides around the country and in 1974 began a high points system, and in both 1974 and 1975 Nizzolan stood top of the league, winning the coveted Manar Trophy for the leading endurance horse of the year, and in 1976 he stood reserve champion because of rider error when I lost my way and earned time penalties. He had the honour of representing the sport of long distance riding in the Parade of Champions at the Horse of the Year Show at Wembley in London in 1975, and appeared in an Arabian extravaganza at London's Olympic arena as the breed's number one endurance horse, as well as at the Arab Horse Society's National Championships. In 1976 he and another horse, Tarquin owned by Margaret Montgomerie, paved the way for Britain in the European endurance rides by taking part in the Hamburg to Hannover 100 miler. Despite not getting an accurate translation of the rules we both survived the distance and some of the rather strange obstacles, including swimming the River Aller 2 km from the finish, and riding as a team finished together, the decision going to Tarquin at vetting the following day with Nizzolan second. It was the first time in Europe for Britain but definitely not the last, as Britain has an enviable European record of wins.

As a 'person' Nizzolan has proved just about the easiest horse to own. Although a stallion he has a nationwide reputation for manners and gentleness. He also imparts his special brand of resilience to his offspring, many excelling in performance fields (see p. 173). One of England's great endurance horses, he is now in retirement except for his wives.

His son Granicus is slowly gaining experience in novice CTRs at the time of writing.

Mapledale Adonis

An Anglo-Arab bred by Mr and Mrs Dinsdale of Througham Court Arabian Stud, Gloucestershire, Mapledale Adonis won the Summer Solstice in 1977. Born in 1964 he was by Zethan out of Ramadi-Azym, but it was not until 1968 that the partnership which earned so many endurance ride victories was born, when Jane Nicholson purchased him as a future performance horse, although at that time, as she says, she did not contemplate riding even 20 miles, let alone 100 in a day. After a hesitant start, when he initially failed the vet who thought that scar tissue affecting the growth of the outside wall of a forefoot would cause problems, he finally settled into New Forest life,

17 Mother and son. Robin Nicholson on Mapledale Adonis, Jane on Wootton Jasper, both 100–mile horses. (Dr R. Marshall)

much as Nizzolan had. In fact throughout most of their competitive years, Nizzolan and Adonis trained together, Jane and I living only 10 miles apart across the Forest which by our mode of reckoning was a forty-five-minute ride away – they were endurance horses in top condition and we often used that distance to measure their fitness. It was also a rare instance where it was as quick by horse across country as by vehicle on a longer route. Adonis' first competitive ride was a Golden Horseshoe Ride (GHR) Qualifier and his second the 1972 Final at Goodwood where he achieved a silver award. Unlike Nizzolan who, other than on rare occasions, only had one rider during his career, Adonis was a true family horse as Jane shared him with her three sons, Robin, Michael and Julian, all of whom piloted him to various successes in his career. An exceptionally generous horse, Adonis' big year came in 1977 with the second running of the Summer Solstice, again over the New Forest, and he finished in a very relaxed manner to win convincingly in a riding time of just over thirteen and a half hours. Subsequently he won the Cheltenham 60 miler as well as being very consistent in CTRs and finishing the season placing high in the Arab Marathon. He held the Manar Trophy for the nation's leading endurance horse in his 100 miler year.

I think that Nizzolan and Adonis benefited tremendously from being able to work together, which they did over many years until I moved from the New Forest. It made light work of the miles, and gave the horses company and zest for work. In his last few years Adonis had a reverse when he hurt his back, but after a prolonged rest was returned successfully to distance work until retirement. Sadly he had to be put down due to cirrhosis of the liver at the age of eighteen, and is much missed by the Nicholson family and his endurance riding friends.

Fforest Orchid

The Summer Solstice 100 changes venue every few years to give variety and also to lessen the load on organizers. Its third running in 1980 was on the very hard, flinty and rolling downland of Sussex with the ride base at Plumpton Racecourse.

Fforest Orchid is a 15.1 hand Appaloosa mare owned by Judy Beaumont, who is well known in both British long distance and driving circles. Initially Fforest Orchid was almost a non-starter in any competitive event, being rescued from an early demise by Judy who has an eye for that something extra in a horse. This paid off because Orchid and Judy became a partnership that meant to win and succeeded repeatedly in whatever sphere they were entered – working hunter, Western showing, hunter trials, CTRs, Golden Horseshoe. But it was in endurance riding that they really shone, serving an apprenticeship in the lower distance of 60 miles before tackling the 100 at Plumpton and winning in a riding time of thirteen and a half hours. The flinty, hard going of the South Downs Way was no deterrent to one of the toughest little horses ever to scythe her way around an endurance course. However, though a tremendous victory, it was just the prelude to bigger things because Orchid and Judy represented Britain in the 1980 French 100 miler at Montcuq, repeating their Plumpton win and, with the recently formed ELDRIC, also giving Britain her first European Champion. Orchid for Britain was tied with Portugal and Judy went to Essen, Germany, for the presentation at the Equitana Horse Fair in March of 1981.

In 1981 this mare continued winning, with three major victories in premier rides to her credit: the Cambridgeshire 75 miler; Peak District 50 miler, and riding again at Montcuq in France she clinched the points to stand European Champion for the second year running. The year 1982 meant a change in lifestyle for the mare as Judy had youngsters coming on, so Orchid was retired and has since produced three superbly marked Appaloosa colt foals to the imported American stallion, R. Mellow Kinsman, whom Judy has also ridden to a GHR gold. It is their offspring Cool Smoke who will be following in his dam's long distance shoes.

Nimrodel

A grey 16 hand mare foaled in 1974, Nimrodel is of mixed breeding but with much Thoroughbred and Trakehner blood close up. Owned by Thea Toomer-Baker, co-editor of the internationally known magazine *Distance Rider*, Nimrodel started as a five year old but it was not until she was eight years old that she really came good, and in what style! Out of six endurance rides entered in 1982 she placed steadily higher up the rankings, finishing her first full season by winning the British Summer Solstice 100 at Plumpton, the Welsh 100 (over two days), and the German Championship 140 miler. The last three classifying as ELDRIC International rides thus gave her an unchallengeable position as European Champion. The following season success piled on success: another 100 Summer Solstice win, another European 100, this time in France, and yet again the European Championship. In 1984 she was narrowly beaten in a fast finish for the Summer Solstice. Indeed Thea says the thing that causes her most concern in Nimrodel's performance is lack of finishing speed, a natural consequence of the heavier conformation of a horse not normally reckoned to be the ideal prospect. Britain quite often produces endurance champions of this calibre (see p. 171).

Nimrodel disappeared from the endurance riding scene in 1985 to raise Thea's next endurance generation, coming back with a bang in 1986 by winning the award for Leading Horse under British Horse Society rules, plus winning the National Championships awarded by *Distance Rider* to the horse and rider gaining most points from rides under both EHPS and BHS rules. In her mercurial career Nimrodel is scheduled for another production event before being back in contention. Both Thea and I are hoping for a world beater, as Nimrodel visited Nizzolan in 1987.

All great horses need a dedicated rider, and with most of Britain's top horses their riders largely come from that 'full-time job' category that has to fit riding into an already full-time schedule. In Thea's case it also includes a 'moonlighting' job as editor of a periodical that is taking up more and more of her crowded time. When asked to what she attributed her success Thea put it down to experience, common sense and a super horse, and also paid tribute to the USA's system of rides for having shown the world what could be achieved. Her long-term aim is to ride a son or daughter of Nimrodel to world championship honours.

18 Nimrodel and Thea Toomer Baker. Twice Summer Solstice winners and twice European Champions.

Tarim

A purebred chestnut Arabian stallion, 15.1 hands high and foaled in 1976 in Wales, was third time lucky in the 1984 Summer Solstice. Tarim made it look so very easy, remaining fresh and eager throughout the whole 100 miles. After two unsuccessful attempts he came back strongly, very fit and very, very fast, breaking the British record held by Nizzolan with a riding time of nine hours, forty-five minutes. His record-breaking ride was over the historical area of Sherwood Forest linked in history and legend with Robin Hood, the real life medieval Earl of Locksley. To crown his win he also achieved the distinction of being awarded the Best Condition award the day following the ride. The following year his rider/owner Val Long was all set to make it a double, and came flying across the finish line in a hotly contested 'run for the wire' with Christine Hull's William. But luck was against them both, as the horses' heart rates failed by a narrow margin to drop sufficiently. Both riders took their disappointment well. The following season Tarim came back with a flourish, making 1986 his year with another Summer Solstice win, to be followed in the autumn by going as a member of the British team to Rome for the first World Endurance Riding Championships. Narrowly missing an individual medal, being placed fourth, he was the highest placing horse in Great Britain's team which came home in triumph as the first ever Team World Champions. His successes earned him Reserve Champion position in the ELDRIC's European Trophy 1986. Unlike many of the well-known endurance horses in Britain Tarim does not contend a very full season of rides, rider Val choosing his events with care, but when the chips are down you can be sure that Tarim will be giving his all.

Kandy Bullard

Kandy Bullard is a brown threequarter Thoroughbred mare foaled in 1972, owned and bred by Jane Welcher from Jane's first endurance horse Victor-

19 Tarim and Val Long, winners Summer Solstice 1984 and 1986. (T. Gillison)

ia. The 1985 win in the Summer Solstice for Kandy was the peak of a long career in the sport, and unusual for two reasons. Owner/rider Jane had ridden in both BHS and EHPS rides for many years, Kandy's dam Victoria taking part in the first 100 miler in 1975. Over the years Jane's horses had always been well to the fore but ridden with extreme consideration, with the horse's welfare uppermost in Jane's tactics. Most competitors, in whatever equestrian sport they participate in, do ride for a win however much they may say they do it for the fun of having a go. Jane is one of the very few that mean exactly what she says. She will not push a horse if she thinks it is in that horse's best long-term interests, so it took a very long time for Kandy to reach her 'glory year'. The year 1985 started well with a gold award on Exmoor's rough and tough Golden Horseshoe Ride, and the Summer Solstice win came as an unlooked for bonus. Kandy was third across the line, but the first horse to pass the veterinary examination, and at the end of the 100 miles she looked so relaxed it appeared she could have gone yet further. The previous year she had been seventh, and in 1986 she was second to Tarim. In a final run in on the last half mile Tarim's speed outdistanced Kandy who, true to her rider's tactics, was not going to be risked at the post.

Jane credits much of her success to husband Bernard who crews for her on all her rides, but it does need a special kind of dedication to get up at 4.30 a.m. every morning in the miserable British winter to exercise horses in the dark before going to a full-time job, and then return in the dark to do stables again.

One aspect of Kandy's training that is unusual is that she is worked in the totally flat and exceptionally dull Fenland reaches of Cambridgeshire (and as I live there too I both know and hate the same problems). It proves that provided the training is meticulous and the knowledge backing it deep, a flatland horse can win the premier endurance rides against horses who have the benefit of ideal training grounds.

Rufus

A bay, unregistered, 950 lb gelding foaled in 1976,

Rufus has been owned by Pat Amies since he was a four year old. Pat started both him and herself in endurance riding with an easy pleasure ride in 1984. Or pleasure for Pat, but Rufus was reluctant to enter – boxing to venues and the return trip proved bothersome at first. Pat admits that once it took twelve people to load Rufus, commenting that 'he can be very bolshy!' In 1985 she started the long road to the Summer Solstice with a season of novice events, during which she realized Rufus' potential and set her sights on a crack at the 100 and the Golden Horseshoe in 1986. However, plans did not work out as well as had been hoped. She just plain forgot to register Rufus in the BHS, so could not even attempt the GHR. However, he qualified easily for the Solstice with two high grades in his required 40-mile CTRs and a third place in the mandatory Endurance Ride, but then, dogged by gremlins, he sustained an injury and had to be withdrawn from the 100. But he still managed to finish the season on a high. At the two-day Red Dragon International 100 in Wales he won the first day's 50-mile leg, and over the two-day 100 placed second in the International class.

Rufus is not an easy horse at the best of times, taking a long time to settle at some rides. Pat's 'brakes' failed her entirely at the Golden Horseshoe in May of 1987. She had just one month to sort this out before the Solstice in June, and as this was the first 100 in one day she had attempted she elected to go for a safe completion – Rufus' brakes willing and operating.

The field included several very fast and well-known horses that Pat was aware would go like smoke so, tucking in with another rider going for completion only, they cruised steadily at 10 mph round the bulk of the 100 mile course. The brakes held well and Rufus stayed cool and collected, vetted well at the 50- and 75-mile marks, and on the last quarter they set off with only twelve riders ahead of them. In the next 15 miles, eight of the twelve went out of contention, and Pat and co-rider Jan Lloyd Rogers on her chestnut pony Honey realized they were in for a place. In the last 10 miles a lot can happen and the pair stuck to their pre-ride plan to take things steadily – in the recent past the 100 has been lost by leading riders pushing too

20 Kandy Bullard and Jane Welcher, 1985 Summer Solstice winners, with some of their trophies. (EMAP)

21 Pat Amies and Rufus. Summer Solstice winners 1987.

hard for a win, and on more than one occasion 'play safe' tactics have secured the Solstice Trophy.

The last few miles of the 100 course was down a training gallop adjacent to the Southwell Race-course venue in Nottinghamshire. Ahead they saw two riders going slowly – numbers two and three? Pushing on they realized that these were riders in the lower distance event killing time before clocking in, so they eased back until the last quarter mile racetrack run-in. Here Pat said she felt bad that having had Jan Lloyd Rogers as her 'brakes' all around the course, she now had an unfair advantage with her larger, faster Rufus, so they delayed the run-in until the final furlong, only to have Rufus, due to rider error – or as Pat terms it 'muggins me' – pull up two yards short of the winning post. Nonetheless elated with her sixth place, she was thunderstruck to learn at the final vetting that her carefully restrained and well-

braked Rufus was indeed the first horse to pass his final vetting, and that two years of hopes and trials, mixed with setbacks both equine and human, had ended with winning the most prestigious event in the British endurance calender.

Pat feels that winning seems a hollow victory when it was at the cost of another horse failing the vet. She certainly should not do so. I too had that feeling when the horse that beat my Nizzolan to the post in a gallop in his 100 year pulled up lame. Lameness occurs well before the vets examine and eliminate. Rufus and Pat Amies truly earned their moment in the Solstice Sun.

EHPS horses and riders

A family affair

Many families in Britain make endurance riding a joint effort, one member riding, usually the wife, while the other half fulfils the less exciting but so necessary function of back-up crew. With the Ware family from Portsmouth, Hampshire, it is a true joint effort, all three members being equally keen to compete. Andrea has the longest history of competitive riding, starting back in 1972 with a black Argentine mare Terasa, soon followed by a partbred Arabian gelding Major Kaftan, but it was only when she had served her apprenticeship that the real successes started with the purchase of the purebred Arab stallion Cairo (1968), bred by Diana Wort by Indriss out of Castanea. He proved an easy horse to train and work, provided he did not get bored. Very important with a distance horse, he loved his food and was a good doer – and in more ways than one, as he placed fifth in the national rankings in his very first year's competition.

The following year Andrea lost Cairo to daughter Jackie, who at age fourteen embarked on a whirlwind year with success following success, sweeping the board in all the junior events and starting an impressive collection of high point trophies. After only one year in junior classes Jackie upgraded herself to the open division, not because she had to, as she still had three more years in the junior rankings, but because she needed the challenge of stiffer competition. Cairo continued to excel and among his major wins were firsts in the Red Dragon Welsh Endurance Ride and the Breamore 50 milers, second in the East Sussex 50, plus being Reserve Arab Champion in 1978, and the following year going one better to take the Championship as well as winning the Junior Championship. Jackie has the distinction of being the youngest rider to win an open endurance class in Britain.

Meanwhile Andrea, having surrendered Cairo, was looking for his replacement and after a season with another purebred stallion, Kazmahal, who won the Manar Trophy for leading horse, purchased the purebred grey gelding Shaaban (1973), bred by Michael Pitt Rivers at Tollard Royal Stud by Vathek out of Shanifah. This horse was to succeed at the very top in just about everything he undertook. He had already won the Novice and Open Championships before the Wares purchased

him and while he was competing was never out of the top six in national rankings. Not content in excelling in EHPS rides he also flew the Ware colours in the BHS Golden Horseshoe rides, giving husband Chris, who up to now had done duty as crew, his introduction to the riding side of the sport. Some introduction it proved to be, with two successive gold awards on the tough course in the Exmoor National Park. Shaaban claimed an International first with a win in the 1981 Levi's Ride and Tie run by the Arab Horse Society, partnered by Nigel Clark and Steve Sowerby who were British National Squad Modern Pentathletes in training for the Olympics. Andrea says she feels the Ride and Tie is just about the most exciting competition they have ever been involved in.

After losing her top horse yet again to another member of the family, she regained him for tackling the 1984 Summer Solstice 100 in which he placed ninth, albeit not being pushed too hard as I remember, but finishing in top condition. He ended the year as the leading Arabian in endurance riding. In the six years Shaaban has owned the Wares he has only once been withdrawn from a ride, but Andrea says he is not an easy horse, being susceptible to tying up so that a careful watch has to be kept on his feed, and so far no remedies have worked. Like his stable companion he also is inclined to get bored during workouts, but leeway is allowed to an old stager, and as Andrea says, 'who can blame him after so many seasons'.

The final member of the Ware stable is Andrea's favourite and latest acquisition, Sunlea Karanina (1976), bred by Mrs A. E. Parker of Sunlea Farm by Makor out of Katriona. A comparative newcomer to distance riding at purchase, with only a few 25 milers to her credit, since 1982 Andrea and the mare have formed a good partnership after initial problems. Karanina did not like being stabled, had her own idea of pace – flat out, and was picky over feed, needing many small feeds to tempt her to eat enough to replace the boundless energy she insisted on using at every opportunity. A rapport has since developed and together their joint names continually appeared in the national rankings, starting with a fourth out of the top six in 1983. In fact Karanina has never been out of the top six, and

22 Cairo and Jackie Ware on the East Hampshire Ride, Queen Elizabeth Country Park, 1979. (Richard Earle)

23 Sunlea Karanina and Andrea Ware on their way to second place in the East Sussex Endurance Ride, 1985. (Tony Ferridge)

has a fistful of different awards to her credit, including the Ghobi Award for perfect condition and the Arab Championship in 1983, a fifth place at the Montcuq 126 miler in France in 1984, and wins and places in Endurance Rides in 1985 plus being a member of the National Team Championship. Not confined to Endurance Rides she also competes regularly in CTRs and has dozens of Grades 1 and 2. While in foal in 1986 she won two championships and one reserve championship and was never out of the ribbons in the show ring. As Andrea puts it, 'Karanina is not just a pretty face!'

To sum up the achievements of the Wares as a family: they are keen competitors but never lose the pure enjoyment offered by the sport. Though as keen as the next neither Andrea nor Jackie will push a horse past its limits. This is best shown by one of the reverses that happen to all top riders. When leading by a full hour in an International ride in Belgium, Karanina had a crashing fall on a slick section of road and on regaining her feet Andrea withdrew her rather than push for a win, even though the mare was still sound and only shaken and bruised. From knowing Andrea I can say that she is very philosophical about the ups and downs of a tough ride, delighted to win but never one to have recriminations of any sort when she does not. Husband Chris, she says, just enjoys the training and taking part in the rides, and stays calm, which no doubt is one reason why Shaaban went so well for him when he introduced Chris to a winning streak. I find the family among the nicest of the current host of competitors, maybe because they see the rides not only as competitions but as chances to meet and make new friends. In addition, the Arab Horse Society need look no further than Chris, Andrea and Jackie as ambassadors for the Arabian breed, as they have successfully produced a string of purebred Arabian winners year after year in all types of competition. Between them Cairo, Shaaban, Kazmahal, and Karanina have covered well over 7000 miles in long distance rides. Some achievement!

Squire Tebeldi

Foaled in 1974, Squire Tebeldi had a more than unusual emergence into endurance riding. Although finishing his first season as a novice in reserve champion position, his career was in jeopardy almost before it started as he was lame at his first ride and ringbone was subsequently diagnosed. Not a very promising prognosis! Happily in the spring of 1980, after six months' rest, he was X-rayed again and given the all clear. Even so, for

this 14.2 hands unregistered chestnut gelding the next two years were unremarkable, except maybe for the sound horsemanship of his owner Sally Scorey (now Grant). Instead of immediately campaigning her now sound 'Beldi', she opted for a very slow build-up programme, taking him easily, entering only a few rides, plus a little Western showing. It was not until 1982 that she felt he had really turned the corner, putting all problems behind him.

Beldi at first glance does not strike one as a horse, or rather pony, that would rank amongst the top level of EHPS endurance horses. He is from the other main group in Britain that does extremely well in the sport – those good, steady, unregistered horses which along with the Arabians make up the bulk of the British endurance riding scene. He is an easy going, compact character who wastes no energy in fussing or fretting, evincing a relaxed manner that put him in the ribbons in Western classes and proved to be the ideal temperament, allied with abundant generosity, when he emerged full time on to the long distance scene.

After a very long apprenticeship in CTR Sally felt Beldi had more to give, and give he did in

24 Squire Tebeldi and Sally Scorey on the Exmoor Golden Horseshoe Ride in 1986. (John Watts Photography)

increasing volume, so that by 1984 his name was regularly in the placings in the longer Endurance Rides; usually among the lower placings but he always finished sound. Sally says: 'I think Beldi is the greatest, especially as he has a large handicap – namely me!' It is true that Sally is not exactly a lightweight, but one of the marks of the real endurance horse is that he can carry a fair weight in proportion to his size, and Sally is only measuring hers against the numbers of featherweight riders in the British rides. Beldi's other drawback is having poor feet, the walls being thin and crumbly and presenting his farrier, Paul Dunning, with the constant problem of keeping shoes on him. So far, with one exception in competition and another in training which caused a setback, he has managed well.

In his first season changing from CTR to ER he completed three 50 milers and two 100 milers and was never unplaced, also coming sixth in the National Championships awarded by *Distance Rider* magazine. In 1985 he continued to improve, going from tenth to fourth in Britain's Summer Solstice 100, to third in the National Championships (*Distance Rider*), and on his first trip abroad to represent Great Britain placing second in the 130 km race at Huy in Belgium, plus being awarded the Best Condition Trophy by a unanimous veterinary decision.

Sally had planned to give Beldi a rest in 1986 as she has a young Arabian waiting to start a long distance career, but the previous year's successes, finishing with a tenth place in the ELDRIC European Trophy, spurred her on to another season. Beldi really was indefatigable, clocking up 960 miles of competition in that one year alone! Also he bettered his Summer Solstice place to a third. Even though Sally admits he lacks the speed to keep with the front runners, achieving an overall speed of 9½ mph is hardly slow, particularly when you realize that the pony does not exactly come from a racing or speed background and that the first two finishers were an Arabian and a three-quarter Thoroughbred. His other 1986 successes included a win in the Cheltenham 75 miler under BHS rules, and many placings in 50 milers run separately by both societies. He was picked to represent Britain at the Rome World Championships,

but by a cruel twist his shelly feet did finally let him down, as he pulled a shoe 6 miles from the finish on a 125-mile ride on stony ground, finishing very slightly and temporarily lame but sufficient to finish Sally's hopes of going to Rome. She commented that such things do happen, but courageously kept going with enough rides under EHPS rules to put Beldi in Reserve Championship position for the Manar Trophy for leading horse of the year.

All in all Squire Tebeldi had indubitably earned his place as one of Britain's best of all time. He has shown consistency and increasing success over many seasons; and he has been considerately ridden, never overfaced or asked for too much. He is what Sharon Saare once called a horse of mine who did not at all look the part but proved he was: 'a sleeper', one that goes unnoticed until he produces top performance in a quiet but very convincing way.

Tarquin

Whether or not he was named for the last Etruscan king to rule Rome, Tarquinius Superbus, this brown gelding certainly deserves the title *superb*. He has extended his rule over the field of British endurance riding for seventeen years, starting with moderate influence as far back as 1970 when he was entered in two GHR qualifying rides. The next two years followed a similar pattern, adding two Silver Horseshoes to a variety of awards gained as an all-rounder. In riding club events he was well to the fore at the Royal Windsor and the Royal International Horse Shows as a valued middle horse in the teams of three competition. Added to this he also turned in award-winning performances in cross country, showjumping, and dressage. Owner Margaret Montgomerie, who is a lecturer at Berkshire College of Agriculture, says he was never brilliant but always gave a dependably sound performance, but I think she underrated her companion as he, or rather they, have proved themselves brilliant in the extreme on the long distance trail.

At first glance, Tarquin definitely does not give the appearance of a top flight endurance horse, and Margaret admits that veterinary surgeons pass

25 Tarquin, twenty-three years young, and Margaret Montgomerie on the South Downs, July 1986. (Alf. Baker)

such a comment and are pleasantly surprised at the end of rides when he is invariably in the ribbons. He stands 15.1 hands high and is of definite heavyweight build, being 1100 lb or more in weight. This extra Margaret says she has never been able to shift. At twenty-four years of age he is still going strong and has what must be the British record number of competitive miles for any horse, his end-of-season running total of 5354 miles in 1986 still being added to. In Britain we do not have the number of events nor the extended annual season of the USA and Australia which enables their riders to clock up so many competitive miles.

There are certainly no other horses still competing in Britain who were well into their distance stride before either of the national endurance societies was even formed. When Tarquin began his career only the BHS offered long distance rides and on a very limited basis. As soon as the EHPS was formed, followed two years later by the BHS Long Distance Riding Group, Tarquin's presence really began to be felt, and the mileage rapidly accumulated. He is not a fast horse, in fact anything but, but he is willing, eminently sensible, able to perform solo or in a group, and his best gait is a mile-eating trot, so that lacking great speed he clips off the miles in such a consistent fashion that he maintains a good rolling average far more easily than horses who spurt and then slow down. Apart from his ample proportions he does have all the inner resources that go to make up the best endurance horses: soundness, equable temperament, generosity, a good doer, and a totally unflappable manner so that no time or energy is wasted in being stupid or flighty.

To tally all his major wins would be very repetitive but there are certain high spots that need to be noted, even in a career that has been a high spot in itself. He has been entered in ten 100-mile rides, some of them 100 milers in one day, some over two and some over three days. He has successfully completed all of them, been awarded Best Condition three times, won three and earned a gold award on another (which equates with a win), and never been unplaced on the other six. Additionally he has four Golden Horseshoes to add to the two early Silver ones, all six awards gained with no veterinary penalties deducted. The only reason he stopped entering GHRs was that Margaret could no longer get time off work to enter, as this ride is always held during the week, whereas most other events are held over weekends.

Tarquin's main EHPS awards, other than 100 miler successes, have been for Leading Horse of the Year, winning the Manar Trophy three times, being reserve twice and third once. The Regent Trophy for High Point Unregistered Horse has been his seven times, and he has been the mainstay of his team which has won the Green Dragon

Team Award five times and been second twice.

Throughout the seventeen years of his endurance rule he has only been absent for two years, when Margaret had the opportunity to work in Canada and he was to all intents retired at the end of 1982. On her return Tarquin by no means intended to stay in retirement, and he completed a full season of rides, eleven events, in 1985, and an even fuller schedule in 1986 with seventeen rides and a season's total of 440 miles – a distance a younger horse might creditably achieve, let alone a veteran of twenty-three.

As a 'person' he is a good companion to have around. In 1976 Margaret and I travelled to Germany to take part in the German Hamburg to Hannover 100-mile ride and I got to know 'himself' quite well in that time. Tarquin and Nizzolan were stabled together and were allowed the run of a pasture and orchard. With the stallion in one and the gelding in the adjacent one, it says much for their temperaments that they got along amicably with only a fence separating them on their daily hour of paddock freedom. For the actual ride they went as a pair as we had agreed to ride as a team, and although very different on the surface we found they matched their way of going admirably. I know I found it a boon to have a companion throughout the ride, which was the first in Europe for both of us – route markings left something to be desired on occasion, and I think the horses benefited from the company. The outcome is well known by now, as Tarquin gave Britain its first outright victory abroad with Nizzolan second behind him. He has represented Great Britain abroad one other time at Montcuq in France, being ninth overall and a member of the British team which gained the gold medal in 1981, when he was eighteen years of age. Had he been younger he would undoubtedly have had many more international successes, but in the early 1980s the ELDRIC with its network of European rides was only making the tentative start that has resulted in a now expanding international endurance scene.

As with many great horses Tarquin has a strong personality and this he imposes by his commanding presence, not needing to resort to the bickerings and bitings of so many lesser equines that are, to put it mildly, a pain in the neck.

Not all of Tarquin's success is due to himself, though, for in different ownership I really do not think he would have achieved even a very small proportion of his international reputation and success. In the field of endurance many potential champions remain unknown for lack of a good rider. Many good horses pushed too hard too soon have a brief hour of glory and then retire from the distance riding scene, burnt out in a year or two. Tarquin's success owes most to the meticulous, dedicated and expert management of his lifetime partner Margaret Montgomerie. She has conserved him over such a very long time and makes sure he leads as sensible a life as is possible. He is not cosseted, nor fed bits of this and bits of that according to the latest advertising push, but is kept stabled in winter and at grass in the summer, his diet including commonsense feeds of oats, barley, sugar beet and grassnuts when in work, with cod liver oil when necessary, and hay ad lib when grass is absent. In competitions he is ridden considerately and with a wealth of expert horsemanship.

Our endurance scene in Great Britain owes a lot to the USA, as Margaret admits, and we in Britain do hear of the national best from the other side of 'the pond'. I wonder, do they know of Britain's Superbus?

An international family of endurance horses

I have mentioned my grey Arabian stallion Nizzolan several times, as he has had a great career in endurance riding in Britain. However, it is not to Nizzolan that I owe my involvement in long distance riding but to Magnet Regent, an American Standardbred Trotter mare of the Peter Volo line whom I purchased as a long yearling more than twenty-five years ago. It was she who gave me my introduction to 100 miling, coping beautifully with the miles and me as a tyro to the sport. During that first 100 miler in 1966 I met Pazzam, a bay gelding, by Nizzam out of Pamela, owned and ridden by Lucille Kenyon who is one of the USA's all-time champions, riding a variety of horses but in particular Pazzam. Together this partnership scored

numerous places and wins in over seventeen 100-mile CTRs, along with three reserve and four grand championship honours. At that time Nizzolan, Pazzam's nephew, had yet to see light of day, and so my first 100s were aboard Magnet Regent.

The following year in 1967 Nizzolan, by Lewisfield Nizzamo (a half-brother of Pazzam) out of an English mare Solange, was born and when he was a yearling both he and Magnet Regent accompanied me on my return to England where long distance riding had just made a tentative start. By the time Nizzolan was three and a half he and Magnet Regent had produced a chestnut filly – Nizette – who in her own right went on to championship honours, although as Hampshire County Champion Showjumper, but later doing well in both 50-mile CTRs and the Arab Marathon. Nizzolan himself began to rack up awards from his five-year-old year, and as I had enough to do keeping him and his stable companion Katchina fit for long distance, Magnet Regent produced a steady succession of colts and fillies, the pairing being what is termed 'a good nick'. Out of the nine offspring, several have been destined for the endurance field in some way or other.

After Nizette the next to go long distance riding was Zoltan (1973), who had a brief career of two years in Britain, placing third in the Novice Championships in 1977 and sixth in the Open Championships in 1978, before moving to France in the new ownership of Cathy Brown. There this grey 15.3 hand gelding came into his own and started ranking high in the French endurance rides, placing and winning on a regular basis. The high spot of his career so far is the 1984 French Lightweight National Championship. He has been back to England to compete, travelled to Austria where he was ridden by the American Darolyn Butler, and was placed fifth overall in Europe in 1985. His last ride in 1986 was representing Britain at the world championships in Rome. So pleased is Cathy with this son of Nizzolan and Magnet Regent that she came to England searching and went back with the youngest of the crop, Panache (1983), who is as yet an unknown quantity. So too is one I have retained, Granicus (1982), who started his career as a five year old and shows promise. He is of similar stamp to Zoltan and if anything a horse with better conformation. Zaritza, the 1976 chestnut daughter of the pair, has been nibbling around the edges of the endurance field and has already excelled herself in the rough and tumble of the Arab Marathon, which is run at racing speed, where she placed fifth and sixth in two attempts, though on one occasion she was hampered by taking the wrong course. But that did not diminish her performance, though it must have been galling to her owner, Rob Llewellyn.

Though the Nizzolan–Magnet Regent cross produces super endurance horses – not to mention producing showjumpers from two breeds, Arabian and Standardbred, considered unlikely to do so: another son, Aquila, won the Welsh Showjumping Championship in 1986 – Nizzolan has not confined passing his endurance qualities on only to Magnet Regent's offspring. He has to my knowledge sired two other British champions, both of whom took the Novice Championship for the EHPS. Both are out of hunter-type mares: the 16.1 hand Nizar, owned by Stephen Humphreys, and Mister Magoo, owned by Peter Favier, who has been doing so much to promote the sport in Britain. In his first season Mister Magoo completed thirteen rides, gaining nine Grade 1s and four Grade 2s, and only accrued a tiny eight points penalty in all that distance. Not a bad start to his distance career.

That this particular family and its branches have

26 Mr Magoo, grey gelding by Nizzolan, with rider/owner Peter Favier. Winners of the 1986 Novice Championship, EHPS.

been so successful is not surprising. The American Standardbred is in my opinion, and I think in the opinion of many American riders, a very tough horse and a super endurance performer. For the endurance antecedents of Nizzolan one needs to check back a few generations. His pedigree carries five lines to Rijm, the sire of Belka who won the 1921 British Arab Horse Society's 300-mile ride when in the ownership of H. V. M. Clark (see p. 144). Also amongst Nizzolan's ancestors can be found full sisters of Ramla, winner of the 310-mile cup of America in 1919. Yet further back we come to Hagar, Lady Anne Blunt's journey mare. I feel proud to have bred, owned and ridden Nizzolan, who I believe to be possibly the most influential sire so far in Great Britain in the field of endurance horses. He and Magnet will be succeeded by son Granicus for England and daughter Panache for France.

The Long Distance Riding Group of the British Horse Society

Among its many equestrian disciplines the British Horse Society (BHS) numbers a section specifically designed to cater for the long distance riding enthusiast. Known as the Long Distance Riding Group (LDRG), it offers a very comprehensive series of rides with a carefully graduated system whereby riders and horses can progress through easy, moderate, more challenging to ultimately extremely tough rides.

The LDRG was formed in 1975 as the BHS recognized the need to promote the sport along the right lines, but the society's involvement in long distance riding went back considerably further to the mid 1960s. With sponsorship from the *Daily Telegraph* newspaper, the Society ran the first Golden Horseshoe Ride with a then top distance of 50 miles. Initially run over Exmoor, in subsequent years it travelled to several venues, but has since returned permanently to Exmoor where Commander Jim Collins, RN Retd, the Chief Warden of the National Park, sets out a different exacting course each year. Still considered the LDRG's premier ride, the Golden Horseshoe event has progressed from 50 to 75 and now to a 100-mile event which is

run over three days, the first being devoted to veterinary examinations and settling in, and the mileage split into two 50-mile sections on successive days.

However, though the Golden Horseshoe Ride is the best known nationally because of its longevity, the LDRG has expanded its activities enormously from the days of a few qualifiers and one final so that there is scarcely a weekend free during the season. This runs from February through to October, with the most active months being the run up to the May Golden Horseshoe with a dozen qualifiers. Subsequently other major rides take place at intervals throughout the peak of the season, when horses already have the benefit of the long training period.

To take advantage of this ride selection, the rider must be a member of the British Horse Society and also a member of the Long Distance Riding Group. The horse must also be entered in the Long Distance Horse Registry each year. The only rides in which the horse may take part without such entry are in Bronze Buckle Qualifying Rides and training rides. Thereafter both rider and horse must be entered in their relevant categories.

The type of events offered by the LDRG are classified as either Bronze, Silver, or Gold series rides, and, with the exception of the three true Endurance Rides, awards are on a graded system according to speed and condition. Horses must be a minimum of four years for Bronze, five years for Silver, and six years for Gold series rides. Riders must be seventeen years or over with the exception of Bronze series and training rides, where juniors ten years and over, accompanied by an adult, may participate.

Bronze series rides for young and inexperienced horses are 20 milers run at 6½ mph, with a final of 30 miles at 7 mph. Once out of this grade the horse steps up to the Silver Stirrup series with qualifying rides of 40 miles at 7 mph and a final of 50 miles at 7½ mph. Achieving a Silver Stirrup means progression to Gold series rides of 75 miles and upwards. It is the rider, not the horse, who needs to qualify with the exception of horses destined for the Golden Horseshoe Ride. For this both horses and riders must qualify on a yearly basis in the

40-mile qualifying rides held throughout the country.

The other major LDRG rides are three Endurance type events where riders are placed individually. These are the Cotswold 100 miler, run from Cheltenham Racecourse in May; the Goodwood International 100 miler held in June, which is one of the qualifying rides for the ELDRIC trophy; and the National Championships run in either late August or early September. Other important events are 'gated rides' run at a minimum average of 6 mph. At designated stops horses are held over until their pulse has dropped to 64 or below. The rider may re-present the horse at ten-minute intervals with a maximum of thirty minutes at any one halt. Once over this time limit the horse is eliminated.

In common with the EHPS, all horses are subject to random dope testing and failure to allow this incurs elimination. But there are certain peripheral rule differences between the two societies. In the LDRG, on all rides of 30 miles and more each rider must have an adult helper to assist en route and at ride base. There are no weight restrictions but the horse must in the opinion of the veterinary surgeons and steward be up to the weight of the rider and equipment. There is no appeal against veterinary decisions and riders are not permitted to discuss their own horse with the veterinary surgeon during the examination. Pulse must drop within thirty minutes after completion of the ride to 64 bpm.

There are two other major differences relating to the actual rides. Although the Goodwood International Ride has individual classifications and is of Endurance category, veterinary penalties are still deducted but are reflected as one penalty equalling one minute of riding time to be added to the total actual riding time. Therefore the fastest horse is not necessarily the winner. The other major difference concerns averaging out the speed over the entire route. On 'gated rides', and also where stipulated in each ride's rules, the minimum average speed must be maintained over each section of the ride. Thus it makes it more difficult to plot one's speed over an unknown route and detailed attention to the map provided, noting con-

tours and roadwork, is essential. All major rides have a pre-ride and route briefing to assist competitors.

Throughout the year the LDRG runs training rides to encourage newcomers, and at least once a year holds a major conference at their headquarters at Stoneleigh in Warwickshire. Periodic training courses are also held at Stoneleigh, and area organizers run events to promote the sport. In common with EHPS the LDRG discourages financial inducements, the riders campaigning for the sheer achievement of seeing their horse(s) in the national rankings. These are gained at the rate of one point per mile at the Bronze Buckle final and Silver Stirrup qualifiers; two points per mile at Silver Stirrup final and Gold qualifiers, and three points per mile at all Gold series rides. To date there are approaching 700 members and these have a packed season of fifty rides to choose from. Many events hold multiple rides in addition to the major class of the day.

LDRG horses and riders

Following are some of the LDRG horses and riders who have attained national and international distinction.

El Askar

Foaled in 1976, El Askar is a 14.3 hand bay purebred Arabian, owned by Carole Tuggey, who showed just about all his opposition a clean pair of heels in 1985 and 1986, and a considerable amount of talent in previous years.

Carole bought El Askar, or Asky as he is known at home, specifically for endurance riding and has finished five very full seasons with an unblemished record of never being eliminated from a ride. This she attributes to several factors, mainly that she took the first years of his competitive work steadily, never asking too much, so that by the time he was asked to do the extensive programme of major rides he was really mature, and not overstressed. She says his best points are amazing stamina and a very good recovery at veterinary checks and after rides. At rest his parameters are 34/8, which is considerably lower than many distance horses. On

<figure>176</figure>

the reverse side she admits that problems do sometimes arise with temperament clashes between them, and for herself she remarks quizzically that finding a comfortable pair of boots is difficult – a vital asset for a rider prepared to slog on foot leading Asky the many miles she did at the 1986 World Championships to make certain of securing the team gold for Britain.

Having a full time job, Carole has to fit in Asky and his training around work hours. She is another, like Jane Welcher, who rises in the wee hours to get the necessary mileage in, although she does say that now he is mature and fit and knows his job she finds it unnecessary to do so many miles in training as before. To add variety and keep him interested she incorporates jumping, dressage and interval training into his routine, a system which has undoubtedly paid off as the successes continue to mount – though where she goes next I do not know.

To date Asky has 2065 miles in competition, starting with a first season total of 170 miles and finishing with 1986s mileage of 475. Within these confines he has sandwiched three Golden Horseshoe awards; three outright wins in the Goodwood International 100 miler in Britain; two successive 200 km rides at Montcuq, France, resulting in a win and a second place, plus a best condition award; a second place in Britain's Breamore 50 miler; and an outright win in the 1985 *Distance Rider* National Championship for points accrued over a season of both EHPS and BHS rides. To add to national honours Asky includes international awards, with a second place in the ELDRIC trophy for 1985, moving up to a win in 1986, as well as being a member of the gold medal World Championship Team. Quite a record; and these are only his major wins! The two salient features of Asky's career are his steady progress up the scale of achievement, accompanied by his absolute soundness over the five-year period it has taken him to reach his peak.

Asked what she would like to see in the way of improvements in the sport Carole said that additional sponsorship and more press coverage were sorely needed. On the subject of influence she feels that France, with their go-ahead attitude and

the vast number of rides they offer, is in the top league, but would like to see an improvement in their general vetting procedures. She sees the world aspect as one needing continual progress but not at the expense of the horses, and would like to see the stricture on lameness tightened up so that there are no degrees and that if a horse is lame in any degree he is eliminated for his own good.

Triella

A bay 15.2 partbred Arabian mare by Count Duval, Triella (1973) has partnered Gill Shutt for eight consecutive seasons. Campaigned mostly in BHS rides this mare has shown marked consistency and soundness, the only problems being an occasional unavoidable lameness caused by picking up hidden broken glass and a nail in her frog – a hazard only too common amongst distance horses who frequently use National Parks where the car-borne tourist is often careless about the detritus he strews around, as I know to my own occasional cost as well.

Gill was reluctant to tally her successes, and indeed admitted to having forgotten many of them, averring that what really mattered was the rapport between her and Triella, or rather Willow as she is fondly called. She paid tribute to the mare's superb stamina, unflappability, perfect manners and ability to make her feel 'like a queen' at competitions, only to reverse the process at home and revert to 'silly filly' antics at the sight of a leaf or a quivering blade of grass. But Gill's memory does not fail her when it comes to what she terms the 'continual nature ramble', with sunrise suffusing mountain and forest; she recalls a veritable encyclopedia of wild flowers on Exmoor; a black-garbed shepherd and his flock in the Cevennes; wild lavender, huge butterflies and the feel of Triella pounding her way through the ruts and boulders of a forest on one of her many jaunts abroad. Gill rides for fun and pastoral pleasure, the sheer joy of a good horse underneath her, and treats as a bonus her mare's string of successes, including four Golden Horseshoes and many high placings in Endurance Rides from 50- to 100-mile duration.

Triella and Gill have been regular members of the British team competing abroad: in Switzerland;

in France, where the team gained a silver medal; and in the Austrian 160 km, for a team bronze and an individual fourth place. Triella stood fifth in the European rankings in 1985, where riders from nine countries compete for honours. Out of the top ten, four places were filled by British horses and riders and another by a British-bred horse ridden by a British rider who lives in France, riding sometimes for that country and sometimes for Britain.

Along the way it is not only Triella who has gained international recognition. Gill recounts the look of amazement on the faces of the Italian team as she galloped past them to the finishing line at Rosenau, Austria. Triella earned a fourth place and Gill a new title of the 'Galloping Grannie', which she says sounds a whole lot more flattering when rendered in Italian.

Rather than push a much-loved horse too far Triella has been retired to stud at her peak, her heir being a purebred Arabian mare who will have to go a long way to earn the accolade awarded Triella by Anthony Pavord, one of Britain's endurance ride veterinarians, who termed her just about the best distance horse he knew.

Pamela James

Riding mostly in BHS events, Pamela James is one of Britain's leading long distance riders. She has represented Great Britain abroad on several occasions with a considerable amount of success. Her best-known mount is Forest Fox (1976), a bay threequarter Thoroughbred mare, whose home-based successes have been an impressive collection of Golden Horseshoe awards, winning a gold in both 1984 and 1985. When the distance was increased to 100 miles she was one of the few to even finish the course, gaining a silver which more than matched in effort the golds of previous years. A gold was also gained in the Welsh 110-mile three-day ride over tough Black Mountain territory, and at Breamore under EHPS Endurance Ride rules she was third in a very strong field going against the clock. However, the highpoint of her career must surely be her sixth place in the Rome World Championships, in conditions of heat that we are

never faced with in temperate Great Britain. She was one of the victorious gold medal team.

Pam says Foxy tends to be lazy in home workouts but is entirely different at an event, becoming very 'lit up' and taking a while to calm down. In common with good distance riders Pam plans her schedule, never overloading a horse with too many events in a season, and believes that the horse benefits from being able to relax with time off between rides. She has to fit training around a full-time job, doing long rides at weekends. Winter training, which starts just before Christmas, includes as many days' hunting as she can fit in. It alleviates the mileage grind, and both she and Foxy enjoy it. Prior to the big rides she aims to do at least two 40-mile Qualifiers, and then she feels the horse is ready to go.

Before Foxy Pam rode a horse called Saxon, and on him learnt her way, very successfully, around the long distance riding scene. Saxon did everything in spite of her, she says. Between them they won a bronze at their first Golden Horseshoe attempt in 1976, followed by golds in 1977, 1978, 1980 and 1981, as well as a Black Mountain Ride gold. Abroad, Saxon also continued to rack up the miles and the awards with a seventh at Montcuq's extremely tough ride in France in 1980, plus a share of the team gold award at the same ride. In 1981 Pam started to make it a habit to be on a gold medal team when Britain won the team award at Huy in Belgium, where Saxon tied for second place and was awarded the Best Condition prize. However, disaster struck in 1982 when he was hit by a tractor and trailer and had to be destroyed.

The future looks bright with Foxy's stablemate, a dark bay Thoroughbred/Welsh Cob cross gelding foaled in 1982. With Pam's sensible routine her new mount will certainly be making a name for himself. She says that much of endurance riding success is luck, but an equal amount is down to solid preparation and not pushing a horse before he is mature enough. In this her horses score as she takes them steadily, giving them two full seasons before attempting the really big rides, relishing the challenge of bringing a new horse steadily and soundly along.

25 Australia

One of the leading nations in the sport of endurance riding started its involvement in a similar fashion to the USA. As America's endurance scene started with the now famous Tevis Cup ride, so Australia's emergence was the staging of the first Quilty 100 miler. In this case the catalyst was a chance remark at a Sydney meeting of the Arab Horse Society, to the effect that 'it was a pity the public were not made aware of the fact Australian horses must rank among the world's best'.

Spurred by that remark and through the medium of his *Hoof and Horns* magazine, R. M. Williams urged the inauguration of an annual 100-mile ride similar in concept to the by then well-established Tevis Cup. Tom Quilty, OBE, a renowned horseman and noted bushman from the remote Kimberleys in Western Australia, gave a handsome gold trophy and his name to the ride, with the veterinary profession providing the vital safeguards, to ensure humane treatment of the horses involved. Like the Tevis, that first Quilty in 1966 was also closely monitored by the RSPCA who were initially dead set against it, but at the finish concurred with the presiding veterinary surgeon in passing the winner fit. He was the Arabian stallion Shalawi, ridden by Hungarian Gabriel Stecher who elected to complete the whole course bareback.

Since that first running of the now world-famous Quilty, which ranks amongst the half dozen toughest of the world's endurance rides, the challenge to prove Australia's horses amongst the world's best has been repeated not once, but many times a year in the widespread net of endurance rides that attract some of the best horsemen and horsewomen in the endurance riding field worldwide. From the countries in which I have had the good fortune to ride in either CTR or ER on 100 milers, among which are the USA, Germany, Britain and Australia, I would definitely rate Australia in the van with both difficulty of course and wealth of experienced horsemen aboard superb horses. To qualify that statement I would only add that I have not yet been privileged to ride a 100 miler in one day in the USA, my events there being confined to Florida and North Carolina at a time when 100 milers were ridden over three days.

Since those not so small beginnings in October 1966 Australian endurance riding has flourished and is today governed by the Australian Endurance Riders Association (AERA), which from a first-year membership of seventy has risen steeply to 2000 and is steadily growing.

Unlike many other nations with long distance riding associations the AERA has only one ride classification – Endurance – and to this end offers in excess of 140 yearly rides nationwide. Entries average out at around forty-five a ride, which is a very healthy state of affairs, and ride distance is a minimum of 50 miles. All judging is by veterinary surgeons and the main criteria used are satisfactory heart rate and soundness. Heart-rate criteria is much stricter in Australia than in other countries. The horse's heart rate must return to 55 or below at the first mandatory checkpoint, and thereafter it must return to 60 or below. There are no degrees of lameness. The horse must move sound or be eliminated. To maintain the sport's clean bill of health random tests are made at the top rides to detect any use of forbidden substances. No financial reward may be offered in the way of prize money at any AERA event, though in some competitions valuable prizes in kind are given, along with trophies, ribbons, sashes, and most often useful and prestigious buckles that commemorate completions of many of the tough rides. To win a Quilty buckle is considered quite an achievement. Perhaps one of the best things about Australian rules are that they are simple and clear cut, and the rides uncomplicated, as compared to some associations that have a plethora of rules and a bewildering number of rides of differing lengths, speeds and types.

The AERA runs a national award scheme in which annual ratings are recorded in several divisions. The main awards allocated on a points basis are for the National Overall Rider; the Lightweight and Heavyweight Riders; and the Overall Horse. Other prestigious awards are for the yearly high kilometre total, the leading horses running up impressive totals – some over 2000 km a year with others pushing them very close. The AERA accords special merit to all Quilty winners, the leading Horse of the Year and the Leading Distance Horse, and they also keep a distance register, the top honours having been held for a considerable time by Juanita, a molly mule owned and ridden by Patsie Sinfield.

The National Championship is now the Quilty 100 miler, for which all riders must have previously qualified by either achieving an earlier Quilty completion buckle, or by having completed one 50-mile Endurance Ride within the previous twelve months with a riding time not more than 50 per cent in excess of the winning time. All horses must be five years of age shown by state of teeth. This safeguards the technical five-year-old registered horse who may be well short of sixty months in age. The maximum riding time allowed for the Quilty is eighteen hours, exclusive of mandatory veterinary holdover checks. All horses must be adequately shod. Prior to implementing a disqualification the rider has the right of appeal to the Ride Head Veterinarian. No rider is permitted to wear spurs or carry a whip.

Originally the Quilty was always held in New South Wales, but is now moved from state to state on a yearly basis, which means that each state has its share of work involved and also that riders from the home state get the occasional chance to compete in this major ride nearer home. Considering Australia's vast landmass this is a definite bonus.

On a regional basis Australia is split into sections, each of the five states having their own Endurance Riding Association with Tasmania making the sixth. Rules pertaining to each state are largely those of the parent body so that riders travelling to rides out of state are assured of consistency in judging criteria. Each state also runs its own series of annual state awards, similar to the national system. In addition to the Quilty and each state's 100 miler, some of the other notable rides are the Winton to Longreach Hall of Fame ride over five days and 250 miles, and the Shazada ride, also 250 miles in five days. The winners of the multiple-day rides are the horses who have the fastest total riding time over the five days. All major rides have a Best Condition award in addition to placing awards and completion buckle, sash or rosette. One point at variance with other associations is that on higher mileage rides young novice horses may compete under the control of an experienced pacemaking rider to ensure they are not overstressed by too fast a tempo.

Horses and riders

From among the ranks of Australian riders there are a great many who have enviable records, and there are legion top equine performers, far too many to include all who have achieved well-merited national recognition, but from amongst their number are several who stand out for consistency over the years.

Juanita

Juanita has two claims to fame on the Australian endurance ride scene. First, she is ranked number one in the Australian distance register: 7857 km to August of 1986; and secondly, she is currently the only mule in Australian endurance competition. Owner Patsie Sinfield from Bringelly just outside Sydney is in the habit of making firsts in Australian endurance riding, being the first rider to campaign a horse, her Arabian gelding Silver Crystal, to 1000 competitive miles. In between Silver Crystal and Juanita came Tahoe, a bay Standardbred gelding with which she had considerable success, his best achievement being a win in the 500-mile 'Bite the Bullet' Sydney to Melbourne ride ridden by friend Colin Adams.

However, for a long time Patsie had been hank-

27 Juanita and Warwick Sinfield, 1983. (Andrew Roberts Photographics)

ering to try a mule and so Juanita was purchased – a bay part-Arabian molly mule barely 14 hands high. With her came the need for different riding tactics; no more long-striding Arabian or powerhouse Standardbred trot, but the shortened stride of a mule who saw no sense in pushing for the front or into the magical top ten groupings of dedicated successful endurance riders. Yet in spite of liking things her own way and rating herself so that in her whole career she has only once been vetted out, she was piling up the miles towards leading the whole of the country in the distance stakes.

En route a major problem was convincing Juanita that Endurance Rides are ridden in successive sections and that mandatory halts are only of short duration. In her first season she thought otherwise, earning laughter, good natured banter and obvious comments as to her origins and inherited stubborness, as rapid reverse gear was the usual preface to second and third legs. But by the

end of that season she was the first mule to earn a coveted Quilty buckle and had successfully completed five endurance rides. To that first Quilty buckle Juanita has added five more, making her one of the few equines to be repeatedly successful on Australia's top ride.

Of her record total, 2000 km have been run over the now well-established New South Wales Shazada Memorial Ride, which has been run each year since 1981 – 400 km in five days and a real test of endurance. On the Shazada course in 1981 Juanita came into her own, forging on and finishing the 400 km in a total riding time of thirty-nine hours, thirty-two minutes, twenty-six seconds – not a winning time by any means, but for a mule who disliked second and third laps she had done ten over the five days and been ridden into the magical top ten with an eighth place, delighting Patsie who was amazed at the awards ceremony to be called up for Best Conditioned and Best Managed trophy.

Juanita has won this trophy three times on the Shazada Ride.

Once having forged her way into the top ten Juanita repeated her efforts in the 1982 Australian Stockman's Hall of Fame endurance ride, Winton to Longreach in southwest Queensland, then run over a distance of 250 km in two days. It meant an excessive amount of hauling for a two-day ride, but the invitation and challenge of competing a now seasoned and nationally known mule in new territory could not be turned down, and Patsie and Juanita again finished in the top ten. A scant month after this ride Patsie handed Juanita over to son Warwick, who partnered her on that and the following year's Shazada. This has proved to be Juanita's favourite stamping ground, as with Warwick aboard they took a sixth place in 1982, and in 1983 bettered it with a fourth as well as clipping off over ten hours on her first Shazada time and winning Best Managed and Best Conditioned for the second time.

The horse closest to Juanita in the distance register as of August 1986 was over 2500 km behind. Juanita's efforts on the distance trail have resulted in her being acclaimed Australian Mule of the Year by the National Association, and this unusual partnership has been photographed for many newspapers and magazines and has made several television appearances. Thoroughly convinced of 'mule power' Patsie has a young mule waiting to take up where Juanita leaves off.

As well as successfully campaigning Juanita and a variety of horses in endurance riding since she saw the first running of the Quilty, Patsie has put a lot into the sport, being on both the New South Wales Endurance Council Committee and on the National Committee for many years. She has been Secretary four times for the Quilty Ride as well as competing, and has given as much and more to the sport as she has taken out, but says it is difficult to find enough people willing to sacrifice the time and energy needed to run the sport as well as to enjoy it. This is a comment echoed in other countries where a dedicated few run the sport enjoyed by a rapidly increasing number of riders.

Glenallon Solomon

A grey 15.2 hands part-Arab gelding, by Diablo out of Bulliluna, owned and partly trained by Don Paton and campaigned mostly by Jenny Oliver, Glenallon Solomon (1975) is a double Australian National Champion, and in Jenny's words 'has it all, except maybe in looks'. He certainly gives endurance riding his all, with a six-year career liberally sprinkled with ride wins. From thirty starts he has twenty-one wins, two seconds and one third. Add nine course records to that, the fastest for 50 miles in two and threequarter hours, and he is a rarity amongst equines, coming out year after year to hold back any opposition, both nationally and in his home state of New South Wales.

Jenny Oliver was hooked on endurance riding after her first attempt with one of her own commercial trail ride horses, and for three years picked the fittest out of her string to use in competition. But it is with Salty, as he is known to his friends, that her name has been combined in a partnership that will be hard to match, and almost impossible to better.

In his six years' endurance work he has never been overfaced, seven events being the maximum number of rides in any one season, which must be a large part of the reason for his continuing supremacy. Too many horses are burnt out too soon, being crowded with excessive mileage and never given the chance to recuperate. Not so Salty. He has an enviable life-style for a horse, turned away

28 Glenallon Solomon (Salty) and Jenny Oliver. Triple Quilty winner.

for six months each year on good grazing, and never stabled even when in training. This starts with a yearly spell chasing brumbies up in Australia's High Country, then on a more mundane level his training steadies to five days a week with a 6- to 20-mile stint per day – again a modest but steady output. Once he is fit and competing he is only ridden about three days a week to keep him ticking over. Jenny does not believe in overworking a horse, saying that though some horses may vet well they can hardly take another step at the end of a ride.

Feeding Salty is simple: wheaten chaff and all the oats he wants, plus his grazing for natural vitamins and minerals. He comes across as a very uncomplicated horse, endowed with a great temperament and possessed of a long-striding easy canter that eats up the whole distance. He also has that essential facility of complete relaxation at vet checks which is so important in a good distance horse, plus the ability to recover rapidly when completely fit. His heart rate varies, but always in the lower range of 22 to 36 at rest, and after the mandatory thirty-minute rest halts averages out at 47 bpm; thus there are no problems in meeting Australia's very strict criteria, which are tougher than in any other country. The only thing Jenny says needs care is that she or owner Don must declare his dropped hip at pre-ride vet checks, otherwise he could be vetted out lame as he steps short with his off-hind leg. Many horses do have a slight gait discrepancy that in no way impairs their performance.

No longer running commercial trail rides, Jenny has worked as a Mothercraft Nurse, but only took jobs on properties where she could take her current distance horse, and she said that most employers were very understanding. Currently a self-employed housepainter in Tumut, her work fits around her endurance riding rather than the other way as with so many riders. Jenny's endurance wins have not been confined to Salty, although he has given her her most prestigious awards. She has been Snowy Mountains Rider of the Year five times; New South Wales Rider of the Year three times; National Rider of the Year twice; and National Distance Mileage Rider of the year

twice. Her own horses have helped her to these awards as Salty's total mileage to the end of the 1986 season is 1717 miles – far below many other great horses, but into that he has packed more major credits than horses with double the distance. Amongst his twenty-one successes his major wins have been the 1985 and 1986 Tom Quilty 100 miler, the two-day Winton to Longreach Event, and a New South Wales State Championship 100 miler. And as this book goes to the publisher Jenny has airmailed me news that Salty has made it three Quiltys in a row, winning the 1987 ride in Tasmania, thus making him a triple champion and a legend in his own lifetime in Australian endurance riding history.

Jenny would not like the sport to turn professional as commercial gain would work to the horses' detriment in favour of the owners' bank balances, but she would like to see greater sponsorship and hopes that the FEI will grant it Olympic status. On the veterinary side she would like to see some of the other endurance riding nations tighten up their veterinary criteria to meet the stricter standards prevailing in Australia.

Andarra Shareef

One of the big guns in world endurance riding by any set of standards, and one of Australia's all-time greats, Andarra Shareef (1973) is a 15.3 hand, 440 kg, grey Anglo-Arab gelding by Shareym out of Mercury. Owner Terry Wood, a solicitor from Kilaben Bay, New South Wales, sent me his partner's record, and very impressive it is. Starting as a five year old he has had eight years of competition, and in that time has logged 4660 km in the official AERA Distance Register and competed in forty-seven rides, the shortest 80 km, the longest 400 km run over five days. He has had sixteen outright wins – four at 80 km; two at 120 km; seven at 100 km; two at 110 km; and one at 400 km. Of these sixteen wins ten were complemented by achieving the Best Condition award. In addition he has also been in the top ten on twenty other occasions. Three of his top tens – a second, a third and a ninth – were in the Quilty 100 miler. Numbers of horses entered in most of the rides were consistently high, sometimes well over 100, so his achievements are of a

29 Andarra Shareef and Terry Woods on the 1985 Quilty. (Andrew Roberts Photographics)

high order, particularly considering Australia has a reputation for producing really tough endurance horses.

Terry says his best win was the 1986 Shazada endurance test over 400 km in which there were ninety-seven entries. Andarra Shareef started the ride weighing in at 440 kg and finished having only lost 5 kg (11 lb) over the whole five days! His heart rate averaged out at 40.9 at the end of the thirty-minute checks, which is only 10.9 above his resting rate of 30. Other memorable wins were the 1984 ACT Brindabella Range 110 km, with a victory two hours ahead of his nearest rival, and with compara-

ble low heart readings; and Barr Topps 100 km, another decisive win by one and a quarter hours to which was added Best Condition. All these wins and places led to accumulating high scores in several national league tables, so that in 1983 and 1984 Andarra Shareef was National Horse of the Year and also national one horse, one rider high scorer, as well as leading state horse for New South Wales. In 1986 he came through with convincing wins for both National and New South Wales Horse of the Year. One very relevant point is that all his awards have been in New South Wales rides, so to win a National Horse Award not once but repeatedly is some achievement, as a travelling horse will have the chance to add out-of-state rides to a total score.

Statistics aside, Terry says Andarra Shareef has that most desirable of endurance horse character-istics – durability. He has never been beaten in a run for the wire in a level start, having a very fleet turn of foot. His fastest finishing time was four hours six minutes over a 100 km course. Allied to this he is an easy horse to train and very intelligent, though his owner does say that he guesses most riders sticking to one horse for so long would find this. I agree entirely, as if the rapport is not there, a rider will not put the necessary work into a horse that is not a pleasure to be with; the endurance then tends to be more on the rider's side.

Although Andarra Shareef is considered by some to be a flat country horse he has competed five times in the Snowy Mountains, racking up four wins! His flatland training is done around Terry's home in the scenic semi-rural areas surrounding Lake Macquarie where there is access to miles of trails and hills. Training consists mainly of short fast workouts, with a total weekly average of be-tween 50 and 80 km. This is augmented by jogging and swimming the horse on a lead rope, the major workouts being the competitions themselves. Andarra Shareef is fed a high grain ration of up to 8 kg (over 17 lb) a day comprising whole oats, cracked corn (maize) and grain mix with additions of vitamins, minerals, calcium, diphosphate, veget-able oil, and electrolytes as needed, as well as lucerne hay ad lib.

Terry says it helps that all the family, his wife

Anne and their three children, are interested in horses. He finds endurance riding a relaxation but admits that having a champion horse keeps his adrenalin flowing. On an outward-looking note he thinks endurance riding has a bright future as it offers riders a chance to test themselves, but that more professional control is needed to protect the horses and to keep the highly competitive rider from drifting away to other areas of equine competition. Sponsorship in Australia is growing, but at present the Rides' Administration is stretched to keep up with the sport's rapid growth.

Bob Sample

Terry Woods has also sent me some personal correspondence between himself and Queensland top endurance rider, Bob Sample, with permission to use the information provided.

Bob Sample's first contact with endurance riding was in 1970. His best-known mount is Sharahd Sheek, a grey three-quarter Arabian gelding, standing 15.2 hands and weighing, when competition fit, 375 kg (827 lb). In addition to Sheek he has trained many other horses for the sport and currently operates a trekking establishment that is a world apart from the normal concept of such places, in that he usually has eight or nine horses capable of competing at top level in the famous Quilty 100 miler. Bob states that his horses are not ridden until four years old and the bulk of their work is steady and slow, most of it in mountains due to his own location.

He is forthright in his opinions, which are backed by nearly two decades of experience. The current wastage of young horses pushed over the top by excessive demands before they are mature appals him. Along with some few top riders I have contacted, he realizes that it takes several years to bring a potential endurance horse to his best, during which time muscles, bones, tendons and ligaments are conditioned and strengthened. Before this is achieved he feels speed should not be asked of young horses. He says that heart and lungs are easier to condition, so that a rider can achieve a quick success, but too much of this early pressure will inevitably result in damage to the horse who has not had sufficient time to repair after a stressful

event. He calls this last factor 'cumulative stress', the build-up of stress and damage in mature as well as young horses through continued competition without the opportunity for rest.

Bob's event horses all receive a very necessary three-month break from riding, and during the competitive season no horse is asked for as much as it will give. After each ride sufficient time to recover from the stress of an event is given, and depending on the event and other factors this could be one week or one month.

Sheek is a prime example of conservative competing, being campaigned for nine years but never being asked to cram the maximum number of rides into any one season.

Bob would like to see the veterinary supervision become even more stringent with criteria such as hydration, sore or tender backs, joints and ligaments being sufficient reason to eliminate a horse from further competition at a specific event rather than the current simpler criteria of adequate recovery rates and gait soundness.

It takes courage to state publicly his feelings that the sport needs a fresh look taken and a tougher set of standards laid down, but it is with thinking and caring riders that the continuing success of the sport of endurance riding rests.

Betty Serpell

Betty Serpell has been dubbed the Quilty Queen for her unequalled record of Quilty 100 miler completions. She took part in the very first ride in 1966 on a tough pony mare, Rusty Miss, whom she described as a working machine and a superb packhorse. Since winning that first Quilty buckle she has raised her total to fourteen, and was the first rider to gain the 1000 mile award for ten Quiltys completed. Nearly all her mounts have been homebred at the family farm in Mitta Mitta, Victoria. With her mainstay, husband Jack who crews for her, she makes a yearly pilgrimage to wherever the Quilty is held. Other of her Quilty mounts have been Scimitar Quick Silver, and the Faraway homebreds, Rikkara, Lutana, Prinera and Reckless. Rikkara, on whom she has done many a distance ride, was the direct result of her first Quilty success: Rusty Miss was the first mare to

30 Betty Serpell, husband Jack and Faraway Rikkara.

complete and won a prize of a service to the purebred Arabian Rikham from Ron and Val Males' Ralvon Stud.

Betty and Jack are two very generous people indeed, hosting a succession of distance riders from around the world. It was Betty who loaned me a mount, her homebred Faraway Lutana, when I rode in the 1977 Quilty while she rode her purebred Arab mare Prinera, and I attribute being able to win my coveted Quilty buckle in large measure to her encouragement and help along the route, which was not without its hazards and lighter side: on a benighted and very steep incline Prinera's bridle fell off leaving Betty without means of control until I replaced it, and soon after I found myself around Lutana's ears when the saddle elected to dive forward on the same descent – in retrospect amusing but not at the time, and thankfully darkness did cover the unedifying sight. Julie Suhr from the USA has also benefited from a

Faraway horse in recent years, doing the 50-mile Taralga Endurance Ride.

After riding the Quilty on a Serpell horse I was lucky enough to stay for a few days at Jack and Betty's farm and see some of her horses who are destined for the distance trail. Before embarking on their endurance careers Betty first takes them on mountain pack trips, leading the young horses so that any misstep in the rugged country she uses is only of danger to the horse until it has learnt to take care of itself. Only then is it ready to care for the rider as well.

She and Jack travel widely in the outback of Australia, hating crowded cities, but revelling in the chance to sample station life. Betty is never happier than when aboard a good Arabian horse and occasional letters recount long days spent working cattle as well as her latest endurance exploits. Over the years the policy of breeding Arabians for performance in a real working system has been vindicated, and Serpell stock have been good ambassadors for the Australian Arab Horse Society. Allied to the breeding goes the training, and Faraway Farm has an excellent reputation and lives up to it. I was greatly encouraged when told that any horse of Serpell breeding and training would go the distance. Betty Serpell has fourteen Quilty buckles to prove it!

26 Austria

Although Austria does not have a specific national association to cater for the sport of endurance riding, it is incorporated into the Bundesfachverrand für Reiten und Fahren in Österreich which governs all sections of equestrian sport. As a member of the ELDRIC Austria is designated under the logo FENA.

As a recognized equestrian discipline endurance riding is relatively new in Austria, the first official ride taking place as recently as 1980. FENA's Chief Officer for endurance riding is Dr Hilde Jarc, herself a very prominent endurance rider in both Austria and further afield in international competitions, and she has been kind enough to fill me in on the state of the sport in her country.

In endurance riding's first officially recognized year membership numbered thirty, and since then it has doubled so that there is now a hard core of sixty active riders, not counting non-riding associates. The number is steadily growing as the sport gains momentum. There are upwards of ten sanctioned rides a year, all of which are of the Endurance category. Judging is done on two levels, that of speed and that of speed and condition, and general ride rules fall into line with the FEI rules for endurance riding (see p. 203). Most rides carry token awards, trophies, rosettes, and so on, with the occasional departure into awarding prize money.

Ride distances vary tremendously with the shortest being a mere 30 km, and the longest 300 km spread over three days, and the number of entries varies from ten to twenty-five per event. However, although Austria is relatively new to endurance riding and numbers are not great she does have the benefit denied some of the peripheral countries in Europe, especially Great Britain, of finding it rather easier to travel horses to surrounding countries, especially Germany which has such a wealth of events to offer. For such a new venture Austria also has a small but good selection of major events, the premier ride being the Vienna to Budapest in three days over 300 km. This is followed in order of importance by the 100 miler Championship ride at Raglitz; the Wienerwald 100 km, and the Frankenau 160 km. At present there are no specific qualifications for entering any of the major rides other than those required by standard rules. Dr Jarc would like to see more sponsorship being awarded to the sport so that endurance riding could continue to grow in Austria, and on a wider basis in Europe. She feels prize money is unnecessary and tends to spoil the sport, but says financial help is really needed for organizers and to enable financially struggling but good riders to reach their potential. As with so many of the less privileged sports, organizers frequently dip deep into their own pockets, and some riders do need the boost of a subsidy to gain the necessary experience in international events.

Horses and riders

Though small in numbers of participating riders Austria does have several horses and riders of national calibre, but the most successful and well-known at home and abroad to date is Hilde Jarc.

Samum and Hilde Jarc

Samum (1969) is a grey, 15 hand gelding weighing approximately 350 kg (770 lb) when in hard training. Of the Arab Shagya breed he was bred in the Styrian Alps and spent his formative years in the mountains, which must account for a certain amount of his hardiness and soundness of wind and limb. Bought at four years of age by Hilde Jarc and husband Andreas he began a very varied career. Once, that is, both riders had managed to direct his exuberance and love of speed into

31 Dr Hilde Jarc and Samum. (Andreas Jarc)

acceptable performance channels. Until he was eleven he participated successfully in dressage, showjumping and eventing, and finally when most distance horses have the bulk of their careers behind them he embarked on what was to prove his most outstanding field of performance – endurance riding.

In his six-year-long second career he totalled 1000 km of competitive work, which though well beneath those of leading horses from other nations is a considerable achievement in a country with a very limited total number of annual events. Initially he went solo, Hilde trying out his capabilities in a mock ride of her own, and finding him admirably suited to the sport persuaded a group of her friends to band together and organize Austria's first endurance rides in 1980. It was really a case of having an ideal prospect and nowhere to compete, so to Samum can be credited the emergence of Austrian endurance riding. For the next two years he reg-

ularly placed in second and third slots, distances being for the most part around the 60-km mark, and it was not until 1982 when Austria had her first 100-km ride that he showed himself at his best. The longer the distance the better he performed: one of the real qualities of the true endurance horse is that the more the pressure is on the better they seem, not really showing themselves superior until most horses have waned.

During the next four years this little horse continued to improve, in 1982 achieving his first international win in a 100-km ride which was also Austria's first international event. In 1983 he made the tremendous leap from a 100- to 300-km ride when the first Vienna to Budapest race was jointly organized by Austria and Hungary. Samum turned in another winning performance in the very fast total riding time for the three days of eighteen hours, forty minutes, being two and a half hours ahead of his nearest rival. Hilde and Andreas then considered retiring him at the peak of his career at fourteen years of age, but were deterred because rumours circulated that the effort of the ride had caused him to break down. I have found in the past that once a horse hits the top, whether it be showing or endurance riding, there are always those ready to carp and cast slurs, and though hurtful it is one of the costs of victory. Fortunately such jealousy is only shown by a few who usually stay ashamedly unnamed. In Austria they were made to eat their words as Samum came back strongly in the 1984 season with a second place in his first 100 miler in a day at Florac, in France, being pipped at the post by a mere thirty seconds, and in 1985 had a fitting close to a remarkable endurance career by winning Austria's first 100 miler and the Open European Championships with riders from eight nations competing.

Hilde credits Samum with having led her to the sport and comments on the deep relationship achieved with her horse which helps counteract the envy shown of his ability. Obviously he is very dear to her and at present she has no thoughts of a replacement, but will continue to participate in the sport by giving back much of the enjoyment gained in her enduring partnership with Samum by continuing to promote the sport for her country.

Endurance riding started as recently as 1980 in Belgium under the guidance of the late André Heinen. Originally it was at its strongest in the southeast of the country, but now it is spreading rapidly northwards. The Belgian Long Distance Riding (BLDR) association is a section of ANTE, the National Association for Equestrian Tourism, and is also affiliated to the Royal Belgian Equestrian Sports Federation (FRBSE). The BLDR association is also a full member of the ELDRIC.

The first Belgian endurance ride took place on 20 April 1980, starting from the Sainte Anne Equestrian Centre at Outrelouxhe, Huy, followed in the same year by three more rides. Over 200 riders nationwide competed in 1986 when the number of rides had increased to sixteen, each event offering several categories of competition. Belgian ride structure is similar to that of Germany and Britain, with horses being eased through the initial years of competition. The Belgian Highway Code requires riders to be fourteen years of age before being permitted on the roads, but junior riders of this age may compete.

Belgian ride categories

Initiation Rides

Run under CTR rules and with distances of between 20 and 30 km covered at speeds between 8 and 15 kph. These are designed to offer those contemplating fuller participation the opportunity to decide if they wish to go further in the sport.

Qualifying Rides

For horses four years of age and upwards. Distances are a minimum of 40 and a maximum of 60 km, and are run at speeds of between 10 and 15 kph. Starting order is either individually or in small groups, with a maximum of three riders at a time and a gap of two minutes between each individual or group. For a ride starting at 9 a.m. all horses must be en route by 11.30 a.m. Judging is on a CTR basis with all horses qualifying that complete within the required time and pass the veterinary examination at the finish. In addition to qualifying awards there are placings for the first five horses judged on a condition basis.

Regional Rides

For horses of five years of age and upwards, qualifying in at least two Qualifying Rides the previous season. Distances are minimum 60 and maximum 80 km. Speed is a minimum of 10 kph and a maximum of 15 to 18 kph, the higher limit being advised in the programme. Judging is on the same basis as for Qualifying Rides.

National Rides

For horses six years of age and upwards that have qualified the previous season in at least two Regional or one National ride. Distances are a minimum of 80 km and a maximum of 160 km per day. For rides run over more than one day the minimum daily distance is 60 km. Judging is as for Endurance Rides with no upward limit on speed, all horses completing who pass the veterinary criteria.

There are no monetary prizes in any Belgian ride. All participants must be paid up members of ANTE and of their National Federation.

For riders' convenience routes must be marked four days prior to the event. Marking must be adequate and changes of direction well positioned and in plenty of time. Distances are marked every 5 km. Riders going off course are eliminated. Rides are based on an average speed of 10 kph and using this as a guide all control posts are closed one hour after the last horse to start should have cleared the post in question. Considering that entries are not of the massive order of American and some heavily subscribed British rides this means that the later starters especially must keep an even pace throughout the ride, watching they do not drop dangerously behind the 10 kph average on any one section. Failure to reach a control post before closure incurs elimination.

Throughout the event riders may dismount and lead their horses if they so desire. Galloping is forbidden on either concrete or asphalt surfaces, and when in sight of the finish it is forbidden to stop and wait. No rider change is permitted once the horse has started on the route. As long as all tack fits well, the only restrictions as to equipment used on the horses are that blinkers and work bandages (*flanelles de travail*) are not allowed. All horses must be shod and each animal will be inspected by a farrier before the start to ensure it is adequately shod. Riders may dress as they please provided it is appropriate to the event. Hard hats are advised, but are not obligatory. Whips and spurs are permitted. Riders are reminded that at all times they must adhere to the Belgian Code of Law.

If any rules are infringed by the rider the BLDR association imposes sanctions. Such infringements are considered by a Ride Jury whose President may also impose sanctions for any abuse of horses, such as pushing an already exhausted horse, misuse of spurs and whips, or aggressive attitude of rider towards the ride authorities. In all cases elimination of the rider will follow. If a rider wishes to appeal against such a decision he/she must put the appeal in writing accompanied by a sum of 500 BFr. If the complaint concerns ride organization it must be lodged before the ride starts. If it concerns something during the ride it must be lodged no more than half an hour after the prize giving. Veterinary controls throughout the Belgian rides are similar to those in other ELDRIC countries. The panel of veterinary judges is in the ratio of one veterinary surgeon to every ten horses. For rides of Regional and National standing all horses must have been vaccinated against tetanus. Horses that come from or are competing in a ride held south of the line of the Sambre and Meuse Rivers

must also have an anti-rabies vaccination. Vaccination cards must be produced.

All horses are examined before the ride, at the finish, and again thirty minutes later. For rides in excess of 40 km there are veterinary examinations en route. The maximum distance between veterinary inspections is 40 km. At mandatory halts there are rest periods of between forty five minutes (minimum) and sixty minutes (maximum). At these halts riders must present a card which has their name, number, horses' name, colour and age inscribed. This is carried throughout the ride and surrendered at the final check. Veterinary criteria are that horses shall recover to a heart rate of 64 or below and respiration of 48 or below by the final check thirty minutes after the finish. Cardiac and respiratory rates are known as Veterinary Criteria 'A'. Other areas of veterinary assessment known as Criteria 'B' are: anomalies in heart or respiratory rhythms, dehydration, congestion of mucous membranes, heatstroke, defective sight, lameness, blemishes (trauma) and doping. All drugs are expressly forbidden and random tests are made to detect their use. Only one veterinary surgeon is needed to judge Criteria 'A'. If the horse fails there is no appeal against the decision. With Criteria 'B' there must be a majority decision by the veterinary panel. Should an equal number of veterinary surgeons favour passing the horse as sound as are against it, then the President of the Ride Jury will pass in favour of the horse. If a rider considers his horse should not have failed Criteria 'B' he may, before the end of the day, present his horse before a commission of three veterinary surgeons appointed by the Council. They must put their decision in writing on the horse's identification card. If a horse fails to pass Criteria 'A' on three successive rides he shall be suspended during the next ten rides, demoted to a lower category and be required to requalify to the higher level. Any rider who rides a horse so disqualified also incurs the same sanction.

A rider who commits any bad breach of conduct such as excessive speed, insufficient training of his/her horse, brutal treatment, and so on, may be barred from entering one or more rides, or be suspended for six or twelve months. He/she may also be permanently barred from competing. If a rider should be unfairly penalized he may be fully reinstated in his right to enter events.

Mares that are three months or more in foal may not be entered in rides, nor may mares with foals at foot.

For all National Rides the horses are examined the day before the ride, and the final vetting is conducted a minimum of five hours after the finish. To pass this examination the horse must satisfy the veterinary surgeon that it is in a condition to go a further distance of 30 km without stress. At the final vetting a Best Condition prize is also awarded.

Where a 'vet gate' voluntary control is used it must be advertised at least 1 km in advance. At the control the rider can present his horse when he wishes during the half hour after his arrival. If he fails to pass the Criteria 'A' test the rider must wait ten minutes and re-present. If he fails again he is eliminated. After passing Criteria 'A' the rider must wait fifteen minutes and present for assessment of gaits. If he is sound he may continue. The time taken at this type of control is considered part of the total riding time, and not as with mandatory halts in addition to riding time.

With a firm base of Regional and National Rides the Belgian calendar has for several years also included two international rides. These are the two-day 150-km ride at Spa in July, and the 130-km ride at Condroz in August, which is run over a very demanding course. The Condroz Ride, starting at the School of Equitation at Gesves, is run under FEI rules. Both rides count towards the ELDRIC Challenge Cup which is decided annually on a points system, with riders competing both nationally and in at least one foreign ELDRIC-sanctioned ride. Belgium, with three other ELDRIC signatories on her borders – Germany, France and the Netherlands – is in an ideal situation to entertain riders from other countries and to send her own best riders to compete in international events.

Among the most prestigious Belgian rides are the Condroz 130-km at Gesves, the FEI International; L'Ardennaise (120 km) at Werbomont, an ELDRIC ride; Wangenie–Charleroi (110 km), an ELDRIC ride; Lesve (100 km), National A ride;

and Theux (70 km in two days), National B ride.

Participation in endurance rides in Belgium has grown steadily. Results from all official rides in 1986 showed a healthy increase, with a total of 200 horses entering rides throughout the season, seventy-two of which qualified in Regional Rides and forty-four in National level competition.

Horses and riders

Belgium, being so small, has yet to run the extensive list of annual rides offered by countries with much larger equestrian populations, but she has riders well able to challenge the best in Europe. A brief look at a few of her horses and riders is offered below.

Dominique Crutzen

One of the best-known Belgian riders, Dominique Crutzen, is partnered by Domino, a grey, 15.2½ hands, half Arabian gelding. He bought the seven year old for general riding purposes and quite by chance found he had an aptitude for endurance riding. In the past three seasons he has covered over 2000 km in Belgian and foreign rides, but covers in excess of 2500 km annually, about half of which are currently in competition. Dominique says Domino's best points are an exceptionally good recovery during events, with rates quickly returning to or near his normal resting values of heart 32, respiration 10. Important for a horse entering the highly competitive arena of European FEI and ELDRIC rides, Domino has a fleet turn of foot which has put him well to the fore in Belgian rides and on more than one occasion gained him high placings abroad. Dominique and Domino placed eleventh in the first World Championships, the only Belgian pair to complete the course, and the first Belgian to complete 100 miles in one day. They have also won at Rambouillet in France. At home he was just pipped at the post at the premier Belgian ride at Condroz in 1986 and finished the season ranking fourth in Europe in the ELDRIC Challenge Trophy.

Asked what led him to take up endurance riding, Dominique said it was because he already owned the ideal prospect in a horse of Arabian breeding and he attributes his successes so far to a thorough understanding between Domino and himself. For the future he sees the sport growing apace in Belgium and centres his own ambitions around training and competing with several horses of his own breeding. He would like to see increased sponsorship and greater involvement of veterinary surgeons. Looking outwards he credits both America and Britain with having given most to the sport.

Beatrice Delvaux

A relative newcomer to endurance riding, in only one year Beatrice Delvaux has had considerable success with her Belgian Trotter Elza (1977), a bay 15.2 hand mare. Initially friends convinced Beatrice to enter for endurance riding. She has to fit her trotter's training around her own working hours, so that exercising is usually done in the afternoons several times a week, with longer rides taking place at weekends. Elza is out by day, stabled at night, and fed on a complete ration. In her first season she gained the Best Condition award in the 70 km National class at the Spa meeting, and placed sixth in the international 130-km class at Condroz against very strong competition. Elza's recovery at rides is rapid, but her *bete noîre* is hot weather. In all her competitions the mare finished in good condition, with the exception of Rome where she tied up and was eliminated. However, it says much for Beatrice's rapid success in home rides that the Belgian national federation included her and Elza in their national team. Beatrice says that in Belgium the sport is still at the amateur stage but improving little by little, and that the same group of people keep on supporting the sport. From her visit to Rome she acknowledges the greater experience of other nations, and in the horses' interests would like to see the 160 km split into a two-day ride. She sees the main advantage of endurance riding as the opportunity really to know one's horse and progress steadily to the top without overstressing it. Her accolade goes to France as the nation that has given most to the sport on several counts, including television and press coverage and veterinary research. On the home front she would like to see an improvement in prizes awarded.

Hermanne Nelly Philippot

Hermanne Nelly Philippot rides a bay purebred Arabian stallion, Sahab Rahhal (1976), raised at his stud, the Haras du Moirmonay at Arville. Sahab Rahhal was bred for performance, but because the Arabian specializes in endurance riding he was especially suited to the new Belgian sport. Monsieur Philippot has only a limited amount of time to devote to endurance riding, as running his stud of twenty-five purebred Arabians is a full-time occupation and he can only take part for four or five months during the year. Sahab Rahhal's yearly training covers approximately 700 km, and his total competition distance is in excess of 900 km. His records show he has exceptionally good recovery in both heart and respiration departments, but the main thing his rider has to watch out for is underfoot going, as the stallion has very sensitive soles.

The spur urging M. Philippot to enter endurance rides was the known ability of the Arabian, his own fortunate circumstances in breeding the horse for the job, and a long-standing interest in the sport. He has had considerable success in the four years he and Sahab Rahhal have competed, the stallion regularly figuring in placings in both Regional and National Rides and winning Best Condition on several occasions. He puts these successes down to the breed's ability, his own stallion's good condition and a sensible mode of riding.

The outlook for Belgian endurance riding he sees as very good, and hopes that the BLDR's major rides will extend distances and be held over several days, and that more 100-mile one-day rides will be run. As a breeder of purebred Arabians he hopes to prove several of his own horses in endurance riding up to National level, and achieve a distance of 1000 km in competition. On a personal level endurance riding gives him a closeness to his horse and the chance to ride regularly, although he feels that at present he has insufficient time for enough training. On a national level he sees the sport as offering promotion to equestrian tourism, and as a dedicated horseman he would like to see more education for newcomers to the sport so that horses are not ruined by ignorance. His accolade goes unreservedly to the USA for giving most to the sport.

Sahab Rahhal stands at public stud and spends a part of his life preparing for the covering season. In his owner's words he is a 'horse for all seasons', and promotes the Arabian breed by his performance. All his endurance training is done on the trail, but he also gives demonstrations and takes part in many other equestrian activities. The stud's policy is to treat each horse as an individual. Each horse is fed a balanced ration, particularly suited to Arabians, high in oats and including mineral salts. The amount fed depends on degree of work and individual metabolism.

Leon Wauters

Leon Wauters only started endurance riding in 1985 but went in at the deep end and with total commitment to the sport. He is partnered by an unregistered piebald gelding called Djahil (1973), who stands 15.1 and weighs 850 lb. Djahil was not bred for endurance riding but when Leon bought him he certainly found himself with no time for anything else. In two seasons he has covered over 8000 km (5000 miles). His annual competitive distance is 1000 km. He has enviably low heart and respiratory rates, is very calm and surefooted, and accepts the presence of other horses without getting excited. He is well built and has a good back – very important in a distance horse. The only drawback is his respiration in very hot weather.

The spur to Leon taking up endurance riding was the presence in his home town of the Belgian champion, and since entering the sport he has racked up an impressive list of achievements with Djahil. These he attributes to training, perseverance and the encouragement given by his coach.

Apart from his successes he gets most enjoyment out of an increasing understanding and rapport with Djahil and aims to finish each ride with Djahil in as good a condition as possible. He does admit that the thing that causes him most trouble is finding enough time to train, but even so he manages to devote about fifty hours a month to Djahil. He rides him around 100 km a week and sometimes exercises him on the lunge. He pays particular attention to his horse's health by having regular vet checks, and is lucky to have a really good farrier.

He says Belgian endurance riding is expanding rapidly, and that world endurance riding is coming closer to having a recognized standard for all countries. France gets his vote as number one, because of the number of rides organized throughout the country and the coverage it gets in the national press. He would like to see more recognition at official level for the sport, and sponsorship of a Belgian national team.

Leon should be proud of his and Djahil's achievements. The results show dedication to the exclusion of all other activities, and amongst them the main credits are: 1985 National Champion; Leading Distance Horse with highest number of competitive kilometres ridden; Leading Horse with highest veterinary score throughout the season; Leading Horse in the Namur–Luxembourg Region. Consistently placing in the National Rides helped to gain the pair these awards. In 1986 Djahil and Leon represented their country both in Rome and in Rambouillet, France, placing tenth, as well as placing in both Belgian international rides. The pair finished well up in the rankings throughout Europe for the ELDRIC Challenge Cup, taking eleventh place out of riders from all the ELDRIC signatories entered.

The Canadian Long Distance Riding Association (CALDRA) was formed in late 1983, and in May 1985 became incorporated as a federal company and was registered with Revenue Canada as an Amateur Athletic Association. However, though the Canadian association is relatively new, the sport of Competitive Trail and Endurance Riding has been gaining popularity since the late 1960s. The number of members since CALDRA's formation in 1983 has grown from an individual membership of forty-one to a current total in excess of ninety, and provincial club membership from five to seven. Provincial clubs represented are British Columbia, Alberta, Manitoba, Ontario, Nova Scotia, New Brunswick and Prince Edward Island. Saskatchewan and Quebec have individual members.

CALDRA's aims, as well as promoting the amateur sport of long distance riding and ensuring that all rides are run humanely, are to educate as wide a spectrum of participants in the sport as possible. This covers not only riders, but clubs and judges. They compile a useful list of veterinary surgeons qualified to judge Competitive Trail and Endurance Rides; lay judges; pulse and respiration technicians; and technical advisers. With the sport now truly international they are actively concerned with developing potentially successful riders to represent Canadian endurance riding in international competitions.

The main driving force in forming a national association has been Nancy Beacon of Flesherton, Ontario, who spearheaded the formation of CALDRA, and is currently its very active President. She is assisted by Angela Markoff from Stouffville, Ontario, in her capacity as Secretary and Treasurer. Both Nancy and Angela are keen competitors and are thus able to offer valid services from a wide base of experience in the actual riding side of the sport – a facet that is sometimes not so evident among other associations' officers.

CALDRA is concerned with promoting all types of long distance riding – Endurance, Competitive Trail, and Ride and Tie – but their main concern lies with Endurance Rides which are run under American Endurance Ride Conference (AERC) rules with a minimum distance of 50 miles.

Their chief veterinary surgeon is Dr James Bryant, DVM, who is Canada's representative on the FEI Endurance Subcommittee and who also officiated in the capacity of veterinary surgeon at the Rome World Endurance Championships in 1986.

At present Canada has no scheme for awards culminating in selecting a national champion, partly because the territory covered by CALDRA is so vast and participation in a broad scheme of rides difficult for members to enter, but they do have a team championship run on Competitive Trail Ride lines. Teams from each province are eligible to compete, the first winners in 1985 being Ontario, with Quebec reserve. This ride was run over two days with a 60-mile course, and in 1986 CALDRA had its first 100-mile three-day CTR, from which team champions were New Brunswick, with Prince Edward Island reserve. To keep the sport in the amateur realm prizes awarded are of token type only. Recognition of success is marked by mileage awards, and for such a young association dedicated involvement is evidenced by several horses and riders passing the 1000 mile mark, with a few clearing the 1500 and 2000 mile barriers.

Canada's progress on a national basis has been rapid. With formation in late 1983 they already had two teams competing at the 1986 North American Championships in California, and Danny Grant on Soliloquy placed a very creditable eighth, while the Canadian West Team placed fourth. Secretary

Angela publishes a quarterly magazine entitled *Going the Distance* in which she keeps the far-flung Canadian endurance scene in touch with regional, national, and international news. In 1986 Canada became a member of the ELDRIC which is now fast changing to a world rather than a European organization.

Horses and riders

Nancy Beacon

The luminary behind Canadian endurance riding is also a rider of note with eighteen years of experience, over 1200 miles in Endurance and a comparable distance in Competitive Trail competition behind her. Nancy Beacon began her distance riding career in 1970 with a horse named Nugget who carried her on her first 100 miler which was run over two days in the mountains of Vermont, USA. Spurred on with a second place in ten hours, thirty-nine minutes, twenty-one seconds, she has trained many horses during the ensuing years and is currently campaigning two: a 15.2 hand Morgan gelding, Trija's Whiperpopper (1971), and a part-bred Arabian gelding, Shamirad (1970). Nancy has a full-time job plus giving much of her 'free' time to furthering CALDRA's interests. In between she conditions and trains her horses, but shares the actual competition with other riders. Given a choice she prefers Endurance to Competitive Trail Riding, preferring the simpler rules, and the excitement that Endurance competitions afford.

Trija's Whiperpopper is the leading horse in the Canadian mileage stakes, having well over 1500 Endurance miles under his girth plus many Competitive Trail and Ride and Tie miles as well. Although Nancy says he is not a racer he has an excellent record for Endurance completions and has well over 500 miles of top tens in a long career starting in 1978, and has qualified for the Purina Race of Champions. Her other horse, Shamirad, is in the top ten list for Ontario's Endurance horses and also has over 1500 Endurance miles, plus many Competitive Trail and Ride and Tie distances recorded. He was successfully partnered by Mike Cottenden in the North American Cham-

pionships in 1986 and was also a member of the Canada East Team. Because of a sensible programme over the years both horses are sound after nearly a decade of competition and still in the forefront of Canadian competitions. It also says much in the way of generosity that Nancy is prepared to surrender the rides on horses she owns and trains in order to act as Chef d'Equipe on Canadian forays into international competition.

As President of CALDRA Nancy sees the overall view of her country's position in the sport and says there is great need for major sponsorship, and also a need for the sport to be accorded a higher profile in the equine world, especially as it is improving all the time and gaining greater support. In Canada itself she says it is going well with a steady increase in popularity.

CDR Soliloquy

A bay 15.1 hand, 910 lb purebred Arabian gelding, CDR Soliloquy was bred by the Cartwright D. Ranch of High River, Alberta, primarily for ranch work. He was snapped up as an endurance prospect by Rob Douglas. As a five year old his endurance career started with a bang. He won all his rides bar one in which he was second, and complemented his winning performances with a succession of Best Condition awards. His second year started well with a win and Best Condition, and then due to a family tragedy Rob Douglas withdrew from competition and sold the horse in August 1985.

New owner Danny Grant, a professional agrologist and real estate appraiser with a horseman's ranching background, was initially interested in campaigning Soliloquy in hotly contested Ride and Ties, closing the 1985 season with races at Calgary and Cranbrook. In 1986 the new partnership gained momentum, putting in around 1200 miles including training and competition, and with Ride and Ties still his priority Danny used Endurance Rides as conditioning sessions. After his first four 1986 races with one first and three seconds, all with Best Condition awards, he was approached by Dr James Bryant with an invitation to join the Canadian national team for the first North American Endurance Championship. Endurance riding

32 Nancy Beacon, the force behind Canadian endurance riding, on her Shamirad. (Visionary Images)

33 Danny Grant and Soliloquy, the top Canadian partnership.

now took precedence. The North American Championship Ride was the first 100 in a day either Soliloquy or Danny had ever attempted, and they placed well – eighth in the prestigious top ten – from a strong field, also giving Canada her first official international success since CALDRA's formation. Spurred by this Danny set his sights on further across-the-border rides, with the Purina Race of Champions and Tevis Cup his goal. He needed one more 100-mile completion to enter the Purina Race but, as so often seems to happen when it matters most, disaster struck. In the only available 100 left in 1986 the Arabian suffered a swollen tendon sheath and was voluntarily pulled at the 85-mile mark. However, another chance was offered to qualify in mid-January 1987 in a 100 miler held in Oregon, and Danny and his veterinarian brother Barrie took the Grant horses, Soliloquy and TG Nadira Wahid, into the −20 °F Oregon weather and qualified in a time of thirteen hours. Apart from the freezing Oregon 100, Soli-

loquy has added other credits to an ever-lengthening list, winning two more 50 milers by mid May 1987, but although winning his May ride he was dogged by ill luck, throwing a shoe and sustaining stress to a suspensory ligament, and Danny has been advised to rest him. At the peak of performance there is always the very real risk of sustaining injury and the real champions take it in their stride. I know of some distance riders of very long standing who never have these setbacks, but they also never really aim high, never put either themselves or their horses to the test, and never achieve anything of real note. Soliloquy has come back before from injury to his hocks and also to a front tendon, neither incident connected with endurance work but sheer accidents – arguments with a fence and a trailer. It takes a champion to retrench and come back a strong winner, and to see a horse through the downs as well as enjoy the highs.

Soliloquy's highs have been of major order in

large measure because of three factors: to produce optimum performance Danny has sought advice on feeding and uses a balanced ration formulated by Gordon Wooden, an animal nutritionist from California, and since switching to this the horse's energy levels have been greatly improved. Added to this en route ride care is meticulous, affording Soliloquy every chance to recoup energy. He has very rapid recoveries, registering a pulse of 60 within five minutes even after an extended period of all-out work. His initial recovery down to the acceptable FEI 64 bpm is even more rapid, coming within a minute of stopping. He is a very competitive horse, able to keep a very fast pace for up to 15 miles at the start of a ride while maintaining a low pulse, and if challenged will accept and forge on at the challenger's pace until it backs off. Slow work, however, tends to make him sluggish as he is essentially a front runner and used to being in the van. When being led or tailed in steep areas he really slows down and Danny says it is best to tail him so he can be encouraged on by swatting with hand or switch. All his wins since Danny has owned him have been when carrying 220 lb or more, and the weight factor is what Danny says causes them most trouble, though by his record it cannot have figured too much as a deciding factor. It is certainly an example to those lightweight riders who complain when having to make up even the very modest weight requirements for certain national or international competitions.

Able to take advantage of American as well as Canadian rides Danny says the USA has given most to the sport, mainly in the tremendous number of events offered, and because it has encouraged the breeding of horses specifically for endurance riding. He thinks both Canadian and world endurance riding is growing slowly and his immediate ambitions centre on competing in the Purina Race of Champions, for which Nadira Wahid is also qualified, the Tevis Cup and eventually the World Championships.

29 Europe (ELDRIC)

The European Long Distance Rides Conference (ELDRIC) was inaugurated in March 1979 at a meeting convened in Germany at the Essen Equitana. Present were representatives from European nations concerned with furthering the sport of endurance riding. Much is owed to the two prime movers in the early efforts to bring European endurance riding under the guidance of a parent body: Hermann Stricker, the then Chairman of the German Long Distance Riding Association, and its Secretary, Penelope Dauster, who continues her efforts today as Secretary to ELDRIC. Since 1981 the ELDRIC President has been Dr Georg Riedler, MD, Chief Haematologist and Oncologist at Lucerne Hospital, Switzerland. He is aided by Vice President Ronald Kydd, well known for his work in the Arabian horse world as a judge of Arabians, three times President of the British Arab Horse Society, and also Secretary of the World Arab Horse Organization.

After that first meeting in Essen, at which I was privileged to represent one of the British associations, the EHPS, the next step was a second meeting in Paris later the same year at which a broad outline of aims was discussed; a European Championship planned with rules laid down; and a guiding committee elected with Monsieur Pierre Passemard of France as President. Initially the countries involved in ELDRIC were Germany, Great Britain, France, Italy, Portugal, Switzerland and Spain, with Poland having a declared interest at the Paris meeting.

Since those early meetings ELDRIC has grown both in numbers of member countries and in the very considerable and desirable influence it exerts on the sport throughout Europe, and indeed now in the rest of the world. The list of European countries counting as full members has since grown to include Austria, Belgium, Holland, Nor-

way and Sweden, with Hungary joining as an associate member. Maybe the greatest measure of ELDRIC's far-reaching involvement has been that the countries where endurance riding has long been established, and to which the world initially looked for guidance, have also become associate members. The American Endurance Ride Conference (AERC) and the Australian Endurance Ride Association (AERA) joined in 1986, and the associations in South Africa, Canada and New Zealand gained associate membership in 1987.

I am much indebted to Penelope Dauster for furnishing me with up-to-date details of ELDRIC. Dr Richard Barsaleau, DVM, one of America's most renowned Endurance Ride veterinary surgeons and a very well known and successful competitor, particularly in the Tevis Cup, finds the world scene in endurance riding in need of standardization, and I think ELDRIC has gone, and is increasingly going, a long way to solving this problem. I know when I took Nizzolan to Germany back in 1976 for the Hamburg to Hannover 100 miler my compatriot, Margaret Montgomerie and I received five different ideas as to what the *specific* rules of the ride were. In the end we just rode, hoping to finish without breaking any rule and getting ourselves eliminated – my German was what I term 'kitchen and shopping German'. Fortunately for us we succeeded in the ride and also in not infringing the rules. Nowadays competitors in all major European events can ride with confidence, knowing that all rides which count for the ELDRIC Trophy fulfil ELDRIC's minimum requirements and are fairly standardized.

In its statutes ELDRIC clearly defines its aims as being:

(1) Promotion of long distance riding as competitive sport;

(2) development, co-ordination and standardization of national long distance riding
rules;

(3) protection of the horses through veterinary
regulations;

(4) international exchange of experience;

(5) organization of the European Championship;

(6) representation of long distance riders at international level, especially in connection
with the FEI.

It has more than fulfilled its undertaking.
International participation has grown steadily, especially since 1982 when for the ELDRIC Championships there were nine rides with five countries
taking part. Since then the number of rides has
risen to eighteen and participating countries to
nine. Though the minimum distance for an
ELDRIC-sanctioned ride is 50 miles, the trend is
for an increasing number of 100 milers as organizing, competing and veterinary expertise develops.

When in 1975 a German team came to Britain
for the first running of the Summer Solstice 100
miler, and Margaret Montgomerie and I reciprocated the following year for the Hamburg to Hannover 100 miler, it was unusual for endurance
horses to travel abroad, but since ELDRIC was
formed it is becoming quite the norm, and along
with the interchange of riders goes the interchange
of ideas to the mutual benefit of the sport and the
horses who give so generously on the long distance
trail.

A degree of standardization of veterinary regulations in all participating countries has been of
undoubted benefit, not only to the riders but to the
horses also. An early ELDRIC regulation was that
should ELDRIC rules and a specific country's
rules differ, the stricter veterinary control would be
used. Now that anomaly seldom occurs, as not only
for sanctioned international rides but for national
events most countries fulfil the ELDRIC minimum requirements.

In addition to tightening up and improving on
the veterinary side of international rides ELDRIC
also holds frequent veterinary seminars where the
endurance veterinary surgeons meet to discuss and

work out any solutions to problems arising in their
sphere at rides. It must surely be to the mutual
advantage of riders, and to veterinarians too, that
the international side of the sport has grown so very
much in size and scope. Not so long ago there were
few veterinarians with an in-depth experience of
adjudicating at endurance rides. Usually entries
were small, thus limiting such experience still
further. Now in the course of a season many endurance ride veterinarians see literally hundreds of
fit horses coming before them. Because of stringent veterinary criteria competitors, for the most
part, take more care to ensure that horses are up to
the demands made of them, and although there is
still a considerable percentage of horses who do
not finish a ride these animals are 'pulled' well
before they reach the stage of injuring themselves.
Riders, knowing this, are tending to proceed in a
more sensible and less cavalier fashion.

Initially, ELDRIC organized the only major international European Championship where riders
were permitted to count the points from a maximum of three international rides, one of which
had to be ridden abroad. This meant that the winning and placing horses were consistently successful and put a premium on seeing that horses were
ridden with knowledge, understanding, and consideration to ensure soundness throughout the
season. This championship is now known as the
European Trophy.

One sphere of ELDRIC's influence has been in
the drafting and recommending of rules for endurance riding with the FEI who since 1983 have
recognized endurance riding as a major equestrian
discipline on a par with showjumping, eventing,
dressage, and so on. Whereas a level of butazolidin
is permitted in other disciplines, the FEI agreed at
ELDRIC's insistence to ban this and any other
such substances from use in endurance riding.
Consequently there has been close rapport between the two bodies and ELDRIC has a permanent representative on the FEI Endurance Subcommittee.

Since 1984 the FEI has held an annual European Championship, and together with the
ELDRIC's European Trophy awarded on a
cumulative points basis, they are the major awards

which riders of international calibre strive for. Because of close liaison and agreement on major rulings many FEI events are also ELDRIC rides.

Ensuring that ride organization is up to scratch is another ELDRIC function. The Executive Committee or one of its representatives visits several venues each year, and should a ride not reach a high enough standard of organization that ride will not be included in the following year's European calendar of events.

All in all, ELDRIC offers, on a very much wider scale, the benefits each national society grants its own members, but with the added attraction that riders from any European member country, and now increasingly riders from further afield, can be sure of meeting conditions very similar to those under which they ride in their own countries. As Americans and Australians and others far afield become keen to ride in Europe ELDRIC can offer assistance and guidance over leasing suitable and sufficiently trained horses. To keep it in the valued amateur realm these 'lease/loans' are normally reciprocal, thus enabling highly competitive and successful riders to broaden their experiences still further.

Though primarily ELDRIC seeks to promote international growth of the sport and to that end now maintains a worldwide communications system with all the major endurance ride societies, it has not lost sight of the very important fact that the majority of riders undertake endurance riding for the sheer pleasure of companionship with their horse and the sense of achievement gained as they cross the finishing line. This recognition of the majority is exemplified by ELDRIC's slogan: 'to finish is to win'.

The FEI has rules which govern seven equestrian disciplines, among which is endurance riding. As the sport becomes more and more international with both individuals and teams competing abroad on a regular basis, particularly in Europe, it has been found advantageous to run international events under the FEI banner. Many European countries' own endurance ride associations follow in principle the FEI rules for their own national events as well as for their international rides. Some countries, although following in the main the FEI rules, differ in minor points, particularly at the lower levels. However, it is now common practice that any ride denoted 'International', in Europe at least, is run to FEI specifications. Other national rides, though open to and welcoming competitors from abroad, do not carry the prefix 'International'.

The FEI's recognition of endurance riding as a major equestrian discipline has gone a long way towards establishing a uniform standard so that no longer will riders be unsure of the exact interpretation of the rules they are riding under. This was an aggravating circumstance in which both myself and others have ridden in the past, where differing rule translations were offered in foreign rides.

Below, thanks to the help of Fritz O. Widmer, Secretary General to the FEI, I am able to give a résumé of the *main* aspects of endurance riding rules established by the FEI.

FEI-sanctioned rides are described as Concours de Raid d'Endurance (CE) and are as follows:

CEF   – Concours de Raid d'Endurance de Frontière
CEA   – Concours de Raid d'Endurance d'Amitié
CEI   – Concours de Raid d'Endurance International
CEIO – Concours de Raid d'Endurance International Official

In Europe only one CEIO per country is permitted each year. Outside Europe two such rides are permitted annually. For a World Championship to be held there must be participants (actual starters) from at least six nations.

All entrants in international competitions under FEI auspices must be nominated by their respective national federations. All horses entered must have been vaccinated against equine influenza and have an up-to-date passport. Competitors may ride a horse belonging to an owner of a different nationality in CEIs, CEAs, and CEFs. In CEIOs any such horses must be leased by the national federation concerned for at least three months and with the FEI Secretary General's approval. Horses and riders must have approved Certificates of Capability to be eligible for FEI World Championship Endurance Rides, and competitors must have a licence before they may compete abroad. Both these documents are issued by the national federations of each country. Sponsorship is in order and the sponsor's 'logo' may be inscribed on the saddle cloth. All other forms of advertising are banned.

Endurance competitions under FEI rules are normally run against the clock. They may also be decided on a set time where penalties are incurred for exceeding the optimum time and for veterinary reasons. However, this must be advised in the schedule. Official international rides may only be run against the clock.

FEI courses must be adequately described in the schedule which must note the type of going and altitude differentials. The most demanding part of the course should not be towards the finish. Competitors must be provided with a route map noting the above plus any hazards and mandatory stops. Not more than 10 per cent roadwork is permitted. The courses must be established one week before and marked at least one day before the event, and distance markers shall be erected every 10 km. Course marking shall be with either red or white boundary flags along the route. At hazards, start and finish, the marking will be by red and white flags and the competitor must proceed with the red flag on his right, the white on his left. Finish line shall be clearly indicated and of sufficient width to enable a fair finish for several horses at a time. Hazards may only be of natural derivation such as ditches, water crossings, steep climbs and so on. An alternative route must be provided around each hazard but each alternative shall not add more than 500 metres to the route.

The minimum distance for FEI rides is 80 km for a one-day ride. At CEIO level the minimum distance is 120 km for a one-day ride. For competitions of more than one day the minimum daily average is 80 km, or for CEIO rides 100 km daily.

Riders may dismount and lead or follow their horses en route but must start and finish mounted. In a set time competition the rules *may* require riders to keep in forward motion during the last part of the ride for a distance no longer than 2 km. Stopping will incur penalties. If a rider is in difficulty at a hazard he/she may not obstruct the passage of another rider. Wilful obstruction incurs elimination.

Outside assistance at rides is forbidden, especially being followed, preceded or accompanied by any person, rider not competing, or vehicle; being assisted at hazards; or cutting wire fences, cutting down trees, or dismantling a fence to permit passage. Also forbidden are radio transmitters to keep competitors advised of how rivals are doing. Exceptions to the 'no assistance' rule are that a competitor may receive help to remount a horse for any reason; catch a loose horse; readjust tack; replace shoes; or be handed any part of equipment. Help is permitted in washing and watering of horses en route. Assistance is permitted at start, finish and at mandatory stops.

The rider's dress is optional but must be appropriate. Hard hats are advised and may be made compulsory by the ride schedule. Whips and spurs will be inspected by the ground jury for suitability. Spurs may be prohibited but if so this must be noted in the schedule. Misuse of either whip or spurs are grounds for elimination, as is the excessive pressing of an exhausted horse. Horse tack is optional with the exception of draw reins which are forbidden. All equipment must fit the horse and be in a safe condition. The schedule must clearly state if there is a minimum weight rule, the rules for weighing in, or the alternative handicap method to be used for those riders not able to make the weight. If there are weight divisions in the event the schedule must state this clearly.

Riders qualify to enter FEI endurance rides from the year in which they celebrate their eighteenth birthday, providing they are nominated by their national federation. Juniors are eligible from the year in which they reach their fourteenth birthday. Horses must be at least six years old. Mares after their fourth month of pregnancy or within nine months after foaling are barred.

A mass start is permitted if the terrain and number of riders permit. If a mass start is not used there will be a draw for starting order. If riders wish and so request at time of entering groups of not more than five riders may start together.

Judging of events is by a panel of veterinarians in the ratio of one veterinary surgeon to each fifteen horses, with a minimum of two veterinary surgeons officiating. There is no appeal against a veterinary decision. At World Championship rides all members of the ground jury and veterinary panel are appointed by the FEI. At other FEI rides at least one of the veterinary panel shall be an official FEI veterinarian. Each national federation shall appoint veterinarians for endurance riding and furnish the list to the FEI for ratification.

The FEI makes provision for random testing for prohibited substances. In endurance rides all such substances are forbidden, and the FEI rules further state that any person (handler, rider) other than a qualified veterinarian, in possession of syringes, needles or such substances will be deemed to have contravened the rule. Injections of electrolytes, vitamins, saline fluids, and so on are forbidden for the duration of the event, except with permission of the veterinary panel. In endurance riding such permission is normally followed by elimination. At official international and World Championship level testing is mandatory, and it is recommended at other rides. A minimum of 5 per cent of horses entered, and in any case at least three horses, must be sampled where mandatory rules apply. At World Championship rides in addition to any random test the first four placed horses are tested, and in the team event one horse from among each of the first four placed teams.

Horses are inspected by a vet prior to, during, and after each ride, and awards are only made to horses passing all the veterinary examinations. During an FEI ride there are mandatory halts at least every 40 km. They may be either of a compulsory rest period, with length determined by the severity of the preceding phase, but with a minimum rest time of forty minutes; or of the 'veterinary gate' type where the rider presents the horse for inspection when he/she deems the time is right within thirty minutes after arrival. The veterinary surgeon may require the horse to be re-presented during the thirty minutes. If the latter system is used it is followed by a timed hold to bring the rest period up to a minimum of forty minutes.

The initial inspection is made on arrival at the venue and is to establish the horse's identity by checking passports and registration papers, to ensure vaccinations are current, and also to ensure the horse is in a fit state of health. At the first veterinary examination heart and respiratory rates are noted, together with any abnormal characteristics. General condition is noted and horses registering an abnormally high temperature will be eliminated. Horses are checked for lameness which is divided into five categories:

(1) Difficult to observe and not consistently apparent, regardless of circumstances;
(2) difficult to observe at a walk or trotting a straight line, but consistently apparent under certain circumstances;
(3) consistently observable at a trot under all circumstances;

(4) marked nodding, hitchy or shortened stride;
(5) minimal weight-bearing in motion and/or rest or inability to move.

Horses evincing lameness greater than Grade 2 are eliminated. If a horse cannot be definitely categorized as lame he must be allowed to proceed. Discrepancies in gait should be noted on the horse's veterinary sheet. Any soreness, lacerations or wounds on either the body, limbs or in the mouth are noted, and if they are deemed likely to be seriously aggravated during the ride the horse is eliminated. Shoeing is not compulsory, but if a horse is shod it should be done correctly and in a state adequate to last the ride. Loss of one or more shoes will not incur elimination. Pads and equiboots (easy boots) are permitted.

At mandatory halts the same criteria are used to establish the horse's ability to proceed. The horse's pulse rate must drop to 64 or below within thirty minutes, and the ride rules *may* say a maximum respiration rate of 36 rpm after the thirty-minute period. If a horse's temperature is 40 °C or more he is eliminated, even if the pulse and respiration rates are not excessive. Excessive fatigue, heat stroke, colic, myopathies and severe dehydration also result in elimination. Any freshly acquired trauma are recorded. If they are severe the horse is eliminated.

At the finish the horse is allowed a thirty-minute recovery time before inspection, when he should meet the necessary criteria as above. The final inspection, which is to determine if the horse is in a fit state to be ridden, is made not less than one hour after the inspection on arrival at the finish for rides of 100 km or less per day. On rides over 100 km per day this inspection takes place not less than five hours after the competitor has completed the course. A decision to eliminate a horse must be made by the veterinary panel or by a majority vote of the panel.

Spot checks may be carried out on all or any horses selected at random throughout the event.

France has one of the longest histories of endurance riding in Europe, but its national body governing the sport was not formally inaugurated until February 1982. Entitled Le Comité National des Raids Equestres d'Endurance (CNREE) it had 210 members in its first year, and this has since risen to well over 1000 active members. Its rapid expansion is shown by the continually increasing number of official rides – 107 in 1986 and 140 in 1987 with the season not yet closed. Originally based in the Centre-Sud Department of France the sport has now spread to many other regions, most of which enter teams in the regional championships, won in 1986 by the team from Aquitaine with runner up Alsace.

The CNREE annual award system covers many categories so that at all stages of the sport incentives are given to promote progress. France is one of the very few nations where financial inducement is offered in the generous cash prizes given at some major events and also for some annual awards.

The CNREE National Championships comprise two divisions: the General Class for riders 75 kg and over, and the Lightweight Division for under 75 kg. The Leading Rider award in both General and Lightweight divisions goes to the rider competing with one or more horses, and the Leading Horse titles to the horses gaining most points in each division. French Championship points can be gained at Allan, Cherveux, Florac, Rambouillet and Montcuq, all of which rank as Grade 1 National Rides. The National Challenge Title is awarded to horses and riders competing in Qualifying, Pre-National (Regional), and Grade 2 National Rides. This annual award is also divided into two classes – leading rider and leading horse. There is also a Long Distance Record with an award going to the horse with the highest number of kilometres covered in Endurance Rides per year, and a similar Kilometre Record going back to

1976. This is headed at present by Hussard de Cazes, a chestnut gelding ridden by Denis Letarte, with well over 2000 km to his credit. A Best Condition Trophy is awarded to the horse with the most points gained in National Rides. In this category France differs from other nations in awarding Best Condition places to several horses per event. As the sport gains momentum more important annual competitions and trophies are being implemented, some regional, and many are backed by generous cash prizes.

French endurance riders are well catered for in both number of events and type of rides, which escalate from easy through to the top level of National and International. They are also kept advised of CNREE news by a quarterly magazine, with a leaflet published in each intervening month.

The two main categories of events are Rides with a Set Speed of between 12 and 15 kph, and Endurance Rides with no maximum speed but with a minimum average speed of 12 kph. The President of the Jury may lower the minimum set speed for rides should the climatic conditions or the severity of the route warrant it. The two categories comprise the following rides:

Rides with a Set Speed
Initiation Rides with a minimum distance 30 km, maximum 40 km; open to horses four years old and over.
Qualifying Rides, minimum distance 60 km, maximum 70 km; horses four years old and over.
Pre-National (Regional) Rides, minimum distance 85 km, maximum 95 km; horses five years old and over.

Endurance Rides
National 1 Rides, 100 to 110 km in one day; open to horses five years old and over.

National 2 rides, 130 to 160 km in one day, or 100 km minimum for rides over more than one day; open to horses six years old and over.

Conditions of entry are as follows: Set Speed Rides are open to riders of twelve years and over. Endurance Rides are only open to riders fourteen years and over. To enter Initiation and Qualifying rides there are no qualifications required of horse and rider other than they be in a fit state to compete and be of the minimum age. Riders under twelve may be allowed to compete provided they are accompanied by a mounted adult.

Horses entered in Pre-National Rides must first have completed two Qualifying Rides. Thereafter they must maintain their qualification status by completing two Qualifying or one National Ride in the current or preceding year. [It seems odd that a higher qualification is required for a lower ride, but this is what is stated in the rules.] Riders must do likewise with the exception that they may spread their qualifications over the two previous years.

Horses entering National Endurance Rides must qualify and maintain qualification on a similar basis. To enter National 2 Rides horses must complete one Pre-National or one National Ride in the current or previous year. Riders must do likewise but may spread their qualification over two years. For National 1 Rides the rules are similar, except the horse may also have his qualification spread over the two previous years.

Other entry requirements are that riders hold an insurance policy for civil and individual cover. With the exception of those entering Initiation Rides, riders must hold a current licence from the CNREE or the French Equestrian Federation and a card from the CNREE showing the qualifications pertaining to rides. They must also hold a medical certificate, and in the case of minors parental authorization. Horses entering rides of Pre-National and National standard must have documents of origin from the stud where they were foaled. If they do not have such registration documents they must have an identification card furnished by and registered with the French Equestrian Federation after ratification by either the stud or a veterinary surgeon. All horses competing must have up-to-date influenza vaccinations.

The general rules which govern both Set Speed and Endurance Rides are as follows. At all rides there must be medical assistance available throughout the entire event and at National Rides an ambulance must also be available. The organizer may not allow the ride to start unless these are present.

Entrants must be advised of the route ten days in advance, and the marking of the route must be in place eight days before the ride. The finish line must be wide enough to avoid risk in case of a fast finish. Distances shall be marked every 5 or 10 km and all control posts must be signed 1 km in advance. Entrants intentionally going off course are eliminated. A time for closing each control post is set and entrants must be advised of this time before the start of the ride. Horses arriving after this time are eliminated and a box will transport them back to base. All riders are provided with a card denoting their name, number, horse's name, age and colour. They must present this at each checkpoint for annotating all veterinary results and observations. It is surrendered at the finish and returned inscribed with the horse's qualification.

Horses must be ridden by the same rider throughout the event. The rider may dismount and lead if he/she considers it necessary. The choice of tack, bridles and bitting is optional. Work bandages, hoods and draw reins are forbidden in all rides. Blinkers are only forbidden in National Rides. Riders' clothing choice is optional but it must be suitable for the event. Hard hats are strongly recommended. The use of whips and spurs is controlled by the ride jury, but they should not be of the kind to cause damage to the horse. If the organizer wishes to forbid the use of spurs such decision must be noted in the ride schedule. There is a minimum weight requirement of 75 kg of which no more than 20 kg may be made up of tack and dead weight. Riders not wishing or able to make up the weight to the required minimum with dead weight will ride in the Lightweight Division.

A farrier will be available at control posts. Horses that are shod will be examined to make sure the shoeing is adequate. Shod horses that lose one or more shoes en route will be able to finish without shoe(s). All types of 'equiboot' are permissible.

Anti-doping controls can be made at any time during the competition. Use of forbidden substances incurs elimination. Rule infractions can also be the cause of eliminations. The President of the Ride Jury may eliminate riders for cruelty to horses, and also for any injurious or aggressive attitude to the judges. If there are any disagreements or complaints over decisions taken on the ride such complaints must be made, accompanied by a fixed deposit, no later than thirty minutes after the proclamation of results. Once the President of the jury, after consultation with jury members, has given his decision there is no appeal against such decision.

Veterinary control is exercised throughout rides by a panel of veterinary surgeons in the ratio of one veterinary surgeon to every fifteen horses. In the case of low entries there will be a minimum of two veterinary surgeons. There should also be an additional veterinary surgeon available for emergency treatment.

Starting order at Set Speed Rides is either in small groups or individually. At Set Speed Rides horses are examined before the ride for general health. Temperature is taken, mucous membrane examined, heart and lungs auscultated; and shoeing, hooves and tendons are inspected and the horse examined at walk and trot. During the ride mandatory halts are located every 30 to 35 km, and the horses are examined on arrival and thirty minutes later when the heart rate must not exceed 64 bpm nor the respiration 48 rpm. Rates exceeding these incur elimination. Each halt is of one hour's duration. Other factors examined are hydration, congestion of mucous membranes, heatstroke, myopathy, lameness tested for at the trot, trauma, and anti-doping as noted earlier. The final examination follows on the same lines. Any horse that the judges consider could be endangered by continuing on course is eliminated. All horses finishing in good time and condition qualify.

The pre-ride veterinary examination for Endurance Rides in the National 1 and 2 categories is similar to the above with the addition that where possible laboratory tests for CPK and haematocrit

are made to determine if the horse is fit enough for the ride. There must be agreement between two veterinary surgeons in order to withdraw a horse. Veterinary controls during the ride are split into two types – Criteria 'A' and Criteria 'B'. Pulse and respiration are registered under Criteria 'A'. The pulse must fall to 64 or below. If the veterinary surgeon notes an elevated respiratory rhythm a rectal temperature will be taken, and if recorded at 40 °C or more the horse is eliminated.

Criteria 'B' checks are for abnormal heart rhythm; respiratory problems; dehydration – where possible a haematocrit test should be done on all horses as close to the 80 km mark as possible; congested mucous membrane; heatstroke; myopathy; lameness. Where lameness is difficult to see and is not consistent under all circumstances elimination is not obligatory. Two veterinary surgeons shall decide whether the horse is to be eliminated or allowed to proceed. To determine this the horse shall be walked and trotted straight for a distance of twenty-five metres, and also in a figure eight at walk and trot. Finally he shall be walked and trotted both mounted and dismounted. If in one or more of these tests the lameness is consistent elimination follows. The horse is also checked for wounds or lacerations in the mouth and on the other parts of the body, and for girth galls or saddle sores. If they are severe the horse is eliminated.

At endurance rides there is either a mass start or riders leave in small groups or individually, but the type of start must be indicated in the ride schedule. The first mandatory halt must be between 25 and 40 km. There must not be more than 40 km between halts. Duration of mandatory halts is sixty minutes. At all mandatory halts and at the finish only one veterinary control is made. The rider chooses the time, within a thirty-minute limit, to present his horse. If the horse does not satisfy the veterinary surgeon it is eliminated.

Horses and riders

France is fortunate, very much more so than other countries, in enjoying generous help, particularly from their long-time sponsors Duquesne-Purina and Les Lunettes Alain du Renon among others. The CNREE also receives greater media and journalistic reportage than other European endurance associations, and French endurance riding is accorded its rightful place as one of the leading equestrian disciplines.

French riders also hold a strong position in European endurance riding, their leading riders frequently appearing well up in the annual ELDRIC Trophy listings. The current French champion, Denis Pesce, riding his great horse, the grey Selle Française (French Saddle Horse) Melfenik, has not only succeeded at home but many times abroad, flying the French flag most notably in Rosenau, Austria and in the Madrid–Lisbon ride, where he placed fourth in a strong international field. Other international awards have been won for France by the following horses and riders.

Melik

A purebred bay Arabian stallion of Polish ancestry, Melik (1976) is owned by Jacques Fellmann. Melik's rider, Dr Michel Laracine, an anaesthetist at Nîmes Hospital, has been a committee member of CNREE since its foundation and has represented France in international rides both at home and abroad, including being captain of the gold medal-winning team at the European Championships in Rosenau, Austria, in 1985. Melik and Dr Laracine have also achieved a third place ranking in the 1985 ELDRIC listing, plus many awards in National 1 Rides at home. As befits a doctor of medicine Dr Laracine pays as much attention to his own physical fitness as that of his equine partner. Melik's own endurance training routine includes regular 20 km workouts, dressage training, and treks over several days judiciously spaced throughout the year. His good points are honesty and knowing his own limits, and a gentle nature and closeness with his rider, and excellent recoveries. Dr Laracine says that on the obverse of the coin he can be somewhat touchy towards other horses, coupling a threat with action.

Kamir II

Françoise Rimbaud and Kamir II have given France many international awards. Kamir II

(1976) is a bay purebred Arabian gelding with over 1500 km to his credit in long distance rides. Amongst his top achievements have been a place on the gold medal-winning team for the 1983 European Trophy, and a fifth place in the European Championships held at Florac in 1984. In 1985 he went on improving to gain a second in the Swiss William Tell Challenge Cup and a first place at Florac. In 1986 Kamir II was the highest-placing French horse in the first World Championships at Rome, placing seventh along with team member Latif ridden by Marie Salome Lux. These two horses secured the World Championship team bronze medal for France, and at the end of the season Françoise and her Arabian placed third in the ELDRIC Trophy listing. Françoise started endurance riding in 1979 on horses owned by Denis Letarte, one of France's leading riders, and started training her own horses in 1982 – first Indigo de Cazes and then Kamir II. She says she finds it difficult to fit the training needed for a top level endurance horse into her busy life, as she has a full-time job. Nevertheless, using all her free time she keeps Kamir II fit with a combination of top class feeding and an intensive training schedule.

Zoltan

Cathy Brown owns both Zoltan and Naquib (see below) and they live in L'Isle Jourdain not far from Montaillou, famous for its historical documentation of the fourteenth-century Cathar movement.

Zoltan is a grey 15.3 hh Standardbred/Arabian gelding bred by the author (see p. 173), and is believed to be the first horse bred specifically for endurance riding in England whose parents were both 100-mile horses. Not an easy character, he treated each ride start as a rodeo session, but later settled after intentionally being given a particularly heavy session on a 60 miler as a cure for his antics. He had two seasons in Britain, doing well in both Novice and Open Championship tables and reaching the top six nationally, before going to France. After a slow start he came into his best years from 1984 onwards. Up to then he had won and placed in a few rides in his first two French seasons and frequently won Best Condition

34 Cathy Brown and Zoltan, 1984 French Lightweight Champion. (Dr R. Marshall)

awards, and finally went on to rack up enough successes to tie for the Lightweight Championship in 1984.

In 1985 he became peripatetic again. In addition to a fistful of rides in France, where he was the leading horse for the number of major rides completed successfully in a season, with two 100 milers and one 125 miler in the short space of ten weeks, he travelled to Breamore in Britain and Rosenau in Austria. The points gained from these rides and his French ones put him fifth overall in the ELDRIC listing. He was pipped at the post for a repeat win of the French Lightweight Championship by a single point, settling for second place. In 1986, after starting with a win, Zoltan turned in enough consistent performances to secure the chance to represent Britain at the World Championships in Rome. There, 50 miles into the 100, disaster struck with a spontaneous fracture of a fore pastern. Up until this accident Zoltan had shown marked consistency over five seasons in France and two in Britain, and had a mileage record well in excess of 1100 miles. He has now totally recovered and Cathy plans to do National rides on him again. In the meantime she has been doing extremely well on her other horse, Naquib.

Naquib

Naquib is a grey purebred Arabian stallion of the Egyptian Hadban Enzahi line which has had such an influence on European Arabian breeding. He had a slow build-up in the first three years of his endurance career. In his third season he was well to the fore, with a win in a 100 km race – Naquib first, the rest nowhere, or at least half an hour behind him. He ended the season on a very high note with a win in the 1986 200 km Montcuq International plus a Best Condition in the Lightweight Division. For this he was ridden by Robert Sedgley, who worked at Cathy's Chateau d'Arques Stud. The year 1987 started well with a good place in the 138 km Allan ride and a win in the Breamore International ride in Britain. Unlike Zoltan, who is a strong horse taking a long time to settle, Naquib has the enviable trait of doing just enough to get by, thus conserving his energy, which when allied to a good strong trot and smooth canter makes for a much less tiring ride. At just over 15 hands and 800 lb when fit he is the ideal build for endurance riding, also possessing the low heart rate so often shown by the very relaxed horse with an unflappable temperament. His only problem is that he tends to 'lose his cool' when mares are around.

Cathy's stud specializes in producing performance horses using Egyptian bloodlines and also

35 Naquib, Cathy Brown's other mount, during the 1987 EHPS Summer Solstice. (John Watts Photography)

horses from proven endurance and racing backgrounds. She describes the French scene as 'fast expanding and very dynamic'. She was first led to endurance riding from a love of riding and open spaces but with the added zest of competition. Her training system relies on progressive work, slow at first and building in length and speed as fitness increases. In competition a good completion is not risked by pushing for a win, although both horses have had their fair share of wins in the very competitive French arena.

In common with many endurance riders I have contacted for this book Cathy feels that the USA has had the most influence on the sport, mainly because of the tremendous depth of veterinary knowledge their ride judges bring to the specialized vetting of endurance rides. Also, and not an aspect many riders have voiced, she would like to see cash prizes become the norm, plus much needed sponsorship for rides. I must say I agree with her on both these counts. Costs are rising fast, and whereas at one time it was relatively inexpensive to campaign a horse in endurance riding, today, particularly with the international scene greatly and rapidly expanding, financial rewards are long overdue, lest the sport become the province of only the affluent. After all, in international rides only the best represent their country, or should. It would be sad to think that for the lack of funds the best had to turn down such an opportunity. With veterinary rules so stringent and completion of a ride depending solely on veterinary criteria being adequately fulfilled, the chance for abuse of the horse in order to line one's pocket would be obviated.

32 Germany

Germany is one of the member nations of the ELDRIC, and in fact its National Association was the prime mover in getting the European parent body off the ground.

Initially known as Verein Deutscher Distanzreiter e.V. it catered for all aspects of long distance riding in Germany. In late 1986 the growing sport of Long Distance Driving was added to its operations and it is now known as Verein Deutscher Distanzreiter und -fahrer e.V.

Founded in 1976 its aims are to support endurance riding and driving in every way by encouraging development of the sport as an independent equestrian discipline. During its ten years' experience, VDD has formulated its own rules for distance riding and driving which are designed to protect the competing horses, and to this end there is close liaison with endurance event veterinary surgeons both at competitions and in a continuing programme of research related to distance riding. VDD sees public relations as an important part of its job, seeking co-operation and communication with the other riding associations in Germany, as well as keeping in contact with as many foreign endurance riding associations as possible.

At present the German association boasts close to 1000 members with membership steadily growing. This shows a rapid growth from the initial number of fifty-five members in 1976. To cater for this growing number there are in the region of 100 events held annually. Many events hold classes for more than one distance, giving a total number of annual German events in excess of 160. This puts Germany on a par with Great Britain in number of rides and popularity of the sport, and also shows a similar growth pattern over the years. There are, however, a greater number of the longer endurance rides held in Germany than in any other of the ELDRIC nations, with possibly the exception of Great Britain whose yearly tally is increasing. Included in the annual schedule of events are more than twenty driving competitions and several Ride and Ties.

Ride structure

This is also similar to that operating in Great Britain. Rides are so designed that novice and young horses are eased into the sport in lower distanced and slower paced events which are run at set speeds. Four categories of ride are open to competitors, and riders of any age may participate:

Einfuhrungsritte (ER)

are introductory rides and run at set speeds only, which may not exceed 12 kph. Distances are between 25 and 39 km, and awards are graded from 1 to 4. Penalties may be awarded against poor pulse and respiration (PR) recovery. Horses must be a minimum of five years of age for ER.

Kurze Distanzritte (KDR)

is the next step up, with rides of 40–59 km in length for one-day rides, and a maximum of 49 km daily if held over more than one day. These rides may be either the set speed rides with PR penalties (similar to British and American CTRs) or they may be run against the clock. Individual placings are permitted in KDRs, and horses must be a minimum of six years of age to participate.

Mittlere Distanzritte (MDR)

are between 60 and 79 km for one-day rides, and 50–59 km daily distance if run over more than one day. They are judged against the clock and horses must be a minimum of six years of age to participate.

Lange Distanzritte (LDR)

are the true Endurance Rides with a minimum distance of 80 km (50 miles) if a one-day ride, and 60 km per day if run over more than one day. Judged against the clock, horses must be at least seven years of age to take part.

The endurance driving events follow the same outline and use the same rules with few exceptions. One is that should one member of a team be vetted out for any reason, the whole team has to be withdrawn. Another is that drivers must be a minimum of fourteen years old, or eighteen years if unaccompanied.

No horse, in either riding or driving, is permitted to enter an event if it has failed to complete a competition within the previous five days. This is a very good safeguard against pushing a horse before he is truly over any ailment and one that could well be adopted by other associations.

Awards in all events are of token value only, being either rosettes, trophies or plaques. Prize money is forbidden, and any gift in kind such as equipment or horseclothing must not be valued at more than twice the entry fee. The cumulative awards for horses and riders are based on distances ridden and are given in increments of 1000 km. The National Championships do not follow the same format each year but are decided at the association's AGM each year. Previously they followed a points system, but have now gone to a one-ride National Championship which is usually held over several days. Currently the distance is 260 km over three days.

Veterinary procedure is similar to that found on many other associations' rides, but it is very clearly laid down. One vet is required for each thirty horses, or part thereof. There is no appeal against a vet's decision, and only horses 'fit to ride' may continue in the ride, or receive awards at ride completion. Interpretation of this rule is that a horse must be able, in the vet's opinion, to finish the distance under a rider without suffering damage or pain. Veterinary checks are a maximum of 25 km apart, and all horses must undergo checks before, during, at the finish, and after the competition. Twenty minutes are allowed for pulse/respiration recovery after a ride and they must drop to a maximum of 64/60 or incur elimination. All MDRs and LDRs must have a rest period during the ride and this must be at the rate of not less than thirty seconds for every kilometre of ride distance. The final check is not less than two hours after finishing a ride, except for LDR where the final check is the day following the ride.

Normal foods, salt and electrolytes are permitted to horses but only orally. Plain water may be used on the horses, but anything else, such as a topical wound ointment, must first receive clearance for use by the officiating veterinary surgeons. The German National Federation pays for up to twenty dope tests annually and it is common practice for winners, and a few horses at random selection, to be tested for forbidden substances. Close control is exerted over riders' behaviour and misuse of spurs and whips, or any other abuse incurs elimination.

Horses and riders do not have to qualify to enter the major endurance rides as the association's rules, particularly in the veterinary department, are stringent enough to protect the horses against being overridden. In particular the minimum age rule offers a very large measure of protection.

I am indebted to Mrs Dauster for providing me with the above information rendered in English, which has saved me considerable time in getting it translated.

Horses and riders

The VDD in the relatively short space of ten years has really grown not only in numbers, but in the comprehensive way it promotes and protects every aspect of German endurance riding, and now driving. German endurance riders have a lot to be thankful for with the very wide range of rides offered to them, and taking advantage of the multiple events Germany has produced many superb horses and dedicated riders who have not confined their riding to Germany alone. Some of them are outlined below.

Crystal Crown, Houari, and Penny Dauster

Penelope Dauster has had an impact on the long distance riding scene in many ways. Her personal endurance riding career spans seventeen years, during which time she has competed on more than a dozen horses, quite a few of which have been 'borrowed' mounts when riding abroad. Somehow she manages to fit her endurance riding, to the tune of over 4000 miles (6762 km), in between acting as Secretary to the ELDRIC and overseeing international affairs for the VDD.

Her current horses are both purebred Arabian geldings bought specifically for endurance riding. The elder, Crystal Crown, has been competing for almost a decade with a running total of nearly 4000 km, and the younger, Houari, has been on the trail since 1983, accruing nearly 2000 competitive kilometres. Both horses' records are impressive by European standards – we do not yet have the vast yearly offerings of major rides that America and Australia enjoy – and Crystal Crown has successfully completed over sixty rides, Houari twenty-six. Including other horses ridden before acquiring her Arabian duo, Penny Dauster has competed in ninety-seven rides, completing eighty-eight. In major rides of 50 miles and over she has achieved ten wins, two high spots being wins in 1982 in both the Swiss 100 miler for the Schnabelsberger Cup and the German Championship riding Crystal Crown. Stablemate Houari has also had his fair share of awards, both at home in Germany with six wins and one abroad at Snapphane in Sweden. However, Penny measures her successes by other criteria than winning, saying that her personal standard of success is measured by the fact that both her horses continue sound after many seasons campaigning – something many riders who burn a horse up in one or two seasons would do well to try and emulate. She attributes her successes to

36 Penny Dauster and Houari at the 1984 FEI European Championships, a member of the Bronze-winning German team.

horsemanship, perseverance – very necessary in an endurance rider – and, a bit too modestly, to lack of stronger competition.

In the horsemanship department I do agree with her very ordinary but sensible methods – the ideal way, I think, of raising a prospective distance horse: stabled at night, paddock freedom by day, with plenty of natural top quality feeds, supplemented by biotin. Progress is steady, breaking horses in at three then turning away. At four horses are hacked lightly, and introduced gradually to competitions at lower levels as five and six year olds, not tackling tough rides until mature at seven years of age. Training is in the order of a sensible 50 miles a week with competitions extra, so horses are neither underworked nor overstressed. All in all it is a sensible, moderate routine that has paid off in horses that stay healthy, sound and successful. Far too many horses are catapulted into competition once the magical age of five is reached, and subsequently pay the penalty by reduction in years of usefulness.

In Crystal Crown she has a very tough little horse, though admits to him being 'bloodyminded' on occasions, but says Houari makes up for it by his superb temperament and comfortable gaits. On a personal level her ambitions are to complete 1000 miles of one-day 100 milers, and with seven already achieved that goal is within close reach; and to do a 150-mile ride in one day, though that may take some time as at present there is no such ride on offer. What Penny does feel would be a retrograde step is the current trend of trying to cut back on the longer distances for international rides, as would the suggestion to employ less stringent veterinary controls at these rides. She says standards must be kept high. It is very important to her that the German ideal of 'to finish is to win' is not lost sight of. Equally important is the need to stress safeguarding horses at both national and international level.

Many riders, even those of international calibre, do not have the experience to assess other than immediate criteria, but Penelope Dauster from her position as the ELDRIC Secretary has a clear picture of how the sport has developed and what the future could, or should, hold. She feels many

countries have contributed to European long distance riding: the USA with its motto, now borrowed by Germany; Australia with its sound vetting rules; Germany, who founded the ELDRIC and kept it going when things were difficult. She gives Great Britain the best accolade of all, saying 'It is an inspiration to everyone as to how the British look after horses'; we certainly do not have an attrition rate worth mentioning in Britain, where it would be very rare to find a rider who will jeopardize a horse's health for a win. She would like to see more veterinary involvement in both research and very importantly at a national level right down to the minor rides.

Contrary to some of my correspondents she would welcome a reduction in prizes at rides, giving the very good reason that the greater the prize the hotter the competition, and the more likely that horses would suffer abuse in a 'run for the wire'. Sponsorship she sees as very necessary for the growing sport, but admits to being adverse to begging, even in a good cause. She would like to see an increase in the number of good riders and dedicated and knowledgeable people coming forward to help run the German society, and says at present under the national system the right type of horse and rider is not being produced. In essence the free way of going, leaving much up to the intelligence of the trained horse, is alien to the dominant aspects of Germanic riding as I see it. It has taken time in Britain, as I know, for a freer way of riding to be accepted – a much needed move away from the stiff methods of British equitation.

With Penny Dauster and many current European riders the right lead is being given.

Klaus Dittrich and Hopauf

One of Germany's best-known long distance partnerships is Klaus Dittrich and Hopauf. Klaus has been involved in endurance riding for twelve years and has well over 7000 competitive kilometres under his horses' girths, much of which has been achieved riding in international competitions representing his country. He has campaigned several horses, but the best known and his current top mount is Hopauf (1976), a chestnut Trakehner gelding standing 15.1½ hands. Bought in 1984,

Hopauf was a chance entry into endurance riding. Klaus did hope to reform the gelding into a distance horse, but first had to contend with the adverse elements of his character which included such anti-social habits as rearing and biting and, as he says, 'liking his own way and failing to co-operate'. In all he had a strong personality that presented more than the usual range of challenges to overcome. To balance these traits Hopauf has a lot of what makes a top endurance horse tick – long stride, excellent parameters of 36/12 at rest and good recovery after stress, solid experience, and that most important asset to a distance horse: un-flappability at competitions. To add to this he is given a sensible routine involving 1300 km a year, of which about 500 km are in actual competition.

As a farmer Klaus is fortunate in being able to take as much time for his and Hopauf's sport as is necessary. He must be one of the few riders whose fitness parallels that of his horse, as his other hobby is top-class athletic competition. Variety marks Hopauf's training, which is a balance between speed and extended mileage workouts, and much of the horse's success is attributable to a sensible calendar of events with plenty of time between competitions, during which he has the benefit of paddock relaxation and a good nutritional level. The rewards have been a string of successes, the once almost unmanageable gelding now channelling his energies into producing an enviable record in German distance riding.

Already no stranger to the winner's circle, having won the German endurance riding championship in 1980, with Hopauf the winner's circle became Klaus' regular spot. Starting with the Trakehner's very first season, three international ride wins – the Trendelburg 100 km in Germany, and the 80-km Laufenthal and 160-km Schnabelsberg Cup, both in Switzerland – gave them the 1984 European Trophy with the highest score of thirty-six points. To prove this was no fluke the pair repeated their success in 1985, by which time the trophy had become known as the ELDRIC Trophy. This time rides entered for the final score were the Erlanden, Germany, 110 km for first place, the Swiss William Tell two-day 100 miler for second place, and two outright wins over

100 miles in one day at Rosenau, Austria, and the Schnabelsberg Cup, Switzerland. In 1986 they made it a hat-trick, winning the Schnabelsberg Cup for the third year in succession, and also winning the Best Condition award. Partnered by Florian Schmidthues Hopauf represented Germany in the first World Endurance Ride Championships in Rome, and even without his usual pilot finished a very creditable fifth.

Klaus says he finds the length of rides fascinating and is stimulated by the tensions of competition. His ambition is to be not only European Champion but to go one better and head the world listings. In 1986, though still accumulating successes on Hopauf, he brought another winner out in Zylanka, who took first place in the Swiss William Tell two-day 100 miler. From past successes in Switzerland I should think that the Dittrich entry serves as a warning to other riders that they have one of the toughest to beat, no matter which horse Klaus is campaigning.

Klaus would like to see more sponsorship awarded to endurance riding, and the introduction of prize money on a regular basis to offset the considerable financial outlay involved for all distance riders who campaign to any great length, particularly in light of the prize money available in other branches of equestrian sport. He also sees America and France as the leading endurance nations because of their greater experience and also the willingness of sponsors in those countries to invest in the sport.

Drago

Drago (1972) and his owner/rider Bernhard Dornsiepen are one of the best-known and best-liked combinations in German endurance riding. Bernhard runs a pony-trekking yard at Eisborn and got his introduction to endurance riding through a friend, taking it up in his mid-forties. His partner Drago, a black 15 hand Welsh Cob cross German Warmblood, was not bought specifically for distance work, but after a two-year initiation period came through in 1981 with a win in the German Championship which at that time was not a one-off ride but the culmination of a season's efforts.

When asked about Drago Bernhard answered

some of the queries with his well-known humour. With tongue in cheek he says his successes over the years were because the others were worse! But joking aside, the pair have had a steady record of achievements in their eight years of competition, and with the exception of two eliminations (*only* two in eight years) have never been below third place. In seriousness Bernhard attributes this to Drago's consistent performance, his enduring qualities on rides and the fact that his horse 'won't go faster than is good for him'. Of course the steady training with no tendency to skip must help, and no pressure is put on Drago in his first months of each season's work, Bernhard bringing him up easily through slow paces until he is fit enough from early March to clip off 20 km an hour several times a week. Total weekly distance is about 100 km and over the season Drago completes about 400 km of actual competition. This steady but sensible output combined with a good rest at the end of each season is the reason why Drago has stayed sound and a threat to all comers for so long. In the five years to 1986 he was only once out of the league table for the ELDRIC Trophy, which is open to riders from all ELDRIC member countries. He and Drago have appeared in the European Rankings more times than any other combination and although Drago has on several occasions won 100 milers in both Germany and Switzerland as well as placing in Austria, his crowning achievement must be his bronze medal at the 1986 Rome World Championships, followed by another bronze in the 1987 European Championships.

Typically and jocularly, when asked about training and feeding Bernhard answered 'Wouldn't you all like to know!' He says it is too complex to deal with in a few words but basically goes through walking and interval training until he arrives at long distance work. On the subject of equine nutrition it seems that Drago calls the shots, as 'he gets what he likes as he is very choosy. THAT'S IT.'

Whatever the training and feeding system it certainly works for Drago. On a more serious note Bernhard is glad to see the German national federation at last recognizing endurance riding as serious competition, but would like to see industry offer more sponsorship to the sport.

Nico

A German Riding Pony of Dülmener cross Arabian breeding, Nico (1975) is owned by Lothar Schenzel, a professional rider. Lothar and his barely 14 hand grey gelding were the 1986 winners of the German Long Distance Riding Championships, the latest achievement in a long line of successes gained over four years. Nico's breeder did not raise him with endurance riding in mind, but Lothar, recognizing his potential, bought him as a likely prospect in spite of saying he wished he could have been a hand taller. Nico makes up for his diminutive stature by having a very tough and enduring nature, a distinctive character, and a highly competitive spirit.

On a yearly basis Lothar covers 8000 km with his distance horses, 500 km of which are in actual competition, but although the yearly total of competitions is relatively small the results are anything but, especially when partnered by Nico. They have competed regularly both at home and abroad and many of Nico's achievements have been outright wins against all comers. Others were winning the *Kleinpferd* (small horse) Division which is a characteristic of some of the German and European rides, where rather than being divided between Light and Heavyweight sections the division is between horse and pony sections. In 1983 he won three *Kleinpferd* Divisions over varying distances, the highspot being the Swiss Schnabelsberg Cup over 100 miles with an outright win, as well as 50- and 80-km events, plus overall first place in the 50-mile Herzberger Endurance Ride. In 1984 Nico again won the Herzberger event, repeated his Schnabelsberger placing and won outright the Vienna to Budapest three-day 300-km ride. His main achievements in 1985 were the Kronshoffritt and a hat trick in the Herzberger ride, where the distance had been upped from 80 to 100 km. Their German Championship win in 1986 was over three days and 260 km in a total riding time of sixteen hours, twelve minutes.

Lothar attributes these successes to having a good, honest little horse, ample time for training allied with those all important correct tactics which play a large part in Nico's campaigning, as he has to be careful over the pony's pulse readings and ride accordingly. Nico also suffers from a hay allergy – a *bête noire* for many distance riders.

Lothar has ridden since he was twelve years old but at that time there was no such thing as endurance riding in Germany. His first mount was an Icelandic horse which fascinated him. At that time this breed was very popular in Germany. After his first horse he had the opportunity to work with a great many, some of which were very difficult, and when he was twenty-three he became a freelance instructor, a few years later, together with his wife, opening his own riding establishment. His involvement with endurance riding started in 1976 when he met Ursula Bruns, a well-known German endurance rider. She kept her own horse in his home town. Since then he says that although he is a professional rider he sometimes finds it difficult to allocate enough time to train adequately for distance riding. Distance riding is his hobby and it gives him the chance to relax and ride very free-moving horses. He was one of Germany's first long distance riders and he has also had the chance to train several horses for the Great American Horse Race held in 1976.

For the future and on a personal level Lothar says that the really big rides interest him most and his aims are high, hoping to go from National to European Champion, along the road to a crack at the supreme honours of a world win. He would like to have the chance to ride at least once more in the Tevis Cup. He feels that the sport is in a healthy state, particularly as it is one aspect of equestrianism that is open to all riders and gives everyone the chance to get to the top of the league. He does all his own distance training except for occasional help given by an assistant when the opportunity arises. He appreciates that the cost of campaigning a horse is extremely high, particularly with no financial awards offsetting expenses, and he would like to see more of the big companies allocating their sponsorship to endurance riding.

Jaco

A dark brown 16 hand gelding from the Hungarian Nonius breed, Jaco (1968) was bought by Hans Endtmann in the early 1970s as a family pleasure horse with no thought of endurance riding in mind. Initially he had a 'nerves' problem, having a compulsion to damage himself, bloodying his head by repeated rammings against the stable wall, or tangling his front hooves in the wall bars. Supplying a rabbit friend settled him, and the long road from thin, hairy, saddle-sored dealer's nag into one of Germany's most consistent endurance horses started. He completed his first distance ride in May 1977 and ten years later in May 1987 he had totalled 7349 km in competitions alone, one of the highest on record in Europe. This does not include the longest trip of all, from Avignon in France to Breisach near Aachen in Germany, nor many other tours or his other mile-eating forte, hunting.

Hans says that Jaco became known as 'Always Second', because although he often tied on time at the finish his horse's pulse used to let him down, never recovering as well as it should. He puts this down either to Jaco's natural tendency or to training conditions. Because of lack of time and limited access to a suitable training environment, apart from a daily hour's exercise after Hans finishes work, Jaco's training rides are also his competitions. Nevertheless, 'Always Second' did break that barrier on many occasions, most notably in 1979 for a win in the 170-km three-day German Championship, and in 1980 for a win in the Hamburg to Hannover 100 miler. There have been many other wins over the years but his main attribute is durability and consistency, especially in the longer rides over 100 km where he consistently placed in the first four. He has three times placed in the European ELDRIC listings – two fourths and a second – and has represented Germany abroad in Holland, France, Belgium and Austria, his best international award being a third place in the Austrian/Hungarian Vienna to Budapest 300-km event in 1984. He has also been in the top ten in Holland and Belgium.

Hans says Jaco's good points are an ideal temperament for a cross-country horse combined with a refusal to pace himself above his natural limits, thus conserving himself over the years. On the debit side, apart from the high pulse readings, he does not like going alone and his upright pasterns make for a hard ride. Also he occasionally interferes, being somewhat base-narrow, though the farrier has corrected this tendency to a great degree over the years. Hans goes on to say that as old age catches up with Jaco there is unfortunately no other horse at present ready to take over from him, but he will continue to do shorter distance rides as long as Jaco remains sound. Also professional and financial commitments limit the number of rides Hans can attend.

With a valid backing of ten very full years of competitions of all types, started when European distance riding was in its infancy, Hans says he would like to see improvements made in the ride rules, particularly where care of the horses is concerned, such as the unnecessary prohibition of alcohol rubs on back and limbs which if their use is not permitted could result in sores from sweat. Also other areas such as doping controls should be tightened up and implemented more often. He also comments that the use of liniments and rubs are not strictly controlled and that ride venues often smell like a chemist's shop.

33 Holland

At the present time endurance riding is only just beginning to gain popularity in Holland and consequently all endurance riding matters are handled by the Nederlandse Ruiter Sport Vereniging (NRSV), which was asked by the Nederlandse Hippische Sportbond to maintain contact with the endurance riding associations of other European countries. To facilitate this Holland became a full member of the ELDRIC and adopted in full the FEI and ELDRIC rules. Their yearly international ride, run under FEI rules, is held at Uddel/Ermelo over a distance of 90 km. Ermelo attracts an entry of approximately thirty riders each year, and because of its relative accessibility has gained entries from overseas riders from Britain, and also from neighbouring Germany and Belgium. Awards at the Ermelo International, and at the other rides held throughout the season, are of token kind only with rosettes and a special plaque to winners. Anneke van Doornik with Sabine is the winner of the two most recent Ermelo rides, and Wicher Wichers riding Royal has both won the Ermelo ride (1985) and represented Holland abroad.

The NRSV also organize three- and four-day riding tours throughout Holland, but these are not of a strictly competitive nature. A recent development is the addition of another major ride into the 1987 European calendar with the 105-km event at Laag Soeren.

Horses and riders

Anneke van Doornik

One of the two outstanding distance riders in Holland at the moment is Anneke van Doornik. She rides a dark brown, 15.2 hand Dutch Warmblood, a half Thoroughbred mare called Sabine (1976) which was bought for general riding purposes. The NRSV three-day pleasure rides covering 40 km a day were Sabine's introduction to the long distance trail and as she enjoyed these jaunts Anneke decided to train her for the one major ride Holland then organized. This was the Ermelo International, and the first year Sabine took part it was still being run as a two-day event of 70 and 30 km. This was in 1982 and since then Sabine and Anneke have entered and completed every year, gaining completion awards in the first two, and at the next three being awarded placings of seventh, tenth, and finally in 1986 emerging the equivalent of the Dutch National Champion with an outright win, covering the 90 km of the now one-day event in a time of five hours. In 1987 Sabine repeated her Ermelo win in the now 100 km ride at an average speed of 15.9 kph.

Training Sabine starts three months before the Ermelo race and Anneke uses lungeing as a considerable part of her routine as well as riding the 30 km of trails around the stables. Early in training she clocks an average speed of 10 kph, only elevating this in the last month with a weekly workout of between 40 and 70 km at 20 kph. She has a full-time job running her own dry cleaning company, so long leisurely rides to accustom the mare to sustained effort are confined to Sundays. Sabine enjoys considerable paddock freedom and the week before the big event work is eased for a mini holiday to bring her to the start in prime fettle. Feeding rations consist of 3 kg (about 6½ lb) split equally between normal rations, which I take to be oats, barley and so on, and a high protein mix fortified with vitamins. Hay is fed according to the state of pasture and several times a week the mare is fed a mash.

Although the mare has only been ridden in a few pleasure and competitive events in Holland she has all the qualities needed to succeed – good mental attitude, willingness, smooth paces, especially at

37 Anneke Van Doornik with Sabine, Dutch National Champions 1986 and 1987.

and assess the results of her training. Naturally she would like to see more competitive events run in Holland, but says it is a problem to organize them in such a small country, especially as the sport is only just gaining popularity and still has only a very small nucleus of keen riders at the present time. However, if Holland follows the pattern of other European countries it should not be long before there is a very healthy growth in both competitors and number of events offered.

Wicher Wichers

Wicher Wichers is at present the only Dutch rider to have competed regularly outside Holland, travelling to Germany for their 100-km Pussade ride in 1985 to place third with his bay gelding Royal (1969), who is a Thoroughbred/Welsh cross. Like Holland's other current top horse Sabine, Royal and his rider started endurance riding by chance. Royal is stabled just outside Groningen in the north of Holland where there is ideal training ground, and Wicher found that both he and Royal enjoyed the opportunity for unlimited riding where it was possible to travel safely at speed. Over the six years of their partnership the pair have covered in the region of 17,000 miles with a yearly stint of 2750 miles in training and 250 miles in competition. In that time they have completed the Ermelo ride six times, and since it has been of international status they have had one win and one second place. The pair have always been in the top ten. Wicher attributes Royal's success to his absolute dependability (110 per cent), bravery, a super trot and a lively but sensible temperament, allied to which he is very good in the heart and respiration department with low resting values and quick recoveries. He is fortunate in having a horse that has no problem area to worry about, Royal always coming home safe and sound, but does admit to a dislike of high temperatures and stony uneven going with their possible adverse effects.

Taking advantage of the limited amount of endurance riding that Holland currently offers Wicher says the sport makes him really appreciate his partnership with Royal, and that it is the most natural way to test a horse's talents and potential.

When asked about the sport's national and in-

the canter, and rapid recoveries. Anneke hopes to get the opportunity to further her experience by representing her country abroad, possibly in Belgium or West Germany which are the closest countries with international rides, although she admits that she may find the going more difficult because of the extremely flat terrain of her home training ground. At present she says the yearly Ermelo ride gives her the chance to test her horse ternational outlook he said Holland will find it difficult to expand to any great extent in the near future because of extremely limited accessibility to suitable trails. The landowners are not so obliging as for instance in Britain, and being a smaller country there are a great many restrictive regulations to contend with when riding out. He says it is very difficult to get sufficient length for even a 100 km course.

On a world basis he fears there is a danger of some riders changing endurance riding into endurance racing, and that this will lead, and he says in some cases has led, to abuse of horses which is the last thing that should happen to our sport. In a similar vein, when asked about the future he feels increased veterinary involvement is vital to improvement; he is averse to sponsorship because of the danger of commercialization which could subsequently lead to hurting the horses. He thinks the current awards schemes without financial involvement are adequate. His views differ in many aspects from those of other international riders, but are more far-seeing than some and have very valid, cogent reasons behind them. He credits the USA and Britain with having had most influence on the sport.

Wicher's own riding career began as a boy, had a long horseless interval, and began again when he felt his career could stand the time and financial involvement. That led to buying Royal, who was then an eight year old and became the family horse, being ridden equally by Wicher and his daughter. Although Royal is ridden all year round his serious endurance training starts in March, with a progressive build-up incorporating a lot of walking, gradually increasing the amount of trotting and also the distances covered. Additionally Royal is put on a treadmill four times a week which Wicher says is boring for him but good for his muscles. Wicher carries a stethoscope on long rides so he can monitor Royal's performance. When Royal is several weeks into his training Wicher uses a fifty-five-

38 Wicher Wichers and Royal, Dutch internationals.

minute trot, five-minute easy canter system, averaging around 17 or 18 kph which they keep up for hours. Feeding is just good quality rations and plenty of them. Because Wicher's business, owning and running a porcelain and crystal shop in Groningen, means frequent absences from home on buying trips, he says he must and can rely on the stable manager, and Royal is fed hay, oats, and something he calls 'Biks', a Dutch prepared horse food. Royal tucks into 8 to 10 kg a day of the oats and 'Biks', with hay ad lib, plus a daily treat of 2 kg of carrots. Obviously his high input enables him to give generously in his demanding yearly output of 3000 miles. Just as obviously his owner's sensible system has meant an enduring partnership with a horse that stays sound.

Endurance riding in Italy is under the auspices of the Associazione Nationale per il Turismo Equestre e per l'Equitazione di Campagna, or ANTE for short. ANTE was formed in 1968 and has approximately 8000 members. Of these 250 are currently involved with Endurance and Competitive Trail riding. The President of ANTE is Professor Vittorio de Sanctis, who is also the President of the FEI Subcommittee for Endurance Riding.

The major annual Italian rides are the Pratoni del Vivaro (160 km); Staffa d'Oro (80 km); Gran Premio di Fondo (500 km over ten days); Torino–Milano (120 km); and the Cannonball Race (80 km). ANTE also runs a considerable number of other rides ranging from 25 to a maximum of 160 km. The National Championships are held over several days, but the date and venue vary each year. The 1986 event was held at Venezia over a three-day period in late June, and the 1987 event changed venue and date to early June in Cesena, Emilia–Romagna. Endurance ride entries average around forty and to participate a rider must obtain a licence by passing an examination of competence. Horses must have up-to-date equine influenza vaccinations and pass the Coggins test. In certain events other vaccinations may be required. Random tests are carried out for forbidden substances.

Prizes are of token value only and awards in most cases go to third place. At ANTE's annual General Assembly awards are made to the winners of the National Championship for Tourism (pleasure category) and to the winner of the National Endurance Championship.

In all competitive rides course conditions must be clearly specified, especially where the going is rough. Roadwork may not exceed 10 per cent of the route. The hardest part of the course shall not occur towards the end of the ride. If hazards are present provision must be made for competitors to view these before the event. They may only be of natural obstacles and must be negotiable. Location of hazards must be described, particularly if they occur in the final stages of the ride, if they are of extended length, and if by-pass alternatives are available. Faults acquired by either a refusal or a fall at a hazard shall be expressed by time penalties according to each event's regulations. Routes must be well marked one week in advance of the event. Yellow markers denote straight on, red a right turn, and white a left turn. The finish line must be clearly marked and have adequate room for several horses moving at speed to do so without prejudice to their chances of a fair finish. Starting procedure must be advised in the schedule and can be either individual, small groups, or a mass start.

There is no appeal against a veterinary decision. The reason for elimination must be furnished to the contestant. Should a horse die during an event the fact must be notified to the Secretary of ANTE with a full report as to the circumstances.

Shoeing is not mandatory, but if a horse is shod it must be in a state adequate to last the ride. Loss of one or more shoe(s) en route shall not be cause for elimination. Dress regulations for riders and tack permissible for the horses are laid down in the National Regulations governing equestrian competitions. Hard hats are mandatory. Whips may not be longer than 75 cm and spurs may not be of a type to cause damage. Excessive use of either whip or spurs, or the continual urging forward of an exhausted horse, are grounds for elimination.

Rides are either of CTR or ER category. CTR rides are a minimum of 25 km. Severity is determined by length and speed in three categories: Category 1, speeds between 7.8 and 12 kph; Category 2, between 9 and 15 kph; Category 3, between 10.2 and 16.2 kph. In Category 3 rides there is the *possibility* of inclusion of a section no longer than 3000 to 4000 metres with ten to fifteen easy natural obstacles which must not be higher than 1 metre, no wider than 1.30 metres at the top or 1.60 metres at the base, and not more than 2 metres wide. Category 4 rides are run at a speed noted in the specific ride's rules but must be of a minimum distance of 50 km per day, whether the ride is run over one or more days. Category 5 rides are the Endurance Rides, which must be a minimum distance of 80 km if the ride is to be held over one day and a minimum of 50 km per day if the ride is held over more than one day. There are to be no natural obstacles nor veterinary penalties in Endurance Rides. All Category 5 rides are National Rides.

In Categories 1 and 2 judging is on a perfect time score plus veterinary penalties; in Category 3 on a perfect time score, veterinary penalties, plus any penalties acquired at obstacles; in Category 4 on a time basis plus veterinary penalties or, if the ride schedule states, on a time score with any penalties converted into time penalties. In team competitions the winner will be the team which has fewest penalties or the shortest total time. In case of a tie the winning team will be the one with the fewest penalties and the least time.

Horses must be at least five years old. In addition to the licence to participate, riders and horses must qualify and go up through the stages, their entry being validated by whichever category of licence they hold. To participate in a Category 3 or 4 ride they must have participated in and successfully completed a ride run by ANTE within the previous twelve months.

In all rides the rider is free to choose the pace and may proceed dismounted but must start and finish mounted, and for the last 500 metres the horse must proceed at either trot or canter or be eliminated. There are no weight restrictions in Categories 1, 2 and 3. In Categories 4 and 5 horses must carry a minimum weight. For men this is 75 kg, ladies and juniors 70 kg. If riders cannot make the weight they may carry extra weights (lead) or penalties expressed in time will be allocated.

Assistance during rides is not allowed, examples being mounting by another rider; exhorting by chasing; pacing by either another (non-competing)

horse or a wheeled vehicle; use of a prepared course; relaying of positions and state of other competitors via radio transmitter. Exceptions which are permitted are assistance with tack; replacing lost shoes; holding a horse during mounting; and help with replacing any equipment; and any normal assistance given by crews at ride venue and at mandatory stops en route.

On arrival at the ride venue there is a veterinary inspection of documents, vaccination and registration papers plus an examination to make sure the horse is in a satisfactory state of health. The first veterinary inspection before the ride concerns pulse, respiration, general condition and locomotor soundness. Horses with raised temperatures or in mediocre condition are eliminated. Checks for lameness are made on a scale of 1 to 5:

(1) lameness difficult to observe;
(2) difficult to observe at walk and trot in a straight line, but observable at times on some ground;
(3) apparent at trot on all going;
(4) marked lameness with shortened stride;
(5) reluctance to bear weight or inability to move.

Horses with lameness in Grade 1 and 2 are allowed to proceed, others are eliminated. Other areas checked include stiffness and saddle sores. If it is considered that either condition will be aggravated by the ride the horse is eliminated.

Each day's ride must be split into two stages separated by a mandatory halt of forty minutes. At mandatory stops similar procedures to the above are carried out. After a thirty-minute rest the horse's heart rate must have dropped to 64 or below or elimination follows. Respiration must have dropped to 36 or below. If the horse's temperature registers 40 °C or above it is eliminated, even if heart and respiration rates are not excessive. Because taking a rectal temperature excites many horses, veterinary surgeons are advised to take this after heart and respiration rates have been established. Lameness above Grade 2 incurs elimination.

After crossing the finish line the horse has thirty

minutes to recover and is then examined as at the first check and mandatory stops. In the case of rides of 100 km the final inspection will not be less than one hour after the finish, and in rides of greater distances not less than five hours after the finish. At this inspection the horse must be in good enough condition to be able to be ridden. If a horse is eliminated it must be by a majority vote of the veterinary officials. If there is a tie the Ride Head Veterinarian's vote will decide.

Although many of the rules are akin to those of other nations, Italy does have some, especially those concerning obstacles in Category 3 rides, that differ widely.

39 Pietro Moneta and Dado, Italian Endurance Champions 1986. (Tucci M)

Horses and riders

Dado

The 1986 Italian Endurance Champion horse was Dado (1973). He is a bay 15.3 hand, 1000 lb Maremmano Migliorato, his dame from a breed that has very ancient lineage tracing to the coveted Gonzagan horses of Renaissance Italy, his sire a Thoroughbred. He has four years' competitive endurance work under his girth. Owner Pietro Moneta says he took up the sport because it gave him the opportunity to spend many hours in his horse's company during competitions. Not bred for endurance riding, Dado really did fall into it by chance, being the prize in a lottery for which Pietro had a $25 ticket! Since his name was literally 'drawn from a hat' he has had many hours of pleasure and satisfaction from the horse, as has Pietro's brother, who trains him. Owing to business commitments Pietro only has the opportunity to ride at weekends.

Italian endurance riding is only now emerging as a national equestrian discipline with relatively few rides being held annually, so Dado's total competition mileage is limited, but nevertheless he is adequately prepared with a yearly 1500 km of training. In four years of competition he has risen steadily up the ladder of achievements from a seventh place at the two-day Rome 150 km in 1983, to a first place and National Championship win at Venezia (Venice) in the three-day 150-km event in June 1986. The partnership have been members of the Italian Team at the European Championships in Austria in 1985 and at the World Championships in Rome in 1986. Pietro hopes to continue to participate at an international level for many years, seeing the events as offering fun and a chance to meet people from all over the world. He attributes his horse's successes to his luck in winning him, followed by the serious training given by his brother. Dado's bonus points are a good resting heart rate, soundness and solid experience, but Pietro admits that his main cause for concern is Dado's tendency to dehydrate on tough rides.

Pietro would like to see an increase in sponsorship given to the sport, plus an improvement in awards and prizes.

35 New Zealand

In the world of endurance riding the New Zealand Endurance and Trail Rides Association Inc. (NZETR) is a fairly new entrant, the national group only having started in 1981. I am grateful to its Secretary, Mrs Hazel McCort, for furnishing me with the association's history as well as details of several of New Zealand's most consistent riders.

The structure differs somewhat from other national associations in that membership is through an affiliated club, with the exception of a few associate members. Although membership is still relatively small the sport's popularity has shown a steady escalation under the national body, growing from four affiliated clubs in 1981 to the present number of fifteen. There are upwards of twenty-four annual rides and distances range from 25 to 160 miles. However, New Zealand has yet to hold a one-day 100 miler, the top mileage at present being held over a two-day span. The three major events each season are the South Island Championship; the North Island Championship; and the National Ride. For the 1985–6 season this last event was held over 75 miles, the highest one-day mileage so far. The National Ride is run alternately in the South and North Islands, and affiliated clubs wishing to host this ride make an early application to the association indicating their willingness and intent, after which it is decided which venue shall be used.

Participation in the major rides is low in numbers, relative to other more established endurance riding countries, but from all the questionnaires completed by the New Zealand riders it is clear that standards are constantly rising in accordance with their associations' aims of promoting the sport and the sportsmanship and horsemanship involved. A very important facet of the governing committee for New Zealand is that both the Secretary and the President are currently very ac-

tive endurance riders themselves, and in my opinion it is vital to any society's sport that the governing body be actively and competitively involved in the sport they seek to govern.

In the vetting procedures for both Endurance and Trail Rides, pulse rates pre-ride and immediately post-ride are over a thirty-second span, but at the final taking thirty minutes after the finish pulse must be taken over a sixty-second count. A veterinary surgeon has it in his discretion to refuse to allow a horse to start that is either in too thin or too gross condition. When being trotted out for gait examination reluctant horses may not be chased forwards, and the length of the lead rope must be at least one metre held loosely. At checks during the ride heart rate must drop to 60 or below at the first check, thereafter to 65 bpm in rides over 80 km and to 60 bpm in rides under 80 km.

Endurance Ride and Trail Ride rules have wide variances. Horses entered in Endurance Rides must be a minimum of five *calendar* years on the day of the ride. In rides under 50 miles the ride is divided into two divisions: Lightweight carrying under 70 kg and Open/Heavyweight carrying 70 kg and over. In rides of 50 miles and over the minimum weight to be carried is 70 kg. Riders may proceed dismounted at any time provided they cross both start and finish line mounted. No punitive means of persuasion are permitted (whips, spurs). Pulse rates are indicated above. Massed starts are mandatory for major rides. Maximum riding times are not to be reduced below a ratio of one hour for every 10 km.

For the North and South Island Championships and the National Ride the *rider* must have qualified over the distance of 25 or 50 miles as appropriate within the previous two-year period. National rides are to be a minimum 25 miles or 50 miles or over, riders qualifying accordingly.

All Endurance Rides are to be run under veterinary supervision, and it is up to the veterinarian(s) to give the Fittest Horse award, choosing from amongst those finishing within fifteen minutes of the winner for every 25 miles. In practice this means a fifteen-minute leeway for a 25 miler, a thirty-minute gap for a 50 miler, and so on. Criteria to be used in determining this award are: the present state of the horse; the time it took to complete the ride; its pulse recovery during the ride; the weight it carried; plus its ability to continue if the ride were longer. It must also be fully shod or hooves protected (easy boots or similar equipment).

A points system is run to determine the winner of Horse and Rider of the Year Award. Points may only be accrued from rides of 50 miles or more. There is also a Kilometre Award for which points count from rides of 40 km (25 miles) and above.

The Trail Riding rules differ considerably from those for Endurance Rides and also in some essentials from those of other countries. Horses need only be three calendar years of age to compete and it is not mandatory to have a veterinarian judge at these rides, though those deputed to judge should be familiar and competent with the correct procedure. The minimum distance for a trail ride is 15 km and the maximum 70 km, though in practice it is evident that most trail rides fall in the 30 to 50 km bracket. Speeds are according to type of terrain to be covered and are stipulated prior to the ride, generally falling in the 4–8 km bracket. There are Novice, Intermediate and Open sections, and weight divisions in each category. Winners and placers are scored out of a maximum of 200 points in seven categories: condition, 40; manners, 15; horsemanship, 25; horsemastership, 50; soundness, 40; way of going, 5; shoeing, 25. Riders may not proceed dismounted, and no assistance is permitted at mandatory stops. No protective gear, bandages, boots, or pads for sole of hoof are permitted. Riders are started at intervals, and on completion of the course must keep their horses moving around while waiting to be vetted, thus ensuring a fair basis for recovery assessment.

From questionnaires completed and returned it seems that most of New Zealand's distance riders would welcome a closer liaison with other endurance riding associations around the world in order to gain advice and keep abreast of current trends. NZETR has recently applied for and been granted association membership of the ELDRIC.

Horses and riders

A brief history is given below of some of New Zealand's leading riders. They do not have the chance to meet and compete against foreign riders as we do in Europe; because of distance Australia, their closest endurance riding nation, is a very expensive journey and so they are rather isolated in their endeavours. However, their aims also are to keep on improving, and I liked the repeated statement that competing and completing were more important than setting record times.

Many of the New Zealand endurance horses come from a working – farming or shepherding – background, taking the odd ride into their stride rather than treating it as the culmination of a specific training regime. Successful horses being used show a wider variation in breed than is usual in most countries where so many of the top horses are predominantly of Arabian or part-Arabian blood.

Muhammad Ali

Known as Cass, Muhammad Ali (1980) is an Anglo-Arab, 15.1 hand chestnut gelding with three years competitive experience to his credit. Bought specifically for endurance riding by Mannie Gall, the NZETR President, Cass had a good lead into the sport, being bred from an endurance mare. The stud service, by an Arabian stallion, was a prize for winning an endurance ride.

To date Cass has successfully completed 460 miles in competition. His first season was beset by that well-known horse problem 'frienditis', causing him to fret at being separated from his mates and being vetted out with high PRs. With a season's experience behind him he then settled well into a successful career and his owner has enjoyed a high rate of success in subsequent rides, rarely placing lower than fourth, and often winning rides up to 60 miles, which is in the higher mileage bracket for New Zealand at present. Among his

40 Muhammad Ali and Mannie Gall winning the 1987 New Zealand National Endurance Ride. (Ron Cooke)

best awards are a second place in the 1986 National Championships over 75 miles, and the prize for Fittest Horse on the day following the ride. This must be gratifying to his owner who says that Cass suffers from several rider-related disabilities, or as he terms it 'weight disadvantages', as Mannie weighs in with tack at over 200 lb, plus riding lopsided due to old and permanent back and hip injuries. The latest information is that Mannie and Muhammad Ali have earned their best award to date in the 1987 National Endurance Ride, held over two days and a 100-mile course, with a win in 9 hours, 32 minutes, 29 seconds.

Managing such consistency must stem from the system of training Cass receives. It is not specifically geared to endurance work but is merely doing the farm chores, as Cass is the station hack and constantly busy with long treks and mustering duties, which in the appropriate season can mount to 200 miles a week, mostly over steep terrain that can go from 300 feet to 2000 feet in less than a mile.

Mannie attributes his success to having a good horse and being able to put a lifetime's experience into effect. He sees the sport as growing substantially and rapidly in the North Island, and some-what more slowly in the South Island, mainly due to sparser population. Initially drawn to endurance riding because he says he had become 'too old, stiff and battle scarred to continue showjumping', allied with a curiosity to see what was over the next hill, he finds the sport rewarding because it offers the chance to do just that as well as giving him opportunities to teach horses to handle themselves in rough country and thus realize their full potential. As President of the association he recognizes the benefits to riders of comradeship, the chance to improve on horsemanship, and also the encouragement of sportsmanship. Concurring with other New Zealand riders he would like to see stricter vetting after rides, and would also like to see the sport attract more sponsorship. His own personal goal is just to keep turning out successful horses regularly and to continue his riding as long as he is physically capable.

Boko

A grey, 15.2 hand gelding, Boko (1979) is another very successful New Zealand horse and from breeding that to me, at any rate, signified he might be a good endurance prospect: he is by a Standard-bred stallion out of a station hack. Owned by Mr W. Parnham, Boko was bought unbroken with endurance riding in mind, but primarily to work for his living as a shepherd's horse. Consequently he receives all his training while working the 60- to 70-mile weekly round of hill shepherding, with additional hill work thrown in. His frequent competitions are by way of a 'busman's holiday'.

On these 'holidays' he has accrued the highest recorded distance in New Zealand which currently stands at 944 km. His main successes have been a string of first places, usually accompanied by the equally important award of Fittest Horse; a second place in the National Championship of 1985 also accompanied by Fittest Horse Award; and the overall win of Horse and Rider of the Year Award for 1985.

Boko's yearly stint runs up to 1700 miles of which only about 300 are in competitions, the rest being spent 'at work'. Mr Parnham says that he is a very strong, sound horse with tons of guts who moves out well at the end of a ride. He does have to

41 W. Parnham and Boko, New Zealand Horse and Rider of the Year in 1985.

guard against Boko giving too much of himself, fretting and wasting energy when inexperienced riders mount a cavalry charge early on in rides – we have the same syndrome in Britain with beginning endurance riders who think it all has to be done in a rush. For the future Mr Parnham aims to keep on competing and completing, but hankers after competing in one of the big rides overseas. His own home scene he sees as on the upgrade with better types of horses competing and turning in increasingly faster times.

Saamien Roland

Saamien Roland (1978) is a grey, 15.3 hand purebred Arabian stallion owned by Lesley Foote, who has been steadily competing with him for five years with a yearly competitive distance of between 150 and 250 miles. Lesley feels that now he is a mature horse he is ready to do more and improve on his many placings. She admits that the only times she has been vetted out was due to lack of thought on her part, as Saamien Roland is a very easy horse who prefers working in a group.

Many owners find it difficult to keep the flesh on super fit endurance horses but Lesley says her Arabian is a good doer who relishes plenty of good feed and can take a high ration without blowing up, but he has to be watched for overindulgence as he tends to pack on the pounds. He is also that ideal endurance mount – a horse who eats, drinks, sleeps, relaxes anywhere.

Involvement in endurance riding was partially responsible for Lesley taking a gamble and giving up a regular schoolteaching job to opt for seasonal work and training other people's horses in order to leave more time for her riding. This is not limited to endurance as Saamien Roland is an all-rounder and adept at jumping and one-day eventing as well.

Lesley says the sport is growing all the time but she would like to see more veterinary involvement and tighter controls at rides to enforce restraint on riders who do not treat their horses as well as they should. She sees a need for greater communication with other endurance riding bodies throughout the world, and for her own personal ambition sets her sights on completing a 100-mile, one-day ride.

Blue Horse

An Anglo-Arab, grey, 15.3 hand gelding, Blue Horse (1980) is New Zealand's current Horse of the Year. He is owned, trained and ridden in competitions by Sandra Mattingley, who initially bought him to sell on after schooling the 'buck out of him'. He had already deposited previous owners and Sandra says 'other owners never really got on with him as Blue can buck "Quite Well"'. However, he has only succeeded in losing her twice and they have achieved a rapport that has resulted in four years of steady progression from Trail to Endurance competition.

Starting in the 1983 season Sandra took him steadily, content to get round and qualify, and in the next year he started to place regularly, the high spot being a second in the South Island Championship. By the 1985–6 season he streaked to the top, racking up enough points to head the horse and rider combination league, placing second again in the South Island Championship and going one better for a win in the National Championship held over 75 miles.

Blue's training programme is extremely systematic, a six out of seven day routine averaging around 12 miles per day, with at least one 25-mile ride a month, and occasionally when not competing a weekend 40 miler. He has an extremely low resting pulse in the mid 20s and this does not elevate dramatically, even when under pressure, being in the low 60s at the end of a fast Endurance Ride. He is calm at vet checks, recovers rapidly, and, another bonus, can happily go it alone for miles without fretting.

Sandra attributes her successes with Blue to having the right horse to start with; learning by trial and error; adequate training preparation; and really knowing the horse inside out. She is lucky in training ground, using mostly hill work to condition Blue, as well as giving him a well-balanced ration of time-tried feedstuffs, plus supplements and electrolytes. The only problem he sometimes runs into and which she has to guard against is dehydration. Sandra is an ultra-lightweight and finds it difficult to make up the dead weight, as she prefers not to use lead for fear of losing it en route

42 Sandra Mattingley and Blue Horse, winners of the New Zealand National Championship.

and being disqualified. Living and working on an 800-acre farm she is fortunate in her own lifestyle, as Blue fits into her daily routine of caring for and training ten horses, breaking youngsters to sell on, and looking after breeding stock. Equally fortunate is her access to plenty of open country and she says New Zealand is great country for endurance rides as it abounds in outback places and you do not need to travel hundreds of miles to get there – comparing that with the flat and dreary British fenland makes me envious.

Her ambitions in endurance riding are to keep Blue going sound and completing well for many seasons, as well as bringing on another young endurance horse. Qualifying at the end is more important to her than fast times, as she sees no point in ruining a good horse just to win one ride. This facet of New Zealand endurance riding comes through with most of my correspondents, and finds an echo in the majority of British riders. While enjoying competition, British riders do not have the 'killer' instinct for a win that characterizes more competitive nations, yet on analysis Britain

shows consistently in international successes. Given time and experience, plus the vital chance to compete outside their own country, New Zealand riders would have the temperamental assets to do well on a world basis while safeguarding their mounts against over usage.

Richmond Proud Texan

Richmond Proud Texan (1980) is a 15.3 hand Appaloosa gelding bred from a proven endurance Appaloosa bloodline, his sire being a stallion imported from the USA and his dam a New Zealand Thoroughbred from a staying line. Hazel McCort, Secretary of NZETR, bought him specifically for endurance as a yearling and has now had two seasons of competition with Tex, wisely waiting until he was mature enough at five years of age before putting him to the test. Before that, during the waiting period, she competed on anything and everything she could so that Tex has profited from her experience gained on other horses.

In his first season he only competed in two 25 milers, but in 1986 had qualified to take part in the major rides, placing second at Waiuku over 62 miles (100 km) and ninth in the National Championship 75 miler. Tex is the first New Zealand Appaloosa to compete successfully in the longer endurance rides. Still in his early career days, he is being competed on sparingly and ridden conservatively, but his preparation at home is none the less thorough with a steady work-in period lasting approximately two months after a complete break in the winter. As the season approaches he is ridden more extensively and does up to a 40-mile training ride as part of his programme each week, the distance increasing as he gets fitter. Hazel is lucky in training ground, having both hills nearby and the beach to use for speed work. Tex's bonus points are inherent soundness; a long stride; and most important in a distance horse a sensible attitude and complete honesty. Hazel says the things that give her most trouble are her personal tendency to dehydrate and Tex's difficulty in coping with heat, but she overcomes this by riding him sensibly, adopting the ELDRIC motto of 'to finish is to win'.

As secretary of NZETR she spends considerable time in the day-to-day affairs of running the association, and says the New Zealand endurance scene is gradually improving and gaining in popularity, but there is considerable room for more such improvement. In common with many endurance riders she recognizes the debt the sport owes to the USA, and also to Australia where a considerable amount of research into stress-related problems in the sport has been done. She would like to see more veterinary involvement in endurance riding and she hopes that through worldwide communications the veterinary scene will improve, as it is very difficult at present to get sufficiently experienced veterinary surgeons to adjudicate at rides. Her own personal ambition is to compete in the Australian Quilty 100 miler riding her own horse!

Dusky Rules

Dusky Rules (1980) is a grey, 15.1 hand Thoroughbred gelding whom Barbara Murray bought for endurance riding as a youngster. In his four competitive seasons he has accumulated 930 competitive kilometres. Although starting very young he was nevertheless taken slowly with very low mileage both in his first season's training and subsequent competitions. In his second season he entered four rides with two wins and a third, and then in the 1985–6 season he was ready to compete on a regular basis in the major rides, never once vetting out and coming home with a high proportion of major placings, including a first and Fittest Horse in a 35 miler, an equal third in the South Island Championship 100 miler (two days), and fourth in the National Championship 75 miler. The 1986–7 season is only part way through at time of writing, and already he has added to his score, ending the first of the season's 100 milers with a third place.

Barbara tallies his good points as clean wind, excellent legs, long, smooth paces, and speed; but on the debit side says he is a difficult horse to settle and for the vet to take pulse readings because of fidgetiness, but says he is becoming better as he matures. Fortunately as the ride progresses he settles, and shows good recovery at the important penultimate and final pulse readings.

Barbara admits that prior to competing on Dusky she had not been very successful, and says it was due to lack of competence on her part, riding ill-judged rides and asking too much too soon from immature horses. Dusky has been slow in maturing, and is not an easy horse to read, but has taught her to take things steadily as he had a tendency to vet out if allowed to rush the first section of rides.

In accord with many of her compatriots she would like to see more veterinary involvement with the sport, and in particular would like to see the New Zealand vets have a chance to be trained by a seasoned endurance veterinary surgeon. America and Australia head her list for dissemination of knowledge on endurance riding, and her current ambition is to ride in the Australian Quilty on her own horse, but sees it as a financial impossibility unless sponsorship is forthcoming. At present the New Zealand rides often give cash prizes and prizes in kind, but the big sponsorships, as with most countries, are still a long way off. She and her partner Kevin are responsible for organizing two of the big New Zealand rides and gaining sponsorship where possible, and Barbara says a breakthrough has recently come in the filming for television of the Homebush, South Island Championship, from which she hopes more sponsorship will follow. On a personal enjoyment level she finds endurance riding gives her the chance of meeting new people and seeing more of her country than would otherwise have been possible, and with down-to-earth honesty says the major impetus to continue persevering came on meeting the right man in her life who was totally involved in the sport.

From such a small selection, even though they are the current leading riders in New Zealand, it is very clear that because of geographical limitations these riders feel somewhat cut off from the rest of the world and what is happening at international level. The New Zealand riders are avid for knowledge, desperately keen to improve, and are doing all they can to widen the base for the sport at home by good promotion. As things are now moving with more interrelation between national associations this should be of great benefit, especially in their recent incorporation into the ELDRIC.

Norway is one of the most recent recruits to modern endurance riding but its earliest records go back to just over a century ago and have a direct bearing on the resurgence of the sport in Norway today.

Just before the turn of the century long distance riding was mainly a sport for cavalry officers, and the first recorded Norwegian endurance ride was a 50-km race won by a Lieutenant Aas on Bijou in a time of one hour, fifty-seven minutes, forty-nine seconds in August 1881. This ride was organized by the Norwegian Officers' Riding Club, which was founded in 1880.

In 1885 by an unusual quirk the death of a young Norwegian cavalry officer gave lasting benefit to endurance riding. Thomas Stang-Michelet had enlisted under the British flag to serve in the Sudan for two years. He travelled to Egypt and took part in a ride with the Bedouins lasting several days before joining his English regiment. He suffered sunstroke and although admitted to military hospital he died from a combination of the sunstroke and typhus. Before he died he willed 20,000 Norwegian kroner to the Norwegian Officers' Riding Club. This money provided the prizes for a 50-km endurance ride in 1886, which was won by E. Jensen riding Guladis in a time of two hours, four minutes, thirty-three seconds. A hundred years later the legacy still provides prize money, and on the hundredth anniversary of the ride the Norwegian Officers' Riding Club voted to support the 80-km ELDRIC ride held at Eidskog, which was won by Annette Haukas on her horse Allanit in a time of four hours, four minutes, fifty-four seconds.

Norwegian endurance riding today is under the aegis of the Norwegian Equestrian Federation (NRYF). It has only been formally organized since 1984 when the NRYF received the FEI rules for endurance riding, and delegated the Three Day Event Committee to undertake this new discipline. The ELDRIC associate member Reidar Naess was asked to help co-ordinate the sport. A small committee was formed and in its first year held one endurance ride under FEI rules at Eidskog, but adapted to the distance of 50 km, and with the main veterinary criteria demanding a pulse recovery to 72 within ten minutes of arrival at each examination station. As with so many countries Arabian horses were to the fore, the first five places being filled by purebreds.

In its formative year NRYF organized a course for distance riding judges and eight candidates went into the next competitive year as qualified endurance judges. Three of these were veterinarians. Still feeling their way, they again organized the Eidskog Ride in 1985, together with several other rides run against the clock under FEI rules. Additional rides of CTR status were run throughout the year but with less stringent rules than those pertaining to Endurance Rides in order to encourage beginners to the sport and stimulate them to try for better performances.

The breakthrough year for Norway was 1986. The NRYF appointed a committee specifically for endurance riding headed by Reidar Naess as Chairman, and Norway became a full member of the ELDRIC. It ran its first ELDRIC ride at Eidskog with two riders from Sweden also competing to give it an international flavour. Endurance Rides increased to three supported by CTR classes, and other pleasure rides without a competitive element gave beginners the chance to become involved.

The prospect for 1987 was extremely good with a very much expanded fixture list, two ELDRIC rides, and many other events offering more challenging rides. All major rides have lower distance classes as well, and the nucleus of Norwegian distance riders is growing rapidly. The Norwegians also organize winter seminars to draw more judges, veterinarians, organizers, and competitors into the sport, and the lengthening list of prospective judges applying for courses shows how the sport is catching on. Also as many of the rides in Sweden are easily available to Norwegian riders the opportunity for participation is multiplied, especially as the two countries' rules at top level are similar, both countries being ELDRIC signatories, and the easier shorter distance rides being comparable in requirements.

An innovation for 1987 was the first championship to be awarded to the horse and rider gaining most points from five rides of 50 km or longer, similar to the ELDRIC system, and on a par with the EHPS of GB where the scores from the horse's best ten results count. Looking ahead, it is hoped to award a National Championship in 1988 from rides of 80 km or longer.

Horses and riders

Reidar Naess

Reidar Naess farms just north of Oslo and has had a lifelong interest in horses, being involved with many of Norway's equestrian associations. He was Chairman of the Norwegian Pony Association for three years (1976–9), and is currently a member of the Norwegian Arabian Horse Society's Executive Committee, a post he has held since 1981. There is a saying in Britain (maybe elsewhere too?!) that if you want to get something done ask a busy person, so when endurance riding became a viable proposition in Norway Reidar Naess was asked to spearhead the new sport. His three current endurance horses are all Arabian.

Saraj (1975), a purebred chestnut mare bred by the Hutchings near Dover, Kent, was imported into Norway in 1978, primarily as a brood mare, but as Reidar became interested in endurance riding she was sidelined to a performance career. As Norway had not yet started endurance riding her first major rides were across the border in Sweden, where she took seventh place in their Karoliner Ride in 1981, and returned to win it in 1982. She has competed three times in the Eidskog Ride,

twice placing third and once winning in 1984. In addition to her endurance riding activities she has had a steady career in dressage, where she is ridden by Lisbeth Eriksen. For four years running – 1983 to 1986 – she won the award for the best Arabian dressage horse in Norway. Prior to her first endurance ride she produced the grey colt Sarin by Ibn Saud, a Swedish Arabian stallion, and she is currently in foal to the Polish bloodline stallion Puszczyk.

Taking over from his dam in the endurance field is Sarin (1980), who has only had limited competition work with Reidar, and who will be ridden for the near future by his stepson, Oddbjorn Berentsen, who learnt the ropes on another of Reidar's Arabians, the grey gelding Skamir (1981), which was imported from Sweden in 1986 and gave thirteen-year-old Oddbjorn his introduction to the sport in two 50-km events, the Furnes and the Askim rides in 1986. He won the Furnes ride and took fourth place in the Askim event.

Birgit and Ellen Marie Woie

Birgit Woie and her daughter Ellen Marie are both committed endurance riders, campaigning the family Arabian Zafra (1979), a grey 14.3 hand mare who has been to the fore in both Swedish and Norwegian rides for the past few years. However, Birgit started her endurance riding on an Arab cross New Forest mare called Farah Dibah on whom she first did the Karoliner Ride. Living and farming with husband Lars near the Swedish border, Birgit and Ellen are in an ideal position to take advantage of the rides run by both countries, Ellen taking over from her mother on the many occasions when Birgit is too busy with behind-the-scenes ride organization. She ran the first Eidskog Ride in 1980 and has repeated it every year except 1983, and as a member of the Norwegian endurance riding committee is responsible for much of the sport's impetus. She is also the first Norwegian rider to make the grade into the European listings, with a fifteenth place in the 1986 ELDRIC Trophy. Their mare Zafra, after producing her first foal in 1984, took to the distance trail and in three seasons has come third, first and second in the Eidskog Ride in Norway, and a completion and a second place in two Karoliner Rides and an eighth place in the Roslags Ride near Stockholm, Sweden.

Norway is entering into endurance riding enthusiastically and the list of riders willing to have a crack at the longer, tougher rides is expanding. Many of the riders compete regularly in both Norway and Sweden, and at present there is a predominance of Arabian blood amongst the horses that are most successful, which must be gratifying to the Norwegian Arabian Horse Society who has helped promote the sport.

Other notable horses currently competing in Norway are Mata Hari, a purebred Arabian owned and ridden by Bjorn Hagin who has been successful with her in the Eidskog and Karoliner Rides; Gabor, a winner in both CTR and Endurance categories in Norway, ridden by Ase Nyang; and Allanit, ridden by Annette Haukas.

37 South Africa

The Endurance Ride Association of South Africa (ERASA) was inaugurated in 1974 and owes much of its early growth to Dirk de Vos, and also to the South African Magazine *Farmer's Weekly* which, for many years, gave financial backing to ERASA's National Championships, the annual 210-km three-day endurance ride held at Fauresmith in the Orange Free State. Each state has its own committee and the four provinces – Natal, Transvaal, Cape, and Orange Free State – run several Pre-Rides leading up to the July Championship. Most rides are 80-km events with the exception of the Hofmeyr 100 miler. Dr J. L. Viljoen, ERASA's Vice President, has provided statistics relating to ERASA which show the steady increase of the sport. From a total of sixty-eight entries in rides held in its inaugural year, by 1986 this count had risen to 999 entries. South African endurance riders also travel fast, the average speed of riders being 18.8 kph, but winning horses need to better that by several kilometres per hour. The purebred Arabian is the most popular horse used in South African endurance riding followed by his partbred kinsman, with other breeds only having a nominal showing. Out of the fifty-six horses that claimed a successful completion in the 1986 National Championship, twenty-one were pure, four Anglo, and seventeen part Arabian. Many studs, particularly those breeding Arabians, are actively promoting stock through the endurance field.

Cash awards or any financial incentives are banned on ERASA rides. If any ERASA member takes part in any ride that offers financial inducement he/she shall lose amateur status and membership of the association will be withdrawn.

ERASA rides are basically of Endurance category, and only rides with a minimum distance of 80 km can count towards Provincial and National Award schemes, or be qualifying rides for the National Championship. Rides of short distances are organized, with completion certificates given for distances of 30 km or above. However, no ride will be considered an Endurance Ride if it is less than 60 km, and this distance is the minimum which counts towards the kilometre distance awards. Rides not classifying as Endurance Rides are nevertheless run under the same rules. Maximum finishing times for the main Endurance Ride distances are: 80 km, seven hours; 160 km, eighteen hours; 210 km, nineteen hours (over three days) – all exclusive of mandatory veterinary halts.

It is suggested that on an 80-km ride there be at least four mandatory veterinary checks – at the start, at 30 km, at 60 km, and at the finish. At every checkpoint the horse's pulse and respiration is taken twenty minutes after arrival; his pulse must fall to a maximum of 70 bpm and there is a suggested maximum respiration of 40 rpm. Any horse with a pulse over 70 bpm is eliminated. Other causes for elimination are excessive dehydration, exhaustion, lameness, signs of illness, thumps, saddle sores and other trauma. Should it be thought necessary blood tests may be run to determine if the horse should be withdrawn. Blood, fecal, or urinary tests may also be run to determine use of forbidden substances. If positive, disqualification follows. Motorized vehicles are banned en route to assist in reducing unhealthy dust and to maintain a greater degree of safety. Back-up crews may follow and give assistance at designated points, but may not accompany their riders en route. Riders may dismount at any time en route but must start and finish each section mounted. Smoking is prohibited.

Horses must be a minimum of four and a half years of age, and horses between four and five years of age must provide either a registration or birth certificate, or have nine permanent incisor teeth erupted. In exceptional circumstances under-age horses may be permitted to enter 30-km rides. In-foal mares are not allowed to participate. All horses must be shod or booted, and if a shoe is lost it must be replaced at the next checkpoint or the horse will be disqualified. At the discretion of the Organizing Committee the shoeing rule may be waived in areas where underfoot going makes unshod travel feasible. Brushing boots, bandages, or other protective coverings are banned. All equipment must be of a humane nature. Spurs are banned. Hard hats, though advised, are not obligatory, the rider accepting responsibility for any accident.

Juniors may participate from the age of ten years on up to sixteen years in Club rides. At sixteen they transfer to the adult section. In National and Provincial rides Juniors must be a minimum of twelve years and remain in the Junior category until they are eighteen years of age. Juniors may only enter provided they are accompanied en route by an adult, and both risk disqualification should they be separated at any time. The distance between them must be 'within hearing distance'. In the event of the adult retiring he must place the Junior rider in the care of another adult and any time lost by either during the handover may not be credited. Similarly if the Junior has to withdraw en route the adult may not proceed until another adult (either mounted or unmounted) has taken over this responsiblity. Again no lost time is credited. A senior may agree to accompany up to three juniors on other than National rides, when he may only accompany two.

There are three weight categories on ERASA endurance rides. Riders weighing in with complete equipment at less than 73 kg may ride at catch weight. However, they may not receive any of the main prizes or placings, or be eligible for Best Condition, nor will they receive either National or Provincial Team points. The distance may be counted for kilometre awards but not for the National Endurance Horse Registry. The largest riding group is in the 73 to 94 kg category. The Heavyweight Class is 95 kg and over. Due to the relatively low number of heavier riders there may not be an individual class for heavyweights, but the weight factor is very much to the fore in deciding the Best Condition Award on 80 km and over rides.

All Juniors ride at catch weight and are judged separately from the seniors. For riders who have to make the weight by carrying lead such addition must be in approved weight bags. Random checks may be carried out either at mandatory halts or en route to ensure that weights have not been discarded. Non-compliance by the rider results in disqualification. If the weights are in order any time lost occasioned by the checking of equipment will be credited to the rider.

The winner of the ride is the horse passing all veterinary examinations and achieving the fastest time over the course. The winner of the Best Condition Award is drawn from the first ten horses to finish within 20 per cent of the winner's time. If there is a field of fewer than fifty horses then the selection for Best Condition will only be from the top 20 per cent of the finishers. Juniors are judged separately for Best Condition. No horse with time penalties is eligible. The award is judged on a maximum points system in three sections:

Weight: the heaviest rider in the qualifying group gets 100 points. All others will have one point deducted for every kilogram lower than the heaviest rider.

Time: the winner on time is credited with 100 points, all others having one point per minute deducted for each minute they finish behind the winner.

Veterinary: fifty points go on pulse where the average of the three riding (working) pulses (taken at mandatory veterinary checks) are averaged out, with 40 bpm being the base. For rates of between 40 to 50 one point per beat is deducted, and for rates of between 51 to 70 two points per beat are deducted. The remaining fifty points are allocated on a grading of 1 – 5 as shown in the table.

	Grading	Multiply by factor	Maximum
Hydration	1–5	× 1	5
Locomotion	1–5	× 3	15
Habitus	1–5	× 3	15
Mucous membranes	1–5	× 2	10
Skin lesions	1–5	× 1	5

Allocation of points for South Africa's Best Condition Award

With no penalty points the rider gets fifty points. Otherwise the penalty points are deducted from fifty points and the balance credited to the rider.

The horse that has the highest score out of the possible 300 is the winner. If there should be two or more horses with five points or less between them then a visual examination may be conducted.

Horses and riders

Eibna Mansour

A chestnut purebred Arabian gelding of the Keheilan Rodan strain, Eibna Mansour (1978) is by Saf Firstaar out of Eibna Sandiana. He was bred by Mijnheer and Mevrouw E. P. Engelbracht at their Brakfontein Stud in the Transvaal, and he is only one of a line of horses carrying the Eibna prefix that have excelled in South African endurance riding.

Bought by Dr Viljoen and campaigned by his daughters Charlene and Lynn, Mansour has had a crowded four-year career, completing twenty-five rides with an average finishing position of third. No ride was shorter than 80 km, and in twelve of them he has been awarded the prize for Best Condition. His early rides in 1983 were all in the junior division, but since then he has been carrying an extra 17 kg to reach the prescribed minimum weight of 73 kg, much of it made up of dead weight. He has completed the Fauresmith National Championship three times, twice with Charlene and

43 Eibna Mansour and Lynn Viljoen, 1986 South African Champions.

once with Lynn. With Charlene riding first as a junior he took fifth place and Best Condition, and then when she rode the following year as a senior he took second place. In 1986, piloted by Lynn, he went one better for an outright win in the record time of eight hours, seventeen minutes, twenty seconds, an average speed of 25.3 kph, although on the first leg he completed the 50 miles at an average speed of 30.1 kph. Dr Viljoen says he is 'a fierce competitor who likes to ride his own ride and is regarded by some of the older riders as somewhat

of a freak'. He warmly praises his daughter for the superb job of conditioning Mansour for his South African record. In the seven-month run up to Fauresmith Lynn and Mansour covered 2700 km in training and competitions.

Enjoying a well-earned rest Mansour, who lives out year round in a very unpampered life-style, is keen to hit the trail in new competitions. His steely fitness clearly showed in excellent recoveries. At no time after the twenty-minute pulse checks did his heart rate show in excess of 54 bpm.

38 Sweden

In 1895 Sweden had a record ride from Jönköping to Stockholm, a distance of 450 km. The race was won by Lieutenant Per Carlberg on his seven-year-old Frey in a time of forty-four hours, twenty-two minutes, thirty seconds to earn a place in Swedish sports history. In the early years of the twentieth century other notable distance rides were recorded by the Swedish military.

The first ride in modern times was the Karoliner Ride, which was started in 1977 with fourteen entries in the 100-km class and forty-one in the 50-km section. It is now international. The ride commemorates Sweden's King Charles XII and two officers who in 1714 rode from Pitesci in Turkey to Strahlsund in Germany – 2400 km in fourteen days.

In 1983 Sweden's emergence into international distance riding was consolidated with a ride named after the guerrillas of the Snapphane district who fought in the Danish/Swedish war of the 1700s. The Snapphane ride started with a 50-mile course and only five entries, but has now built to a 75-mile course Endurance Ride with lower-distance supporting classes.

The sport is progressing with more riders involved, steadily rising standards, and new rides coming into the yearly calendar. Sweden's endurance riding comes under the aegis of the Swedish National Equestrian Federation (SRC) and has the same standing as all other equestrian disciplines in the country. Endurance riding has received a tremendous boost with the projected staging of the 1990 World Equestrian Games in Stockholm, where the third running of the World Championship 100-Mile Ride Endurance event will be held.

For many years Louise Hermelin from Krontorp has been the enthusiastic force behind endurance riding in Sweden and much of its current success is the result of her consistent efforts. Appointed by the SRC she is the country's official representative to the ELDRIC Committee (as well as being a committee member) and the liaison with all other regional organizers for anything concerning this discipline. The same system pertains for all other disciplines, such as dressage, one-day eventing and jumping. Under SRC rules every competitive rider and all horses entering rides of 50 km or more must have a licence to compete. The horse's licence is issued once and is valid for its entire lifetime. The rider must apply on an annual basis for a licence which is only issued to members of clubs affiliated to the Swedish Federation. Such licences entitle both horse and rider to enter all disciplines – at variance with the BHS who require a membership fee and registration for the horse for each discipline.

The basic rules for Sweden are as follows. All rides of 80 km or over run in Sweden are of the Endurance category and run to FEI standards, with the pulse requirement being 64 bpm or less thirty minutes after the rides finish. However, to safeguard horses competing in lower distances Swedish rules operate a pulse requirement of 60 maximum. For rides under 50 km the 'vet gate' system is used, where a ten-minute stop can be used after presenting the horse for pulse check. This is used to encourage more responsible riding.

The rules provide for several classes of ride:

Category A Minimum distance 120 km. If held over more than one day, minimum daily distance is 100 km.

Category B 80 to 120 km per day. If held over more than one day the minimum daily distance is 80 km.

Category C 50 to 79 km in one day.

Category D Rides under 50 km.

On the longer distance rides the mandatory veterinary stops must be between 25 and 40 km (maximum) apart, and the number of such stops are dictated by the severity of the course. Duration of stops is a minimum of forty minutes, maximum sixty minutes. Pulse readings are taken thirty minutes after arrival at stops. For entry into the longer distanced rides horses must be a minimum of six years of age. Novice horses entering the lower distance rides (Category D) need only be five years of age, if the rides are styled 'Education' classes.

The schedule must advise the terrain, particularly if it is hilly. There may not be more than 10 per cent of hard-surfaced going and the most difficult part of the course shall not be towards the end. Each rider shall be provided with a map of the course which must be adequately marked with red and white flags, chalk and so on. Hazards must be noted on the map, and bypass routes provided that do not add more than 500 metres to the course. The finish must be wide enough for several horses to cross at one time. It must be well marked. Route markers are placed every 10 km. Riders should be able to check the course the day before, and on the day may dismount and lead their horses, but must start and finish the route mounted.

Riders must wear hard hats with chin-strap affixed. There are no tack restrictions with the exception that blinkers and hoods are not allowed. Reins must be attached to bit or hackamore. All horses must be shod. Whips must not be more than 75 cm long. Any abuse via whips, or spurring, or over-driving of the horse shall be reason for disqualification.

All rides run under the FEI rulings are run against the clock, and in the lower distanced rides of CTR nature which come outside this bracket the organizer is responsible for indicating in the schedule the speed to be used and maximum time allowed for any particular ride. The organizer must also state for CTR rides any penalties to be allocated and the method of marking such penalties.

En route the rider may not receive assistance from outside, other than at mandatory stops. Examples of forbidden help, and also the examples of permitted assistance, are according to the lines laid down in the FEI rulings.

All horses are given a pre-ride examination the day before to check on health, vaccinations, and identity papers. Veterinary examinations take place before, during and after the ride and there are two veterinary surgeons and one director in the adjudicatory panel, in addition to qualified pulse and respiration personnel. Penalties, where applicable, are given for bad condition. Reasons for elimination include hyperventilating; high temperature of 40 °C and over, even if the pulse and respiration are not elevated; and lameness. If the veterinary surgeon is not sure as to the lameness the horse is trotted twice in each direction, and if he is still not sure the horse is allowed to proceed. Horses are not permitted to be chased up at veterinary examinations. There is no appeal against a veterinary decision.

At present the growth of all equestrian activities is rocketing in Sweden, particularly endurance riding. The main rides in Sweden's distance riding calendar are the Göinge Ride (80 or 100 km); the Roslags Ride (120 km); the Snapphane (120 km); and the Karoliner (100 km). Of these the Roslags, the Snapphane and the Karoliner are the ones which carry international status, with one being selected each year for the Swedish National Championship as well. In 1987 it was held at Roslags and won by Hans Wallman on Miss China. All rides have shorter distance events incorporated into the ride schedules. Clubs new to endurance riding are only permitted to organize the lower distance, easier rides (Categories C and D) until they gain more experience. In 1987 prize money in modest sums was introduced for the Roslags International. As yet numbers entered in Sweden's longer distanced rides are small, as the sport, although increasing, has as yet only a growing nucleus of riders prepared for the demands of endurance riding. But it is proposed to increase ride distances steadily until 1990 so that within its own borders Sweden can offer competitors the chance of gaining experience in the 100 milers that are so much to the fore in the well-established endurance countries. This is particularly important for both Sweden and Norway, as geographically they are possibly in a less favourable position even than Britain for competing abroad; in addition to a sea crossing they are situated right at the northern tip of Europe. Many of the central Europeans such as the Germans, Austrians and Swiss, and the Belgians and the Dutch, though having to travel a moderate distance, are considerably closer to many of the international rides.

Horses and riders

From among the top Swedish riders Louise Hermelin and Sture Landqvist have had considerable success. Both ride purebred Arabians.

Louise Hermelin

Louise Hermelin has been involved with endurance riding for ten years and is the Swedish Equestrian Federation's international representative responsible for all internal and external matters allied to the sport. It is to her enthusiasm that much of Sweden's recent progress is due, and she is concerned to prove to Swedish riders that endurance riding need not be too time consuming but can be satisfactorily attempted by riders prepared to give it an honest try.

On her own home front, as well as being involved in organization she is one of Sweden's top endurance riders and one of the few who have competed abroad representing her country. Her first distance horse was the grey partbred Arabian Herkules, now into his twenties. Louise was present when he was born, and at sixteen years of age in his seventh season of distance work he was still game enough to tackle one of Europe's toughest rides, the 300 km Vienna to Budapest three-day ride in 1983, finishing sixth out of a field of forty-seven.

After Herkules' retirement she campaigned the grey purebred gelding Navarino by the Egyptian stallion Shakhs. In two seasons Navarino did well, always being in the placings except for a single instance of being vetted out. He has now gone on to eventing where his insatiable eagerness allied with a bright happy nature should enable him to make a good transition to a second career. Her current number one horse is very different. Another Arabian, the grey 15 hand mare Sheesmira (1979) has a very easy-going even lazy manner and is hard to

keep interested in training. However, she is a good mover, has comfortable gaits, loves competition and – that very important element in an endurance horse's makeup – she remains calm. As a novice, Sheesmira started in exemplary fashion, doing four major rides in her first season – Snapphane, Roslags and Karoliner in Sweden, and Eidskog in Norway just across the border. She was in fact the only horse from either country to complete in all four rides in one season – not bad for a novice. She was partnered throughout by Louise's friend Lena Linneaus. In 1987 she gained further successful experience: third at Roslags, fifth at the Karoliner, and a competition in her first 100 miler at the European Championships at Erlangen in West Germany. Sheesmira's back-up will be Marab, whom Louise bred herself. He is a purebred gelding born in 1982 by Mamluk out of Lady Socks and he starts the 1988 season with limited competition as a novice.

Louise is a farmer who also breeds Arabians. She believes in keeping her distance horses in as natural an environment as possible, turned out in large paddocks but with plenty of standard feeding, incorporating oats, hay and lucerne. She says it is vital to know each animal's idiosyncracies, to treat each as an individual, and to take into the training a thorough knowledge of what you are doing and why. Her own interest in endurance riding comes from the simple statement that she 'loves it and feels great after the ride is over, and that it brings her close to her horse whilst giving something worthwhile to train for'. Her aims are to maintain consistency with the same horses year after year as she initially did with Herkules. She concurs with Sture Landqvist on wishing that greater sponsorship was available to further the sport, and in according USA prime place in the league of endurance nations, but to this adds Australia and Great Britain.

Sture Landqvist

Sture Landqvist is the 1986 Swedish National Champion endurance rider, and his mount is the grey, 14.3 hand Arabian stallion Alfar (1977).

Alfar was not bought for endurance riding, only taking it up in 1983 as Sweden began to expand her

44 Louise Hermelin and Herkules, Swedish finishers in the 1983 Vienna to Budapest ride.

45 Sture Landqvist and Alfar, 1986 Swedish National Champions.

programme for endurance riding. As with so many good Arabians he is an all-round performer, being equally well versed in dressage, jumping and driving, but when the chance came to add yet another category to Alfar's achievements Sture entered him in the 1983 Snapphane Ride on a trial basis and was delighted with a sixth place. In 1984 he was entered again and won at Snapphane, repeating the win in 1986, also adding a victory in the Karoliner Ride, thus more than proving his ability as an endurance horse and adding to his value as a breeding stallion. Sture attributes these successes to Alfar being a fine horse who is well trained, and also to his enviably low heart rate both before and during competition. His temperament is good and there are no worrying aspects to watch out for during competition except on the occasions when mares are in season during a ride.

As the sport is becoming very popular in Sweden

Alfar will no doubt continue to add to his endurance, English pleasure and driving successes, as well as pass on his ability. He is fortunate in having a rider who can devote sufficient time really to campaign a horse adequately. Sture and his wife run an Arabian stud at Risarp and Sture is also involved as a licensed amateur trainer in racing and harness trotting. Alfar's endurance training, amongst his many other activities, includes a steady low daily mileage to keep him ticking over, with some extended training rides in the build-up period before major competitions. Nutrition is time-tried, good quality oats and hay, with some molasses added. His rider's main ambition is to be selected for the Swedish National Team. In common with many endurance riders Sture pays tribute to the USA as having contributed most to the worldwide scene of endurance riding.

Switzerland began organized distance riding in September 1978 with the founding of the Schweizerische Distanzreiter Vereinigung (SDV). In its first year SDV had thirty-three members, the number rising to over 200 active members in 1987. In 1981 SDV became a member of the Swiss Central Organization for Horse Sports (SZP). Switzerland was a founder member of the ELDRIC and in 1981 Dr Georg Riedler from Ebikon became its President.

SDV offers nine annual events, some of which have multiple classes. Annual awards are a National Championship in both the Endurance and Competitive Trail category, and points for these can be gained at three major rides: the Schnabelsberg Cup (160 km in one day); the William Tell (160 km in two days); and the Winterthur (80 km in one day). These events also run CTR classes. Scoring is on a points basis and the highest score achieved over the three rides determines the winner. Points are awarded for starting, kilometres ridden, and placing. Ratings go to fifteenth place in both championships. Additionally there are kilometre awards in increments of 500 km. These are awarded to the riders riding the greatest number of kilometres regardless of number of horses, and to the horses achieving the greatest distance. Presently Dr Riedler heads the rider list with over 2700 km achieved on two horses, and Magic, a partbred Arabian owned by Franz Imhof, holds the kilometre record for horses with 1856 km behind him at the end of the 1986 season. To these figures must be added the 650 km Madrid–Lisbon ride, ridden early in 1987 in which both placed.

Prizes are of token value only with plaques and rosettes given to successful riders. The veterinary guidance for SDV is in the hands of Dr Andreas P. Gygax, who is the association's veterinary adviser.

Switzerland offers four ride categories. Elevator Rides (DRF) are similar to the Pleasure Rides run by some other associations. Speed used and distance ridden is optional, and they are a good medium for training and testing horses under competition conditions. There are veterinary examinations at the finish of the rides. Ride and Ties are run under rules similar to those operating in the USA; and the two main categories of ride are the Kombinierte Langstreckenprufung (KLP) which are Competitive Trail Rides, and the Distanzrennen (DR) or Endurance Rides.

KLP rides

They are split into three sections:

Kurze Distanzritte

of between 30 and 40 km, ridden at a maximum speed of 12 kph with a maximum time allowance of one and a half times the ideal time, e.g. 8 kph. Open to horses five years and over.

Mittlere Distanzritte

of between 41 and 79 km ridden at a maximum speed of 15 kph. Maximum time allowance as above. Open to horses five years and over.

Lange Distanzritte

of 80 km or more in one day, or an average of 60 km a day for rides of more than one day. Ridden at a maximum speed of 15 kph with maximum time allowance as above. Open to horses six years and over.

All horses must be vaccinated against equine influenza. Denerved horses and in-foal mares are not allowed to compete.

Junior riders must be at least ten years old and

until they are fourteen years of age must be accompanied by an adult.

Riders' dress is optional but should be suitable for the event, and hard hats are advised. Whether or not spurs and/or whips can be used is decided by the organizer, and if allowed any misuse of same incurs elimination. Horses' equipment is also optional but should fit well and be in good condition. Anything which restricts the horse's breathing is banned. All horses are to be adequately shod or booted (easy boots or similar equipment).

When unattended stallions must be double secured by halter and neckrope. Riders are allowed to care for their horses when stabled at the ride base. In cases of emergency where treatment is necessary the veterinary surgeon can proceed and then decide whether to deduct penalties or to eliminate the horse. Internal or topical medication is not generally allowed and then only with the permission of the veterinary judges. Wet bandages and poultices are allowed. Minerals, dextrose and vitamins are permitted via natural methods, but not by injection. Tests for forbidden substances via blood, urine or saliva can be made. If they are positive the owner bears the cost; if negative the costs are born by SDV.

Outside help during the ride is not permitted except in the case of illness, loose horses, holding horses, and at mandatory rest stops. Further help in CTRs is forbidden.

Reasons for eliminating horses are: lameness, coughing, depression, insufficient bodily condition, bad shoeing, treatment of the horse with medication if the medication can positively influence the horse's performance, and if a false declaration about the horse's health is given.

Reasons for disqualifying riders are: galloping on asphalt or cement; mistreatment of horses; cheating (for example, clipping parts of the route).

Before the start of the ride there is an obligatory briefing of all competitors. According to the number of entries the ride may be split into a section for small horses (148 cm or under) and large horses. Starting order can be either singly, or in small groups of up to three riders. In CTRs dismounting or standing still with the intention of achieving an ideal time or a better pulse and respiration count

are forbidden. Dismounting and leading on hard going, asphalt, concrete or similar footing, or on steep uphill and downhill gradients is permitted. The organizer indicates where such places are.

In all middle and long distance CTRs there is a mandatory halt of a minimum of one hour. The total time of halts is determined at the rate of a minimum of one minute per kilometre. The number and duration of pauses are according to the ride distance and severity. In distances of less than 40 km the pause shall be in the middle of the ride. Examination of horses is in order of arrival at halts where a firm footing must be available. Horses over the time limit are penalized at the rate of one point per minute. An excess time of thirty seconds or under is permitted. All horses are examined untacked before the ride. Trotting up on a halter is obligatory. All blemishes are noted. The veterinary surgeon decides if the horse is in a condition to start.

Controls on the ride are as the above detailed stops, and from 1987 all halts are of the 'vet gate' type. If after between ten and thirty minutes the PR rate falls to 50/30 no penalty points are deducted. If the rates are higher penalties are deducted at the rate of one point for every two beats or respirations above that limit. If after thirty minutes they are higher than 64/48 the horse is eliminated. After the thirty minutes the horse must be trotted up on a halter.

Spot checks can be made en route. If they are, there will be a fifteen-minute obligatory halt which will be deducted from the riding time. If after ten minutes the rates are over 72 the rider waits a further five minutes and the horse is checked again. This will be repeated if the values still do not fall to 72/72 or below. If the horse fails again the rider waits a further twenty-five minutes and this time is not deducted from riding time. If the horse fails yet again he is eliminated. If the horse has to wait five minutes he is penalized two points, and a further two points for the second five-minute hold. The third twenty-five-minute hold is a further ten penalties. Maximum time at a spot check hold is forty-five minutes.

In KLPs riders start with a maximum 200 points: 100 for the horses, and 100 for horsemanship which is judged by riding judges. The horse is judged on condition (70 per cent); health (20 per cent) and care (10 per cent). Horsemanship is judged on various qualities: general care, in-hand handling, riding skill, tack, pacing of ride, manners of horse, safety in riding and fairness (sportsmanship). The winning and placing horses are those that have the highest score after horse, rider, and time penalties have been totalled.

DR rides

Endurance Rides (DRs) have many of the same general rules pertaining to tack, rider's clothing, reasons for elimination and disqualification, age of riders, doping, in-foal or denerved horses, and so on. The main differences are as follows. Horses shall be a minimum of six years of age. The judging is on speed only, provided the horse satisfies veterinary criteria. There are no penalty points deducted during an Endurance Ride. The type of start is decided by the organizer. At mandatory pauses which are now of 'vet gate' type the horse's pulse must fall to 64 or below within thirty minutes of arrival at the checkpoint. There are also examinations at halts for general condition, lameness, and depression. There is no laid down respiratory guide, though this would be noted under general condition.

End-of-ride check is the same. The final check, also on the same basis, is five hours after all horses are in. The Best Condition prize is awarded to the horse in the best condition from among the first ten finishers who have completed the course in a time no greater than 10 to 15 per cent in excess of the winner.

On Endurance Rides the competitors are permitted help from their crews throughout the ride and are also permitted to dismount and lead at any time en route.

Appeals against a veterinary and/or rider judge's decision are not allowed. Appeals against an organizer's decision to impose disqualification on a rider must be made within an hour of prizegiving and be accompanied by a deposit of 50 SFr. which is returned if the appeal is upheld by the Sanctions Commission.

Horses and riders

Marquise

Marquise (1977) is a brown, 15.2 hand part Arabian mare bought by Fritz Müller especially for endurance riding. In four years of competition she has proved extremely consistent, clocking up around 400 km of competitive distance each year. Fritz says her good points are an efficient and smooth gallop, allied with staying power and good parameters, plus an obvious enjoyment of the long distance trail. She is also enviably calm. The only black spot is a sensitivity to hard ground. Already an enthusiastic rider Fritz is also a long distance runner and said after beieng introduced to endurance riding it was the obvious sport for him. With a job as a college teacher and politician he has plenty of time to train, or more honestly says that because he enjoys the sport he takes the time and is fortunately blessed with an understanding wife. For him endurance riding's special appeal is the teamwork between horse and rider and the intrinsic fairness of such a challenging sport. He applies much the same principle to endurance ride training as to the training of a long distance runner, working consistently four times a week and including interval training and workouts at different speeds.

Marquise works happily on a general diet with no special additives. She has achieved considerable success with placings in lower distance rides and many Ride and Tie firsts and seconds, but her best achievements have been in the 100 km and over rides, starting with a third in the 1985 Schnabelsberg Cup, and finishing that season by earning enough points to win the Swiss Championship and to qualify for the World Championship in Rome. Unfortunately in 1986 the mare suffered a very bad accident with a car, but has since made a full recovery and will be back on the trail.

Fritz puts his mare's successes down to serious and consistent training of both horse and rider, pointing out that the rider has to be trained too, a point often not considered sufficiently. He feels that the Swiss basis for endurance riding is too small and not producing enough good riders, and that international experience is too limited. He would like to see all the endurance ride rules adjusted, and feels that for distances over 100 km the race element of the ride wanes and the event becomes one of mere endurance. He was much influenced by the great American Race of 1976 after reading a book by a Swiss competitor in that race, and he accords the USA first place in world ranking.

Magic

A grey 16.1½ hand partbred Arabian gelding owned by Franz Imhof, Magic (1977) has the highest number of competitive kilometres credited to a Swiss horse, with over 2400. His yearly training incorporates 2400 km of which 500 are competitive, with the exception of 1987 which he opened with the longest European ride to be held to date – the Madrid to Lisbon 650 km endurance ride held over eight days, in which Magic placed twelfth from an international field.

Franz bred Magic himself, though not initially as an endurance horse, but by the time he was interested in the competitive challenge of endurance riding Magic was just about old enough to compete and has had a consistent career for the past five years. Franz rides mostly because he likes the companionship of his own horse, who he says is a one-person horse very attached to his rider, and because of the opportunity to enjoy the 'great outdoors'. Not highly competitive, Franz says his ambitions are to finish in the middle, not necessarily for any major prize but to go according to how both he and Magic feel. Nevertheless they have had their fair share of prizes and successes competing abroad for Switzerland on several occasions: the 1983 Vienna to Budapest 300 km; the 1986 World Championship in Rome for a twelfth place; plus the Madrid–Lisbon 1987 race. In Switzerland's Schnabelsberg Cup they have placed eighth, third, fourth and third respectively, and Magic has been runner-up for the Swiss Championship in 1985 and third in 1986. The pair have also been placed twice in the European ELDRIC Trophy, taking ninth place in 1983 and moving up to fifth place in Europe in 1986.

Franz is lucky with Magic who is keen to go on and has no troublesome spots to worry about en route, though he does occasionally have to watch out for colic. On Swiss endurance riding he says it is only at the beginning of its development, but that the overall world endurance scene is very good, and pays tribute to some of the foreign rides, especially the Madrid–Lisbon ride, and in fact puts Portugal number one in his estimation for the perfect organization of a great, long ride. He would like to see more veterinary involvement in the sport and says the veterinarians should protect the animals but not be narrow minded. He spends all his spare time, taken from running his bookshop, on his endurance riding, and on average trains three times a week according to the situation. Magic is fed nothing special, just good oats, minerals, and ad lib grazing.

Björn

Björn (1973) is a dun Norwegian Fjord gelding just over 14.2 hands high bred by current owner Peter Baumgartner, who has had horses all his life. He started endurance riding in 1977 as a natural consequence of interest in all endurance sports, and because he wanted to see what his horse could achieve in a sphere they both enjoyed.

Though smaller than most endurance horses, mostly competing in the *Kleinpferd* section, Björn is no slouch when it comes to a race, holding the record for the 100-km Schnabelsberg Ride for *Kleinpferde*. In addition to showing many first places his ride diary is sprinkled with awards for Best Condition and Best *Kleinpferd*, and Peter credits teamwork and mental attitude of the rider as the reason Björn has been so successful. The pony's best points are surefootedness and strong legs, with a good low heart rate as well, but he does tend to brush when tired and Peter says he does not drink well on the trail.

Björn is out at grass during the day and fed extra concentrates and vitamins during intensive training. This is thorough and consistent, three to four times a week with periods varying from one hour to four hours, and over the year he covers around 2500 km of which 500 km are competitive. Peter says endurance riding needs to become more popular in Switzerland and that the Swiss CTR system needs changing. He would like to see more sponsorship come into the sport and entry fees reduced, with better stabling offered for horses at rides rather than big prizes, although as an afterthought he would also like to have his cake and eat it too, and hopes for bigger prizes in addition to the other improvements. He feels the USA leads the world, saying that they are more adventurous and have a more positive mental attitude to endurance riding.

Dr Georg F. Riedler

Dr Riedler is one of the most consistent of the Swiss riders and has been a major influence on European endurance riding since 1981 when elected President of the ELDRIC. He is a physician and head of the Haematology and Oncology Department at Lucerne Hospital, but from an extremely busy schedule still devotes considerable time to the sport, split between his duties as ELDRIC President and his own riding.

At present Dr Riedler is compaigning a 15.3 hand Shagya Arab gelding, Gazal (1979), who was bred in Babolna, Hungary, and bought specifically for endurance riding. Dr Riedler is no stranger to sports competition, especially those involving an endurance element. He already has the National Orienteering Championship to his credit, as well as being a top-class contender in cross-country skiing, so it was almost inevitable that when Switzerland became involved in endurance riding Dr Riedler should take it up. He is currently the leading distance rider in Switzerland with over 3400 km to his credit, 1500 of which have been achieved with Gazal. His yearly training consists of around 3000 km including competitions, which in 1986 totalled 780 km. To open the 1987 season he, as well as compatriot Franz Imhof, added the eight-day Madrid–Lisbon ride to his score, placing thirteenth in a tough field. He has piloted Gazal on several other international rides as well: his own country's Schnabelsberg Cup and the Lucerne William Tell Challenge, and the Cavalcata Aleramica in Italy, placing in the top ten in the William

Tell and Italian rides, which gained him a European ranking of ninth place for 1986. Because of his crowded schedule Dr Riedler says he does not have as much time as he would wish for training and therefore it is important to recognize his own limits. He sets his aims at good completions rather than all-out pace for winning.

Gazal's good points are that he is an independent horse with both physical and mental strength, who also has good heart/respiration rates. Although he is of Arabian blood Dr Riedler says that the training and conditioning he receives is of greater importance than ideal breeding. He is ridden, according to the state of the competition season, three to seven times a week, with low mileage in the early stages rising to over 100 miles a week at peak periods. He is routinely at grass for the bulk of the day, and his feeding is of a normal molassed grain mixture with vitamins added prior to events, plus hay as needed. During the winter months, apart from a very little riding, Dr Riedler gives Gazal a well-earned break.

As President of the ELDRIC Dr Riedler is in a position to see more clearly than most the overall view of endurance riding. For Switzerland he says it has yet to be developed, and for the world that it is in need of more promotion, which the ELDRIC tries to do in Europe by keeping contact with riders and other endurance associations, national federations, and with veterinary surgeons who are involved with endurance riding. He says cooperation between riders and associations is essential if the sport is to become strong and popular, and that it is vital to get the right image of caring riders and organizers across to dispel any doubts that endurance riding harms the horses. More sponsorship and veterinary involvement is necessary. As with so many riders, and in his case with a great understanding of the wider aspects of the sport, he gives the USA his accolade of excellence, saying it has a long history in the sport, the most experience, and also many experienced veterinary surgeons who are also active endurance riders.

The Tevis Cup

Without a doubt the world's best-known 100-mile endurance ride is the Western States 100 Miles One-Day Ride from Squaw Valley, Nevada to Auburn, California. Pioneered back in 1955 by the late and famous Wendell Robie, it was the first such ride to be run to find if the twentieth-century trail horse matched his earlier counterpart of California's nineteeth-century Gold Rush days.

Following that first ride on 8 August 1955, the ride has been run every year since, with abundant proof that today's horses possess the stamina, endurance, and trail savvy of those earlier mounts made famous by the Wells Fargo and Pony Express riders of the mid 1800s.

In addition to testing today's horses the Tevis Ride, in commemorating the history of the Wells Fargo and later Pony Express Trail, has itself made history, not only in America but in every country where 100 milers are now run. Almost all 100 milers use the rules for the Tevis Cup as the framework on which they build their own National Championship events. Great Britain unashamedly 'lifted' the rules in toto in 1975, as the best possible guide to running successfully Britain's first 100 miles in one day event, which was organized by the Endurance Horse and Pony Society of Great Britain.

The Tevis Cup is run each year on the Plain's Indians' 'Full of the Riding Moon', which gives it a sliding date between mid-July and early August. The trail is that used by the gold and silver miners of the 1840s and 1850s, running from the site of the Nevada silver lodes across the Sierra Nevada to the site of the ancient Californian gold mines. In its 100 miles of wilderness trail, jealously guarded and consistently conserved as a riding and hiking route, it goes through, up and over, down, and across some of the most beautiful and most challenging terrain that the two states can offer.

With its two prestigious awards it echoes the history of the Gold Rush. To the winner of the ride goes the Tevis Cup, honouring both today's riders and Lloyd Tevis, long-time President of the Wells Fargo Company. With the Haggin Cup for the best conditioned horse amongst the first ten finishers, James B. Haggin, pioneer, associate and friend of Lloyd Tevis, is fittingly remembered as an eminent breeder of first-class horses raced to national championship honours.

Huge entries of 200 plus are fielded for the Tevis Cup, all coming under the stringent rules administered by a panel of veterinary surgeons whose job it is to see no horse is damaged by undue exertion. Though not needing to qualify in other rides to enter, all entries are screened before acceptance. Horses (and mules) five years and over and serviceably sound are eligible to compete, and to be in contention for the Tevis and Haggin Cups each horse must carry a minimum of 165 lb. Those riders wishing to go for the coveted Tevis Buckle may elect to ride at catch weight. There are no monetary prizes. Regulations govern procedure during the ride and no horse may be overridden, left unattended, or in any way abused, and the organizers welcome and appreciate the attendance of the SPCA officers. Use of any drugs is forbidden and riders must submit their horses for testing if so required. Detection of or refusal to allow a test for drugs incurs elimination. Electrolytes, salt, water, feed and vitamins are permitted orally only. Horses must not have had any prohibited medication administered within seventy-two hours prior to the ride.

The 100 miles must be completed within twenty-four hours, inclusive of mandatory rest stops, which occur twice for one hour each at Robinson Flat and Michigan Bluff, with other spot checks at designated areas throughout the trail. At the one-hour stops horses must satisfy the team of veterinary surgeons that they are in a fit condition to proceed. Any horse showing signs of SDF, or any other deleterious signs, will be held over at the spot checks until he has recovered, or if he fails to do so he will be withdrawn to safeguard his health. Throughout the ride there is no appeal against a veterinary surgeon's decision, and any rider attempting to proceed against instructions is liable to be prosecuted by the SPCA.

Once across the finish line at Auburn Fairgrounds the horses have forty-five minutes to recover, and are then thoroughly examined using the same veterinary criteria that obtained at the hourly mandatory stops. Any horse not passing this check in a condition 'fit to continue' is eliminated. The fastest 'fit to continue' horse is the winner of the Tevis Cup. The first ten finishers are eligible for the James B. Haggin Cup for Best Condition and these are rejudged the following morning. The horses are re-assessed, ridden at walk, trot, canter on both reins; their willingness and locomotor ability are noted. The horse considered to be the most outstanding is awarded the trophy. To all other successful finishers goes the silver buckle depicting artist Hansen's Pony Express Rider at full gallop.

Many riders compete in the Tevis Cup on a regular basis and over twenty have achieved the 1000 mile buckle for riding ten Tevis trails. Others, not content with that, go on for yet more buckles. Amongst these several stand out even more than their fellow riders: Wendell Robie, who won the Tevis Cup four times, twice with Bandos and twice with Bandos' daughter Molla; Lincoln Mansfield with sixteen completion buckles; Donna Fitzgerald who won the Cup no less than six times with her superlative Witezarif; and Julie Suhr, who though not a Tevis Cup winner has won its Haggin Cup three times with HCC Gazal. I have frequently paid tribute to the Arabian in this book, but in the results of the Tevis Cup he stands out as the horse to ride if you want a hope of getting near the winner. Thirty of the thirty-two races have been won by horses of Arab blood.

The Tevis is also the magnet that draws top

international riders to pit their horsemanship against the Sierras, and riders from many countries accept the challenge in the hopes of returning home with a Tevis buckle. As international participation increases more foreigners will attempt and win their buckles, and more Tevis riders will travel to far-off lands to compete, though few will emulate Cassandra Schuler, who at first try in Europe returned home with the first World Championship to add to her many Tevis awards.

Tevis horses and riders

Wendell T. Robie (1895–1984)

A name that lives in American legend is that of Wendell T. Robie; a man who will be remembered for his many great achievements, and by today's endurance riders for the vision he had over thirty years ago of what endurance riding could and should be: rapport with one's horse; companionship on the trail; and the opportunity to share the incomparable scenery which he enjoyed on his home territory. His legacy to today's riders is 100 miles of virgin territory, the trail of the Western States Trail Ride. The world-renowned Tevis Cup crosses country still largely preserved as it was in the days of the Pony Express more than 120 years ago; 100 miles of conservationists' and riders' territory.

By education a forester, by dedication both conservationist and horseman, it was Wendell who in 1955 had the vision to show that even in our softer age a horse was still capable of the old-time rigours. He and a group of friends, in spite of animal rights inspectors, showed that twentieth-century man and horse were still capable of withstanding stresses and strains with no ill effects. From that first 100 miler has grown the tremendously popular sport of modern endurance riding.

Wendell Robie's Lake Tahoe to Auburn ride captured the riding public's imagination and from then on his name has been entwined with what became the challenging Tevis Cup Western States Trail Ride. For twenty-five years Wendell guided the ever-expanding 100 miler, and in that time rode the route himself thirteen times, winning it on

46 Wendell Robie in action on the Tevis Trail, negotiating the famous Cougar Rock. (Western States Trail Foundation)

four occasions and being awarded the Haggin Cup when he rode his Arabian stallion Siri.

From his stallion Bandos, bought for endurance riding, and winner of the first two events, stems a host of sucessful horses. His own mare Molla and stallion Siri were Bandos' get. Additionally there are many more Bandos get and linear descendants who have been successful in the Tevis and other endurance rides and this horse must have had more influence on the breeding of endurance horses than any other in America, by blood and reputation. Man and horse alike have left an indelible stamp on modern endurance riding.

It took determination to see the sport established and without Wendell Robie's generosity in time, effort and finance endurance riding today would

not be so successful. He has had a far-reaching influence, way beyond the hills and mountains of his beloved Nevada and California; when I ask 'What country do you feel has influenced endurance riding most?' I am repeatedly given the answer USA. Without the guiding influence and generosity of that one individual America would not now hold her world pre-eminence. Wendell's generosity, though, started at home. A keen competitor himself, he also loaned horses to other riders after taking care to be personally involved with the horses from start to finish – breeding them, training and ultimately seeing them campaigned to success after success.

With his passing he did not leave a void, but an inheritance that prospers throughout the riding world and spans many countries, many continents.

Richard B. Barsaleau, DVM

Not many endurance riders have such wide-based experience as Richard B. Barsaleau, DVM, from Loomis, California. He is known on three fronts: successful competitor; very experienced veterinary judge; and writer of distinction who shares his accumulated knowledge of breeding, training, competing, and veterinary judging through revealing articles in many equestrian publications.

In twenty-five years' involvement with endurance riding he has seen and helped the sport grow. He has used a variety of horses, particularly those of Arabian blood, and from curiosity to see what the Thoroughbred could do when it was relatively unknown on the endurance trail he became well known as a serious contender aboard the bay, 16 hand, 1100 lb mare Liftaway, who traces to that very compact little chestnut, Hyperion, winner of two classics – the English Derby and the St Leger.

Other good horses in the Barsaleau stable have been the two partbred Arabians, Good Trip, a bay, 15 hand, 1000 lb mare, and The Red Camel, a chestnut, 16.2 hand, 1100 lb gelding. All were either chosen or bred specifically as using horses, with endurance riding in mind as the natural purpose for which horses were best suited.

Fitting in competitions and training must be no easy task for a very busy veterinarian, who is also in demand as a judge at rides and horseshows, yet sandwiched in there is a consistent yearly average of 1600 miles' training, though now due to other commitments actual competition rarely tops much more than 300 miles. Over the years considerable successes have been accumulated and Dr Barsaleau was the first veterinarian to achieve his 1000 mile buckle for completing ten Tevis Cup rides, three times placing in the top ten. This is a double credit to his horses and the manner in which they are trained, bearing in mind that including tack they carry in excess of 200 lb, which must put them

47 Dr R. Barsaleau, DVM, and Good Trip in the 1968 Tevis Cup. (Charles Barrieau)

at a disadvantage in the speed stakes. In Australia at the Quilty Hundred, where I briefly met him, he placed first of the Heavyweights riding Rockybar Samal, a five-year-old Arabian loaned to him by R. M. Williams of the Rockybar Stud and owner of Australia's top equestrian magazine, *Hoofs and Horns*.

Dr Barsaleau follows a steady programme of training, using sound common (as well as veterinary) sense. A believer in regular moderate mileage rather than infrequent hard spells, he covers in the region of forty miles per week, with a build-up of slow work in natural terrain, often riding one horse and leading another, especially youngsters. He places stress on breeding the right stock with good feet and legs, and, very necessary for hill work, his horses also have good saddle holding withers. No horse is campaigned until he is mature enough to tackle the stresses involved, and throughout preparation attitude, appetite and aptitude are monitored. Feeding is classic with oats, barley, corn and lucerne (alfafa) hay. A horse off his food is never ridden, neither is one that evinces even a slight tendency to hoof or leg problems.

For the future Dr Barsaleau sees the sport continuing to grow and an increase of interrelation and communication between the endurance associations of other countries. He considers standardization of rules throughout the world as being of paramount importance.

As a rider in the Heavyweight division he continues to demonstrate that judicious pacing can bring his horses in fit, eager, and – very importantly – hungry. He does admit, though, that the lightweight riders have an advantage over the heavyweight riders and to that end would like to see an improvement made in the categories at rides, so that weight divisions are generally introduced for a fairer assessment of finishing horses.

As a veterinary judge he would like to see more veterinary surgeons participating as riders, so that they acquire the experience of knowing just how an endurance horse feels on the trail. Thus equipped they would be able to offer more competent services at rides. A practitioner of what he preaches, he has more than 3000 miles of successful endurance competitions behind him.

Julie Suhr and HCC Gazal

One of the best known twosomes in endurance riding in the USA today is Julie Suhr and HCC Gazal – or it should really be a threesome, because Julie says that without husband Bob none of it would have been possible. How many of the really top partnerships have that silent supportive partner behind them?

Julie's emergence into endurance riding goes back twenty-three years, starting when she was forty years old, when with children leaving home she had more free time and needed the challenge of something new. Endurance riding fitted the bill, though she is the first to admit that her debut was hardly promising with a mare able to, as she puts it, 'trot *Three Whole Miles*'. She was therefore ready for the Tevis. Needless to say neither of them made it past the first vet check, but the following year on a borrowed Arabian she earned her first completion award, and in the succeeding years she has crept steadily through the field to be amongst the front runners. In the last few years she has placed sixth, fourth, second and third on her beloved Gazal. What is more important, Gazal is the triple winner of the coveted Haggin Cup for Best Condition, and his achievement is an all-time record for this trophy.

Gazal (1975) is a 15.1 hand bay gelding that Julie and Bob bought specifically for endurance riding on the recommendation of a friend. His successes come as no surprise as he was raised by the Hyannis Cattle Company, breeders of many a top endurance horse.

From her correspondence with me about Gazal it is obvious that he is a very special person, and his main attributes are simply overwhelming class allied with a superb temperament that makes him a delight to work with. He is fortunate in having not only very low pulse and respiration rates, but also rapid recovery from stress, so that little time is spent in vet gates at rides. Julie says she feels he has yet to be tested in his athletic maximum, and that although her friends think he is very competitive the real reason for his continued success is that he just adores company and hates being left by a passing horse. This may be a small part of the story,

48 HCC Gazal and Julie Suhr, triple winners of the Haggin Cup for Best Condition on the Tevis Ride, competing in 1981. (Hughes)

but surely the real reason is a rare partnership and an owner who resists the temptation to keep asking the ultimate from such a willing horse. The result is that in several seasons of endurance work Gazal has 5650 miles under his girth, and he is still 100 per cent sound – a tribute to both Julie and Bob who also partners Gazal on occasion, the most memorable being the 1986 250-mile Pony Express

Ride where they achieved the fastest time and overall Best Condition on the five-day ride. Julie mentions with pride that Bob had never ridden a horse until he was fifty, competed in his first endurance ride, the Tevis at fifty-nine, and aged sixty-eight shows the rest of the field the way home, proving that endurance riding really is a sport for everyone regardless of age.

In her own endurance riding career Julie has ridden over 10,032 miles on a variety of horses, and says she does not ride for points, believing it better to conserve a horse with a limited number of well-spaced rides, rather than ride it into the ground in a wastefully short career – a syndrome that is not confined to any one country. Obviously, along with many international endurance riders, she sees the true endurance horse as that champion who campaigns well over many years and comes through happy and sound.

Julie and Bob have competed on four continents – in France on the Florac 100 miler; South Africa on the Fauresmith 130 miler; and in the 50 miler at Taralga, Australia. Consequently they are in a better position than most to assess endurance riding on a world basis, and say they have nothing but good feelings about its continuing success, particularly now that the FEI have accepted it as a separate discipline.

Julie has three main ambitions left in endurance riding. The first is to earn her 2000 mile Tevis buckle. Currently she is on number seventeen and leads the field for the greatest number of completions achieved. The second is that she hopes to achieve these on Gazal and have him still 100 per cent sound, but I think the best ambition, and the clue to her generous character, is that she hopes Gazal lives as long as her other two retired endurance horses, who are in sound and happy retirement at twenty-seven and twenty-eight years old respectively.

Would that all riders repaid their equine partners for their years of unstinting generosity on the endurance trail!

The Fitzgeralds and Witezarif

It is a little difficult to put into a 'cameo' a detailed analysis of the Fizgerald family's successes. To anyone in American endurance riding the Fitzgerald name is synonymous with achievement, and to those of my readers who are unfamiliar with New World endurance rides the Fitzgeralds must be the foremost family in the sport, and have been for a period spanning almost thirty years. Along the way Pat and Donna have been partnered by a whole string of super horses, most of which have been of pure or part Arabian breeding.

In his long distance career Pat has competed on at least thirty horses and Donna on fourteen. Their completion records clearly show that soundness and durability are the hallmark stamping Fitzgerald horses, as many of their mounts have very long and impressive careers. Between them the husband and wife team have racked up thirty Tevis Cup buckles, with son Mike adding to the score. Additionally other awards, many of them wins, have been accrued on 100 milers in eighteen other locations, not to mention the in-between 50 milers which go to make up an extensive endurance calendar. Pat has a total mileage in excess of 11,000, and Donna over 8000. The most outstanding fact is that the same horses are repeatedly successful; a few names that strike one from amongst the records are Ken, Pat's mount and winner of the Tevis Cup in 1962 and still going strong in 1969; Quist, ridden mainly by Pat but occasionally by Donna, son Mike and daughter Heidi over a five-year span; Halanad, a strong contender in 100 milers over a twelve-year period; Darito, an all-around family horse brought out in 1978 and still competing today; and of course the incomparable Witezarif, Donna's partner from 1970 and still competing today.

A purebred Arabian, this little bay gelding by Witezar traces to the famous Polish stallion Ofir. He was brought to the Fitzgerald ranch in 1968 as a five year old to be sold on if possible. Straight away Donna took a liking to the little bay, but Pat considered the asking price too high even though Witezarif immediately impressed them with his performance, carrying Pat easily over any ground, no matter how rough or steep. However, it took two seasons, four 100 milers with three different riders, in which he showed a glimmer of his potential with places and a win with Best Condition thrown

49 Pat Fitzgerald and Ken winning the Tevis Cup in 1962.

in, before Pat succumbed and wrote out the cheque that secured Witezarif. He immediately gave him to Donna.

Donna admits to a shaky start on the little bay, riding him too hard and too fast and running out of steam at 85 miles on their first ride together, but says it was the most valuable lesson she ever learnt. Thereafter with the bond growing stronger the pair started on a cruise to the top, with three straight wins in the 1970 season, including their first Tevis Cup. Subsequently Witezarif treated the Tevis Cup as if it was his own, winning it on five further occasions and once finishing second, a record that is likely to stand unbroken. The Tevis Cup only accounts for a moderate percentage of this horse's successes as he accrued an additional eight 100-miler wins, including the Bonanza Ox Trail ride that is considered by some to be the toughest of all. In all he completed seventy-five rides, twenty-six

of them 100 milers, and was first past the post on nineteen occasions. Speaking of him at twenty-four years of age Donna says she hopes to do a few more 50 milers on him, veterinary advice permitting, and add to his already mammoth lifetime total of well over 5000 successful competition miles.

To replace Witezarif she looked for a horse of similar breeding and for several seasons she and Pat campaigned his close relative, Hyannis Cattle Company's Rusmaleto. This chestnut gelding also proved his worth with a steady list of completions, places, and three 100 wins, but sadly developed arthritis in a fore-limb on the sesamoid where the suspensory passes over it. After showing such promise it was devastating, particularly as Donna in particular had worked up a rapport with the horse. She had twice had the chance to exchange Rusmaleto and turned it down, but when the third offer came from the vendor to take him back and

50 Donna Fitzgerald and Witezarif, five times winner of the Tevis Cup, attacking Cougar Rock to come equal first in 1976.

replace him with a similarly bred colt Donna leapt at the chance, even though it meant being without a top horse while the youngster grew into his strength.

Endurance riding is one of the few sports where riders can make repeated come-backs. Indeed, they never really leave the scene, but are often forced to wait in the wings between the retiring old stager and the time it takes their future mount to grow up. I have known several such riders who hit the top and then have an enforced absence due to the youth of the horse they are convinced is worth waiting for. In Donna's case I doubt anything will

replace Witezarif, but the 1990s will doubtless be seeing her name well to the fore again as her new colt matures and hits the trail.

The North American Trail Ride Conference

NATRC was instituted in 1961 and has a current membership of 1300 plus. It caters for the long distance rider who elects to enter CTRs, where a great number of factors are assessed to determine winners. Although speed is involved it is only one of the important criteria, as opposed to being the main object as in Endurance Rides. The NATRC has divided the country into six regions which effectively cover the whole area, giving prospective CTR riders opportunities to ride in one of the many sanctioned rides.

The NATRC is very explicit in every aspect of its organization, putting out an extremely comprehensive rule book, so drafted that there is no chance of ambiguity in meaning or interpretation of rules. It also publishes a detailed Judges' Manual, adherence to which is mandatory for any of the veterinary or horsemanship judges who officiate on NATRC rides. The judging system also provides a selective process of enrolment on to the Judges' Panels which requires judges in both categories to have at least five references, one of which must be from an approved NATRC judge (of whichever category they are applying for) before they can even be considered. Then follows an apprenticeship period for both veterinarians and horsemanship judges. NATRC encourages veterinarian judges to have practical, that is, actual competitive, experience of the association's rides. Prospective horsemanship judges must have sufficient competitive experience before applying. It is a pity that, in Europe particularly, NATRC judges qualifications are not more often demanded.

The NATRC's stated 'aims' are:

(1) to stimulate greater interest in the breeding and use of good horses possessed of stamina and hardiness and qualified to make good mounts for trail use;
(2) to demonstrate the value of type and soundness in the proper selection of horses for competitive riding;
(3) to learn and demonstrate the proper methods of training and conditioning horses for competitive riding;
(4) to encourage good horsemanship as related to trail riding;
(5) to demonstrate the best methods of caring for horses during and after long rides without the aid of artificial methods or stimulants.

Their competitive rides are structured around the above considerations as are their adjudicating systems. Rides fall into one of three categories, each split into divisions.

Type AA Ride consists of three consecutive days of riding with total distances of 80–90 miles. Open Division horses only.
Type A Ride entails two consecutive days of riding with total mileage of 50–60.
Type B Ride entails one day with distance 25–40 miles.

These distances are for the Open Divisions for horses sixty months of age and upwards. Novice Division rides are for horses four to five years of age with a minimum age of forty-eight months (that is from date of foaling, not 1 January in the case of registered horses; for unregistered horses the state of tooth eruption determines minimum age). Mileage in Novice Divisions is a maximum of two-thirds of the Open Division classes, or 20 miles per day. The Open Division has separate classes for Heavyweight (190 lb and over); Lightweight (130 lb and less than 190 lb); and Juniors, who ride at catch weight. Juniors must be a minimum of ten years of age and they may not ride stallions. The Novice Division may also offer similarly divided classes. Open Division rides are ridden between 4 and 6 mph and Novice Rides between 3½ and 5 mph. Various elements determine time permitted on any ride, such as weather, ground condition and difficulty of terrain.

General rules applying to all classes include the following. No drugs of any type may be administered to the horse and entry into the ride constitutes agreement to testing for forbidden substances. By definition refusal of such permission incurs elimination. Normal feeds, supplements, electrolytes, salts, minerals, and water may be given orally only. Should any horse require veterinary intervention and treatment, such as intravenous fluid, that horse is automatically eliminated. Ice may not be used to reduce oedemas or fever in limbs.

Shoeing is optional. However, shoes must be no more than one inch wide (web) at the toe nor more than three-quarter inch wide at the heel. Pads are forbidden other than rim pads, which shall be flush with the width of the shoe and not more than three-sixteenths of an inch thick. If a horse casts a shoe he may be fitted with an easyboot (or similar protection) but relinquishes the chance to go for other than completion award and points. Type of tack is optional, but a saddle must be used, and all equipment must fit the horse. Protective equipment such as overreach, brushing, scalping or knee boots are forbidden.

Judging of any NATRC ride falls into two broad categories: veterinary judging and horsemanship judging, and there are at least two qualified judges at each ride, each dealing with their own province but closely interrelating and consulting together throughout the ride. There is no appeal against a judge's decision unless said judge has breached a rule.

The veterinary judging is split into four categories, each according to its relevance carrying a percentage of the 100 mark total: condition, 40 per cent; soundness, 40 per cent; way of going, 5 per cent; manners, 15 per cent. The veterinary judging is a continuing analysis of the horse's performance with plusses and minuses over the whole of the ride and accent placed on the horse's ability both to withstand and to recover from stress. To this end pulse and respiration, with accent on the former, are prime points of reference. Horses are checked on arrival, the morning of the first day, at least twice each day en route for a pulse and respiratory evaluation, at the finish of each day, and again after a designated cooling out period and at the end of the ride. One anomaly in the rules that does strike me occurs in the judging of soundness. A lame horse is not permitted to start a ride, but under a sub-heading 'Lameness' there are degress of lameness, many of which do not incur elimination but attract penalty marks for a horse going lame en route but not significantly enough to be eliminated. Conceivably a lame horse could figure in the awards for a completion, and if not enough finishers in that class are left to fill the six places even in the actual placings. In Britain and Australia there are no degrees of lameness. The horse is either lame or not lame. Elsewhere criteria are

assessed differently: some countries follow Britain, others use a scale of 1 to 5 as per the FEI standards.

The horsemanship criteria in NATRC rides are split into grooming, 20 per cent; trail equitation, 50 per cent; trail care, 30 per cent. Under each sub-heading comes anything whatsoever to do with the riding, care of the horse at base and en route, handling under saddle, in hand, and during stable care, so that at the end of the ride the horsemanship evaluation is a very analytical picture of every aspect of the rider's ability on or around his mount.

After 10 pm at night horses may not be attended by riders/owners except in the case of emergency when such visitation shall be reported to ride management. Failure to report such attention may incur penalties at the judges' discretion.

On NATRC rides not much escapes the eagle eyes of the judges and awards can be considered well merited. They are not obligatory under all circumstances, and if in the judges' opinion, for instance, a first place in a low number class with less than six entries is not warranted it is not given. Awards have to be earnt by valid performance. However, awards are generous, going to sixth place in each class in each division in both the horse and horsemanship sections. There is also an overall winner from amongst the open classes for the Sweepstakes or highest point horse on the ride.

There are also annual awards based on points accumulated throughout the season. The two main awards are the National Sweepstakes Championship for the President's Cup, going to the horse with the highest score nationwide in the Open Division; and the Grand Champion High Average Award, going to the horse achieving the highest average score from amongst all the rides he has entered. The horse is required to start on a minimum of eight rides, two of which must be either out of state or out of region, or if preferred one out of state and one out of region. Other awards given are National Championships, which depend on the horse accruing enough high places and points before he is so designated. This is at variance with other countries where a National Champion is the horse that is his country's leading horse for a specific year. Under NATRC rules there could be several National Champions per year. Each region also awards its own High Point and Championship awards, and the NATRC encourages horses to be ridden consistently over a considerable time by offering 1000 mile awards. Parallel to this is the rider mileage scheme, but this may be achieved on a number of horses, the rider not the horse gaining the award.

For those riders wishing challenge but not the constant need to look over their shoulders and keep up a really fast pace, NATRC offers a very comprehensive schedule of events efficiently planned and well judged.

NATRC horses and riders

Arab Incognito

Arab Incognito's story can be classified by the English saying, 'Good things come in small packages', as he is just a shade under 14 hands. Nito owns the Tate family – Rip, Linda, and son Ripley – in particular laying claim to Ripley whom he introduced to Competitive Trail Riding in 1982. Nito was four and Ripley ten and both were in their first Novice ride under NATRC rules, and Nito started as he meant to go on by winning the Sweepstakes.

The following year the little red dun, half Arabian with Appaloosa markings was sidelined while the family moved from Wichita Falls to Waxahachie, Texas, which gave Nito time to mature. In 1984 the pair started to capitalize on their earlier good start, taking part in sixteen rides in the NATRC Open Division, ending the season by accumulating sufficient points to win Junior Horsemanship for Ripley, National Junior Horse of the Year for Nito, plus National High Point Half Arabian, and for Ripley the 4–H Awards (similar to the Young Farmer's Club in Britain). He was also runner up for NATRC's President's Cup, and fourth in the Grand Championship Division – not

51 Ripley Tate (aged fourteen) and Arab Incognito on a 90–mile ride in 1985.

bad for a six-year-old pony and a twelve-year-old boy. In 1985 a similar result was produced, except that he stood down to Mara Khan who pipped him at the post for the Half Arabian High Point. By the end of 1985 the pair had ridden 1510 miles in CTR competitions, but for the immediate future their ways had to part, as the horsemanship judges were commenting that a rapidly shooting up Ripley at five foot eleven was too big for his horse, even though he was a lightweight rider. Linda commented that Nito is not small, but only takes up a little space.

Meanwhile, while Ripley was stamping the Junior Division – and a fistful of others – with Nito's and his brand, the rest of the family also campaigned horses successfully. Father Rip, a professional farrier, campaigned another half Arabian named Tejas with considerable success, achieving his 1000-mile merit award in 1985, a

52 Linda Tate and Sea Pride, reserve in the 1985 National Lightweight Awards. (Kerry)

National Championship and an overall sixth place nationally in the Heavyweight Division, plus a third in Heavyweight Horsemanship. Mother Linda's partner was Sea Pride, an Arabian cross Saddlebred that had upgraded from a 1984 Novice Division to the 1985 Open and completed nineteen rides. In spite of being beset with pasture injuries he finished the season with a Reserve National Lightweight Award.

In 1986 there was a general but successful switch around of mounts. Linda took over Nito, riding him in the Lightweight Division, though she says Ripley never lets her forget he is on loan until he is old enough to ride unaccompanied in Endurance Rides. With Linda Nito won the National Grand Championship with the highest average score ever recorded over the season's entries. He also won National High Point Half Arabian Award again. Meanwhile Ripley was partnering Judy Collier's purebred Arabian Czar of Ole', entering nine rides and winning the Junior National Championship, a third overall placing at the end-of-year National Awards, plus a second in the National year-end horsemanship rankings.

Nito finished the 1986 season with well over 3170 CTR miles, and the decision was taken to campaign him in Endurance Rides in 1987 where so far he has shown the 'big 'uns' a clean pair of heels on many occasions. At the time of writing he has accrued 440 successful Endurance miles in seven rides, two wins at 50, a second at 60, a third at 50 (this after Linda tried to catch a horse for a thrown rider for fifteen minutes, and because of the confusion of the lost time and a last-minute change of trail the placing was lowered to a technical eighth), a second at 75, and he crossed the line ahead in a 105 miler. I think Linda will be loth to give Nito back to Ripley for the 1988 season, when at sixteen he can ride unaccompanied in rides run by the American Endurance Ride Conference (see p. 267).

Waiting in the wings to prove themselves are a young purebred Arabian for Linda and an Appendix Quarter Horse of predominantly Thoroughbred blood for Rip. This horse has gone some way to doing just this with many wins and places already.

As a family the Tates have a superb aggregate of wins and places, but their mainstay is the little half Arabian who was originally bought to be a working hunter pony but proved to be far more suited to the distance trail – though he did have the class to win ribbons in the show arena as well. On the CTR and ER trail his qualities show best in a good, long 16 hand horse stride, a remarkable ability to recover to near resting rate pulse and respiration, and a good dose of common sense allied with meticulous training for trail work. He trailers easily, eats well at home and away, and is just about the best horse to have along – more like a dog than a horse, Linda says, though for my money I would find a horse preferable to have along any day, especially a companion of Nito's stamp. Linda says that the only thing she has to watch out for is not to get Nito too fit as he gets 'lit up' at check stops when he should be resting. For the change from CTR to ER she now does a bit more in-between event work at more elevated speeds. Nito has adapted well to the transition.

In summing up Linda says, 'He is a blessing that only a horse person could appreciate, and that if you own one like him in a lifetime you're extremely lucky.' I think others with their own super horse will concur.

Sharon Saare

It was back in 1976 that I met Sharon Saare, whose reputation had preceded her to England as one of America's all-round endurance people. On a much needed holiday taken in Europe she made a detour for a 'busman's' section of her vacation and rode a little gelding of mine called Katchina in a Devonshire CTR, placing fourth in the Open Division.

Riding strange horses, however, is nothing to Sharon as in her equestrian career she has ridden over 4000 and she says 'I get acquainted fairly rapidly'. What was evident, though, was that acquaintance in her case meant a real rapport with Katchina, who was no stranger himself to a legion of riders, having introduced many to both competitive riding and to Western showing. But I wager that on this occasion he did appreciate the empathy and rapport that emanated from his American guest.

In the annals of Competitive Trail and Endurance Riding there are riders who have made their individual mark in the 'winner's enclosure' riding one superlative horse over a period of years, or sometimes a variety of mounts throughout a distinguished career. Sharon Saare, with a quiver of successes, has made her contribution as an educator in the field of endurance riding. Her endurance career was prefaced by a very long stint in the show ring. In spite of many successes with good horses, showing eventually lost both challenge and variety, performance being largely constrained to endless circling. In endurance riding Sharon saw a fresh sport that gave a chance to 'everyman' and 'everyhorse'. Success could not be bought with a fat cheque. Only dedication and putting the effort into preparing a horse would ensure finishing, let alone winning or placing in a ride. In short, endurance riding offered a fresh challenge, a new approach to training. In common with many endurance riders, Sharon quickly became hooked, the habit reinforced by racking up a considerable array of awards, just a sample of which were Best Condition in the Bonanza Ox Trail 100, three Tevis buckles, a whole range of 100 mile buckles, and many 50 mile endurance achievements, often finishing in the top ten.

But it is as an educator that she has made her greatest contribution to the sport and many future endurance riders will have cause to be grateful to her. With her endurance career starting in the mid 1960s when the sport was in its infancy, she was in a position to observe all aspects of competitive rides, both CTR and Endurance. From her long experience as an all-rounder, including running a huge sales operation handling thousands of horses, she was able to make objective criticisms of what she saw on many rides – both positive and negative. While the sport was feeling its way it was often hampered by objections levied by various humane societies which had a very poor understanding of the demands made on the horses and therefore propounded invalid judgments. Despite this the sport was beginning to attract large numbers of competitors, many of whom had no real knowledge of true horsemanship, let alone the stringent demands endurance riding would make on themselves and their mounts. Sharon saw there was a real need to educate riders into a proper awareness of ride demands, and she also had the foresight to understand that unless said riders were enlightened and standards were improved the booming sport could crash.

In 1971 Sharon helped the Appaloosa Horse Club produce a film about endurance riding using an actual competition – the Drakes Bay 50 miler at the Point Reyes National Seashore in California. This was followed in 1972 and 1973 by a busy period of writing. That there was a crying need for education was proved by the acclaim with which her books were received. She wrote two books for the Appaloosa Horse Club in which every aspect of the sport was set out clearly and succinctly, and these were followed by a best-seller for Farnam Inc., the largest equine products company in the USA.

Following on the success of her books came an offer of funding for a nationwide educational seminar and clinic tour. It was decision time, and a very difficult one for Sharon to make as she also had a dual prospect of competing on a full-time basis. She frankly admits that she wanted to compete, but also knew it was a crucial time for the sport – a make or break situation – and she finally opted for 'evangelizing', as she terms it. Opportunities would occur along the way to compete on borrowed horses, and this in itself would enlarge her pool of knowledge about stress on many levels as she rode a tremendous variety of mounts, some of which were well prepared, some adequately so, and others marginally. It also broadened the scope of her seminars and clinics as she had first-hand experience of all aspects of the sport and was able to advise accurately; not as so many do from the standpoint of an onlooker. These rides in a multitude of locations also gave her an opportunity to assess the shortcomings of much of the saddlery in use, which in turn led to the patenting of her own hugely successful Saare Saddle, designed with both horse and rider comfort, durability, and saftey combined.

Her yearly itinerary for over more than a decade included a minimum of 30,000 miles travel, which sometimes peaked at 60,000, and encompassed a network of forty-five states as well as engagements as visiting lecturer in Canada, Mexico, Australia and Hungary.

Possibly the best-known horse she rode was an Appaloosa called Easter Ute, owned by actor James Drury of *The Virginian* Western television series, but among the roll call of mounts Sharon numbers Arabians, Appaloosas, Quarter Horses, my own Heinz 57 Katchina, an Australian Brumbie cross, many grade (unregistered) horses, a Standardbred and several partbred Arabians. For preference she likes a mature horse, eight to twelve years old, and a middle of the road type around 15 hands weighing approximately 960–980 lb. Many riders achieve a bond with their special horse, but it takes a special rider to work in harmony with anything that is offered and from such a very wide number of breeds and types.

In between travelling and lecturing she has managed to notch up a considerable competition mileage, approaching 3000 miles, 2000 on record with the American Endurance Ride Conference alone. Now that 'evangelizing' is over she plans to devote more time to competing, hoping that an old injury from a car crash will not prevent her from full participation in the big ones. A taste of a return to competition was a 60 km ride in Germany in 1985, and the future rests with a new horse and, it is hoped, personal fitness.

Patriotically she pays tribute to the USA as being in the van where dissemination of knowledge about the sport is concerned and sees a good future for it. In the USA alone there are now over 500 rides a year. In a hands-across-the-water agreement we both see the sport as an excellent way to breed the right type of horse, irrespective of breed. If its conformation and disposition are not right it will not succeed in the rigours of endurance riding, and if the condition carried is too fine or too gross it will inevitably suffer excess stress. Endurance riding is going a long way to undoing the bad effect the false values of the show ring has encouraged.

One other aspect of this many-talented horsewoman that has been of inestimable value to today's and future generations of riders is Sharon's involvement in securing continuing use of open land for horses. Without strong representation

53 Sharon Saare and Easter Ute at Cougar Rock in the 1967 Tevis Cup.

much of the American countryside, as is common in England, would disappear under developers' concrete. A tribute to her efforts and one of the high points of a multi-faceted career was recognition by the US Forest Service, with a seventy-fifth Anniversary Award for 'outstanding service in appreciation of your significant contribution to Forestry and Conservation'.

But surely the best reward for an educator is seeing the results of her many years' work in lecturing and writing pay off in the steady rise in standards throughout not only the USA but the rest of the world which has looked to America for ground rules in endurance riding. In this she is more than justified in feeling great pleasure.

The American Endurance Ride Conference

AERC dates from 1972 when in its first year 695 riders competed in twenty-four rides. Initially any-one who entered a sanctioned ride was considered a member. Paid-up membership came later, but although competitions are still open to all, only paid-up AERC members are eligible for the prestigious array of awards the AERC bestows at each annual convention.

Since its inception AERC has grown rapidly and membership stands at well over the 2200 mark, while the ride list has expanded to over 700. The network of rides covers the whole country, which is sectioned into eight regions, each having its own set of yearly awards in addition to AERC's National Awards. For horses going from CTR into ER there is a graduated system. Limited Distance Category Rides range from 25 to 35 miles, before elevating to Endurance where rides go across the whole spectrum from 50 to 150 miles. The 50 milers are most popular with several hundred a year, followed by nearly a hundred 100 milers, then 75 milers.

With such a wealth to choose from it certainly

places AERC at the forefront of world endurance riding, so it was no surprise that the first world champion (see later) came from among its ranks. Other countries with a shorter history of organized endurance riding can be proud of many of their horses and riders with distinguished performance records, but where most of their leading riders/horses currently hover around the 1000 competitive mile mark with only a few in the multiple thousand mile bracket, AERC's ranks is bursting at its seams with 1000 mile horses and riders; it has well over 500 horses listed as 1000 milers, over a hundred of whom will break into the 2000 mile category in less than a season's further campaigning. Then there are the specialists whose mileage rockets year by year in 1000 mile increments and reaches the climax with the grade horse Bandit, owned and ridden by Smokey Killen throughout an endurance career totalling well in excess of 13,000 miles.

There are many differences apparent in the endurance scene in America as compared with, say, Britain (and with much of Europe), and many factors lead America, and in particular AERC, into pre-eminence in the sport. Without wishing to place any factor as paramount there are some that highlight this, one of the most relevant being space. America, a vast country, offers unlimited riding space which those of us on the other side of the Atlantic, for the most part, can only dream of. Also the concept of trail riding is very much closer to the American way of farm life, in places still an integral part of it. The bane of all but a few British endurance riders is the very high percentage of unavoidable roadwork involved, which cuts both rhythm and speed. America, except in a few locales, has a year-round event calendar, whereas on the other side of 'the Pond' at least five months of the year are 'closed season' due to weather, lack of daylight – dangerous on those unavoidable highways at night – and inaccessability of much of our riding country (farmers do not grant permission so readily if a large event entry could carve up their land under winter mud conditions).

A very big plus where AERC scores is that amongst its ranks of dedicated riders there is a fair sprinkling of practising veterinary surgeons who would be very quick to ensure changes were made in ride structure should they not be in the horses' best interests. European veterinary surgeons are dedicated and hardworking at endurance rides but they mostly lack that vital ingredient – experience from the back of the horse in endurance competition. This too applies to the governing bodies of many endurance associations. From the AERC records it is obvious that all major officers, including Regional Directors, have a considerable 'from the saddle' experience, mostly ranging in the thousands of practical and enlightening miles. Many riders also sit on European committees, but far too many committee members do not know endurance riding from that all-important point of view – the extended mileage ahead viewed from between the horse's ears.

To compete in an AERC ride the horse must be at least sixty calendar months of age, unlike some countries where the age is taken as of 1 January. Endurance Rides, as opposed to Limited Distance Rides, are a minimum of 50 miles. Where multiple rides are offered at an event a rider may elect to upgrade from a shorter distance to the higher distance on the day, but to place in the longer distance ride competitors must be travelling in the van of the lower distance event. This safeguards the declared higher distance riders from having an 'unknown' entrant acquiring an unfair advantage over them and upsetting their strategy.

Strict veterinary control obtains throughout all AERC events and differs in one respect from many other national associations, in that the veterinary criteria to be used are announced prior to each ride, rather than being laid down 'hard and fast' in the rules. This means that local climatic conditions can be taken into consideration when setting heart and respiration limits. All horses must pass a pre-ride and a one hour post-ride veterinary check, plus as many en route examinations as are deemed necessary. Veterinary surgeons may place any horse under restraint if they feel it is being pushed above safe limits. No veterinary decision may be overturned by Ride Management.

There is no maximum speed on endurance rides, but the minimum speed is typically 5 mph, or twelve hours for a 50 miler, and so on. Entered horses may not be paced by an unentered or with-drawn horse, nor by a vehicle. The only such rating may be by another horse entered in the ride. No testing for forbidden substances is done by the AERC, but the State of California does random tests and publishes a list of prohibited drugs which is the AERC guide. Use of such drugs will result in disqualification from the ride and further penal-ties, such as barring the rider from future competi-tion and/or removing any mileage and points credit from the award system.

The list of major awards within the AERC framework is based on a points system, as well as the mileage recognition as detailed above. There are two AERC divisions – Senior and Junior. Juniors are riders under sixteen years of age who must be accompanied by an adult en route. The only exceptions to this rule are that fourteen year olds with an AERC endurance mileage of 500 miles or more may, with parental and ride manage-ment consent, ride unaccompanied. The Senior Division rides are divided into Heavy, Middle and Lightweight sections depending on riders' body weight at the beginning of the season. This again differs from other associations where the weight is deemed to be rider plus equipment. In addition to placing awards at each ride there is also a Best Condition award chosen from amongst the top ten finishers on each ride, regardless of which division or weight category they are in.

AERC horses and riders

Darolyn Butler

Darolyn Butler was lucky to be born into a family whose life centred around ranching and horses, acquiring her first pony by the time she was three. Living in Oklahoma, which is host state to the yearly Quarter Horse World Championships, she naturally gravitated towards the Quarter Horse scene. As a teenager she entered barrel races and showed successfully under stock saddle, plus adding Rodeo Queen crowns to her performance credits which included a win in the Horsemanship Division in the Miss Rodeo America Pageant in 1971 when she was twenty-one. In her mid-

twenties she had a brief flat race career aboard Quarter Horses, but at the core of her equestrian activities there was a hankering to ride the open spaces away from show ring glitz and knife-edge competition.

The catalyst that turned her from successful show to champion endurance rider was a magazine article on the Tevis Cup. Fired by an exuberant determination she made the transition rapidly, starting at the top, not working her way through painstaking years of novice classes, and on only her fourth ride tackled the Western States 100 Mile Endurance Ride. Even more of a challenge, her husband Pat picked up the gauntlet and made the 1981 Tevis Cup his first ever endurance ride. Riding leased horses, they finished ninety-fourth and ninety-fifth in a field of 250 starters, and Darolyn says that although they were proud of themselves at their first 100 miler success, because they were so new to the sport they did not really realize just what an achievement it was. She pays tribute to Dr Barsaleau and Wendell Robie who encouraged them on their break-in to endurance riding, Dr Barsaleau by dragging them both up the Tevis trails in a pre-run preparation of what to expect on the day.

Within a year the Quarter Horses had mostly gone, their places being taken by Arabian and part-Arabian horses. For the next twelve months, as their home state of Texas had only extremely lim-ited endurance ride events, they travelled far for out-of-state experience. In 1982 the string of en-durance ride successes began, as with a purebred and an Anglo-Arab Darolyn and Pat were well to the fore in Central Region AERC rankings. Then came the first of the champions.

Karram Rou Fad, better known as Uno, was a bay, purebred, not very typy Arabian whom his erstwhile lawyer owner had tried unsuccessfully to turn into a show horse. His rangy, athletic frame was better suited on the distance trail, especially in closely wooded, tricky going where Darolyn found he could really fly over the ground, gaining so much time that he outdistanced his fleeter rivals repeatedly. In his full 1984 season the seven-year-old entered twenty-two rides, never being elimin-ated and accumulating enough points to emerge

54 Darolyn Butler and Karram Rou Fad, National Champion and Best Condition Champion in 1984.

National Champion and Best Condition Champion. Out of the twenty-two starts at distances from 50 to 105 miles Uno scored twelve wins, four of them in 100 milers out of five 100 mile rides, plus nine Best Condition awards. He never placed lower than fourth. Hitting the top had proved no obstacle to combined determination and the future looked good for Uno and Darolyn, and then disaster struck. Temporarily boarded away from home to be available for Pat to compete on while he was working in Dallas, Uno was inadvertently poisoned by ingesting blister beetles infesting alfafa hay.

His successor Thunder Road was entirely different in all but one respect – both horses had drive and toughness. Thunder Road, an unregistered grey Arabian, had a reputation for wildness and stubborness, and although Darolyn has channelled his wildness productively along the distance trail he still indulges in an occasional bucking spree, even after two years of hard usage and 3000 miles that have stamped his image on AERC records. Darolyn says he is the toughest horse she has ever ridden, and the roughest. He is also accident prone and is constantly recovering from minor 'incidents' and one major setback. Lightning never strikes twice, so the old saw goes, but blister beetles did. Thanks to rapid recognition of symptoms and equally rapid treatment Thunder Road pulled through and five weeks later was back in contention. He stands 14.3 hands and weighs around 830 lb, is compact with rugged limbs and large hooves, and again is a very untypy Arabian

that is naturally athletic, with that blessing for endurance horses – a very rapid recovery to an acceptable heart rate no matter what the stresses.

Darolyn admits to going more by her instinct about a horse and how he strikes her as a prospect than by analytical assesssment of pros and cons, and in choosing Thunder Road the instinct paid off. He has proved almost invincible, whether in 50 milers or in double the distance, and he shot to AERC National Champion in 1986 with a string of wins that started at the beginning of December 1985, and will be almost impossible to better by one horse in a single season. Out of twenty-nine events he recorded twenty-four wins and fourteen Best Conditions, and towards the end of the season when just needing points he was eased back for completions in the Great Texas Horse Race, only needing to compete on three of the five days. The period that stands out most, and will I am sure strike awe, particularly in Europe where 100 milers are very thin on the ground at present, is 18 October to 8 November 1986, during which time he competed in four 100 milers on successive weekends, winning all four.

Somewhere in between rides Darolyn and Pat find time to run a family enterprise producing equestrian videos for home and overseas. These educational films cover aspects of the horse world ranging from English and Western showing to rodeos. Naturally they specialize in the booming sport of endurance riding where folk now realize an educational groundwork is vital. Occasionally Darolyn writes for magazines, mainly on endurance topics and her own special training system in a concise style where she outlines what makes her horses tick: well-balanced diet, adequate training, neither too much nor too little, saying that frequently riders fall into these errors, particularly that of overtraining. She advises competitors to ride with common sense; to weigh up the opposition; to think out their tactics and not allow themselves to be pushed into riding someone else's race; and above all to save that little bit for when it is needed. Then the horse can go again and again, just like her Thunder Road who did it repeatedly in top form for a twelvemonth, and came out strong and ready for the next season.

55 Darolyn Butler and Thunder Road, AERC National Champion in 1986.

Rushcreek Lad

Rushcreek Lad is a grey Arabian gelding who has set a new record in the USA. In 1987 his owner Trilby Pederson, a fifty-three-year-old mother of six who lives in Los Gatos, California, has shown what the sport of endurance riding is all about. In twelve months she and Rushcreek Lad have competed in seventy-four endurance rides, completing seventh-three of them. They have travelled 4260 miles on the hoof, and in the horsetrailer many tens of thousands of miles, even competing as far as 2500 miles away from home base. In all that mileage she has not won one ride, yet ended this fantastic season as the AERC National Champion. At the end of his competitive year Rushcreek Lad was 100 per cent sound due to Trilby's conservative manner of riding. It was her policy to just complete, never risking her horse for a chance win, and it paid off as other riders with winning times

would often develop unsoundnesses that kept them out of future contention. I am indebted to Julie Suhr for this late addition as the book was almost on the presses when her letter arrived. She says that it opens up a new concept for the USA of miles, not wins, counting, yet in Britain it has always been the miles that were just as important as the wins!

World Champions 1986

Finally, to finish my roundup of endurance riding nations with their top riders and horses, there is the partnership that showed where the sport can lead in the popularity explosion that marks this toughest of equestrian disciplines.

Shiko's Omar and Cassandra Schuler flew the American flag over the Pratoni del Vivaro in Rome in September 1986. Together they had won the first World Endurance Riding Championship over

56 1986 World Champions, Cassandra Schuler and Shiko's Omar.

the sweltering 100 mile route through the Italian countryside. It had taken just under eleven hours (ten hours, fifty minutes, thirty seconds) to win for America, but the obverse of that gleaming Gold Medal was Omar's eight years of dedicated care, training and judicious campaigning by his owner Claude Pacheco and rider Sandy Schuler, both veterinarians.

Shiko's Omar, a chestnut, 15.3 hand, 1100 lb purebred Arabian gelding was purchased as a four year old mainly because of his all-around athletic ability. He received a good mental and physical grounding in dressage training, and all systems were tested with considerable racetrack galloping. As a four year old he was entered in one 30 miler, and then in the ensuing years completed a few rides a year until 1983 when he was mature enough to tackle the 100s. Omar does not have the massive mileage for his eight years' campaign, but his 1500 plus miles have great validity, being in top rides against the country's best. Sandy says she finds it difficult to understand riders who campaign horses at myriad minor rides chasing annual national championships, and feels the sport would be better served if a different system were used to honour great horses. Maybe taking a leaf out of the EHPS of GB's book wouldn't be a bad idea – after all, in its early years the EHPS based itself entirely on American expertise. EHPS championships are only taken from the ten best results per year for each category.

Since 1983 Omar and Sandy's achievements in top 100s have been impressive, his main attribute being consistency. He could be counted on to achieve a top ten ranking – sixth in the 1984 Tevis, third the next year; first and Best Condition in the Swanton Pacific 100 in 1985; and in 1986 as well as being World Champion he took a seventh in the Purina Race of Champions, which is only open to the top ranked 100 mile endurance horses in America, and fifth in the North American Championships.

Sandy runs a one-woman equine practice in Petaluma, California, and says that the Northern Californian situation with its flourishing endurance riding community offers good competition with well-filled rides that enjoy good management and excellent veterinary care for horses. Her training ground is mostly hilly with rises of 1000 to 1500 feet, minimal flat ground, and considerable rocky underfoot conditions. In these conditions, ideal from the point of view of those riders constrained to flat areas, Sandy trains a variety of horses for the distance trail, preferring Arab or Arab crosses with good straight limbs, big feet, plenty of bone, and good movement. As a horsewoman and veterinary surgeon she appreciates the need for a slow build-up with any competition horse, saying it takes several years to produce a top-flight horse. Taken slowly at first with two or three rides a week for young horses, they receive months and if necessary a year to two of preparation before they ever see the competitive side of life. Thereafter they are ridden on average around three times a week – two short spells and one extended ride. Each horse has a moderate competition load, enough to test but not overstress it, accomplishing four to six rides per year, and rarely being asked to do more than one ride a month. Feeding is simple – oats and alfalfa hay ad lib, with hard rations of barley, maize, and Purina mixed feed according to work and body maintenance. Also in the Californian climate horses need not be stabled at night as in the more rigorous Northern European climate, and Sandy says she experienced some problems with Omar getting used to being stabled in Rome, whereas at home he is at liberty. A major plus in her endurance horses' lives is that each one has an annual holiday from work. Too many horses are never given the chance to replenish mental and physical energy banks.

On this regime Omar produced his winning performance at Rome and it must be the reason that he is still sound and set to go after eight seasons. On Rome itself Sandy says that even months after her win she was not sure it had sunk in properly that she and Omar are World Champions. She looks back on the event as an adventure full of excitement, but one that needed considerable adjustment. Feed proved a problem, and she had to fall back on emergency rations of alfafa pellets which the American team brought with them, as Italian hay was unsuitable. Humidity proved a problem too, as high as 85 per cent, and with temperatures in the eighties the horses sweltered their way around the course, which after the Californian hills Sandy said she found much flatter and with too much roadwork – the bane of most European riders. As a conservative rider Sandy, although excited and honoured to be chosen to go, had not considered winning, feeling it was better to cruise in with a horse in good condition than to push for a win and take too much out of the horse. On this occasion, feeling Omar strong underneath her and recovering well at checks she was prepared to ask the question. At the 80 mile mark she felt confident that Omar could beat the British horse El Askar, who was tiring fast. The only other horse that posed a latent threat was Bernhard Dornsiepen's Drago, a much slower horse than Omar, who had no chance of catching the fleet Arabian. Apart from the final veterinary check Omar was home and dry, finishing with plenty of reserve and having to be held to a trot.

With a background of riding horses since a child, where she first showed in Stock Seat Equitation, then switched to English style on acquiring a hunter, Sandy was introduced to endurance riding in 1976 by another veterinary surgeon, Dr Cory Soltan, DVM, who is also a top endurance rider. Since then she has logged over 5000 miles in successful competition, so is qualified to give valid comment on the world situation which she sees as in its infancy with accompanying growing pains, but nevertheless headed in the right direction. She particularly approves of the stricter FEI rulings and applauds the move to more 100 milers, feeling they are better on the horses, needing more diligent training and better horsemanship than the too fast 50s. The stricter FEI controls encourage competitors to ride more conservatively, and therefore promote better horsemanship. For the same reason she prefers the more difficult rides which force riders to conserve their horses. On the minus side she realizes that each ride will assume too much importance with competition intensified as riders aim for places on national teams.

Her own and Omar's endurance future? Omar has had the six months holiday promised him on his return from the World Championships and is set to go, but Sandy will campaign him sparingly, saving him for the big races – the Purina Race of Champions in 1987, and the next World Championships on home territory in Virginia in 1988.

Useful addresses

Great Britain
The Endurance Horse and Pony Society of Great Britain. *Membership Secretary*: Ossie Hare, Mill House, Mill Lane, Stoke Bruerne, Northamptonshire NN12 7SH, England.

The British Horse Society Long Distance Riding Group. The British Horse Society, British Equestrian Centre, Stoneleigh, Kenilworth, Warwickshire CV8 2LR, England.

Australia
The Australian Endurance Riders' Association. *President*: Bernard Harris, Box 235, Gawler, S.A. 5118, Australia. *Secretary*: Pauline de Marchi, c/o same address.

Austria
Bundesfachverband für Reiten und Fahren in Österreich, Prinz-Eugen-Strasse 14/1/6a, A-1040 Wien, Austria. *Chief Officer for Endurance Riding*: Dr Hilde Jarc.

Belgium

Belgian Long Distance Riding. *Secretary*: Jacques Ghislain, Aux Fontaines 108 B, 4133 Clermont, Engis, Belgium.

Canada
Canadian Long Distance Riding Association Inc. *President*: Nancy Beacon, RR#2, Flesherton, Ontario, NOC IEO, Canada. *Secretary*: Angela Markoff, RR#3, Stouffville, Ontario, L4A 7X4, Canada.

European Long Distance Rides Conference
President: Dr Georg F. Riedler, Sonnenterrasse 25, CH–6030 Ebikon, Switzerland. *Secretary*:

Penelope Dauster, Pfarrstrasse 7, D–6272 Niedernhausen, West Germany.

Fédération Equestre Internationale
Secretary General: Fritz O. Widmer, Schosshaldenstrasse 32, PO Box CH–3000 Berne 32, Switzerland.

France
Comité National des Raids Equestres d'Endurance. *Secretary*: J. Robin, Seneuil, 79410 Chervaux, France.

Germany
Verein Deutscher Distanzreiter und -fahrer e.V. Baumschule 4–6, D–4554 Ankum, West Germany.

Holland
Nederlandse Ruiter Sport Vereniging. *Secretary*: J. Brouwer, Box 507, NL–2300 Am Leiden, Netherlands.

Italy
Associazione Nazionale per il Turismo Equestre e per l'Equitazione di Campagna. Largo Messico, 13 – 00198, Roma, Italy.

New Zealand
New Zealand Endurance and Trail Riders Association Inc. *Secretary*: Hazel McCort, Craig Road, RD3, Waiuku, New Zealand.

Norway
Norges Rytterforbund. *Secretary*: S. E. Berg, Hanger Siolevei 1, N–1351 Rud, Norway. *Chairman LDR Committee*: Reidar Naess, Ramstad, N–1481 Li, nr Oslo, Norway.

South Africa
Endurance Ride Association of South Africa. *President*: H. Smith, 46 Tessebe Avenue, 0181 Monument Park, Pretoria, South Africa.

Sweden
Svenska Ridsportens Centralforbund. Sandhamnsgatan 39, S–115 28, Stockholm, Sweden. *Chief Officer for Endurance Riding*: Louise Hermelin.

Switzerland
Schweizerische Distanzreiter Vereinigung. *Secretary*: Werner Egloff, Walterswilerstrasse 1025, 5745 Safenwil, Switzerland.

United States of America
American Endurance Ride Conference. *National Office*: 701 High Street, Suite 203, Auburn, California 95603, USA.

North American Trail Ride Conference. PO Box 20315, El Cajon, California 92021, USA.

The Western States Trail Foundation (*Tevis Cup*). PO Box 5110, Auburn, California 95604, USA.

Conversion tables

1. Miles to kilometres

Miles	Kilometres	Kilometres	Miles
1	1.6	1	0.6
5	8.0	5	3.1
10	16.1	10	6.2
25	40.2	25	15.5
50	80.5	50	31.1
75	120.7	75	46.6
100	160.9	100	62.1
120	193.1	120	74.5
150	241.4	150	93.2

2. Fahrenheit to centigrade (celsius)

Fahrenheit	Centigrade	Centigrade	Fahrenheit
−40	−40	−20	−4
0	−17.8	0	32
32	0	10	50
60	15.6	20	68
80	26.7	30	86
100	37.8	40	104

3. Pounds to kilograms

Pounds	Kilograms	Kilograms	Pounds
1	0.453	1	2.205
5	2.265	5	11.023
10	4.53	10	22.046
20	9.06	15	33.069
100	45.3	25	55.115
150	67.9	50	110.25
200	90.6	100	220.5

4. Inches (yards, hands) to centimetres

Inches	Centimetres	Centimetres	Inches
36 (1 yd)	91	100	39 (3 ft 3)
56 (14 hands)	142	150	59 (14.3 hands)
60 (15 hands)	152	160	63 (15.3 hands)
64 (16 hands)	163	170	67 (16.3 hands)
72 (2 yds)	182	200	78 (6 ft 6)

Bibliography

Anderson, R. C. and J. M. *Quicksilver*. David and Charles, 1973.

Balsdon, J. P. V. D. *Life and Leisure in Ancient Rome*. Bodley Head, 1969.

Birley, A. *Marcus Aurelius*. Eyre and Spottiswoode, 1966.

Brown, Dee. *Bury My Heart at Wounded Knee*. Barrie and Jenkins, 1970.

Carlson, G. P. Professor of Medicine, School of Veterinary Medicine, University of California, Davis, California.

Chair, Somerset de. *The Legend of the Yellow River*. Constable, 1979.

Chambers, J. *The Devil's Horsemen*. Weidenfeld and Nicolson, 1979.

Chevalier, Raymond. *Roman Roads*. Trans. from the French by N. H. Field. Batsford, 1976.

Cook, J. M. *The Persian Empire*. J. M. Dent and Sons, 1983.

Cotterell, A. *The Encyclopaedia of Ancient Civilizations*. Windward, 1980.

Cunninghame Graham, R. S. *Horses of the Conquest*. Heinemann, 1930.

Dio Cassius. *The Roman History: the Reign of Augustus*. Penguin Classics, 1987

Distance Rider Magazine. Edited by Thea Toomer Baker and Tony Ferridge.

Dupuy, E. and T. *Encyclopaedia of Military History*. Janes, 1970.

Eadie, J. W. The Development of Roman Mailed Cavalry. *Journal of Roman Studies* 57 (1967), pp. 161–73.

Gall, Sandy. Independent Television News. *Viewpoint* (11 November 1986) and personal communication.

Haddle, J. *The Complete Book of the Appaloosa*. Barnes and Co., 1975.

Haines, F. *Appaloosa*. Arco, 1963.

Herodotus. *The Histories*. Penguin Classics, 1974.

Homer. *The Iliad*. Penguin Classics, 1986.

Holder, P. A. *The Roman Army in Britain*. Batsford, 1982.

Humble, Richard. *Warfare in the Ancient World*. Guild Publishing, 1980.

Huxley, E. *Scott of the Antarctic*. Weidenfeld and Nicolson, 1977.

Hyland, A. *Endurance Riding*. Pelham, 1974; Lipincott, 1975.

Jones, Lt C. [1808] *Diary of the Corunna Campaign*. Gale and Polden, 1936.

Keller, W. *The Bible as History*. Hodder and Stoughton, rev. edn 1956.

Kilby, E. Article in *Equus Magazine*. August 1986.

Machin Goodall, D. *The Flight of the East Prussian Horses*. David and Charles, 1973.

Maso, L. B. Del. *Rome of the Caesars*. Bonechi Edizione.

Millar, Fergus. *The Roman Empire and Its Neighbours*. Chapter 'Sarmatians' by Tamara Talbot Rice. Weidenfeld and Nicolson, 1967.

Moorhouse, G. *To the Frontier*. Hodder and Stoughton, 1985.

Olivova, V. *Sports and Games in the Ancient World*. Orbis, 1984.

Pfalser, I. L. Ancient Asian Pony Express. *Western Horseman*, December 1973.

Pliny (the Elder). *The Natural History*. Loeb Classics, 1964.

Polo, M. *The Travels of Marco Polo*. Trans. Teresa Waugh. Sidgwick and Jackson, 1984.

Randers Pehrson. J. D. *Barbarians and Romans*. Croom Helm, 1983.

Ramsay. The Roman Post. *Journal of Roman Studies*.

Renault, M. *The Nature of Alexander*. Allen Lane, 1975.

Richardson, B. and D. *The Appaloosa*. Arco, 1969.

Ridgeway, William. *The Origin and Influence of the*

Thoroughbred Horse. Cambridge University Press, 1905.

Ronay, G. *The Tartar Khan's Englishman*. Cassell, 1978.

Rose, R. J. Equine Clinic, College of Veterinary Medicine, University of Sydney, Australia.

Roux, G. *Iraq*. Penguin Classics, 1976.

Saggs, H. W. G. *The Might that was Assyria*. Sidgwick and Jackson, 1984.

Savill, A. *Alexander the Great and His Time*. Rockliffe, 1966.

Savours, A. *Scott's Last Voyage*. Sidgwick and Jackson, 1974.

Settle, R. W. and M. L. *Saddle and Spurs*. Stackpole, 1955.

Snow, David H. Animal Health Trust, Equine Research Station, Newmarket.

Steere, James H. DVM. Novato, California.

Stobart, J. C. *The Grandeur that was Rome*. Sidgwick and Jackson, 1961.

Suetonius. *The Twelve Caesars*. Trans. R. Graves. Penguin Classics, 1975.

Tacitus. *The Histories*. Penguin Classics, 1984.

Tschiffely, A. F. *Southern Cross to Pole Star*. Heinemann, 1933.

Vernam, Glenn. *Man on Horseback*. Harper and Row, 1964.

Wentworth, Lady. *The Authentic Arabian*. George Allen and Unwin, 1945.

Woodham Smith, C. *The Reason Why*. Constable, 1953.

Xenephon. *The Art of Horsemanship*. Trans. M. H. Morgan. J. A. Allen, 1979.

Select index

This index includes the main names and topics covered, and page reference is given to the first or major occurrence in the text.

Rule changes

These pages are provided for noting annual rule changes which may take place in the various societies.

STRONGMAN

MY STORY

Eddie 'The Beast' Hall

Virgin BOOKS

1 3 5 7 9 10 8 6 4 2

Virgin Books, an imprint of Ebury Publishing,
20 Vauxhall Bridge Road,
London SW1V 2SA

Virgin Books is part of the Penguin Random House group of companies
whose addresses can be found at global.penguinrandomhouse.com

Penguin
Random House
UK

Pictures courtesy of Eddie Hall and Family, except for photo section p14
© Uchit Vadher, p15 © Alex Whitehead/SWpix.com, p15, p16 © Rick Findler

First published by Virgin Books in 2017

www.penguin.co.uk

A CIP catalogue record for this book is available from the British Library

HB ISBN 9780753548707
TPB ISBN 9780753548981

Typeset in India by Integra Software Services Pvt. Ltd, Pondicherry

Printed and bound in Great Britain by Clays Ltd, St Ives PLC

Penguin Random House is committed to a sustainable
future for our business, our readers and our planet.
This book is made from Forest Stewardship Council®
certified paper.

For Nan and Alex

CONTENTS

CONTENTS

PROLOGUE

9 July 2016, 7.45 p.m.
World Deadlift Championship, First Direct Arena, Leeds

'Fifteen minutes to go, Eddie.'

'Yeah, all right. Fuck off, will you?'

'Is there anything you need?'

'Yeah, there is: for you to fuck off. Don't worry, dickhead. I'll be ready.'

This is one of the few occasions when swearing doesn't get me into a shit load of trouble. They know what I'm like backstage at a competition and so it's water off a duck's back. I'll still apologise later. It's at the end of the night when the fines start being dished out and it's usually because somebody's been daft enough to stick a microphone in front of me.

'So, Eddie. How do you feel about winning Britain's Strongest Man?'

'Fucking excellent, brother.'

'CUT!'

I've already been in trouble once tonight. A few minutes ago I pulled 465kg (1,025 lb), which, although just a stepping stone to the main event, is still a new world record. After the lift the presenter, Colin Bryce, asked me what I was going to do next. 'Unleash the beast,' was what I meant to say, but when I opened my mouth and started speaking, a word beginning with F found its way into the sentence. The crowd also know what I'm like and they thought it was hilarious.

I don't do it to impress anybody or to piss anybody off. I do it because, rightly or wrongly, it's part of who I am and it's almost impossible for me to deviate from that. There is no 'Eddie Zero', I'm afraid. No low-calorie alternative. I'm full fat, mate, and – much to my mum's regret and embarrassment – another word beginning with F.

In fifteen minutes' time, at precisely 8 p.m., I will pull 500kg (1,102 lb) in front of 10,000 people and in doing so become the first human being in the history of the world to lift half a tonne. Let me say that again, boys and girls: half a tonne. That's about the same weight as an overfed racehorse.

Notice I've left out the words 'attempt to', by the way. The definition of the word attempt is 'to make an effort to achieve', which means there is always a possibility of failure. Not tonight. Not here. This, my friend, is history in the making and ensuring such occurrences take place is the reason I have been put on this earth. Some people are here to build houses and work in banks, and some people are here to change the world.

Being a foul-mouthed history-making cheeky behemoth does come at a cost, however. Ever since agreeing to do the lift I have had to virtually ignore my wife and kids and over the last six months I have spent no more than a few hours in their company. That in itself has obviously been a massive sacrifice for all of us, but in truth it's just the tip of the iceberg. My daily routine has been to eat, sleep, train, recover and repeat, and in addition to a couple of short but extremely severe bouts of depression, which I think were triggered by stress and isolation, I have gradually become less mobile. This is because, in order to lift such a massive weight, I have had to put on an extra 15kg (33 lb) in weight and right now I am just over thirty-one stone. My God, it's been hard though. I have suffered all kinds of pain over the years but preparing for this has been a different kind of hell and even now I am in a very, very dark place.

As I sit quietly in the dressing room I suddenly belch, and am reminded of what I had for my dinner – or lunch, if you're posh. Whilst everyone else will have been tucking into sandwiches or burgers, I was in a restaurant ordering a mouth-watering lump of fat taken straight from a massive joint of gammon. In terms of taste it was probably one of the most disgusting meals I've ever eaten, but in terms of calories, it was the dog's. About 4,000, all told.

You see, to me, when it comes to milestones, the half-tonne deadlift is right up there with the four-minute mile and if anybody ever manages to break the record once I've smashed it – and they will – it will be my record they're breaking. Let's face it, nobody gives a damn who holds the current record for running a mile, and why would they? Whoever holds the record is simply clinging to the coattails of greatness. The only name that matters when it comes to running the mile is Roger Bannister, and why? Because he proved the naysayers wrong and did what everyone said was impossible. He became – and remains – the benchmark and regardless of the fact that the record he set is now slow in comparison to today's athletes, it is the only one we really care about. He walks (or runs) on a higher plane to the rest and in a few minutes' time he'll have to make some room – quite a bit of room, actually – for me.

The reason this is relevant now is because the only person in this entire arena who thinks I'm going to pull this lift is me. Some of my mates probably think I have a chance, but the bookies are offering odds of 25/1 and so have me down as a complete no-hoper. That's fine though. Other people's doubt is my biggest motivation and the fact that the no's are unanimous makes it a forgone conclusion as far as I'm concerned.

'OK, we're ready for you, Eddie.'

'Come on then, fucker, lead the way.'

After a quick detour to a disabled toilet, which I'll explain later, my three-man entourage and I make our way to the stage. As we pass the other athletes one or two of them shout, 'Good luck, Ed,' but I know not one of them thinks I can do it. Seeing them all staring at me is like a last-minute shot of adrenalin.

One man not staring at me from the pool of athletes, but whose words echo through my mind, is four-time World's Strongest Man, Brian Shaw. Brian should be here, but he pulled out of the event announcing that 500kg was ridiculous. In fact, the current World's Strongest Man had publicly proclaimed that 480kg (1,058 lb) was the absolute max he thought was doable by anyone.

As we walk on I over Žydrūnas Savickas – arguably the strongest men in history – voicing his concerns about the feat I'm about to attempt. 'What happens to the human body at such a weight,' he says. 'I am not sure we are designed to handle that amount. It is a little dangerous but we shall see.'

I respect both men but I will make them eat their words.

We're almost at the stage now and I can hear the MC warming up the crowd. This is supposed to be the support event for Europe's Strongest Man but it should be the other way around. Whoever wins that title won't be making history. They won't be on Roger Bannister's higher plane.

As I walk through the curtain onto the stage the first thing I see is the crowd, all 10,000 of them. The biggest audience ever for a strongman event. A hit of smelling salts brings that familiar wild, yet strangely pleasurable pain burning through my skull. I gesture to the crowd to make some noise and they respond with a deafening roar. This, right now, is the deepest, darkest moment of my life.

Over the past twenty years only 9kg (20 lb) has been added to the world deadlift record. What am I going to add? 35kg (77 lb)? Bloody hell.

As I bend down and put the straps around my hands everything goes quiet. I'm locked in now. I am in the zone, as they say. I've visualised this moment a thousand times and I've practiced it a thousand more. Rep after rep of drills, hour after hour of training in the gym has led me to this moment. I'll hear the crowd again once I've locked my back out, but for the next ten seconds or so it's just me and the bar.

As I find my grip, I see, just fleetingly, a picture of my family in my mind's eye. It's a quick but important reminder of exactly why I'm doing this.

I'm happy with the grip now, so am ready to go.

OK, Roger. Shove up a bit, mate. It's time to make some history.

CHAPTER 1
Eight Pounds, Fourteen Ounces

Believe it or not, give or take a pound or two, my weight has always matched my age (or at least it did until I hit twenty-nine stone). So at the time of writing I'm nearly thirty years old and a nice healthy thirty-odd stone. At six foot three inches I'm quite a noticeable presence in a confined space, shall we say.

When they meet me, a lot of people say that they can't imagine me being anything other than big, so these first few chapters are going to be a bit of a revelation to some. It's the same when Mum and Dad get the photograph albums out. Whoever's unlucky enough to be shown them will see one of me as a kid messing about on a beach or something, and then say, 'Naaaa. That can't be Eddie!' It gets on my tits sometimes.

Anyway, you can check this with my mum if you like but at birth, I, Edward Stephen Hall, weighed eight pounds and fourteen ounces exactly, having been born at North Staffs Maternity Hospital to Stephen and Helen Hall at 4.59 p.m.

on Friday 15 January 1988. According to the internet I share a birthday with Martin Luther King Jr and the rapper Pitbull, which actually makes perfect sense: a man who inspired millions and a success story who's named after an angry and potentially dangerous dog. I'll take that. What is perhaps more relevant is the fact that I seem to be the only sportsperson of note to have been born on 15 January 1988. As somebody who doesn't like sharing things – especially titles, world records and podiums – that suits me down to the ground.

According to Mum and Dad I was a very happy and easygoing baby who loved being cuddled; particularly by Mum and her own mum, Nan. Nan was an amazing woman and when I started getting into trouble she was one of the only people who could get through to me. More about that later.

I have two older brothers, Alex and James, and while Mum and Nan wanted to hug me, those two wanted to kill me. I don't think there was any jealousy involved, like there is in some cases. They just saw a fat little shit move into the house and decided they were going to kick his ass.

One of the earliest examples of this reprehensible behaviour happened when I was just a few weeks old. My brother, James, who today plays professional rugby for Bristol yet still weighs a mere eighteen stone, decided to lift me up by my neck and then drop me on the floor, and because he was only about eighteen months old he obviously got away with it. I'd like to see him try that now. In fact, I'd like to see anybody try it. My eldest brother, Alex, who was three when I was born and is now about a foot shorter (ha ha), probably did the same and worse when nobody else was looking and so the fact that I made it to nine months is a miracle.

The reason I mention this particular age is that it heralded my first visit back to a hospital, yet strangely enough it had nothing to do with either of my homicidal siblings. The problem started when I suddenly began sleeping about twenty-three hours a day. Although Mum and Dad must have been relieved by this, it obviously wasn't normal and so I was taken into hospital to have a few tests. The diagnosis was severe anaemia and once they managed to get a bit more iron into me I was fine. Children and babies are especially susceptible to anaemia during periods of rapid growth and so looking back I'm surprised I didn't get it every week.

By the time I was about a year old I could punch, bite and elbow and by eighteen months I'd started kicking, stamping and headbutting. This might sound a little bit hardcore to some people but it was simply a matter of survival. A quick argument would take place first – an accusation of some kind probably, or just an insult – and then, once we'd got all that preliminary crap out of the way, it would be straight down to business – BOOM! It was toddler warfare. We'd start off in the living room, punching, kicking and throwing each other off the furniture and then once we'd become tired of using our limbs to inflict injury we'd go looking for weapons. Things like remote controls were always the first to hand but the damage you could do with one of those was limited so in an act of desperation we'd try picking up chairs or even the bloody coffee table. There was a lot of shouting, a shit load of swearing and lots of cries of 'AAAAAAAAAAARGH!'

Once we'd exhausted the living room a natural break would occur when we'd catch our breath and try to think of the location of some suitable – and preferably lethal – weaponry. One by one we'd go darting off to wherever the arms were concealed and then once we were all tooled up and back in the room it would start again.

'Right you bastard! Now I'm going to kill you. AAAAAAAARGH!'

I remember our dad used to have a replica samurai sword and whoever managed to get their hands on that first obviously had the upper hand. Or the upper cut, if you like. We used to chase each other around the house with this and the only thing that prevented us from taking a swipe and probably killing each other was the fact that it weighed quite a bit so we couldn't swing it properly. Eventually Dad realised what was happening and locked the thing away and it's a damn good job he did as I shudder to think what might have happened otherwise.

Our mum must have had the patience of a stadium full of saints when dealing with us. As we became older and stronger it obviously became more and more difficult to split us up and so in the end she would just put each of us in one of the bedrooms hoping that we'd play quietly. She should have done that from the off, really. Either that or just sedated us.

Unfortunately, this boisterous behaviour wasn't just confined to home and even a quick trip to the shops would often turn nasty. I know that all brothers fight a bit but that's all we ever did. There was never any downtime. Or, if there was, it was simply the calm before the next storm. Mum and Dad recently reminded me of a day trip to Blackpool we tried to make in the early 1990s. Notice I say 'tried' to make. Apparently, we had an Austin Montego at the time which means sod all to me but one of the reasons Mum and Dad had bought the car was because it had two rear-facing seats in the boot so that me, Alex and James wouldn't have to sit next to each other. Nice try! It was going to take more than a couple of rear-facing seats to stop the war. Even though we weren't able to hit each other we could still have a go verbally. And we did. Threats of what we'd do to each other once we reached Blackpool began being issued before we'd even left our road and by the time we reached junction 19 of the M6, which was about twenty-five miles from home, Dad had had enough.

'THAT'S IT! WE'RE GOING HOME.'

At first I think we thought it was just an idle threat and so we carried on. It wasn't, though. Dad was serious, and who can blame him? Sure enough, he came off at junction 19, went straight around the roundabout, and started heading back to Stoke.

'I'm not putting up with that for another eighty miles,' he said. 'No way!'

In an act of defiance, Alex, James and I bawled our fucking eyes out all the way home and made far more noise than we had done arguing. Poor Dad was at the end of his tether by the time we got back and he had to lock himself in a room for a few hours. I'm surprised he didn't stay there longer. So much for a family day out.

Despite the aggro, we have always been a very close family – very pro each other – and, although I didn't know it at the time, the fighting would pay dividends once I was let loose onto the streets. Since the pottery industry disappeared, Stoke-on-Trent has become quite a deprived area. In order to survive, you have two choices: hide away and keep yourself to yourself or become street-wise and be prepared to put the boot in when necessary. I obviously chose the latter and if I hadn't had that apprenticeship in extreme violence and savagery I'd have found it very, very hard indeed.

Something that really exemplifies my choice – not to mention my mindset, back then – is the content of my very earliest memory. I must have been about three and a half years old and still at nursery and I remember this kid came up to me and started pissing me off. I can't remember what he did exactly but I remember telling him to fuck off. Even then I was using some pretty industrial language but that was the norm, not just in our house, but in the entire city. The kid went off to get a teacher and after I'd been duly reprimanded the little bastard slyly said something else to me and so I headbutted him and gave him a black eye. Headbutting has always been a speciality of mine and even at three and a half years old I was up there with the best of them. I may not have been very tall at the time but put me on a box and I could have floored an adult. Fortunately, that's not my only memory from childhood, but it's definitely my earliest. A psychologist would probably have a field day with something like that.

I think what also helped in preparing me for life on the streets was the fact that at home there was never any hiding place. So regardless of what age you were you had no choice other than to stand there and defend yourself. It didn't matter what the other one had in his hands (bar a samurai sword!); you had to put your head down and have a go, and that's exactly what we did. Once again it was fight or flight and the latter was never, ever an option – nor would you ever want to take it. Even when Mum put us in different rooms we'd still walk around like miniature caged beasts, shouting and banging on the doors. There was no retreat, no surrender, and very little by way of defence. It was as if we'd all been stuck in attack mode.

One of the things that encouraged us to behave like that, I think, was the fact that we never established a dialogue between us. So instead of saying 'Can I play with that toy?' or 'Are you going to eat that fish finger?', we simply took the toy or ate the fish finger. The victim would obviously respond to this in kind and there you would have it – constant fucking chaos! Mum and Dad used to intervene occasionally, but even then, we'd be back scrapping within a few seconds.

Mum, who is one of the world's greatest human beings, was always the peacemaker – encouraging us to shake hands and be nice to each other – and Dad was the loud authoritarian character who would just explode when he'd had enough. He's a big lad, my old man – about six foot two inches – and once he'd reached his cut-off point you knew about it. In that respect, I'm exactly the same as him, as when I do lose my rag I go nuclear, but because I've also inherited some of Mum's patience I can generally prevent myself from getting into trouble. Well, sometimes.

The other thing, apart from aggro – and a bit of love, it has to be said – that was prevalent in the Hall household was competition, and that too has served me well over the years, although more so since I took up sport.

It was there from day one really and, again, it was all a result of good old-fashioned sibling rivalry. According to Mum, I'd watch James and Alex walking when I was baby and as soon as I was able to copy them, I was off. What eventually changed was the fact that, instead of simply wanting to emulate my brothers, I wanted to beat the bastards, and so that obviously added to the tension within the household. If they ran to the end of the garden in ten seconds, I'd want to do it in nine, and if they jumped off a wall, I'd have to find a higher one. It became a bit of an obsession with me.

What also made things interesting was our height. I'm taller than James and Alex (Alex is about five foot eleven inches, James is six foot and I'm six foot three inches) and from the age of about five until I got to high school we were all roughly the same height. This meant that nobody was at a disadvantage. It also presented us with another opportunity to piss each other off and for a time that became the big motivator. Fortunately, we started to appreciate how futile that was and so we began to concentrate on our own ambitions. The rivalry was always bubbling somewhere underneath though.

Genetically, I think we have my mother to thank for our competitiveness as – in addition to retraining to become a firefighter a few years ago after spending years teaching kids with special needs – she's also started competing in Iron Man Triathlons. For those of you who don't know, this consists of a 2.4-mile swim, a 112-mile bike ride and then a full marathon. That takes some serious training and dedication and she's more than a match for it. Part of Mum's motivation is a simple desire to keep fit but she's certainly not there just to make up the numbers and that, I think, is really what drives her on.

I've never asked her about this but if I were a betting man – and I am – I'd say that one of the reasons Mum sometimes left the three of us to get on with trying to compete with each other (and it did become a bit ridiculous at times) was because she was hoping we'd develop a desire to succeed. If that *was* her modus operandi, it worked. But what separates me from Alex and James is the fact that I've always taken this hunger to achieve to ridiculous extremes. In fact, that's a pretty accurate description for me. A ridiculous extreme.

Anyway, let's get onto Dad.

Since becoming a strongman I've had to sacrifice all kinds of things – time with my family being the most troublesome and upsetting – but this is really small fry to what my old man has given up. He worked as a health and safety officer in the same factory for over twenty-five years and because of the hours he worked we hardly ever saw him. Even when we did see Dad he was stressed out; a direct consequence of coming home from a job that was repetitive and unchallenging and going straight into a warzone.

He didn't have time for hobbies or anything and because he's got a good brain on him that must have been extremely stifling. There was no 'me time' for Dad and no shed to disappear to. Because he remained dedicated to his job we were not only able to live in a nice house and never want for anything, but we were also free to get out there and try to realise our potential, knowing that – unless it was something dangerous or stupid – we would always receive his and Mum's full support. Basically, we got everything Dad should have had but couldn't, which is why I cringe sometimes when I think about the way we used to behave. Fancy walking into that, day after day. Some lesser men wouldn't have come home, but not Dad. He was obviously a glutton for punishment – thank God.

The saving grace with regards to our relationship with Dad was our annual family holiday, and because of his endeavours we were able to go to some really special places. It was the one time during the year we'd be able to spend time with him in a relaxed atmosphere. Portugal always seemed to be our family's destination of choice back then and we'd spend all day every day just chilling by the pool, having barbecues and lazing on the beach. Even the fighting used to lessen a bit during these special times and that was solely because we were all so pleased to see Dad carefree and happy for a while. He was a completely different person on holiday and that change in mood was wonderfully contagious.

Once we were back home, things would return to normal pretty quickly and before you could say 'seconds out, round one', the three amigos would be making up for lost time by smashing remote controls over each other's head, issuing death threats and making our ever-patient mother's life an absolute misery. I expect Dad was relieved to get back to work.

As well as spending some quality time with my family, those holidays taught me a very important lesson in life and that is to be grateful for what you have and to always look for the positives, however well hidden they are. The human brain will generally err toward the negative and that can often cloud your better judgement. That's something that's helped me, not just as a human being but as an athlete. When your brain's telling you that something's crap and that your life's a pile of shit, the chances are the thought is exactly that, a pile of shit.

I think Mum and Dad knew that one day the fighting would come to an end and, bar moving us all to a sodding zoo, there was bugger all they could do about it until then. Sure enough, when we got to our early teens – or when I did – we gave up fighting almost overnight and suddenly started talking to one another. We became mates, I suppose, and it's been exactly the same ever since. We still had our moments, of course, but because we'd finally learned how to talk to one another and show an interest in each other's lives, the fighting was usually averted and conversations took place instead. Pretty sweary ones, it has to be said, but conversations just the same. I remember thinking to myself after talking to Alex one day, *Wow! My brother's not a snivelling arsehole after all. He's actually OK.*

But if that was a revelation for the three of us – and it was – what must it have been like for Mum and Dad? To be honest, I think it was just a massive relief. In fact, it probably knocked years off them. Like an early retirement! They're great though, and all three of us think the sun shines out of their fu … We think the world of them.

CHAPTER 2
Injury Time

Believe it or not, one of my first talents as a young child was having injuries and accidents. In fact, if I ever have to write a CV it's something I'll probably include.

CURRENT JOB: PROFESSIONAL STRONGMAN

SPECIAL SKILLS: STABBING MYSELF AND FALLING ARSE OVER TIT

All kids have accidents, of course, but from the age of about four onwards I seemed to develop a knack, and although this may sound strange I think I became addicted to them. It won't surprise you to know that one of my very first injuries, which was definitely *not* an accident, was perpetrated by the only person I can honestly say that I was scared of as a small child – my brother James. He was an absolute headcase from the year dot and as well as being my hero, in a way (as was Alex), he was also my nemesis.

The injury James inflicted on me was caused by him throwing ice in my face, the bastard. It was close range too, so there was never any question of it being an accident. The only thing I do question is whether or not he sharpened the ice before he threw it because it made a real mess of my face and I had stitches everywhere.

How much of it was already within me I'm not altogether sure, but these unending battles with James either established or aroused in me an almost impenetrable sense of bravery, which, on some occasions, has enabled me to take on multitudes of men without even batting an eyelid. I can honestly say that since overcoming my fear of fighting James I have never once gone into a scrap feeling scared, regardless of the numbers or the situation. Excited? Oh yes. Exhilarated? Definitely. But that raw emotion of fear, which can often be crippling, is something that deserted me long ago and was immediately replaced by a feeling of self-assurance. I actually felt invincible from the age of about four, which is ridiculous when you think about it. This is something that has been growing within me ever since then and as well as becoming an intrinsic part of my weaponry it is probably the one thing that separates me from my competitors in strongman. That, and being absolutely fucking excellent, of course. People may only have been calling me 'The Beast' for the last couple of years, but I think I've been one for least twenty-five.

My next mishap of note involves me falling out of a tree and although you might think this quite a standard childhood injury, I can promise you it was anything but.

James was with me – naturally – and I think we'd challenged each other as to who could climb the highest. Because I was now confident *and* competitive, I just kept on going while James had the good sense to stop. Even when I knew I'd climbed higher than he had and I was running out of tree, I refused to stop. Eventually one of the branches snapped and down I came. I must have fallen at least thirty or forty feet and the faster I fell the harder I hit the branches, and the closer I got to the ground the bigger and harder the branches became. By the time I eventually landed I was in all kinds of agony, and as well as a broken arm I had bumps on my head the size of bull's testicles and was covered in about a hundred bruises.

My immediate reaction was to call to James and ask him to get Mum and Dad, but as he ran off in the direction of the house I suddenly started to laugh. I had never, ever felt pain like it before yet in a strange sort of way I almost enjoyed it. I remember saying to myself, *This is fucking brilliant!* I'd just fallen out of a massive tree and had survived. It felt like an achievement.

A minute or so later, as I started to relive what had happened, an overwhelming sense of excitement surged through my body, almost cancelling out the pain, and I swear that if I had been physically able to I would have climbed the tree and done it again.

Does that make me sound a bit weird? I suppose it does but then I probably am a bit. You have to be, if you're going to be me.

The next incident is a little bit gorier and took place on a family holiday to Portugal when I was five. As well as Mum,

Dad and the three of us brothers, we also had Dad's parents with us, Grandad and Grandma, and as far as I remember the first few days were great: it was red hot and the pool was massive. Or at least it was to me.

One afternoon, about four or five days into the holiday, Grandad decided he wanted an orange and proceeded to peel one in the kitchen, with me watching him, unobserved. I don't think I'd ever seen anybody peel an orange with a knife before and remember thinking, *Good skills, Grandad!* I was amazed by the way the skin came off in one continuous twirl and it can't have taken him more than a few seconds. Shortly after he'd finished he left the room and I decided to give it a go myself. After taking an orange from the fruit bowl I pulled up a stool from the breakfast bar, took the knife from the sink and as I tried to stick the knife into the orange, it went straight through my left hand. Within about a second the orange was blood-red and there were people absolutely everywhere. It was chaos. The knife Grandad had used was thin and razor sharp so it was never going to end happily. That said, it went through my hand very easily and so when Dad pulled it out it wasn't a problem.

As opposed to taking me to hospital, which would have meant claiming on the insurance, my grandma stitched up my hand using a very fine needle and I don't remember there being any tears at all. In fact, she coped very well! Well done, Grandma. It honestly didn't bother me though and because the gash wasn't too big the pain was minimal. Most kids would have been vomiting and screaming their little arses off but it was water off a duck's back to me. I'm not trying to make myself sound tough, by the way. I'm not into all that bollocks and I've got nothing whatsoever to prove. It was just the way I was. It's always the inconvenience of being injured that bothers me most, as opposed to the injury itself.

A few days later, whilst still in Portugal, we were about to go for a walk and as I was sat on the tiled floor putting on my sandals, my dad, who was wearing clogs at the time – although don't ask me why – stood on one of my fingers by mistake and completely ripped off my fingernail. Imagine a size 11 solid wood clog with about sixteen stone of man standing in it suddenly landing on your fingernail. That particular episode was definitely less enjoyable than the tree or the orange and I remember getting a kick up the arse for calling Dad a ... something quite rude.

From the point of view of simply staying alive, the worst thing that could have happened to me at this time was finding somebody even more dangerous to emulate than James and Alex, but that's exactly what did happen.

In truth, it was only a character from a film, but the man who played him went on to become my biggest inspiration outside of my family. As well as being lucky enough to have met the great man in later life, I was also proud to have him present at two of my deadlift records; he was actually at my side cheering me on at both of them. He is the incredible Mr Arnold Schwarzenegger and when I was about five years old his most iconic film role gave me somewhere to channel all of this confidence, energy and bravery that was running through my five-stone frame. I almost died in the process, but it felt great!

The fictional character in question is obviously the Terminator and over the years I must have watched the film at least a hundred times. I actually think it was still an eighteen certificate back then so I started watching it a good thirteen years early. Mum and Dad would have had a fit if they'd found out but I'm so glad they didn't.

Like millions of other kids, I wanted to *be* Arnolds Schwarzenegger's seemingly indestructible cybernetic android and after becoming completely and utterly obsessed with the character I set about trying to copy him and even made up some of my own stunts. These included throwing myself off bikes at high speed, jumping off high walls and trying to land on one foot, and even throwing myself out of trees instead of just falling out of them. Looking back it must have seemed like I had some kind of death wish but I remember feeling so pumped up at having something to aim towards.

Mmmmm. I think I needed to go to school!

CHAPTER 3
Educating Eddie

I think my parents were hoping that school might tame me a bit and, despite me not being the ideal pupil, it probably did for the first few months. I was obviously out of my comfort zone a bit and without my brothers being there I had to establish myself as an individual.

Educationally I was a bit of a paradox, I suppose, because as well as being easily distracted I was also the one most willing to try. Regardless of whether I knew the answer or not I would always be the first to put my hand up when the teacher asked a question. If I didn't know the answer, I'd just guess – but I had to be the first. I obviously wasn't a shy boy but my main motivation wasn't getting the question right, it was seeking the approval of others. So whenever I did manage to answer a question correctly and was congratulated by the teacher I'd almost explode with pride. That's something that has never left me. Even today, if I win a competition, a text from my mum saying 'Well done son, I'm proud of you' will mean more to me than any trophy. Making people proud or pleased, however trivial the situation or the circumstances, is the main reason I do what I do.

With regards to my behaviour at primary school, let's just say that it was a game of two halves. My first school, Friarswood, is undoubtedly a wonderful educational establishment now but twenty-odd years ago my group of mates would be there telling the teachers to fuck off. Every break time there'd be a big group of us – seven, eight and nine year olds – smoking behind the bike sheds and fighting each other … these were the kids I always gravitated towards and them to me.

It wasn't that I necessarily liked many of them. They were just a lot more exciting than the bright kids and the one thing I couldn't live without was excitement. When I was with my brothers there was never, ever a dull moment and when they both went to school I was bored shitless. Being with kids full-time again made me want to try to replicate what my brothers and I had at home. Although it was never the same as it was with Alex and James, it was better than sitting on my own or with a load of uncool boffins.

The only real bright spot throughout my entire sentence at Friarswood was my reception teacher, Mrs Vivian Mills. She was like a beacon of positivity and calmness in a period of my life that I considered to be a massive inconvenience, but because she only taught me during my first year at the school her influence sadly wore off pretty quickly. When Mrs Mills spoke, everybody sat up and listened. Not because she was commanding (although she was), but because she always had something interesting to say. That much I do remember. Unbeknownst to me, Mrs Mills must have followed my progress in strongman and when I finally went professional back in 2014 she tracked me down and handed me a cheque for £200.

'I read that you'd gone professional Eddie,' she said giving me a peck on the cheek. 'So here's something to help you on your way.'

It was fabulous seeing her again and was an amazing gesture. That's the mark of the woman and people like her change lives. Luckily for me, she wasn't the only person who was to have a positive influence on me during these years.

One of my parents' many attempts at giving me an interest other than roughhousing and inflicting injury was offering me piano lessons when I was nine. I don't mind admitting that I was horrified when they first suggested it. I was a miniature thug for Christ's sake, whose hobbies included smashing bottles over people's heads and using four-letter words beginning with F and C. I couldn't think of anything more diametrically opposed to what I enjoyed doing than learning a flaming instrument, which was probably the reason Mum and Dad tried to get me into it. Piano lessons! I could have died.

My teacher, who lived on our street, was called Mrs Winder and she and her husband had lived in the area for years. She must have been in her sixties at the time and when I turned up for my first lesson I was, not to put too fine a point on it, somewhat lacking in enthusiasm.

'You must be Eddie,' she said on opening the door. 'Come on in.'

Mrs Winder had a very kind face and from the moment I set eyes on her I felt completely at ease. This wasn't how I was used to feeling when I met new people. Something was obviously wrong.

'Before we start, let's have a quick chat,' said Mrs Winder. 'I want to know all about you.'

Again, that wasn't how people spoke to me.

'All right then,' I said. 'What do you want to know?'

After asking me some questions about school and stuff, Mrs Winder turned the conversation to music.

'Do you like music, Eddie?' she said.

I just shrugged. 'Only the Beatles,' I answered truthfully. 'Mum and Dad used to play them in the car.'

'OK then. Let's see if we can find something you like.'

By this time I remember thinking that I didn't want to play the piano or listen to music, I just wanted to carry on talking to Mrs Winder. I've always enjoyed the company of older people and there was something about her I really liked.

'Tell me what you think of this,' she said, before picking out some music and sitting down at the piano.

The tune she played was 'Love Me Do' by the Beatles and I grinned from ear to ear as I began to recognise what she was playing.

'It's the Beatles,' I said approvingly.

'That's right,' said Mrs Winder. 'If you practise hard enough you might be able to play that one day.'

That was all the incentive I needed and over the next two years or so I became quite a proficient little pianist. Impatient, but then isn't every child when they start learning a new instrument? In the end I could turn my hand to most styles of music but I always ended up playing either the Beatles or John Lennon. 'Imagine' was my favourite. It still is.

What was even more enjoyable than the music – and, in all honesty, was the reason I stuck it out for so long – was my unique friendship with Mrs Winder. It might sound slightly ridiculous to some people but going to her house became one of the highlights of my week and, as much as I enjoyed tickling the ivories and paying homage to the Fab Four, it was the conversation running alongside that fired me and caught my imagination. Mrs Winder and I would talk throughout each lesson and I'd tell her things that I wouldn't dream of telling my parents, or even my friends for that matter. No subject ever seemed to be off limits and I knew that whatever truths or revelations I divulged would never go any further. Mrs Winder knew that I was a bit of a tearaway but there was obviously something about me she liked and knowing that made me feel great.

The lessons were like a cross between a confessional and a counselling session and in hindsight I should have carried them on into adulthood. In fact, if you're still alive, Mrs Winder, get in touch!

Domestically, there was only one person who could bring out the best in me without trying, and that was Nan my mum's mum. As much as I love my parents, they obviously represented authority and because they had to spend so much of their time telling me off and answering letters from school, our relationship was often fraught.

Being with Nan, though, was like being wrapped in a warm blanket. Whenever I was with her all the anger I felt just disappeared. In every other situation there'd be aggro of some kind bubbling underneath but with her it was different. I could never scowl at my nan like I'd scowl at Mum and Dad. It was just unthinkable. I only smiled when I was with her.

Occasionally she'd offer me little bits of advice and if she'd heard about me being naughty she'd smile at me and say, 'Eeee, what have you been up to now, Eddie?' She never judged me. In fact, I don't remember Nan ever judging anybody.

What she gave me more than anything was unconditional love and for somebody who pissed a lot of people off and had a lot of things going on in his head that was incredibly important. It didn't matter how many people I'd infuriated or how aggrieved I felt, Nan's love would wash it all away. She was my lifeblood.

By the time I got to Year Five at Friarswood I'd burned my bridges so badly that I had to be moved to a different school. My confidence, or should I say cockiness, had been over-flowing again since I'd found my feet there and together with limitless amounts of courage, a mouth like an open sewer and an overwhelming compulsion to piss people off I had officially become public enemy number one. If my parents hadn't moved me when they did I'd either have been expelled by the headmaster, bumped off by a contract killer hired by the PTA, or set upon by a group of desperate, rabid teachers.

The straw that broke the camel's back was probably fighting. It had always been a problem for me at Friarswood but by the time I'd been there a few years it had become an epidemic and each and every playtime I'd be involved in some kind of gang warfare somewhere in the school. Unfortunately this would often follow me back into the classroom and that's when the trouble really started. You see, the kids I fought at school were the same kids I fought outside of school and so there was a constant undercurrent of hostility there that would occasionally morph into violence. We're not talking about simple fisticuffs here. Even at six or seven we were using bottles and large pieces of wood. Anything we could get out hands on, basically, and I used to love every single second of it. I genuinely was the proverbial little bastard, I'm afraid, but as a firm believer in karma it was all part and parcel of becoming who I am today. That's my excuse, anyway.

The next school daft enough to have me was Westlands Primary School in Newcastle-under-Lyme but my experiences there were very different to Friarswood with regards to the teachers, the pupils and everyone's general behaviour and the contrast took me by surprise.

Chapter 3

My own teacher especially, Mr Stirland, was on a completely different level to any adult I'd ever met before and the effect he had on me was both immediate and profound. Together with my reception teacher Mrs Mills, my nan, and one or two others, he was one of a select few adults who was able to influence me as a child and prevent me from acting like a prick. He was one of those teachers that you never, ever forget and he was actually the first, after my nan, to discipline me using words that weren't either shouted or screamed. He simply spoke in a soft but commanding voice.

At first I didn't know what the bloody hell to do. I think I'd probably told him to fuck off or something, but instead of receiving the usual tirade in return he just sat me down and talked to me. Funnily enough, it was actually *what* he said that made a difference, not how he said it. He explained in a consultative yet authoritative manner why it wasn't appropriate for me to behave in that way, and by the time he'd finished, I felt about two inches high. It was a revelation in a way and, although it didn't stop me from swearing at adults ever again, he made me pick and choose my moments. Mr Stirland also never seemed to get angry, which took the wind out of my sails, and he had a command of the English language that most of us could never dream of having. Instead of writing books, he used his gift to control – and then educate – little arseholes like me.

Although they'd often tried, nobody had ever really got the better of me before, either physically or verbally, so not only did I respect Mr Stirland massively for having achieved that, I always did as he asked. He didn't just introduce me to a different kind of behaviour, he introduced me to a different kind of *being*. He showed me there were bright people who used their brains instead of their fists in life.

From an educational point of view, Mr Stirland was again a revelation. As well as making me appreciate the importance of studying, he made it both interesting and fun. At Friarswood I'd always been seen as a potentially smart kid who just wouldn't apply himself, but because of the way Mr Stirland controlled me – and he did actually control the way I behaved – I very quickly started realising some of this potential. I could still be a little bit unruly at times and was often extremely cheeky, but that was par for the course. Mr Stirland was a teacher with gentle touch and an impressive vocabulary, not a fucking miracle worker.

One thing that also made a big difference to me was the fact that I had to call Mr Stirland 'sir'. That was the norm at Westlands and it set a precedent with me, one that I enjoyed being a part of. A lot of people won't believe this but I actually have a tremendous amount of respect for discipline, providing it's explained to me concisely and I consider it to be fair. Present me with the opposite, however, and I'll kick up a massive fuss. Not because I'm difficult, but because I refuse to take shit from people.

Over the next year or so, Westlands Primary School became a kind of educational enclave for me and after just a few weeks of being there I repaid Mr Stirland's faith and hard work by getting myself in the top sets for everything. I went from being a little shit to a scholar and it was a very satisfying transformation.

Whilst me infiltrating the top sets at school was a miracle to some people, to others it was an abomination. Some of the brighter pupils thought I was a bit of a dickhead (although they didn't say as much) and once I started invading their territory they were horrified.

'How the hell did someone like you make it into Set One?' one of them asked me. 'You're always misbehaving.'

My reply was typically to the point.

'Because I'm fucking clever.'

It was true, I was, but the best was yet to come. About half way through Year Six the top seven or eight pupils from my year were invited to take the exam to attend one of the local private schools and I was one of them. This, I think, was the final insult to those boffins who disapproved of me and when word got around I could see that they were absolutely disgusted. Things like this weren't meant to happen to people like me, and that, brothers and sisters, could actually end up being my epitaph! Proving people wrong has actually become a bit of an addiction to me and even back then it felt absolutely fantastic. But what felt even better than getting one over on those dickheads was finding my feet as a human being – or starting to – and realising that there were other avenues worth exploring apart from just messing about.

I think most kids have got it in them to do well at school, providing they're in the right environment and surrounded by the right people. Unfortunately, not all of them are lucky enough to have those essentials but I'm living proof that they can make a real difference to a child. If I'd stayed at Friarswood, God knows where I'd have ended up. Behind bars, probably. There was still time for me to mess things up, though, as I'd prove at high school. My problem was that in order to stay on the straight and narrow I needed Mr Stirland to be there twenty-four hours a day and that was obviously never going to happen.

One thing that did help to reinforce Mr Stirland's influence on me was joining the Cubs. I'd already been a Beaver from the age of six until eight but I remember Cubs being much more fun and once I started going to Westlands it almost became an extension of school. A lot of my new classmates went to Cubs and so that too gave me an incentive to calm down a bit and behave. One thing I noticed at Cubs, more than I did school, was that because I was big and because I liked a fight, a lot of kids tended to gravitate towards me. Even at the age of eight I was very much the alpha male. I definitely thrived on that kind of attention and adulation and it was something that I was very keen to build on and preserve. Part of that was down to simply wanting to be the top dog, and the other part was wanting people's approval. Whenever we went camping I always wanted to be the one who put up the tent and built the fire and the reward for me pushing myself forward and doing that was the aforementioned approval. That made me a very happy boy.

CHAPTER 4

Swimming Against the Stream

Unfortunately, school and Cubs only took up about half of my waking hours, which meant there was still plenty of time for me to get myself into trouble. In this respect I never, ever wasted a minute and as the battles got harder, so did I. Despite my persona in the classroom and in the church hall, my natural setting was and always had been 'head case', and unfortunately no amount of outdoor activity or academia could overshadow that. 'A loose cannon' was how one teacher once referred to me and even though I couldn't stand the old bugger he'd hit the nail on the head.

Fortunately, there was still one final saving grace that took up just enough of that spare time to keep me out of the correction centres. It's something I became obsessed with for a while and am still good at to this day, although given the size of me you might not think so. That something is swimming and for a while I was one of the country's brightest young hopes. As well as setting records here, there and everywhere, and winning loads of gold medals, I was tipped as being a future Olympian. Sadly, my slightly wayward personality and inability to conform – or in other words, my big gob – prevented me from taking it as far as it could have gone and I think it's something my parents still regret.

According to Mum, I first started swimming way back in 1990 on one of our treasured holidays to Portugal. Back then, during the last two weeks in June, there was something called the Potters' Fortnight, which was Stoke's version of the Wakes Week holiday, and Grandad and Grandma had treated us all to a fortnight away. This would have been our very first holiday as a family and even though I was just two years old I was already trying to emulate my brothers in the pool. They were both good swimmers and in order to match them I would first have to become armband-free. To me this wasn't a problem but to Mum it was, and every time I jumped into the swimming pool and ripped them off she would scoop me out and put them back on again. This battle of aquatic attrition went on for absolutely ages – it happened about twenty times, apparently – until eventually Mum just said, 'Right then, you. I've had enough of this. Sink or swim.' And apparently, I swam. Well, I say I swam. It was probably more of a doggie paddle really, but it was a start.

Mum's actually a qualified swimming instructor and although she's taught one or two kids who've been able to swim at two, it definitely wasn't the norm. I don't think it was natural ability that enabled me to stay afloat, although that did come into effect later on. Instead the main impetus definitely came from a desire to catch up with my brothers. But what's more significant to the present day, and in particular to becoming a strongman, is that I managed to do it all on my own. Working things out for myself and being a self-starter have been the foundations on which I have been able to build my career as a strongman and that self-contained attitude was as important to me as a kid as it is today.

Swimming, as well as being my hobby, was the only sport I was ever interested in as a child. In fact, it was my life. Even when I was just five years old I remember seeing all the other kids running home after school and while they were all sitting around playing on their PlayStation eating cornflakes I'd be down the pool for an hour and a half swimming my arse off. Up and down I went, night after night after night. It didn't matter what the weather was like or what was on TV, swimming was all I thought about. I still turned into a savage again the moment I left the pool but for as long as I was in the water the people of Newcastle could walk about in relative safely.

Although I was part of a club from the age of five, I started competitive swimming from the age of about eight. Once again I took it all very, very seriously and always made sure that I learned from my experiences. I remember missing lunch once for some reason one day and although the difference wasn't massive I was definitely below par at training, so from then on I made sure that I never missed a meal. Following on from that I started watching what I ate, so even at eight and nine I was eating and training like an athlete. Or at least like I thought an athlete should. I remember reading interviews with Mark Foster and the more I read the more obsessed I became and the more obsessed I became the more I started altering my behaviour. I didn't tell my parents or my swimmimg teacher about this. I just got on with it. The first thing I did each morning after getting out of bed was a ten-minute stretch, which Mark Foster had said was important for mobility. Well, if it was good enough for Mark, it was good enough for me. I'm not sure why I didn't want anybody else to know but I remember teaching myself to stretch very, very quietly. It isn't possible for me to do anything by halves and because of my obsessive nature and relentless determination to improve that always put me ahead of the game.

Once again, one of the main motivations in me becoming the next Mark Foster was that desire to beat my brothers; they were both really good competitive swimmers so I threw myself into yet another self-induced war of sibling attrition. By this point I don't think James and Alex could have given a toss about our sibling rivalry but I'm afraid I wasn't letting go quite so easily. Looking back, my obsession was probably bordering on being unhealthy. I certainly don't regret it because it's helped me get where I am, but I've never met anybody as obsessed with coming first as me. Even then I never, ever needed motivating. Everything came from within.

I think the advantage of having two older brothers for heroes is that the ultimate goal of becoming as good as them was always attainable. You don't get that with the David Beckhams of this world. That kind of hero is almost untouchable really, and getting to where they are is always difficult to envisage. My two idols were usually in their bedrooms, farting and carrying on.

I remember going to training sessions with my brothers and some other lads and if I didn't win every single length I'd go off on one. Sometimes I'd cry and sometimes I'd shake with anger. I was even physically sick once; that was how much it meant to me. It would just make me try harder and as soon as I got home I'd run upstairs to my bedroom and work out what I had to do to improve. For a young lad I was ridiculously focused, if a little bit unstable!

I started winning races at the club almost from day one and the euphoria I felt when people congratulated me was like nothing I'd ever experienced before. All somebody had to say was 'Well done, Eddie' and I'd be floating on air. Whoever said it would get a mile-wide smile and that alone would give me enough impetus to want to win again. I mean *really* want to win. Nothing I have ever drunk, eaten or smoked before has ever had such a dramatically pleasing effect and I can't see that ever changing. There's something very life-affirming about making people happy.

Competitive swimming played a big role in making me who I am today, and I can honestly say I loved it. Unfortunately, though, I also had the little matter of school to attend to. My primary school years were coming to an end and now high school was rearing its ugly head on the horizon. But first, a little holiday ...

CHAPTER 5
The School of Hard Knocks

A few months before I started at high school we went on a two-week family holiday to Kenya. Yes, you heard right. Although we lived on a nice street we were probably the ones with the least amount of money, and while everyone was driving around in Mercs and the like we still had our clapped-out Austin Montego. What a shitheap that was! But it was all a case of priorities: instead of Mum and Dad spending their hard-earned cash on a new car, which my brothers and I would only have ended up wrecking, they decided to take us away to nice places and make some memories.

Kenya, though. That was a very different ball game and I was ridiculously excited when they told us. The reason I'm mentioning it is because – as well as it being the best holiday we ever had as a family – it also taught me a life lesson that, if I'm totally honest, gave me a much-needed kick up the arse.

What happened was this. While we were out in Africa we were invited by our rep, who was Kenyan, to play football at one of the local schools and afterwards somebody handed me a packet of sweets. Within about two seconds I had a hundred hands in my face and a few seconds after that, no sweets. At the time I was a bit angry and complained to the person who'd handed them to me.

'Hey,' I said to him. 'I didn't have one of those sweets.'

Straightaway he looked at me as if I was stupid. 'They weren't for you,' he said. 'They were for them.'

Like most kids who are brought up in places like the UK, I was full of my own self-importance but that changed the way I thought and made me pull my head out of my arse. Apparently the world didn't revolve around me after all. It was a small incident but it made a big impression on me.

This wasn't the only experience that created a lasting memory for me on that holiday. While we were there we went on safari and saw elephants, lions and giraffes in the wild, but the highlight for me actually happened at a zoo. We were in the reptile house and one of the keepers told me to cup my hands and hold them out. Then he handed me an egg.

'Be very, very careful with it,' he said. 'If you keep it warm, it might hatch.'

'What's inside it?' I asked him.

'It's a crocodile,' he said.

Just then the bloody egg began to hatch and within about thirty seconds I had a newborn crocodile lying in the palm of my hand! Things like that don't happen in Stoke. Although I did have a dead rat thrown at me once.

Anyway, I can't avoid high school any longer so we may as well crack on with it.

Somebody asked me the other day if, after leaving primary school, I felt ready to go to high school, and I replied, 'Is anybody ever ready?' Going from being top dog to the lowest of the low is hard to take and in my case the thought of starting all over again *and* being in education for another five years filled me with dread. The inspirational Mr Stirland had a new batch of idiots to teach and my new place of learning made Friarswood Primary look like a Swiss finishing school. The importance of learning hadn't left me yet but I hated my new high school. I thought it was dog rough.

When I started at high school, James was in Year Nine and if he hadn't been there I would have been in a lot of trouble. Kids in the older years were always picking fights with the biggest guys in the years below and I would have been just what they were looking for. James, who had a fierce reputation but did very well in class, prevented that from happening, which meant I could crack on and make some new friends. These, not surprisingly, were all the kids who used to get caught smoking and that became the status quo for the entire time I was there. Although I wasn't much of a smoker myself, I did enjoy the odd spliff and for the first couple of years at high school – that is, when I was around eleven and twelve

– I did little else. Even after school, the first thing we'd do was go straight to the park to get wasted, which was daft really because that wasn't me at all. I did it partly because it was something I wanted to experience but the main reason was because I was desperate to fit in. These were the people I'd chosen to hang out with and, as mad as it might sound, I gave them exactly the same commitment I'd given to training. I got stuck in! I was also the alpha male, remember, and was naturally compelled to lead from the front. There were one or two kids who were slightly taller than me in class but because of my endeavours in the swimming pool I was built like the proverbial brick shithouse and had already been the proud owner of a six-pack for about four years. I must have been at least five foot eleven inches when I started at high school so aesthetically I had the same physical attributes as an adult; I was just broader-shouldered and generally thinner.

A few years previously, while I was at Friarswood Primary, some of the pupils accused me of taking performance enhancing drugs because I was so ripped. The name-calling went on for weeks on end but to me it was simply a tribute to what I'd achieved. Every time one of them shouted something I just smiled my well-developed little arse off. They thought I needed to take drugs to look like I did and that made me feel unique. I remember thinking, *Fucking right, mate, I am something special!*

It's often been said, usually in a negative way, that people who are driven can be quite narcissistic. But I think it's a requirement rather than a trait and it doesn't necessarily mean you're a prick. Do I have an excessive interest in myself and my physical appearance, which, according to the dictionary, are the attributes that signify a narcissist? Well, of course I do, and have done from a very early age. My body and my personality are my livelihood, though, so it's no different from a greengrocer harping on about how great his shop is.

The best two examples I can think of with regards to people who have made this characteristic work for them are Muhammad Ali and the aforementioned Arnold Schwarzenegger.

I remember watching Arnold Schwarzenegger's film *Pumping Iron* many moons ago. It's a docudrama that follow's Arnie's journey to the 1975 Mr Olympia competition, which was being held in South Africa. I first saw it at the age of eleven and it made a huge impression on me. In the film, Arnie openly uses psychological warfare to intimidate his opponents and get under their skin. He had decided to go public as a narcissist and so instead of just being quietly confident like the other contenders he started broadcasting it to anyone who'd listen. I was completely flabbergasted by the way he spoke to people. Another one who plays similar kinds of mind games is José Mourinho. Providing you're as good as you say you are – and he, Ali and Arnold most certainly are – you have a good chance of making it work for you. OK, so you might make one or two enemies, but in actual fact the only real enemies you make are the people who you defeat, so in my opinion it's a job well done.

So by the age of eleven I was already an arrogant little bastard with an allegation of taking performance enhancing drug abuse to my name. Watching Arnold Schwarzenegger made me fall in love with being in love with myself, if that makes sense, and it's now a big part of who I am.

This insight is all fairly retrospective, by the way, as I only found out what a narcissist was a couple of years ago. Somebody called me one on social media one day and when I looked it up in the dictionary I was cock-a-fucking-hoop. I didn't reply to the prat who posted it but I remember thinking, *On the fucking nail, dickhead.* The fact that he'd called me a narcissist meant that I'd got to him in some way and that just made me happy.

It's the narcissists with no self-awareness who are the ones who annoy people and gyms are absolutely full of them. The lads with a fake tan and the Gucci vest and trainers who only train their chest and biceps. We all know a few of them and the chances are there might be one or two reading this book. Well, if you are one of those hitherto oblivious narcissists, stop being a twat and start making it work for you. And give over with the fake tan. You look like an idiot!!

Anyway, back to high school (if we must). Even though I didn't like the place and was in with the wrong crowd I still managed to utilise some of my academic potential and without trying I again managed to force myself into the top set for every single subject. I was also the class clown and so even in class all I did was dick around. Once again this vexed the arse off the poor devils who had to strive to achieve academic excellence and when their frustrations came to the fore I used to enjoy perfecting my cockiness on them. They used to get so worked up, bless them.

'Oi, Eddie. You misbehave, dick around and call everyone a twat, yet you're in all the top sets. How the hell do you do it?'

'Natural talent, mate. Some of us have it, and some of us don't. Actually, quite a few of you don't.'

This was my apprenticeship for becoming the man I am today. Fortunately, it's something you can never perfect which means you can always enjoy trying.

I felt really let down by some of my teachers at my high school. Not all of but enough were able to rid me of any remnants of enthusiasm or aptitude I may have had. In some of my more benevolent moments I have tried to persuade myself that they might have had their enthusiasm knocked out of them by teaching unruly kids for years but some of them seemed to enjoy putting pupils down. Actually, there were two in particular who, if I saw them in the street today, I'd have to stop myself from punching them in the back of the head. They seemed to go out of their way to make my life a misery and for a time they were very successful. They were always putting me down and it was as if they wanted me to fail. They know who they are and if either of them are reading this, thanks for the contribution and I hope you paid full price!

Bright or not, I still had plenty of wobbles in my early years at high school but was kept on the straight and narrow, or

my unique version of the straight and narrow, by an exasperated supply teacher who I could tell wanted to kill me. He
was quite calm normally, which was a novelty, and had short
dark hair and a beard. Hands up, I admit I behaved like an
absolute dick for this man but for the first few lessons he said
nothing and just glared at me. I didn't do anything especially
bad, by the way, it was just the usual clowning around. There
is such a thing as having too much of a good thing though
and at the end of what must have been the fourth or fifth
lesson with him he asked me to stay behind. I was obviously
quite used to this and as he was only a supply teacher and not
one of our regulars I was expecting a quick reprimand. How
wrong can you be!

When the last pupil bar me had left the classroom he got
up, shut the door, walked over to where I was sitting and
proceeded to tear me a brand-new arsehole. The language he
used was even worse than mine and as he prodded me in the
chest I could tell by the look in his eyes that all he wanted
to do was take me by the scruff of the neck and shake me
until my head fell off. Fortunately for me he just carried on
prodding but what really held my interest was the fact that
the words coming out of his mouth belied his physical slight-
ness. He didn't seem remotely intimidated. 'What the fuck are
you doing?' he said. 'Seriously, Eddie, what the fuck are you
doing? Why are you making my life a misery and why are you
acting like a dick? You do realise by acting like this you're
fucking up everyone else's chances, don't you?'

At first I was really taken aback. I'd had teachers swear at me before but never so vociferously. I had it in my head at the time that I wanted to be a swimmer when I left school and so I didn't bother applying myself to my schoolwork at all. I was convinced I'd be going to the Olympics or whatever so I didn't really give a shit. This was my answer when he asked me if I realised what I was doing.

'You honestly think you're going to make a living from being a swimmer, Eddie,' he said. 'OK, so what if it doesn't work out? What if you get injured? What are you going to do then?'

I just shrugged when he said that, but it was definitely hitting home.

'You cannot rely on something as tenuous as swimming, Eddie, and do you know why I'm telling you this? Because you're obviously a really bright kid and if you stopped being a prat for just one second and decided to knuckle down a bit you could have a go at being a swimmer with a plan B in place. You've only got one chance, Eddie. Don't fuck it up.'

Since becoming a strongman I've been on the end of some astonishing inspirational talks, usually from my mate and fellow strongman, Rob Frampton, and this had exactly the same effect. A lot of other kids would have reported him for swearing and being a bit physical but this bloke was going out of his way to make a positive difference to my future and my God, his words hit home.

I don't even know this bloke's name, more's the pity, but I came out of that classroom a changed kid. OK, I didn't become a prefect overnight or anything, but I did knuckle down a bit for a while and tried to stop buggering up everyone else's chances. I must admit it was hard as I enjoyed making people laugh but from that day I had learned what was more important.

The subject I enjoyed and excelled at most was maths and it's something that has paid dividends as a strongman. A lot of the other kids used to hate it and could never understand its relevance but to me it seemed obvious. If somebody said, 'Why do we have to learn about angles on a triangle?' I'd reply, 'Because if you're an architect you need to be able to work out how high a roof needs to be.' That's obviously quite a crude example, but you get my drift. Maths made sense to me and it's added real value to my life as a strongman.

Today I use it for things like degrees and leverage, but in addition to that it helps me with calorie counting and working out the lengths of bars. The one that impresses people most is being able to convert pounds to kilograms, or vice versa. I don't need a calculator. It's just pops up in my head and I can do it in a flash.

568 lb = 257 kilos

See!

So if there are any aspiring strongmen or strongwomen reading this, for heaven's sake, make sure you knuckle down and get your GCSEs. You won't regret it.

CHAPTER 6

A (Swimming) Star in the Making

By the time I was twelve years old (and twelve stone) I was actually in quite a good place for a change. I was doing well at school, I'd cut down on my cannabis intake and was even having fewer fights. This would have been the same time that peace broke out between me and my brothers and to top it all off, my swimming career was coming along very nicely.

That supply teacher's lecture had had a very strange snowball effect on my mindset because the confidence I'd gained from working hard at school, and creating a safety net for if the swimming went tits up, actually gave me even more confidence in the pool. This allowed me to relax more and helped me to perform better. It was a proper paradox all right, but one that I gratefully accepted.

The only people who were suffering on my behalf now were my parents – but just for a change it was down to something I was doing right, as opposed to any misdemeanours. I was now completely dedicated to swimming, which meant they were having to take me training at all hours, and because they had such punishing jobs I could tell that it was killing them. Neither of them ever complained but I remember glancing over at them sometimes as we drove towards the swimming pool and they looked exhausted. The most punishing of these sessions started at 5.30 a.m., which meant we had to be up and out by 5 a.m. I wasn't especially happy about this either but it was purgatory to Mum and Dad.

The dedication required by young competitive swimmers is obviously significant but the same could also be said for the parents. Fancy giving up almost every bloody weekend just so your kid can go swimming. You can't really get pissed the night before a competition because the chances are you'll have to drive to God knows where at silly o'clock in the morning and then once you're there you'll be sat on your arse twiddling your thumbs for hours on end. It's a seriously hard life and because the sport's so popular and competitive, only a tiny, tiny fraction of young hopefuls make it to the Nationals, which is short for the National Age Group Championships. At the time that was my own personal ambition and even though I stood a good chance of qualifying there was no way it was going to be at the expense of my parents' sanity. I'd caused them enough grief over the years and it was about time I started paying back some of their love and dedication.

I think I'd just finished watching *The Terminator* again for what must have been about the fifteenth time and, feeling pumped-up and inspired as I always did by the end, I found

Mum and Dad and told them I had an announcement to make. God only knows what they thought I was going to say. I'd already nearly given Mum a heart attack by borrowing Dad's hair clippers and giving myself a Mohican (school were not happy!) and I think she thought I'd had something pierced or, worse, had a tattoo done. Me, have a tattoo or get something pierced? What a ridiculous suggestion.

Once I'd got Mum and Dad together I informed them of my plans.

'From now on I'm going to make my own way to training in the morning and I'll do the same for the evening session. Oh yes. And I'm going to win every single freestyle event at the 2001 Nationals.'

As statements go this was bold to say the least but Mum and Dad hardly batted an eyelid. They knew exactly how good I was and, in my own self-assured little mind, attaining the required qualifying times would be a mere formality.

Sure enough, I managed to qualify for every single race – the 50m, 100m, 200m, 400m and the 1500m – and my God, did I train for it. The regime was three and a half hours a day, five days a week, with competitions at weekends. As fit and driven as I undoubtedly was, it was damn hard work.

After getting up at 5 a.m. I'd cycle into Newcastle town centre, which was about two miles, and do a full-on ninety-minute session. Then, in the evening, I'd make the same journey again and do another two hours. My coach was a man called Arnold Faulkner who was the Head Coach at

Newcastle Swimming Club. He must have been in his fifties when I first got to know him and he had short grey hair and wore glasses. The best way of describing Arnold back then in terms of personality was firm but fair and he was the person who taught me the importance of consistency. He didn't get through to everyone though and I remember there were two other swimmers in the group who, for whatever reason, only used to turn up to the morning sessions once or maybe twice a week. While this understandably exasperated Arnold it used to infuriate me, as even though I cycled in I never missed a session. So to try and teach them a lesson, and to make them feel inadequate, I began playing games with them. Whenever they did turn up for the morning session I'd allow them to beat me, which obviously lulled them into a false sense of superiority. Then, come the weekend and the competitions, I'd completely annihilate them. They were obviously a bit miffed by this but as opposed to doing something about it they just stood there looking like dickheads week after week and carried on turning up when they wanted.

I think Arnold was secretly pleased that these lads didn't always turn up because if ever I needed an illustration of the rewards that consistency brings, that was it. Being a budding alpha male also meant that I was forever looking for opportunities to prove myself over the next man, and in that respect, it was manna from heaven. But by far the best part of training for the Nationals, or just training in general really, was feeling myself improve. What a fucking thrill that was, and still is! Back then I obviously had fewer distractions so the feelings of euphoria it gave me were very, very pure and in the run-up to the 2001 Nationals they were my lifeblood. These days it's slightly different because there are so many different factors to consider, such is the pressure of being a professional sportsman, but it still gives me a massive high. If I hadn't been so driven and confident it wouldn't have felt nearly as good because it wouldn't have meant as much, so discovering what was at the end of the rainbow was a very, very nice surprise. The ultimate reward, I suppose.

Arnold was actually the one who put the idea in my head about making my own way to training. The reason he suggested it was because one morning neither Mum or Dad had been able to take me in for some reason and, instead of getting on my bike or catching a bus, I skipped the session. The next time I saw him, Arnold said to me, 'You could make that problem go away if you cycled in. What do you think, Eddie?' This immediately got me thinking about what it was doing to Mum and Dad and a week or so later I made my announcement.

As well as being a very shrewd motivator, Arnold inspired absolute trust in me. If he said swim 100 metres in fifty-five seconds, I would swim 100 metres in fifty-five seconds, and then, if he said swim it in a minute, I'd swim it in a minute. In different circumstances, I might have questioned some-body for asking me to post a slower time, but because it was Arnold I never did. At the end of every training session he'd get us all together for a chat and whatever instructions he gave us became gospel to me. If he said we weren't drinking enough fluids, I'd start drinking more immediately and then turn up to the next session with a two-litre bottle of water in my hand; partly because I wanted to impress him, if I'm being honest, but mainly because I trusted him and relied on him to help me improve.

This might sound slightly conceited to some but because I was Arnold's star pupil, certainly with regards to commitment, but also ability and potential (OK, that does sound conceited!), I'm pretty sure he started building the training sessions around me, for the simple reason he thought I stood the best chance of success. I don't know if any of the other kids noticed it but I did. He knew he was backing a winner.

CHAPTER 7
Game Plan Emerges in Pool

Remember in one of the previous chapters I explained how I was inspired by Schwarzenegger's narcissistic persona in *Pumping Iron*, and how I started to try my own hand at projecting self-belief and unsettling my opponents? These mind games – i.e. behaviour that winds up the competition and gives me a mental edge – actually originated at swimming competitions and unfortunately they got me into all kinds of bloody trouble.

Visually, I already stuck out like a sore thumb because of my Mohican and as well as being an above-average swimmer I was also the best-looking. Easily the best-looking! Even so, this still wasn't enough for me so, as I'd done with the lads who used to skip the morning sessions, I started having some fun with my competitors. The main difference was that instead of just pissing off a couple of dickheads for a laugh like I had before, I did it because A) I wanted to fuck with my opponents' heads and gain an advantage, just like

Arnold and Ali, and B) because I was a show-off who not only enjoyed being the centre of attention but loved making people laugh. Actually, there's a C too. As you know, I also had a problem with conforming, so if an opportunity ever arose to stick two fingers up at the establishment I would grab it by the neck and shake it until I'd pissed off as many people as I could. I was the scourge of competitive swimming for a while. Seriously!

When it came to unsettling my opponents, I took my cue from Arnie. I always employed a three-pronged attack that would take place before, during and after a race and because I always won, the kids having to race me gradually became demoralised. With their performances becoming poorer, I soon became invincible.

As we lined up before a race I'd start shouting things like, 'This is going to be fucking easy,' which none of them used to like. Then, just for a bit of fun, I'd start shadow boxing and making Tarzan calls. This was the clincher really because all of a sudden, their attention was on me instead of the forthcoming race, which meant that mentally I already had them in the palm of my hand. Once the race had started, I'd always keep a metre or so behind the leaders, which made them all extremely nervous. And then, right at the last minute, I'd speed up and finish them off. The moment these also-rans were out of the pool I'd be on them, saying things like, 'I told you. Absolutely no chance, mate!' The poor fuckers didn't know what had hit them.

I'm obviously not as blasé as that these days but I still like to put my gob to good use and am more than happy to give someone the finger halfway through an event if I fancy it; partly to remind them I'm there, of course, but also to let them know that they're about to lose. People just don't know how to react to that kind of behaviour and long may that continue. Some individuals hate me for it, but they're just the people who let it get to them most. They're my prey, I suppose.

Despite the gamesmanships being a little bit unorthodox it was all within the rules and so there was bugger all anybody could do about it. I was wanted in several counties by various different kids, parents and officials, but that meant it was having the desired effect and so I just carried on. Not one of them had ever experienced anybody like me before. The thing that stopped anybody from complaining, I think, was that they all knew I was the best. If anyone had decided to kick up a fuss it would have seemed like jealousy or sour grapes. It was bordering on genius when you think about it because I was just a kid. Arnold Schwarzenegger may have been my inspiration but I still had to put meat on the bones, so to speak, and it all happened very naturally.

When it came to acting the fool, that was even more contentious, but instead of breaking any actual rules it was more a case of me forgetting things like common decency. Allow me to explain.

While at a big swimming gala in Wolverhampton one day I was standing in a room at the top of the building next to the scoreboard and quickly noticed that, whenever the scores went up, everyone down below looked up in unison. The room I was in had a viewing area and so, in addition to me being able to see the crowd, they could all see me. This gave me an idea. After the next race when the scores were about to go up I got as close to the scoreboard as I could. Then, about a second before the scores went up, I turned around and pulled a moonie. I might not have been able to see the reaction to me showing my arse to the great and the good of the West Midlands swimming fraternity (although I wish I could), but I could most certainly hear it and it was exactly as you'd expect.

Unfortunately for me and our team, the president of the Amateur Swimming Association was in town that day and within about ten minutes of me pulling down my trunks the entire team had been threatened with disqualification. Personally I thought that was a bit OTT but you know what these official types are like. No sense of humour! Fortunately for everyone concerned, my coach Arnold was as proficient in acts of diplomacy as he was recognising talent in the pool, so thanks to him disaster was averted. I still don't know how I would have reacted had the president of the ASA followed through with his threat because I'd always got away with being mischievous. It wouldn't have ended well though and knowing me I'd have either given him a repeat performance or turned around and shown him the other side. I had a habit of doing that too, I'm afraid.

The escapade that got the biggest laugh happened at another swimming gala and involved me borrowing a garment from a young lady. Whenever I made my way to the pool at a gala the first thing I did was look for my parents (all kids do it) but on this particular occasion I was keener than ever to spot them. This was because, unlike all the other competitors, I was wearing a bathrobe. When Mum and Dad saw me wearing it they looked absolutely terrified, and with good reason. They knew I was up to something but obviously had no idea what it was. Mum's told me later that her biggest fear was that I had nothing on underneath and when I was called onto the blocks she and Dad had already made their way to the aisle seats so they could make a quick getaway if need be.

When my name was eventually called out I slowly and provocatively undid the bathrobe to reveal that I was wearing Becky Dulson's swimsuit. Becky was a team mate of mine and because she had a spare swimsuit with her that day I had asked if I could borrow it. The entire place erupted when I finally took off the bathrobe but I don't think anybody was particularly surprised. I was famous for pulling stunts like that and I think that, like Mum, they were just relieved I wasn't bollock naked. That's still an ambition of mine, though. If you ever see me at a strongman event dressed in a bathrobe, run like fuck.

I kept the swimsuit on, by the way, and won the race easily, which probably prevented me from getting into trouble. It was just another normal day at the pool really.

Talking of putting the wind up my parents, which I've actu-ally turned into a bit of an art over the years, it was about this time that I got my nipple pierced and once again I chose to break it to them with as much drama as I could muster.

I'd already asked them both if I could have my ears pierced but they'd said I wasn't allowed until I was sixteen and had left school. As it turned out I ended up leaving school well before I was sixteen (or was I pushed? You'll find out soon enough), but even though I'd been banned from having my ears pierced, nobody ever said anything about nipples. It was quite fashion-able then and so just for a laugh I got it done one day while I was out on the piss with some mates. It hurt like hell though! After that, at swimming, I'd had to wear a plaster over my nipple and Mum had asked me once or twice what was wrong. 'Oh, nothing,' I fibbed. 'I just caught it on something.' Well, I had caught it on something. A bloody piercing machine!

A few days later, Mum was in the kitchen on her own one afternoon and so before Dad got home I thought I'd break it to her so that she could tell him later on my behalf.

'Mum,' I said shiftily. 'You know you said I couldn't have my ears pierced?'

Once again, the look on Mum's face represented the horror of things to come, or things she *thought* were to come, and as I slowly began taking my T-shirt off she stood there looking at me through squinted eyes.

'What have you done?' she said. 'Please tell me it's not a tattoo!'

'It's worse than that,' I said, trying to wind her up even more.

Once the nipple ring was revealed, Mum let out groan. 'Oh my good God!' she said. 'Don't tell your dad. He'll go mad!'

As it turned out, Dad didn't go mad at all so it was all a bit of an anti-climax. They were obviously saving their outrage up for when I got my tattoos.

When Arnold and I eventually travelled to Ponds Forge in Sheffield for the 2001 Nationals I don't mind admitting that, inside at least, I was absolutely bricking it. I was still super-confident and shockingly arrogant but it was like going into the unknown and that was seriously daunting. Also, I don't think I'd ever been pitched against the best of the best in anything before and so this was the ultimate test for me. It was the ultimate test for everyone, I suppose.

It's no exaggeration to say that in order to get to the National finals you have to beat, or be better than, literally tens of thousands of kids and whoever ultimately triumphs is the best our country has to offer in their category and age group. That is one serious accolade when you think about it and fortunately for me the size of the prize far outweighed the anxiety I was feeling. Arnold also reminded me that everybody there would be anxious and that also made a difference. What made the biggest difference though was that I knew, in my heart of hearts, that I was the most talented swimmer in the building. Other people obviously didn't believe that but who cared what they thought? I believed it and Arnold believed it, and by the time I was called to the blocks for my first race I was ready to give my opponents the aquatic equivalent of a right good kicking.

Sure enough, an hour or so later I was the proud owner of four golds medals, a silver medal and two – count 'em – two new British records. The results were as follows:

50m freestyle, 26:43 – 1st
100m freestyle, 57:01 – 1st
200m freestyle, 2:04 – 2nd
400m freestyle, 4:19.02 – 1st
1500m freestyle, 17:31.86 – 1st

The only reason I didn't win the 200m is because my arm touched one of the ropes and that cost me about half a second. Otherwise, I'd have been able to keep my original promise to Mum and Dad and win the lot. Never mind, though. Four out of five wasn't bad for a first attempt, he said modestly.

At the time, I actually remember trying to blame Mum for the silver, but she wasn't having any of it. For breakfast that morning she'd given me something different to what I usually had and as a self-confessed creature of habit who found it hard to accept that he may have made a mistake, I pointed the finger at Mum's last-minute catering alteration. I forget exactly what she said to me but it definitely ended with 'off'.

Winning four golds and a silver at the same championship was as rare as rocking-horse shit but what was even more remarkable was that times I triumphed with were faster than many of the older age groups. The icing on the cake though, if my memory serves me correctly, was hearing that my time of 26:43 in the 50m had beaten the record held by Mark Foster. I'd beaten my hero. Actually, I think I'd thrashed him!

If I was a confident young lad going in to the 2001 Nationals, I was felt unconquerable coming out. I remember thinking to myself that every single piece of advice Arnold had given me, and everything I'd done to try and better myself, had now been vindicated. There's a photo in this book of me, Arnold and the medals and I never tire of looking at it. What an amazing day.

CHAPTER 8
Putting the Boot into Boot Camp

As is so often way, I soon became a victim of my own success and not long after triumphing at the 2001 Nationals I was selected for what was called the World Class Potential Programme. This was basically a residential boot camp that took place quarterly, which was attended by some of the country's finest young swimmers as well as top-notch coaches who had been flown in from all over the world. Coaches who were used to training Olympians, by the way, as opposed to over-confident, cross-dressing, moonie-pulling trouble-makers with Mohicans.

The person who was most pleased with me being picked for the World Class Potential Programme, apart from Mum and Dad, was Arnold, and that's completely understandable. To him it was the ultimate compliment – a kid he'd trained being earmarked for greatness – whereas to me it was the beginning of the end. From the very moment I enrolled on the programme I was given a new training regime that was to be implemented and overseen by Arnold and to say that I disagreed with the content of the programme would be a gross understatement. In all, I had to swim about 50,000 metres every week but instead of concentrating on swimming freestyle like you'd expect I was spending just as much time swimming backstroke, breast stroke and butterfly – none of which I really enjoyed and none of which were any use to me.

All of a sudden, everything had become very, very serious and business-like and once I began being annoyed by it, I very quickly began to hate it. I remember feeling gutted that things had changed and couldn't for the life of me understand why they'd had to go and spoil it all. Arnold and I had done unbelievably well up to now and we had medals and records to prove it. I obviously appreciate that changes would have to be made in order for me to progress, but because the modifications were so stark, and because it was all done in such a dull, militarised fashion, I decided to go to war.

One of the more light-hearted examples of my belligerence took place at Loughborough University during one of these boot camps and involved a swimming pool that had a viewing area underneath and to the sides, enabling the coaching staff to observe you swimming. Half way through a training session one day I decided to have a bit of fun. Dad was in attendance that morning, although not at the pool, and as the coaches all stood there waiting for me to pass I decided to whip off my trunks (yes, I know, again!) and give them something more interesting to observe. Unfortunately for Dad, the coaches always filmed these training sessions and an hour or so later he was called into one of the offices and shown a film of me basically skinny dipping. Obviously, that embarrassed him somewhat but at the time I couldn't have given two shits.

What upset me most about all this was that Arnold had become completely taken in by the new regime. Once again that's entirely understandable. To him, working with all these Olympic coaches was like hitting the big time but instead of him continuing to be his own man – and a very forceful and independent one at that – he just turned into a puppet for these Olympic pricks.

The boot camps themselves were all run with military precision We always got up at 5 a.m. and after a nice two-hour swim we'd have breakfast. After that we'd do gym work followed by something like yoga and then we'd break for lunch. The afternoons always started with a nice bit of body conditioning and to round off the day you'd have another two-hour swim. It was the same every day, by the way, and the discipline was as military in style as the precision. This, I'm afraid, is why things really started going belly-up. All I wanted to do when I turned up to one of these boot camps was get into a bloody fight. Not a physical fight, but a verbal one. Once again, I don't mind things like rules and discipline, providing you can convince me that they're all there for the greater good. This would have been unthinkable to the coaching staff because as far as they were concerned we were just commodities: teenage swimming machines who were there to work and do exactly as we were told.

They had this system where, if you were late for a training session or a meal or whatever, you were given a black tick and if you got three black ticks you were sent home. I was thirteen years of age when I entered this programme and you don't treat thirteen-year-olds like that, for Christ's sake. Or at least I don't think you should. First of all you earn the respect of the pupils, as Arnold had with me, and then, providing you do a good job of teaching them, you shouldn't need to enforce a load of demeaning and preposterous rules. Having a punishment system like that in place and then ramming it down people's throats all the time means that you're obviously expecting the worst from them and, in my case, that immediately put me on the back foot. Why not show a bit of trust first, and then, if someone does step out of line, have a quick word? It's not rocket science.

These big-time coaches didn't give a toss about my well-being or about who I was or what made me tick. All they cared about was me sticking to a training programme and abiding by the rules. To them I wasn't a human being. I was a potential medal winner who'd help them reach a target. Had I chosen to surrender my character and become one of their robots, the chances are I'd have made it to the Olympics. In fact, I know I would. To me, though, it wasn't worth the sacrifice. Instead of being the plucky self-starter who promised his parents he'd win at the Nationals, I'd have been part of some Olympic production line. Worst of all I'd have been betraying my true self and even if I had won a gold medal at the Olympics I'd have derived no satisfaction from it whatsoever. I really mean that. It doesn't matter how big the prize is, the most important thing is being true to yourself.

When it came to working with Arnold day to day I still went through the motions, but deep down inside I knew that it was all bollocks and so I no longer gave him 100 per cent. I just couldn't. He seemed to be a totally different person to me and thanks to the new training regime every ounce of enjoyment had been stripped away. As opposed to being passionate about my training, Arnold had become almost fanatical. The longer it went on the more distance there was between us.

This first started manifesting itself at the 2002 Nationals at Ponds Forge. I still came away with two golds but because I was now on the World Class Potential Programme and part of the junior elite I'd been expected to at least match last year's performance. The fact that I didn't pissed a lot of people off, not least Arnold. He obviously had to report back to the WCPP and as well as questioning my commitment and ability they may well have questioned his, too.

Unsurprisingly, this resulted in a series of arguments between Arnold and me and as I became more and more uninterested in proceedings, and as Arnold became more frustrated, the arguments got worse.

At the end of a training session Arnold would say, 'Why are you pissing about, Ed? What the hell's up with you?' And I'd reply, 'Well, what the hell's up with you? You've completely changed, Arnold!' It was petty crap really.

One day the inevitable happened and it all came to a head. It was at the end of an afternoon session and after receiving yet another one of Arnold's rollockings I said something I perhaps shouldn't have and then after Arnold had done the same I told him this was no longer for me. The following day I changed swimming clubs from Newcastle to COSACCS, which stands for the City of Stoke on Trent Swimming Club, although you'd never know from the initials! From my first session with COSACCS I immediately fell in love with swimming all over again. The atmosphere was so relaxed and everybody seemed happy.

Me leaving Newcastle was a big kick in the teeth for Arnold as I was obviously his star pupil and even today I feel sorry about the way it ended. If it isn't broken, though, why mend it? Modify it, if you have to, but by making it unrecognisable I'd forgotten where the initial success came from and once that had happened, I was gone.

My coach at COSSACS was a man called Greg Clark, who is still in charge there, and although I never got my edge back in the pool he allowed me to be myself and we had an excellent working relationship. He understood that trying to change me would only ever lead to trouble and he told me that apparently Mark Foster had had a very similar personality. The difference between Mark and me, though, is that there was evidently a limit to his intransigence; where he was prepared to make certain compromises in order to succeed, I was not. In fact, looking back, the only compromise I made during my swimming career was taking my foot off the gas so I could start enjoying the sport again, so in that respect it made me the worst possible kind of competitor.

At about the same time as Arnold and I parted ways I decided to say a fond farewell to the World Class Potential Programme. This was going to be fun.

The person in charge of the World Class Potential Programme was an Australian man called Bill Sweetenham and it's safe to say that he and I never really got on. He was the National Performance Director for the Great Britain swimming team from 2000 till 2007 and he was head of the Argentinian national swimming team for several years until 2014. He was the one who'd come up with all that black tick bollocks and I couldn't stand the man. To me he was the reason I no longer enjoyed swimming and I'd been itching to tell him what I thought of him since the off.

This opportunity to press my self-destruct button eventually arose at one of the boot camps. As usual, not long after we arrived, one of Sweetenham's lackeys came around and gave us all the 'three black ticks and you're out' lecture. There were no words of welcome or encouragement, just threats of what would happen if we didn't toe the line.

After having this read to us yet again something inside me clicked and I thought to myself, *Naah, this isn't for me. As far as I'm concerned you can all go and fuck yourselves.* The button had now been pressed and there was no turning back.

Although some of the other kids there were OK they were all quite posh and so I didn't really click with any of them. On top of that they were all good little boys and girls who'd obviously been beaten into submission and to tell the truth I just felt sorry for them. Being a promising swimmer back then was a very, very miserable existence.

My first act of defiance took place in the hotel we were staying at but the results far exceeded my expectations. I'd decided to spark up a cigarette in my room, knowing full well that somebody would tell the coaches, but instead of hearing a knock at the door and receiving a black tick an alarm went off and the entire hotel had to be evacuated. I remember standing in the car park surrounded by hundreds of people thinking gleefully, *I am in so much fucking trouble!*

Not surprisingly, Sweetenham and his coaching monkeys went absolutely apeshit and so within hours of arriving I'd already been given two black ticks. Two! Why I wasn't sent home there and then amazes me but not long after being given the ticks I had another knock at my door. 'Mr Sweetenham would like to see you in his hotel room now,' said a very stern-looking coach. This was my big opportunity.

'I'll tell you what,' I said. 'Tell that fat twat that he can come and see me.'

Five minutes later I was no longer a member of the World Class Potential Programme and had been removed indefinitely from Mr Sweetenham's Christmas card list. It was sad that it had to end that way but I'd far sooner get kicked out for calling the man who'd spoilt it all a twat than have my parents write him a letter. There was no way I was just going to leave that programme voluntarily. I had to be given the boot.

But before we move on from swimming I just wanted to tell you about one of the more enjoyable experiences I had in a pool, which happened just after my fourteenth birthday. I could have left it with me calling Sweetenham a twat but over the years I've had far more good times than bad in the water and I think I need to emphasise that and not leave the subject on a downer. Incidentally, if there are any budding strength athletes reading this who don't currently swim, then take my advice and do it. The benefits it will have, not just on your performance but on your health in general, are many and varied and if I hadn't had it as a platform there's no way I'd be where I am today. Just make sure you wear the right costume and if anyone tries to piss around with your training routine tell them to do one.

Anyway, back to my happy swimming memory. I'm not sure if it still happens today but every March at Fenton Manor Pool in Stoke they used to hold a 5k swimathon to raise money for charity. If memory serves me correctly it was all part of something national and a few weeks after it had taken place the people with the best times in each category were all invited to a dinner and a presentation. I have no idea how many people took part in the swimathon countrywide, but as it was such a massive event there must have been hundreds or maybe thousands in each category. Because I was back in love with the sport (although not for long), I was well up for it. I didn't train for that distance but I was as fit as a butcher's dog and knew I was more than a match for it.

The time I eventually posted in the thirteen to fifteen age category was one hour, one minute and fifteen seconds and at the risk of sounding like a big-head I completely annihilated the rest of the country. Seriously, that's quick. No other child came close to that time and I'm pretty sure it was the fastest overall. According to one or two swimming websites a 5k swim should take most fitness swimmers between ninety minutes and two hours so that gives you a good idea of how fast it was.

The gala dinner and presentation was held at Butlin's in Minehead and we – as in me, Mum and Dad – had an all-expenses-paid weekend there. I'd never been able to take my parents anywhere before and so being able to treat them was fantastic. Better still, it didn't cost me a penny!

On the Saturday night the Butlin's Redcoats started off proceedings with a big show and then after dinner Duncan Goodhew presented all the awards. I got a photo, of course, which pleased me no end, but it was only at the dinner that I realised how big a deal it was and that made it better still. It was a very proud moment.

One of the primary reasons I wanted to do well at the 5k swimathon was because, just a few weeks previously, my nan had been diagnosed with acute lymphoblastic leukaemia. She was very ill when she started treatment and in all kinds of pain.

This was the first time in my young life that I'd had to deal with the prospect of losing somebody dear to me and the fact that it was Nan made it especially hard to bear. She could always bring out the best in me no matter what the situation, for the simple reason that I knew how much she loved me. Because of this, and because of the amount of pain she was in, I desperately wanted to take Nan's mind off things and at the same time make her proud of me. I knew I could be a pain in the arse sometimes and so wanted to compensate her. I seem to have a habit of doing that!

I think it worked, though, and when Nan found out that I'd won the swimathon she was in floods of tears, and because she was in floods of tears, so was I. Unfortunately Nan was too ill to come to the presentation, but even so, she knew I'd done it for her and that meant everything to me.

CHAPTER 9

Losing My Way (and Finding It)

Despite the successful swimathon, Nan's diagnosis hit me harder than I originally thought and marked the start of what was a difficult couple of years. The worst, in fact. By this point the swimming was starting to go tits up and with that on the wane and Nan being ill I'm afraid I started reverting to my former self. Or should I say, a version of my former self. I was a couple of years older now and instead of just fighting and smoking weed I was now drinking booze like it was going out of fashion and this took the fighting element to a completely different level.

My brothers will bear witness to this but when I started going off the rails I could drink a full bottle of whisky in a single night, no problem. Sometimes more. Because I was so fit, and because I was also a big lad, it didn't affect me as much as it would most people and so in order to get completely off my face and forget about everything I had to down stupid amounts. That was why I did it, because I wanted to block out Nan's diagnosis, and it worked an absolute treat. I'd drink and then slowly but surely everything would seem OK. For a time. The real problem was the volume of sprits I was drinking, and I'm not just talking about the alcoholic volume, although that was definitely a contributing factor. You see, the more I drank the higher my tolerance became and the higher my tolerance became the more I drank. The result of this vicious intoxicating circle was more violence and after a while all I wanted to do was hurt people. For a time I became a seriously fucked-up individual (some people would say I still am!) and, as well as inducing in me some pretty serious bouts of depression and anxiety, the situation also led to some serious injuries.

Probably the worst of these happened about halfway through 2002 and the reason for the fight, I'm now very ashamed to say, was a pair of my brother's stinking trainers. The other person involved was an eighteen-year-old guy who lived near us. He'd nicked my brother's trainers from our doorstep one day and then a few nights later while I was out on the lash he turned up and started bragging about it. 'Hey, your lad's trainers are comfortable,' he laughed, and I remember saying, or slurring, 'Piss off, you creepy fucker.' By this point I'd already had well over a bottle of scotch and although my alcohol tolerance level was high I was now barely able to stand up. Even so, I still offered to fight the weirdo but instead of jumping up and giving him a kicking like I would have if I were sober, I just fell back on my arse. I was bolloxed.

Now I don't remember any of this but this dickhead obviously saw an opportunity while I was drunk and so as I was sitting there out of my head he took a run-up and kicked me full-on in the face. To this day, and this is God's honest truth, he is the only person who has ever got the better of me in a fight and I had to be battered for it to happen.

If somebody takes a run-up at you and toe-punts you in the face – even a soft-arsed prick like that – it's going to make a mess. Sure enough, my face was now far from perfect and as well as having a very badly broken nose, which had to be reconstructed, I also had to have endoscopic sinus surgery so that I could breathe properly. Mum and Dad were not happy, but then I wasn't exactly over the moon. I'd been a pretty good-looking lad until then and for a while afterwards I looked like the Elephant Man.

The one positive thing to come out of 2002 (apart from the swimathon), and it's a pretty significant one when you think about it, was that it was the year I first joined a gym, and no prizes for guessing who my inspiration was. Step right up, Mr Arnold Schwarzenegger. You remember the scene in *The Terminator* sequel when he walks up to those dickheads and says, 'I need your clothes, your boots and your motorcycle.' Well, I was watching that one day when all of a sudden I thought, *I could look like that if I put my mind to it*. This was a genuine defining moment for me and once again I gathered my parents around me so I could announce my intentions.

'Mum, Dad,' I said. 'I'm going to have a body like Arnold Schwarzenegger.' I think I said previously that Mum and Dad never once derided my ambitions and whenever I told them something like this they'd just nod and say, 'OK, son. You'd better crack on with it then.'

The gym I joined was Total Fitness and even though I was fourteen and you weren't supposed to lift weights until you were eighteen I still managed to blag my way in. This was something I became an expert at in my teens. I definitely looked a lot older than I was and because I was tall and broad the gym owners assumed I knew what I was doing. And I did, to a certain extent, because I'd seen people train before. But anything I didn't know I just picked up while I was there. I seemed to click more with adults than I did with kids and everyone was very helpful. Just to put my size into perspective, Dad was about six foot two inches and fourteen stone at the time and I was an inch shorter but the same weight. From the word go I behaved, looked and trained like a fully grown adult and pretty soon I was lifting weights like one. Everything was in place: I had a super-strong heart, a massive lung capacity and there wasn't an ounce of fat on me, and because I was also quite young I put muscle on very easily. I was just built for it.

From a mental point of view this was exactly what I needed and so I gave it my all. You already know there are no half measures with me but going to the gym gave me a purpose in life, and with things like swimming going tits up and school about to do the same I needed a purpose more than ever.

Ah yes, my education. I was hoping you'd forgotten about that.

CHAPTER 10
Downhill to Expulsion

As life outside of school began to deteriorate after Nan's diagnosis, life inside school followed pretty much the same path. It was a mixture, really, of fights, detentions, isolations, suspensions, lunchtime spliffs and lots and lots of bad language. The majority of the isolations and detentions came from telling teachers to fuck off and the suspensions usually resulted from fights. I'd fight anybody, regardless of year, and slowly but surely I helped to create an epidemic. I'm getting a feeling of déjà vu here. Are you? Some of the stuff we did you'd go to prison for these days but back then you could get away with a lot at high school. Or at least you could at ours. I'm certainly not proud of it. In fact, I'm completely and utterly ashamed and always cite my behaviour at school as being the benchmark of how not to live your life.

The environment, as I've already said, wasn't really conducive to getting a good education but I'd already proved that I could rise above that and so the only person to blame for things going tits up was me. I really was a complete dickhead, to be honest, and if I'd been the headmaster I'd have fired me into fucking space. As it was, they only fired me as far as home but it was enough to rid the school of one of its most troublesome pupils.

I was so, so angry though. That is the all-pervading emotion I remember feeling back then and it was as if I'd become possessed. I was the original Mr Angry! When you wake up in the morning the first thing you do is look at the clock, right? Well, when I woke up, the first thing I did was experience a sudden rush of anger and to stop it getting worse I'd have to lie in bed for a few minutes. The worst bit was feeling the veins on the side of my head throbbing and sometimes I honestly thought my head was going to explode. It was terrifying. The more I wanted it to go away, the angrier and more frustrated I became. It was yet another vicious circle.

Nan's diagnosis was definitely the catalyst for my fury but the alcohol and everything else made it much worse. Looking back it was like a series of unfortunate events, culminating in my expulsion from school. First Nan was diagnosed, then the swimming started going belly up. After that I started drinking, which is when the depression and anxiety appeared, and once I started fighting again all hope was lost.

By the way, I should say that Mum and Dad had absolutely no idea that all this was going on. They know now, of course, and they knew about the suspensions from school and the depression; but as far as all the drinking and a lot of the fighting were concerned, they were completely unaware. This isn't because they were bad parents, by the way. Anything but. It's because, like most people with problems or addictions, I became very adept at hiding them and when I eventually told Mum and Dad what had been going on they were flabbergasted. And upset, it has to be said.

The depression and anxiety would stay with me until my late teens, and you might be surprised when I tell you what finally released me from it. But like a lot of things in my life, it was something I felt I had to deal with on my own (I did take Prozac for a while but it made me feel worse) and for a lad in his mid-teens with more issues than a soap opera, that was no mean feat. The anxiety was crippling at times. I would be assailed by an overwhelming feeling that everything in my life was going wrong, and because there was so much backing up the idea that this was actually the case, the anxiety very quickly span out of control.

The depression, though. That was something far more disturbing. It first started manifesting itself when I began having thoughts about being shit and worthless. Fairly textbook, I suppose. Then, as they became a regular fixture, I started having thoughts about killing myself. Sometimes I could barely move it was so bad and I've never cried so much in my entire life. Whenever I thought about my nan a feeling of desperation would hit me like a truck. Then, as that began to subside, sadness would take over. That's when the crying would start, followed by the suicidal thoughts. Third in line would be anger and after that it would be booze, fights and trouble.

Just when I thought that things couldn't get any worse I went out one night, got pissed, pulled a girl and ended up getting her pregnant. What an absolute twat! When she told me I was completely devastated and it amplified the depression and anxiety ten-fold. All I did during this time was cry, drink and fight, and as far as my thinking mind was concerned any hopes of me having a bright future had disappeared. Gone forever, and all because of a drunken shag.

Eventually both mine and the girl's families met up and it was decided that the best thing for everyone concerned would be a termination. It's not my proudest moment by any stretch of the imagination but because of where I was at the time mentally and what it might have done to me had it gone ahead, it was definitely the right thing to do. More importantly, though, the girl involved was only my age and far too young to become a mother.

The relief I felt once that was sorted out was deep and it actually gave me a platform to recover, although only a very small one. In any case, because of my self-belief, and maybe even my narcissism, I never took the suicidal thoughts seriously enough to act on them. Deep down I guess I always knew there was hope. Come on, what would the world do without me, for heaven's sake? I don't mind admitting, though, that the depression and anxiety absolutely flattened me and if I hadn't had that intrinsic self-belief bubbling away underneath all the alcohol and the suicidal thoughts I might well have ended up travelling to a much darker place. Thank God I'm a bighead!

Chapter 10

Anyway, I know you're dying to find out how I got expelled, so without any further ado, let's crack on.

There was this lad at school. I can't really tell you what he's called but even his name still makes my temples twitch! Although he was as big as me he was a right flabby fucker and I absolutely detested him, and him me. There were two reasons for this: first, he was a massive bully and used to go around smacking up geeks, and second, we were seen as the two hardest lads in the school, and as you know I do not like sharing titles. It was the bullying that used to piss me off the most. I'm not saying I was perfect by any means, but I would only ever fight people who were up for it or who mouthed off and I certainly didn't go around attacking geeks. The lad was a complete coward and if there's one thing I hate more than flabby fuckers who think they're hard, it's flabby fuckers who attack geeks. It's not on, pal!

The longer this went on, the more I wanted to hurt this prick. So eventually I devised a plan where I could get him on his own and teach him a lesson.

It was snowing at the time and the plan was for one of my mates to throw a snowball at this lads and then run off into the woods. Sensing an opportunity to hit somebody smaller than him, he would then follow my mate, hoping to catch him. Ha, ha! No chance. Once he was in the woods I would then appear from behind a tree and challenge him to a scrap. Easy really.

These sorts of things don't always go according to plan but on this particular occasion it went like a dream. Or a

88

nightmare, for one flabby fucker. My mate threw the snow-ball at this lad and hit him on the back on the head. He then chased my mate into the woods, I appeared and, *voilà*, one scrap waiting to happen. I was so up for this fight it was unreal and after about twenty seconds it all came to an end when I headbutted him and knocked his front teeth out. My only regret was that he didn't put up more of a fight but despite our similarity in size he was wheezing like an asthmatic after a few seconds.

Although the fight took place outside the school it was during the lunch break and so still deemed as being in school time. This meant that one of the first people to hear about it was the headmaster. I knew what was going to happen; it was the final straw. Sure enough, the following day my parents were informed that I'd been expelled and, in a way, I think they were relieved. I certainly was. Mum and Dad knew I had problems and to be honest my head was like a fucking hamster's wheel at that time. The noise was non-stop! In order to complete my GCSEs and not end up in borstal I needed the least number of distractions as possible, not to mention fewer fellow fifteen-year-olds, and so expulsion was actually the best thing for me and definitely the best thing for the school. In fact, I bet they got the bunting out when I walked through the gates for the last time.

As soon as I was expelled from school, some home tuition was arranged and from then until the end of Year Eleven I was basically left to my own devices. I didn't take the piss, though, and when I wasn't being tutored I was usually down the gym. A lot of people assume that home tuition is something either tree huggers or posh people use for their kids, but in the Stoke area circa 2003 it was a luxury reserved mainly for kids who had either been expelled or for kids who had serious issues. Kids like me, basically!

In fact the home tuition worked really well for me and I ended up getting better GCSE grades than any of my friends at school. This was partly down to my tutor, Keith. He's one of that select band of adults I told you about who managed to influence me, and without him I'm not sure I'd have done half as well as I did.

If my parents were around, Keith would come to our house to tutor me but if they weren't we'd have to meet somewhere public. Bearing in mind the kind of kids they were tutoring this rule was probably put in place to protect the tutors rather than the pupils and whenever I did meet Keith in a public place this theory was pretty much borne out. I'd always turn up early which meant I'd see Keith with the pupils he had prior to me and over the months I saw him get screamed at, kicked, punched and spat on. How the hell he put up with it all is something I will never be able to fathom but by the time I sat down he was calm and ready to go. Most people would have murdered the little bastards, and from what I could see they'd have been doing the world a favour.

Because I liked Keith I had no problem working for him, and after seeing him being abused like that I wanted to give the man a break. But it was how he treated me that had the biggest effect and, a bit like that supply teacher, he genuinely seemed to care. Keith obviously knew the background of why I'd been expelled but he never judged me and he never held it against me. What he did do, apart from getting me through my GCSEs, was to say things that rejuvenated me and made me feel positive about the future.

One day after a lesson he said, 'Do you know, Eddie, you're totally different to the other kids I teach. You're polite, well behaved and you've got a brain. You may have a few issues but I have no doubt whatsoever that you will overcome these and become a success.'

I must have had a seventy-four-inch chest after he said that, at least! This wasn't just a script though, or if it was he was a bloody good actor. Keith knew full well that the direction of my life was in the balance and he wanted to do everything he possibly could to push me the right way. I have no doubt whatsoever that he'd have tried doing the same with all the other kids but I also know that, in many cases, he'd have been fighting a losing battle. Kids like me – the ones who were redeemable – were probably the reason he got out of bed in the morning and there was no fucking way I was going to let him down.

CHAPTER 11
Twenty Police, Two Brothers

Thanks to Keith, and a bit of hard work, I came away from full-time education with seven A–C-grade GCSEs including an A in Physical Education and a B in Maths. I hadn't suddenly become a budding academic or a paragon of virtue, but I was now a proud, well-balanced and reasonably well-educated young man who, after some extremely trying times, had gone some way to repaying the efforts of a handful of incredibly special adults: Mum, Dad, Nan, Mrs Mills, Mr Stirland, Keith (sorry for not remembering your surname, Keith), and the supply teacher whose name also unfortunately escapes me. It's all very well having faith in yourself, but having the faith of people you respect and/or love is the umbrella under which it all sits.

By the time I took my GCSEs you could easily have mistaken me for a thirty-year-old man. I was about six foot two inches, sixteen stone, and I had a skinhead, a pierced nipple and scars all over me. I looked as rough as a nut! But because of what had happened over the last couple of years I also had both the personality and the character to match my mature appearance and looking back I definitely benefited from all that independence. Who cares if it was enforced?

Two other things I benefited from back then, and do now, were my parents' work ethic, which has always been impressive, and a morbid fear of being skint. The latter had been with me since high school and – coupled with an entrepreneurial spirit, a bit of nous and a few decent contacts – I took more money from my fellow pupils than the lady working the till in the dinner hall.

I started off by selling cigarettes, which were easy to get hold of, and I'd sell one for 50p. Bearing in mind they were probably about £3 a pack back then that's not a bad mark-up and right from Year Seven I was like a walking tobacconist. 'Two Lambert & Butler? Yeah, OK. That's a quid. Go on then, piss off.' I was like a cross between Del Boy and Charles Bronson.

Once the entrepreneur in me had started coming to the fore I moved on to selling dodgy PlayStation games and was chipping consoles left right and centre. After that I started selling pirate DVDs. In my four and a bit years at high school I must have made thousands.

Despite all the crap going on in my life, this made me realise that there were very few people in the world who were willing, or able, to be the ones who would provide the products and services needed in whatever environment you were in. As well as opening my eyes, it helped me to spot the opportunities.

Now I was out in the big wide world these qualities would be just what I needed and they'd start coming into play in about a year; or, in the case of this book, a page or two. In the meantime, I decided to enrol on a three-year course in electrical engineering at the local college. I'm not entirely sure why I chose electrical engineering, apart from having a vague interest in the subject, and I was planning to explore how I'd use the qualification as I progressed. I had one or two ideas in my head but to be honest the whole thing was a compromise really. I had to do something.

After about three weeks of being a budding electrical engineer I started to lose interest and as well as being bored shitless I could feel the walls closing in around me. There was certainly more freedom at the college than there had been at high school but everything else was the same and pretty soon I hated it. I think I lasted three months in all but by the end I was literally banging the doors down. I felt like I'd been re-institutionalised and I promised myself then that I would never, ever darken the door of full-time education again. I could get by without it, and it could certainly get by without me.

By this point I was hitting the gym quite hard and as I started lifting more, I obviously started eating more and using things like protein supplements, and, as many of you know, these don't come cheap. I hated being dependent on anybody, least of all Mum and Dad, and so I needed to find some money quickly.

Luckily, Mum saw an advert in a local paper one day advertising for an apprentice truck mechanic in a place called Cobridge, and so straightaway I applied. There were two apprenticeships up for grabs, and there were about fifteen applicants in all. This was the first time I'd ever been to a job interview, and although it's not something I particularly enjoyed I felt like it had gone well. I've always had a knack of being able to get on somebody's wavelength pretty quickly. You could put the most boring prat in the world in front of me and I guarantee that within five minutes I'll have found out what makes them tick and will be telling them jokes about stamp collecting or whatever.

I came away from that apprenticeship interview with a bit of a spring in my step and when Mum asked me how it had gone I informed her that I was more than quietly confident. I treated it like a competition, which I suppose it was, and despite not being desperate to become a truck mechanic, I desperately wanted to beat the other applicants. A few days later I received a letter telling me I'd done just that, so a week or two after that I finally made my debut in the world of legitimate employment as an apprentice HGV mechanic at LEX Commercial, Cobridge. It was never going to make me a millionaire but I ended up enjoying it: it was mentally and physically challenging enough to keep me interested and got me used to a routine. With overtime, I'd sometimes work up to fifty hours a week and with the twenty or so I spent in the gym that left little time for socialising. This was actually a godsend, as when I did find time to go out it nearly always ended in – yes, you guessed it – trouble.

As with my transgressions at the swimming boot camps, I could offer you dozens of cringe-worthy examples of my less-than perfect behaviour on the streets of Stoke, but for my mum's sake I'm just going to stick with the one. It's a bloody good one though.

I was still sixteen at the time and because I hadn't been out in a while my brother James suggested that we go out on the piss together. Bearing in mind our temperaments, this probably wasn't the wisest of proposals and we ended up taking on half the Stoke constabulary. We actually did OK, as it goes.

Up until about two in the morning we'd had a really good laugh and hadn't had a sniff of trouble all night. Then, as we were standing outside a nightclub, this bird, who was absolutely shitfaced, started gobbing off at James and calling him all kinds of shit. We'd both had a few and because this woman was three sheets to the wind we just told her to shut the fuck up. Unfortunately, she decided to ignore our advice and after another ten minutes or so of listening to her gobbing off, James and I started giving her some back. She looked a right state so we had plenty of ammunition.

Anyway, as we were all exchanging pleasantries an officer of the law stepped up and tried to intervene. At first I was relieved because I thought he might shut her up but instead of telling her to do one he started having a pop at James.

Whether or not this policeman was related to the woman I'm not sure, but she was evidently a lot more pissed than we were and also a damn sight more aggressive, so if anyone should have been reprimanded, it was her. This, I'm afraid to say, is when the fierier side of our temperaments started pushing themselves to the fore and before you could say 'somebody put a bag over this no-mark's head' we were surrounded by police officers.

Remember ages ago I talked about me, James and Alex being like miniature caged beasts whenever Mum put us in separate rooms? Well, as well as being caged once again we were now much, much bigger and as well as having about fifteen pints swilling around inside us we were getting really fucked off. Even though this woman was still swearing her arse off and trying to goad James, she still hadn't even been told to shut up by the police. We, on the other hand, were surrounded by about ten of them and every time James or I swore back at this gobby woman we were threatened with arrest.

'Hang on a second,' I said. 'She's has just called you a twat and you don't even bat an eyelid. What the fucking hell's up with you?'

'Swear like that once more, sir,' said the copper, 'and we'll lock you up.'

Never mind the woman goading us. The police were doing a far better job!

In the end, we'd had enough and so after being threatened again with arrest while this woman just carried on swearing and what have you, we told the police that they could fuck right off.

This was obviously exactly what they'd had been trying to engineer, and with a few lads egging us on from the pavement we readied ourselves for a bit of a ruck. James must have been about twenty-two stone at the time and because it was late in the year I'd have been touching seventeen. The police must have known we weren't going to come quietly so why the fuck they wound us up like that I have no idea. They must have fancied us.

After we'd sworn at them one of them stepped forward and tried to arrest James but as he did I grabbed him, threw him across the road and told him to fuck off. By this time all you could see were police officers and all you could hear were sirens. If you'd only just arrived in the area you'd have been forgiven for thinking there was a full-blown riot taking place.

For the next ten minutes or so small groups of police would move in and try to arrest us and every time they did we'd push them away or pick them up and chuck them into the road. It was a bit like a game you'd play at Cubs, but with a tiny bit more violence and more flashing lights. May the good Lord forgive me but it was absolutely fucking excellent. It also shut that woman up, which was a bonus.

Eventually the police got fed up with being pushed and thrown, which was a shame, and so split into two groups;

one for me and one for James. Then, once they'd got themselves ready, they charged at us and began the unenviable task
of trying to restrain us. According to one or two mates who
witnessed the fracas it was pretty spectacular and it took about
fifteen minutes for them to get us handcuffed and into the van.

Incidentally, the reason I sound so casual about what
happened isn't because I don't have any respect for law and
order. It's because I didn't like the way we were treated by the
police and in my opinion they set out to get a reaction. All we
did was stand up for ourselves and not let them shit on us, so
yes, I quite enjoyed it.

A few weeks later James and I were up in court and got a
reprimand. For as long as I live I will never forget what the
judge said to us. He said:

'James and Edward Hall. What you did was not big and it
certainly was not clever. You do realise it took over twenty
police officers to restrain you? I for one don't think that's very
impressive.'

I remember standing there grinning to myself, thinking,
I fucking do! Twenty's an incredible number. Don't get me
wrong, I certainly wasn't proud of getting arrested. I was just
impressed by the way it happened.

CHAPTER 12
Getting Back on Track

By the time I was seventeen I'd cleaned up my act a bit and although I was hitting the gym harder than ever I still had no ambitions to become a strongman. Since being expelled I'd gradually cut out the drinking and, not surprisingly, this had had a positive effect on my depression. It was still there, but with my self-esteem making a comeback it had far less to go at.

The reason I was pushing harder gym, apart from wanting to look like Arnie, was the fact that I'd started doing some door work and I wanted to look as big and imposing as humanly possible. Actually, I think I'd always wanted to look as big as humanly possible but this gave me an excuse.

Even then, I knew that I was easily the strongest man in my gym and probably in the entire area. This was a big boost for me confidence-wise – a powerful realisation – and made me feel similar to how I feel when I win a strongman competition. I'll let you choose which one.

Some of you might be wondering how I knew that I was the strongest man in Stoke when I was just seventeen, and as a man who likes to back up his claims I'll be only too happy to tell you.

The first time I ever did a max bench press, which I did at seventeen, I pressed 180kg (397 lb) and my first ever max squat was a quarter of a tonne, or 250kg (551 lb). Not too shabby. My first ever max deadlift, which is obviously what I'm most famous for and took place at the same time, was 260kg (573 lb), which is over half the current world record held by that bearded bloke with the Mohican. Suave bastard.

Even today, I can count on the fingers of one hand the amount of people who can deadlift over 200kg (441 lb) at my gym, never mind 260kg. Anything over 200kg is a big deal if you're into lifting weights and so maxing 260kg on debut was fucking unbelievable.

Whilst I may not have been able to dedicate as much time to the gym as I did to my two jobs – that simply wasn't possible – I definitely spent more time thinking about it and the more I thought, the more I researched, and the more I was able to hone what I was doing and improve. I was also no slouch when it came to asking for advice and being surrounded by so many older and more experienced people was a big advantage. One of my very first gym partners was a local man in his forties who was a bodybuilder and powerlifter. He'd been training since before I was born and was obviously full of good advice. I was like a sponge in that respect and just soaked it all up.

The reason I started doing door work was because I was always skint and this was in small part down to all the money

I was spending on things like extra food, supplements, gym membership and equipment. Even then I was probably shelling out a good £80 a week on extra food and the same again on supplements. It doesn't take a mathematician to work out that a lad taking home about a grand a month won't have much left after spending that kind of money. So despite the fact that there weren't that many hours left in the day I thought I'd try to make the few that there were supplement my supplements, so to speak. Scraping by was never going be enough for me and I always needed to feel like I was progressing in life.

Yet again I wasn't really supposed to be working as a doorman at seventeen (you had to be at least eighteen) but because of my size and my character I got away with it. After blagging my way on to a door supervision course I started off working as an in-house doorman at several nightclubs four or five nights a week.

As well as extra money, the door work provided me with a bit of a social life and not being able to drink on the job meant it never interfered with the gym or with my apprenticeship. I was a bit tired sometimes the following day but at that age it doesn't matter. Don't worry, I hadn't turned into a complete teetotaller. I just drank occasionally.

I remember seeing all my friends from high school turn up to these nightclubs on a Friday and Saturday night and I'd watch them blow all their money and get completely off their heads. This used to happen week after week after week and it reinforced my desire to better myself, both physically and fiscally. I used to think, *Why would you do that to yourself? Why would you blow all your fucking money in one night?* It felt to me that as everyone else was going backwards, or at best treading water, I was moving forwards. The only things I ever had on a Sunday morning were a clear head and a bulging bank balance. To me that was very, very satisfying and was all the confirmation I needed that I was doing the right thing. I actually became a bit of a paragon of virtue for a while and whenever I got talking to friends who were in that 'work, get fucked and become skint' rut, I'd try to tell them, without sounding too pious, that there was an alternative. Nobody ever listened. Rather sadly, they ended up becoming my motivation because their apathy and stagnation used to scare the living shit out of me. The wider the gap between us, the better.

After working in-house at these clubs for few months I started becoming annoyed by the fact that it was always me who had to sort out things like cover for people who couldn't be arsed to turn up. I didn't ask for this responsibility, by the way, it just happened. I was reliable and always very professional so I was treated like a head doorman. This got me thinking that as opposed to doing it for free, maybe I should set up my own company, and that's what I did. I charged the venues so much per week and instead of doing it as a favour I shouldered all the hassle officially and got paid for it. It's bizarre, when you think about it. At seventeen years of age I was breaking up fights, throwing out drunks and telling groups of rowdy women to behave themselves. Then, just a few months later, I was employing a load of men twice my age and running the door of the majority of nightclubs in Stoke. If any of the doormen ever put a foot out of line I'd bollock them but I was always considered to be a very fair boss and never had much trouble. Every Friday night I'd visit all the clubs to give the men their wages and because they were self-employed and paid their own taxes I had bugger-all paperwork to deal with. It was easy really. But once again somebody had to come up with the idea and on this occasion, it was me.

One of the most amusing things about this situation, certainly given my age and also my past, was that in addition to liaising with the venue owners on an almost daily basis, who were all two or three times my age, I also had to liaise with the police about local troublemakers. Fortunately, none of them seemed to recognise me so it never became an issue but I remember thinking on several occasions while I was talking to them, *I'm sure I threw you into a road once.*

Despite the temptation, and I *was* tempted to say something, I was never unprofessional with any of the people I worked with and with some damn good money coming in (I must have been the wealthiest seventeen-year-old in Stoke), I was now able to splash out on some of the finer things in life, including a nice black BMW 3-series. I'd passed my driving test not long after my seventeenth birthday and managed to keep the BMW an entire four months before writing it off. It happened not long before my eighteenth birthday and was the first time I'd ever driven in icy conditions. Naturally, I was your archetypal boy racer so I saw ice more as an accelerant than a hazard and no allowances were made. This went quite well for the first couple of days but after channelling Ayrton Senna one afternoon I completely misjudged a roundabout, drove straight over it and then wrapped the car around a lamp post. It was like the time I fell out of that tree all those years ago. I'd almost killed myself yet all I could do was laugh. The rush was amazing!

Because my insurance was about £1,500 I didn't bother claiming on it and bought a clapped-out Fiesta just to get around in. It didn't have the same performance as the BMW but it was a hell of a lot safer.

Unfortunately, my addiction to speed was never going to be quashed by a prang in a Beamer and not too long after that I developed a passion for quad bikes. The first one I bought was a bog-standard Yamaha 250cc and after ripping the engine out I replaced it with a GSXR 600 from a superbike and stuck a turbo on it from a Subaru Impreza. Mark my words, this thing was fucking evil and because it had about 225 brake horsepower on the dyno I had to put drag swing arms on it to stop it wheeling, which it did in every gear. It also had racing suspension, racing tyres, racing brakes and everything was chrome dipped. It looked the absolute dog's bollocks and all in all I must have spent about £15,000 on it. It was my pride and joy.

Despite having laughed in the face of death one or twice up till then this quad bike was in a different league: it put me right inside its mouth and halfway down its fucking throat. It was just ridiculous. One day I got home after a near-miss that almost killed me and thought, *If I carry on driving that thing I'll be dead in a week*. You can't drive something like that slowly. It's all or nothing. And there was no way in the world I was going to fanny around in it at 30mph. That'd be like hiring a big bastard like me to move fucking pencils. No, it had to go unfortunately so that evening I put it on Ebay. Let it kill some other fucker!

I kind of made light of it before but I was working some unbelievable hours back then. For starters, my apprenticeship took up at least fifty hours a week (sometimes more if I had to work weekends) and my door work was at least another twenty. Add to that the twenty I spent training and you've got the best part of a hundred-hour week. I know they say that all work and no play makes Jack a dull boy but I absolutely loved it. I loved my day job, I loved being financially sound, I loved the social life that the gym and the door work gave me, and I loved the status they gave me too. I was the strongest bloke in the gym and I was the man who ran the doors in the nightclubs. It was exactly where any self-respecting young alpha male would want to be.

Even Nan seemed to perk up a bit for a while. Since being expelled we'd spent a lot of time together and despite being tired a lot of the time I think she was buoyed by my transformation. It wasn't going to save her, unfortunately, but it definitely made her happy, and if Nan was happy, so was I.

In hindsight, the only thing I regret missing out on from that period are some aspects of a more conventional social life for a man of my age: weekends away with the lads and stag dos. Apart from the very occasional night out, which would have been once every six months, I never once allowed myself to become distracted. At the end of the day if I had gone out on the piss more I'd only have got into trouble, and as a fine upstanding member of the community (ahem), I couldn't afford to do that. I was quite the little businessman really and it was only matter of time before I moved into even bigger and better things.

CHAPTER 13
Body Beautiful

Apart from my Mohican, my beard, my size, my sheer unbelievable brilliance and of course my modesty, I'm probably best known – visually, at least – for my tattoos. Though the effect that my very first tattoo had on my long-suffering mother, had I known it beforehand, would have made me think twice about having it done.

Whenever I'd spoken to my dad about tattoos he'd always echoed what his dad, my orange-slicing grandad, had told him: 'While you're living under my roof there'll be no drugs, no police and no tattoos.' I don't think he was really bothered either way but he repeated it just the same.

Rightly or wrongly (although it's usually wrongly with me), I'd already contravened two-thirds of that regulation and so it seemed a pity not to go for the hat-trick.

It all started off with a little bit of self-imposed peer pressure. As well as being a doorman and a truck mechanic, I was also an eighteen-stone body builder and without wanting to appear like a complete conformist, I seemed to be the only person in all three of these environments who didn't have any tattoos.

That's about as far as the conformity went though and so instead of following the crowd and getting a tattoo of a bulldog or whatever, I went the whole hog and got a Celtic tribal band that went from my elbow, up my arm, over my back, and then down to the other elbow. It took about forty hours in all and although it smarted a bit at times I was as happy as a pig in shit with the result and in my opinion it looks fantastic. That's me all over though. If I was going to get a tattoo done like everyone else, I could never get a tattoo like everyone else's, if you see what I mean. It had to be something different and it had to be something noticeable, otherwise, what's the point? These days people seem to enjoy having the same tattoos and haircuts and the big craze at the moment is having a short back-and-sides and a tattoo sleeve on your left arm. My gym's absolutely full of them. I know exactly how good it can feel fitting in, but when it comes to things like cutting my hair and putting a load of permanent ink on my skin, I prefer to be a forerunner as opposed to a follower. You lads carry on, though. Don't mind me.

It's something I actually thought about long and hard and the more I thought about it the more determined I became that whatever tattoos I got should match my personality. They had to be big, and they had to be bold.

Unfortunately, my poor mum wasn't quite as pleased with my body art as I was and the first time she saw it she burst into tears. Just for a split-second I thought it might be because she liked it, but when she cried 'Oh my God, Eddie, what the bloody hell have you done?' I knew that perhaps she wasn't exactly enamoured by it and I was left feeling a tiny bit crestfallen. I still catch her scowling at my tattoos sometimes, but in all honesty, I think she's grown to like them. She'd never, ever admit it though. Dad, on the other hand, has gone one better and has had one done himself. If this paragraph makes it into the final book, incidentally, I'll be amazed – because, unlike his youngest son, Dad hasn't told his mum yet. Go easy on him, Grandma. He's a good lad really.

If I had a tenner for every time I've been called a paradox over the years I'd be able to put down a deposit on a house, and that's exactly what I did after having my first tattoo. Most people would go to the pub; I bought a house.

I had about ten grand in the bank at the time, which was about enough for a deposit, and apart from wanting my independence I knew for a fact that your average eighteen-year-old would never be able to afford to buy their own place and that made me feel like I was achieving something. I can find competition in pretty much anything!

The house I ended up buying is the house I live in today and it cost me the grand total of £115,000. That might not be very much by today's standards but it felt like an absolute fortune at the time and my God did I feel grown up. I remember thinking to myself, *I've just spent over a hundred grand. What the fuck!*

Less than a year later I ended up buying a second house, which is just a hundred yards up the road, but this was purely an investment decision. The idea came from a bloke I worked with at LEX Cobridge, who, without wanting to sound rude, was a bit of a wise fool. He was one of those people who seemed to know something about everything, without being a bullshitter, but despite offering lots of good advice and he rarely practised what he preached and so never benefited himself. I just don't think he had either the guts or the drive to follow any of it through, which is shame.

Anyway, he started going on about pensions one day and said, 'Why would you put 5 per cent of your wages into a pension scheme for thirty years, just so they can give you £200 a week when you retire? Buying a house is a much better idea.' This seemed to make perfect sense to me because as well as a house paying for itself via the rent it generates, and so not really costing you anything, you'd be able to cash it in whenever you liked. Being tied in to something like a pension scheme filled me with the same dread as being tied into a job for the rest of my life. It wasn't for me.

Anyway, before you start thinking I'm too sensible I should tell you about how I got another rather noticeable feature of my appearance. As well as my tattoos, the other thing people ask me about most with regards to my stunning good looks is the scar that runs over my left eye. Because it runs directly over the middle of my eye, and because it is very noticeable, some people think it's either make-up, which is bollocks, or that it was done deliberately, which is just beyond bollocks. I mean, come on. Regardless of how hard it might make you look, who in their right mind would get somebody to knife them across the eye?

In actual fact the scar was attained during an altercation that took place on Valentine's Day around the same time as I got my first tattoo, and, as with so many things, it isn't something I'm particularly proud of. I was out with a few mates of mine at a nightclub in Hanley and as well as being three sheets to the wind I was also wearing one of those Superman T-shirts (one of these days Superman's going to get caught wearing an Eddie Hall T-shirt!). Anyway, at about one o'clock in the morning this prat walked up to me and said: 'Oi, Superman. Reckon you're hard?'

Being me I replied, 'Actually, dickhead, yes, I do.'

'You want to prove it?' he said.

'Why not? Wherever you like.'

I then followed this knobhead out of the nightclub and as he walked his mates started joining him. *Here we go,* I thought. *Another fanny who can't fight his own battles.*

By the time we got out of the nightclub there were about twelve of these idiots and by the time we reached the road they all seemed to be carrying hand tools. Things like hammers and stuff. At first I thought they might all have been carpenters, but I was wrong. They were just tools.

The fight only lasted five or ten minutes but during the commotion one of them attacked me with a Stanley knife and that was the result. I only noticed it the next day and instead of going to the doctors I just left it to heal up. I was more concerned with my hands and my forehead. They were in a right fucking state! My knuckles were pitch black from where I'd been smacking these twats and the front of my head was covered in lumps from where I'd been headbutting them. I looked like a frigging Dalek! The eye was almost secondary really and became more noticeable once it had healed up. Before that it was just a wound so could have been an accident. People are fascinated by scars. Especially when you look like me.

These days I'm obviously a reformed character but I still get the odd prat asking to take me out occasionally. The only difference these days is that they're all on social media so they're probably hundreds or even thousands of miles away. Proper tough guys! I get things like 'I could do you with one punch, mate,' or 'You wouldn't last two minutes with me.' After having a laugh I just block them. There's no use getting involved. Best leave them in fantasy land.

While we're here I may as well go through the rest of my scar collection.

The other one people ask me about is at the top of my right cheek and it was a present from my brother James, bless him. We'd been having a scrap one day (after I'd been winding him up) and because there weren't any samurai swords knocking about the place he threw a piece of ice at me instead. Some of the things we used to do to each other you wouldn't do to your worst enemy. We've actually beaten each other unconscious before. As kids! It's crazy.

The next one's just above my lip but because of my beard you can't really see it. That was a result of being hit with a knuckle duster by one of James's friends and it actually made a hole in my face. This idiot used to get on my nerves and one day I got so fed up with him that I called him outside. We got split up after a couple of minutes but as I was walking away he shouted, 'Hey, Eddie,' and when I turned around he hit me just below my nose. You could see my teeth through the hole. It was gross! I didn't go down though and before I went to A&E I managed to get the boot into him a couple of times.

Last but not least is the scar on my eyebrow. That happened while I was snowboarding with some mates one day (in Stoke by the way, not the Alps). As we were trundling through the snow we came across a group of lads. Naturally, I couldn't resist mouthing off to them but before I could get an answer one of them hit me with a spade. My eyebrow looked like a fucking sausage and it took me a good few minutes to get my bearings.

Served me right really.

CHAPTER 14

Beginnings and Endings

The autumn of 2007 is a pivotal time in my life for two very different reasons. First, on 2 September, I entered my first strongman competition, which, bearing in mind what I do for a living, is pretty damn pivotal.

It was actually my brother James who first suggested I enter it and it was in reaction to my size. In fact, I think his exact words were: 'You've got to do something with all that fucking muscle, Ed!' I was lifting some ridiculous weights by this point and so I agreed. It was just for shits and giggles really but because there was competition involved that made it interesting. The advert for the event read as follows:

NOVICE STRONGMAN EVENT
2 September 2007
The Fitness Factory, Unit 5, Burnham Business Centre,
Blannel Street, Burnley, BB11 4AJ

Athlete Registration 11 a.m. Start time 12 p.m.

Entrance fee – £10 to include competition T-shirt

Top three athletes receive competition trophy, next four competition medal

1st prize – £75 voucher *

2nd prize – £50 voucher *

3rd prize – £25 voucher *

* vouchers redeemable in Muscle Mass Supplements shop

CLOSING DATE FOR ENTRY 24TH AUGUST 2007

HEAD REFEREE – FORMER BSM MICK GOSLING

GUEST APPEARANCE AND TROPHIES PRESENTED BY MARK FELIX

THE EVENTS

1. Truck Pull: 7.5-tonne (16,500 lb) truck pull. 20 metres course. Time limit 75 seconds.

2. The Log Lift: 90kg (198 lb) for reps in 75 seconds.

3. Farmer's Walk: 90kg in each hand. 40 metres with turn. 75-second time limit.40-MINUTE BREAK

4. Deadlift: 190kg (418 lb) for reps. Time limit 75 seconds.

5. Tyre Flip: 350kg (771 lb) tyre to be flipped 8 times. 90-second time limit.

6. The Medley: 60kg (132 lb) barrel carried 20 metres, 90kg farmer's walk carried 20 metres, 100kg (220 lb) chain drag 20 metres.

This will be a very good show for first timers. Well organised with prizes. Come on guys, give it go.

I turned up to the event with no agenda and no idea what I was doing. Was I a fan of strongman then? Yes, I suppose I was really. I knew who the main protagonists were, people like Terry Hollands and Mariusz Pudzianowski. If you lifted weights they were the blokes you looked up to and when I found out Mark Felix was giving out the prizes I remember being quite excited. I'd met plenty of famous footballers before through door work but because I couldn't give a shit about the sport that never impressed me. They were just a bunch of rich idiots in my eyes. Mark Felix, though? He was one of the best deadlifters on the planet at the time and that did impress me. He was somebody I admired and wanted to meet. Terry Hollands was also doing really well then and because of his success there was a bit of a buzz around the sport. I was only there for a laugh though, and didn't know a tyre flip from a farmer's walk. Seriously! I had to ask for advice on almost every event. Where do I hold it? Where do I stand? What do I do? Apart from the standard deadlift I was new to it all and I remember people laughed at me for wearing weight-lifting gloves. I asked the referee once or twice if I was allowed and honestly, it was as if I'd farted the national anthem! I also remember doing the truck pull wearing standard Caterpillar boots, which was novel. None of the gear, no idea! It all took place in a car park somewhere in Burnley and there were probably about a hundred people there.

I can't remember the details of how I performed in each event but I definitely ended up finishing fifth out of fifteen.

This was OK bearing in mind I was so inexperienced and getting to meet Mark Felix was the icing on the cake. One thing I do remember from that day is noticing the difference in build between me and the other competitors. Although I was quite a big lad I was also very defined, whereas the others were a lot bigger and bulkier. Vanity was still part of my motivation then, but if somebody with the wrong build and no experience could come fifth in a competition, what would happen if they sacrificed their vanity for bulk and then gave it another go? I'd definitely got the taste for it.

Before I had a chance to do anything about it, though, something happened that was to break my heart and put all my other thoughts into perspective. The second reason why autumn 2007 is so pivotal took place on Monday 22 October and it is still the bitterest pill I have ever had to swallow. It was the death of my nan, who had been living with leukaemia for the last five years. I touched earlier on the closeness of our relationship but since her diagnosis that had deepened and she was so much more than just a grandparent. She was my friend, my confidante, my carer, and even my unofficial parole officer! I know it's quite an overused expression these days but more than anything, Nan was my rock. It must have been hard not to judge somebody as difficult and screwed up as me, but she never did. Not once.

My depression and anxiety had started soon after Nan was diagnosed which demonstrates just how much she meant to me. At the time, losing her would have been the worst thing that could have happened in my life and over the past five years I'd had to learn to live with the fear of that happening, just as Nan had learned to live with her leukaemia. The prognosis, and the condition, was obviously very different for me. I was young and strong and underneath all that crap going on inside my head was somebody normal-ish waiting to get out. And he would get out, eventually. For poor Nan, the condition and the prognosis were far bleaker and how the hell she held on for as long as she did amazes me. My God, I'm grateful for it. Leukaemia's one of those diseases that can kill you in a day, if it can, but Nan wasn't having any of it. She was made of sterner stuff and I'll always be enormously proud of her bravery.

This is the first time I have ever recounted the full story of my nan's passing and to be honest I've been dreading it. But it's got to be done.

It happened on a Monday, and because I'd been working the doors all weekend I'd decided to take the day off work. I remember feeling absolutely fucking knackered and in addition to this I'd had a big row with my girlfriend Laura the day before and was feeling very down and alone. Then, later in the morning, I received a telephone call from the hospital saying that my nan had been admitted, she was alone, and would I like to come up immediately.

My initial reaction to her admission was anger, because she'd expressly asked to die at home and the fact that this might be denied her infuriated me. Unfortunately, my grandad had very severe dementia at the time and, after finding her unconscious on the couch, he instinctively called an ambulance. Grandad had then started to panic and so while a neighbour looked after him, the paramedics took Nan to hospital.

When I got there I saw my nan very briefly before being asked to wait in a room. She was surrounded by people and when a doctor came to speak to me I was told that she was very, very weak and would probably die. He then asked me if I'd like them to resuscitate her and I said that we should respect her wishes and let her die with at least some dignity. That was so, so difficult for me because all I wanted Nan to do was live, but this wasn't about me, was it? This was about her and if she wasn't able to die at home like she wished, it was up to me, with the doctor's help of course, to ensure that she died as peacefully and painlessly as possible.

Straight after speaking to the doctor I went into Nan's room, sat by her side, held her hand and told her how much I loved her. Together with my parents, she had always been my most voracious supporter and whatever mistakes I'd made in life, Nan always believed I'd come good. Emotionally, she had underwritten every dream I'd ever had and so before she passed away I decided that we would share one more.

'Do you know what, Nan,' I whispered to her. 'One day I'm going to become the strongest man on Earth and when I do, you're going to be the proudest nan there's ever been.'

About a minute later, Nan slipped away and about five minutes after that the doctor pronounced her dead. The fact that I was there for Nan when she passed still means the absolute world to me and if she'd died all alone I don't think I'd ever have been able to forgive myself. I'm convinced she hung on, so I could be with her in her final moments.

For the next half an hour or so I just sat on Nan's bed, hugging her. Then, one of the nurses reminded me that perhaps I should make a few telephone calls and let people know, which I did. After that they moved Nan into a room where I could be alone with her and again I just sat there hugging her and asking her to come back. Many of you reading this will know what I mean but the realisation that you'll never see somebody again and the desperation that accompanies that is extraordinary and for a time I just couldn't get my head around it. We're not programmed to understand things like eternity and every time I remembered that I would never, ever see my nan again I'd experience a moment of blind panic, followed by a pang of overwhelming sadness.

My poor mum was having a final interview to become a fire fighter that day and Nan must have died while she was about halfway through the questioning. With Mum's phone being turned off I obviously couldn't get hold of her and so left messages instead. Once she eventually got back to me I told her what had happened and she was absolutely beside herself. I tried to reassure Mum that it had all been very peaceful but like me she was disappointed that Nan hadn't been able to die at home. It certainly wasn't anybody's fault but she'd been so adamant and I think we felt like we'd let her down a bit.

Almost as soon as Nan had passed I could feel what was left of my depression and anxiety lift, and, in a way, I'd almost been expecting it to. Had Nan known what I'd been going through and why, she'd have been absolutely devastated, but love can manifest itself in odd ways sometimes and while she was alive it was my way of expressing my grief at her illness. Why I couldn't have shed the odd tear like everyone else I'm not sure, but then, I don't do things by halves, do I? If I'm going to get upset when one of my favourite people gets leukaemia I'm going to do it properly!

Now she'd passed away, the depression and anxiety had been replaced by feelings of extreme sadness which meant I could mourn my nan, get on with my life, and, most importantly of all, remember all the fantastic times we'd had together. That's exactly what Nan would have wanted.

A much-needed highpoint after losing my nan was a request by my old swimming teacher, Greg Clarke, to come out of retirement and help out COSSACS in a medley race at a swimming competition in Wolverhampton. Greg said, 'Come on, mate. Let's have a laugh and see what you can do. See if the magic's still there.' Greg knew exactly how competitive I was and even though I hadn't swum for a couple for years I thought, *Why the hell not?* I'd get to see some old friends and regardless what had happened with Bill Sweetenham and, more regrettably, Arnold, I'd enjoyed my swimming days massively and I could certainly use a bit of enjoyment again after Nan's passing.

When it came to the race I even surprised myself and managed the 50-metre freestyle in just 25.8 seconds. Bearing in mind the current world record is 20.91 seconds that's pretty fucking amazing, especially when you consider my size. Being about twenty stone meant I was twice as big as every other swimmer there and so all things considered perhaps I should have considered returning to the sport. No flaming chance! The sport would have closed down if it thought I was returning. It was nice to dip my toes back in, though. I still get interviewed about swimming, by the way, and just recently I had about four or five pages in the *Swimming Times*.

By the time I was twenty years of age then I had a good job, my own business, two houses, a BMW Z3, a growing collection of amazing tattoos and a fifth place trophy won at a novice strongman competition in darkest Burnley. Who could ask for more? My apprenticeship had come to an end at LEX Cobridge but I still felt like an apprentice there, so I managed to get a job looking after a fleet of trucks at Robert Wiseman Dairies. As well as a certain amount of autonomy, the new job meant that my wages virtually doubled overnight. The trucks were also a lot cleaner and we had a great team spirit.

Everything was going well but even with all these distractions I thought a lot about Nan's passing. It was a watershed moment in my life and one that I will never forget. But life has a way of grabbing you by the balls sometimes and reminding you – rather forcibly – that with every end there is a beginning. And exactly one year after Nan died, I was to have a new beginning of my own.

CHAPTER 15
Baby on Board

On 28 October 2008, a year to the day after my nan passed, something happened that was to change my life forever. My daughter Layla, whose birth was obviously expected but certainly hadn't been planned, was born weighing six pounds and seven ounces, and with her came a brand new me. I remember I was obsessed with who was the hardest lad at high school. In fact, in the whole of bloody Stoke! That's not a healthy ambition for Christ's sake, and look where it got me. All of a sudden, the only thing that mattered in the world was Layla and it won't surprise you to know that I took fatherhood very, very seriously. Out went the sporty BMW Z3, and in came a family-friendly BMW X5. I even started working harder, which was barely possible, and I became totally focused. I suddenly had a reason for working hard and working out, apart from just bettering myself, and I had a goal, which was to be a good dad and to make Layla proud.

For the first time ever I began taking pride in myself, which is something I'd always found difficult. I'd sometimes taken pride in what I'd achieved, such as winning golds at the Nationals and deadlifting 260kg (573 lb), but that's a different thing altogether. One is all about you, and the other is all about what you can do. In order to take pride in yourself you first have to accept who you are, and with the depression now gone that was much, much easier to do. Nobody's perfect, but all in all I wasn't a bad lad and if taking pride in yourself means trying to be a better person, which I believe it does, I was going to give it my best shot; not just for the sake of my new-born daughter, but for the sake of me and for everyone around me.

Layla's mum, by the way, Laura, who I'm no longer with, had been my girlfriend since high school and we'd stayed together until I was about eighteen. Then, when I'd just turned twenty, we got back together again for a short time and the result of that reunion was Layla. I was able to be there for the birth, although I only came in right at the end, and it completely knocked me for six. It doesn't matter what you think you've achieved in life or how much money you've earned; watching a new life come into the world, one that you've helped to produce, moves you on to a much higher plane in my opinion.

As a result of me trying to take pride in myself I went from being somebody who was generally feared in the town and whose presence spelt trouble, to somebody who was respected and who was seen as being a bit of a gentle giant. Don't worry, I hadn't suddenly turned into Cliff Richard, and there was definitely no epiphany going on. I simply resolved to *try* to set a good example to my daughter and make her proud of me.

Nine years on and I still live by exactly the same rule, the only difference being that I now have two kids and a wife, so that's three times the motivation. That's how I look at it, anyway. When people who want to talk to me about strongman ask me what my goal in life is, I always say, 'To win the World's Strongest Man.' That's what they expect me to say and from a professional point of view it's correct. What I don't tell them is that by winning the World's Strongest Man I'll help maintain my ultimate goal of making my family proud of me. But what then? Having pride in yourself and being a good person is something you have to work at over an entire lifetime and so once that's out of the way I'll be onto something else. There's no destination, just a journey. And hopefully, a long one.

For all my talk of setting examples, I was still only twenty years of age when Layla arrived and when it came to my relationship with Laura it was one area where I'm afraid I failed to live up to my own hype. I used to receive a hell of lot of attention from women while I was working the doors and to be honest with you the temptation became too much. Laura and I had also been together for a long time, on and off, and it was the first and only relationship either of us had ever had. I think I was bored really. Not with Laura, but with the relationship. I know some of you will think I'm a bit of a hypocrite after what I said about setting examples, but I did say that I was no angel.

Layla's going to be nine this year and although she doesn't live with us she's only a minute up the road and we've got a very, very good relationship. I'm her hero, which I have to admit makes my sixty-eight-inch chest swell with pride. It hasn't always been easy and until I turned professional as a strongman my relationship with Layla had become a casualty of my all-or-nothing nature; the all being strongman, and the nothing being my relationships. Making people you love proud of you is all good and well, but when your efforts start to destroy those relationships something has to give.

Nevertheless, becoming a strongman became a huge focus for me at this time and, rightly or wrongly, I threw myself into it 100 per cent in my usual fashion. If I was going to be a strongman and make my new daughter proud of me, I was going to be the best fucking strongman she'd ever seen.

CHAPTER 16
Going National

Since entering the novice competition in Burnley I'd been like a man possessed and as well as upping my training a lot I'd started eating for England. There was no science behind it at the time. I just upped absolutely everything! I still wasn't expressly training for strongman at this point, by the way. That would come much later. I was just going through the usual muscle groups. In fact, the only specific training I'd done so far was when I attended a strongman camp at a gym in Stoke. I honestly couldn't tell you why this was the case and it's madness when you think about it. I just don't think it occurred to me. I'd just turn up to a competition, compete in all the strongman events, and then go back to just lifting weights in the gym. Talk about missing a trick!

With regards to how dedicated I felt, it was a carbon copy of what had happened with the swimming, except there was no Arnold Faulkner or Greg Clarke to help me. This was actually a positive, in the sense that I had nobody to fall out with, but not having any advice or experience to hand obviously wasn't ideal and the result of that was I was actually training to be a bodybuilder and not a strongman. This slowly evolved and although I carried on training as a bodybuilder I also started training all the strongman events. This meant that if I was training legs, for instance, I'd also do a farmer's walk. Or, if I was training chest, I'd do a log press.

In hindsight, this wasn't as bad as it sounds because if there's one environment I thrive in it's 'me against the world', and that's exactly what it felt like. I might well have been at the bottom of the ladder but as opposed to worrying about what I didn't have, I got off my arse and started researching and asking for help. That's one of the things I love about strongman: you're completely self-contained, and apart from physios and the like, the only people you can really fall back on in the sport are your fellow strongmen. I have to admit I found this quite difficult early on because I can be wary of other people – especially the competition – but once you learn to relax a bit and you realise you're in the same boat it's fine. At the end of the day you're not asking them out on a fucking date or anything, you're just helping each other out, and because the sport's not exactly rolling in cash we rely on each other to a point and that's a good thing.

The first competition I entered after Burnley took place in Northwich in Cheshire and I think it was a qualifier for England's Strongest Man, although I could be wrong. The reason I remember it so well is because I was competing against Mark Felix and the events were as follows:

- Hand-over-hand Vehicle Pull – 2-tonne 4x4, 70-second time limit
- Vehicle Lift – on frame, as many lifts as possible in 70 seconds
- 85kg (187 lb) Steel Log Lift – as many overhead lifts as possible in 70 seconds, head to head
- 150kg (331 lb) Conan's Wheel (lift and walk in a circle) – as many revolutions as possible
- Barrel Load – barrel ranging from 70–100kg (154 – 220 lb), loaded onto the back of a pick-up truck, fastest time wins
- Digger Bucket Lift – 60-metre course, furthest distance in fastest time

As well as beating Mark on a couple of events, the steel log lift being one of them, I lost to him by just three points. This was a defining moment for me because Mark had been a regular contender at the World's Strongest Man finals for a number of years and so was part of the elite. Beating him, even in two events, made me sit back and think seriously about my future. I was just twenty-one years of age and I'd been pipped at the post by one of the strongest men in the world in just my second competition. What would happen if I really gave this my all? I thought to myself, *I've got a fucking shot here. I could get to the finals of World's Strongest Man.* It still didn't click to start training the events properly, though. Berk!

There you go, brothers and sisters. If you ever want somebody to blame for me being a strongman, look no further than

Mr Mark Felix. I get on well with all the lads, but Mark's a really, really nice guy. He's very quiet, so we don't have much in common in that respect. He's one of the best though.

In July 2009, I entered the inaugural Staffordshire's Strongest Man competition in the market town of Leek and finished third overall. This was yet another defining moment in a way because as well as out-performing the majority of my more experienced rivals it was local to where I lived. An awful lot of people turned up to cheer me on: friends from school and mates from both of my jobs and from the gym. This was a massive boost for me because it resulted in recognition and you know how important that is to me. The only thing that pissed me off about the competition was the fact that I failed to win – but I knew it was only a matter of time.

Funnily enough, I came across a report on the competition the other day that was published in the *Stoke Sentinel* and as it was my first mention as a strongman I thought I'd include it.

The winner of the first-ever Staffordshire Strongest Man contest is ... from the Black Country.

Wayne Russell took first prize after winning the inaugural competition during Saturday's Leek and District Show.

He overcame nine other competitors, including Crewe's Wayne Tunstall and Newcastle's Ed Hall, who finished second and third.

In a remarkable test of strength the strongmen
had to:

Lift a 105-kilo log as many times as they could;

Try to complete a 20-metre course while carrying
120 kilos in each hand;

Lift the back of a 280-kilo van for as long as
possible;

Flip a 400-kilo, 5ft 8in-high tyre;

Lift five stones of various weights onto platforms of
differing heights in the quickest time.

After winning, 36-year-old Wayne Russell said: 'It
was a good event. I was confident I would do well.'

Wayne Tunstall was disappointed not to win but has
just come back from injury. The 28-year-old, who is
the reigning London's Strongest Man, Derbyshire's
Strongest Man and UK Strongest Man North of
England, said: 'I'm disappointed not to win but I've
only just come back from an injury, so I'm pleased
with how I've done.'

Bouncer Ed Hall, aged 21, who lives in the
Westlands, said: 'I think it will be a great event
to have every year, and there's been quite a lot of
interest from the public.'

Crewe plasterer Simon Daniels came ninth in his
first-ever strongman contest. The 37-year-old said: 'It's
been a good event, especially considering it's the first
one. I'll train hard this year and come back again.'

Noting that this is shorter than the original version – assume that's deliberate but in case it wasn't...!

That's the first and last time I include a report on me coming third. Never again!

But did you notice the difference in age between me and most of the other competitors? They were all seasoned campaigners whereas I was just a pup. Nobody knew who the bloody hell I was when I came onto the scene and with my tattoos and my Mohican they probably thought I was a right tosspot. In fact, I remember the way some of them used to look at me and they definitely weren't wishing me well. In reality, I wanted them to think I was a no-hoper as it made proving them wrong all the more satisfying; it was probably the first time in strongman that I started actively playing mind games with my competitors.

The last competition I entered in 2009, which was the annual Strongman of the North competition, gave me my first taste of injury in the sport yet still yielded a highly respectable seventh position. At the time I remember being disgusted with myself for finishing seventh but that was simply down to frustration and inexperience. Injuries are part and parcel of what we do and you have to learn to accept them. More importantly, though, you have to learn to go easy on yourself both physically and mentally and the more you beat yourself up about an injury the more detrimental it will become. For the last fifteen months I'd literally been going from strength to strength and when my knee suddenly went halfway through the competition I thought it was the end of the world. These days, as frustrating as an injury can be, I always try to take something positive from it. This might just be an opportunity to rest up for a few days but I'm always on the lookout for some preventative strategies and if I can figure out how I can prevent that injury from that happening again, it could actually end up being a worthwhile experience.

At the end of my first full year in strongman I had two podiums to my name, a knee injury and a lowly seventh. But they were just the headlines and despite looking OK on paper they belied an even more positive scenario. I was twenty-one years of age and twenty-one stone and, as well as a steely determination and almost unlimited amounts of energy, I had enough natural talent to keep *The X Factor* going for a hundred fucking years. Sooner or later all this would start coming to the fore and I promised myself that this time next year the world of strongman would have a new star in the making. I might not be top of the game yet, but when I turned up to an event the other lads would know exactly who I was and what's more they'd take me seriously. That was my immediate ambition at the end of 2009 and only a nutcase would have bet against me.

The first few months of 2010 were relatively slow strongman-wise but the competitions I did enter all yielded firsts – or, if I was injured or having an off-day, the odd second. Even when I did come second, I'd just become even hungrier, so either way I was walking away with a win.

These were all either local or regional shows but what I really wanted a crack at was one of the nationals. That's the only way I could progress now, and I knew that success in the sport was a forgone conclusion. Not because I said it would be, but because I'd worked my fucking arse off doing one hour of cardio and four hours weight training every single day.

My opportunity finally came at the start of May and began with a telephone call from a mate of mine called Dave Meer. Dave, who's a fellow Staffordshire lad, was an experienced strongman and unfortunately he'd had to pull out of the England's Strongest Man competition through injury.

'I'm going to put your name forward as a replacement, if you're game,' said Dave. 'You'll have to qualify, of course.'

'A mere formality, Mr Meer,' I replied.

After thanking Dave very much I put the phone down and immediately began thinking about what was to come. England's Strongest Man (now defunct), whilst not being the most prestigious competition on the circuit, always had a cracking pedigree and past winners included the likes of Terry Hollands, Laurence Shahlaei, Eddy Ellwood and Jamie Reeves, who'd won World's Strongest Man back in 1989. What really excited me was that whoever won the competition would be promised safe passage through to the following year's UK's Strongest Man competition, and that's when things started getting interesting. This was the break I'd been waiting for and there was no way I was going to balls it up.

Sure enough, I pissed the regional qualifier and so with that safely out of the way it was all eyes on the final. This took place in Teesside on Sunday 12 September, almost three years to the day after making my debut in Burnley, and to me that was not only a good omen, but a perfect indicator of exactly how far I'd come in the sport.

The final took place at the Old Billingham Business Centre, Chapel Road in Billingham and the events were as follows:

1: 28-tonne (61,729 lb) truck pull over 25 metres
2: Log lift, 130kg (286 lb)
3: Flip, carry and drag
4: Axle deadlift
5: Loading

The competitors, while not being part of the elite, were still some of the best in the country and the difference in class to the kind of competitors I'd been used to was noticeable. These boys were massive and as well as there being several who were taller than me, there were one or two who were touching thirty stone. What a fucking eye-opener! It didn't make me feel intimidated, exactly, because I knew I had the measure of them. What it did do, though, was give me an extra gear and because of that extra gear I ended up winning the competition by half a point. Half a fucking point! At the end of the day I wouldn't have cared if it had been an eighth of a frigging point, just so long as I won.

Once again, I came away from that competition thinking, *If I can win a national at twenty-two, what will I be able to do when I'm twenty-three?* My progression had been quite organic so far, and I had to be careful not to rush things. I was still very young but with three years' experience already under my belt I was also no longer a novice. With my immediate ambitions now met, I had to start thinking about some new ones. Well, it would obviously be the UK's Strongest Man next, but then what? Maybe qualifying for the World's? Nah, that would be impossible. Wouldn't it?

CHAPTER 17
My Better Half

Despite all the momentum that was building around my strongman career at that time, there was something else that occurred in 2010 that was to have an even more lasting effect in my life. The most important thing to happen to me during this period, apart from meeting Mark Felix and spending a Sunday afternoon in Teesside, was meeting my wife, Alex.

Anybody who knows me, or who has seen my documentary, *Eddie: Strongman,* will have some idea of what this woman means to me and how important she is to my very existence, but I'd like to expand on that slightly and at the same time explain how she helps me day to day. Don't worry, there's no need to get your violins out, but at the risk of sounding like a cliché I believe it's true when they say that behind every great man there is, more often than not, a much greater woman. Mark my words, they don't come much greater than mine. Some of you still might be wondering what this has got to do with being a strongman and once you've finished this chapter I hope you'll realise that it had everything to do with it.

Chapter 17

Being a strongman, as I've already intimated, can be a very solitary existence. Some of that's self-imposed, of course, and some of it isn't. But every time you emerge from that isolation – whether it be returning from a competition, recovering from an injury or just coming back from the gym – having somebody there who will always be 'pro-you' no matter what is as important as any amount of dedication or endeavour. In fact, to a certain extent you rely on that person to even exist; partly because they often inspire you to succeed – which Alex does, together with our kids – and partly because you can't be dedicated or enterprising without having a solid home life. For me, that's the platform from which I achieve greatness and Alex both creates and maintains that. I've often said to people, either in person or on social media, that they should never, ever underestimate me or what I can achieve, and the person who gives me the power to say that – and mean it – is my wife.

I first met Alex at the beginning of 2010. I was obviously still working the doors and as well as being a bachelor with his own house I also had a hot tub. In fact, I was probably the closest thing to a playboy Newcastle had ever seen and some weeks I'd hold hot tub parties in the garden. George Clooney in Saint-Tropez I was not, but after having a few in town, my mates and I would invite a load of girls back and we'd all have a bloody good time. Would I like to elaborate on that? Absolutely not. Suffice to say these parties could often go on for a very long time and more often than not I'd wake up to find mates asleep on the lawn and all kinds of everything in the bloody hot tub.

Then one night a mate of mine rang up and asked me what I was doing. 'There's a few of us getting pissed in the hot tub,' I said to him. 'Why not come over, and while you're there, bring a couple of girls with you? The more the merrier.'

Although these hot tub parties only lasted a few months (in total, not individually!), they represented the closest thing I'd ever had to a regular social life and looking back they were absolutely tremendous. Seriously, if you're a young lad who wants to know why you should work your arse off, there's your fucking answer! Get yourself a good job – or two, if you can manage it – then buy a house and invest in a hot tub. You won't regret it.

Anyway, when this mate of mine eventually arrived, he had two girls with him and one of these was Alex. Although she was local to the area I'd never met her before and although she knew who I was it was only by reputation. I've never asked Alex if that was a good or a bad thing and I don't think I want to know.

This may sound like a line but honestly, Alex was very different to any girl I'd ever met before and we hit it off imme-diately. Usually, and forgive me if this sounds conceited, which it does, but nine times out of ten it was the girls who came on to me and so historically I'd never had to put much effort in.

With Alex, it was a bit of an about-change and because I really fancied her I decided to turn on the charm. I'm not sure if she noticed but I definitely gave it my all. She's a big girl, about six foot tall, and that's one of the things that really attracted me to her. That, and her sparkling personality, of course! In all seriousness, she really did, and does, float my boat massively in that department and I remember being amazed at how caring she seemed. The initial attraction, though, for both of us, was our height and build and by the time she got out of Mr Lover's hot tub we'd arranged our first date.

Over the following weeks Alex and I went all over the place and it's fair to say we became inseparable. She must have thought all her Christmasses had come at once when I suggested we go jet skiing one day.

'Where to?' she asked, probably expecting me to say Majorca or somewhere.

'Colwyn Bay,' I replied.

I must say that Alex managed to hide her disappointment very well and she even managed to say, 'Ooh, that sounds nice.'

My dad had a jet ski at the time that he used at Colwyn Bay and before I started working my arse off for a living I used to use it quite a bit. We actually had a really good day up there and because it was a jet ski I thought would be in keeping with my playboy image. Hot tubs in Staffordshire and jet skis in North Wales. It was pretty serious stuff.

Within a year of meeting Alex I'd already decided that she was going to marry me. She didn't know it yet, but she was, and so all I had to do was tell her. Having never proposed to anybody before, and being an incurable romantic, I knew that it had to be something special – and, if I was going to stick to my 'all-or-nothing' rule, something truly spectacular. Getting on one knee in Paris was never going to be good enough for me so I had to start thinking.

I forget where the idea came to me exactly but it was pretty convoluted and involved an aeroplane, some very large signage, my dad, my mum, my future wife (I hoped), my future in-laws, one of her grandparents, and me. It had more elements to it than you could wave a stick at but providing my dad remembered how to fly the plane, and providing my mum had put the signage out and had reminded Alex's dad and nan to stand outside and wave at the right time, then nothing could go wrong. Oh yes, and Alex had to be looking in the right direction at exactly the right time – AND, she had to say yes. Piece of piss.

The idea was that my dad, who'd had his pilot's licence a few years, would take Alex and I out for a nice romantic flight together from an airfield about an hour away from where we lived, which, as the crow flies, was just a few minutes or so from Alex's parents' house. 'I'll tell you what,' I said to Alex. 'Why don't we fly over your parents' house?' to which she replied, 'Yeah, OK.'

While all this was going on my mum was on Alex's parents' lawn laying out a huge canopy that read:

ALEX
WILL YOU MARRY ME?
X

All we had to do now was get my dad to fly over the house, which would be easy, and then get Alex to look down at her parents' lawn, which wouldn't be so easy.

Because Alex had been really busy at work (she works for a recruitment company) she hadn't seen either her dad or her nan in ages and so as an extra touch I asked them if they'd mind standing on the lawn and waving when we flew past. I'd already asked her dad's permission to marry Alex, which he'd given me, and I was so glad that he agreed to be involved. He and Alex's nan did wave, bless them. And then they waved again. I don't know how many times I had to ask my dad to fly over Alex's parents' house but it must have been three or four. 'Oh, look down there, Alex,' I kept saying. 'Isn't that your parents' house?' She just wasn't interested.

When Alex eventually did look down and saw the proposal, and her dad and nan, she was in tears. So before she could say no, I slid the ring onto her finger, gave her a kiss and told her that I loved her. Funnily enough, she never did give me a formal 'yes' to the proposal but I'm pretty sure she'd have said something by now.

We got married about a year later and so within two years of first meeting me over a steamy hot tub in Newcastle, Alex had become my wife. By the time we tied the knot she was already about eight months pregnant with our son Max so there was very nearly an extra guest.

When it came to the stag do I decided to keep it quite low-key and although we all had plenty to drink we had a few days to recuperate before the big day. There's nothing worse than people turning up to their own wedding pissed. Isn't that right, Eddie Hall! Unfortunately, I made the almost fatal error of going out for 'just a few beers' the night before the wedding and ended up forgetting concepts like 'bed' and 'sleep' and went straight to the church still pissed. This, as you can imagine, went down like an atlas stone at a basketball game and neither Alex nor any of her family or friends – nor any of mine, come to think of it – were in the slightest bit impressed. God knows what I must have smelt like, but it can't have been very nice.

Because I don't drink very often I tend to go a bit mad sometimes and my tolerance level has actually increased since my whisky drinking days. Because I'm so big it takes about ten pints to even have an effect on me, and at least twenty to send me on my way, plus four or five shots. This isn't some macho brag, by the way. I weigh over thirty stone, remember, and consume about 80,000 calories a week. Getting me pissed is like trying to fill a bucket with a hole in it.

Because of my faux pas I hadn't even written my speech, if you can believe it. Being this disorganised was a completely new experience to me. Fancy leaving it till your wedding day to find out what it's like – what a tit! It went OK in the end but it was the first and last time I've blagged something so important. Funnily enough, the reception was held in a marquee on Alex's parents' lawn and I think returning to the scene of the crime helped to improve matters. We all ended up having a fantastic day, no thanks to me.

Alex has been by my side since I first won England's Strongest Man and her role, with regards to strongman, is multi-dimensional and it takes in every aspect of what I do: the training, the recovery, the diet. Alex makes all my meals, and there's a lot more to that than just shoving some ingredients into a pan. There's a real science to it and Alex has bossed that on my behalf. She still works, by the way, so it's time she has to make for herself. Actually, it's time she makes for me. But by far the most vital contribution Alex makes to my career is all the emotional support she gives me, and believe me, my emotions match my frame. They're not small! I can go from nought to sixty in about a second and a half and when I lose it, I fucking lose it. Before meeting Alex the only person who could tame me and talk sense into me was Nan, so the fact that somebody has replaced her makes me a very lucky man. It doesn't matter how bad the problem seems or how insurmountable the challenge, Alex helps me see through all the crap and helps me to focus again. It's fair to say that if I didn't have her fighting my corner I wouldn't be where I am today.

There are a great many sayings and mottos that have become lost in the land of clichés over the years, and sadly this renders them almost stale and meaningless. There is one saying in particular though that I would like to liberate from this verbal scrapheap because it sums up exactly how I feel about Alex and offers a true and accurate description of the effect she has had on my life. That saying is 'She is the best thing that has ever happened to me', and if nobody else wants it, I'm happy to keep it for her. For Alex.

CHAPTER 18

Introducing the Spartan

Right, enough of all that soppy bollocks. Let's get back to business. I think 2011 and 2012 is when I came of age as a strongman, both in terms of success and ability, but also in terms of character and personality. The more successful I became, the more bombastic I became, and by the time I arrived in Belfast to compete at UK's Strongest Man in August 2011, I'd established myself not only as one of the best strongmen in the UK, but also one of the most famous. Or should I say infamous? The fame was in fact completely premeditated, because although it was quite natural for me to beat my chest and play up to the audience and the cameras, it was also necessary in order to A) get me some recognition and separate me from the crowd, B) help promote the sport, and C) make me some damn money.

Let me start from the beginning.

When I came back from winning England's Strongest Man, my first national title, I was expecting, rather naively perhaps, to receive at least some recognition; either a 'well done' from my mates, a call from a journalist or maybe an offer of some sponsorship. Not a fucking peep. The final was on a Sunday, and when I went into work on the Monday nobody said a thing and there were certainly no journalists creeping around the garage, let alone potential sponsors. It didn't seem to matter to anybody.

Don't get me wrong, I wasn't expecting John Inverdale to be kissing my arse or for Nike and Coca-Cola to be waving contracts in my face, but I had it in my head that by winning a national title – one of only two, at the time – I'd at the very least have the local paper giving me a call. The silence was absolutely deafening and it put me on a massive downer; it's one that I still get to this day after a show, and for similar reasons.

On the Tuesday I called the local paper and asked to speak to the sport's editor. He obviously had no idea that I'd won England's Strongest Man, and why on earth would he? He took all the details and said he'd run something in a day or two. On the Thursday I bought a copy of the paper and there, on page 26, in the bottom right-hand corner, was a paragraph made up of three short sentences under the tiny headline: 'Local Man Wins Strongman Competition'. What really got my goat was that on the previous page there was a three-quarter-page report on a six-year-old winning a fucking badminton competition. Little Timmy beats a few locals and he gets three-quarters of a page. Eddie Hall wins England's Strongest Man – almost killing himself in the process – and gets three frigging sentences. What an absolute kick in the dick.

I had three choices at this point: I either jacked it in and went and did something else, carried on whinging, or did something about it – i.e. grabbed the sport by its fucking neck and shook it until people started noticing me. I knew that the sport of strongman was well loved in the UK, and I also knew that the one thing it was lacking, apart from money and regular TV exposure, were characters, and without those characters that was never, ever going to change.

When I started swimming all those years ago I very quickly realised that the person who gets noticed (by the crowd, at least) isn't the one who puts in the best time, it's the one who shouts and screams the loudest. They're the people the crowd want to see and they're the ones they remember. It obviously isn't as prevalent in swimming as it is in other sports because it's so time-driven, but whenever I used to get called onto the blocks at a swimming competition, everybody used to stop what they were doing and look at me – and the reason they did that wasn't just the enormous bulge in my trunks, it was because I was the one who stood out from the crowd and made a big fucking noise. The fact that I was also a damn good swimmer made sure they kept their eyes on me in the pool, but even if I'd been an also-ran, I'd still have been the one they recognised the next time around. Even back then I knew, deep down, that one day this would be the making of me and would help me to separate myself from everyone else, not just in terms of recognition, but also performance. And, because of the mental effect my persona has had on my competitors – i.e. getting into their heads – that's often been the case. Clever, isn't it? I'm just a fucking genius.

Something else that interested me at that time was WWF. Not the wrestling itself, necessarily, but its protagonists. Once again it was a case of 'who shouts loudest gets the most attention' and that's what fascinated me. The guys who'd created brands around themselves were not only the ones receiving the most attention and signing the most autographs, they were also the ones making the most cash – and the longer I spent in strongman the more anxious I became to try to emulate that. We're all absolutely enormous for Christ's sake, and because we lift heavy things for a living and say 'AAAAARGH' a lot, we're crying out to be characterised.

Believe it or not, the Beast, as I'm known now, is the second persona I've had in strongman. The first, which I got from the film *300*, was the Spartan, and it served me well for about three or four years. I already had the Mohican from my swimming days, and with the beard, which I'd grown as soon as I was able, and the tattoos, I definitely had the look of a Spartan about me. Watching the film sealed the deal.

When I first started calling myself the Spartan, which was about 2011, some of the more established strongmen began taking the piss out of me on social media. I was still the new boy back then and for a time I was a bit of a laughing stock. Not to the spectators, by the way. They lapped it up, which is why I became so popular, so quickly. Some of my colleagues, though, were less than impressed and comments such as 'What a dickhead' and 'This guy's making himself look like a fool' started appearing on a certain website beginning with the letter F.

Oh, how things change.

About a year ago I was having a conversation with some people within the strongman industry about why my persona had caught on and why I had so many followers on social media. I wasn't bragging about it or anything. We were just talking about it as being a success story within strongman. Suddenly, one of the people who'd slagged me off piped up and suggested that all strongmen should give themselves a brand and while they were at it they should all start kicking and screaming a bit more. Well, you could have knocked me down with a fucking feather. I'm afraid I just had to say something. 'Hang on,' I said. 'I've been doing this since 2011 and if memory serves me correctly you were one of the first people to call me a dickhead and claim that I was making a fool of myself.' After that silence prevailed, not surprisingly.

These days, a lot of the upcoming amateur strongmen are giving themselves stage names and building brands and I think that's fantastic. After all, imitation is the sincerest form of flattery and as the man who pioneered the idea within the sport of strongman, I take that as a massive compliment. Because we perform in arenas now, as opposed to car parks, giving yourself a stage name and trying to create a brand is almost a necessity, especially if we're going to turn strongman into the sporting equivalent of WWF, which I believe is possible. I don't think the established guys should bother, though. Especially ones who called me a dickhead.

At the end of the day, you need to remember that ultimately you're there to entertain the audience, so you need to put on a bit of a show. And you have to be adaptable. For instance, English audiences like a little bit of humility, whereas Scottish audiences don't. They just want you to beat your chest and say that you're going to annihilate the competition, whereas English audiences want you to talk about how much you respect your opponent. I'm fine with both, but the alpha male in me will always enjoy the former a lot more. Scottish audiences are also harder to make laugh than the English, so again, you have to adapt and alter what you say. That's not necessarily a good thing for me, though, as the harder I try the more I swear.

The issue of money, as with the alter ego, also came to light when I entered UK's Strongest Man in 2011. Bearing in mind this was a televised event and Britain's flagship competition at the time, what do you think the winner got? Fifty grand? No chance. OK, ten then? Try taking away eight from that. That's right, you got £2,000 for winning UK's Strongest Man in 2011, which at the time wasn't even a month's wages for me. The trouble was that everybody just accepted it and so even the strongmen who did manage to win the odd competition were barely breaking even, which meant the rest were obviously losing money. How is a sport – which, remember, is no stranger to success – supposed to be taken seriously when even its most successful protagonists haven't got a pot to piss in?

Once again, I could easily have said, *Fuck this for a game of soldiers, I'm going to do something else.* But what would be the point in that? I already had two good jobs and if I'd wanted to rest on my laurels and become Mr Average I'd have done it years ago. Something had to change though and instead of the TV companies just paying a few quid for the rights and not giving a dick about the sport, a new idea was needed. Something mutually beneficial where the first priority would be the advancement of strongman and where the strongmen themselves would be remunerated, incentivised and made to feel involved. I wanted to be a partner in strongman, not a fucking pawn.

But all that was in the future. In the meantime, I had a competition to win. When I arrived in Belfast to compete at UK's Strongest Man, my ambition as a strongman was actually to be the best in the British Isles. Whenever I decide to do something and then start telling people about that ambition, such as cleaning up at the Nationals or having a body like Arnold Schwarzenegger's, it's because I consider it to be attainable. There's no point going public about a pipe dream, because the chances are you'll make yourself look like a twat. The reason I hadn't even thought about becoming World's Strongest Man

With my beautiful
mum, Helen, on
the day I was born
– 15 January 1988.

Me at five months old.
Mum always said I was
a happy baby.

My first bike. I was a pro
rider straight off. The bike
was a hand-me-down –
always a problem of being
a younger brother.

Me at nursery.

My brothers and me on Dad's pride and joy. One brother, unnamed, took it for a ride at 15 and binned it. You can guess what followed!

My first means of transport at 16.

On holiday in Portugal, 1993. We were always dressed the same on holidays and I will cherish these memories forever.

Aged 10 on my first day at a new school – the last school had had enough of me!

My brothers and me swimming on holiday in Portugal.

1995: I broke my arm falling out of a tree the day before we flew out on a holiday to Portugal. Nothing stopped me swimming.

1995: We were always trying to prove who was strongest, my brothers and I.

National Swimming Championships 2001: Arnold knew I was good but I don't think he expected four golds and a silver medal. Following this success, I was enrolled onto the World Class Potential Programme.

My first real feature in the local paper. I felt like a celeb.

Future star: Ed Hall.   Photo: PAUL PICKARD.

NEWCASTLE star Ed Hall has been identified as one of the country's brightest prospects.

The 13-year-old has been selected for the world class potential programme organised by British Swimming and will attend training weekends at Leeds international pool during the next four months.

Hall will be joined at the camps by Newcastle swimming coach Arnold Faulkner who will help train the youngsters.

Hall's selection follows his phenomenal success at the national championships this year where he claimed four titles and set a new British record.

Here I am, aged 14 and weighing 14 stone. This was taken after completing Swimathon, a 5km charity swim in support of cancer. I completed the course in 1:01:15.

I was 16 and 16 stone when this picture of me was taken. I am taking part in my last National Swimming Championship in Sheffield, 2004.

2002: Me, Nan and
Grandad Jackson after
winning four golds at
the Nationals. This was
a proud moment for all
the family.

Our family jet ski
was responsible for
many great memories,
including (nearly)
getting lost at sea.

My first car, a
BMW 316. I was
17 and the coolest
kid on the block.

At 14, I started lifting weights during my training to help keep me out of trouble.

My brothers and me after our charity swimathon. We would always do our bit for charity and we're holding our certificate of recognition here.

July 2003: 15 and 15 stone.

Burnley 2007: My first ever tyre flip in my first Strongman Competition, aged 19.

Burnley 2007: Mark Felix, the first World's Strongest Man competitor I met.

Teen shows his strength

TEENAGE strongman Edward Hall finished in a respectable fifth place after battling through the rounds in his first contest.

The 19-year-old, of Eleanor Crescent, in the Westlands, went up against other musclemen at the event in Burnley.

In heavy rainfall, the truck mechanic gritted his teeth through events including the tyre flip, log lift and truck pull.

It was Edward's first big strongman event and he has now developed a taste for it.

He said: "I saw the advert and everyone kept encouraging me to take part.

"I will definitely do more, I'd eventually like to get to the World Strongest Man competition"

Also taking part was fellow competitor Mark Hill, of Bucknall, who finished in eighth position.

He added: "I was very pleased with that, as there were a fair few experienced competitors."

December 2010: The first competition where I began to show confidence and showboat – hence topless.

Family gathering on the occasion of my son's christening.

On a family holiday in Portugal. My brothers and I have had over twenty years of practice lining up for family pictures, as you can see from these.

June 2012: The day
I married my queen.
Alex was eight months
pregnant with Max. I'm
a very happy man here.

My first family photo
shoot. I think the kids
look so nice here.

Winning my first UK's Strongest Man competition. I set a record of 1m 18s whilst holding 20kg in each arm.

The 2014 Deadlift Championships at Europe's Strongest Man. This is the moment I dropped the World Record Deadlift... bad times!

Redemption. World Recor
462kg at the Arnold
Classic, Melbourne 2015.

Photo shoot for a new
clothing line, Xplosive
Ape. I am usually free
for modelling jobs,
by the way.

Chatting with my new
pal Arnie... *I'll be back!*

Pulling an ancient double-decker bus at Europe's Strongest Man 2017. A very hard pull.

One of my many brutal physio sessions, it often brings tears to my eyes.

Me and Mo during one of our many catch-up meetings, running over business ventures and appearances.

Here's me in the hyperbaric chamber that I built myself. Alex, my wife, is taking the picture.

Sitting in 9ºC water to aid recovery. My balls would disappear but it was all worth it!

Pushing the limits with a 500kg World-Record-breaking deadlift. To this day, this is the most dangerous thing I have ever done.

(although I had dreamed about qualifying for the competition), is because it was unknown territory and if I'm ever unsure about what, or who, I'm up against, I'm not going to start mouthing off. Some of you might find that hard to believe, but it's true. I'm confident and cocky, not daft and dopey. I might let my mouth run away with me sometimes but I rarely set myself up for a fall. I obviously knew what the field was, going into the competition, and I was confident of winning.

The competition was held over three days and the events were as follows:

Day 1

Duck walk and drag 40-foot lorry and trailer 20 metres x 1 competitor

Strongman flag hoist, five flags to be hoisted x 2 competitors

Human wheelbarrow, 20 metres, 90 seconds timed, 1 competitor

Arm wrestling x 2 competitors

Day 2

Deadlift car hold, straps, maximum x 2 competitors

Conan's torture circle, 360 degrees, 90 seconds x 1 competitor

Axe barbarian crucifix maximum hold x 2 competitors

Tyre flip, 20 metres, 90 seconds, 3 competitors

Final

Arm over arm anchor and chain, 20 metres, 90 seconds x 4 competitors

Axle for maximum x 1 competitor

Ultimate strongman shield carry, distance carried x 2 competitors

Squat for reps, 90 seconds x 1 competitor

Stones of strength, 100kg–160kg (220–353 lb)

I watched a recording of this competition the other day and my God did I stick out like a sore thumb. But in a good way. Most of the other competitors are big, bald and quite sedate, whereas I'm like a white B.A. Baracus on fucking acid. What an absolute gobshite! At the end of one of the arm-wrestling bouts, which I won beating a former Irish arm-wrestling champion, I let out this huge evil laugh and then screamed something that sounded like 'OOOOOJAAAAH!' My opponent was not impressed. A lad called Rob Drennan beat me in the final of that event and as he's getting the better of me I'm shouting and screaming like somebody's sawing my fucking leg off. That was how desperate I was to win.

They interviewed me at the start of the competition and who do I begin rabbiting on about? Arnold Schwarzenegger. 'What's your big ambition?' the presenter asked me, and I said, 'To be on television like Arnold Schwarzenegger.' When he looked at me like I was a cock, I shrugged my shoulders and said, 'Well, it could happen!' That was my first televised event, and it has to be said I looked like a natural.

During the truck pull, which I won, all you can hear is Alex shouting, 'COME ON, EDDIE!' She almost drowns out the bloody commentators. This, I'm afraid, became a bit of a bugbear of mine and over the years it started to get more and more annoying. It's not just Alex, by the way. In fact, my mum's the worst. She's only about five foot three inches, but she's got a voice like an amplified foghorn in the bottom of the Grand Canyon. Don't get me wrong, I absolutely love having my friends and family around me, but because I recognise their voices it can be distracting when I hear them during events. This came to a head at World's Strongest Man a couple of years ago when, half way through the truck pull, I started hearing this voice. 'Take little steps, Eddie!' it said. 'Take little steps!' It was Mum and the more I tuned into her voice the more annoyed I became.

Because the TV cameras were on me I obviously couldn't say anything but inside I was shouting, 'WILL YOU SHUT THE FUCK UP, MOTHER! I AM TAKING LITTLE FUCKING STEPS AND I'M TRYING TO PULL A MASSIVE FUCKING TRUCK!'

She obviously meant well, bless her, but after that I set a rule that friends and family had to remain silent during competitions, especially during a bloody truck pull. Little steps my arse!

I ended up winning UK's Strongest Man by half a point and went back home a reasonably happy man. It was televised later in the year and I got a real buzz out of telling all my mates I was going to be on TV. If I hadn't won though, I wouldn't have told a soul.

CHAPTER 19
Losing a Contest

In early 2012, I got meningitis. As you do. I was at work one day and as I was levering a bar down to test a suspension bush the bar slipped and smashed me in the nose. It was a bit of a mess but I carried on working. I'm dead hard, me!

Two days later I came down with a really bad headache at work. It was so bad, in fact, that I could hardly see anything and so I ended leaving about an hour early. Not that hard, then!

On the journey home, the lights from the oncoming traffic set the headache off again and when I got home I just collapsed on the sofa. Fortunately, my mum came over about half an hour later to drop something off and when she saw me on the sofa I was completely non-responsive. Couldn't speak, couldn't move, nothing.

Mum called an ambulance and after having a few tests at the hospital they confirmed that I had bacterial meningitis. Alex was pregnant with Max at the time and I was terrified I'd given it to her. Apparently, meningitis can lie dormant in your nose and if it gets disturbed it can become active quite quickly. Not everybody has it, but if you have and you have a nose injury you could be in trouble. I was off work for about two months in all and it really put me back.

This was the catalyst for making me give up the door work and as soon as I was back on my feet I sold the business. Despite the meningitis my immune system hadn't been firing on all cylinders so a near-death experience was exactly what I needed. It was a bit extreme though!

My first competition of 2012 took place in March and was a Giants Live event called the Melbourne Classic (now the Arnold Classic). Whoever finished inside the top three got immediate passage through to World's Strongest Man which was taking place that September. In the end I finished fourth, but a guy called Colin Bryce, who runs Giants Live with Darren Sadler, was so impressed by my performance that he took me to one side after the competition and told me that he'd make sure I won qualification. This was a colossal boost for me because I was confident that by the time September came around I'd have shortened the gap between me and the world's elite. With that being my only barometer it was imperative that I made it to Los Angeles, which is where the competition was being held.

Colin did have one issue, though. I was now starting to bulk up a lot and if I wasn't working or training, I was either eating or thinking about eating. Obviously, I needed to get bigger, but at the same time I had to try to maintain my fitness and mobility. Static power's important, but roughly half the events at World's Strongest Man require movement and if I wanted to challenge the athletes who were, perhaps, more genetically gifted than I was, I couldn't afford to have any weaknesses. When Colin told me that he intended to get me to Los Angeles he questioned whether my mobility was up to scratch and to be brutally honest, no, it probably wasn't. This is because I still wasn't training for strongman and so all I did from a training point of view was to lift weights.

Even so, I was still quite taken aback by Colin's comment and so parried it by informing him that I used to be a national swimming champion (which obviously requires a certain amount of mobility) and that I still held several records. I could tell by the look on his face that he thought this was bullshit and so I thought, Right then, Mr Bryce. Not only will I prove to you that I can move well with weights, but I will also prove that I was once the toast of the swimming world. Until I pulled that moonie and called Sweetenham a fat twat, of course.

Sure enough, when we finally got to LA I pulled out some of my press cuttings and very proudly handed them to Colin. He actually knows Mark Foster and when I'd told him that I'd broken one or two of Mark's records he once again thought I was pulling his plonker. I'll never forget the look on his face when he started reading the articles. While Colin's eyes started widening, a self-satisfied grin began permeating my face, which, if it could have been translated into words, would have said, 'What do you think about that then, eh?'

One of the reasons I was so keen for Colin to read those articles is because he was somebody I looked up to and admired. I may be a narcissist with a big gob but there are certain people in the world who make me want to shut up and listen, and Colin's one of them. It's the same with strongmen. I made a point, around this time, actually, of getting to know people like Brian, Thor and Big Z, for the simple reason that they were the best and I wanted to feed off their success. I also get on really well with them, which helps. Some strongmen would probably feel either intimidated or deflated by hanging around with people who are on a different level to them, but not me. If I was ever going to match, or perhaps even better, these inspirational behemoths, I had to know what made them tick, and, over the years, I've picked up all kinds of stuff – everything from eating habits, through to how they respond to certain situations and how they prepare for certain events. You can't always tell what they're thinking, of course, but being close to them means you often get a pretty good idea. Conversely, I think they've also picked things up from me. Especially since I've moved up to their level of size and strength. I've definitely taught them one or two new words!

When it comes to sport, Colin has been there, done that and bought the T-shirt; as well as being a former Olympic bobsledder he also spent time as a strongman and is one of the best sporting commentators there is. Ever since I first met Colin all he's wanted to do is help the athletes get on and he's advised me in every aspect of my life, from how to train to how I should conduct myself. Intellectually, he's a powerhouse but what I take away most from our relationship, apart from his friendship, is his wisdom. Colin has this knack of pulling things he's either heard or read out of thin air just at the right time and he's a constant source of inspiration.

A few years ago, Colin spent some time with Mike Tyson and when he asked him what Muhammad Ali had over everyone else he said that Muhammad Ali was the only one prepared to swim into dark waters.

'What do you mean, dark waters?' I asked Colin.

'Well,' he said, 'if all the greatest boxers swam out to sea, Muhammad Ali would be the one who'd keep swimming no matter what. He'd be the only one willing to swim into dark waters.'

That story of Colin's stuck with me big time and it describes my attitude to a T. To get where I want to be I am prepared to swim into the very darkest waters and regardless of what I do in life that will never change.

Funnily enough, that's not the only story that resonates with me that came out of this conversation between Colin and Mike Tyson. When the two of them got on to the subject of Ali calling himself the greatest, Tyson told Colin that Ali pinched that saying from a wrestler who was around in the 1940s called Gorgeous George. Being a good wrestler wasn't enough for Gorgeous George and so he invented a persona for himself that he knew would piss off his opponents. Back then, men were supposed to be men, so in order to have the most impact, George started turning up to fights wearing frilly bathrobes and platinum blonde wigs. He even used to enter the ring to Elgar's 'Pomp and Circumstance'. Not only would this infuriate the other wrestlers but it also gave George an immediate advantage. There was no way in the world his opponents could lose to a man dressed like that but because he was so effeminate they were afraid of going anywhere near him. It was absolute genius when you think about it and he turned the hitherto niche sport of wrestling into a huge hit. Apparently Muhammad Ali had seen George camping it up on TV one day, saying, 'I'm the greatest.' This obviously struck a chord with Ali and the rest, as they say, is history. That's where he got his big-talking public persona from and helped to make him a star.

When Colin told me this story everything just clicked into place and I could see how much of my own behaviour mirrored that of Gorgeous George's. I remembered how that public persona had come instinctively to me back when I was starting out as a swimmer – the bragging, the mind games, the flamboyant entrances ... even the cross-dressing! Obviously like George and Muhammad Ali (or Cassius Clay, as he was then), I had to back up the showmanship with talent and ability, but the character also helped to give me the edge. Yet again, Colin had helped to give me an insight into my own personality.

When I found out I'd qualified for the 2012 World's Strongest Man I almost exploded. For a start it was going to be held in Los Angeles, which is somewhere I'd always wanted to go, and at the time, qualifying for the competition represented the sum of my ambitions within strongman. I'd make a judgement as to whether I'd alter this ambition after the competition had taken place, but in the meantime, I was just happy to be taking part.

I'll tell you something, though, it was a good job I had built my ambitions around what I knew, because when I got to the hotel and had a good look at the competition I felt like a little girl. I was twenty-four stone, for Christ's sake, but I genuinely felt minuscule. Every single athlete seemed to be huge and when I first saw people like Brian Shaw, Hafþór (Thor) Björnsson and Žydrūnas Savickas in the flesh, I almost packed up and started hitching a ride home. Not only were these blokes tall, especially Brian and Thor, but they were also as heavy as fuck and they were all about thirty stone. A six-stone difference might not sound like much to some people, but when you add to that a height difference of about six or seven inches, things start taking on a new light. Actually, those two mammoth freaks usually block out most of the light!

I suppose it was another Arnold Schwarzenegger moment in a way, but this time it was in triplicate, and, it was in the flesh. These three athletes have all taken the title of the World's Strongest Man and were so far and away better than everybody else it was ridiculous.

Despite feeling like a Jack Russell nipping at their heels I still thought I had it in me to get through my qualifying group and at least make it to the final, but unfortunately it wasn't to be. I did win a couple of events – the Viking press and the squat – which I was pleased with, but it was a difficult group to get out of and at the end of the day I was neither big enough nor good enough to progress, and finished the group in fourth place. Normally they use things like barrels for weights in the Viking press but this time they were using quad bikes and given my history I was always going to win that. It was a pyrrhic victory though and sometimes you have to hold your hands up and admit defeat. It's not something I find easy but once I get over the disappointment, the first thing I do is start looking for positives, and in this case, they weren't too difficult to find. I was still young and, although I wasn't big enough or good enough at the time, I had the makings of becoming a true behemoth, in every respect.

One thing I remember at the end of the competition was watching a photograph being taken with six different winners of the competition. There was Big Z, Brian Shaw, Bill Kazmaier, Magnús Ver Magnússon, Svend Karlsen and Phil Pfister.

I remember standing behind the cameraman thinking, *what an absolute fucking privilege*. Everybody – all the athletes and crew – were in awe of these guys and it was a great moment. Privilege aside, my one overriding emotion as I stood there watching them all was envy. Pure envy. What a motivation though.

Competitively, World's Strongest Man 2012 really opened up the world of strongman for me. In fact, it was like discovering a whole new continent. One populated by ugly-looking giants from America, Iceland and Lithuania, who ate, breathed and slept strongman; and who, unless I did something about it, would swallow me for breakfast every day of the fucking week. It was sink or swim time again. And, as per usual, I had three choices: give it all up and be happy mending trucks, consolidate my position as the strongest man in Britain, or start eating like a horse, training like a maniac and swinging from the chandeliers before finally mixing it with the big boys. It was time to start building the beast!

The rest of 2012 was a bit up and down really. I won UK's Strongest Man again, and won convincingly. Then I made my debut at Europe's Strongest Man at Headingley Stadium in Leeds, and it was like the Worlds all over again. I certainly didn't perform to my best but with Thor and Žydrūnas in the line-up it was a reminder not only of where I needed to be, but where I would be once I'd finished. I was now training specifically for strongman, at last, and that was already paying dividends. It had taken me a while but instead of just lifting weights I was training each specific event. The equipment didn't always match, but it was a step in the right direction.

CHAPTER 20
A Dramatic Arrival

Before we move on to 2013, there's one more event from 2012 that I have to tell you about, although it's nothing to do with strongman. This was a thousand times more stressful, although on the up-side I didn't have to lift a finger. The event in question was the birth of my son, Maximus, who was born on 10 July.

Maximus had been planned; Alex and I had even spoken about having kids on the day I asked her to marry me. We'd chatted about all aspects of our future that day and in celebration of our new life together Alex came off the pill the next day. About three months later she sat me down and told me she was pregnant, so as well as being a planned baby, he was a bloody quick one too. He ended up arriving four weeks after our wedding day.

Unlike I had with Layla, I actually managed to attend the birth from the start this time around. But the labour itself was very long and about half way through I actually went away to train for a few hours. That might sound a bit off to some people but hey, life goes on. That's my job and if I don't train,

I don't get paid. The midwife said I had plenty of time so while Alex was panting away in the hospital, I was pumping away in the gym.

A few hours later I was back in the hospital with Alex and because I was knackered after training I crashed on the floor and started nodding off. Suddenly, I heard an alarm going off and when I opened my eyes all I could see were red flashing lights and Alex being wheeled off by some nurses. I leapt to my feet to follow them, and fortunately one of the nurses waited behind for me to tell me what was happening in response to my frantic questions. Apparently there was a problem with Maximus's heartbeat and they were going to have to give Alex a caesarian. Poor Alex had lost consciousness by now and even though I was only peering in through a window in the door she seemed to be in a really bad way. These few minutes were some of the worst of my entire life and for all that time – which felt like eternity – I honestly thought I was losing them both. The feeling of helplessness was unbearable and when I eventually heard Maximus scream for the very first time, after being delivered by caesarean section, I almost collapsed with relief. It was like being pulled out of a fiery pit.

About five minutes later I was allowed into the delivery room and was able to hold Maximus for the first time. Alex was still unconscious at this point and although they'd told me several times that she was going to be OK I was still as nervous as hell. Not only do I love Alex to pieces but I need her, and now Maximus needed her. I'm not sure how I would have coped being a single parent but I wouldn't have fancied my chances much. I'm OK lifting weights on my own but bringing up children is much bigger task. Probably the biggest.

Fortunately, the doctors were right and a few minutes later Alex came around. She was still very poorly but she was alive, which was the main thing. Is it possible to measure extreme relief? Well, if anyone ever wants an example of somebody who is literally on their knees with it, then look no further than me on 10 July 2012.

The one thing people always want to know about Maximus is where we got his name from and because I'm tremendously proud of it I'm always only too happy to tell them. The first thing they usually always say is, 'Only you could call your son Maximus, Eddie!' and that's fucking bang on. Come on, it's the coolest name on the planet, right? I first got the idea when I watched the film *Gladiator* and that would have been in my mid-teens. I was obsessed by the film, just like I was obsessed by *The Terminator*, and when I first watched Russell Crowe introduce himself as Maximus Decimus Meridius, I remember thinking, *Fuck me, that is a proper fucking name!* It was pure power. At that moment I promised myself that if ever I had a son I would called him Maximus. I wasn't bothered about the other two names. They sounded like diseases.

Whatever Maximus ends up doing in life, and I know it's going to be something special, the moment he shakes a person's hand and says, 'Hi, I'm Maximus, how do you do,' they're going to think to themselves, *Wow, what a great name*. And, if he ends up being a big lad like his dad, which he probably will be, it'll make it even more impressive. I hope to God he doesn't end up being five foot five inches and about ten stone with a name like that!

When Alex was pregnant with Maximus we went and had a scan and when they told us what sex he was I was like a kid at Christmas. I'd kept on saying to the nurse who was doing the scan, 'It'd better be a boy. Seriously, it'd better be a fucking boy!' God only knows what she thought I was going to do if it hadn't been. I actually think I'd have just sulked for a bit. It's not that I have anything against girls, by the way. Layla's testament to that. Let's face it, though, there are only so many future boyfriends you can beat up, so us having a boy was better, and safer, for everyone concerned. Will I be a protective father? What do you think! Of course I will. I'll be fair though and I've promised Layla that she'll be allowed to date boys the moment she turns fifty.

The effect Maximus's birth had on me was very similar to Layla's in that it reminded me of my responsibilities and prevented me from acting like a prick. It wasn't as if I'd fallen off the wagon completely, but it was a timely reminder all the same, and because of this I became a lot more self-aware. By now I'd given up working the doors and so my only source of income was the day job. This was obviously a positive with regards to my family life but the effect it had on my bank balance was anything but. Despite Alex also bringing in a wage, the lack of decent income was starting to bother me. Food alone was now costing about £250 a week and that was just for me! I couldn't let it get to me. Only two things mattered now: succeeding in strongman and making my young family happy and proud. It was a self-fulfilling ambition, potentially.

However, there was a danger with this ambition that was always present too: that the very process of me attempting to become the strongest man on the planet wouldn't make my family being happy and proud, but it would have the opposite effect on them. It was something I was going to have to learn how to manage the hard way over the next few years.

CHAPTER 21

Planes, Trains and Automobiles

Worlds's Strongest Man 2013 was an experience I will never, ever forget, and for all kinds of reasons. Good and bad. It started off with me almost murdering a Chinese teacher on a plane, and finished with me being the eleventh strongest man on Earth. But before we get into all that, let me tell you about something that, as I've become bigger, has caused me no end of bloody problems. Namely, travel. The bane of my life.

I think I first noticed it becoming a problem when I was about nineteen years old, and so nineteen stone. That was the point I realised that things like cars, trains and aeroplanes hadn't been designed for people like me. I seemed to have outgrown pretty much everything and the more I travelled, the more I noticed it, and the more I noticed it, the more it got on my frigging nerves.

Even short flights can be a nightmare and after only an hour on a plane I'll already be suffering from swollen feet, a bad back and swollen legs. Sometimes my feet actually double in size which makes it impossible for me to put my trainers on afterwards.

As I've become bigger so have the problems, and since I hit about twenty-four stone it's become almost impossible to get around easily, whether I'm travelling by train, plane or coach. When it comes to cars I have to buy American models and at the moment I'm driving a big Chrysler 300. Even that's become a struggle; in addition to having to lean away from the door pillars constantly it's murder on my back. They also cost a fortune to run, but then isn't that the rule? The bigger you get the more fuel you need.

This isn't just a rambling complaint, by the way. I'm just telling you what it's like. If I were that bothered I wouldn't have chosen to live my life this way, but this is what I do. You could stick me on ten-hour flight with no sleep, and I'd still get off and break a world record. In fact, I did once. I'll tell you about that in a bit.

The mode of transport that causes me the most amount of hassle, and the one I'll do literally anything to avoid (although that's difficult), is air travel. And, as I alluded to earlier, as well as almost being the death of me, both physically and mentally, it has pushed me to the brink of committing homicide – not just once, but on numerous occasions. That would make an interesting interview:

'So, Eddie. What would you like to do if you weren't a strongman?'

'I'd like to kill people on aeroplanes.'

Take April this year, for instance. I had to go to Frankfurt for an Expo and when I got to the gate at Manchester Airport I was denied access because of my size. 'You'll need to buy an extra seat, sir,' said the jobsworth in charge, 'Otherwise you will not be flying with us today.' Everything was too much trouble for this arsehole but instead of hammering him into the ground like I should have and then letting out an evil laugh, I just took a deep breath, shot him a look that said, 'Next time, wanker,' and then called the sponsor and asked them to buy me another ticket, which they did. I'll tell you what though, he was right. Even with two seats I only had about a centimetre either side of me and virtually no bollock space. Some of you might have seen this on my documentary but the acid test for me with regards to how I cope on a flight is how much bollock space I've got. If my balls can breathe, I can cope with just about anything. If they can't, somebody will probably die, and it won't be me.

Long-haul flights are obviously the nadir of my travelling life and before I board any plane for a long-haul flight there are two things I simply have to do: swallow a handful of diarrhoea tablets, and take a good long shit. Taking a dump on an aeroplane is almost a physical impossibility for me. In fact, the only way it might work is if I reversed in, but that's a big if. One thing I wouldn't be able to do is close the door and as somebody who eats around 12,000 calories a day you would not want to be within fifty yards of me when I'm on the throne.

Then, there's the small issue of cleaning up after myself, which I'd have to do in the aisle. Not a nice image, is it? I don't mind, but I have a strange feeling that the other passengers might just be reaching for the oxygen, if not the sick bags.

When I was on the flight to Frankfurt I had to go for a piss but because the toilet was so small I had to pee with the door ajar. One of the hostesses was horrified at this and started having a go at me.

'Sir!' she said. 'You can't do that. It's against the law.'

'What the hell do you expect me to do?' I said to her. 'I need a piss, for Christ's sake. If you want to try and close the door behind me, go ahead.'

This air hostess did try and it must have been hilarious watching her. She couldn't do it though.

To be fair, most people are quite good-humoured when it comes to this sort of thing and generally I rub along well with the airline staff. Occasionally though, you'll get a jobsworth and when that happens, sparks usually fly, and when sparks fly, I get into trouble. Whenever I'm going through security I always ask if I can go through the FastTrack lane because of the pain in my back and generally they give me the nod. 'Yes, of course, sir. Off you go. No one's looking.' When I'm in heavy training I can't stand for long and even after five minutes in a queue my back will be in agony. This before I've even got on the plane.

There was one little Hitler though (I won't say where) and when I asked him if I could slip into the FastTrack lane and told him why he actually said to me, 'Come along now, sir. I hear this sort of thing all the time and I don't believe a word of it. You'll have to stay in line like everyone else.'

I really was suffering by this point but instead of clocking him one I just said, 'Thanks for fuck all, mate,' and then I got back in line. However, apparently you're not allowed to say the word 'fuck' to scroats like that so once I'd walked through the metal detector I was stopped by a load of guards who all but strip-searched me. In fact, the only thing they didn't do was stick a finger up my arse. If they had, they'd have had to cancel all flights.

Why can't you just keep your fucking mouth shut? I thought to myself. In my defence, though, it was four o'clock in the morning, I was getting asked for selfies and autographs left, right, and centre, and I was in a tremendous amount of pain.

That too is something that is part and parcel of being a strongman and if I don't wake up in the morning experiencing some kind of pain or soreness I know that I haven't been training hard enough. It's as simple as that. I'm not talking about a muscle strain or a twisted ankle. I'm talking about your entire body telling you to fuck off constantly. Even as I'm writing this, my back's throbbing like you wouldn't believe and I've got shooting pains going down my left arm. Anybody else would be running to A&E if they had this but if you're a strongman it's as normal as getting a hard on, but not nearly as much fun.

There's a part in my documentary where Geoff Capes reels off all the injuries he's had over the years and what he suffers from today, and it's a truly frightening list. This is on top of the usual stuff like strains, pulls and tears, by the way. He's had a new hip, operations on his knees, abdominal operations, problems with his vertebra and compressed nerves on his spine. Geoff finishes his litany of injuries by saying, 'Basically, I'm buggered,' and although it's quite a funny moment, he means it. He really is buggered.

The pain probably started when I was about fifteen or sixteen, and, like everything, it's just amplified as I've become bigger. Think about it. I'm ripping my muscles on a daily basis and so my body's usually awash with lactic acid.

Anyway, let's get on this plane to the World's Strongest Man competition in China.

As I said, I almost ended up killing a teacher on this flight, but with very, very good reason. The man was a disgusting arsehole and how the hell he ended up in charge of a load of children I'll never know.

We didn't get off to the best of starts because when I asked him – very nicely, I might add – if he'd mind swapping seats so that I could have the aisle seat he just shook his head once and didn't even look at me. This was a fourteen-hour flight we were about to embark on and even though there were just two of us in these seats, I was the one with my shoulder pushed up against the side of the plane with no bollock space and no room to stretch my legs. Teach, on the other hand, who was about three foot six inches tall, was free to stretch his legs out to touch the other side of the aisle, had they been long enough.

The next thing this arsehole started doing was farting. I even said to him at one point, 'You dirty little bastard,' but I think he took that as a compliment.

Every single air mile bestowed on me a new level of hatred for man. Whenever he wanted to attract the stewardess's attention, instead of pushing the button or catching the stewardess's eye politely as she passed in the accepted manner, he'd shout and start waving his hand.

And few hours into the flight he started spitting in the aisle. I'm not talking about spitting out orange pips. This man was hoiking up greenies like you would not believe. None of the airline staff seemed to give a shit, by the way, which concerned me slightly.

By the time we reached Sanya I was capable of just about anything and when I got up to disembark the plane, my feet were the size of melons and my body felt like it'd been in a twelve-round boxing match. This obviously made my mood even worse so from the moment I got out of my seat until we started queueing at passport control I walked about an inch behind this dickhead and as well as growling at him I started telling him what I was going to do to him. Of course he knew full well that I was there and by the time we got to passport control he'd got up to a canter and was almost shitting himself. I'm afraid I can't really repeat what I said to him but put it this way, if words alone could kill a man he'd have turned inside out and then burst into flames.

Unfortunately, my travelling companion's behaviour seemed to be representative of the general population and if I'd been given a pound for every time I saw somebody gobbing in the street I'd have been able to get a private plane home.

My spirits were not lifted by the accommodation, when I finally arrived at it. It's changed now, fortunately, but at the time the organisation of the World's Strongest Man had room for improvement. Luckily, Giants Live, who now run the qualifying events for World's Strongest Man, including Europe's Strongest Man and Britain's Strongest Man, are starting to incentivise us. They are growing the sport and that's my biggest motivation too. One of the reasons Giants Live are able to do this is because they stage their events in arenas and the ticket money is used to remunerate the athletes, which obviously motivates us to do well. They also sell the TV rights to the competitions, which helps generate more money, and everybody is happy.

CHAPTER 22

Making a Big Impression in Hungary

Despite not getting through to the final at World's Strongest Man 2013, I only missed out by half a point, and as well as winning three events in my heat, I was first reserve for the final. So, within just a year of completely flunking World's Strongest Man and feeling totally out of my depth, I'd elevated myself to become the eleventh strongest man on the planet. Not bad, I guess. The improvement had been perfect really – steady and organic – and the only thing I was slightly disappointed about was the fact that it had taken me so long for the penny to drop so that I shifted my training from just weights, to weights and actual events. By now I'd invested in some serious strongman equipment, such as a yoke, a log and some atlas stones, and I'd also changed gyms. The place I was at originally was just a bog-standard gym that was part of a chain, whereas the new place, Strength Asylum, majors in things like strongman, powerlifting and bodybuilding. I've been there ever since. They allow me to keep all my equipment on-site which means I can train strongman events whenever I like. Except the truck pull, that is. For that I have to borrow a lorry from a local skip company (Jumbo Skips in Newcastle-under-Lyme) and then pull it around a trading estate. Oh, the glamour!

Speaking of glamour, it took me a total of thirty hours to get back to the UK from China and by the time I walked through my front door I was literally on my knees. It was great seeing Alex and the kids but I felt like a fucking zombie. The following morning I was due to catch a flight to Belfast to defend my UK's Strongest Man crown and as I got into bed that night I was ready to abdicate. Fuck me, was I tired. By the time I woke up, all thoughts of abdication had vanished and the only things running through my head were Alex, the kids, and thoughts about the next World's Strongest Man competition. It was now another year until the next tournament and if I wanted to see another improvement I'd have to get my head down. It was going to be tough but I was confident that within two years there would be four men vying for the title of World's Strongest Man, not three, and one of them would be a narky bearded twat from Stoke.

But for now my most pressing urgency was my home title to defend. By the time I boarded the plane for Belfast I was like a man possessed and was so confident in my abilities that I'm pretty sure I could have flown the plane myself. In fact, I know I could. I can fly a plane, by the way. It's a piece of piss.

Once again, I've watched a couple of recordings of this tournament and you can see I'm absolutely on the frigging money.

Very, very businesslike. I don't waste a drop of energy, so there's no showboating, and subsequently, I make mincemeat of the opposition. What actually helped was knowing that I was going to be tired. That made me sharp. This was my third UK's Strongest Man title on the bounce and although it wasn't the World's, it still felt fantastic. One thing I'd forgotten about until I watched the recording back was the fact that instead of winning a nice trophy like you would at most strongman events, you get a glass vase! I think they might have got them muddled up with a sewing competition or something. When the titles are running at the end of the show and I'm standing on the podium trying to look hard, you can't help noticing that instead of holding aloft a miniature statue of Charles Atlas or whatever, I'm trying to hide a nice piece of glassware.

Anyway, job done, so you'd think at this point I could relax slightly, right? Wrong. There was one more tournament in 2013, which was memorable for all the wrong reasons. As well as visiting Hungary for the first time, which was nice, I caused a diplomatic incident that had Colin Bryce apologising, not only to the Hungarian parliament, but also to the President himself.

I know you're not surprised but I'm going to tell you anyway. This was a Giants Live event, which meant it was also a qualifier for the Worlds, and the two big names in attendance were me and the American, Mike Burke. Sure enough, Mike and I finished first and second respectively, but as opposed to just turning up, competing, and then pissing off again, like we normally did, we were invited by the sports minister to go on a tour of the Hungarian houses of parliament. As well as being a fan of strongman, this man was also a two-time Olympic champion and because Colin had said that it would be rude to refuse the invitation I reluctantly agreed. It's not that I didn't want to go (honest!), I just hated being on my feet for too long and it just wasn't my kind of thing. But because my mentor said it was the right thing to do, I grabbed my bum bag and off we went.

I have to say that this sports minister guy was really welcoming and the first ten minutes or so were actually quite interesting. After that it all became a bit boring and by the time we reached the chamber where the National Assembly of Hungary sits I was looking for a distraction. Luckily, or unluckily if you're Hungarian or Colin Bryce, a large group of Japanese tourists suddenly appeared in the chamber and without even thinking I ran off down the stairs and made my way to what turned out to be the President's lectern; somewhere only the President is allowed to go. In order to get to the lectern I had to pass two very heavily armed guards but as I approached them at speed their jaws just dropped, so instead of getting shot, I got through. It was all going well so far and now I'd caught the Japanese tourists' attention I was determined to give them a show.

As soon as I got to the lectern I ripped off my vest and started a full posing routine, showing off all the different muscle groups. The poor sports minister was in a state of shock by this time but the Japanese tourists were lapping it up and all you could hear, apart from the odd gasp, were cameras going off. It was straight out of *Pumping Iron*, really. Very professional.

Not being an actual bodybuilder, I eventually ran out of poses, but because my public wanted more, I decided to give them more. *I know*, I thought. *I'll do a Usain Bolt pose. That's quite current.*

Within a second I was attempting what I thought was an Usain Bolt pose, but because I hadn't got it quite right the Hungarian sports minister and virtually everyone else there, apart from Colin and the Japanese, mistook it for a Nazi salute. When Colin realised what the sports minister and gathered dignitaries were all thinking he shat his pants and he still describes it as 'that awful, awful moment'. You don't have to be a historian to know that Hungary was once invaded by the Nazis and although time's obviously a great healer the last thing they were expecting was an unintentional reminder via a topless strongman at the President's lectern. It was not one of my greatest moments and as well as writing several letters of apology, Colin also had to speak directly to the President. Fortunately for me, one of our cameramen had been filming the tour and so we were able to prove that it definitely wasn't a Nazi salute, just a crude Usain Bolt pose.

I really do think we should move on now. Certainly out of Hungary!

CHAPTER 23
Doncaster to L.A.

Although every year has been pivotal in its own way, 2014 was make or break and it's the closest I've ever come to jacking it all in. Up until then I'd always been what you'd call an enthusiastic amateur, I suppose, which is what the majority of strongmen still are. There are a few full-time professionals, but although there aren't many there were enough then to keep me from getting my hands on the only trophy I genuinely dreamt about winning. Remain an enthusiastic amateur and the best I could ever hope for, realistically, was a domestic trophy or two and a finals place at World's Strongest Man. Not a podium though. In order to achieve that I would need to become a professional but to become a professional I would need sponsors who were willing to give me cash.

Those sorts of negotiations were beyond me so what I actually needed more than anything was a manager. But where do I get a …? You get the picture. It was all a bit overwhelming. For the time being, I had to put these thoughts on hold but they were very much in the back of my mind as I entered my next competitions.

The year got off to a fantastic start as it marked my first ever win at Britain's Strongest Man, which is the UK's longest running and most prestigious competition. The first man to win it back in 1979 was the great Geoff Capes and since then two other World's Strongest Man winners, Gary Taylor and Jamie Reeves, had won the competition plus my two mates, Terry Hollands and Laurence Shahlaei. The competition had taken a break between 2009 and 2011 and after Laurence dominated the first two years back it was my turn to take over. It might not be an international trophy but Britain's Strongest Man is one of the sport's biggest domestic competitions, and with a qualification place for World's Strongest Man up for grabs I was desperate to show my dominance.

The competition took place on March 16 at the Doncaster Dome and the events were as follows:

1. Farmer's walk and duck walk medley (130kg–140kg (286–308 lb) farmer's; 200kg (441 lb) duck walk – 20 metres each)
2. Log lift for reps – 150kg (331 lb)
3. Deadlift for reps – 340kg (750 lb)
4. Dumbbell for reps – 100kg (220 lb)
5. Conan's Wheel
6. Loading race – sacks and barrels

There were nine competitors from Great Britain in total: Terry Hollands, Laurence Shahlaei, Mark Felix, Graham Hicks, Ben

Kelsey, Lloyd Renals, Simon Jonston, Brian Irwin and myself. Plus there were a further three international competitors: Kevin Larsen from Norway, Marco Guidi from Italy and Daniel Garcia from Gibraltar. Not a soft line-up, by any means.

I finished up standing top middle on the podium with Graham Hicks to my right and Laurence Shahlaei to my left. In the athletes meeting prior to the competition all the athletes had kept calling out who they thought was going to win each event and, because they all seemed to be unanimous, and because they didn't mention me, it got under my skin. Not one person had me down for a single win so it was the perfect motivation. It's also why I gave Laurence Shahlaei the middle finger as I was completing the final event. Everybody had him down as the overall winner and I wasn't having any of it. It was a good day's work, all in all.

As the biggest win of my career this did my profile no harm whatsoever and when World's Strongest Man came along just a week or so later I had companies falling over themselves to sponsor me. The trouble was they were all offering kit as opposed to cash and, as much as I appreciated their support, it wasn't going to afford me the opportunity to achieve parity with the three professionals who all but ruled the sport: Thor Björnsson, Brian Shaw and Žydrūnas Savickas.

I know I keep banging on about money, incidentally, but I've always felt the need to shout about it. It was very simply a matter of survival at the beginning. But as I've gradually become a bigger box office draw, it's become more about realising my worth and getting my fair share.

I did a few seminars a couple of years ago and I remember somebody asking me what the prize money was for World's Strongest Man. When I told them the winner got $45,000 I could see their jaws dropping. 'Is that all?' they said. 'You easily could earn that doing a normal job.' You can see why cash sponsorship was a necessity.

Despite the difficulties with turning pro still hanging over my head, my immediate goal was to focus on reaching the finals of World's Strongest Man. When I arrived in Los Angeles for the qualifiers I was bigger and stronger than I'd ever been. In fact, I was almost the finished article. A good performance here and perhaps some cash might materialise.

In the very first event I managed to injure my right bicep when picking up a sack but fortunately it wasn't serious. Even so, I still finished that event last and already had my work cut out. Once again, I've watched this heat back and for some reason I seem to be on my best behaviour. There isn't quite so much bravado as normal and I even wish one of the other competitors luck, which isn't like me. To be honest I think the injury made me nervous and because I'd come so close the year before I think I was feeling the pressure a bit. Fortunately, as the heat progressed, I gained confidence and ended up finishing second behind

Jerry Pritchett, who was the man I'd wished luck. The only reason I didn't win the group was because I didn't need to. First and second went through and by the time we got to the atlas stones I'd done enough. What mattered was that, at the third time of asking, I was at last through to the final of World's Strongest Man.

The first event of the final took place on the beautiful Venice Beach ... but that's where the positives end, I'm afraid. It was a loading race – three huge tyres weighing 100kg each – and the thing that scuppered me was not only my technique, but also the fact that we were having to carry these things on sand. Just walking on sand is hard enough but when you're trying to run while carrying a massive tractor tyre it tends to present problems. Each of us had our own technique and unfortunately mine was shit. Unlike everyone else, who tried to carry it over their shoulder, I decided to get inside the tyre and then carry it like some enormous hula hoop, but as hard as I tried to remain upright I just kept on falling arse over tit. It had worked in the familiarisation session! One event down and out of a field of twelve I lay last on one point. Oh dear. Actually, oh bollocks!

The next event, the circus medley which is axle press and circus dumbbell, was a slight improvement and I ended up finishing mid-table. This left me ninth overall which was, quite frankly, appalling, but highlighted perfectly the gulf that existed between me and the top three (the rest didn't matter). I so wanted to be in that club.

The next event, which was the keg toss, demonstrated not only the top tier's dominance, but also how being a lanky freak like Brian or Thor can give you an advantage at certain events. That's taking nothing away from their strength, by the way. It's just a fact. Even so, their performances were absolutely astonishing and I came away half wanting to ask for their autographs, and half wanting to kill them. I should have killed them really!

You had two throw eight kegs in all over a bar – two at 40 lb, two at 45 lb, two at 50 lb and two at 55 lb – and the bar was set at six metres. Brian Shaw stepped up and did all eight in just under seventeen seconds. This performance was just astounding and when Brian stood on the sidelines waiting to watch Thor he must have thought he had it in the bag. I say in the documentary that Thor's like a kid who's been locked in a shed for twenty-six years and then released, and that's absolutely bob on. He chucked all eight of those kegs in 16.35 seconds and if you're wondering if that's fast, just you try picking up twenty or thirty kilograms and then imagine having to throw it over six metres in the air. You'd have to do it eight times, of course. The look on Brian's face was an absolute picture and we were all saying the same thing, basically: how in the name of Odin's arse did you do that?

The final three events told a similar story as far as I was concerned, and because of a litany of errors (all of which I learned from), I would only excel in one of them. That was the squat lift and the only man who managed to beat me was the eventual winner, Žydrūnas Savickas. Once again, I finished mid-table and despite being envious of what I was witnessing I was learning a massive amount. I went home to Stoke hungrier than ever to go professional and start realising my true potential.

CHAPTER 24
Deadlift Drama

I had almost five months until the next big event and spent all of that time either mending trucks, training, eating, sleeping or looking for sponsors and which meant I had precious little time for the wife and kids. This is a running theme throughout this book and gets a whole lot worse later on. Even though we'd been married just a couple of years, Alex's patience was already starting to run thin and it's not difficult to see why. My excuse for being AWOL was that I was doing it for her and the kids and that once I'd won World's Strongest Man everything would be different. That's all good and well when you're starting out but once reality sets in it can turn sour. Despite all my promises, I think Alex was having difficulty seeing the light at the end of the tunnel. To me there was no doubt I was going to get there but there's only so many times you can say to somebody, 'It won't be like this forever, I promise.'

One thing that I hoped would instil some belief in Alex was Europe's Strongest Man and in particular the world deadlift championships, which was the warm-up event. As somebody who excelled at the deadlift this was the chance for me to bag a world record, which once again would heighten my profile and enable me to get closer to my ambition.

The venue for both these competitions was Headingley Rugby Stadium and with an audience of 5,000-plus – and, as the current holder of the title of Britain's and UK's Strongest Man – I knew that the crowd would be right behind me.

The night before I hardly got a wink of sleep as I was a bit nervous but I actually got out of bed feeling OK, I'm not advocating insomnia as an aid for achieving success but some-times it can help sharpen the mind and body and fortunately this was one of these occasions.

The deadlift world record is the only one that really matters in strongman, as despite being a relatively simple exercise it's the one that uses all the muscle groups and exemplifies what strongmen do: see who can lift the most weight. I'd smashed it in the gym on several occasions and was itching for the opportunity to make it mine.

The first round was 400kg (881 lb) (the current world record was 460kg (1,013 lb) and I pulled it as a speed rep. Benedikt 'Benni' Magnússon also did well but I was the only one who pulled it like a toy. By the way, it wasn't that long ago that 400kg would have been a new world record so this demonstrates just how far strongman has come over the past ten years or so. Or, if you want a more exact marker, since I came on the scene.

If you watch it on the documentary there's no strain what-soever on that initial lift and I stomp off the platform like a man possessed. It was one of the first times I remember actually feeding off a crowd and the moment I locked it out they went mad. Because it had been so easy they knew what was coming and the energy they were creating was like having an extra limb.

Next up was 420kg (925 lb), which is when we started having one or two casualties. That was to be expected as a lot of the athletes wanted to save themselves for the main event, but in my case, this *was* the main event.

Round three was up to 435kg (959 lb) and about an inch before locking it out I tripped backwards and dropped the bar. Fortunately, I still had time to go again but from an 'energy expended' point of view it meant I was one lift ahead of everyone else. Even so, I still pulled it and in doing so managed to set a new British record. This, again, is when I noticed the incredible power of the crowd and when I locked out the lift I stood there, soaking it all in, and even gestured to sports presenter Caroline Pearce and the Channel 5 film crew up to come and have a word with me. Well, if you're going to showboat you may as well do it on camera – *and* while giving an interview.

By the end of round three, Loz Shahlaei had matched my record 435kg and so going into round four we had me; Loz; Benni Magnússon; the Austrian, Martin Wildauer; and Yorkshireman Andy Bolton, who was the first man ever to deadlift a thousand pounds. The weight we were attempting was 445kg (981 lb).

Unfortunately, Loz tore his lat while attempting his lift and, with Wildauer and Bolton not getting anywhere near, that just left Benni and I. Because I'd done the extra lift everybody thought I'd be exhausted, and, given the amount of sleep I'd had (or hadn't had), perhaps I should have been. Tired or not, I walked onto that platform swimming in confidence and with the help of about one hundred and ten decibels of noise I lifted that bar in about two seconds flat. Once I'd locked it out and referee Magnús Ver Magnússon's hand had gone down, I suddenly felt a swathe of what can only be described as industrial-strength joy flooding through my body and as the crowd stood up and went mental I just stood there with the lift locked out and shouted, 'Oh *fuck* yeah!' Watch the documentary and read my lips. It's not difficult! What an unbelievable feeling.

Next up was 461kg (1,016 lb), which would be a new world record – the heaviest weight anybody had ever lifted in the history of the world. For the last few years Benni had dominated the deadlift scene and although he was still obviously one of the best I knew I could do him. I just knew it. He was at the height of his powers whereas I was improving all the time.

Benni went up first for the record and despite struggling midway through for a few seconds he pulled it relatively quickly and, more importantly, he pulled it cleanly. As much as I don't like seeing Benni pull world records, watching his reaction was a treat. Because he's Icelandic I have no idea what the fucking hell he's saying, but once he puts the bar down he jumps forward and starts screaming at the bloody audience.

Now it was my turn. Taking to the platform, all I could hear in front of me were the crowd shouting, 'Come on, Eddie.' It was almost as if all 5,000 of them were taking it in turns with each one being a bit too impatient to wait for the other to finish. The lift itself was a different animal to the others and represented a massive jump. This was necessary, as going up by two or three kilograms would have taken about ten bloody lifts.

As I started to raise the bar I knew I had enough in the tank but it was going to be close. *Just pick the fucking thing up, Eddie*, I thought. *You cannot let him beat you.* Once it was at the top of my thighs I knew I had done it and all in all it took me about six seconds to lock it out, which isn't too shabby really. As I did so the noise just got louder and louder but there was going to be no showboating this time. All I wanted to see was Magnus's hand go down so I could claim my share of the record. It seemed to take an age but eventually it did, which meant the lift was good. I may only have had a share of a world record, I thought. But it was better than nothing.

And then it happened.

In what I can only describe as being a last-minute attempt at showmanship I dropped the bar, and the moment I did so Magnus put his arm back out, and waved it once from left to right. That meant disqualification.

I must have watched this back a thousand times (I really must be a glutton for punishment!) and the look on my face says it all. It was as though life itself had come to an end very,

very abruptly and I remember experiencing a pang of desperation. It was almost like an electric shock.

The night before at the athletes' meeting, Magnus, who was the chief referee, had said, 'I want you to lower the bar, don't drop it,' and to be honest, I just don't think I was listening. Rule or no rule, what fucked me off at the time was that it made no difference to the lift itself and so, as there was so much riding on it, why not just give me the lift? It was a good lift, so why not? In hindsight, yes of course I should have listened and put the fucking bar down nicely but situations like this are what make me so incredibly fascinating. Rightly or wrongly, I felt enormously aggrieved straight after the lift and as well as shedding a few tears I also shouted one or two naughty words into something that looked suspiciously like a microphone. Once again, I'd like to apologise for that as there were kids present but there was so, so much riding on that lift. To have it taken away from me *after* I'd locked it out was the ultimate kick in the dick.

In an interview in the physio room afterwards I said that I didn't really care about the disqualification and that in my eyes I was still a world record holder. I even said I was happy! But that was just me trying to save face. At the end of the day, I'd fucked up big time and what happened afterwards, which was a bout of full-blown depression, wasn't nice for anyone.

The last time I'd experienced what I consider to be a true period of depression, as opposed to the downer I go on after a competition, was when my nan had been suffering from leukaemia, and unfortunately this was pretty damn close to that. I felt destroyed inside and for a week or two afterwards I could hardly bring myself to speak to anybody. Even Alex. She and I are a partnership and I suppose I felt like I'd let her and the kids down. Worst of all, I was starting to have feelings of self-doubt. It didn't matter how much Alex or my parents believed in me, if *I* didn't think I could do it any more I knew I may as well just jack it in right now.

It's actually quite childish in a way but the epicentre of my resentment was having the record for a few seconds and then having it taken away from me. It was like a toddler having its toy snatched off him. If I'd failed the lift I'd still have had the motivation to come back and do it again but because I'd already done it, that motivation had been replaced by sadness and indignation. And they're not the emotions you really need when you're about to lift heavy weights!

After remaining silent for a week or so, Alex sat me down for a chat. It wasn't that I didn't want to speak to her, I just didn't feel able to. Even so, I wasn't required to say a word on this occasion as she was the one doing the talking. Her rallying call, which was exactly what I needed, went something like this:

'Have you any idea what you achieved at Headingley a couple of weeks ago? Any idea at all? You, together with Benni, lifted more weight than any other person who has ever walked the Earth. Do you know how amazing that is? You always talk about wanting to be the best, but the fact of the matter is, you already are! Don't you realise that, Eddie, you already are the best in the world. Dropping the bar was unfortunate but it shouldn't affect your strength, physical or mental. The Eddie I know would learn from this, take the positives and come out fighting. Don't allow this to spoil your career, Eddie. Please!'

As Alex had started talking I'd been slumped on the sofa, which is where I'd been for the last two weeks. I was only really half listening at first but after a few seconds something inside me clicked and the more she talked the more it seemed to make sense. By the time Alex said the words 'come out fighting', I was sitting bolt upright on the sofa and with a bit of warming up I could probably have lifted 470kg (1,036 lb) there and then.

'God, you're right,' I said. 'What the fuck have I been doing?'

'Never mind that. Just go out there and do what you do best.'

For the last two weeks, I'd felt like the most badly served person in the world, yet in fact I was one of the luckiest. More importantly, I was also one of the strongest people in the world – potentially *the* strongest – and it was time to start making people aware of that fact.

CHAPTER 25
Mighty Mo

The biggest priority now in my attempt for world domination was to get the freedom, and the cash, to go pro. And so, as opposed to moping around the house feeling sorry for myself and getting on everyone's tits, I hit the gym and started putting myself about in front of Stoke's business community.

The first event I attended was a charity darts match at Stoke City's stadium in October 2014. The former World Darts Champion Adrian Lewis was taking part, as were several members of the football team, and as I was a local celebrity I'd been invited. Fortunately for me the organisers had asked if they could introduce me to the crowd and ask me a few questions and given what I was after, I obviously agreed. As a shop window this event was invaluable, as in addition to me probably being unknown to quite a few of the people present, there was enough money in the room to raise the *Titanic*.

Sure enough, as I walked onto the stage most of the room seemed to gasp and before the MC started speaking, all I could hear were people saying things like, 'Look at the size of him!' and 'Is he that the strongman who's been on TV?'

It was an ideal situation really and so in order not to bugger things up I decided not to swear.

Unbeknownst to me, sitting in the room that night was a local businessman called Mo Chaudry. He owns WaterWorld in Stoke which is the largest waterpark in the UK, and, as well as once appearing on Channel 4's *Secret Millionaire*, he'd also advised the great Phil Taylor at the start of his career. More importantly, Mo's father, who had moved to the UK from Pakistan in the 1960s, had once been an old-fashioned stone-lifting strongman and even Mo himself had been a powerlifter and a weightlifter at university and had been a medallist at the British student championships. According to him, he was quite taken aback when he saw me at the event but because he was entertaining guests he never got a chance to say hello.

Fast forward a few months and I was at a spa and fitness club I'd recently joined in Newcastle called M-Club. I use the place for swimming mainly, but also some rehabilitation. One day the manager came in and said that the owner of M-Club would like to set up a meeting with me and when I asked why he was a bit vague. To cut a long story short, the owner in question was Mo and he's since admitted to me that one of the reason he wanted to see me was because he was afraid I'd scare his customers away. Charming! I think he was worried I'd be utilising the gym and was having visions of me using his customers as dumbbells. He needn't have worried. As much as I love going to M-Club, the gym is a bit, how do I say, underequipped for me.

Once Mo was satisfied that his customers weren't going to be used as weights, we started talking about my career. Without me even telling him that I was intending to go professional, he said that it would be essential if I ever wanted to progress.

'I saw you on TV over Christmas on *World's Strongest Man*,' he said. 'Do you know the difference between you and the big three? Apart from them being professional?'

'No,' I replied.

'You're in awe of them,' he said. 'I could tell by the way you looked at them.'

This bloke was sharp. I was in awe of Žydrūnas, Brian and Thor, as well you know, but nobody but me had ever noticed before.

'So, Eddie,' said Mo. 'How are you going to become the World's Strongest Man?'

'By going professional,' I replied.

'And how are you going to do that?'

'God only knows,' I said. 'I've got plenty of sponsorship opportunities. The problem is, none of them are offering cash.'

'OK,' said Mo. 'If you go professional, do you honestly think you could win World's Strongest Man?'

'Without any doubt,' I replied. 'All I need is a chance.'

Mo paused for a few seconds and then smiled.

'All right then,' he said. 'I'm going to give it to you.'

'What do you mean?' I said. I was feeling a bit slow that day.

'I'm going to sponsor you,' said Mo. 'I'm going to under-write everything. Your mortgage, your bills, everything. I'll look for sponsors first, but if they don't materialise I'll pay for everything myself. How does three years sound? Will that be enough time?'

This all happened within about fifteen minutes.

'Well, yes,' I said, completely and utterly stunned. 'That should fine.'

'You've inspired me, Eddie,' Mo said. 'As far as I'm concerned you can hand in your notice at work first thing tomorrow morning.'

Because this had all happened so quickly I was honestly worried he hadn't thought it through properly.

'But what about living expenses?' I asked. 'It's not just a case of covering my bills.'

'I realise that,' he said. 'You work out exactly how much you need and I'll sort it,' he said.

It was an incredible offer but this is so typical of the guy. As with Colin Bryce, he just wanted to help me from the off and because of that I never once felt exploited. It was all about what he could do for me, not what I could do for him. It was the very opposite approach of how it felt with the World Class Potential Programme back in my swimming days.

However, a few days later when I went to Mo's office to sign the contract, I said, 'I'm sorry, Mo. I really appreciate your offer but I'm afraid I'm not going to sign this.'

'Why ever not, Eddie?' said Mo, quite rightly flabbergasted.

'Because I want you to represent me, as well as sponsor me,' I said.

The look on Mo's face was a picture. It went from extreme shock to out-and-out confusion in about two seconds.

'What do you mean you want me to represent you?' he said.

'Just that,' I replied. 'I want you to manage me. I've done some research on you and I've come to the conclusion that you're the best person to take me to the top.'

Before going to his office to sign I'd asked a lot of people about Mo and each and every one of them had said just that. He's the best person to take you to the top. Remaining self-contained was important to me – but as a strongman, not as a businessman. I was about to become a professional and I knew full well that as I progressed my profile would grow, as would the opportunities. I needed somebody to manage all that so I could concentrate on getting strong. In that respect, I was in the same situation as before I met Mo, just a step up.

'What do you think?' I said to him.

There was a pause.

'OK then,' he replied. 'Let's have an adventure.'

CHAPTER 26
Occupation: Strongman

I was now one of a very small and elite group of people: a professional strongman. It's not an occupation you see advertised down the job centre very often and, as I think you'll have gathered, it's not exactly a structured career. Everything I know about what it takes to be a top athlete in this event is what I've taught myself. So what does life as a professional strongman actually involve?

Well, first off, you have to eat a lot. And I mean *a lot*.

Many people dream about being able to eat as much food as they like but for me that's a reality. The only difference is that I don't dream about it. I have nightmares.

Last week alone I spent over £300 on food (that's for me alone) and I'll be doing the same thing every week now until I get to World's Strongest Man. That's my life. I sleep, I eat, I train and I recover. There's little deviation. But what would you say the most taxing of the four is?

Well, it's certainly not sleep. Saying that, due to my size I do have something called sleep apnea, which can result in me stopping breathing while I'm asleep. To help combat this I have to wear a CPAP mask in bed and although it's not ideal I wouldn't consider it to be an issue.

Training too, whilst being hard work, is over and done with in about four hours and because of the sense of achievement I get, I could hardly describe it as being taxing. I do get a bit bored of it sometimes and on some days I find it hard to go. Once I'm there, though, it's fine and at the end of the day it constitutes about 95 per cent of my social life.

Recovery is probably easier than sleeping really, apart from some of the physio, and because that's so pro-active that also give me a light sense of achievement. So, the most taxing aspect of my everyday life as a strongman is definitely food. You see, when I'm not eating the food, I'm buying it, and when I'm not buying the food, I'm researching how I can improve my diet. Seriously, brothers and sisters, consuming what I do really is all-consuming.

With food, like training, it's all about consistency, and if you miss a meal, believe it or not, you won't be as hungry for your next meal. It's all about keeping an equilibrium and if there's one thing a stomach doesn't like, it's surprises.

If you think all this eating doesn't leave me much time for anything else, you'd be right. People often ask me what hobbies I do in my spare time, but the fact of the matter is I don't have any hobbies, or any spare time. Remember what

I said earlier about having never been on any benders with the lads? Well, it's exactly the same with hobbies. And holidays, come to think of it. Alex and I have been together seven years now and we have never had a holiday. We didn't even have a honeymoon. That's pretty appalling when you think about it, but since we've been together I've hardly had time to breathe, let alone pack my bags and go and relax for a couple of weeks.

The closest I've ever come to having a hobby is when I called in at a fishing shop in Hanley about six or seven months ago and bought myself a fishing rod, some tackle and some bait. The intention was to grab a couple of hours each week (which you'd think would be doable) but it's all still in the boot of my car and will probably be there forever. It's a shame really as I was looking forward to giving it a go, but the fact is that while I'm competing at this level my life is not my own. That's just the way it is. What makes that worse is that my life doesn't belong to Alex or the kids either, and sometimes I'll spend no more than a couple of hours with them in a week. The only connection I have with normality is watching television, as boring as that sounds. That's what I do to relax and that's what I do when I spend time with my kids. Usually I'm too knackered to do anything else, and so, rightly or wrongly, it ticks an awful lot of boxes.

Horror films are my thing and if ever I do have an hour or two to myself I'll stick on a zombie film or an episode or two of *The Walking Dead*. Basically, anything with an apocalyptic theme to it. A lot of people equate watching films and television to escapism, and it's the same for me. The difference is that I like escaping to what might be the end of the world as opposed to a school full of fucking wizards. Where I get that from I have no idea, but it seems to suit my personality. I think I must be addicted to adversity (or is it aggro?), because it's a running theme with everything I do.

As for the training, most of it is done in the gym, of course, but I still do swim whenever I can. I normally go to the pool at least once a week, usually on a Sunday afternoon, and I do what's called HIIT training, where I try to keep my heart rate above 150 beats per minute for about fifty minutes. The way I do that is to do two twenty-five-metre lengths in the pool at a very fast pace. It usually takes me about forty seconds to do two lengths. Then I'll have about one minute and twenty seconds' rest. As that time comes to an end, when my heart rate's dropping to about 145 to 150, I go again. This way I'm always keeping my heart rate above 145 to 150 for fifty minutes. That increases your cardiovascular system massively. It also helps mobility in my shoulders and my spine.

As I said earlier, swimming keeps me mobile and that's why I'm one of the most flexible guys in strongman. Even at thirty-plus stone I can still get my palms on the floor without bending my legs and with the overhead events I can get my hands behind my head to press, no problem. A lot of my opponents can't do this because they're too muscle-bound, but I've found swimming has prevented that from happening to me. I still do mostly freestyle but if I get to a point where I'm really out of breath, I'll perhaps do a bit of breaststroke to recover a bit quicker. I can still swim fifty metres in under thirty seconds, which, if I do say so myself, is fucking impressive.

But of course it's the gym where I spend what feels like the majority of my life so I thought I'd finish off this chapter with a few stories about life in the gym, including the time my eyeball popped out. This part is not for the faint-hearted so if you're a bit sensitive it's probably best to move on.

I dread to think how many hours I've spent in the gym over the years but a rough estimate would be about 10,000 hours, which is just over a year. Bearing in mind I've only been going to the gym for the last fourteen years, that's a significant amount of time, and to be honest I've experienced all kinds of stuff there. Some of it good, some of it bad, some of it disturbing, and some of it painful. Let's face it, it's the last two you're most interested in so without further ado let me tell you the full story of how my eyeball popped out.

I would have been about eighteen or nineteen years old at the time and was pushing a thousand kilos on a leg press. Because I was always at the gym, my mates would often drop in to see me and on this particular day I was feeling a bit cocky.

'Why don't you sit on the leg press?' I said to two mates, which they did. 'Right, watch this, lads,' I said to the remaining group. 'I will now push a thousand kilos plus these two dickheads.'

Being a bit of a showman (or should I say show-off?), I decided to do the whole screaming and grimacing bit. The vast majority of this was obviously for effect, but what I also did was keep my eyes wide open which you're not supposed to do. Always keep your eyes squinted or even closed when you either lift or push, I'd always been told, but because I was young, naïve and knew better than everybody else this obviously didn't apply to me.

After four reps I was on the verge of winning an Oscar but then on the fifth something happened. When I say it was all for show, what I mean is that I was just exaggerating everything but in actual fact it was a bloody big weight. This was going to be my final rep but before I could lock it out I heard a popping sound from my right eye socket and then felt my eyeball pushing hard against my eyelids. I didn't feel any pain exactly but I knew something was up and so let down the weight as quick as I could.

Visually, this injury was on a par with something out of *Zombie Flesh Eaters* and the reaction of my mates was hilarious.

'OH MY GOD!' they all screamed as they ran away. 'YOUR EYE'S COME OUT! EDDIE, YOUR FUCKING EYE'S COME OUT!'

I was used to looking in the mirror as I trained but that was normally to admire my incredible physique and boyish good looks. Recoiling in horror was something I hadn't really anticipated but that was exactly what was happening. Fuck me, I looked strange. Very carefully I started pushing my eyeball back in but once it was there I couldn't see a damn thing.

'It's just dark,' I said to my mates, who had crept back to watch in appalled fascination.

'Don't worry,' they reassured me. 'It'll come back. Why don't you go again?'

Honestly, only a lunatic would take medical advice from this lot.

'Yeah, fuck it,' I said. 'Come on, somebody get back on.'

It took about two hours for my sight to come back but because I was young and daft I just assumed it would. I also did about three more sets and all in all it wasn't a bad workout. To be honest, it's not a story I used to tell very often for the simple reason that it only happened once and its novelty value in the gym lasted no longer than about ten minutes. It was only when somebody asked me about my mishaps in the gym that it came to mind, so I mentioned the story in my documentary and it's been a favourite ever since.

A far more common occurrence when training weights (usually when you're doing things like leg presses and squats) is shitting yourself. We've all done it at some stage. In fact, you could say it's the original rite of passage. I bet you're really glad I've mentioned this.

There is actually an art to keeping everything in while you're mid-rep but it's one that doesn't come easily, so to speak. The most dangerous time for me when it comes to shitting my pants is when I'm on the way back up from a squat, which is ironic really, as in the confines of a toilet that usually means I've just had one. The trick is to listen to your body, and the more you listen, the more you know when you need to go. It's just like training in that respect.

Something less messy but far more dangerous is passing out, and, once again, the art to practising prevention both begins and ends by listening to your body. Oh yes, and breathing! You have to remember to breathe.

The first time I ever passed out I was doing front squats. I had a bar across the front of my shoulders with my arms crossed holding the bar in and I think I had five plates on each side. Once again, I'd have been about eighteen or nineteen, which is when I started lifting heavier weights, and after doing about four reps the next thing I remember is waking up on my back. I don't remember feeling dizzy or anything. All I remember is waking up on my back with my legs folded behind me at the knees and the bar across my neck. Basically, I'd folded myself in half!

I think this was probably down to technique, or lack of it; I must have been resting the weight on my neck. This meant I was impeding some of my main arteries and so after a while I just went. That was seriously fucking scary! The thing is, you have to be so, so careful lifting weights, which is why I've included a list of dos and don'ts in this book for anybody who isn't sure. All I would add to that list is: if you're ever unsure whether you're doing anything right or if something doesn't feel right, for God's sake, stop what you're doing and ask! Be cocky and confident by all means, but make sure you use it to your advantage.

I've also passed out during deadlifts a few times, and, as with me shitting myself, it always happens on the way up. Actually, with a deadlift, it usually happens at the very end of the rep.

It doesn't matter what I'm lifting, I always hold my breath for maximum stability and sometimes that's my downfall. Yet again, it's all about listening to your body and so the longer you do this the more attuned you become to its needs and capabilities. Mark my words, I do not recommend anybody reading this book to hold their breath while they're lifting weights. To do so, you have to be completely in touch with your body (or as much as you can be) and even then, you are taking risks that may not be worth it.

All in all, then, being a professional strongman isn't a career that would suit anyone. It's only for those who really are prepared to sacrifice their life for their ambition, who have a burning drive to be the best and to challenge their body to the limit on a daily basis. Or just the nutcases, depending on how you want to look at it.

Anyway, back to the story. You want to know how Mo Chaudry's gamble on me worked out, don't you? Suddenly it seemed like even more was riding on my success ...

CHAPTER 27

Attempting the Arnolds

Luckily for Mo – or, should I say, Mo's bank balance – he was able to find enough sponsors who were willing to pay me cash and I'm happy to say that each and every one of them has stayed with me. It's the perfect arrangement, really: they enable me to train full time and in return they get the best of me.

The first major international competition I entered after going pro was the Arnold Classic in America, Arnold Schwarzenegger's own strongman competition. If ever there was an event tailor-made for me to win, it was this. I mean, come on. How often have I mentioned Arnold Schwarzenegger in this book so far? Fucking loads! The man's a God to me and so to say I was looking forward to competing in his competition would be a gross understatement. But it was also intimidating – not because of the prospect of meeting my hero for the first time, although that did give me a few sleepless nights, the kind you have on Christmas Eve – no, it was because of the reputation of the competition itself. The Arnolds, as it's known, is widely considered to be the most challenging strongman contest on earth and although it doesn't have the cachet of World's Strongest Man it carries more prize money and is certainly the most intense.

The competition itself is part of the Arnold Sports Festival, a multi-sport event consisting of various competitions including professional bodybuilding (the Arnold Classic) and strongman (the Arnold Strongman Classic). Set up in the late 1980s, it's become one of the biggest sporting festivals on the planet and now has events all over the world.

What surprised me most of all were the amount of people there. Until then I'd been used to competing in front of, at most, five thousand, and when I first walked into the exhibition centre in Columbus, Ohio, it almost took my breath away. Apparently there are over a quarter of a million people who attend this event each year and a fair chunk of these are strongman fans.

I actually found the enormity of the event quite intimidating at first and I was completely out of my comfort zone. I just wasn't used to being around so many people. I soon adjusted to it though and when I was finally introduced to the crowd for the first time it was like being at the MGM Grand. The MC was pure Las Vegas!

'Our next competitor, from England – Eddie Hall! Twenty-seven years old, six foot three inches tall and weighing 385 lb. FOUR TIMES UK's Strongest Man!'

Each competitor has to walk on carrying their home nation flag and then stand in a line facing the audience. We do the same at all the Giant's Live events and it looks great.

Since 2003, Žydrūnas Savickas has won this title no fewer than eight times and behind him is Brian Shaw on three. A lot of people credit Žydrūnas as being the strongest man who's ever lived and after the first event on the first day I wouldn't have disagreed with them.

The event in question was the Austrian Oak, which is basically a log press (i.e. lifting a log-shaped bar above your head – not exactly easy as it's an awkward shape to hold), First up was Benni Magnússon. He had a good go but couldn't get the last ten inches. Up next was Thor and he barely got it above his head. This thing was fucking heavy, by the way: 405 lb (205kg)! After him was Brian Shaw, who didn't fare much better, and after two more disappointed hopefuls it was my turn. My first event at my first Arnold Classic. Nervous? I was crapping myself! There must have been at least 10,000 people there but as always I went out there with the intention of giving it absolutely everything.

Just getting this thing onto your chest takes up a massive amount of energy and by the time I was ready to push for a lift I already felt half gone. Even so I pushed for all I was worth and on my first attempt I was about the same as Benni. This wasn't good enough so because I still had time I decided to go again. This time it came up a bit easier and so without fannying around I went straight for the lift. I was literally about an inch away from locking it out but I just didn't have it in me. Bollocks! I certainly wasn't happy but that thing was just absolute immense.

Last up was Žydrūnas and because of his reputation everyone had stayed back to see if he could do it. Thor, Brian, me ... we were all standing by the side of the stage hoping he'd be having an off day. He wasn't. He walked onto the stage, picked it up like it was a fucking twig and then lifted it in about two seconds flat. I'd seen enough.

Next up was the frame walk, which was set on an incline, and once again I struggled for some reason. I can't put my finger on it. I just wasn't at the races.

When I got back to my hotel room that evening I was both pissed off and miffed. Finishing the first day in eighth after two of my best events was not a good start but tomorrow was another day. Thank God!

Fortunately, after having a good night's sleep and a bit of a word with myself I felt cracking the next day and arrived at the exhibition centre absolutely full of it. The first event was the tyre deadlift and after getting rid of the also-rans it was just me and Brian Shaw in the final. The best I managed was 1,111 lb but he pipped me by pulling 1,117 lb. It was an improvement on yesterday but I still didn't feel right.

Going into the final event I was in fourth place but five points off the lead. The event in question was the circus dumbbell and again, it should have been another strong event for me. I can't remember where I finished in the event itself but what I do remember is lining up at the end of the final day for the presentation. This time I was dreading hearing that MC's voice as I knew what he was going to say.

'In sixth place, Eddie Hall.'

You wanker!

I was now one of the few full-time professional strongmen in the world and this was just dog shit. I'd let myself down. The only surprise bigger than me finishing sixth was Thor finishing seventh, so at least I wasn't alone. I remember commiserating with the big man directly after the presentation and between the two of us we could have depressed a roomful of pissed-up monkeys. Brian fucking Shaw won the competition, the gangly American freak. I remember looking on at Brian as Arnold Schwarzenegger (yes, I know!) handed him the trophy and his cheque. The word 'envy' doesn't even come close to covering the emotions I felt at that moment, but if you tried adding things like resentfulness, anger and hatred to the list, you'd be about half way. I love Brian but at that moment in time I wanted to rip off his head and shit down his neck.

As I walked away from the exhibition centre in Columbus, Ohio, with my cheque for $6,000, I wondered if I would ever get to meet my hero. I'd managed to grab a quick photo with him at the competition but hadn't said a word to him and had simply been one of thousands. That wasn't my style at all. I wanted to impress Arnold and make him notice me. I wanted him to want to speak to me.

Thanks to Colin Bryce, a new world record and some very tired athletes, that opportunity would come a lot sooner than I thought.

CHAPTER 28
The Beast is Let Loose

The day after the Arnold Classic I got on a plane and flew to Melbourne for the Australian version of the same competition. It took three flights in all and after spending thirty hours in the air I finally arrived in Australia. The longest of the three flights, which lasted seventeen hours, was actually the most comfortable but even so I was in fucking bits by the time I arrived at the hotel and so was looking forward to having a couple of days' rest.

I arrived in Melbourne on the Friday and we weren't meant to be competing until 11 a.m. on Sunday. Then, right out of the blue, the promoter of the event told Colin Bryce, who was running the strongman competition, that the start had been moved forward to 11 a.m. on Saturday. The reason it had been moved was because Arnold Schwarzenegger was supposed to be attending the first event, which was the deadlift, and for some reason he was turning up a day early. To try to impress Arnold, this promoter had promised him a world record attempt at deadlift and by all accounts the great man was looking forward to it.

The problem this presented to Colin was finding somebody who was willing to go for the record. Everybody was obviously knackered from travelling and competing for deadlift to max in a standard strongman event is a lot different to going for a world record as not only is there a little bit more pressure involved, but the weight is obviously increasing. The first person Colin tried was Brian Shaw but he refused, as did everyone. It was hardly surprising, given the notice involved. This would have been about 11 p.m. and so just twelve hours before the attempt. I'd already spoken to Colin when I'd arrived and he knew how exhausted I was. Even so, he decided to give me a try.

'Yeah, I'll give it a go, mate,' I said. It must have been the jet lag.

The posters for the Arnold competitions always have a bodybuilder at the centre and because our sport was always seen as the poor relation I decided to help out. There was also the prospect of meeting my hero, of course, but my primary motivation, if I'm honest, was just to help out Colin.

The reason Arnold was interested in seeing a world record attempt at deadlift was because he himself used to be a powerlifter, which I wasn't aware of. According to Colin he'd pulled 720 lb (327kg) back in the late 1960s, which is some weight.

The following morning, at about 10.50 a.m., I was all ready to go. Actually that's a lie because I felt like shit. What I mean is that I'd just finished the main deadlift event and if I was going to go for a world record it would have to happen quickly. I'd actually had a shocker in the event, by the way, and had struggled on 360kg (793 lb). So how the fuck I was going to lift 462kg (1,018) was a mystery.

Then, all of a sudden, the promoter received a phone call from a rather doubtful Arnold Schwarzenegger. 'Are you sure you've got somebody who can pull 1,019 lb?' he said. 'With a real bar?'

'Yes,' said the promoter. 'And he has to lift now.'

'OK,' said Arnold. 'Hang on. I'll be there in five minutes.'

Thirty minutes later we're still sitting there like lemons and so in the end I said, 'Look, Colin. I'm getting cold now. I've got to go for it. At least let's give the crowd a bit of a show.'

The world deadlift record was still held by Benni Magnússon and you all know the history behind that. I knew I had to give it another go to lay to rest the demons from my disqualified previous attempt. Also Colin and the promoter were having a nightmare and so the least I could do was help them make the best of a bad job. I may not have had my hero there to watch me but I felt this was my chance to step up.

As I was psyching myself up, Colin received a text from Arnold. 'On my way,' it said.

'Eddie, Eddie, Eddie!' he screamed. 'Arnold's on his way. He'll be here any second.'

'OK, I'm ready,' I told him.

Arnold or no Arnold, by the time I got myself into position, I could see that Colin had done a fantastic job warming up the crowd. Because of the noise they were making I was starting to feel strong again. They were only standing just a few yards behind me and there was so much energy. I obviously didn't realise the significance of it then, but when Colin went to introduce me he said: 'From Stoke-on-Trent, to take the world record by one kilogram! Lifting 1019 lb! Eddie "THE BEAST" Hall!' It was the first time anyone had called me that. The moment he said it the crowd started chanting, 'Beast, Beast, Beast!' and as I locked on, put on my straps and the prepared to lift, that was all I could hear. Fuck me, I felt strong now. I felt like I'd had fifteen hours' kip.

Unbeknownst to me, just as I started lifting the bar, Arnold Schwarzenegger walked up with his entourage and although I wasn't aware of it he stood beside me and started shouting in my ear. There'd been doubt in my mind right up until a second or so into the lift but as I started to pull northwards I could actually feel myself getting stronger and stronger. Then before you could say, 'I need your clothes, your boots and your motorcycle,' I was standing with Arnold Schwarzenegger at my side having become the first man ever to lift 1,019 lb. Fucking get in there!

After putting – not dropping – the bar down, I took off my straps and went mental for a minute and as well as jumping around and shouting 'YES!' and 'AAAAARGH!' a lot, I screamed the word 'LIGHTWEIGHTS!', which was obviously directed at those athletes who'd chosen not to attempt the record. Sorry, but I just couldn't resist.

The first person to come up and congratulated me was Arnold – or Arnie, to his mates. He actually touched me! Which is surprising really, as I was covered in fucking sweat. The first thing he said was, 'Wow, you really are a beast!' and from then on, that was it – the name stuck. *Fuck the Spartan*, I said to myself. *If Arnold says I'm a beast, I'm a beast!*

I think I've had several 'best days of my life' in this book, but until the next one comes along I'm claiming this one to be it. I honestly couldn't believe it. The first time I'd noticed Arnold was present was when I'd almost locked out the lift. I suddenly saw these purple loafers to the right of me and I remember thinking, *Who the hell wears purple loafers?*

After congratulating me, Arnold interviewed me for the TV cameras and that was just astonishing. The first question he asked me was how much training I did, and so I told him that it was 365 days a year and then I explained what had happened at Headingley with the disqualification. By this time I was starting to well up because all I could think about was how close I'd come to jacking it all in, and all because of a disqualified lift. After what had just happened – and what was actually happening – that was one scary thought. The two people who'd had made this possible, apart from me, were Alex, who had persuaded me not to give up, and Mo Chaudry, who'd given me the opportunity to go full time.

Looking back, what I actually find equally scary is the thought of what might have happened had Magnus given me the lift. For starters I'd have shared the world record with Benni Magnússon, and I don't like sharing. What I find even more disturbing is the thought of me not having that hunger – that madness, even – that the disqualification eventually sparked after Alex had got through to me.

After telling Arnold my life story and explaining how I'd come back from the brink, he said, 'You're a winner, a champion, somebody who has failed in various different lifts, but every time you've got up again. That's what winners do. They don't stay down, they get up and they get going. Congratulations, and I hope you'll say [this is where I had to join in] – I'LL BE BACK!'

CHAPTER 29
Life in the Spotlight

That year, 2014, was the year I realised I was famous and I remember thinking to myself, *At last, some recognition!* By now I'd appeared on all kinds of TV shows (not only strongman) and it had got to the point where I was recognised pretty much everywhere I went. This was, and is, extremely gratifying for me, but I think the game changer in terms of being recognised was the advent of selfies. I used to have this notion when I was younger that if and when I ever became famous I'd be stopped and asked for an autograph or a chat. It never entered my head that I'd be asked to have my photo taken and I don't mind admitting that it took some getting used to. To make things simpler I decided to use just one pose, which I pull for all selfies regardless of who's taking it. And before you ask, no, it's not a Usain Bolt!

One of the only times I don't like having my photo taken is when I'm out with my family, which, as you know, is about as rare as rocking-horse shit. I also don't like being asked if I'm in pain, so don't ever ask me for a selfie if I'm standing in a queue at an airport! Generally speaking though, I love it, and what I like most of all is that people usually have something nice to say. That does make everything worthwhile some days, and it can make a big difference to how I feel. Some young lad coming up and saying, 'Hey Eddie, I'm a really big fan of yours,' can give you just enough encouragement to make it through to the following day. It really is that simple.

On the rare occasions when I refuse to have a selfie taken I'm called all kinds of names on social media and whoever's been refused will usually mutter something derogatory as they walk away. If I'm in restaurant with my family and I'm about to put a Yorkshire pudding in my mouth, what the hell do you expect? Some people just don't get it.

Me and the wife and kids were going to Alton Towers a few weeks ago and so before we went I decided to take action. We'd been to West Midlands Safari Park a few months before that and while we were sitting having a drink I must have been asked for a photo about twenty times. Given my size, I might not be the most famous man in the world but I'm definitely one of the most conspicuous. When you see me coming it must be like Mr Stay Puft from *Ghostbusters*. Either that or a barrage balloon. I don't stand a chance.

When I say I took action before we went to Alton Towers, what I mean is that I asked my mum if I could borrow her beanie hat. She looked at me as if I was mad and when I attempted to put it on it was like trying to cover the moon with a tablecloth. In the end I wore a hoodie and some sunglasses, but it made no difference whatsoever. Sure enough, within about ten minutes of being there I was mobbed and so we ended up coming home. That's obviously not ideal but what can you do? If I'd wanted to have a quiet life I should have become a librarian.

I think the most embarrassing situation I've ever been in, certainly with regards to being recognised, happened at an Expo I attended a few years ago. I won't say where or when it was for the sake of the person involved, but I'm telling you now it was a damn close shave and involved an incredible piece of acting.

I'd been asked to do a photoshoot at this Expo that involved me picking up some girls and balancing them on my shoulder. It's something I get asked to do a lot, not surprisingly, and a couple of weeks ago I even had the Lord Mayor of Stoke on my shoulders. Anyway, just after I'd finished this photoshoot a couple of girls came up to me and asked me if I could do the same with them. Their boyfriends were already poised with cameras and so I thought, *Yeah, why the hell not?* They only weighed about eight stone wet through and so I'd hardly notice they were there. Thirty seconds later another two girls came up and asked the same, so I obliged. I did feel a bit like a fucking fairground ride by this point but hey ho, it's nice to give something back. Once the two girls were safely on the ground I shouted, 'Who's next?' but before I could stand up straight again I managed to catch a glimpse of the lower half of the person next in the queue. And thank fuck I did. She was standing with her back to me and as well as having calves the size of rugby balls, she had thighs like rubber dinghies and an arse that should really have had its own time zone. Quick as a flash I grabbed my back and started grimacing.

'Oh fuck,' I cried. 'My back!'

As I pretended to try to straighten myself without success, this girl and her boyfriend approached me and asked me if I was OK.

'I was in a competition a few days ago,' I lied. 'And I'm still a bit sore. I'll be OK. No more lifting gorgeous women, though. Sorry, love.'

The poor girl looked absolutely gutted but what could I do? It wasn't her weight that was the problem. It was getting it from the ground onto my shoulders, and then keeping it there. I'm a strongman, not a fucking pendulum ride!

Funnily enough, it was at this Expo that I entered my first, and last, nail-hammering competition, which resulted in me experiencing something that, hitherto, had been alien to me: humiliation. Throughout my years in strongman – and in swimming – I'd had everything thrown at me: I'd been sent home, reprimanded, shouted at, disqualified, fined, docked points and even beaten on one or two occasions. But never humiliated. Then, at this Expo, somebody thought that because I was big and strong I'd be ideal as a nail hammerer. And they were right, in the first instance. The prize for winning this competition was two tickets to the British Moto GP at Silverstone as well as qualification to the final of the British Nail-Hammering Championship. Who knew there was such a thing? (I certainly didn't.) And first prize for winning that was a brand-new motorbike worth a cool £10,000. Dad was with me at this Expo and I remember saying to him, ''Ere. I'm going to have that fucking bike. Watch this.'

All you had to do was hammer a ten-inch nail into a piece of hardwood and whoever did it the quickest, won. Dad had already had a go and to be fair to him he was one of the fastest yet. About fifteen seconds, if memory serves. I think I was one of the last people to attempt it and I remember picking up the nail, resting it on the block, and within three hits it was flush with the wood. BANG, BANG, BANG! Job done. After soaking up the applause, I looked at Dad, winked, and said, rather presumptuously, 'Dad, how do you fancy going to Silverstone to pick up my new bike?' Dad's a big motorbike man and I knew he'd be up for going to the GP. 'OK, son,' he said. 'I'll tag along.'

About a month later Dad and I were on our way to Silverstone for the Grand Prix weekend and the competition. I'd already decided what I was going to do with the bike: sell it, and pocket the cash. What I was going to do with the cash I still hadn't decided, but I'd already told Alex it was coming in. 'Ten big ones, honey,' I'd said to her. 'And all for knocking in a fucking nail.'

When Dad and I got to where they were having the competition there was an actual Moto GP bike on display in the room and because everyone was taking photographs of me I decided to pick up the bike and pose with it. You should have seen the looks on the organisers' faces. What a picture! As I was hoisting it aloft, Dad sidled up to me and whispered, 'That bike's worth a quarter of a million pounds. For fuck's sake, don't drop it!'

There were ten people in the final of this British Nail Hammering Championship and I was the biggest by half a foot and at least ten stone. It was in the bag.

First up was a lad from North Yorkshire. I forget his name (let's call him Jim Smith), but I'll never forget his occupation.

'First up,' said the man with the mic, 'is Mr Jim Smith from North Yorkshire. Occupation: farrier.'

I looked at Dad and said, 'What the fuck's a farrier, Dad?'

For some reason he looked worried. 'Somebody who knocks in nails for a living, son,' he said.

'Yeah, but he's only about five foot nine inches. Nothing to worry about.'

Unbeknownst to me, the hardwood had been replaced by a kind of laminate block, which was about ten times harder, and as opposed to whacking the nail as hard as he could, this bloke was tapping it very quickly. It was going in, but only slowly.

'Fuck me, Dad,' I said. 'He's taking forever. Why doesn't he just whack it?'

Dad didn't say a word and just stood there with his arms folded.

'Next up,' said the man with the mic, 'is Mr Mike Green from Dorset. Occupation: farrier.'

Yet again, this bloke was only knee high to a grasshopper.

'I'm a bit worried about this,' said Dad.

'Don't be,' I replied. 'Have you seen how fast they are? I'll piss it.'

As it turned out, the first four contestants were all farriers and as well as their styles being identical, their times were all similar too. Even so, I was still confident that power would prevail and when I walked up to the block and picked up my nail I was as confident as I'd ever been. *Watch this*, I said to myself.

As I tried to rest the nail on the block it started sliding around. *Strange,* I thought. *Seems a bit hard to me.* At the Expo I'd managed to make a tiny hole with the nail that had kept it in place. This time though, it was a lot more difficult.

'Ready?' said the time keeper. 'Three, two, one, GO!'

I lifted up the hammer, and with all the power I could muster I brought it down on top of the nail. 'BANG!'

Instead of penetrating the block, the nail stayed exactly where it was and just bent slightly. 'Bollocks!' I said. I picked up another nail and tried again but this time it flew off the table. *What the hell's going on?* I thought. *This stuff's like steel!*

Anyway, to cut a pitifully long story short I didn't win the motorbike and the farriers, one of whom did win it, obviously knew exactly what they were doing. Good for them.

As opposed to hanging around for the Grand Prix, which was the following day, I called Mum straight after the competition and told her that she could come and take my place. I was just appalled with myself.

Getting back to fame briefly, the thing that really pisses me off, although it doesn't happen any more, is when people come to my house. I have a zero-tolerance policy when it comes to this sort of thing and the last person who tried it got a fucking battering. It was in 2014 and we were sitting at home having a quiet evening when somebody did a knock and run. Although I didn't get out in time to catch them, I'd had CCTV installed and so went to have a look. It was actually a gang of local teenagers who I recognised, but because they all had hoodies on, I couldn't pinpoint who did it. Anyway, I knew full well that they all hung out in the park and so I climbed into my car and drove up there.

As expected, every single one of the little bastards was there and when they saw me walking towards them they panicked. Fortunately, I didn't have to run as there was only one way out and so once I was in position I gave them the full SP. 'Right then, fuckers,' I began. 'Which one of you bastards knocked on my door and ran off?' Obviously, nobody said a word and everyone just shrugged their shoulders. 'I'll tell you what,' I said. 'If you don't tell me who did it I'm going to smack every single one of you. Did you get that? You will all leave here with a black eye.' There was probably about twelve of them in total and the moment I'd finished talking they all pointed to this one kid. 'Right then, you,' I said, before picking him up by the scruff of the neck. 'You're coming with me.'

Believe it or not I can be quite menacing when I want to be and by the time I'd got this kid into my car he was absolutely cacking himself. In fact, he was actually whimpering.

'All I'm going to do,' I said to him, 'is take you back to my house and you're going to apologise to my wife, and if you don't, I'm going to strangle you.'

The apology Alex received was sincere (although the delivery was a bit stuttery) and when he finally finished talking I kicked him up the arse and sent him on his way.

You see, to me, stuff like that is crossing the line, both literally and metaphorically. My wife and kids live in that house and if you start doing things like that there's a chance you might scare them or, worse still, put them in danger. I might not be the greatest dad or husband on the planet but I'll stop at nothing to make sure they're safe.

Anyway, let's get back to the story. Becoming famous was (generally) a nice side-effect of my work as a professional strongman, but the real business was to keep hauling myself further up the ladder to the top ...

CHAPTER 30
Captured on Camera

Four weeks after returning home from Melbourne I was back on a plane to Malaysia for the 2015 World's Strongest Man. Even though I'd only been pro for a few months it had already started paying dividends and I was confident that, if I hadn't caught the top three, I'd at least have made ground on them. In terms of a result, anything better than sixth would do, but because of the progress I'd made I was confident of finishing at least fourth.

Without wanting to sound like a bighead, qualifying was a piece of piss and by the time the final arrived I was bigger and stronger than I'd ever been. The problem was, so were Brian, Thor and Žydrūnas. Actually, at almost forty years of age, Žydrūnas Savickas was probably just a fraction past his best at this point. Even so, he was still the most experienced strongman there and only a fool would have written him off.

The competition finished with Brian first on fifty-three points, Žydrūnas second on forty-nine and a half (I told you!), Thor third on forty-nine, and me fourth on forty-five and a half. Brian Shaw was on imperious form that year and although I didn't win an event outright, I did manage to whip Thor's ass on the atlas stones, which not many people can claim to have done. As this was the finale of the competition, I was determined to do well and I only just got beaten by Brian on time.

What gave me the most amount of satisfaction that year was the knowledge that I was now knocking on the door of the top three and everything I'd prophesised prior to becoming a professional was starting to come true.

The only thing that wasn't working out was my home life. I'd had this notion that, once I'd gone full time, I'd be able to devote more time to my family. Fat chance! As well as obviously spending more time in the gym, I was also spending more time recovering – which could be anything from having physio to hot and cold treatments – and that's something that takes up an awful lot of time. Then you have eating. I was now well on my way to being thirty stone and that takes time – and preparation. So, if I wasn't eating or sleeping, I was training, and if I wasn't training, I was either recovering or researching. Somewhere in between all that I had to try and fit in my sponsor commitments, not to mention the media, so actually, I was probably spending less time with the family than I had when I was a truck mechanic. The only difference was that we had a plan now, something to aim for, and that – for the time being, at least – was papering over the cracks.

The last major strongman event of 2015 was Europe's Strongest Man, which, as always, kicked off with the

World Deadlift Championships. Unfortunately, I ended up sustaining an injury during the main event but managed to win the World Deadlift Championships in style. By now, I was starting to pull away from the crowd at deadlift and nobody in the world could come anywhere near me. I knew it, and so did they. I was already the best there had ever been.

In the end, I broke my own world record by a kilogram. Oh, and I did it as a speed rep. You watch any other strongman lift anything over 430kg (948 lb) and the majority will be as slow as an eight-day clock and close to fucking dying. Not me. This is what I live for.

Anyway, just to prove how fucking fantastic I was, here are the results from the World Deadlift Championships that year:

1. Eddie Hall 463kg/1020 lb: New World Record
2. Hafthor Björnsson 450kg/992 lb
3. Jerry Prichett and Rauno Heinla 435kg/959 lb
4. Andy Bolton 420kg/925 lb
5. Terry Hollands, Krzystophe Radzikowski, Mark Felix, Dainis Zageris, Matjaz Belsak, 400kg/881 lb
6. Dimitar Savitinov 360kg/793 lb

That wasn't the only good thing that came out of this year either. You may have noticed but throughout the book I keep on referring to 'the documentary'. For those of you who aren't aware, it's called *Eddie – Strongman*, it's absolutely fucking amazing, it's on Netflix and on DVD, and it was released towards the end of 2015.

The brainchild behind the documentary, Matt Bell, isn't a child, but he definitely has a brain, as when he decided a few years ago that he wanted to make a documentary about a strongman, he chose me. As I said, the man's not daft.

Matt had been a presenter on *UK's Strongest Man* for a couple of years but really he was a film maker and when he first approached me back in 2012 I was surprised, but I was definitely interested. I obviously wasn't sure if anything would come of it – such is the world of film-making – but it was definitely worth a punt. First and foremost, I trusted Matt and I liked him. I was also flattered; as you know, I like having my feathers stroked.

The first thing we had to sort out was the money, or rather Matt did. We generated the majority of it via crowd-funding but Matt also put a lot of his own money in and we managed to get one or two sponsors. When filming began at the start of 2013 I was surprised by how full on it was. There were only usually one or two people present – Matt and one other – but they were there all the frigging time and after a week or so I remember thinking, *What the fucking hell have I done?* When somebody says, 'We'll be following you all the time,' you don't take them literally. Or at least I didn't. Matt had gone to great lengths to explain everything, though, so it was my own fault. I was just going to have to get used to it.

The premiere was as posh as fuck and took place at the Mayfair Hotel in London on 19 December 2015. There's a private cinema there that holds about 200 people and after the screening we did a Q&A on stage before getting absolutely trollicd. It was a hell of a night, and, all credit to Mr Bell, it's one hell of a film. Since then it's been picked up by Netflix and has been on there ever since. In fact, it even trended on Netflix for several months so God knows how many people have seen it. There is talk of there being a sequel to the documentary, but I can't say any more at the moment. Don't bet against it happening.

Talking of bets. I'm just about to have one on myself.

CHAPTER 31
Preparing to Lift Half a Tonne

The idea to attempt a half-tonne deadlift first came about directly after the 2015 World Deadlift Championships (which was the support event for Europe's Strongest Man) where I'd broken the world record by pulling 463kg (1,020 lb). I'm pretty sure this is on camera somewhere but I remember saying to Colin Bryce after the show that if he could find a backer who'd be willing to put up the cash, I would pull half a tonne at next year's event. Now, I know for a fact that Colin didn't think I could pull 500kg (1,102 lb) at the time (nobody in the world did apart from me), but he obviously thought it would make a good spectacle and so without pissing around he found a backer and told me we were on.

At the time, such a lift was considered to be impossible and I remember reading discussions on strength forums entitled, 'Will we ever see a 1,100-lb deadlift?' Every single person who replied to that initial question said no, it would never happen, and thinking about it sensibly, you can understand why.

Since time immemorial, if somebody had attempted to break the world deadlift record they'd probably go up by 1kg (2.2 lb), which is what the likes of Benni and I had been doing for a couple of years. It wasn't something that happened every day, and because not all attempts were successful it was obviously a very gradual progression. Going up by a massive 37kg (82 lb), or about 8 per cent, was beyond ridiculous but what sealed the deal and made everyone assume it was impossible wasn't the increase, it was the weight itself. Half a tonne is the equivalent of a very heavy racehorse and, to the vast majority of sane human beings, that was beyond the possibilities of man.

It was these pundits' certainty – their unequivocalness – that first caught my imagination. The more people told me that a half-tonne deadlift couldn't be done, the more I told myself it could.

As a challenge this ticked so many boxes for me. First, but not foremost, it had a good lump of cash attached to it and as a professional strongman that was music to my ears. Secondly, I'd be doing something that nobody had ever done before in the history of the world and that in itself floated my boat big-time. Do you know that since time began, over 110 billion people have walked the Earth? If I did manage to lift half a tonne off the ground I'd be making history, and it didn't matter how many people either matched it or bettered me in the future, I'd always be the first. That's the difference between something like this and winning World's Strongest Man. Winning that title means you follow in the footsteps of some amazing athletes and it means you'll always be part of what is a very special club. That's just it, though, you're part of a club. One of many. Following in other people's footsteps doesn't make you a history maker. The last tick-box, and by far the biggest, was that it provided me with the ultimate motivation – that nobody in the world (that I was aware of) thought it was possible. That really is my lifeblood.

When I eventually went public with my intentions, the reactions from people were perfect: a mixture of negativity and incredulity. I knew I could find encouragement if I needed it (and I was sure I'd be needing some on the night), but for the time being I was quite happy feeding off all the pisstakers and naysayers. Their negativity fuelled my positivity and if it hadn't been for so many people doubting me I don't think I'd have been arsed. Seriously. If everyone had turned around to me and said, 'Do you know what, Ed, I reckon you're going to pull that half a tonne,' I'd never have attempted it. Proving myself right is fantastic, but proving others wrong is even better.

The icing on the cake was seeing Brian Shaw and Žydrūnas Savickas, two of the strongest men who've ever lived, both come out and say that it couldn't be done. They didn't take the piss or anything, they were just giving their honest beliefs. I remember Brian saying that he simply thought it wasn't possible, whereas Žydrūnas thought it could only end in injury. Maybe he was right?

The only distractions I'd had leading up to the lift, apart from a few personal appearances, had been Britain's Strongest

Man, so I'd been able to remain pretty focused. I'd worked out that in order for me to support 500kg I would have to weigh at least 185kg (408 lb). That meant putting on over 15kg (33 lb) in the final six months. I did it, just, but a lot of that went on in the final few weeks. From the second I woke up until the moment I went to bed I would either have food in my mouth, in my hand, or within reaching distance. There was no science behind the 185kg, by the way, it was just an educated guess. I needed something to work towards, and 35 per cent of the weight I was lifting seemed about right.

That's one of the mad things about my sport; we don't have any coaches or advisors. Given what we do in the gym and at competitions that's absolutely ridiculous. I was looking at the event list for World's Strongest Man the other day and I thought to myself, *In a few weeks*' time I'm going to be on the other side of the world doing Viking presses, tyre flips, truck pulls and atlas stones at the biggest strength event on the planet yet I have never been coached in any one of these events. Now you can look at that in one of two ways: you can either you shake your head and think, *That's a disgrace! Why doesn't the sport do more?* Or you can see it as an opportunity and work out how you can change things for the better. Welcome to the Eddie Hall school of strongman! It could happen.

That's another paradox. Successful strongmen, on the whole, are bright guys, and the reason I know that is because we're left to our own devices so we have to figure it out for ourselves if we want to do well. It doesn't matter how much natural talent you have, if you can't work out how to train properly, refine your technique and work out what food to eat, you're going to get left behind. It's not just survival of the fittest, it's survival of the sharpest.

Let me give you a quick example of exactly how this culture of self-sufficiency has worked for me. About a year ago I was in Sweden doing a guest appearance at an expo and about half way through I was told by the organisers that in ten minutes' time I'd be required to do a demonstration deadlift of 400kg (881 lb). It wasn't anybody's fault but unfortunately this hadn't been communicated to me so I told them that I wasn't ready.

'Don't worry, Eddie,' they said. 'We'll get you ready.'

About two minutes later this bloke walks in carrying what looked like an enormous car buffer. 'What the hell's that?' I asked him.

'Watch this,' he said, and before I could say another word he started working my back and warming me up with this huge car buffer.

'How's that?' he asked.

'Fucking unbelievable,' I replied. 'Better than any warm up I could ever do.'

It was astonishing. Five minutes later I went out into the hall, pulled the 400kg and I was fine. Job done. The moment I got back home I went straight out and bought one of these things and it's now become an important part of my warm-up routine. If I'd been surrounded by coaches and the like I would never have discovered that machine and the fact that I did makes me appreciate my autonomy even more.

Something else that's made a big difference to me lately, although this is actually quite specialist, is a mouth guard. The idea, in layman's terms, is that if your jaw's moving about a lot then your body follows suit. Keep your jaw fixed, however, and you will remain far more stable and balanced. Believe me it works and is worth at least a couple of extra reps.

Something that you'll all have seen strongmen use over the years are smelling salts. Even though we know what's coming they work purely via the element of surprise. Honestly, taking a good sniff of that stuff is like being slapped in the face and the reason strongmen pull so many ridiculous faces when we take a sniff of smelling salts is because it makes us want to kill somebody! Once you've had some of that you can lift pretty much anything. Or at least you feel like you can.

Although deadlift was already part of my training routine, I started refining and modernising the sessions from the moment the attempt was confirmed, which was about a year before. Each week I'd alternate between heavy lifting and speed, and then, at the end of every quarter, I'd go for a new personal best. Thursdays were deadlift day and so as soon as I arrived at the gym I'd go straight to the deadlift platform. To warm up for deadlift I always do what's called a 'pyramid up' – one plate ten reps, two plates eight reps, etc. – and then I stretch. I cannot emphasise enough the importance of stretching, regardless of what you do in the gym. Fail to do it properly and as well as never realising your full potential you're bound to do yourself an injury. A lot of people just can't be arsed and that's madness. Take my word for it, when it comes to training it's as essential as the exercise itself.

All the way through this session I would be eating bananas and drinking cranberry juice. Fast-acting sugars, basically. Once the heavy lifting started I would then eat lumps of steak between each lift. This provided me with natural proteins, natural BCAAs and natural fats. As far as I know I'm the only person who does this but I'd definitely recommend it. It obviously costs a bit but it's worth the investment.

Before I went professional I could only manage one heavy-lifting session every two weeks as that was the time it took my body to recover. A deadlift, remember, is the only exercise that uses every part of your body, so it makes sense. Everything kills! After going pro, I discovered things like hot and cold treatments and massage. Each one reduced my recovery time, so the more I added to the programme, the quicker I could start lifting again. Once again there's a cost attached to it but I don't view that as a barrier, I view it as a motivation. If it's the right thing to do you can always find a way.

Despite all the massages and ice baths etc., I was in constant pain, especially during the last few weeks before the record attempt. Getting out of bed to eat in the morning was absolutely excruciating and it took me every minute of the time I had between getting up and going to the gym to prepare myself for the next session. Even at home I had to try to block myself off, so despite living with my family physically, we had to be separated emotionally. I know that's not ideal, especially when you have small children, but that's the way it had to be. Mentally, I was in a very, very dark place leading up to the lift, so even if I had been able to communicate with my family I would probably either have screamed at them or burst out crying. I'm not sure if it was a depression, exactly. It was just somewhere I had to go. Strangely enough, that actually formed part of my motivation, as I knew it would only last until the lift. Do the job right and it would evaporate immediately. Fail, and it might stay.

Not one aspect of this practice is healthy, of course, but it's what I had to do. Alex and I have been through hell over the last seven years – or rather, I've put her through hell – but what keeps us together is the fact that she knows I'm doing it all for us. Completing the lift would go some way to offering us financial security but I have to admit that I hadn't envisaged it being quite so intense. Alex and I have been on the verge of splitting up several times and the vast majority of women would probably have walked out long ago. It certainly hasn't been easy. It rarely is with me.

About two weeks prior to the lift I started having heart palpitations. This was obviously down to the pressure, but the more I had the palpitations the more I thought something was wrong and so it became self-perpetuating. It was all my own fault. I'd created so much hype within the strength community that, should I not manage the lift, I'd be a complete laughing stock. So despite being in perfect shape (apart from the heart!), I now had an element of doubt. Paradoxically, this was probably as essential to my final preparations as confidence itself. Why? Because with over-confidence comes complacency and in order to prevent complacency from creeping in you have to maintain self-awareness. Believe me, a seed or two of doubt can do wonders for your self-awareness. The perspective isn't always balanced, but at least you're looking in the right direction.

I'd made an awful lot of claims in my time but, God willing, I'd always managed to back them up. This one was different, though, as basically I was attempting to separate myself from every other strongman who had ever lived. I was trying to create my own exclusive club. One that, regardless of which way it went, would only ever have one member: the first man to lift half a tonne – or, the first man to fail to lift half a tonne. One was quite desirable; the other, not so much.

Now I had only one day to go before the attempt. The next day would be the day I went down in history, or died trying.

CHAPTER 32
The Day of the Dead(lift)

The day before the event I drove up to Leeds in silence. I often do that as it helps me to focus and plan, and on this occasion there was only one thing to focus on but a lot to plan. For a start, I was beginning to worry whether I'd be able to sleep that night and so somewhere on the M1 I started to devise a strategy. Actually, it was more a concoction really and involved 1000mg of tramadol (the maximum dose is usually 500mg) and about three shots of whisky. Sometimes a bit of insomnia can keep you sharp but this was different. Had I not taken anything I know for a fact that I wouldn't have slept a wink and bearing in mind what I was attempting that would have spelled disaster. Fortunately, the whisky and the tramadol worked a treat and when I woke up the following morning I felt like a new man. I started shitting myself again soon after, but the first five minutes or so were great!

Incidentally, the previous day I'd gone out into Leeds and bought myself twenty litres of Lucozade, as you do, and by the time I went to bed that night, every single bottle was empty. I drink something similar prior to every event and for a time afterwards my entire body glistens and swells up. What's even more amazing, on that occasion, is that despite consuming such a vast amount of liquid I didn't go to the toilet once. Every drop was absorbed and used.

The first thing I did that morning was have a protein shake. Actually, it's the first thing I do every morning! Then, after napping for another hour I went out and had the biggest, fattiest fried breakfast you have ever seen in your life. I think I had six or seven sausages, five big rashers of bacon, four eggs, loads of mushrooms, four hash browns, some tomatoes and baked beans. Then, at about 10 a.m., I went out again and had a huge bowl of porridge. It was more a bucket really. After stretching off I went back to bed and had a couple of hours' kip. I do always sleep, by the way, when I go back to bed. I don't just sit there and watch TV. It's an essential part of my recovery.

For lunch, I went to an all-you-can-eat meat restaurant and asked the chef to cook me off any fat he had from either pork or gammon. Nice image, isn't it? Just thinking about it makes me want to puke, but at 9 calories per gram it was worth about 4,000 calories. It looked, tasted and smelt absolutely rank and the chef must have thought I had some kind of weird fetish. I tried to explain what I wanted it for but as I was talking he just walked slowly backwards.

By this time, Rich, my physio had arrived, so, after spending another hour in bed and then eating some flapjacks, I got up and had a nice long physio session before heading off to the arena. I always like to arrive at these places at least half an hour before everyone else as it gives me the chance to acclimatise. Something else I do which nobody else does is spend some time in the arena while it's empty. Then, when people start arriving, I periodically wander out there again. This prevents me from becoming either nervous or overcome by the amount of people present and, as well as helping me get used to the noise, it allows me to utilise the energy the crowd can generate. I've seen dozens of athletes walk out in front of a full arena and it scares them half to death. Just for a moment they forget what they're actually there for and by the time they've pulled themselves together they've lost a lot of impetus.

Something else I have to watch out for are changes in temperature. Because of the amount of isotonic liquids I drink I'm boiling hot before a competition and am like a massive ball of energy. It's important that I maintain that heat and keep all the energy in, so sharp changes in temperature, especially lower temperatures, are a definite no-no.

With regards to contact, I hardly speak to a soul in the lead-up to a lift or a competition. In fact, on this particular occasion I decided to put my earphones in. The music I always listen to is Eminem, which takes me back to my very early high school days. That was a time when I didn't give a shit about anything, so as well as keeping me focused it helps level me out emotionally. A few happy memories are just what you need sometimes.

If anyone comes to talk to me prior to an event I always shake my head and look away but on this occasion, apart from the people on my team, no one came anywhere near me. There was one occasion when somebody did disturb me and unfortunately they bore the full brunt of my anger. It happened in the gym, just before I was due to attempt a 400kg (881 lb) squat. As usual, I'd been stomping up and down like a dinosaur psyching myself up. Then the last thing I did before attempting the squat was look in the mirror, have a few words with myself and sniff some smelling salts. As I'm standing there telling myself how fucking strong I am, this kid walked up and tapped me on the back. Because I was so massively revved up I just ignored him but the stupid prat tried again. This time I'm afraid I just lost it and backhanded him. I didn't look, I just smacked him in the face. After that he must have gone scampering off and I did my lift. I said to my training partner Luke afterwards, 'Who the fuck was that tapping me on the shoulder?'

'No idea,' he said. 'But you proper smacked him in the face.'

I obviously felt pretty bad about it afterwards but at the end of the day I was focused and ready to lift. If you're daft enough to tap me on the shoulder when I'm in the zone, for fuck's sake don't do it a second time!

One thing I noticed as I was warming up at the arena was that all eyes were on me. Every single athlete and crew member was just staring at me. There was also silence, which there never usually is. At last, I think some doubt was creeping in. Not for me, but for them. If they thought I hadn't stood a chance they'd have been carrying on as usual, but backstage at the Leeds Arena at 7 p.m. on Saturday 9 July 2016 you could have heard a fucking pin drop.

The three athletes who were competing at the World Deadlift Championship were me, Benni Magnússon and Jerry Pritchett, and all three of us had agreed to go for the 500kg (1,102 lb). The other athletes present were obviously there for Europe's Strongest Man but to be honest there seemed to be more interest in the lift. This was history, remember.

As the three of us were doing a few warm-up lifts, I remember thinking, *Have either of these two got it in them to lift 500kg?* Benni seemed to be getting very worked up prior to lifting 300kg (661 lb). He was literally shaking with anger. It was only a warm-up though, so what was the point in that? He also lifted it very, very quickly, so as opposed to warming up, what he was actually doing was expending some of his energy and adrenalin.

A few minutes later, while he was still pumped up, Benni came up to me and as well as telling me I wouldn't lift the 500kg, he also said he'd lift more than me that day. Even though we were rivals, Benni and I had trained together once or twice and generally we got on very well. There was a difference between us, though, and that difference was exemplified right there and then. 'Do you know what I see in your eyes, Benni?' I said to him. 'I see me lifting 500kg.' The moment I said that, Benni's head lowered and his body language completely changed. I knew he wouldn't get anywhere near me, and certainly nowhere near 500kg. The thing is, so did he. I didn't want to head-fuck Benni but it had to be done. It was just me and the bar now.

When it came to the running order I asked to be first out and for two simple reasons. First and foremost, I wanted to be the first man to lift 500kg. I was adamant that neither Benni nor Jerry (ice cream, anyone?) were up to it but I still wanted an insurance policy. And secondly, I didn't want to see anyone else fail. Normally that might have spurred me on but Žydrūnas Savickas had been right when he said there was a high chance of injury and the last thing I wanted to see was somebody tearing a hamstring off. That would have put me off completely.

The night before at the athletes meeting, Benni and I had almost come to blows over who would pull first. It was proper handbags! I'd said to the promoters that I wanted to go first and straightaway Benni said that he did. 'Why the fuck should you go first?' I said. 'The 500kg was my idea and at the end of the day I'm the one who's got the best chance of lifting it.' Naturally, Benni didn't quite agree with me and for the next thirty minutes or so we carried on arguing. 'Let's toss a coin,' suggested one of the promoters. 'Fuck your coin,' I said. 'I'm going first and that's that.' In the end I think I managed to wear Benni down because after what must have been about forty-five minutes he held his hands up and said, 'If it means that much to you, go first!' I think I must have bored him into submission.

Now at last we were almost ready to go. Backstage, Benni and Jerry lifted 380kg (838 lb) and 400kg (881 lb) to warm up (I opted out). The first lift we needed to do onstage was 420kg (925 lb). I walked out into the spotlights, Colin Bryce introduced me to the crowd and the moment he said my name the entire place just erupted. It was a real hairs-on-the-back-of-your-neck moment.

About ten seconds later, I'd pulled the 420kg and after winking at the camera I walked off stage thinking, *That didn't take long*. It was a fucking speed rep! The next lift was 440kg (970 lb), which I decided to skip, and after that it was going to be 465kg (1,025 lb), which would be a new world record. Once again, I walked onstage to thunderous applause and to show my appreciation I pulled it as a speed rep again. Seriously, you watch it back on YouTube. Blink and you'll miss it. After me it was Jerry and Benni's turn, and fair play to them, they pulled it too. They didn't manage to speed rep it, but they were good lifts.

By this point I knew for a fact that I was going to pull 500kg and the only things worrying me now were Benni and Jerry. The deal was that, regardless of who went first, if more than one person pulled it we'd have to share the record and that was obviously only fair. Was there a chance they might lift it too? Christ, I hoped not. I wanted to keep all the glory for myself and as awful as it might sound I remember willing them to fail.

Apart from the ice cream brothers preying on my mind, in the minutes leading up to the lift everything was perfect. My team especially were textbook and I couldn't have wished to have had better people around me. They were Rich, my physio; Luke, my training partner; Rob Frampton, the strongman; and Andy Parker, who owns my gym. All four of these guys are friends of mine but as importantly, with regards to the situation, they're the most positive people you could ever meet, especially Rob Frampton. After he'd finished talking to me I could have walked on fucking water. That man can seriously empower people.

While Rob was massaging my ego and putting chalk on my hands, I had Rich massaging my legs, Andy putting my belt on and Luke sorting out my mouth guard. All this had been planned beforehand, by the way. The idea being that I wouldn't have to think about anything other than the lift. I couldn't wait to get out there now.

At about 7.45 p.m. a crew member came into my room to ask me politely if there was anything I needed. As per my usual practice, I told him in no uncertain terms to fuck off. The people at Giants Live know what I'm like at events and it was nothing personal. In fact, I think they expect it now. The last thing to go on was my T-shirt with my sponsors on. Now I was ready.

'We've still got a few minutes,' said Rob. 'I'll tell you what. Let's go for a walk.'

To get a bit of peace and quiet we all decamped to a disabled toilet where Rob carried on speaking the gospel. I needed to be in a confined space with positive people and this was our only option. Not very glamorous I know, but it's who you're with that's important, not where you are. As Rob spoke I stared at myself in the mirror. Normally when I'm trying to psych myself up I'll start thinking about very dark things. Things that make me angry. The psychology behind this is quite obvious as the angrier I become, the more adrenalin I have running through my veins. Once I'm incandescent with rage, I'll stare at myself and say, 'Now.' That's all. 'Now.' Less is definitely more in these situations.

By the time our impromptu motivational get-together had come to an end I was on the brink of spontaneously combusting. Without any further ado, I turned around, kicked open the door and we made our way to the stage.

Once we were stage-side, the lads started checking everything and making sure I was happy. I was. I was good to go. The crowd had been absolutely fantastic all night but as I walked out to the bar they seemed to go quiet all of a sudden. Perhaps they were nervous?

'Come on, you buggers!' I remember shouting, and then I gestured. 'Give us a hand!'

Fortunately their response was both loud and immediate but as I was standing there taking it all in I started to have what some people might call an out-of-body experience. It was bizarre, but all I could see for about five seconds was me, in position, locking out the lift. I was about fifty yards away looking down at the stage, and all I saw was me. It was self-belief TV.

Once the vision of me had gone and I was back in the arena I locked onto the bar, doing up my straps and checking my breathing. Then I got my feet and shoulders in line. *Right then, Eddie*, I thought. *Time to go*. I took a big breath and then another. The moment that second breath was completely in I tensed up momentarily, let it out, and then went to take what would have to be the biggest breath of my entire life. I don't know how many cubic centimetres of air I took into my lungs but it was enough to blow up a bouncy castle. Once that breath was held I started pulling the bar in towards my shins. My eyes were closed now and I couldn't hear a thing. As the bar slammed against my shins I leaned back, put all the weight into my arse and as I rolled forward I remember thinking to myself, *For fuck's sake Eddie, try and make it look easy!* How ridiculous is that? Here I am, about to try and lift half a tonne, and all I'm bothered about is how it looks!

From the moment I took the strain I knew I had enough power to nail it. My entire body had been quite loose until then but the moment I started to lift, all the energy came together and it just went BOOM! You can actually see the bar shudder at this point and as it's coming up I'm standing there thinking, *I've got this. I've fucking got it!* Internally I was laughing my arse off. Not because I was happy, although I was. Oh no. This was an evil laugh! A laugh that signified my revenge. As I locked out the lift I remember shouting, 'Fuck you!' which was directed at every single person who'd said it couldn't be done. It could be done, but only by one man.

The next thing I remember is waking up looking at a massive pool of blood. My blood, apparently. There must have been about a litre of it, but as well as it streaming out of my nose it was also coming out of my ears and even my eyes. My beard was drenched in it.

As the medics came in and started taking my belt and the straps off, my body started convulsing. I was also going in and out of consciousness at this point so for the first twenty seconds or so I had no control over my body. The first voice I remember hearing was one of the medics saying, 'You've got to get up, Ed. You've got to get up and let people know you're OK.' As he was saying this two other medics were busy wiping blood out of my eyes and ears.

Once I was fully conscious again I decided I'd had enough of this attention and so once they'd finished cleaning me up I started telling them all to fuck off. This took everyone by surprise and they scattered like school children. It was such an emotional moment though and the more conscious I became of my surroundings the more I realised what I'd just achieved. From that moment on it was just a groundswell of emotions. A culmination of spending twelve months in hell. I remember looking at the 10,000 people in front of me and it was unbelievable. People were either crying, cheering or just standing there with their mouths open. Either way, what I think we were experiencing was a variation of exactly the same thing: a mixture of extreme joy and shock.

Colin Bryce, who is never normally short of a few words, was just standing there looking at me and shaking his head. Colin Bryce has almost as much faith in my abilities as I do and by the day of the competition I reckon he was one of the few people who thought I could do it. He always told me I could, and I love him for that, but if truth be known there was only one person in the world who really believed I could pull that lift a year ago and he'd just lost a litre or so of blood in the process. The point at which that changed was when I pulled 465kg as a speed rep and once that happened you could feel the atmosphere change in the arena. Before that it had been one of enthusiasm. Everyone had been enjoying themselves and who knows, they might even see a world record. But the moment I pulled that lift everything flipped and all that enthusiasm changed to expectation. Now they were expecting not just a world record, but *the* world record. That memory of me standing there looking at the audience's faces is one of the most vivid I have and it will stay with me for the rest of my life.

One of the first people to congratulate me after the lift was Benni. Both he and Jerry attempted the lift after me as arranged, and although Benni had managed to get it off the ground it was only by a few inches. Poor Jerry ended up pulling a hamstring during his attempt and so in some ways Žydrūnas had been proved right.

'I knew you were going to pull it,' Benni said to me. 'I just didn't realise you were going to pull it so fast, you fucking freak!'

Bearing in mind we'd been adversaries for a couple of years that was a really sweet thing to do and if I'd had the energy

I'd have given him a big hug. As it was, I was well and truly F.U.C.K.E.D. and had hit a rather large wall. My skin was now so pale it seemed almost transparent and even twenty minutes after the lift my heart rate was still just over 160. That's nothing, though. Ever since he arrived, the doctor, who said I shouldn't have been alive, had been trying to take my blood pressure but according to him it was so high it was off the charts. He estimated that twenty minutes after the lift it was about 300 over 180, which is beyond dangerous. That's the reason I'd started bleeding out of so many orifices. 'All that blood has got to go somewhere, Eddie,' the doctor had said. 'If it hadn't come out of your nose, your eyes and your ears, your heart would probably have exploded.' That made me feel miles better!

Actually, I was starting to feel a lot worse again and despite them feeding me lots of sugars and carbs I was back to being in and out of consciousness. This was different, though, almost as if I was stoned, and as well as me thinking I had massive hands everyone around me seemed to have two heads. It was all very trippy!

About two hours later I was just about able to stand up, but only just. Medically, it had been the scariest two hours of my life and was my body's way of telling me I'd had a very narrow escape. The only thing I can compare it to was the time I fell out of that tree when I was a kid. This time though there was no laughter and no adrenalin. It was as if my life had been draining away. I never, ever want to feel like that again.

I know you're going to want to know how much money I got for the lift but I'm afraid I can't tell you. What I will tell you is that a few months before I had a bet on myself with a famous online bookmaker. Their odds of 25/1 looked quite attractive so I decided to have a punt. Once again, I couldn't possibly tell you what the stake was but let's just say I took full advantage of the odds.

Funnily enough, about the time I put the bet on I was talking to the Lithuanian strongman, Vytautas Lalas. He'd come over to Stoke for a competition we were both appearing in and he said to me, 'Eddie, do you honestly think you can pull 500kg?'

'Seriously, Vytautas,' I said. 'I will pull that weight. I've just had a big bet on myself and if you've got any sense you'll do the same.'

'Honestly?' he said.

'Look, mate,' I said to him. 'If you put £5,000 on you'll get about £125,000 back. Trust me.'

'OK,' he said. 'I'm doing it!'

I haven't seen Vytautas since then so have no idea if he did or not. I bet he fucking didn't.

The following day was Max's fourth birthday party and I don't mind admitting that it brought me down to earth with an almighty thud. We must have had about forty people in the house that day and apart from a couple of them saying, 'Well done, Ed,' nobody said a frigging word. Yes, OK, I know it was Max's party. The night before I'd experienced the biggest high of my life and normality was difficult to deal with. In the end I asked Rich to give me a massage so while everyone was downstairs on the bouncy castle he got to work on my back. What a state that was in. Rich said it felt like two pieces of steel.

What ended up easing my transition back to normality this time around was the amount of coverage it received worldwide. To this day, I have never seen anything like it in strongman, regardless of the event, and there's been nothing like it since. Even World's Strongest Man doesn't receive this kind of exposure. As well as trending on Facebook and Twitter it even made the news on ESPN America! That might sound a bit trivial to some people but for a niche sport like strongman it's a massive achievement. A big, big thing.

Speaking of World's Strongest Man, that was my next competition. In five weeks' time!

CHAPTER 33
Two Fingers

After the lift, I stayed away from the gym for a week and instead concentrated on my recovery. The majority of these sessions were physio, hot and cold treatments, or stretching, and after every session I felt better and better. Never had I been so in need of rehabilitation and that week was just amazing. I could actually feel my body coming back to life.

By the time I went back to the gym the following Monday I had exactly four weeks to prepare for World's Strongest Man. I was over the depression now and in addition to looking forward to appearing at the World's I was able to appreciate the enormity of what I'd achieved. Obliterating the world record like that amplified my self-confidence like you wouldn't believe and as opposed to just strolling into the gym like I'd always done, I was now trotting! All I wanted to do was train, train, train, and so basically, I increased everything. I increased my training, my food, my physio and my hot and colds. I'd just become the first man ever to lift half a tonne and without wanting to sound like a bighead, although I probably will, I was the most famous strongman on the planet. If I wanted to maintain that position and do justice to the lift – and to my reputation – I had to act accordingly. Best of all, I actually *wanted* to do this. For the first time in a while I was actually enjoying being a strongman.

By the time I got on that plane to Botswana there was no doubt in my mind that I was going to win 2016 World's Strongest Man. My plan was that when I won the competition I would retire from it immediately and then consolidate my position as the best in Britain. I'd do other things too, hopefully, but when I boarded that plane in August 2016 what I thought I was doing was attending my own semi-retirement party. I had all our holidays planned and because Alex had, and has, been through so much on my behalf, I was looking forward to treating her like a queen. Best of all, we were finally going to have that honeymoon we'd never had. The excitement I felt was incredible because you know how important it is for me to follow through on my promises. This one was the biggest of them all and to be honest the ambition had been going on for quite some time. Because there was no doubt in my mind that I would win, I'm afraid I'd lulled myself into a state of blissful ignorance and if there was ever a time when I could have done with those seeds of doubt I mentioned earlier it was now. What is it they say? Be careful what you wish for? Unfortunately this had disaster written all over it.

Botswana seemed like an amazing place and I wished I'd had time to have a look around. The hotel we stayed at was by a lake that was full of crocodiles and hippos and so that was a surreal experience. Especially for somebody more used to seeing shopping trollies in shitty canals! The only thing that worried me slightly while flying in to Botswana was the temperature. The average temperature there in August is about twenty-eight degrees Centigrade, whereas in Stoke it's probably more like eight. It hadn't been a problem in Los Angeles the year before but these things can differ massively and competing in hot temperatures was just about the only thing I hadn't trained for. In the end it was fine as there was a bit of a breeze and all in all I think I do quite well in the heat.

The day before the heats began I was still walking around in fairyland. I was bigger than I'd ever been before, strong as fuck, swimming in confidence, and on the verge of achieving my dream. Then, that afternoon, I went to what's called a familiarisation session, which basically gives the athletes a chance to familiarise themselves with the equipment. The only kit I wasn't sure of was the stuff they were using in the loading event so I made a beeline for that. It was supposed to be the first event in the heats, and you had to load four barrels onto a platform for time. It's standard stuff but I wanted to make sure I knew what I was handling.

When I picked up the barrel it felt fine and so I had a quick run with it. Yep, no problems there. Then I thought, *I know, I'll just try and throw it onto my shoulder and see if that makes it easier to carry.* Don't ask me why I did this, I just did. But as I went to throw it up I heard the most horrendous crack. Everyone in the entire yard stopped what they were doing and looked. I was wearing a glove at the time and when I took it off the ring finger and the middle finger on my left hand were at least five times their usual size. Colin Bryce was with me and I just saw his jaw drop.

'Colin,' I said to him. 'I'm out. That's it. I'm out.'

After that both of us just looked at each other in a state of incredulity. What the fuck had I just done? I couldn't believe how stupid I'd been. Both my fingers had been dislocated but because it had never happened to me before I didn't have the knowhow to protect myself.

You had to grip the barrel with a flat hand and unfortunately when I tried to throw it onto my shoulder the very end of my fingers had got caught underneath the rim. The rest of my fingers were straight and so with all that stress on the tendons they just went snap.

Despite being gutted beyond belief I decided to carry on with the competition. A lot of that was down to pressure, mainly from myself. The vast majority of people in my position would have buggered off home. This was my life, though. My career. I didn't have a job to go back to like most strongmen so I had to stay put and try to make it work. There was a pride element, too. I'd never walked away from anything in my life and I wasn't going to start now. The telephone call to Alex was devastating and although she did her best to sound philosophical I could tell that she was gutted. She must have been thinking, *Oh hell. Another year of this!*

Do you know, I'm trying to put a gloss on this situation because actually, it didn't turn out too bad. That's just not good enough for me, though. Even if I hadn't got carried away with the whole retirement thing I'd still have been devastated at not being able to win. That's what hurt most, I think: competing when I knew that I couldn't win the title. It was like going for a walk around the Yorkshire Dales with a couple of electrodes strapped to your bollocks.

In my qualifying group I had Nick Best, Grzegorz Szymański and Adam Bishop, so some big strong lads. Even so, I still managed to win the group by five clear points so I went into the final with a glimmer of hope. Only a glimmer.

The day before the final took place, the organisers of World's Strongest Man asked me, Brian and Thor if we'd mind visiting a hospital to make a few speeches and hand out some prizes. Sorry, but why on earth would you ask three athletes who are about to compete in the final of a competition to visit a hospital full of sick people? Under normal circumstances I'd have been first on the bus but the way my luck was going I'd have come away with malaria or something. It didn't make any sense to me and so I'm afraid I had to decline.

The first event in the final was the frame carry and because it wasn't one of my strongest events I had trained my fucking arse off for it. I'd even brought in a grip specialist who'd visited my gym twice a week for five months and without exaggerating my grip was just phenomenal. This bloke had cost me an absolute fortune but because I needed the help, it was worth it. I also knew that the rest of the field thought I didn't stand a chance in this event so I'd been itching to prove them wrong. But that was before the accident. Now, the only thing that was itching was my arse.

When the whistle went I locked on and when I tried to pick it up both my fingers dislocated again. The pain was excruciating – like nothing I'd ever experienced – and I'm surprised I didn't faint. I knew that every other athlete would have points after this and I was buggered if I was going to be alone on zero. As long as I managed to pick it up I'd be awarded one point and so after pulling myself together and preparing for the pain, I did just that. I may have finished last, but at least I wasn't pointless.

That smidgen of hope I mentioned had evaporated by now and from here on in it was all a matter of pride. I might not have been able to win the war, but I could still come out fighting in a battle or two. The next event was the circus barbell to overhead. This was usually a good event for me but because I couldn't grip the bar properly I knew I'd have difficulty. As well as being dislocated, my fingers were ridiculously swollen, so even if I did manage to lift the barbell off the ground I'd have to put all the pressure on my right. I don't know how the fucking hell I did it but even with all that going on I still managed eight reps and ended up coming joint first with Thor. In training I'd been doing ten reps so I should have bloody won it.

Event three was deadlift for max and after everyone else had dropped out it was left to me and Brian Shaw to fight it out. This was like a dream come true for me because not only is Brian one of the greatest strongmen who's ever lived, he's also the most professional athlete I've ever come into contact with. Going toe to toe with him in the final of World's Strongest Man – a title he'd already won three times, by the way – was a big moment for me. Nobody's taught me more in the world of strongman than Brian and I'm proud to call him a friend.

As I said, his professionalism is second to none and if there's a device out there that will help improve your grip, even by 1 per cent, Brian will have it before anyone else knows it's even out there. He would spend his last dollar on becoming stronger, and his dedication to the sport, and to becoming the best ever, is forensic. I'm exactly the same in that respect but that's only because of him. I've picked things up from loads of athletes over the years but Brian's the only one I've actually imitated. Before I met him, if somebody had ever suggested that I need to spend £50 a week on physio I'd have told them to fuck off. Nobody I knew spent £50 a week on physio and even the very thought of it was just ludicrous. What Brian did was tell me *why* I should spend that kind of money and made me see it as an investment, not a cost. Only a prat would ignore his expertise. These days I spend nearly £200 a week on physio and although that's almost a wage to some people, it's a necessity to me. Even if I wasn't a pro and couldn't really afford it I'd get a paper round or something to pay for it. I might even be persuaded to sell my body! Whatever I spend,

I know I'll make it back ten-fold. That's the way you've got to look at it.

Because of where I was in the points I knew that I couldn't win the competition so I said to Brian, 'Look, rather than us both risking injury for the sake of half a point, why don't we shake hands and draw this event,' and he agreed. To me it didn't make any difference but to Brian it obviously did so he snapped my hand off. Would I have beaten him if I'd carried on? Well, of course I would. Do you know anybody on the planet who can live with me at deadlift? My mentality had changed momentarily and because I could no longer win the actual contest it was as close as I'd ever come to throwing in the towel.

The next event, which took place the following day, was the plane pull. Not the truck pull, but the plane pull! A C-130 Hercules Air Transporter, to be exact, weighing a colossal forty-five tonnes? It's not everyday you're asked to pull a plane twenty-five metres and I was looking forward to it.

This was meant to be a timed event to see who could finish the course fastest, but with nobody managing to complete the course it was all down to distance. Even though the fingers were a factor and made me drop the rope, I still managed third place behind Thor and Brian Shaw. In fact, I ended up finishing just six centimetres behind Brian.

After that event I lay fourth behind Brian, Thor and the very talented Georgian lad, Konstantine Janashia. To be honest, I couldn't believe how well I'd done, but I was still pissed off at not being able to contend.

The fifth and penultimate event was the kettlebell throw and I finished fourth, just behind Jean-François Caron. This again was affected by my fingers and at the end of each throw I was in absolute agony. It was a sadist's paradise! In training I'd done six in around fifty seconds but on this occasion I managed just five in 56.92. A good effort but not much else. I would never have beaten Brian and Thor at this event but I might just have snatched third. Shoulda woulda coulda ...

Going into the last event I was one point off third and about eight points off the lead. Bar Thor and Brian dropping down dead and leaving me their points in their wills, the best I could hope for was a podium finish – my first at World's Strongest Man. You see the efforts I'm going to to make this sound positive!

In order to secure third, I had to beat Janashia on the atlas stones and that's exactly what I did. I threw the first four up as quickly as I could and then once I saw that Janashia was struggling I put up the fifth up at my leisure.

Now then. Do I think that if I hadn't had the accident I would have won World's Strongest Man 2016? Yes, of course I do. And that's not because I'm deluded or anything. It's a simple case of mathematics. Based on what I'd done in training, if I'd been fit and Brian and Thor had finished on the same points I would have won the competition. The thing is, I didn't, did I, so basically it's a complete load of bollocks. Anything can happen during a competition and the last thing I was going to do was become obsessed with what might have happened had I not been a silly twat at the familiarisation session. Life's too fucking short for all that crap.

In all seriousness I was extremely pissed off at coming third and when I stood on the podium and looked up at Thor and Brian I thought, *What a load of absolute wank*. I should have been standing in the middle. I'd still have been smaller than Thor and Brian but at least I'd have had a bigger trophy. I'm trying to decide if I was feeling sorry for myself and to be honest I probably was. I still had that overriding desire to come first, which was obviously at odds with where I was on the podium, but I couldn't help thinking that I'd been dealt a bad hand – pardon the pun.

That evening, Brian Shaw and I went out for a meal and I remember saying to him that I should have done a lot better. What I also said is that even if I had done better, I don't think I'd have beaten him. That really wasn't like me at all. All this magnanimous bollocks had to stop!

When I arrived back in Stoke the atmosphere was flat to say the least. My usual grievances of a lack of recognition and difficulty in adjusting to normal life had been superseded by an overwhelming sense of disappointment; not just for me but for Alex too. Everything I'd sensed over the phone was true and when I saw her face for the first time it spelled just three words – *not another year*. She obviously didn't say as much but it was written all over her. I felt the same, but for slightly different reasons. For me the biggest problem, apart from not being able to keep my promise to Alex, was being so fucking heavy. Over the past twelve months or so I'd been swimming in some very dark waters and I also had to think about my future health. At six foot three inches I'm not small, but I'm nowhere near tall enough to carry thirty-one or thirty-two stone. Not on an ongoing basis and certainly not while I was putting my body under so much pressure. Because of all the swimming I've done in the past my heart is extremely healthy but by carrying so much weight I knew I was abusing that advantage daily. Sooner or later it was going to catch up with me and at the time it was starting to become a worry.

Over the next week or so, Alex and I talked a lot about the future and I managed to persuade her to give me one more year. The sacrifices she makes, not to mention the effort she puts in, are equal to mine and so I knew if it didn't happen it would be the end of us. For a start I'd be a nightmare to live with and despite all the positive aspects of our relationship, the negative ones – all the sacrifices she makes and all the promises I've failed to keep – would cast too big a shadow over our relationship. I love Alex more than anyone else on Earth but ultimately I knew that could be our downfall. Letting her down doesn't just kill her, it kills me too. The next nine months were going to be crucial.

CHAPTER 34
The Here And Now

In about a week's time I'll be flying out to Botswana for World's Strongest Man, so before I lose my temper sitting on a plane for twenty-four fucking hours I'll just bring you up to date with what's been going on and tell you about all the preparation I've been doing. As I write this chapter it's now the middle of May 2017, and I've still got everything to play for.

From a competition point of view it's been up and down and if you were basing my chances of winning World's Strongest Man on the last two competitions it would be in the balance. The first one, which took place in March 2017, was Britain's Strongest Man at the Doncaster Dome. As Britain's most prestigious strongman event this was extremely important to me and after holding the title every year since 2014 I was obviously mad keen to retain it.

Well, to say I had a good day would be an understatement, because as well as winning three of the five events I finished the competition 14.5 points ahead of second place. That's a ridiculously impressive lead and proves that I'm the best in Britain by a long, long way.

On top of the prize money for the event I also won a motor-bike and at the end of the competition I rode it out of the Doncaster Dome in front of the crowd, burned some rubber, and then rode back in again. Any chance to show off.

Next on the agenda was Europe's Strongest Man at Leeds Arena. That took place on April Fool's Day, and, given my performance, it was very, very apt. This was always going to be a two-way battle between me and Thor and to be honest with you, I thought I was going to whip his fucking ass. This assessment was based on how I'd improved since last year, but what it didn't consider was how Thor might also have improved. Unfortunately for me, he had, and to be honest with you, I had seriously underestimated him. Like me, he'd obviously upped his game and he's definitely stronger than last year. A lot stronger. Everybody knows what Thor is capable of and if he gets it right in training, he could be one of the best there's ever been. Although the competition was tight – just two points in the end – he was definitely the better man and I was far from being my best. Not even breaking the world axle press record, which I did towards the start of the competition, could cheer me up and all in all it was a bad day at the office.

My only excuse for delivering such a lacklustre perfor-mance, apart from some stress at home, was the heart attack I'd had about ten days before. Well, it felt like a fucking heart attack! While having my bloods done one day I was told that I was a little bit low on potassium. 'Just eat a few bananas or take a supplement for a week' was the advice I was given, and really, that should have been that.

Because it was so close to Europe's Strongest Man I'm afraid I panicked a bit and as opposed to doing what I'd been told and either taking a supplement or eating a few bananas, I took lots of supplements *and* ate mountains of lovely bananas. Little did I know that by taking in too much potassium I was in danger of giving myself a heart attack. It didn't take long for me to find out.

After I'd been popping supplements and gorging on bananas a few days I started getting cramps all over my body. My arms and legs were the worst but I even got them in my bloody eyes. Fuck, that was painful. After that I started twitching everywhere and because I thought it was all down to having low potassium I ate more bananas and popped even more pills.

A few days later, this would have been about 20 March, I got into bed about 11 p.m. and the moment I lay down, my heart started beating at about a hundred miles an hour. *That's not right,* I thought. *I'm not stressed about anything and all I'm doing is resting.* After putting a finger pulse oximeter on, it came up with a reading of 140 beats per minute. Bear in mind a normal resting heart rate is 60 to 100 beats per minute, less if you're very fit. 'I'm going to sit downstairs for a bit,' I said to Alex. 'Something's not right.'

Things like this had happened before and so I wasn't too worried. Sure enough, about ten minutes later, my heartbeat started to drop. The thing is, it didn't stop dropping and within about ten minutes it was down to 30 beats a minute. 'Alex, call an ambulance,' I said in a panic. My left arm had now started tingling and when I started getting pins and needles down it I thought I was fucked. The paramedics arrived in about five minutes flat, by which time my heartbeat had gone back up to about 120. After running some tests, they told me that my potassium levels were dangerously high and that my heart had gone into spasm. That's when I realised what had happened. *What a fucking berk,* I thought. *I've almost bloody killed myself.*

The paramedics recommended that I go into hospital for some treatment but before I agreed I asked them for a media block. I didn't want people seeing me with wires sticking out of my chest, especially so close to a competition, so before we set off they rang the hospital to see if it would be OK. 'I'll pay for the private room,' I said. 'And anything else that's necessary.'

I have no idea why, but for some unknown reason the matron or the sister or whoever said no to the media block. They had rooms, according to the paramedics, but the answer was still no. 'Well, I'm afraid I can't go in then,' I said to them. 'It'd be a nightmare.' They tried to persuade me otherwise but I was having none of it. In the end, I just sat up and flushed the potassium out by drinking gallons and gallons of water and after about seven or eight hours my heart rate started normalising again. The next day I couldn't train and it took me a good two or three days after that to feel normal again. It taught me a lesson. Just fucking listen!

Europe's Strongest Man took place about a month and a half ago now, and it's enabled me to make a few tweaks and get that little bit closer to where I need to be. Seriously, if Thor puts in a performance like that at World's Strongest Man I'm going to have a serious problem on my hands. Given how confident I usually am that may sound a bit defeatist. It's not meant to be; I know I can still beat Thor. He knows that too. The problem is, he can also beat me, so it'll all be down to who's best on the day.

That show, by the way, had an audience of over 11,000, which as far as I know is one of the largest ever in strongman. I haven't included many adverts in this book but if there's anyone reading this who has never been to a strongman event before then take my advice and go. As a form of family entertainment it's got everything and, unlike football or any of that bollocks, there are no boring bits. It's all full-on action and if you go to one that I'm involved in, all the better. Our sport is now bigger than it's ever been and if you're reading this you must at least have an interest. Seriously, if you haven't been to one before, just go. You'll absolutely love it.

You remember I mentioned the Las Vegas-style introductions at the Arnold Classic? Well, Colin Bryce is getting quite good at that and because the competitions are becoming so big we decided to make the introductions a little bit more interesting. As I'm called 'The Beast' I suggested to Colin that we should play on that a bit. 'What do you have in mind?' he said. 'How about some massive chains and a mask?' I suggested. I have no idea what Colin *thought* I was going to suggest, but one thing I do know is, it wasn't that. Fortunately he quickly warmed to the idea and a couple of days later my costume arrived. 'Now all I need is some music to go with it,' I said to him. 'You just leave that to me,' he said. The result had the audience on their feet and if you tune into the competition later in the year when it's televised you'll see exactly what Colin and I came up with. I did suggest taking the mask and chains with me to World's Strongest Man but apparently they've been confiscated. Probably a good thing.

The only scare I've had recently took place about ten days ago at the start of May, but fortunately it turned out to be blessing in disguise.

Once a year, all strongmen have to have an ECG and when I went for mine it detected what's called a suboccipital decompression, which causes heart rate variability. What the doctor couldn't understand was that my blood pressure was 120 over 60, which, for a thirty-stone man, is just ridiculous. Ridiculous in a good way, I should add. He checked it about ten times just to make sure but it still came out the same.

The results of the ECG went straight back to the governing body's medical team who told me that until the decompression had been explained I wouldn't be able to compete. They also instructed me to have an echocardiogram as soon as possible. With only three weeks to go I was terrified and instead of waiting for an appointment with the NHS, which would have taken years, I booked in with my local Nuffield hospital.

After the echocardiogram, which seemed to take an age, the doctor said I had the most efficient heart he'd ever come across and because it was so efficient even the smallest anomaly would be flagged as a problem.

'Tell the governing body that, and quick!' I asked him. 'I'm supposed to fly in a couple of weeks.'

Damaging my heart has always been a worry for me, especially since I've been this big, so receiving the news that my heart was so healthy has done me the power of good. It's like I've been given permission to push that little bit harder.

That just about brings us up to the present day. As I'm sitting here now I am genuinely more focused and positive than I have ever been in my entire life. About strongman, that is. From the moment I get up until the moment I get to bed all I can visualise is lifting that trophy. Thor and Brian are beside me, still towering over me of course, but I'm in the middle. I am the fucking winner. I've always said that unless I die or unless a doctor tells me to stop, I will become World's Strongest Man. I honestly can't remember the first time I said that, but I'll tell you one thing, I have never been so sure of it in my entire life.

I have got a lot of injuries at the moment. In fact, I'm riddled with them. The difference is between now and last year is that not one of them will affect any of the events I'll be competing in. There is a slight shoulder problem that worries me a bit but I'm confident I'll get that sorted before I go.

The events at this year's World's Strongest Man suit me down to the ground so I've never stood a better chance of winning. Three of the events should be bankers for me: the squat, the deadlift and the Viking press. If I win those three events like I should do, all I have to do is get a top three finish in the remaining three. If I do that I will be crowned 2017 World's Strongest Man. Do the other three events worry me? To be honest, they do, a little bit. But this is where those seeds of doubt I mentioned earlier come in useful. Winning the first three events might turn out to be a lot easier than coming second or third in the second three. Then again, it could be the other way around. The second three events, by the way, are the plane pull, the tyre flip and drag, and the atlas stones. In the absence of any aeroplanes in Newcastle, I've been using a lorry from that local skip company again to train that, and when it comes to the tyre I've managed to source the exact same one they'll be using in the competition. A drag's a drag, so all you need to do to train that is pick up a T-bar and drag some weight. Believe it or not I don't actually train for atlas stones. It's just a case of grunting that stone from A to B and as long as you use the right tacky, which is the stuff we put on our forearms – and, as long you're strong enough, of course – then you should be OK. There are actually all kinds of tacky, and which type you use depends on the temperature. That's why I always carry a thermometer to competitions.

The most essential thing I'll be taking with me this year to World's Strongest Man is Rich, my sports therapist. All in, that's going to cost me about six or seven grand but it's worth every single penny. A lot of people will think I'm mad for doing it but he's the best there is and so when I lift that trophy it'll be the best six or seven grand I've ever spent. At Europe's a few weeks ago, and at Britain's, I was the only strongman who brought his own physio. In fact, because it was so fast-paced at Europe's, I had two. Each was handed their own sheet of paper at the beginning of the night telling them exactly what to do and when. All I had to do was lie there and let them get on with it. There are physios available at strongman events but if they don't know your body it just doesn't work. For me, anyway. Some might call that being anal but I call it professional.

One of the many differences between this year's World's Strongest Man and earlier events is that this year every single base has been covered. There are no – repeat, no – excuses. If I get beaten at this year's competition it will be down to either strength, bad luck or injury, and I obviously can't legislate for the last two. I simply have to deliver.

It's fair to say it's become an obsession and you would not believe the lengths I've gone to. Actually, by now you probably would. I'm going to tell you anyway.

Do any of you know what hyperbaric oxygen therapy (HBOT) is? It's a medical treatment that enhances the body's natural healing process and it takes place in what's called a hyperbaric chamber. While you're in there you inhale pure oxygen and you're able to increase and control the atmospheric pressure. I usually have it at about 22psi which is about one and a half atmospheric pressures. That's the equivalent to being twenty metres under water and the atmospheric pressure forces the oxygen into your muscles and opens all your capillaries and arteries. That's a layman's description, by the way.

To put the effectiveness of the therapy into perspective, one hours' in a hyperbaric chamber is the equivalent to twelve hours' recovery time. And, the less time I need to spend recovering, the more time I can spend training. It's that simple.

A hyperbaric chamber would normally cost at least a hundred grand but it's basically a rolled piece of steel with a Perspex window in it and, because I'm quite a practical person, I decided to build my own. It's now in my gym at the bottom of my garden and it's a hell of a piece of kit. You've got to be so, so careful what you take in there (no jewellery or mobiles, etc) and to be honest it's as boring as hell. I usually do about an hour and a half a day.

Training too has gone up a gear and I've almost killed myself at least twice. I remember one instance on the leg press. I was doing over a thousand kilos and after doing eight reps all I remember is waking up with the weights about an inch from my chest. Fuck knows how I managed to extract myself, but I did. That was a scary one. I also passed out while training the log press one day and it smashed against the back of my head. How many fucks did I give? Not one.

In the powerlifting world, i.e. squat, deadlift and bench, I was doing weights that would make the best in the world look second rate. I was benching 265kg (584 lb) for six reps and the British record is only 250kg (551 lb). In the squat, I was doing 345kg (761 lb) for ten plus reps and the British record is 380kg (838 ln). But that's only one rep. The deadlift speaks for itself but the person closest to me in Britain is Loz Shahlaei on 435kg (959 lb). That's a 65kg difference! That's how strong I had to be.

After I'd built the hyperbaric chamber and had bought myself new hot and cold tubs, which again are essential for recovery, I was on the verge of being skint. If Alex had known how bad things were, she'd have gone apeshit. I had to do it though. Everything I have, financially, physically and mentally, has gone into winning this competition. I think I'd sell my house if I'd needed to. I've definitely sold my soul.

NO – FUCKING – EXCUSES.

I'll tell you what. Let me just take you through a typical day in the run up to this competition. You honestly won't believe it.

2 a.m. – Get up. Eat some steak and drink a litre of protein shake.

7 a.m. – Get up and have another protein shake. This time with spinach, ice cream, nuts, butter, protein powders, raspberries and blueberries.

9 a.m. – Get up and have a full English breakfast. Five or six of everything. Wash it down with a litre of cranberry juice.

9.45 a.m. – Go out for a brisk walk.

10 a.m. – Eat 100g cashew nuts and drink half a litre of protein shake.

10.15 a.m. – Back to bed. Because I'm in training I'll be knackered so I won't just lie there. I'll be fast asleep.

12.30 p.m. – Get up and start cooking dinner which will either be spaghetti bolognaise or chicken, rice and pasta. I'll also have half a large cheesecake for pudding and a litre of cranberry juice. That meal alone will be at least 3,500 calories.

1.30 p.m. – Back to sleep.

3.10 p.m. – Get up, pack for the gym and start eating again. Tuna sandwich, flapjack, bananas, beef jerky and two large bottles of Lucozade.

3.30 p.m. – Set off to the gym and carry on eating. Flapjacks, nuts and bananas.

3.45 p.m. – Start training my fucking arse off. No time limit. I train until I drop and if I don't pass out I will definitely vomit at some point during the session. It's as simple as that. Everything's become so extreme. All the way through I'm eating things like steak and beef jerky and I'll drink at least three litres of cranberry juice. How I don't actually look like a fucking cranberry I have no idea.

8 p.m. – At the end of the session I'll drink a litre of full fat milk with two scoops of protein powder. Then, I'll drink a litre of coconut water.

8.15 p.m. – Drive straight to M-Club and stretch off for half an hour. Every muscle group. After that I'll alternate between the sauna and the cold tub.

9.30 p.m. – Back home for tea. Steak, chicken, pasta, curry. Something like that. Then I'll have the other half of the cheesecake. That'll be at least another 3,000 calories.

10.15 p.m. – Alex will go to bed and I'll go to the hyperbaric chamber for ninety minutes. Because of the noise it's impossible to fall asleep so I just lie there in the dark.

11.45 p.m. – Have a quick snack, something like a protein bar, then try and get some sleep before I'm up again.

There. Not exactly a ride on the big dipper, is it? This has been my life every day now for the last six months and as extreme as it might seem I've actually become used to it. Eating to the point of vomiting is the bit I dislike the most and once I've finally won this competition I'll definitely cut back.

She's given me permission to say this, but the only thing that's been really difficult over the last six months has been my relationship with Alex. Since coming back from World's Strongest Man 2016 it's been on a downward spiral and given what I've already told you it's not difficult to see why. As well as holding a job down she's had to do everything; clean the house, take Max to school, do the shopping – the lot. Worst of all she's had a husband who may as well have been on another planet. The only time I spend with her and the kids is a couple of hours on a Saturday but because I'm knackered I can't go anywhere. To be honest it's been making her ill, but what can I do? I can't give up now. I've come too far. I keep saying to her, 'It's only a few more weeks. After that, I promise things will change.' I don't think she listens to me anymore. Who can blame her?

Quite a few people – very daring people – have been asking me what I'll do if I don't win this year's competition and I haven't been able to answer. All I know is that I stand to lose everything, and when I say everything, I obviously don't mean my house and my fucking car. I mean my family. The only thing I can liken it to is when a soldier leaves the army. You hear all kinds of horror stories about those poor men and women not being able to adjust and that's exactly what I'm scared of. The only difference between me and them is that if it goes tits up for me it will be all my own fault.

The thing that a lot of people have trouble understanding, and I'm one of them, is the self-destructive nature of what I do. I mean, come on. Why would anyone subject their bodies, and their minds, to such ridiculous amounts of punishment, while at the same time alienating their family? It's actually quite irrational when you think about it, but then that's strongman. Apart from wanting to lift more weight than the next man, nothing really makes sense.

I said in the documentary that the only reason I was doing this was for Alex and the kids, but am I? Am I really? Do I want to make them proud or do I want to be the centre of attention? If I'm being brutally honest I'd say both. The difference is that I might actually be able to live without being the centre of attention. What I can't live without is my family.

What gives me hope is that my desire to be congratulated is part nature, part nurture. I've always been a show-off, as you know, and from the moment I stepped onto the blocks at my first swimming gala I've been trying to wrap myself in layer after layer of acknowledgement and approval. That, my friends, is my one and only addiction, and providing I can handle losing some of it, then Alex and I might, just might, be OK.

But I'm not going to lose though, am I?

Anyway, I'll see you all in Botswana.

CHAPTER 35
Botswana Diary

Thursday 18 May 2017

You remember I mentioned not being able to legislate for luck or injury? Well, fortunately I haven't been injured yet, but if my luck carries on like this it won't be long before I am. I've been in Botswana for a day now and everything that could have gone wrong, has.

Let's start with the journey, shall we? We didn't fly until about 7 p.m. and so I spent the first half of the day packing, eating, stretching and having a bit of physio. At about 4 p.m. we set off to the airport and from the moment we arrived there everything seemed to go wrong.

For once, I'd actually paid to go in the priority lanes at security yet everyone who wasn't in the priority lanes seemed to get through before me. It's a good job I didn't swear at anybody because this time they'd probably have given me a full cavity body search!

After posing for about a hundred photographs, which I didn't mind, I made my way to the business class lounge where I was hoping to have a meal. Business class? This was more like dog class. The food there was absolutely disgusting and so because of that I ended up missing a meal. I'm not the fussiest eater in the world but this was beyond the pale. *No matter,* I thought. *There'll be plenty of food on the planes.*

We were catching three flights in all – Manchester to Paris, Paris to Johannesburg, and Johannesburg to Gaborone, which is the capital of Botswana. The first flight went fine, although there was no food. *Never mind,* I thought. *The next flight is where business class kicks in, so not long to wait.*

After going through security for a second time and then posing for another twenty photographs, I finally made my way to the gate for the flight to Johannesburg. The plane was a 747. As I boarded I handed the steward my ticket and he very kindly said he'd show me to my seat, which, according to him, was right at the front of the plane. As he led on, I quickly realised that he was taking me into economy class instead by mistake but by the time I managed to attract his attention it was too late.

'Oh, I'm so sorry, sir,' he said. 'You're obviously supposed to be in business class.'

'Yes, I know I am,' I replied through gritted teeth.

'Well,' said the steward. 'I'm afraid it's quite a journey. You need to go right to the back of the plane, up the stairs, and walk back to the very front of the plane. Your seat is directly above us.'

What an absolute fucking dickhead.

Because all the passengers were trying to put their hand luggage into the overhead lockers it took me thirty-five minutes to get from there to my seat and I ended up being the very last person to sit down. I was first on, for fuck's sake!

One of the most important things I take with me on a night flight is my sleep apnea machine, as if I fall asleep without it I can actually die. Even if I'm not planning on going to sleep I can still drop off and so unless I'm eating I have to wear it. Anyway, as I started to unpack my stuff I quickly realised that I didn't have the mask for my machine, which meant I couldn't use it. I must have lost it going through security or something but without it I couldn't fly.

'Excuse me,' I said to one of the stewards. 'I've left my sleep apnea mask in security, and without it I can't fly.'

'What do you mean, you can't fly?' This one was a bit of a grumpy twat.

'I mean, that if I fly without it, I could die.'

'Well,' he said. 'What do you want us to do about it?' Fuck knows what they were like in economy. They probably carried tasers or something.

'I've got a spare one in my luggage, but that's obviously in the hold. Somebody's going to have to get it, I'm afraid.'

'Oh, no, no, no,' he said. 'I'm afraid that's impossible.'

'Well, I can't fly without it, and I'm certainly not getting off. It's up to you. I'll just stay standing here until it arrives.'

Fortunately the captain agreed to them finding it but because it took about twenty-five minutes we ended up missing our slot. We obviously took off but thanks to me we were almost an hour late. Three hundred and sixty people all delayed by a thirty-one-stone strongman with a potentially deadly sleep disorder. You couldn't make it up.

By the time they found the mask I'd become so worked up that I was on the brink of collapsing and I was pouring with bloody sweat. For some reason the air conditioning wasn't working and unfortunately they couldn't fix it, which meant I just carried on sweating. World's Strongest Man was going to be a walk in the fucking park compared to this.

Once we were finally in the air I took a couple of painkillers, put my mask on, and tried to get some sleep, but because it was so hot I found it impossible. I'd have stripped off but all I was wearing was a pair of shorts and a vest.

To make matters worse, the bloke who was sitting next to me had a really bad cold and so as well as preventing me from resting with all his coughing and spluttering, he was also putting me at risk of getting ill. Once again the food was shit and so that was now three meals I'd missed. Thank fuck I'd packed plenty of snacks.

After pissing about in Johannesburg for a couple of hours, I found out that Rich, my physio, had been put on a later flight to Gaborone. So, as I was driving us both to the hotel, I'd have to wait for him. Ninety fucking minutes I was sitting there, and that was after I'd been to sort out the hire car.

By this point I don't think I'd ever been as stressed in my entire life. I'm surprised I haven't needed fucking therapy! Perhaps I do?

By the time we eventually got to the hotel all the other athletes had checked in, eaten, bought a load of Gatorade and were relaxing in the pool. I, on the other hand, was standing there in reception feeling like a slightly malnourished gorilla who'd been locked in a fucking sauna for twenty-four hours and had his bananas pinched.

After unpacking and having a shower, I went to the shop, bought a shedload of Gatorade, necked that, and then went to have a meal in the athletes' tent. I think I said earlier in the book that conditions for the athletes at World's Strongest Man had improved in recent years. Well, I'm afraid I have no choice than to take that back. Or at least some of it. The food in that tent was absolutely vile and I wouldn't feed it to my dog. I have got a dog, by the way. It's a Labrador pup called Jack. Anyway, for as long as I'm here I'm going to be eating out.

There's only been one problem with regards to the competition so far, but potentially it's a big one. I bumped into Colin Bryce soon after arriving and he was standing with a man from Scania. They're providing the tyres for the flip and drag event in the final and after showing me a photo of the tyres we're going to be using I've realised that I've been training with the wrong one. Fuck knows how it's happened but the one I've been using has a different tread *and* it's about 80kg

(176 lb) lighter. Nothing I can do about it now. Because of all the stress, not to mention the tyre fiasco and being fed dog food, I've kind of lost my appetite, which isn't good. What a twenty-four hours it's been. We've got the medicals tomorrow, and then the media. Time to get some rest.

Saturday 20 May 2017

Well, that was fucking fun. After a good night's kip I had some physio before making my way down for the medicals and the media. Despite us all being given a schedule for both, most of the athletes just seemed to roll up when it suited them. Like a dickhead I decided to do the same but I got there just as it was starting to piss them off. 'Go away, look at your schedule, and come back at your allotted time,' was the advice they gave me. Fair enough!

In between the medical and the media I went to the familiarisation yard, which was all fine. Apart from the tyre everything's OK and after coming out of there I could feel my appetite coming back, thank God. I've eaten jack shit in the last couple of days, compared to what I should be eating, and have got some serious catching up to do.

My favourite part of the day was the media. Sometimes I can be quite humble in an interview but this time I came out all guns blazing and was as cocky as fuck in all of them. The first question they all asked me was, 'How do you think you're going to do, Eddie?' And I gave every single one exactly the same answer, which was, 'I've already won, mate.' These people all thought I was joking and after asking for a serious answer they got the same one back. 'I'll tell you again. I've already won this.'

The reason I made that claim wasn't just because I thought it was true. It was because I wanted it to get into the heads of the other athletes and so by making such an outrageous statement I knew that the media would ask them about it. 'Eddie Hall says he's already won the title. What do you think about that?' I'm just an evil fucking genius.

The only other athlete who has scared me so far is Brian. Thor looks fit and so does Žydrūnas, but Brian looks immense. Stupidly, I went and asked him how much he weighs and at the moment he's just over thirty-three stone. Two hundred and ten fucking kilograms! I think Thor's the same as me, about thirty-one, so there isn't much in it.

There's something different about Thor. I know the competition hasn't started yet but he just doesn't seem as confident as he usually is. Perhaps it's just nerves?

Funnily enough I've been watching some videos of Thor training the events for this year's competition and he's looked absolutely fucking colossal especially in the deadlift, the squat and the overhead.

Sunday 21 May 2017

I've spent most of today trying to fuck with Brian Shaw's head. Not in a bad way. I've just been trying to wind him up a bit and plant a few seeds. I'd do the same to Thor if I could get anywhere near him, but he's got an entourage of about thirty people. He's like Leonardo Di fucking Caprio.

The task of trying to emasculate or intimidate somebody as big and powerful as Brian isn't easy, but I've had a lot of fun trying. First of all I started asking him what he thought of the events, but in a really cocky manner. 'How do you think you'll do in the squat, Brian?' I asked him. 'Not your strongest event, is it? And how about the deadlift? That's probably one of my best at the moment. I should piss that.'

After giving him some massive man slaps on the back I started saying, 'Do you know what, Brian. I reckon I'm going to win this year. In fact, I think I'm going to piss it. How do you think you're going to do, Brian? Confident? You must think you have a chance.' My campaign was absolutely relentless and in the end, I even cupcaked him. Cupcaking Brian Shaw, though! You've got to be fucking brave to do that. Brave or stupid. I think I'm probably both.

The thing is, the more I tried winding Brian up the less he reacted, and the less he reacted the more I knew I was getting to him. If people react, they're on the same page as you are, but if they don't, that page has been turned. Will definitely try it again.

Actually, while we're on the subject of winding up the competition, I can tell you that one of the biggest and funniest paradoxes within strongman is the fact that, despite us all being giants who do manly things and shout 'AAAAARGH!' a lot, it's actually one of the bitchiest sports on the planet. Because it's so niche there aren't that many athletes and because we spend so much time together, everybody's connected via Facebook. It's like living in a village, I suppose, but with that comes a bit of a village mentality. Everybody knows what everyone else is either thinking or doing and so sometimes it gets a bit daft.

A strongman would never slag off another strongman to his face, by the way. Heck no. What they do instead is get a friend of theirs to post something derogatory and then hope it gets back to the person for whom it's intended, which it usually does. It's like Chinese whispers really, and a lot of it has to do with either jealousy or fear.

Take this competition, for instance. I've heard that some people think the events have been chosen to suit me and one or two have even been complaining that it's a fix. What an absolute load of bollocks. For years now, many of the events have favoured taller athletes. For instance, keg toss, power stairs, and atlas stones on six-foot plinths. Nobody ever said a thing about them favouring taller athletes, or if they did, I never heard them. Remember what I said about fear and jealousy? They know that I'm the real deal and because they're scared of what I can achieve – and, let's face it, they have good reason to be – they're already looking for excuses. I suppose it is the ultimate compliment in a way but boy does it get on my tits. The problem is that nobody will ever come out and say something to my face whereas that's the only way I can communicate. If I've got a problem with somebody I'll tell them, and if I think something's unfair, I'll tell the powers that be. If you want to make an omelette you've got to break some eggs and if people can't handle that then tough.

Monday 22 May 2017

First day of the heats today and it started off with a fucking disaster. The event was the load and drag, and for some reason the lane I was in was a lot grittier than others and I ended up finishing fourth. This isn't an excuse, by the way, as every person who used that lane did poorly.

I've had loads of people messaging me and asking how I've done but I can't bring myself to tell them. The expectation is starting to become overwhelming. It's my own fault, I suppose. After all, I create the hype. That's the easy bit though. Anyway, tomorrow's another day.

Tuesday 23 May 2017

Normal service has resumed, thank fuck!

Today was the log press and the only man in my group who came anywhere near me was the Polish lad, Mateusz Kieliszkowski. He and I competed alongside each other and after knocking out five reps very quickly I stood back and waited for him to catch up. Once he got five I lifted a sixth and once he got six I lifted a seventh. It was all about conserving energy for me. We ran out of time in the end and finished on seven each. Should have been watching the clock.

Next up was the bus pull and as well as winning my group I also finished faster than all the other athletes, including Thor. This is normally one of his best events and beating him has really boosted my confidence. Especially as that's one of the three other events I didn't think I could win. As importantly, it will have planted a seed in Thor's head and I know for a fact he'll be fucked off. The question is, how will he respond? If he lets it get to him he'll capitulate, but the chances are he'll come out fighting. Unfortunately, they're going to be swapping the bus for a fucking plane in the final, but the main thing is he's beatable. I know it, and so does he.

I spoke to Alex earlier and told her about yesterday. I was hesitant at first because I didn't want to make her nervous but the results today seemed to reassure her. And me, as it goes. She's worried though, I can tell. Really worried. I reiterated my promise to her but I'm starting to get the feeling that she's fed up with hearing it. I obviously can't blame her for that but until I produce the goods it's all I have to offer. What also frustrates her is being stuck at home while I'm competing abroad, and that's another thing that will change once I've won. Just so long as she doesn't cheer me on or start shouting advice. Fuck no.

Wednesday 24 May 2017

Deadlift day!

What a result. Not one person in my group could deadlift and so I won the event with just four reps. Kieliszkowski, who came second, did three in about fifty seconds and I pulled my four in just under ten. Every other group winner had to pull about eight or nine which means they've all had to expend twice as much energy.

Next up was the gold bullion toss (similar to the keg toss) and I only had to throw three to win the group. Best of all, whoever was winning the groups going into the last event didn't have to take part, which means I got to conserve even more energy. That said, so did the other winners.

It's hard not to get carried away by this but I've got such a good feeling about the final; if I can get past the worry, that is. As I said, as long as I win the deadlift, the squat and the Viking press, I know I'll be home and dry. OK, maybe I should rephrase that. I *hope* I'll be home and dry.

The only other people I've been watching so far have been Brian and Thor and from what I've seen so far, Brian poses the bigger threat. As well as being enormous he definitely looks more comfortable. We'll see.

Saturday 27 May 2017

Something funny happened first thing this morning. I got shat on by a bird! I was out having a stroll and all of a sudden some landed on my arm. Not much, but enough to make me call after the perpetrator! At first, I was mildly horrified but then it reminded me of something.

Back in 2014 I was competing in Malaysia in a round of the Strongman Champion's League. Me and Thor had been swapping first and second place all the way through and after the final event we were tied on points. In this situation, you go on what's called countback, which is who had the best positions overall. Unfortunately for me, in one of the events he'd been third and I'd been fourth so he beat me by one placing.

A few days before that we'd all been to an exotic bird park and half way through the day one of them had shat down Thor's back. Everybody pissed themselves, naturally, but after the event had finished he came up to me and said, 'When that bird shat on me, I knew it was for a reason.' 'Really?' I said. 'You're putting the win down to bird shit?'

I have to admit I was confused at the time but after getting shat on this morning maybe there's something in it? I'll try anything.

It's about two hours before the first event of the final and over the last two and a half days I've done nothing but eat, stretch, hydrate, have physio and relax. I did have a problem with sciatica a few days ago and once I realised it was my mattress I went out and bought a better one. Everything's so cheap here and, sure enough, I was fine the next morning. Brian Shaw was complaining of a similar problem and once I told him what I'd done he went out and did the same. I could have stayed quiet I suppose and let him suffer, but I'm not completely evil.

I also had a bit of a problem with stiff hips yesterday, which was down to having a tight quad. This produced a brief, but nevertheless serious scare, as when I was in my room with my leg on a chair trying to stretch the quad I suddenly heard, and felt, an almighty snap. For a second I thought I might have done myself some damage but instead it fixed the problem. It was painful – snapping a quad usually is – but my movement has improved ten-fold.

Well, that's what I've been doing physically. Mentally, I've been going off my box with worry and my head's been like a hamster's wheel. The closer the final gets the more in touch I become with the rest of my life and I'd be surprised if there's a single worst-case scenario I haven't thought of yet. In terms of severity they normally range from grave to catastrophic, and unfortunately this destructive train of thought has kept me from sleeping. I even had to call out the doctor the other day and get him to prescribe me some diazepam. I only took the diazepam last night and fortunately it gave me the best night's sleep ever. I'm still worrying my fucking arse off, but at least I can do it with my eyes open today. My confidence and strength are still there, bubbling away underneath, but all I can actually *feel* is fear. Over the next two days I will have six opportunities to save the rest of my life. That may sound a bit overdramatic but that's what my head is telling me. Six events that will define my future.

Right. I've got to be down in reception in a bit so I'd better get my shit together. Wish me luck.

Sunday 28 May 2017 – COMPETITION FINISHED

I've managed to escape the press for a few minutes but have been told by the organisers that I'm not allowed to give details of what has just happened. The competition isn't televised until Christmas and obviously they want as many people to tune in as possible. That's fair enough. One thing I am allowed to do is give you an indication of who won the competition, and in order to do that I will write just four words:

I kept my promise.

Acknowledgements

As far as I know I'm one of the first strongmen to write an auto-biography so it only makes sense that I thank those responsible first. They are, James Hogg, who helped me write the book. My publisher, Lorna Russell at Virgin Books, and my literary agent, Tim Bates. Thanks guys. It's been a great experience.

Next, I'd like to say a special thank you to three people who made a big difference in my early life. They are: Vivienne Mills, my first and favourite teacher – and, my first sponsor! Arnold Faulkner, my swimming coach and the man who taught me how to become a champion. And Greg Clarke, my second swimming coach and the man who taught me how to enjoy the fruits of my labours. I know I wasn't the easiest pupil so thanks for your perseverance.

I dread to think how long I've spent in the gym over the years and if it wasn't for these three lads it would have been a lot less enjoyable. They are Andy Parker at Strength Asylum, Bazza Bailey at Ultimate Fitness, and last but not least, my long-suffering training partner, Luke Fullbrook. Thanks lads.

A few years ago, I was approached by a very confident TV presenter called Matt Bell who wanted to make a documentary on my life. The resulting film, *Eddie: Strongman*, is something I'm very proud of and I'm pleased to say he's become a good friend. Well done mate and here's to the sequel!

If it hadn't been for my manager, Mo Chaudry, I wouldn't be where I am today. It's as simple as that. He was the one who made it possible for me to go full-time and all in all I think things have gone reasonably well. Mo, I will always be very, very grateful.

These days an athlete is nothing without his sponsors and it's a department in which I have been blessed. In no particular order, I'd like to thank Phil Blakeman at Blakeman's; Chris and Dave Johnson at the Pulse Group; Chris Butler; Wayne Walker at Wayne Walker Meats; Uchit Vadher at Xplosive Ape; Peter Wright at Wright's Pies; Ray, James and John at Jumbo Skips; and everyone at Protein Dynamix, MUHDO and Alpha Bottle. Thank you all for your support.

Before I move on to my family I'd just like to say thank you to the boys and girls at Giants Live – in particular Darren Sadler and Colin Bryce – and also to my good friend Neil Pickup. I'm lucky to have such good friends within the sport I love.

Over the years I've tested the patience of every member of my immediate family and in a variety of different ways. I'm anything but predictable!

Luckily for me each and every one of them has stuck with me through thick and thin, and because of that I worship the ground they walk on. They are: my brothers James and Alex, my children Layla and Maximus, my Mum and Dad, Helen and Stephen, and my wife Alex. Seriously. Words cannot express my admiration.

This book is in memory of Sheila Jackson, David Jackson and Reginald Hall.

Eddie Hall's Competition Record

Amateur competitions

2007 Burnley Novice Strongman	5th
2008 Blackburn Novice Strongman	7th
2009 Staffordshire's Strongest Man	3rd
2009 North UK's Strongest Man	7th
2010 North UK's Strongest Man	2nd
2011 NEC Birmingham Strongest Man	2nd

Britain's Strongest Man

2014 Britain's Strongest Man	1st
2015 Britain's Strongest Man	1st
2016 Britain's Strongest Man	1st
2017 Britain's Strongest Man	1st

England's Strongest Man

2010 England's Strongest Man (Elite)	1st
2011 England's Strongest Man (UKSC)	1st

Europe's Strongest Man

2012 Europe's Strongest Man	8th
2017 Europe's Strongest Man	2nd

Giants Live

Giants Live 2012 (Australia)	4th
Giants Live 2013 (Hungary)	2nd
Giants Live 2014 (Hungary)	3rd

UK's Strongest Man

2011 UK's Strongest Man	1st
2012 UK's Strongest Man	1st
2013 UK's Strongest Man	1st
2014 UK's Strongest Man	1st
2015 UK's Strongest Man	1st
2016 UK's Strongest Man	1st

World's Strongest Man

2012 World's Strongest Man	Qualified
2013 World's Strongest Man	Qualified
2014 World's Strongest Man	6th
2015 World's Strongest Man	4th
2016 World's Strongest Man	3rd
2017 World's Strongest Man	1st

Index

EH indicates Eddie Hall.

Index

Index